# THE AMERICAN SYSTEM

# GEORGE F. COLE

THE UNIVERSITY OF CONNECTICUT

# OF CRIMINAL JUSTICE

## SEVENTH EDITION

WADSWORTH PUBLISHING COMPANY

I(T)P  An International Thomson Publishing Company

Belmont ~ Albany ~ Bonn ~ Boston ~ Cincinnati ~ Detroit ~ London ~ Madrid ~ Melbourne
Mexico City ~ New York ~ Paris ~ San Francisco ~ Singapore ~ Tokyo ~ Toronto ~ Washington

| | |
|---|---|
| CRIMINAL JUSTICE EDITOR | Sabra Horne |
| DEVELOPMENT EDITORS | Janet M. Hunter and John Bergez |
| ASSISTANT EDITOR | Jason Moore |
| EDITORIAL ASSISTANT | Jessica Monday |
| PRODUCTION EDITOR | Deborah Cogan |
| TEXT AND COVER DESIGNER | Cloyce Wall |
| PRINT BUYER | Randy Hurst |
| ART EDITOR | Kevin Berry |
| PERMISSIONS EDITOR | Jeanne Bosschart |
| COPY EDITOR | Judith McKibben |
| PHOTO RESEARCH | Photosynthesis |
| TECHNICAL ILLUSTRATIONS | Precision Graphics |
| COVER PHOTO | © Tim Flach, Tony Stone Worldwide |
| COMPOSITION | Brandon Carson, Wadsworth Digital Productions |
| COLOR SEPARATION | Color Tech |
| PRINTER | Quebecor Printing/Hawkins |

**Library of Congress Cataloging-in-Publication Data**

Cole, George F., 1935–
    The American system of criminal justice / George F.
Cole—7th ed.
        p.   cm.
    Includes bibliographical references and index.
    ISBN 0-534-24048-8
    1.  Criminal justice, Administration of—United States
        I.  Title
KF9223.C648   1995
345.73' 05—dc20
[347.3055]                                                94-11411

**For more information, contact:**

**Wadsworth Publishing Company**
10 Davis Drive, Belmont, California 94002, USA

**International Thomson Publishing Europe**
Berkshire House 168-173
High Holborn, London, WC1V 7AA, England

**Thomas Nelson Australia**
102 Dodds Street
South Melbourne 3205, Victoria, Australia

**Nelson Canada**
1120 Birchmont Road
Scarborough, Ontario, Canada M1K 5G4

**International Thomson Editores**
Campos Eliseos 385, Piso 7
Col. Polcano, 11560 México D.F. México

**International Thomson Publishing GmbH**
Königswinterer Strasse 418, 53227 Bonn, Germany

**International Thomson Publishing Asia**
221 Henderson Road
#05-10 Henderson Building, Singapore 0315

**International Thomson Publishing Japan**
Hirakawacho Kyowa Building, 3F
2-2-1 Hirakawacho
Chiyoda-ku, Tokyo 102, Japan

# BRIEF CONTENTS

CONTENTS

# The Criminal
# Justice Process

# Police

## 4   Police   132

# Courts

# 8  Defense Attorney  300

# 9  Pretrial Processes  328

# 10 Court 364

# 11 Trial and Posttrial Processes 398

# PART FOUR

## Corrections

**PART FIVE**

# The Juvenile Justice System

*To the 20th Anniversary Edition*
*by Gilbert Geis, University of California, Irvine*

**It is uncommon for a social science textbook to persist** through seven editions and over two decades. It is even more uncommon for it to do so with unabated intellectual vigor and vitality and with unremitting attention to the most recent and most compelling developments in its field. George F. Cole's *The American System of Criminal Justice* has done both of these things.

Revising textbooks is a curious business. Authors often anguish over what to omit and what to include between one edition and the next. The conscientious writer must maintain constant vigilance to discover the new idea, the better statement, the more gripping vignette that tellingly makes a general point. Some writers become a bit lazy and make merely cosmetic changes, an update here and there and a bevy of new footnotes reflecting later publications. There is no question in which of these camps the present text belongs. This seventh edition offers a thorough rewrite of the previous one and a comprehensive restructuring of the chapters, even as it continues the intellectual traditions that have marked this text from its inception.

These intellectual underpinnings are worth elaborating upon, because they illuminate the special character of this book. When first issued twenty years ago, *The American System of Criminal Justice* imposed coherence upon a field of study that was barely out of its academic swaddling clothes. In the early 1960s the study of crime was still something of a wayward enterprise in college and university settings. There were stray criminology and corrections courses in sociology units, where they were regarded, along with offerings in marriage and the family, as rather unpretty parts of the department curriculum, tolerated only because they generated considerable student enrollments. At the same time, many two- and four-year colleges and some universities offered degrees in what usually was called police science. Enrollment generally was confined to law enforcement personnel hoping to improve their position in their department. Courses typically were taught by retired or moonlighting police officers, and

classes had a considerable tendency to devolve into interesting but rather pedagogically beside-the-point exchanges of war stories offered up from the work experiences of the professors and the students.

This situation began to change with the establishment in 1968 of the Law Enforcement Assistance Administration (LEAA) under President Lyndon B. Johnson. This agency provided substantial subsidies to persons enrolled in criminal justice classes and set up heavily funded programs for research on crime and criminal justice. Academic institutions responded to the subsidies offered by LEAA by beefing up existing police science programs and inaugurating new programs in criminal justice. Younger students enrolled and demanded sterner and heartier intellectual fare, so that courses began not only to draw upon law enforcement materials but also to consider the information from law and the social and administrative sciences.

When LEAA scholarship funds were withdrawn after about a decade, many expected that there would be a stark retreat in criminal justice education. Instead, the field continued to grow dramatically. First-rate doctoral programs that had been established at the State University of New York, Albany, and at Rutgers University flourished. Innumerable undergraduate programs continued to be inaugurated under a wide variety of academic housing arrangements.

It was against this backdrop that the first edition of *The American System of Criminal Justice* appeared in 1975. The text provided what was essential to the integrity of a new field in its drive to gain intellectual respectability: coherence, rigor, scholarly sophistication. It cannot be proven, but it seems to me likely, that the appearance of this textbook contributed significantly to the growth and vitality that have come to mark the academic study of criminal justice. It did so in part by demonstrating—as it continues to demonstrate forcefully—that information and insights from the diverse social sciences can be blended with research about the operation of the criminal justice system to provide a deeper and intellectually sound understanding of that system.

In addition to exhibiting the interdisciplinary and empirical character of the field, *The American System of Criminal Justice* highlights the fundamental theme that criminal justice is a complex social system that itself is a part of the wider social, political, and economic systems of the country. Students who learn about criminal justice from this text will appreciate that we cannot comprehend criminal justice without thoroughly understanding the larger contexts in which it is practiced.

A third noteworthy contribution is Cole's emphasis on the issues of public policy inherent in any society's attempt to deal with crime. A political scientist by training, Cole is especially attuned to these issues. Furthermore, he enriches students' understanding of policy questions, and of the American democratic system in general, through instructive comparisons with the systems, procedures, and customs of other societies. American academic work has rightly been accused of being too parochial and failing at times to appreciate the value of other ways of doing things. This is not an accusation that can be leveled at this text.

All of this sounds sophisticated and complex, and it is—yet one of George Cole's gifts is the ability to make such nuanced understanding accessible to a broad range of students. One of the virtues that immediately stand out for me in this volume is its straightforward and uncluttered prose style. Ernest Hemingway, perhaps the greatest of recent stylists writing in the English language, used to say that the trick was to know and understand everything about your subject, and then to exercise restraint and present only enough to convey the essentials. If you do this job well, Hemingway said, readers will know that what is before them is both an accurate and an aesthetically pleasing portrait of the subject. Another outstanding writer, Robert Penn Warren, offered a further guideline: "The real academic job is to absorb an idea, to put it into perspective along with other ideas, not to dilute it with lingo."

Cole carries out these dictums with consummate skill. Take, as one example, the pithy statement about early tactics of prison management: "The Quaker method aimed to produce honest persons whereas the New York system sought to mold obedient citizens." Or that on policing in the inner city: "The ghetto resident thinks of the police as an army of occupation and the police think of themselves as combat soldiers."

Cole does not flail about and offer a potpourri of contradictory studies, then point to the methodological flaws in each, and conclude that the matter remains unresolved and that more and better research needs to be carried out. Instead, he absorbs the body of work on the point being considered and highlights for students those conclusions that are significant. And he does so with a very sure sense of what is important and how each part fits in with the remainder of the information he offers regarding the American system of criminal justice. There are no detours onto side streets whose only attraction is that some fad or other has led to the production of a sizable body of largely irrelevant information.

In brief, this edition, like its forebears, is an extraordinarily good book—well written, thoroughly informed, and fair. And for all its academic rigor, there are heroes enough throughout the book. Cole has a keen appreciation, for example, of the enormous pressures Americans put on their police to do a job that contains so many contradictory demands: for service, for kindness, for toughness, for bravery, for ingenuity, for wisdom. Even as he challenges readers to understand the system of criminal justice *as a system*, he does not lose sight—or permit his readers to lose sight—of the human side of the story.

Many students who first learn about criminal justice from this text will find jobs in that field of work after they graduate. Some of those who used the earliest editions already are established in executive positions in the police, probation, and the courts. The lessons conveyed by *The American System of Criminal Justice* should be for them not only of academic importance but of direct practical significance. Besides, in itself, the realm of criminal justice is monumentally important. "The quality of a nation's civilization," Walter Schaefer, an eminent jurist, once declared, "can be largely measured by the methods it uses in the enforcement of the criminal law." These methods—their virtues and their shortcomings—have been dealt with in estimable fashion for twenty years and through seven editions of *The American System of Criminal Justice*.

*Gilbert Geis*
*University of California, Irvine*

**Instructors of criminal justice enjoy an advantage** that many of their colleagues in other disciplines might envy. Most students come to the introductory course intrigued by the prospect of learning about crime and the operation of the criminal justice system. Many of them are optimistic about the role they may one day play in allocating justice, either as citizens or in a career with the police, courts, or corrections. All have been exposed to a great deal of information—and misinformation—about criminal justice through the news and entertainment media. Whatever their views, few are indifferent to the subject they are about to explore.

Like all newcomers to a field, however, introductory students in criminal justice need, first, *a solid foundation* of valid information about the subject and, second, *a way to think about* this information. They need conceptual tools that enable them not only to absorb a large body of factual content but also to process that information critically, reflect on it, and extend their learning beyond the classroom. Providing both the essential content and the critical tools is the dual aim of this text.

## Approach of This Text: Three Key Themes

When the first edition of *The American System of Criminal Justice* was published in 1975, it embodied three assumptions about the future direction of criminal justice as a discipline and the way that the introductory course should be taught:

- *The field of criminal justice is interdisciplinary,* with research contributions from criminology, sociology, law, history, psychology, and political science.

- *Criminal justice involves public policies* that are developed within the political framework of the democratic process.

- *The concept of social system* is an essential tool for explaining and analyzing the way criminal justice is administered in practice.

This approach has met with a degree of acceptance that has been gratifying, humbling, and challenging. Instructors at hundreds of colleges and universities throughout the nation have embraced it, and over the years more than a half million of their students have used the book. Yet no textbook author can afford to rest on his or her laurels, particularly in a field as dynamic as criminal justice. The social scene changes, research multiplies, theoretical perspectives are modified, and new policies are promulgated while old ones fall out of favor. Not least, students and their needs change as well. Accordingly, I have taken the opportunity to make this seventh edition of the "Eagle" even more current, vital, cohesive, and appealing to students and instructors alike.

## Highlights of the Seventh Edition

This has been a major revision effort in both content and presentation. Users of the sixth edition will immediately see significant changes in organization, including a streamlining of Part I, a reorganization of the discussion of policing, and an additional chapter on corrections. Beyond these major changes the organization of each chapter has been examined and in many cases improved.

In addition to structural changes, each chapter has been thoroughly updated in content, research citations, examples, and emphasis. The text has been rewritten on a line-by-line basis to ensure that descriptions are succinct and clear, that chapters and sections are cohesive, and that students are guided to the text's special features so that they perceive these features as significant and related to the context in which they occur. The introduction of full color clarifies and enhances the many graphs and figures while lending new vitality to the text, photographs, and illustrations. I hope that these changes make this seventh edition even more usable and "teachable" than its predecessors. Let me summarize its principal features in terms of the two goals introduced earlier—to promote content mastery and thoughtful learning.

## Content Mastery: Organization, Coverage, and Study Aids

Although the basic plan of the text will be familiar to current users, this edition embodies several important changes. Similarly, study and review aids have been revised and enhanced.

**A More Streamlined and Cohesive Introduction to the Field**   Part I has been shortened by one chapter and reorganized to provide a more concise and cohesive overview of the text and of the course. Chapter 1 now gives a complete overview of the criminal justice system and how it is studied. Importantly, this chapter now makes explicit for students the three themes that have long been recognized by instructors: that the study of criminal justice is interdisicplinary, that the administration of criminal justice inevitably involves politics and issues of public policy, and that the concept of system is the best way to understand the way criminal justice works in the real world.

Students are then introduced to the idea that analysis of the crime problem requires an understanding of the strengths and weaknesses of our measures of criminality, victimization, and criminal justice effectiveness. Chapter 2 explores this issue by showing how these measures are derived and the safeguards that must be taken if the data are to inform analysis accurately. To complete the overview of the field, Chapter 3 introduces the concept of criminal law.

**Improved Coverage of Policing**   Major changes are taking place in American policing as the law enforcement/crime fighter emphasis is supplemented by a greater focus on community policing and problem solving. Part II (Chapters 4, 5, and 6) has been reoriented to illustrate this shift in police operations.

**Updated and Expanded Coverage of Corrections**   With prison crowding and overwhelming probation caseloads has come a search for intermediate punishments that are more restrictive than probation but less restrictive than incarceration. Part IV has been thoroughly revised to reflect these and other shifts. Chapter 12 (sentencing) and a new Chapter 14 (probation and intermediate sanctions) introduce such innovative sanctions as intensive probation supervision, home confinement, boot camp, and restitution. In addition, recent research on the governing of prisons challenges many of the assumptions of the past. Chapter 15 (goals and management of prisons) has been rewritten to show the importance of governance in maintaining secure, safe, and humane prisons.

**Study and Review Aids**   To help students identify and master core concepts, the text provides several study and review aids:

- *Chapter outlines* preview the structure of each chapter.
- *Opening vignettes* introduce the chapter topic, often with a high-interest anecdote or episode.
- *Questions for Inquiry* highlight the chapter's key topics and themes.
- *Chapter Summaries and Questions for Review* reinforce key concepts and provide checks on learning.
- A new appendix on *understanding statistical graphs and charts* is designed to help readers interpret the data presented in the text.

**Enhanced Graphics Program**   Today's students have been greatly influenced by television. They are attuned to colorful images that convey not only information but also values and emotions. In this edition a group of outstanding graphic artists and photo researchers have helped to develop an extensive program of full-color illustrations. Illuminating quantitative data have been converted into bar graphs, pie charts, and other graphic forms; written summaries of the graphic presentations make them easier to grasp. Special care has been taken with regard to the placement of photographs so that the images and captions are tied directly to the message of the text.

## Promoting Critical Understanding

The features just described should enable any diligent student to master the essential content of the introductory course. While such mastery is no small achievement, most of us aim higher: we want our students, whether future criminal justice professionals or simply future citizens, to be capable of taking a more thoughtful and critical approach to issues of crime and justice than they did at the start of the course. To this end, the text provides several features intended to help students learn *how to think* about the field.

**Thematic Emphases**  As noted at the beginning of the preface, a gratifying number of instructors have welcomed the three key assumptions that have guided the writing of this book. In the past these assumptions were mostly implicit; in this edition I try to "give them away" to students as well.

The idea that *criminal justice is interdisciplinary* is now explored in words and graphics in Chapter 1. In subsequent chapters, students will recognize that the research cited is drawn from a number of disciplines. The interdisciplinary character of the field is further reinforced by the many sidebar *Biographies* of important figures in the history of criminal justice.

*The role of politics and policy* in criminal justice is also presented in Chapter 1 and developed through examples and explicit discussions throughout the text. For example, the text explores the political atmosphere surrounding the "three strikes and you're out" proposals and the treatment of the crime of rape and its victims. Throughout the book, students are reminded that the definition of behaviors as criminal, the funding of criminal justice operations, and the election of judges and prosecutors all result from decisions that are politically influenced.

Finally, the *system perspective* on the administration of criminal justice is an explicit theme not only in Chapter 1 but also in many of the ensuing chapters. It is reinforced graphically a number of times with illustrations that remind students of exchange relationships, the flow of decision making, and the way the criminal justice system is itself embedded in a larger governmental and societal context.

**Close-Ups and Other Real-Life Examples**  It is not enough to understand criminal justice in a purely theoretical way. Not only for the sake of interest but also for a balanced understanding, students need a wealth of illustrations showing how theory plays out in practice and what the human implications of policies and procedures are. In addition to the many examples in the text, *Close-Up* features in each chapter are drawn from newspapers, court decisions, first-person accounts, and similar sources. In this edition, the Close-Ups are more smoothly integrated into the context so that students see their pertinence more readily.

**A Question of Ethics**  Criminal justice requires that decisions be made within the framework of law but also consistent with the ethical norms of American society. In each chapter *A Question of Ethics* scenarios place students in the context of decision makers faced with a problem involving ethics. The aim is to make students aware of the many ethical dilemmas faced by criminal justice personnel and the types of questions that they may have to answer if they assume a role in the system.

**Comparative Perspectives**  With the move toward more global thinking in academia and society at large, students are exhibiting a new interest in learning more about criminal justice systems in other parts of the world. Many chapters of this edition include a *Comparative Perspective* section that describes a component of criminal justice in another country. In addition to broadening students' conceptual horizons, these sections encourage a more critical appreciation of the system many Americans take for granted. By learning about others, we learn more about ourselves.

## Supplements

An extensive package of supplemental aids accompanies this text.

### Instructor's Resource Manual and Computerized Test Bank

A full-fledged Instructor's Resource Manual has been developed by Professor Christopher Smith, School of Criminal Justice, Michigan State University. New to this edition are lists of resources, lecture outlines, and testing suggestions that will help time-pressed teachers to more effectively communicate with their students. Each chapter has multiple-choice and true-false test items as well as sample essay questions. The Instructor's Resource Manual is backed up by a computerized test bank available for IBM-PCs or compatibles and Macintosh computers.

### Transparencies

To bring the graphic portions of the text to the classroom, full-color transparencies for overhead projection are provided. These transparencies help instructors to thoroughly discuss concepts and research findings with students.

### Study Guide

A more extensive Study Guide has been developed for this edition. Because students learn in different ways, a variety of pedagogical aids are included to help them. Each chapter is outlined, major terms are defined, summaries are given, and sample tests are provided.

## A Group Effort

It is not possible to be expert about all portions of the criminal justice system. Any author needs help in covering new developments and ensuring that research findings are correctly interpreted. This revision has greatly benefited from the advice of two sets of scholars. Each read the

manuscript from a different perspective. One group was asked to comment on the entire manuscript, with an emphasis on its organization and pedagogical usefulness. These reviewers were chosen from the wide range of colleges and universities throughout the country that have used previous editions, so their comments were especially useful with regard to presentation, levels of student abilities, and the requirements of the introductory courses at their institutions. A second group of reviewers are nationally recognized experts in the field, and they focused on the areas in which they specialize. Their many comments helped me avoid errors and drew my attention to points in the literature that had been neglected. The names of all the reviewers can be found at the end of this preface.

A large number of students and instructors who used the sixth edition also contributed abundantly to this revision. Several hundred readers returned the questionnaire included in the last edition. Their comments provided crucial practical feedback, as did those made to me personally when I lectured in criminal justice classes around the country.

I have also been assisted in writing this edition by a diverse group of associates. Chief among them are development editors John Bergez and Jan Hunter, and copyeditor Judith McKibben. Because early in the process it was decided to do a major reshaping of the book, their help was most valuable. The project has benefited much from the careful work of Deborah Cogan, production editor. Cloyce Wall designed the interior of the book and developed the extensive photographic and art programs. And the following reviewers contributed valuable comments: Paul C. Friday, The University of North Carolina at Charlotte; Armand P. Hernandez, Arizona State University; Ida Johnson, The University of Alabama; Barbara J. Keith, Rio Hondo College; William M. Nixon, Eastern Kentucky University; Rudy Prine, Valdosta State University; Walter F. Ruger, Nassau Community College; Vince J. Webb, The University of Nebraska; and Ralph Weisheit, Illinois State University. Ultimately, however, the full responsibility for the book is mine alone.

*George F. Cole*

**W**elcome to *The American System of Criminal Justice*! I wrote this book with the overriding objective of presenting you with a clear picture of the *reality* of crime and justice in the United States. I think you will find that picture sometimes familiar and sometimes surprising, on occasion disturbing and yet in many ways reassuring. Above all, I think you will find it a fascinating subject to study.

Fascinating—and important as well. Whether you are contemplating a career in criminal justice or a related field, or simply want to be a more informed participant in our democracy, you will find that issues of crime and justice touch upon your life and the lives of those around you. All citizens—not just judges, police officers, attorneys, defendants, and prisoners—have a stake in the way criminal justice is administered and the measures society deems appropriate to combat crime.

In this book I hope to take you beyond sensationalized and oversimplified accounts you may have encountered about how police, courts, and corrections function in the United States. To become educated about this subject, you need a solid base of reliable information. But you also need a way to *think about* that information—a set of conceptual tools for analyzing and interpreting what you read and hear about criminal justice. In this book I have tried to provide both the information and the tools.

In the next seven pages I will explain how the text works and how you can get the most out of it. The study of criminal justice has enthralled me for many years; I hope this book passes on some of that fascination to you.

*George F. Cole*

George F. Cole

# Organizing Your Study

To organize your study effectively, take advantage of the *consistent format of each chapter.*

## Criminal Justice and the Rule of Law

**Chapter Outlines** present an overview of the topics to be covered that you can use as a framework for study and review.

3

The veteran Milwaukee police officers were understandably shocked when, in August 1991, they opened the freezer in Jeffrey Dahmer's apartment and found two human heads in a refrigerator, two in a freezer, and seven others boiled clean. In the basement they found an acid-filled blue barrel of body parts. Investigators soon learned the full extent of Dahmer's crimes. The thirty-one-year-old laborer confessed to the police how he lured young men and boys from gay bars to his apartment where he drugged and killed them, had sex with their corpses, dissected and cannibalized the bodies.

Is there any question that Dahmer was insane when he committed these crimes? If he does not meet the legal definition of insanity, who does? As Richard Moran has noted, "All the defense really has to do is describe the contents of his refrigerator and freezer. Normal murderers do not mutilate their victims, nor do they display their heads or hearts. Cannibalism is not an alternative lifestyle, nor is necrophilia just some odd sexual preference."[1] However, the Wisconsin jury that convicted

89

**Opening Vignettes** offer brief real-life stories that set the stage for the chapter subject.

...defense that he was not guilty by reason of men-...er will be incarcerated for the rest of his life.
...eal with people such as Jeffrey Dahmer? In re-...rles Manson, "Son of Sam" David Berkowitz, ...enry Lee Lucas have come to public attention. ...ose behavior almost rivaled that of Hannibal ...e movie *Silence of the Lambs.* Although the facts ...doubt, the defendants' legal responsibility for ...rrific aspects of their crimes became an issue. ...committed their crimes? Were their rights pro-...om arrest to trial? What is an appropriate pun-...als?

...mer serves to remind us that even when some-...nstrous behavior, it is law that is at the base of ....Law governs the conduct of officials, and law ...citizens. Law thus performs two functions: (1) ...that are labeled criminal, and (2) it describes ...ed under our adversarial system by those with ...nforcement, adjudication, and corrections. Per-...f committing an illegal act unless the state is ...ditions specified in the law were met and that ...y the law were followed. Moreover it must be ...as **legally responsible** for the act as illustrated

...v criminal justice operates as an administrative ...ical and social forces; now the third necessary ingredient of our analysis—law—must be examined. This chapter explores the two aspects of criminal law: the substantive criminal law and the law of criminal procedure.

### Questions for Inquiry

- What are the foundations and sources of American criminal law?
- How does the substantive criminal law define crime and the legal responsibility of the accused?
- How does the procedural criminal law define the rights of the accused and processes that must be observed in dealing with a case?
- What are the major interpretations of the criminal justice amendments of the Constitution by the U.S. Supreme Court?

### Foundations of Criminal Law

In our system of justice, violators of society's rules are prosecuted and tried according to laws. Not all behavior that is offensive or considered deviant is criminal behavior. Only behaviors proscribed by the criminal code are illegal. We have seen that in different locations and times, dif-

**Questions for Inquiry** focus your attention on the key points to be explored in the chapter.

## Running Glossary

defines the terminology of the field. Definitions of terms are placed in the margins, next to the first appearance of the term (in boldface type) in the text. These terms are also defined at the end of the book in the main glossary. The page number on which the term is first defined appears in boldface type in the index.

---

**clearance rate**
The percentage of crimes known to the police that they believe they have solved through an arrest: a statistic used as a measure of a police department's productivity.

**reactive**
Occurring in response to a stimulus, such as police activity in response to notification that a crime has been committed.

**proactive**
An active search for offenders on the part of the police in the absence of reports of violations of the law. Arrests for crimes without victims are usually proactive.

The **clearance rate**—the percentage of crimes known to the police that they believe they have solved through an arrest—is a basic measure of police performance as they deal with citizens. The clearance rate varies with each category of offense. In such **reactive** situations as burglary, the rate of apprehension is extremely low, only about 14 percent; much greater success is experienced with violent crimes (46 percent), in which the victims tend to know their assailants.[41] Arrests made through **proactive** police operations against prostitution, gambling, and drug traffic have a clearance rate, theoretically, of 100 percent.

The arrest of a person often results in the clearance of other reported offenses because the police make it a practice to connect arrested persons with similar, unsolved crimes when they can. Interrogation and lineups are standard procedures, as is the lesser-known operation of simply assigning unsolved crimes in the department's records to the defendant. Acknowledgment by offenders that they committed prior but unsolved crimes is often part of the bargain when guilty pleas are entered. Professional thieves know that they can gain favors from the police in exchange for "confessing" to unsolved crimes that they may not have committed.

### Police Discretion

Discretion is a characteristic of organizations. Whether in the corporate structure of General Motors or in the bureaucracy of a state welfare department, officials are given the authority to base decisions on their own

---

U.S. Constitution but they can provide *more*. It may be that during the new era of conservativism on the Supreme Court, state courts will continue the civil liberties revolution begun by Chief Justice Warren.

### Summary

Only behaviors proscribed by the criminal law are illegal. The criminal law embodies descriptions not only of the forbidden behavior and the punishments to be administered but also of the ways in which justice officials must deal with defendants. The criminal law is thus divided into substantive and procedural law. The criminal law may be found in constitutions, statutes, case law, and administrative regulations.

Substantive law concerns the question, "What is illegal?" For every criminal charge, it must be shown that the behavior of the accused was consistent with the seven principles that define crime. Defenses such as self-defense, necessity, and insanity may be used to show that the accused was not legally responsible for the offense. Every crime is classified as either a misdemeanor or a felony.

Procedural law focuses on how the law is enforced. The manner in which evidence is collected, the admission of witnesses' statements at trial, the judge's charge to the jury, and the rights of prisoners are only a few of the matters in which the procedural law stipulates what can and cannot be done. Since 1961, we have seen a major expansion of the rights of defendants through decisions by the U.S. Supreme Court. Interpretations by the justices of the Fourth, Fifth, Sixth, and Eighth Amendments have required the states to conform to these protections.

Many people believe that the substantive law and the rules of procedure have become so intricate that criminals escape punishment, court proceedings are unnecessarily drawn out, and the police are unable to do their job. Others contend that law and due process are essential for a just society. These positions remind us of the values summarized in the Due Process and Crime Control models and of the tensions existing between the rule of law and the administration of justice.

### Questions for Review

1  What two functions does law perform? What are the two major divisions of the law?

2  What are the sources of the criminal law? Where would you find it?

3  List the seven principles of criminal law theory.

4  What is meant by *mens rea*? Give examples of defenses that may be used by defendants in which they deny that *mens rea* existed when the crime was committed.

5  What is meant by the "incorporation" of the Fourteenth Amendment to the U.S. Constitution?

### Key Terms and Cases

administrative regulations
case law
civil forfeiture
civil law
common law
constitution
double jeopardy
entrapment
exclusionary rule
fundamental fairness

inchoate crimes
incorporation
legal responsibility
*mens rea*
procedural criminal law
procedural due process
self-incrimination
statutes
strict liability

substantive criminal law
*Barron v. Baltimore*
*Escobedo v. Illinois*
*Gideon v. Wainwright*
*Mapp v. Ohio*
*Miranda v. Arizona*
*Powell v. Alabama*

### For Further Reading

Fletcher, George P. *A Crime of Self Defense: Bernhard Goetz and the Law on Trial.* New York: Free Press, 1988. An insightful examination of the legal issues involved in the Goetz case.

Katz, Leo. *Bad Acts and Guilty Minds.* Chicago: University of Chicago Press, 1987. Exploration of questions raised by the insanity defense.

Lewis, Anthony. *Gideon's Trumpet.* New York: Vintage Books, 1964. A classic examination of the case of *Gideon v. Wainwright* showing the process by which the issues came to the U.S. Supreme Court.

Morris, Norval. *Madness and the Criminal Law.* Chicago: University of Chicago Press, 1982. A stimulating and controversial examination of the insanity defense by a leading criminal justice scholar.

Simpson, Alfred W. Bain. *Cannibalism and the Common Law.* Chicago: University of Chicago Press, 1984. Exciting study of the case of *The Queen v. Dudley and Stephens* showing that there were many such incidents during the age of sail where punishment did not follow.

Wolfe, Linda. *Wasted: The Preppie Murder Case.* New York: Simon and Schuster, 1989. An in-depth examination of the arrest and trial of Robert Chambers for the murder of Jennifer Levin.

### Notes

1  Richard Moran, "His Insanity Plea Can't Free Dahmer," *Boston Globe*, 2 February 1992, 60.

2  *New York Times*, 20 September 1991, A–1.

3  *Miller v. United States*, 78 U.S. 268 (1871).

---

## Summary

offers a capsulized version of the chapter's major ideas.

## Questions for Review

allow you to test your understanding of specific material and express what *you* think about aspects of the criminal justice system.

## Key Terms and Cases

provide a quick means of testing your knowledge.

## For Further Reading

suggests up-to-date sources of information to assist with independent study or with research papers.

# Understanding the Realities of Crime and Justice

Several features of this book are designed to give you a vivid picture of the way the criminal justice system really works. In addition to the elements on these pages, **Appendix B, Understanding and Using Criminal Justice Data**, explains how to read graphs and other visual presentations. As you will discover, criminal justice is an empirical science that uses systematic techniques to collect and analyze information. By learning how to study and extrapolate from the data presented in charts and graphs, you will become a more skilled student of criminal justice.

## Real-Life Examples

—both historical and contemporary— are included throughout the book to help you envision and reflect upon the human implications of criminal justice policy. After all, the study of criminal justice is the study of real human beings in dramatic, sometimes life-and-death situations.

during one era found to be acceptable in another? Such issues need discussing because a theory explaining the sources of criminal law will have an important impact on assumptions concerning the nature of crime and the causes of criminal behavior.

A number of theories have been developed to explain the focus and functions of criminal laws and the social processes by which they evolve. These ideas can be divided into the consensus model and the conflict model.

The Salem witch trials of 1692 illustrate Durkheim's view that deviance tightens community bonds. To what extent is the prosecution of Dr. Jack Kevorkian, charged with assisting his patients in committing suicide, a contemporary example of consensus theory?

### Consensus: Law as an Expression of Values

The **consensus model** holds that criminal law reflects societal va... go beyond the immediate interests of particular groups and ind... Law is thus an expression of the social consciousness of the whol...

Consensus theory has been greatly influenced by the pioneer... ologist Emile Durkheim (see the accompanying Biography), wh... that groups in society—black and white, rich and poor—might... sorts of different interests but have underlying agreements on t... ues. From this perspective, laws are necessary to establish mor... aries in order to differentiate good members of the community... Legislators, as representatives of the people, formalize these val... criminal law. The law thus reflects the kind of conduct that a co... considers, at a particular time, to be "sufficiently condemnable"... legal punishments. From this perspective criminal law may be v... "a barometer of the moral and social thinking of a community."

As an example of consensus theories in action, we can loo... Puritan Massachusetts. Kai Erikson argues in the book *Waywar...* that three serious "crime waves" in seventeenth-century Mass... helped the colonists define the values of their society. During eac... periods—the Antinomian controversy of 1636, the Quaker pers...

**Chapter Two:** Crime, Victimization, and Cr...

## Graphics

are essential parts of the presentation in this book and require close study. The many flowcharts, graphs, tables, photographs, and other visual aids are carefully designed and captioned to illuminate the text.

**Figure 5.8**
**The felony apprehension process**
Apprehension of a felony suspect may result from a sequence of actions taken in response to the crime by patrol officers and detectives. Coordination of police response is important in solving major crimes.

3   *Follow-up investigation:* After a crime has been detected and a preliminary investigation has been made, a detective determines further action. In a typical big-city department, incident reports from the previous day are analyzed immediately the next morning. Assignments are distributed to individual investigators according to their specialties. These investigators study the information, weigh each informational factor, and determine whether the factors are sufficient to indicate that the crime can be solved.

A study of the Kansas City (Missouri) Police Department showed that although homicide, rape, and suicide received considerable attention, fewer than 50 percent of all reported crimes received more than a minimal half-hour investigation by detectives. In many of these cases, detectives merely reported the facts discovered by the patrol officers during the preliminary investigations.[43]

Detectives must make several discretionary decisions concerning any investigation. As already noted, a decision must be made about whether the preliminary investigation has produced enough information to warrant a follow-up investigation. Decisions also must be made about the crime categories that should receive special attention and whether an investigation should be discontinued. Steven Brandl found that in burglary and robbery follow-up investigations the value of the lost property and the detective's expectation that the case would be resolved through an arrest were the primary factors influencing the amount of time and effort spent in solving the crime.[44]

When a full-scale investigation is thought warranted, a wider search—referred to as a "cold" search—for evidence or weapons is undertaken: witnesses may be reinterviewed, contact made with inform-

**192**   **Part Two:** Police

the work of the police, although attitudes differ significantly by race (see Figure 6.4). Even in economically depressed inner-city areas where the police may be viewed as the tools of an unjust society, most inhabitants see them as protectors of their persons and property. Indeed, "the single most striking fact about the attitudes of citizens, black and white, toward the police is that in general these attitudes are positive, not negative."[16] Despite these findings, the police themselves do not believe that the public regards their vocation as honorable or their work as just. They feel that they are looked upon with suspicion, in part because they have been given the authority to use force to ensure compliance. Some scholars have argued that police cynicism increases their desire to use force on citizens.[17]

Throughout the publications of police organizations runs the theme that the public is extremely critical of law enforcement agents. But the general public is not the only group that is unappreciative of the police; other actors in the criminal justice system are often cited. Lawyers, prosecutors, and judges demean the officer's status by failing to treat the police with professional respect and by not dealing seriously with offenders whose behavior may have endangered the patrol officer. Part of the burden of being a police officer is that one is beset by self-doubt about professional status and worth in the public mind. This burden heightens the pressures on individual officers to isolate themselves within the police community.

Because they believe that the public is hostile to them and that the nature of law work aggravates the hostility, the police tend to separate themselves from the public, developing strong in-group ties. The police culture also encourages the strong bonding that commonly occurs among people who deal with violence. This solidarity "permits fallible men to perform an arduous and difficult task, and ... places the highest value upon the obligation to back up and support a fellow officer."[18]

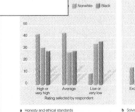

a  Honesty and ethical standards          b  Solving crime

**228**   **Part Two:** Police

## Close-Ups

complement the text discussion by presenting
provocative accounts from journalists, prisoners,
judges, attorneys, and others that allow you to
see the reality of the criminal justice system from
a variety of perspectives.

## Biographies

highlight the careers of influential
figures from many disciplines who have
contributed to the development of the
field of criminal justice.

### Battered Women, Reluctant Police

As Joanne Tremins was moving some belongings out
of her ramshackle house on South Main Street [Torrington,
Connecticut], her 350-pound husband ran over, grabbed the family cat and strangled it in front of Tremins and her children.

For more than three years, Tremins said, she had complained
to Torrington police about beatings and threats from her husband.
Instead of arresting him, she said, the police acted "like marriage
counselors."

The cat attack finally prompted police to arrest Jeffrey Tremins
on a minor charge of cruelty to animals. But four days later, outside a
local cafe, he repeatedly punched his wife in the face and smashed
her against a wall, fracturing her nose and causing lacerations and
contusions to her face and left arm.

That Joanne Tremins is suing this New England town of 34,000
is not without historical irony. For it was here that Tracey Thurman ...
won a $2 million judgment against the police department in a federal
civil rights case that has revolutionized law enforcement attitudes toward domestic violence.

The Thurman case marked the first time that a battered woman
was allowed to sue police in federal court for failing to protect her
from her husband. The ruling held that such a failure amounts to sex
discrimination and violates the Fourteenth Amendment.

The resulting spate of lawsuits has prompted police departments nationwide to reexamine their long-standing reluctance to

make arrests in domestic assault cases, particularly
when the wife refuses to press charges. State and
local lawmakers, facing soaring municipal insurance
costs, are also taking notice.

Here in hilly Torrington ... Police Chief Mahlon
C. Sabo said [the Thurman case] had a "devastating" effect
on the town and his seventy-member force. "The police somehow, over the years, became the mediators," said Sabo. "There was a
feeling that it's between husband and wife. In most cases, after the officer left, the wife usually got battered around for calling the police in
the first place."

Although the law now requires them to make arrests, police officers here said, the courts toss out many domestic cases for the same
reason that long hampered police.

"Unfortunately, many women just want the case dropped and
fail to recognize they're in a dangerous situation," said Anthony J.
Salius, director of the family division of Connecticut Superior Court.
"If she really doesn't want to prosecute, it's very difficult to have a
trial because we don't have a witness."

Nearly five years after the attack by her estranged husband,
Tracey Thurman remains scarred and partially paralyzed from multiple stab wounds to the chest, neck and face. Charles Thurman was
sentenced to fourteen years in prison.

For eight months before the stabbing, Thurman repeatedly
threatened his wife and their son, two. He worked at Skee's Diner, a
few blocks from police headquarters, and repeatedly boasted to policemen he was serving that he intended to kill his wife, according to
the lawsuit.

---

For too long, criminal justice agencies, and perhaps society as a whole,
viewed domestic violence as a "private" affair best settled within the family (see the Close-Up "Battered Women, Reluctant Police"). Concern was
often expressed that official involvement would only make the situation
more difficult for the victim because she would have to face the possibility of reprisal.

From the viewpoint of most police departments, domestic violence
was thought to be a "no-win" situation in which officers responding to
calls for help were often set upon by one or both disputants. If an arrest
was made, the police found that the victim often refused to cooperate
with a prosecution arising from the incident. Further, entering a residence
to handle such an emotion-laden incident was thought to be more dangerous than answering calls to investigate "real" criminal behavior. The
belief was widespread that intervention in family disputes was a leading

---

**Cesare Lombroso**

**B**orn in Verona, Italy, in 1836, Cesare
Lombroso became one of the most eulo-
gized and attacked criminologists of all
time. His work brought about a shift from
a legalistic preoccupation with crime to
a scientific study of the criminal.

As a professor of psychiatry and
criminal anthropology at the University
of Pavia from 1862 to 1876, Lombroso
founded the biological school of criminology, often referred to as the Italian
school. Lombroso maintained that certain people are born criminals. These
"throwbacks" to a more primitive stage
of human evolution can be identified
by physical characteristics. He believed, too, that crime is the result of a
disease that can be inherited or
brought on by social factors. The work
of Lombroso and his followers encouraged the development of more humane
treatment programs for criminals.
Lombroso's ideas are best expressed
in *Criminal Man* (1876), *The Female
Offender* (1895), and *Crime: Its Causes
and Remedies* (1912).

It is important to underst...
sation because their assumpti...
laws are enforced, guilt or in...
punished. As we examine eac...
sider the implications for crim...
For example, if biological the...
then governmental policies...
through genetic analysis and...
adopted. On the other hand, th...
lead to governmental policies...
ucation, and provide job train...

### Biological Explanations

Cesare Lombroso's (1836–1909...
in the physical characteristics...
from the law-abiding citizen (s...
lieved that offenders are *born*...
more primitive and savage p...
culty adjusting to modern soci...
cial incompetence and by the r...
the criminal is thrust into illeg...

With the development of...
physical characteristics to the i...
intelligence level and mental...
believed that criminals commit...
logical urges they inherited f...
nologists with this orientation...
the correspondence between t...
ily members.

Two studies published in...
titious name of Jukes and the...
dence that genetic deficiencie...
succeeding generations to lives...
than one thousand descendant...
he dubbed the "mother of cri...
pers, 60 thieves, 7 murderers,...
eases, 50 prostitutes, and ot...
collected by Henry H. Godda...
family, a group of relatives...
Kallikak, contained more crim...
marriage into a "good" family...

These early studies have b...
seriously in their time. In many states crime-control policies were enacted
to require that habitual offenders be sterilized, which was done under the
assumption that crime could be controlled if hereditary factors were not
transmitted. This practice was declared unconstitutional by the U.S.
Supreme Court in *Skinner* v. *Oklahoma* (1942).[42]

# Thinking Critically About Crime and Justice

Three key themes introduced in Chapter 1 take you beyond mastering factual content to a more critical appreciation of criminal justice in the United States. In addition, **Comparative Perspectives** and **A Question of Ethics** discussions allow you to compare the American system of criminal justice with practices in other countries and to probe difficult ethical questions faced by police, prosecutors, and others.

## Criminal justice is an interdisciplinary science.

Among the principal disciplines that contribute to the study of crime and justice are history, economics, political science, psychology, sociology, criminology, and law. This convergence of perspectives helps to make criminal justice a fascinating course of study for scholars and students of many backgrounds and interests.

## Criminal justice inevitably involves issues of public policy and therefore politics.

Some officials of the criminal justice system, such as many judges and district attorneys, are elected to their offices. More broadly, in a democratic society, issues such as crime rates, the rights of accused criminals and victims of crime, and the merits of the death penalty are inescapably political.

## The concept of *system* is an essential tool for understanding how criminal justice is administered in practice.

Throughout the text, a systems perspective illuminates the way decisions are actually made in criminal justice, including why suspects are arrested or let go, convicted or acquitted at trial, kept in prison or released on probation or parole.

**Figure 1.1**
**Criminal justice: an interdisciplinary social science**
We can understand the interdisciplinary nature of criminal justice by examining the theoretical orientation of each field and examples of its research contributions.

**HISTORY**

**Theoretical Orientation**
Examination of social forces as they have influenced the development of criminal justice institutions and processes.

**Research Examples**
• David Rothman, *Discovery of the Asylum.* Invention of the penitentiary in 1830 shifted punishment to institutions and away from community corrections.
• Eric H. Monkkonen, *Police in Urban America, 1860–1920.* Urban police used to provide a number of social services in addition to crime control. Policies during this period emphasized the importance of the police maintaining close links to the community.

**PSYCHOLOGY**

**Theoretical Orientation**
The influence of the human organism, especially neurological factors and personality, on criminal behavior.

**Research Examples**
• Hans Jurgen Eysenck, *Crime and Personality.* Conscience is instrumental in making us behave in moral and socially acceptable ways. Rehabilitative treatments can help criminals modify their behavior.
• Karl Menninger, *The Crime of Punishment.* Criminal behavior is an illness of the mind. Offenders should be treated by medical practitioners, and prisons should be transformed into treatment centers.

**ECONOMICS**

**Theoretical Orientation**
Application of economic principles to criminal behavior and the instruments of criminal justice.

**Research Examples**
• Gary Becker, "Crime and Punishment: An Economic Analysis." An economic framework can be used to make decisions about the allocation of criminal justice resources.
• Peter Reuter, *Disorganized Crime: The Economics of the Visible Hand.* Bookmaking, numbers, and loan-sharking provide markets for the distribution of illegal goods. The violence and corruption of the Mafia is generally defeated by the "invisible hand" of the market.

**POLITICAL SCIENCE**

**LAW/JURISPRUDENCE**

**Theoretical Orientation**
The role of law in the administration of justice.

**Research Examples**
• Norval Morris, *Madness and the Criminal Law.* This examination of the insanity defense sets forth principles for dealing with the mentally ill who have committed crimes.
• Andrew von Hirsch, *Doing Justice: The Choice of Punishments.* There should be a return to retribution (deserved punishment) as the goal of the criminal sanction.

**SOCIOLOGY/CRIMINOLOGY**

**Theoretical Orientation**
Analysis of social and cultural influences on criminal behavior and the agencies of justice.

**Research Examples**
• Gresham Sykes, *The Society of Captives.* Prisoners form their own society with values, norms, and roles. The pains of incarceration cause inmates to adapt to their environment.
• Gary Kleck, *Point Blank: Guns and Violence in America.* Gun control policies will not reduce violence unless stricter background checks, owner registration, and dealer licensing are required.

**Theoretical Orientation**
The impact of politics on the administration of justice.

**Research Examples**
• James Q. Wilson, *Varieties of Police Behavior.* Politics influences policing mainly through the selection of police executives. Political factors influence the style of policing in various types of communities.
• John Dilulio, Jr. *Governing Prisons.* Rather than depending on inmate leadership to maintain control, prison managers should invest time and energy in their position.

**Comparative Perspectives sections** provide a new way of looking at the American system by contrasting it with criminal justice practices in other countries.

## Corporal Punishment in Singapore

A Singapore court's decision to sentence an American teenager, Michael Fay, to receive a flogging for vandalizing cars with spray paint produced a predictable nod of approval from many Singaporeans, long accustomed to their government's firm hand. For many Americans the punishment seemed unduly harsh, yet others expressed the view that this might be the answer to our crime problem.

Fay was sentenced to six strokes of the cane; four months in prison; and a $2,230 fine after pleading guilty to two counts of vandalism, two counts of mischief, and one count of possessing stolen property. Canings, the term for floggings, in Singapore are carried out by a jailer trained in martial arts who uses a moistened, four-foot rattan cane. The offender is stripped, bound by the hands and feet to a wooden trestle. Pads covering his kidneys and groin are the only protection from the cane. Should he pass out, a doctor will revive him before the caning continues. The wounds generally take two weeks to heal; scarring is permanent.

(2) searches during field interrogation, (3) searches of automobiles under special conditions, (4) seizures of evidence that is in "plain view," and (5) searches when consent is given. As we see in A Question of Ethics, warrantless searches raise a number of ethical concerns in police work.

*Incident to a Lawful Arrest*   When an officer has observed a crime or believes that one has been committed, an arrest may be made and a search conducted without a warrant. It is the fact of the lawful arrest that justifies the exception to the Fourth Amendment.[63] In part, the rationale for this exception is the possibility that the suspect will destroy evidence unless swift action is taken. But in *Chimel v. California* (1969), the Supreme Court also said that such a search is limited to the person of the arrestee and the area within the arrestee's "immediate control," defined as that area "from within which he might [obtain] a weapon or something that could have been used as evidence against him" in order to destroy it.[64] Thus, if the police are holding a person in one room of a house, they are not authorized to search and seize property in another part of the house, away from the suspect's physical presence.

*Field Interrogation*   The police often stop and interrogate persons without knowing any facts to justify an arrest. Clearly, much police activity involves interrogating people who are acting suspiciously or who are disturbing the public order. These street encounters, often called "threshold inquiries," allow for brief questioning and frisking: patting down the outside of the suspect's clothing to ascertain whether there is a concealed weapon.

In the case of *Terry v. Ohio* (1968), the Supreme Court upheld the stop-and-frisk procedure.[65] Here, a police officer noticed two men taking turns looking into a store window and then conferring. A third man joined them. Suspecting that a crime was about to be committed, the officer confronted them, removed pistols from two of the men, and charged them with carrying concealed weapons. The court ruled that it was a constitutional search since the officer had stopped them for the purpose of detention or interrogation and that, because he believed he was dealing with armed and dangerous individuals, the frisk could be conducted for his own safety or that of others.

On the basis of *Terry* and subsequent decisions, it is now accepted that a police officer is justified in stopping and questioning an individual

*A Question of Ethics*

Officer Mike Groton knocked on the apartment door. He and fellow officer Howard Reece had gone to this rundown part of town to arrest Richard Watson on the basis of evidence from an informer that Watson was a major drug seller. "Police officers, open up," said Groton. The door opened slowly, and a small, tense woman peered into the hallway.

"Ma'am, we have a warrant for the arrest of Richard Watson. Is he here?"

"No. I don't know any Watson," was the answer.

"Well, let us in so that we can see for ourselves."

Groton and Reece entered the apartment. Reece quickly proceeded to a back bedroom. The window leading to a fire escape was open and the bed looked as though someone had left it in a rush. Reece started to poke around the room, opening bureau drawers and searching the closet. In the back of the closet he noticed a woman's pocketbook hanging on a hook. He opened it and found three glassine packages of a white powder.

"Hey Mike, look what I found," he called. Groton came into the bedroom. "Looks like heroin to me," said Reece. "Too bad we can't use it."

"Why can't we use it? This is the place."

"But the warrant only specified the arrest of Watson. It didn't say anything about searching his closet."

"Let's just keep those packets. When we catch him we can 'find' it in his pocket."

What are the issues here? Can the officers keep the heroin packets? Is bending the rules acceptable in some circumstances? If so, do these circumstances warrant it? What should the officers do?

nt of good time that can be earned varies among the y from five to ten days a month. The amounts are written codes of some states and stipulated in department of cordirectives in others. In some states, when ninety days of arned, they are vested; that is, they cannot be taken away re misbehavior. Prisoners who then violate the rules risk s not vested.

Sentences   In accord with the goal of rehabilitation, ed corrections for much of the past half century, state legdopted indeterminate (often termed *indefinite*) sentences. the notion that correctional personnel must be given the ake a release decision on the grounds of successful treates with indeterminate sentences stipulate a minimum and ount of time to be served in prison: one to five years, three to twenty years, one year to life, and so on. At the time of e offender knows only the range and that he or she will gible for parole at some point after the minimum term me) has been served.

*Terry v. Ohio* (1968)
A police officer may stop and frisk an individual if it is reasonable to suspect that a crime has been committed.

**A Question of Ethics boxes** explore the ethical dilemmas that arise within the administration of justice and emphasize that the criminal justice system requires not only that decisions be made within the framework of the law but also that such decisions must be consistent with the ethical norms of society.

# To Further Support Your Learning...

STUDY GUIDE    CHRISTOPHER E. SMITH

THE

AMERICAN

SYSTEM

OF

*CRIMINAL JUSTICE*

SEVENTH EDITION

GEORGE F. COLE

**The Study Guide**
(by Christopher E. Smith, Michigan State University) accompanying this text offers learning objectives; an outline; and review exercises that highlight major terms, case law, significant individuals, and key discussions and concepts related to each chapter of the text. Ask your campus bookstore manager to order a copy of this highly recommended learning tool for you.

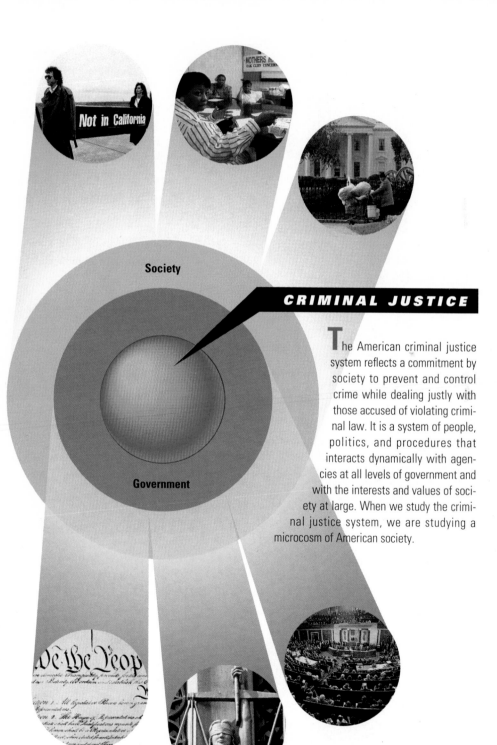

**Society**

**Government**

## CRIMINAL JUSTICE

The American criminal justice system reflects a commitment by society to prevent and control crime while dealing justly with those accused of violating criminal law. It is a system of people, politics, and procedures that interacts dynamically with agencies at all levels of government and with the interests and values of society at large. When we study the criminal justice system, we are studying a microcosm of American society.

# The Criminal Justice Process

The American system of criminal justice is a response to a problem that has required attention in all societies from time immemorial: crime. In order to understand how the system works and why crime persists despite our best efforts to control it, we need to examine both the nature of criminal behavior and the functioning of the justice system itself. As we will see, the reality of crime and justice involves much more than "cops and robbers," the details of legal codes, and the penalties prescribed for lawbreaking. From defining what behavior counts as criminal to determining the fate of those offenders who are caught, the process of criminal justice is a *social* process that is subject to many influences other than written law.

Part 1 introduces the study of this process and provides a broad framework within which to analyze how our society—through its police, courts, and corrections—attempts to deal with the age-old problem of crime.

PART ONE

# Crime and Justice in America

**Newspaper headlines tell the story: "Killings Soar in Big Cities Across U.S.," "Shopowners Demand Foot Patrol," "Drug Turf War Yields Violence," "Neighbors Unite Against Crime," "Prison Population Reaches New High."** Television news programs depict urban neighborhoods ravaged by drugs and crime, small towns where shootouts have occurred, and frightened citizens expressing fears about leaving their homes at night.

One might hope that citizens of the "land of the free" could live without having to devote great physical and psychological energies, let alone resources, to personal protection; but for many Americans the possibility of being victimized by criminals is ever present. When in 1973 the National Advisory Commission on Criminal Justice Standards and Goals set as a target the reduction of crime over the ensuing ten years, it stated that a time would come in the immediate future when

- A couple can walk in the evening in their neighborhood without fear of assault and robbery.
- A family can go away for the weekend without fear of returning to a house ransacked by burglars.
- A woman can take a night job without fear of being raped on her way to or from work.
- Every citizen can live without fear of being brutalized by unknown assailants.[1]

More than two decades later, however, these goals are more elusive than ever.

The study of criminal justice offers a fascinating examination of a crucial social problem. It is a challenge to a democracy to develop policies that deal with **crime** while still preserving the ideals of the rule of law and justice. Chapter 1 presents the three themes of this book: (1) crime and justice are public policy issues, (2) criminal justice is an interdisciplinary social science, and (3) criminal justice can best be analyzed as a social system. To build a foundation for the chapters that follow, we will look at the goals and organization of the criminal justice system and at the flow of decision making as a person is arrested and moved through the system. Concepts such as system and exchange will aid our understanding. As you read this chapter be aware that we will seek to answer a series of questions.

**crime**
A specific act of commission or omission in violation of the law, for which a punishment is prescribed.

## Questions for Inquiry

- How are public policies regarding crime formed?
- What disciplines contribute to criminal justice as an academic and research field of study?
- What are the goals of the criminal justice system?
- How is criminal justice pursued in the federal system of government in the United States?
- What are the major characteristics of criminal justice as a social system?
- What are the primary agencies of criminal justice in the United States and how do they interrelate?
- What is the flow of decision making from arrest to correction and release?
- How do the Crime Control and Due Process models of criminal justice help us understand the reality of the system?

## Crime and Justice as Public Policy Issues

Crime and justice are crucial policy issues in a country such as the United States where there is a tension between the need to maintain public order and security and the need to protect such precious values as individual liberties, the rule of law, and democratic government. Although there is widespread agreement in American society that crime is a serious problem, there is no consensus on how to deal with it. Some people believe that the answer lies in stricter enforcement of the law through the expansion of police forces and the enactment of punitive measures that will result in the swift and certain punishment of criminals. The holders of this conservative view, politically dominant during the 1980s, argue that we must strengthen crime control, which they assert has been undermined by U.S. Supreme Court rulings and liberal programs that have weakened traditional values of responsibility and family. In opposition to this view are those who argue that the strengthening of crime control has endangered the cherished values of due process and justice. Liberals say that such an approach is ineffective in reducing crime and that the answer lies in reshaping the lives of individual offenders and changing the social conditions from which criminal behavior springs.

## The Politics of Crime and Justice

Although we may argue the pros and cons of various criminal justice policies, we must recognize that they are developed in the political arena at the national, state, and local levels. That crime is a political issue was shown in the 1988 presidential campaign between Republican George Bush and Democratic challenger Michael Dukakis, then governor of Massachusetts. Much to the chagrin of the Dukakis camp, a Bush television campaign commercial pictured convicted murderer Willie Horton, a man who had walked away from a Massachusetts prison furlough program and traveled to Maryland, where he raped a woman and assaulted her husband. In the minds of many Americans, Willie Horton epitomized their concerns and fears about crime, especially that committed by minorities. Many argued that Horton's criminality was possible because of the policies of liberal politicians who were "soft" on crime. As a result, many commentators believe, the public response to the Horton commercial contributed significantly to Dukakis's defeat.

The impact of Willie Horton on presidential politics is one of the more dramatic illustrations of the relationship between criminal justice and politics. But just as important are the more "routine" linkages. Penal codes and the budgets of criminal justice agencies are passed by legislators who are responsive to the voters. Congress appropriates millions to assist states and cities to wage the war on drugs but prohibits any expenditures on legal counsel for poor defendants. At state and local levels, many criminal justice officials are elected, rather than appointed, and decisions by the police, prosecution, judiciary, and corrections are influenced by community concerns. Candidates for public office often use the issue of law and order to gain votes. A city council may increase the budget of the police while cutting back on appropriations for social services.

In short, at every level of government criminal justice involves public policy decisions that are deeply affected by politics. If we think of justice as a "good" (that is, as a kind of product) created by the legal system, then we can say that **political considerations** explain, to a large extent, *who* gets *how much* of that good and *in what ways* within the setting of the local community.

**political considerations**
Matters taken into account in the formulation of public policies and the making of choices among competing values—who gets what portion of the good (justice) produced by the system, when, and how.

## Controlling Crime in a Democracy

More important than the distinctions between liberal and conservative approaches to crime policies is the necessity that any approach to crime be developed within the context of American democratic ideals. The way we control crime represents a basic test of our ideals. The administration of justice in a democracy can be distinguished from that in an authoritarian state by the extent and form of protections provided for the accused as guilt is determined and punishment is imposed.

Perhaps the most important question confronting American society is how to control crime while preserving the rule of law and the elements of freedom and justice that define a democracy. Citizens cannot enjoy their freedom, for example, if they are afraid to walk the streets and must spend a lot to protect themselves against crime. By the same token, freedom is too precious to be infringed upon by unconstitutional actions of law enforcement agencies or by citizens taking the law into their own hands. Similarly, those wrongly accused of crime do not receive justice if they are convicted; offenders who have paid their debt to society do not receive justice if they are treated as ex-cons rather than as citizens. Though much of our crime problem would disappear if the police were to receive a massive allocation of resources and if limitations on their actions were removed, such a public policy would create a police state and a loss of freedom and justice.

Just as governmental policies with regard to foreign affairs, health care, and education are developed in the political arena, so too are those designed to deal with the crime problem. At every level of government we can see the linkage between politics and criminal justice. That is to be expected in a democracy where policies in the public interest emerge through the actions of citizens and their representatives. As one of the major themes of this text, policy issues will be explored in succeeding chapters.

The political and policy dimensions of the problem of crime suggest that the understanding of criminal justice can involve contributions from diverse fields of study such as political science, economics, and history. This point brings us to a second major theme of this book, that the study of criminal justice is an *interdisciplinary* social science.

## Criminal Justice as an Interdisciplinary Social Science

**criminologist**
A scholar who uses the scientific method to study the nature, cause, amount, and control of criminal behavior.

The contemporary study of criminal justice is an academic, research, and policy field that is differentiated from previous scientific attention to the problem of crime by three characteristics. First, criminal justice is interdisciplinary. In the mid-1960s, the study of crime and justice, previously the domain of **criminologists**, was suddenly infused with scholars from such disciplines as political science, history, law, economics, and psychology. Although some members of these disciplines had been associated with earlier criminological approaches, the vast proportion brought to their new study many theories, concepts, and research methodologies from their parent field. A second characteristic is the extension of the field to include all aspects of crime and the administration of justice. Whereas earlier the primary focus had been on criminal behavior and its correction, contemporary scholars study all the organizations and processes that constitute the criminal justice system. Finally, the mission of the criminal justice field includes developing explanatory theory and applying that theory to crime and justice policies.

This shift in the focus and boundaries of criminal justice studies was spurred by the 1967 report of the President's Commission on Law Enforcement and Administration of Justice.[2] The commission was created by President Lyndon Johnson when the public became concerned about rising crime rates during the mid-1960s. For the first time a prestigious national commission analyzed the administration of criminal justice as an interrelated system and not as a set of separate entities. This analysis served to broaden the perspective of investigators. Crime was no longer viewed as a problem primarily for the police. The establishment of the Law Enforcement Assistance Administration (LEAA) in 1969 and the appropriation by Congress of funds for research on crime and justice encouraged new efforts to determine the basis of criminal behavior, to understand decision-making processes within the administration of justice, and to evaluate crime-reduction policies. A large number of scholars were thereby encouraged to devote their energies to the crime problem.

The interdisciplinary nature of criminal justice that has emerged during the past twenty-five years can be understood by recognizing the essential components of the field, summarized in Figure 1.1. Because crime involves human behavior, key research findings and concepts have been drawn from the behavioral and social sciences of *sociology* and *psychology* as well as from *history*. Because the institutions of criminal justice (police, courts, corrections) compose an organizational system, useful concepts have come from the *administrative sciences* (public administration, management). Of course, criminal justice operates under law; accordingly, its boundaries are formed by the actions of legislators and the decisions of judges, so that *legal studies* are an indispensable part of the discipline. As an arm of government, criminal justice operates within the political context, with policies, resources, and officials emerging through electoral, legislative, and executive processes; accordingly, *political science* contributes important insights. Finally, *economics* contributes principles such as cost/benefit ratios, which are applied to our understanding of criminal behavior, organizational incentives, and deterrence. The individual contributions and perspectives of these disciplines have made criminal justice a dynamic field.

It is important to understand the tasks that scholars in criminal justice have undertaken. The press and the public may decry the perceived rise in crime, and reformers may argue for changes in how justice is administered, but to deal with the issues of crime and justice effectively we must base our decisions on knowledge rather than on mere opinion or belief. The field of criminal justice aims to supply knowledge based on sound principles of social science.

**Figure 1.1**
**Criminal justice: an interdisciplinary social science**
We can understand the interdisciplinary nature of criminal justice by examining the theoretical orientation of each field and examples of its research contributions.

### HISTORY

**Theoretical Orientation**
Examination of social forces as they have influenced the development of criminal justice institutions and processes.

**Research Examples**
• David Rothman, *Discovery of the Asylum*. Invention of the penitentiary in 1830 shifted punishment to institutions and away from community corrections.
• Eric H. Monkkonen, *Police in Urban America, 1860–1920*. Urban police used to provide a number of social services in addition to crime control. Policies during this period emphasized the importance of the police maintaining close links to the community.

### PSYCHOLOGY

**Theoretical Orientation**
The influence of the human organism, especially neurological factors and personality, on criminal behavior.

**Research Examples**
• Hans Jurgen Eysenck, *Crime and Personality*. Conscience is instrumental in making us behave in moral and socially acceptable ways. Rehabilitative treatments can help criminals modify their behavior.
• Karl Menninger, *The Crime of Punishment*. Criminal behavior is an illness of the mind. Offenders should be treated by medical practitioners, and prisons should be transformed into treatment centers.

### ECONOMICS

**Theoretical Orientation**
Application of economic principles to criminal behavior and the instruments of criminal justice.

**Research Examples**
• Gary Becker, "Crime and Punishment: An Economic Analysis." An economic framework can be used to make decisions about the allocation of criminal justice resources.
• Peter Reuter, *Disorganized Crime: The Economics of the Visible Hand*. Bookmaking, numbers, and loan-sharking provide markets for the distribution of illegal goods. The violence and corruption of the Mafia is generally defeated by the "invisible hand" of the market.

### LAW/JURISPRUDENCE

**Theoretical Orientation**
The role of law in the administration of justice.

**Research Examples**
• Norval Morris, *Madness and the Criminal Law*. This examination of the insanity defense sets forth principles for dealing with the mentally ill who have committed crimes.
• Andrew von Hirsch, *Doing Justice: The Choice of Punishments*. There should be a return to retribution (deserved punishment) as the goal of the criminal sanction.

### SOCIOLOGY/CRIMINOLOGY

**Theoretical Orientation**
Analysis of social and cultural influences on criminal behavior and the agencies of justice.

**Research Examples**
• Gresham Sykes, *The Society of Captives*. Prisoners form their own society with values, norms, and roles. The pains of incarceration cause inmates to adapt to their environment.
• Gary Kleck, *Point Blank: Guns and Violence in America*. Gun control policies will not reduce violence unless stricter background checks, owner registration, and dealer licensing are required.

### POLITICAL SCIENCE

**Theoretical Orientation**
The impact of politics on the administration of justice.

**Research Examples**
• James Q. Wilson, *Varieties of Police Behavior*. Politics influences policing mainly through the selection of police executives. Political factors influence the style of policing in various types of communities.
• John Dilulio, Jr. *Governing Prisons*. Rather than depending on inmate leadership to maintain control, prison managers should invest time and energy in their position.

First, we must know something about the causes of crime and the effects of efforts to control it. Second, we need to learn how the criminal justice system operates in dispensing justice, not in theory, but in real life. That means we must carefully examine the history and operations of the police, courts, and corrections and the social forces that created them. The reality of criminal justice in the United States will shock many people, but only when we understand how the justice machinery functions can we make realistic proposals for change.

The description of criminal justice as a social system is important, but criminal justice specialists have a third task; they must also be able to analyze *why* the process operates as it does. They must draw on the literature of a wide range of scholarly disciplines to coalesce theories and concepts that will help them comprehend reality and predict the probable course of future actions. Social analysis is an ongoing search to determine why people act as they do. When the roles played by the multitude of actors in the vast criminal justice system are understood, new and different approaches can be explored to achieve the goal of maintaining both order and human freedom.

## Goals of Criminal Justice

Having now seen that the study of criminal justice is an interdisciplinary social science, we turn to a first look at the system of criminal justice in the United States. We begin our inquiry by asking what goals the system serves. Although these goals may seem straightforward, it can be difficult to specify exactly what they mean in practice.

In 1967 the President's Commission on Law Enforcement and Administration of Justice described the criminal justice system as an apparatus society uses to "enforce the standards of conduct necessary to protect individuals and the community."[3] This statement serves as the basis for our discussion of the goals of the criminal justice system. Although there is much debate on the purposes of criminal justice, three goals are prominent: doing justice, controlling crime, and preventing crime. We will look at each of these goals and then consider some of the implications for the operations of the system.

### Doing Justice

We must first recognize that *doing justice* is the basis for the system. Without a system founded on *justice* there would be little difference between criminal justice in the United States and that in authoritarian countries. Doing justice assumes fairness. It requires that the rights of individuals be upheld and that persons be given what they deserve by virtue of their criminal conduct as judged by the law. Thus doing justice at least implies that (1) offenders will be held fully accountable for their actions, (2) the rights of persons who have contact with the system will be protected, (3) like offenses will be treated alike, and (4) officials will take into account relevant differences among offenders and offenses.[4]

The goals of controlling and preventing crime cannot be accomplished solely by the police, courts, and corrections. All citizens must be involved.

The requirement of doing justice is a tall order, and many will point to defects in the American system. Justice demands that the rights of both the accused and actual offenders be upheld, that officials follow procedures defined by the law, that punishments be designed to give offenders what they deserve, and that officials be allowed to individualize the way they handle cases. In a democracy, a system that places as paramount the doing of justice is viewed by citizens as legitimate and is thus able to pursue the secondary goals of controlling and preventing crime.

## Controlling Crime

The criminal justice system is designed to control crime by apprehending, prosecuting, convicting, and punishing those members of the community who do not live according to the law. An important constraint on the system in our society, however, is that efforts to control crime must be carried out within the framework of law. The criminal law not only defines what is illegal but also outlines the rights of citizens and prescribes the procedures that officials must use as they attempt to achieve the system's goals.

In any city or town we can see the goal of crime control being actively pursued: a police officer walking a beat, a patrol car racing through a darkened street, an arrest being made outside a neighborhood bar, lawyers advocating points of law before a judge, probation officers visiting clients, and the forbidding gloom of a maximum security prison. Taking action against wrongdoers helps to control crime, but the system must also employ strategies to prevent crimes from happening.

## Preventing Crime

The criminal justice goal of preventing crime can be achieved through various strategies. Perhaps most important is the deterring effect of both the doing justice and crime control goals. The actions of the police, courts, and corrections not only punish those individuals who violate the law, but, in so doing, also provide examples that are likely to deter others from committing wrongful acts. As will be discussed extensively in Chapter 12, deterrence is a much-disputed concept, but it is assumed to be a major factor in crime prevention. For example, a racing patrol car not only is responding to a crime situation; the presence of the police vehicle also serves as a warning that law enforcement is at hand. It is difficult, however, to prove scientifically that deterrence succeeds because it is impossible to show how many people do not commit crimes due to the threat of sanctions. Many law-abiding people might refrain from criminal behavior for other reasons than deterrence.

Crime prevention is also dependent upon the actions of citizens. Unfortunately, many Americans do not take the steps necessary to protect themselves and their property. People often leave homes and vehicles unlocked, do not use alarm systems, and walk in dangerous unlighted areas. By not taking simple precautions to prevent criminality, Americans can become crime victims.

Citizens must be actively engaged in preventing crime, although they do not have the authority to enforce the law. Society has given this responsibility to the criminal justice system. Thus, citizens must rely upon the police to stop criminals; they cannot take the law into their own hands (see A Question of Ethics).

The ways in which American institutions have evolved to achieve the goals of doing justice, controlling crime, and preventing crime lead to a series of choices. In the pursuit of criminal justice goals, decisions must be made that reflect legal, political, social, and moral values. As we try to understand the system, we must be aware of the possible conflicts among these values and the implications of choosing one value over another. The tasks assigned to the criminal justice system could be eased considerably if they were clearly determined so that citizens and officials

### A Question of Ethics

After his jewelry store had been burglarized for the third time in less than six months, Tom Henderson was frustrated. The police were of little help, merely telling him that they would have a patrol officer keep watch during nightly rounds. Tom had added new locks and an electronic security system. After unlocking his shop one morning he saw that he had been cleaned out again. He looked around the store to see how the thief had entered, as the door was locked and evidently the security alarm had not sounded. Suddenly he noticed that the glass in a skylight was broken.

"Damn, I'll fix him this time," cursed Henderson.

That evening after replacing the glass, he stripped the insulation from an electric cord and strung it around and across the frame of the skylight. He pulled the cord into a socket, locked the store, and went home.

Two weeks later when he entered the store and flipped the light switch nothing happened. He walked toward the fuse box. It was then that he noticed the burned body lying on the floor below the skylight.

What are the limits to which a person can go to "protect his castle"? If the police are unable to solve a crime problem, then is it ethical for individuals to take matters into their own hands?

could act with a precise understanding of their responsibilities and obligations. Making such easy translations of wishes into reality is not characteristic of human institutions.

## Criminal Justice in a Federal System

We have already noted that criminal justice is an inherently political institution. How does the political system of the United States influence the enforcement of the law, the trying of defendants, and the correction of offenders?

Of primary importance in the American system of criminal justice is the federal governmental structure created in 1789 with the ratification of the U.S. Constitution. The Constitution created a delicate political agreement. The national government was given certain powers—to raise an army, to coin money, to make treaties with foreign countries, and so forth. All other powers were retained by the states. In particular, nowhere in the Constitution are there specific references to criminal justice agencies of the national government. Yet we all are familiar with the Federal Bureau of Investigation (FBI). In addition, criminal cases are often tried in United States district courts, which are federal courts, and the Federal Bureau of Prisons operates institutions from coast to coast. Nevertheless, most criminal justice activity actually occurs at the local level. Next we look more closely at how the federal system affects the administration of justice in the United States.

### Two Justice Systems

The United States has two distinct criminal justice systems—national and state. Both systems are involved in enforcing laws, trying criminal cases, and punishing offenders, but they do so on different authority, and their activities vary greatly in scope. Criminal laws are written and enforced primarily by agencies of the states (including counties and municipalities), yet the rights of defendants are protected by the constitutions of both state and national governments. Although approximately 85 percent of criminal cases are heard in state courts, certain offenses—drug violations and transportation of a kidnap victim across state lines, for example—are violations of both state and federal laws.

### Jurisdictional Division

As a consequence of the bargain worked out at the Constitutional Convention in 1787, general police power was kept by the states. No national police force with broad enforcement powers may be established in the United States. The national government does have police agencies such as the FBI, the Drug Enforcement Administration, and the Secret Service,

Unlike France, where all police officers are employed by the national government, most officers in the United States are employed by state and local governments. What differences might this make for policing in the two countries?

but they are authorized to enforce only certain laws pertaining to specific powers granted to Congress. Since Congress has the power to coin money, for example, it also has the authority to provide for detecting and apprehending counterfeiters, functions that are performed by the Secret Service of the Department of the Treasury. The FBI, a branch of the Department of Justice, is responsible for investigating all violations of federal laws with the exception of those assigned by Congress to other departments. The FBI has jurisdiction over fewer than two hundred criminal matters, including such offenses as kidnapping, extortion, interstate transportation of stolen motor vehicles, and treason.

The role of criminal justice agencies following the assassination of President John F. Kennedy in November 1963 further illustrates the federal-state division of jurisdiction. Because Congress had not made killing the president of the United States a federal offense, the suspect Lee Harvey Oswald, would have been brought to trial under the laws of Texas had he lived (Oswald was shot to death by nightclub operator Jack Ruby shortly after his arrest). The U.S. Secret Service had the job of protecting the president, but apprehension of the killer was the formal responsibility of the Dallas police and other Texas law enforcement agencies.

As the constant movement of people and goods across state lines has become an integral part of American life, federal involvement in the criminal justice system has increased. The assumption that acts committed in one state will have no effect on the citizens of another state is no longer useful. In the area of organized crime, for example, crime families and gangs deal with drugs, pornography, and gambling on a national scale.

Congress has passed laws designed to allow the FBI to investigate situations in which local police forces are likely to be less effective. Thus, under the National Stolen Property Act, the FBI is authorized to investigate thefts exceeding five thousand dollars in value when the stolen property is likely to have been taken across state lines. In such circumstances, disputes over jurisdiction may occur because the offense is a violation of

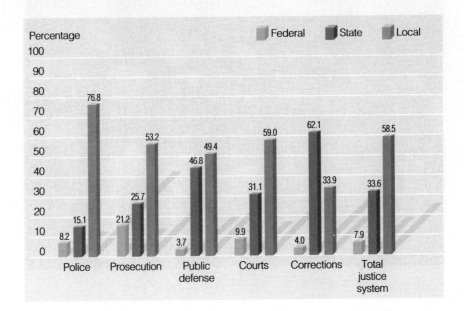

**Figure 1.2**
**Percentage (rounded) of criminal justice employees at each level of government**
The administration of criminal justice in the United States is very much a local affair as can be seen from these employment figures. It is only in corrections where the state, rather than municipalities, employs a greater percentage.

SOURCE: U.S. Department of Justice, Bureau of Justice Statistics, *Bulletin* (September 1993).

*both* state and national laws. The court to which a case is brought may be determined by the law enforcement agency that makes the arrest. In some cases, such as the prosecution of the Los Angeles police officers accused of the 1991 beating of Rodney King that was immortalized on videotape, defendants may be tried under state law and then retried in the federal courts for a violation of the laws of the national government. In most instances, however, the two systems respect each other's jurisdictions.

It is important to emphasize that the American system of criminal justice is decentralized. As Figure 1.2 notes, two-thirds of all criminal justice employees work for local units of government. With the exception of corrections employees, the majority of workers in all of the subunits of the criminal justice system—police, judicial, prosecution, public defense—are tied to local government. Likewise, the costs of criminal justice are distributed in varying proportions among the federal, state, county, and municipal governments, as shown in Figure 1.3. It is in the states and communities that laws are enforced and violators are brought to justice. Consequently, the formal structure and actual processes are greatly affected by local norms and pressures—that is, by the needs and demands of influential local people and by the community's interpretation of the extent to which the laws should be enforced.

## Criminal Justice as a System

To achieve the goals of criminal justice, many and varied organizational subunits, each with its own personnel, functions, and responsibilities, have been developed. If we were to look at an organizational chart, we might assume that criminal justice is an orderly continuum in which a variety of professionals act upon the accused in the interests of society.

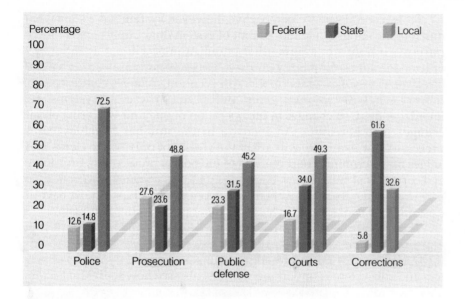

Figure 1.3
**What are the costs of criminal justice services and who pays for them?**
State and local governments bear the major costs of criminal justice services.

SOURCE: U.S. Department of Justice, Bureau of Justice Statistics, *Bulletin* (September 1992), 3.

But if we are to understand the administration of criminal justice, we must look beyond the formal organizational chart, such as the one found in the opening section of this book, to see how the system really works. To assist us in this task, we can use the social science concept of **system**, which helps us arrive at an overall, or macro, view of the administration of justice. It can help clarify how criminal justice functions by giving us an opportunity to analyze each of the organizations of criminal justice and their relationships to each other.

Criminal justice as a system is the third theme of this book. Thus criminal justice involves issues of public policy that are studied using the concepts and methods of various social science disciplines. In addition, the concept of *system* helps us to recognize that the agencies and processes of criminal justice are linked. One result is that the actions of the police, for example, have an impact on the other parts of the system—prosecution, courts, and corrections.

Exchange relationships influence decisions throughout the criminal justice system.

## Criminal Justice from a System Perspective

Critics often say that criminal justice is a "non-system." They make this charge because they do not think the administration of justice in America conforms with the formal blueprints or organizational charts that outline the process or with the traditional notions of how the system is *supposed* to work.

From a social science perspective, however, **system** has a somewhat different meaning. While the concept of system does imply some unity of purpose, it does not assume that organizations will act as rationally ordered machines. Criminal justice is a living system composed of a number of parts or subsystems—police, prosecution, defense, courts, corrections—each with its own goals and needs. These subsystems are interdependent, so changes in the operation of one unit will bring about changes in other units. An increase in the number of felony cases processed, for example, will affect the work not only of the clerks and judges of the criminal court but also of the police, prosecution, probation, and correctional subsystems. For criminal justice to achieve its goals, each part must make its own distinctive contribution. Each part must have at least minimal contact with at least one other part in order to function.

The system perspective allows us to examine criminal justice not only at the macro level of organizations but also at the micro level of individual and group behavior. Although understanding the dynamics of system and subsystem is important, we must also see how individual actors play their roles. The criminal justice system, of course, consists of a great many persons whose jobs require them to perform specific tasks. A key tool for analysis of the relationships among individual decision makers is the concept of **exchange**. This concept allows us to examine interpersonal behavior as resulting from the evaluation by individuals of the costs and rewards of one course of action over an alternative course.

**Plea bargaining** is probably the most obvious example of an exchange relationship. In about 90 percent of criminal cases, the defendant's fate is not determined through a trial, but rather through a bargain worked out between the defense attorney and the prosecutor in which the defendant agrees to plead guilty in exchange for a reduction of charges. As a result of this exchange, the defendant achieves a lower sentence and the attorneys move the case in an expeditious manner. Thus each of the major participants achieves desired goals.

Such face-to-face relationships are found throughout the criminal justice system. The concept of exchange makes us aware that decisions are the products of interactions among individuals and that the major sub-

**Figure 1.4**
**Exchange relationships between prosecutors and others**
The prosecutor's decisions are influenced by the relationships that are maintained with other criminal justice agencies, governmental units, and community influentials.

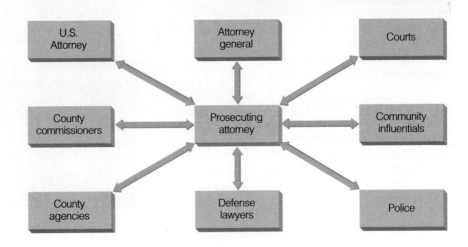

systems—police, prosecutor, court, and corrections—are tied together by the actions of individual decision makers. Figure 1.4 presents selected exchange relationships between a prosecuting attorney and others.

The concepts of system and exchange are closely linked, and their value as tools for the analysis of criminal justice cannot be overemphasized. In this book, these concepts serve as the organizing framework to describe individual subsystems and actors. Let us further explore the special characteristics of the criminal justice system that make it unique.

## Characteristics of the Criminal Justice System

Any organization—be it a university, General Motors, or the Seattle Police Department—can be described in terms of the functions it performs, the names of the principal actors, the value of the resources it produces, and the special ways its tasks are pursued. Four special attributes—discretion, resource dependence, sequential tasks, and filtering—characterize the work of the criminal justice system. Other organizations contain one or more of these features, but few contain all four.

**Discretion**  At all levels of the justice process there is a high degree of **discretion**, the ability of officials to act according to their own judgment and conscience (see Table 1.1). The fact that discretion exists throughout the criminal justice system may seem odd given that our country is ruled by law and has created procedures to ensure that decisions are made in accordance with that law. However, instead of a mechanistic system in which law preempts human decision making, criminal justice is a system in which the participants—police officer, prosecutor, judge, and correctional official—may consider a wide variety of circumstances and exercise many options as they dispose of a case. The need for discretionary power has been justified primarily on two counts: resources and justice. If every violation of the law, for example, were to be processed formally, the costs would be staggering. Additionally, criminal justice practitioners believe that in many cases justice can be more fully achieved through informal procedures. For example, a judge may believe that justice is better served if a sex offender is sent to a mental hospital rather than to prison. Because our system professes to promote individualized justice it must allow for the use of discretion.

**Resource Dependence**  Like other public service organizations, criminal justice does not produce its own resources—for example, its budget, staff, and equipment—but is dependent on others for them. It must therefore develop special links with people responsible for the allocation of resources—that is, the political decision makers. Criminal justice actors must be responsive to the legislators, mayors, and city council

**discretion**
The authority to make decisions without reference to specific rules or facts, using instead one's own judgment; allows for individualization and informality in the administration of justice.

Police officers have the discretion to consider the circumstances of a situation before acting. How is the exercise of discretion consistent with the rule of law?

members who hold the power of the purse. Ultimately, it is decisions by the community through its political leaders that influence the level of funding for criminal justice activities.

**Sequential Tasks**   Every part of the criminal justice system has distinct tasks that are carried out sequentially. Because a high degree of interdependence characterizes the system, the actions of one part of the system directly affect the work of the other parts. The courts can deal only with the cases brought to them by the prosecutor, who can deal only with persons arrested by the police. Not every person arrested, however, arrives in the courtroom.

**Filtering**   The criminal justice process may be viewed as a **filtering process** through which cases are screened: some are advanced to the next level of decision making, and others are either rejected or the conditions under which they are processed are changed. As shown in Figure 1.5, persons who have been arrested may be filtered out of the system at various points. Note that very few of the suspects arrested are prosecuted, tried, and convicted. At each stage decisions are made by officials as to which cases will proceed to the next level. Some arrestees are released because the police decide that a crime has not been committed or that the evidence is not sound. The prosecutor may drop charges thinking that conviction will not be possible or that justice would be better served through diversion. Great numbers of those indicted will plead guilty, the judge may dismiss the charges against others, the jury may acquit a few defendants, while most of those who go to trial will be found guilty. The "funnel-like" nature of the criminal justice system results in many cases entering at the top but only a few resulting in conviction and punishment.

To summarize, the administration of criminal justice is a system composed of a set of interdependent parts (subsystems). This system has four distinguishing characteristics: (1) discretion, (2) resource dependence, (3) sequential tasks, and (4) filtering. Using this framework for analysis, we look next at the primary agencies of criminal justice in the United States, and we then examine the flow of decision making within the system.

---

**filtering process**
A screening operation; a process by which criminal justice officials screen out some cases while advancing others to the next level of decision making.

**Table 1.1**
**Who exercises discretion?**
Discretion is exercised by various individuals throughout the criminal justice system. What influences these decisions?

SOURCE: U.S. Department of Justice, *Report to the Nation on Crime and Justice*, 2d ed. (Washington, D.C.: Government Printing Office, 1988), 59.

| These Criminal Justice Officials... | ...Must Often Decide Whether, or How, to: |
|---|---|
| Police | Enforce specific laws |
| | Investigate specific crimes |
| | Search people, vicinities, buildings |
| | Arrest or detain people |
| Prosecutors | File charges or petitions for adjudication |
| | Seek indictments |
| | Drop cases |
| | Reduce charges |
| Judges or magistrates | Set bail or conditions for release |
| | Accept pleas |
| | Determine delinquency |
| | Dismiss charges |
| | Impose sentence |
| | Revoke probation |
| Correctional officials | Assign to type of correctional facility |
| | Award privileges |
| | Punish for infractions of discipline |
| | Determine date and conditions of parole |
| | Revoke parole |

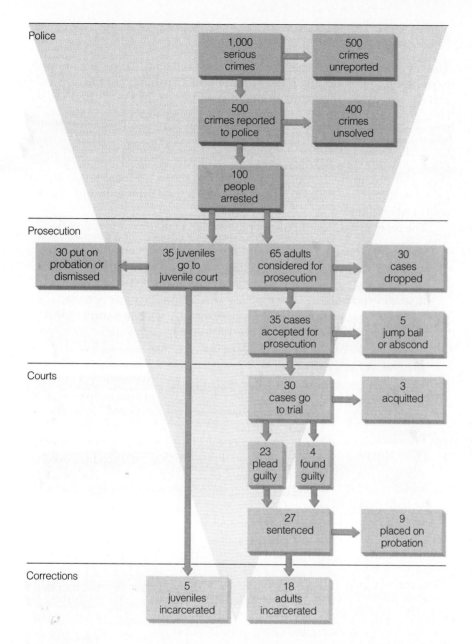

Police

| 1,000 serious crimes | → | 500 crimes unreported |

500 crimes reported to police → 400 crimes unsolved

100 people arrested

Prosecution

30 put on probation or dismissed ← 35 juveniles go to juvenile court | 65 adults considered for prosecution → 30 cases dropped

35 cases accepted for prosecution → 5 jump bail or abscond

Courts

30 cases go to trial → 3 acquitted

23 plead guilty | 4 found guilty

27 sentenced → 9 placed on probation

Corrections

5 juveniles incarcerated | 18 adults incarcerated

**Figure 1.5**
**Criminal justice as a filtering process**
Decisions made at each point of the criminal justice system result in some cases being dropped while others are passed to the next decisional point. Are you surprised by the small portion of cases that remain?

SOURCE: Data from this figure have been drawn from many sources including: U.S. Department of Justice, *Sourcebook of Criminal Justice Statistics, 1992* (Washington, D.C.: Government Printing Office, 1993) and Bureau of Justice Statistics, *Bulletin* (January 1988, February 1989).

## The Primary Agencies of Criminal Justice

The criminal justice system encompasses a major commitment on the part of American society to deal with persons who are accused of criminal law violations. The subsystems encompassing the police, prosecution and defense, courts, and corrections consist of over sixty thousand public and private agencies with an annual budget of over $74 billion and almost 1.7 million employees.[5] Let us review the major components of the criminal justice system and their functions.

## Police

The complexity and fragmentation of the criminal justice system are perhaps best understood given the number and jurisdiction of the approximately seventeen thousand public organizations in the United States engaged in law enforcement activities. The police function is dominated by local governments, as seen in the fact that the entire federal government has only fifty law enforcement agencies while each state government (except Hawaii) has one; the bulk of agencies are dispersed throughout counties, cities, and towns. At state and local levels these agencies have over 840,000 employees and a total annual budget in excess of $41 billion.[6]

The responsibilities of police organizations fall into four categories.

1  *Keeping the peace.* This broad and most important mandate, or command by the people, involves the protection of rights and persons in a wide variety of situations, ranging from street-corner brawls to domestic quarrels.

2  *Apprehending law violators and combating crime.* This responsibility is the one the public most often associates with police work, though it accounts for only a small portion of the time and resources of law enforcement agencies.

3  *Engaging in crime prevention.* By educating the public about the threat of crime and by reducing the number of situations in which crimes are most likely to be committed, the police can lower the incidence of crime.

4  *Providing a variety of social services.* In fulfilling these obligations, a police officer recovers stolen property, directs traffic, provides emergency medical aid, pulls cats from trees, and helps people locked out of their dwellings.

## Courts

**dual court system**
A system consisting of a separate judicial structure for each state in addition to a national structure. Each case is tried in a court of the same jurisdiction as that of the law or laws broken.

Although we may talk about the judiciary, the United States has a **dual court system**, consisting of a separate judicial structure for each state in addition to a national structure. Each system has its own series of courts, and the U.S. Supreme Court is the body where the two systems merge. Yet the Supreme Court does not have the right to review all decisions of state courts in criminal cases. It will hear only those cases that involve a federal law or those that claim one or more rights guaranteed by the Constitution were denied during the state criminal proceeding.

With a dual court system, interpretation of the law can vary from state to state. Although states may have laws that are similarly worded, none of the state courts interprets the laws exactly the same. To some extent these variations reflect diverse social and political conditions. They may also represent attempts by state courts to solve similar problems by different means. But the diversity of legal doctrine results primarily from fragmentation of the court system. Within the framework of each jurisdiction, judges have the discretion to apply the law as they believe it should be applied until they are overruled by a higher court. The criminal law of auto theft, for example, thus depends not only on the laws written by the fifty state legislatures or by Congress but also on the development of interpretation in the judicial system of each state and of the federal government.

The **adjudication** procedures of each state have evolved through a blend of legislative enactments and judicial interpretation of both state and federal laws. Decisions made by criminal justice actors may be challenged as violating defendants' rights under the laws or the constitution of the particular state or under the U.S. Constitution.

**adjudication**
The process of determining the guilt or innocence of a defendant.

## Corrections

On any given day approximately four million Americans are under the care of the corrections system. Unlike agencies of the police and the courts, a "typical" correctional agency or activity is difficult to describe. The great variety of correctional institutions and programs are provided by public and private organizations, involving federal, state, and local governments, and are carried out in many different community and closed settings.

The average citizen probably equates corrections with prisons, but only about a third of convicted offenders are actually incarcerated; the remainder are supervised within the community. Probation and parole have long been parts of the enterprise, as have community-based halfway houses, work release programs, and supervised activities.

The federal government, all the states, most counties, and all but the smallest cities are engaged in the corrections enterprise. Increasingly, nonprofit private organizations such as the YMCA have contracted with governments to perform correctional services. Of late, for-profit businesses have undertaken the construction and administration of prisons through contracts with governments.

The police, courts, and corrections are the primary agencies of criminal justice in the United States. Each of these organizations is a part, or subsystem, of the criminal justice system. Each subsystem is linked to the other two subsystems, and the actions of each affect the others. These interrelationships can be seen as we examine the flow of decision making within the criminal justice system.

## The Flow of Decision Making in the Criminal Justice System

The disposition of cases in the criminal justice system involves a series of decisions made by officials—for example, police officers, prosecutors, judges, probation officers, and wardens—who decide whether a case will progress to the next point or will be dropped from the system. Although the flowchart of criminal justice decision making shown in Figure 1.6 appears streamlined, with cases entering at the top and moving swiftly toward disposition at the bottom, the route is long and has many detours.

At each step, officials exercise discretion in ways that influence a defendant's fate. Many cases are filtered out of the system, others are forwarded to the next decision maker, and still others are dealt with through informal processes.

Moreover, the flowchart does not include the influences of the social relations of the actors or the political environment within which the sys-

**Figure 1.6**
**The flow of decision making in the criminal justice system**
Each criminal justice agency is responsible for a portion of the decision-making system. Thus the police, prosecution, courts, and corrections are bound together through a series of exchange relationships.

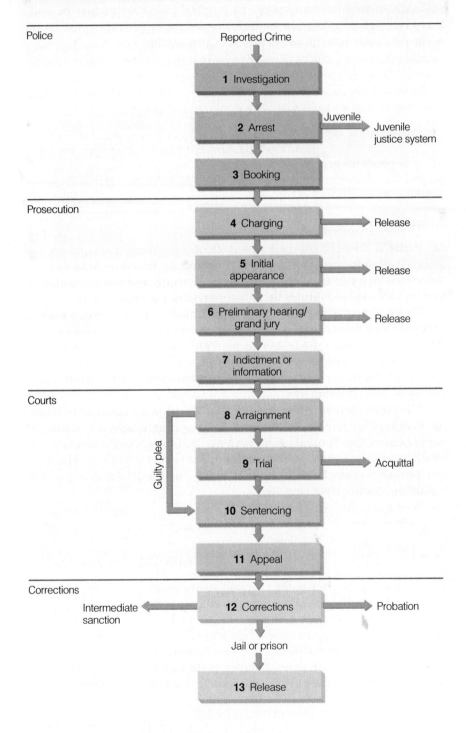

tem operates. As we follow the thirteen steps of the criminal justice system remember that the formal procedures outlined may not always depict reality.

## The Thirteen Steps in the Decision-Making Process

The criminal justice system can be understood as consisting of thirteen major steps of law enforcement, adjudication, and corrections. The system looks like an assembly line where decisions are made about defendants—the raw material of the process. As these steps are described keep in mind the conceptual devices discussed earlier: system, discretion, sequential tasks, filtering, and exchange. The terms used and the sequence of the steps vary in some parts of the United States, but the flow of decision making shown in Figure 1.6 is illustrative of the general process.

**1** *Investigation.* The process begins when the police believe that a crime has been committed and an investigation is initiated. The police are normally dependent on a member of the community to report the offense; only under atypical circumstances are the police able to observe illegal behavior. Most crimes have already been committed and their perpetrators have left the scene before the police arrive, so law enforcement is at an initial disadvantage.

**2** *Arrest.* If the police find enough evidence indicating that a particular person has committed a crime, then an arrest may be made. **Arrest** involves taking a person into custody, which not only restricts the suspect's freedom but also constitutes the initial steps toward prosecution.

Under some conditions, arrests may be made on the basis of a **warrant**—that is, an order issued by a judge who has received information pointing toward a particular person as the offender. In practice, most arrests are made without warrants. In some states, police officers may issue a summons or citation that orders a person to appear in court on a particular date, thus eliminating the need to hold the suspect physically until case disposition.

**3** *Booking.* The immediate effect of arrest is that the suspect is usually transported to a police station for booking, the procedure by which an administrative record is made of the arrest. When booked, the suspect may be fingerprinted, photographed, interrogated, and placed in a lineup for identification by the victim or witnesses. All suspects must also be given a "Miranda warning"—that they have the right to counsel, that they may remain silent, and that any statement they make may later be used against them. Bail may be set.

**4** *Charging.* Prosecuting attorneys provide the key link between the police and the courts. Their responsibility is to take the facts of the situation provided by the police and determine whether there is reasonable cause to believe that an offense was committed and whether the suspect committed it. The decision to charge is crucial because it sets in motion adjudication of the case.

**arrest**
The physical taking of a person into custody on the ground that there is probable cause to believe that he or she has committed a criminal offense. Police may use only reasonable physical force in making an arrest. The purpose of the arrest is to hold the accused for a court proceeding.

**warrant**
A court order authorizing police officials to take certain actions, for example, to arrest suspects or to search premises.

**5** *Initial Appearance.* Within a reasonable time after arrest, suspects must be brought for an initial appearance before a judge to be given formal notice of the charge on which they are being held, to be advised of their rights, and to be given the opportunity to post bail. Here the judge determines if there is sufficient evidence to hold the suspect for further criminal processing. If there is not sufficient evidence, then the case will be dismissed.

The purpose of bail is to permit the accused to be released while awaiting trial. To ensure that the person will be in court at the appointed time, surety (or pledge), usually in the form of money or a bond, is required. In almost all jurisdictions, the amount of bail is based primarily on the judge's perception of the seriousness of the crime and the defendant's record. For accused persons who lack the necessary money for bail, a bondsman (a person who lends such cash) may provide the financing. Suspects may also be released on their own recognizance—a promise to appear in court at a later date—when the crime is minor and when it can be shown that they have ties in the community. In a limited number of cases bail may be denied and the accused detained because he or she is viewed as a threat to the community.

**6** *Preliminary Hearing/Grand Jury.* Even after suspects have been arrested, booked, and brought before a magistrate to be notified of the charge and advised of their rights, the evidence and probability of conviction must be evaluated before a decision is made that they should be held for prosecution. The preliminary hearing, used in about half the states, allows a judge to determine whether probable cause exists to believe that the accused committed a known crime within the jurisdiction of the court. If the judge does not find probable cause, the case is dismissed. If there is sufficient evidence, the accused is bound over for arraignment on an **information**. In the federal system and in states with grand juries, the prosecutor appears before this body of laypersons who decide if there is enough evidence to allow the prosecutor to file an **indictment** (see Figure 1.7). The preliminary hearing and grand jury deliberations are designed to prevent hasty and malicious prosecutions, to protect persons from mistakenly being humiliated in public, and to discover if there are substantial grounds upon which a prosecution may be based.

**7** *Indictment/Information.* If, as a result of the preliminary hearing or grand jury, an information or indictment is granted, then the prosecutor prepares the formal charging document and enters it before the court.

**8** *Arraignment.* The accused person is then taken before a judge to hear the indictment or information read and is asked to enter a plea. Defendants may plead guilty or not guilty or, in some states, stand mute. If an accused pleads guilty, the judge must determine whether the plea is made voluntarily and whether the person has full knowledge of the possible consequences of the action. Should the guilty plea be accepted, a trial is not necessary and sentencing follows.

**9** *Trial.* For the relatively small percentage of defendants who plead not guilty, the right to a trial by an impartial jury is guaranteed by the Sixth Amendment, but this right has been interpreted as an absolute require-

**information**
A document charging an individual with a specific crime. It is prepared by a prosecuting attorney and presented to a court at a preliminary hearing.

**indictment**
A document returned by a grand jury as a "true bill" charging an individual with a specific crime on the basis of a determination of probable cause as presented by a prosecuting attorney.

Grand jury indictment required: all crimes
Grand jury indictment required: all felonies
Grand jury indictment optional
Capital crimes only
Grand jury lacks authority to indict

ment only when imprisonment for more than six months may result. In many jurisdictions, lesser charges do not command a jury. The use of juries is required in only a small number of cases; most trials are summary or bench trials—that is, they are conducted before a judge without a jury. Because of the high portion of guilty pleas, it is estimated that only 10 to 15 percent of cases go to trial and that approximately 5 percent are heard by juries. Whether a criminal trial is held before a judge alone or before a judge and jury, the procedures are similar and are prescribed by law. A defendant may be found guilty only if the evidence proves beyond a reasonable doubt that he or she committed the offense.

**10** *Sentencing*. Judges have the responsibility of imposing sentences. During sentencing, attention is focused on the offender; the intent is to make the sentence suitable to the particular offender within the requirements of the law and in accordance with the retribution and rehabilitation goals of the criminal justice system. Although criminal codes place limitations on sentences, the judge still has the discretion to consider alternatives: suspension, probation, prison, or intermediate sanction, for example.

**11** *Appeal*. Defendants found guilty may appeal their conviction to a higher court. An appeal is based on claims that the rules of procedure

**Figure 1.7**
**Grand jury requirements**
States used the grand jury for different offenses and in different ways. This once-important part of the system has grown less so during the twentieth century.

SOURCE: U.S. Department of Justice, *Report to the Nation on Crime and Justice*, 2d ed. (Washington, D.C.: Government Printing Office, 1988), 72.

The public often equates corrections with prisons, yet only about a third of convicted offenders are incarcerated. Two thirds of offenders are on probation or parole in the community.

were not properly followed by criminal justice officials or that the law forbidding the behavior that resulted in the charge is unconstitutional. The number of criminal trial verdicts appealed is small in comparison with the total number of convictions, and about 80 percent of such appeals result in an affirmation of the lower court decision.

**12** *Corrections.* Execution of the court's sentence is the responsibility of the correctional subsystem. Probation, intermediate sanctions, and incarceration are the sanctions most generally imposed.

Probation allows convicted offenders to serve their sentences in the community under supervision. It is used instead of incarceration especially for the young, first offenders, and offenders convicted of minor violations. The conditions of probation require that offenders observe certain rules—be employed, maintain an orderly life, go to school—and that they report to their supervising officer as required. Violations of the conditions of probation may result in its cancellation by the judge and the imposition of a prison sentence.

Intermediate sanctions have been created in recent years. These are viewed as more restrictive than probation but less restrictive than incarceration. Intensive probation supervision, boot camp, home confinement, and community service are several forms of intermediate sanctions.

Regardless of the reasons used to justify incarceration, prisons exist to segregate the criminal from the rest of society. Offenders convicted of misdemeanors usually serve their time in city or county jails, while felons serve their time in state prisons. Isolation from the community is probably the most overbearing characteristic of incarceration. Visits from family members and correspondence are restricted, and supervision is ever present. In the name of internal security, prison officials justify unannounced searches and rigid discipline among inmates.

**13** *Release.* Upon completion of his or her sentence, the offender will be released. Release may be granted by serving the full sentence imposed by the court or by returning to the community under supervision of a parole officer. Parolees remain under supervision until the length of time represented by their maximum sentence has expired or for a period as specified by law. Parole may be revoked and the person returned to prison if the conditions of parole are not fulfilled or if the parolee commits another crime.

To give a real-life example of the system in operation, the following Close-Up, excerpted from *Newsweek* magazine, describes the experience of Donald Payne, a young man from Chicago who is arrested, prosecuted, convicted, sentenced, and punished for charges incurred when he attempted to hold up a liquor store.

## The People versus Donald Payne

An 18-year-old named Donald Payne came hand-cuffed and sullen into the Chicago courthouse—a tall, spidery, black dropout charged with the attempted armed robbery and attempted murder of a white liquor-store owner, Joe Castelli, in a "changing" fringe neighborhood. The police report told it simply: "... victim stated that two male Negroes entered his store and the taller of the two came out with a gun and announced that this is a holdup, 'give me all of your money.' With this the victim ... walked away from the area of the cash register. When he did this, the smaller offender shouted 'shoot him.' The taller offender aimed the pistol at him and pulled the trigger about two or three times. The weapon failed to fire. The offenders then fled...."

Nobody knows, really, why the street swallows up so many of them. Poverty in the midst of affluence is surely part of it, and color in the midst of whiteness; so are heroin and broken homes and the sheer get-it-now impulsiveness of life in so empty and so chancy a place as a ghetto. But no one can say which ones will go wrong—why a Donald Payne, for example, will get in trouble while three brothers and two sisters come up straight....

### Investigation

Patrolman Joe Higgins nosed his unmarked squad car through the night places of [Chicago's] Gresham police district, watching the alleys and storefronts slide past, half-listening to the low staccato of the radio, exchanging shorthand grunts with his partner, Tom Cullen, slouched low in the seat beside him. They had been riding for three humdrum hours when, shortly after 9 P.M., they picked up the call: gunfire in the street up in the north reaches of the district. The two cops glanced at one another. Cullen got the mike out of the glove compartment and radioed: "Six-sixty going in." Higgins hit the accelerator and snaked through the sluggish night traffic toward Shop-Rite Liquors—and the middle of his own neighborhood....

It was near first light when they spotted the car, parked in a deserted industrial area with two runaways, 13 and 17 years old, curled up asleep inside. The two patrolmen rousted the boys, searched the car—and found the blue-steel .25 under a jacket in the front seat. One of the boys, thoroughly scared, led them to a 17-year-old named James Hamilton who admitted having driven the car but not having gone into the store. Hamilton led them to his kid cousin, Frank, who admitted having gone into the store but not having handled the gun or clicked the trigger. And Frank Hamilton led them to Donald Payne.

### Arrest

And so, red-eyed and bone-weary, Higgins and Cullen, along with a district sergeant and two robbery detectives, went to the little green-and-white frame house in Roseland at 9 A.M. and rang the bell. Payne's sister let them in and pointed the way upstairs.

Payne was sleeping when the cops crowded into his little attic bedroom and he came awake cool and mean. "Get moving," someone said. "You're under arrest."...

They marched him out in handcuffs past his mother, took him to the district station and shackled him to a chair while one of the officers started tapping out an arrest report.... The cops put Payne into a little back room. Castelli [the liquor-store owner] picked him out—and that, for the cops, was enough.

### Booking

Payne was taken to the South Side branch police headquarters to be booked, then led before a magistrate who set bond [bail] at $10,000. The bond is a paper figure: the Chicago courts require only 10 percent cash. But Payne didn't have it, and by mid-afternoon he was on his way by police van to the Cook County Jail....

### The Defender

Public Defender Connie Xinos disliked Donald Payne from the beginning. They met in the prisoners' lockup behind Judge Fitzgerald's courtroom, and all Xinos had to go on then was the police report and Payne's public-defender questionnaire ("All I know is I was arrested for attempted murder on August 5") and that insinuating half smile. *He did it*, Xinos thought; all of them except the scared children and the street-wise old pros swear they are innocent, but you get a feeling....

Xinos is 30, the son of a Greek cafeteria owner bred in the white Chicago suburbs, a stumpy young bachelor with quizzical eyes, a shock of straight, dark hair and a Marine Reserve pin glinting gold in the lapel of his three-piece suit. He came to the building a year out of John Marshall Law School, hoping for a job as an assistant state's attorney but hungry enough for steady pay and trial experience to settle for what he could get....

Xinos learned fast.... "It's our court," Xinos says. "It's like a family. Me, the prosecutors, the judges, we're all friends. I drink with the prosecutors. I give the judge a Christmas present, he gives me a Christmas present." And you learn technique. The evidence game. The little touches: "The defendant should smile a lot." The big disparities: which judge gives eighteen months for a wife-killing and which one gives twenty to forty years. How to make time and the caseload work for you. "The last thing you want to do is rush to trial. You let the case ride. Everybody gets friendly. A case is continued ten to fifteen times, and nobody cares any more. The victims don't care."

Everybody just wants to get rid of the case." Then you can plead your man guilty and deal for reduced charges or probation or short time. You swing....

The ones you can't [forget] are the few you plead guilty when you really believe they are innocent: "When you're scared of losing. When they've got a case and you believe your guy but you lose your faith in the jury system. You get scared, and he gets scared and you plead him." But the Donald Paynes—the great majority of his cases—are different. Xinos never liked Payne; Payne fought him, and Xinos much prefers the pros who tell you, "Hey, public defender, I killed the f——er, now get me off." Xinos thought Payne should plead guilty and go for short time. But Payne clung to Standard Alibi Number Umpty-one ("I was home at the time this was supposed to have broke out") and demanded a trial, so Xinos gave him the best shot he could.

## The Jail

He clambered down out of the van with the rest of the day's catch and was marched through a tunnel into a white-tiled basement receiving area. He was questioned, lectured, classified, stripped, showered, photographed, fingerprinted, X-rayed for TB, bloodtested for VD and handed a mimeographed sheet of rules of the Cook County jail. He was issued a wristband, an ID card and a ceiling ticket, led upstairs and checked into a tiny 4-by-8 cell with an open toilet, a double bunk, two sheets, a blanket and a roommate. The door slammed shut, and Donald Payne—charged with but still presumed innocent of attempted robbery and attempted murder—began nearly four and a half months behind bars waiting for his trial....

All the while, his case inched through the courts. Illinois requires that the state bring an accused man to trial within 120 days or turn him loose—a deadline that eases the worst of the courthouse delays and the jailhouse jam-ups that afflict other cities. But the average wait in jail still drags out to six or seven months, occasionally because the state asks for more time (it can get one sixty-day extension for good cause), more often because delay can be the best defense strategy in an overloaded system. Evidence goes stale; witnesses disappear or lose interest; cases pile up; prosecutors are tempted to bargain. "You could get twenty years on this thing," Constantine Xinos, the assistant public defender who drew Donald Payne, told him when they met. "Don't be in a hurry to go to trial."

## Preliminary Hearing/Grand Jury

Waiting naturally comes easier to a man out on bail than to one behind bars, but Payne sat and waited. On August 24, nineteen days after his arrest, he went ... to the basement tunnel to the courthouse, stripped naked for a search, then dressed and was led upstairs for a hearing in Room 402—Violence Court.... Payne waited in the lockup until a clerk bellowed his name, then stood before Judge John Hechinger in a ragged semicircle with his mother, the cops, the vic-

tims, Assistant State Attorney Walter Parrish and Assistant Public Defender Connie Xinos, and listened to the prosecution briefly rehearse the facts of the case....

Judge Hechinger ordered Payne held for the grand jury. The day in court lasted a matter of minutes; Payne was shuffled back through the lockup, the nude search, the basement tunnel and into [the jail] again.

## Indictment

On September 18, word came over that the grand jury had indicted him for attempted armed robbery (gun) and attempted murder, and the case shortly thereafter was assigned to Circuit Judge Richard Fitzgerald for trial....

## Arraignment

Everybody kept trying to talk him out of his trial. "Plead guilty, jackass, you could get ten to twenty for this," Xinos whispered when they finally got to trial. *Ain't no need for that,* said Payne. "You really want a jury?" the assistant state's attorney, Walter Parrish, teased him. "Or you want to plead?" *I want my trial,* said Payne. Everything in the building says cop out, make a deal, take the short time....

The pressures to plead are sometimes cruel, the risks of going to trial high and well-advertised.... Still, Payne insisted, and Xinos painstakingly put a defense together. He opened with a pair of preliminary motions, one arguing that the pistol was inadmissible because the evidence tying it to Payne was hearsay, the other contending that the police should have offered Payne a lawyer at the line-up but didn't. The witnesses straggled in for a hearing on December 1. Joe Castelli took the stand, and Patrolman Cullen, and, for a few monosyllabic moments, Payne himself. Had anyone advised him of his rights to a lawyer? "No." Or let him make a phone call? "No." But another of the arresting officers, Robert Krueger, said that Payne had been told of his rights—and such swearing contests almost always are decided in favor of the police. Everybody admired Xinos's energy and craftsmanship. Nevertheless, Fitzgerald denied both of the defense motions and docketed the case for trial on December 14.

## Trial

And so they all gathered that wintry Monday in Fitzgerald's sixth-floor courtroom, a great dim cave with marbled and oak-paneled walls, pitted linoleum floors and judge, jury, lawyers, defendant and a gallery so widely separated that nobody could hear anything without microphones.

*Jury Selection*  Choosing a jury took two hours that day, two the next morning. Parrish [the state's attorney] worked without a shopping list. "I know some lawyers say fat people are jolly and Germans are strict," he says, "but none of that's true in my experience. If you get twelve people who say they'll listen, you're all right."

But Xinos is a hunch player. He got two blacks on the jury and was particularly pleased with one of them, a light-skinned Urban League member who looked as if she might be sympathetic. And he deliberately let one hard hat sit on the panel. Xinos had a point to make about the pistol—you couldn't click it more than once without pulling back the slide to cock it—and the hard hat looked as if he knew guns.

*Presentation of the State's Case*    That afternoon, slowly and methodically, Parrish began to put on his case. He opened with the victims, and Castelli laid the story on the record: "About ten after 9, the gentleman walked in…. He had a small-caliber pistol…. I edged away…. The other lad came up to me and he said, 'Shoot him, shoot him, shoot him.'… The first youth pointed the gun at me and fired three times or four—at least I heard three clicks." And the gunman—did Castelli see him in court?

"Yes I do, sir."

"And would you point him out, please?"

Castelli gestured toward the single table shared by the prosecution and defense. "That," he said, "is Donald Payne."

*Presentation of the Defense's Case*    But Xinos, in his opening argument, had promised to alibi Payne—his mother was prepared to testify for him—and now, on cross-examination, he picked skillfully at Parrish's case. Playing to his hard hat on the jury, he asked Castelli whether the stick-up man had one or two hands on the gun. "Only one, sir," said Castelli. "And was that trigger pulled in rapid succession—click-click-click?" Xinos pressed. "Yes, sir," said Castelli, and Xinos had his point: it takes two hands to keep pulling the slide and clicking the trigger.

Next came Patrolman Joe Higgins, who remembered, under Xinos's pointed cross-examination, that Castelli had described the gunman as weighing 185 pounds—30 more than Payne carries on his spindly 6-foot-1 frame. Payne had nearly botched that point by wearing a billowy, cape-shaped jacket to court, but Xinos persuaded him to fold it up and sit on it so the jurors could see how bony he really was. The 30-pound misunderstanding undercut Castelli's identification of Payne—and suddenly the People and their lawyer, Walter Parrish, were in trouble….

What [Parrish] had in *People* vs. *Payne* was the Hamilton boys, the two cousins through whom the police had tracked Payne. Parrish had hoped he wouldn't have to put them on the stand. "It was a risk," he said later. "They could have hurt us. They could have got up there and suddenly said Donald wasn't there." But he was behind and knew it. He needed Frank Hamilton to place Payne inside the store, James to connect him with the car and the pistol. So, that afternoon, he ordered up subpoenas for the Hamiltons. "We know how to scramble," said his young assistant, Joe Poduska. "That's the name of the game."

*Plea Bargaining*    The subpoenas were being typed when Connie Xinos happened into the state's attorney's office to socialize—*it's like a family*—and saw them in the typewriter. Xinos went cold. He had talked to the mother of one of the Hamiltons; he knew their testimony could hurt. So, next morning, he headed first thing to Parrish's austere second-floor cubicle—and found the Hamiltons there. "We're going to testify," they told Xinos, "and we're going to tell the truth."

Xinos took Parrish aside. "Let's get rid of this case," he said.

"It's Christmas," Parrish said amiably. "I'm a reasonable man."

"What do you want?" Xinos asked.

"I was thinking about three to eight."

"One to five," said Xinos.

"You got it."

*It's an absolute gift*, Xinos thought, and he took it to Payne in the lockup. "I can get you one to five," he said. Payne said no. Xinos thought fast. It was a dead-bang case—the kind Clarence Darrow couldn't pull out—and it was good for a big rattle, maybe ten to twenty years. Xinos went back downstairs, got the Hamiltons and sat them down with Payne in [Judge] Fitzgerald's library. "They rapped," he remembers, "and one of them said, 'Donald—you mean you told them you weren't *there*?' I told him again I could get him one to five. They said, 'Maybe you ought to take it, Donald.' I said, 'You may get ten to twenty going on with the trial.' And he said, 'Well, even if I take one to five, I'm not guilty.' That's when I knew he would go."

But would Fitzgerald buy it? Xinos was worried…. But Fitzgerald agreed to talk, and the ritual began to unfold….

Fitzgerald scanned Parrish's prep sheet, outlining the state case. Xinos told him glumly about the Hamiltons. "We look beat," he conceded.

"Walter," asked the judge, "what do you want?"

"I don't want to hurt the kid," Parrish said. "I talked to Connie, and we thought one to five."

They talked about Payne's record—his jobs, his family, his old gas-station burglary rap. "Two years' probation," Xinos put in hopefully. "That's nothing." Fitzgerald pondered it all. He had no probation report … and no psychological workup; sentencing in most American courts comes down to a matter of instinct. Fitzgerald's instincts told him one to five was a long time for Payne to serve—and a wide enough spread to encourage him to reform and get out early….

"Will he take it?" the judge asked Xinos.

"I'll go back and see," Xinos replied. He ducked out to the lockup and put the offer to Payne.

"Let's do it," Payne said. "Right now."

## Sentencing

A light snow was falling when they brought him back into court, grinning slightly, walking his diddybop walk. A bailiff led him to a table below Fitzgerald's high bench. His mother slipped into place beside

Illinois' Joliet Prison.

him. The judge led him through the prescribed catechism establishing that he understood what he was doing and that no one had forced him to do it. Payne's "yesses" were barely audible in the cavernous room. [Judge Fitzgerald then imposed the sentence agreed to as part of the plea agreement.]…

And then it was over. Fitzgerald called the jurors in and dismissed them. They knew nothing of the events that had buried Donald; they sat there for a moment looking stunned.…

### Prison

You can write to your lawyer, your preacher and six other people, the sergeant was saying.… No. 69656, born Donald Payne, sat half listening in the front row in his gray prison coveralls, his eyes idling over the chapel wall from the flag to the sunny poster—GOOD MORNING WORLD.…

Joliet [Prison] is a way station for Payne. He may wind up at Pontiac, where most younger offenders do their time; he would prefer the company of older men at Stateville.… He says that in either event he will stick to his cell and go for early parole. "When I get out," he told his mother once in jail, "I'll be in church every day." Yet the odds do not necessarily favor this outcome: though the Illinois prisons have made progress toward cutting down on recidivism, a fifth to a third of their alumni get in trouble again before they have been out even a year. "Well," said Payne, smiling that half-smile at a visitor during his first days as No. 69656, "I'm startin' my time now and I'm on my way home."

The Menendez brothers were tried for the murder of their wealthy parents in 1994. Highly visible cases like this one do not give an accurate picture of the criminal justice system as a whole.

## The Criminal Justice Wedding Cake

The linear, or assembly-line, depiction of the criminal justice process that we have just examined can give the impression that all cases are treated equally. What is not revealed is the degree of importance accorded to each case by the agencies and actors in the process and the ways in which a case's importance influences the allocation of justice.

Samuel Walker has suggested that although the flowchart is a notable aid to our understanding, we must recognize that different kinds of cases are handled in different fashions.[7] He suggests that the nature of a case has much to do with how criminal justice officials and the public react to it. Some cases achieve a high level of visibility, either because of the notoriety of the defendant or victim or because of the heinous nature of the crime. At the other extreme are those "run-of-the-mill cases" involving unknown persons who are

charged with committing minor crimes. Walker suggests that we regard the criminal justice process as a cake with tapered layers, like those of a wedding cake (see Figure 1.8).

Layer 1 consists of those very few "celebrated" cases that are exceptional, receive great public attention, result in a jury trial, and often run into extended appeals. The cases of mass murderer Charles Manson, would-be presidential assassin John Hinckley, socialite Claus von Bulow, and serial killer Jeffrey Dahmer are in this category. Not all cases in Layer 1 achieve national notoriety; from time to time local crimes, especially cases of murder and rape, are treated in this manner. The celebrated cases are like morality plays. Too often, however, the public assumes that all criminal cases are handled in this manner.

Layer 2 consists of **felonies** that are deemed to be serious by officials: crimes of violence committed by persons with long criminal records against victims unknown to them. These are the cases that the police and the prosecutors consider important from the perspective of crime control and that usually result in "tough" sentences.

Layer 3 also consists of felonies, but the crimes and the offenders are of lesser concern than those in Layer 2. They may involve the same offenses as in Layer 2, but the offender may have no record, and the victim may have had a prior relationship with the accused. When such cases occur, the primary goal of criminal justice officials is to dispose of them quickly. For this reason, many are filtered out of the system and plea bargaining is encouraged.

Layer 4 is made up of **misdemeanors**. About 90 percent of all cases handled in the criminal justice system are found in this layer. They concern offenses such as public drunkenness, shoplifting, prostitution, disturbing the peace, and motor vehicle violations. Looked upon by officials as the "garbage" of the system, these cases are adjudicated in the lower courts, where speed is essential, trials are rare, processes are informal, and fines, probation, or short jail sentences result. Assembly-line justice reigns.

Walker's conception is a useful corrective to the flowchart perception of the system. Cases are not treated equally: some are viewed as very important by criminal justice officials, others as merely part of a mass that must be processed. When one knows the nature of a case, one can predict with some degree of confidence the way it will be handled and its outcome. Later we will emphasize the differential treatment of cases: for now the wedding cake analogy underscores the fact that officials' conceptions of what is "important" determine how cases are dealt with.

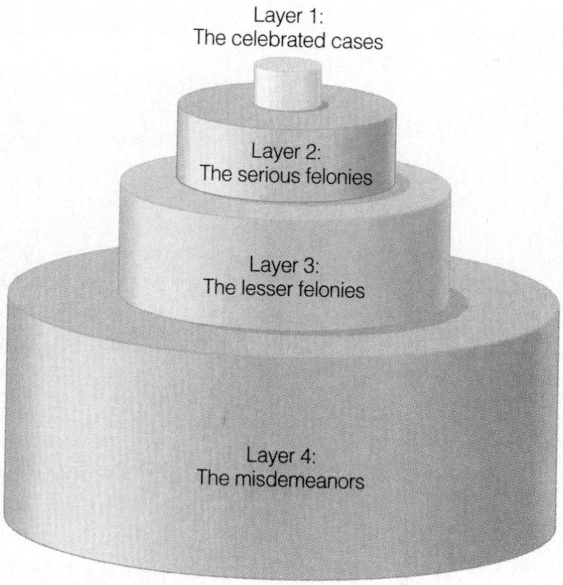

Layer 1:
The celebrated cases

Layer 2:
The serious felonies

Layer 3:
The lesser felonies

Layer 4:
The misdemeanors

**Figure 1.8**
**The criminal justice wedding cake**
This figure emphasizes the fact that different cases are treated in different ways. Only a very few cases are played out in the full dramatic "L.A. Law" style; the greatest number are handled administratively through plea bargaining and dismissals.

SOURCE: Drawn from Samuel Walker, *Sense and Nonsense about Crime Policy*, 2d. ed. (Pacific Grove, Calif.: Brooks/Cole, 1989), 22–27.

**felonies**
Serious crimes usually carrying a penalty of death or incarceration for more than one year.

**misdemeanors**
Offenses less serious than felonies and usually punishable by incarceration of no more than a year, probation, or intermediate sanction.

# Crime Control versus Due Process

Scholars often use **models** to organize their thinking about a subject and to guide their research, since models are ideal types that clearly characterize the values and goals that underlie a system. In one of the most important contributions to systematic thought on the administration of criminal justice, Herbert Packer describes two competing schemes: the Crime Control Model and the Due Process Model.[8] These models articulate two ways of examining the goals and procedures of the criminal justice system; they represent opposing views of how the criminal law *ought* to operate. Packer likens the Crime Control Model to an assembly line and the Due Process Model to an obstacle course and describes them as polar extremes, the endpoints of a continuum.

The behavior of criminal justice decision makers is influenced by its administrative structure and by the values of the American culture. These values provide legitimacy and justification for the ways in which criminal behavior is controlled and defendants' cases are judged. Packer recognizes that the administration of criminal justice operates within the contemporary American society, such as respect for the rule of law and the maintenance of civil rights and liberties, and is therefore influenced by cultural forces that, in turn, determine the usefulness of the models. In addition, no one actor or law enforcement subsystem functions totally in accordance with either of the models; elements of both are found throughout the system. The values expressed within the two models describe the tensions within the process.

## Crime Control: Order as a Value

Underlying the **Crime Control Model** is the proposition that the repression of criminal conduct is the most important function to be performed by the criminal justice system. As Packer points out, to achieve liberty for all citizens to interact freely as members of society, the Crime Control Model requires that primary attention be paid to efficiency in screening suspects, determining guilt, and applying appropriate sanctions to the convicted.

In the context of this model, efficiency of operation requires that the system have the capacity to apprehend, try, convict, and dispose of a high proportion of criminal offenders whose offenses become known. Because of the magnitude of criminal behavior and the limited resources given to law enforcement agencies, emphasis must be placed on speed and finality. Accordingly, there must be a high rate of arrests, a sifting out of the innocent, and conviction of offenders, all of which depend on informality, uniformity, and the minimizing of occasions for challenge. Probable guilt is administratively determined primarily on the basis of the police investigation, and those cases unlikely to end in conviction are filtered out. At each successive stage, from arrest to preliminary hearing, arraignment, and courtroom trial, a series of routinized procedures is used by a variety of judicial actors to determine whether the accused should move to the next level. Rather than stressing the combative elements of the courtroom, this model notes that bargaining between the state and the accused occurs at several points. The ritual of the courtroom is enacted in a small number of cases; the remaining cases are disposed of through negotiations over the charges and usually end with defendants' pleas of guilty. Thus Packer likens decision making under the Crime Control Model to an assembly-line process. That is, an endless stream of cases moves past fixed stations where workers in the system perform the small but essential operations that bring each case closer to being the finished product, a closed file.

## Due Process: Law as a Value

If the Crime Control Model looks like an assembly line, the **Due Process Model** resembles an obstacle course. Although likewise valuing human freedom, the Due Process Model questions the reliability of fact-finding. Because people are notoriously poor observers of disturbing events, the possibility of the police and prosecutors—the main Crime Control Model decision makers—committing an error is very high. Persons should be termed *criminal* and deprived of their freedom only on the basis of reliable information. To minimize error, hurdles must be erected so that the power of government can be used against the accused only when it has been proved beyond doubt that the defendant committed the crime in question. The best method to determine guilt or innocence is to test the evidence through an adversarial proceeding. The model assumes, then, that persons are innocent until proved guilty, that they have the opportunity to discredit the cases brought against them, and that an impartial judge and jury are summoned to decide the outcome. The assumption that the defendant is innocent until proved guilty is emphasized by Packer as having a far-reaching impact on the criminal justice system.

According to the Due Process Model the state must prove in a procedurally regular manner that the person is guilty of the crime as charged. Prosecutors must prove their cases under various procedural restraints that deal with the admissibility of evidence, the burden of proof, the requirement that guilt be proved beyond a reasonable doubt, and so forth. Forcing the state to prove its case in an adjudicative context protects the citizens from undeserved criminal sanction. In the Due Process Model, the possibility that a few who may be factually guilty will remain free outweighs the possibilities in the Crime Control Model for governmental power to be abused, the innocent to be incarcerated, and society's freedom to be endangered. Table 1.2 compares the basic elements of these two models.

> **Due Process Model**
> A model of the criminal justice system that assumes freedom is so important that every effort must be made to ensure that criminal justice decisions are based on reliable information; it emphasizes the adversarial process, the rights of defendants, and formal decision-making procedures.

## Reality: Crime Control or Due Process?

If someone from a foreign country should ask you to describe the way the U.S. criminal justice process functions, what would you say? Which of the value models would you use in your explanation?

**Table 1.2**

**Due process model and crime control model compared**

What other comparisons can be made between the two models?

| | Goal | Value | Process | Major Decision Point | Basis of Decision Making |
|---|---|---|---|---|---|
| **Due Process Model** | Preserve individual liberties | Reliability | Adversarial | Courtroom | Law |
| **Crime Control Model** | Repress crime | Efficiency | Administrative | Police, pretrial processes | Discretion |

The public's idea of democracy probably leads to an understanding of the criminal justice system in accordance with the ideals of the Due Process Model. According to this view, principles, not personal discretion, control the actions of police officers, judges, and prosecutors. Criminal justice is thus seen as an ongoing, mechanical process in which violations of laws are discovered, defendants are indicted, and punishments are imposed, with little reference either to the organizational needs of the system or to the personalization of justice. This perspective gives little opportunity for discretion in the criminal justice machine, and any attempt to induce flexibility must be carried out *sub rosa* (in confidence).

Unlike the values expressed in the Due Process Model, in which decisions are made in the courtroom as a result of adversarial conflict, the reality of criminal justice in America is more comparable to the Crime Control Model, in which guilt is administratively determined early in the process and cases are disposed of through negotiation. Rather than an emphasis on discovering the truth so that the innocent may be separated from the guilty, the Crime Control Model assumes that those arrested by the police have committed *some* criminal act. Accordingly, efforts are made to select a charge that the accused will plead guilty to and that will result in an appropriate sentence.

## Summary

Crime and justice are high on the agenda of national priorities. An important theme of this book is that criminal justice involves issues of public policy. Because the United States is a democracy, policies and programs for dealing with crime are developed in the political arena with input from citizens, elected representatives, and government officials. Unlike criminal justice in authoritarian countries, in democracies crime is controlled within the framework of law.

As an academic discipline, criminal justice emerged in the late 1960s as a result of the report of the President's Commission on Law Enforcement and Administration of Justice and the Omnibus Crime Control Act of 1968. A second theme of this book is that the study of criminal justice is an interdisciplinary field, with scholars from such disciplines as economics, history, law, political science, psychology, and sociology each viewing crime and the administration of justice through their own conceptual and theoretical lenses. This interplay of disciplines makes criminal justice a vibrant field.

The goal of criminal justice is to maintain justice while controlling and preventing crime. The administration of criminal justice is carried out within the framework of the federal system of government, which means that most agencies and resources devoted to the pursuit of criminal justice goals reside at the local level. The national government deals with violations of the federal criminal code while state and local governments deal with violations of state laws.

Students of criminal justice must be able to analyze the problem of crime and the administration of justice. A framework based on the concept of *system* helps us to understand the dynamic processes of the criminal justice system. The concepts of discretion, sequential tasks, resource dependence, filtering, and exchange further assist our analysis. The criminal justice system is composed of the subsystems of the police, courts, and corrections. The system processes defendants through a series of thirteen legally required steps in which officials exercise discretion to determine whether a case will be dropped from the system or transferred to the next step. Although a linear, or assembly-line, model of criminal justice helps us understand the system, an important corrective is the analogy of criminal justice as a wedding cake with layers of cases being treated differently.

Two ways of conceptualizing the criminal justice system are the Due Process Model and the Crime Control Model. These tools help us analyze how and why cases progress through the system. Although most citizens probably think of criminal justice in terms of the Due Process Model, the reality of the system is closer to the Crime Control Model. As one scholar has written:

It is in the day-to-day practices and policies of the processing agencies that the law is put into effect, and it is out of the struggle to perform their tasks in ways which maximize rewards and minimize strains for the organization and the individuals involved that the legal processing agencies shape the law.[9]

The fact that criminal justice is a social system embedded in a larger governmental and social context is a third theme of this text. Throughout the book we will be concerned with the actual operation of the American criminal justice system and with the links among law, politics, and administration in the prevention and control of crime.

## Questions for Review

1 How do politics influence the criminal justice system?
2 What academic disciplines have been major contributors to the study of criminal justice?

3   What are the goals of the criminal justice system?

4   What is meant by the concept of system? How is the administration of criminal justice a system?

5   What are the thirteen steps in the criminal justice decision-making process?

6   Why does Walker suggest that the criminal justice wedding cake is a better depiction of reality than a linear model of the system?

7   What are the major elements of Packer's Due Process Model and Crime Control Model?

## Key Terms

adjudication

arrest

crime

Crime Control Model

criminologist

discretion

dual court system

Due Process Model

exchange

felony

filtering process

indictment

information

misdemeanor

model

plea bargain

political considerations

system

warrant

## For Further Reading

Currie, Elliott. *Confronting Crime*. New York: Pantheon, 1985. A critique of conservative and liberal arguments about crime with particular emphasis on the work of James Q. Wilson. Urges development of social and economic programs to reduce crime.

Friedman, Lawrence M. *Crime and Punishment in American History*. New York: Basic Books, 1993. A historical overview of criminal justice from colonial times. Argues that the evolution of criminal justice reflects transformations in America's character.

Huff, C. Ronald. *Gangs in America*. Newbury Park, Calif.: Sage, 1990. An outstanding collection of essays concerning gangs, gang violence, and public policy.

Packer, Herbert L. *The Limits of the Criminal Sanction*. Stanford, Calif.: Stanford University Press, 1968. A classic examination of many of the assumptions underlying the American system of criminal justice.

Wilson, James Q. *Thinking about Crime*. 2d ed. New York: Basic Books, 1983. Argues for policies to improve the criminal justice system and thus reduce crime. Examines various law enforcement, sentencing, and correctional strategies.

# Notes

1. U.S. National Advisory Commission on Criminal Justice Standards and Goals, *A National Strategy to Reduce Crime* (Washington, D.C.: Government Printing Office, 1973), 1.

2. U.S. President's Commission on Law Enforcement and Administration of Justice, *The Challenge of Crime in a Free Society* (Washington, D.C.: Government Printing Office, 1967).

3. U.S. President's Commission on Law Enforcement and Administration of Justice, *The Challenge of Crime in a Free Society* (Washington, D.C.: Government Printing Office, 1967), 7.

4. John J. DiIulio, Jr., "Rethinking the Criminal Justice System: Toward a New Paradigm," *Performance Measures for the Criminal Justice System* (Washington, D.C.: Bureau of Justice Statistics, 1993), 10.

5. U.S. Department of Justice, Bureau of Justice Statistics, *Bulletin* (October 1992), 2.

6. U.S. Department of Justice, Bureau of Justice Statistics, *Bulletin* (July 1993).

7. Samuel Walker, *Sense and Nonsense about Crime: A Policy Guide*, 2d ed. (Pacific Grove, Calif.: Brooks/Cole, 1989), 22.

8. Herbert L. Packer, *The Limits of the Criminal Sanction* (Stanford, Calif.: Stanford University Press, 1968). For alternative models see John Griffiths, "Ideology in Criminal Procedures or a 'Third Model' of the Criminal Process," *Yale Law Journal* 79 (1970): 359; Thomas E. Reed and Larry K. Gaines, "Criminal Justice Models as a Function of Ideological Images: A Social Learning Alternative to Packer," *International Journal of Comparative and Applied Criminal Justice* (Winter 1982): 213.

9. William Chambliss, ed., *Crime and the Legal Process* (New York: McGraw-Hill, 1969), 86.

# Crime, Victimization, and Criminal Behavior

**Rape.** The very harshness of the word conveys the violence of the deed and the intensity of the fear and disgust with which society has traditionally viewed this crime. From ancient times, when developing cultures first became concerned about the purity of bloodlines and about what they regarded as the theft of property (the woman's virtue-value) and created regulations to govern sexual relationships, rape has been a taboo that has evolved into a formal offense.

Although forcible rape is generally understood to be sexual intercourse by a male with a female who is not his wife against her will and under conditions of threat or force, different countries have variously defined the offense and stipulated the penalties. For example, in England a decision of the House of Lords ruled that "if a man believes that a woman is consenting to sex, he cannot be convicted of rape, no matter how unreasonable his belief may be."[1] In some areas of the world rape is not charged if certain classes of women, such as servants, are involved. Forcible rape is an accepted form of sexual relations for unmarried males among the Gusii, a large tribe in Kenya.[2] In Western countries legal distinctions are often made among rape, forcible rape, and statutory rape, on the basis of such factors as the age of the female, the level of force employed, and the nature of the sexual conduct.

In the United States, before the rise of the women's movement, some states required that the victim's word be confirmed by evidence provided by some other person, a requirement that obviously could be difficult to meet. Moreover, defense counsel could make reference to the victim's past sexual conduct even though victims would regard their sexual experiences as irrelevant to the alleged crime.[3] In yet another change brought about by pressure from feminist organizations, some legislatures have changed their penal codes to allow wives to accuse their husbands of rape.

The variety of definitions of rape and evidential requirements for establishing that rape has occurred helps remind us that laws are written by human beings. They emerge from human experience and they are administered by humans. Thus disagreements often occur concerning the exact nature of the behavior that is legally defined as criminal.

In this chapter we first examine how crime is defined and measured, next look at crime victimization, and then examine theories on the causes of crime. As we strive to understand what crime is, and why it occurs, we will begin to see some of the complexities that make dealing with the "crime problem" such a challenging endeavor.

## Questions for Inquiry

- What are the sources of criminal law?
- What are the major types of crimes in the United States?
- How much crime is there and how is crime measured?
- Who are the victims of crime?
- What theories have criminologists developed to explain criminal behavior?

## Sources of Criminal Law

Many students ask, "Why is it illegal for me to smoke marijuana but legal for me to consume alcohol?" If the answer is that marijuana might be addictive, could lead to the use of more potent drugs, and is generally thought to be detrimental to health, then students may point out that alcoholism is a major social problem, that beer may whet one's thirst for hard liquor, and that heart and liver disorders, not to mention highway fatalities, are caused by overindulgence of alcohol. If the argument persists, an exasperated "clincher" might be "because pot smoking is against the law, and that's that!"

Why does the law declare some types of human behavior criminal and not others? What social forces are brought to bear on legislators as they write the criminal code? Why are activities that are labeled criminal

during one era found to be acceptable in another? Such issues need discussing because a theory explaining the sources of criminal law will have an important impact on assumptions concerning the nature of crime and the causes of criminal behavior.

A number of theories have been developed to explain the focus and functions of criminal laws and the social processes by which they evolve. These ideas can be divided into the consensus model and the conflict model.

## Consensus: Law as an Expression of Values

The **consensus model** holds that criminal law reflects societal values that go beyond the immediate interests of particular groups and individuals. Law is thus an expression of the social consciousness of the whole society.

Consensus theory has been greatly influenced by the pioneering sociologist Emile Durkheim (see the accompanying Biography), who argued that groups in society—black and white, rich and poor—might have all sorts of different interests but have underlying agreements on basic values. From this perspective, laws are necessary to establish moral boundaries in order to differentiate good members of the community from bad. Legislators, as representatives of the people, formalize these values in the criminal law. The law thus reflects the kind of conduct that a community considers, at a particular time, to be "sufficiently condemnable" to impose legal punishments. From this perspective criminal law may be viewed as "a barometer of the moral and social thinking of a community."[4]

As an example of consensus theories in action, we can look back to Puritan Massachusetts. Kai Erikson argues in the book *Wayward Puritans* that three serious "crime waves" in seventeenth-century Massachusetts helped the colonists define the values of their society. During each of these periods—the Antinomian controversy of 1636, the Quaker persecutions

The Salem witch trials of 1692 illustrate Durkheim's view that deviance tightens community bonds. To what extent is the prosecution of Dr. Jack Kevorkian, charged with assisting his patients in committing suicide, a contemporary example of consensus theory?

**consensus model**
A legal model that asserts that criminal law, as an expression of the social consciousness of the whole society, reflects values that transcend the immediate interests of particular groups and individuals.

of the late 1650s, and the witchcraft hysteria of 1692—the Massachusetts Bay colonists labeled as criminal certain behaviors that challenged church authority (disturbing the congregation, absence from church, contempt of the ministry). By arousing the public to these "crimes," the Puritan leadership was better able to set the boundaries of their society, to clarify their doctrines, and to renew community norms.

Erikson's fascinating study is based on Durkheim's idea that crime is a natural social activity and performs an important function. In Durkheim's view, violations of **norms** unite people in anger and indignation; that is, when a deviant breaks the rules of conduct that the rest of the community holds in high respect, citizens can come together to express their outrage.[5]

**norm**
Societal expectations concerning behavior.

Crime, then, creates a sense of mutuality or community because it supplies a focus for group feeling. Much like a war or some other emergency, deviance makes people more alert to their shared interests and values. To what extent do we label groups in our own society as criminal because they are viewed as violating important social norms and values?

Consensus theorists posit that there is agreement in the United States on the moral values that are formalized in criminal law. But many observers question whether this is possible given the multiplicity of racial, ethnic, and religious groups in contemporary American society. A national public opinion survey concerning the severity of various crimes sheds some light on this question.[6] The people interviewed were asked to rank the seriousness of 204 illegal events. The results (see Table 2.1) showed that there was generally broad agreement on the severity of specific crimes. Differences were noted, however, in that crime victims scored the acts higher than did nonvictims, and the severity ratings assigned by blacks and other minority-group members were generally lower than those assigned by whites. The consensus perspective seems to hold true for certain crimes, but not for others.

## Conflict: Law as an Expression of Power

**conflict model**
A legal model that asserts that the political power of interest groups and elites influences the content of criminal law.

In contrast to the view of the criminal code as a product of the society's value consensus, another approach emphasizes that the power of the dominant social groups influences the content of the code. Persons holding to this **conflict model** argue that a state or nation is better characterized by diversity and conflict than by consensus and stability. According to this model, people generally pursue their own goals, and these interests reflect the diversity of their membership in subgroups based on race, social class, age, and economic level. A second point made by conflict theorists is that the law is framed by the most powerful interests and is seldom the product of the values of the whole society.[7]

In this view, power, force, and constraint, rather than common values, are the basic organizing principles of society. Since there are unequal distributions of political influence, some groups will have greater access to decision makers and will use their influence to ensure that legislation is enacted to protect their interests. According to this approach, wrongful acts are characteristic of all classes in society, and the powerful not

| Severity Score | Ten Most Serious Offenses | Severity Score | Ten Least Serious Offenses |
|---|---|---|---|
| 72.1 | Planting a bomb in a public building. The bomb explodes and twenty people are killed. | 1.3 | Two persons willingly engage in a homosexual act. |
| 52.8 | A man forcibly rapes a woman. As a result of physical injuries, she dies. | 1.1 | Disturbing the neighborhood with loud, noisy behavior. |
| 43.2 | Robbing a victim at gunpoint. The victim struggles and is shot to death. | 1.1 | Taking bets on the numbers. |
| 39.2 | A man stabs his wife. As a result, she dies. | 1.1 | A group continues to hang around a corner after being told to break up by a police officer. |
| 35.7 | Stabbing a victim to death. | .9 | A youngster under sixteen runs away from home. |
| 35.6 | Intentionally injuring a victim. As a result, the victim dies. | .8 | Being drunk in public. |
| 33.8 | Running a narcotics ring. | .7 | A youngster under sixteen breaks a curfew law by being on the street after the hour permitted by law. |
| 27.9 | A woman stabs her husband. As a result, he dies. | .6 | Trespassing in the backyard of a private home. |
| 26.3 | An armed person skyjacks an airplane and demands to be flown to another country. | .3 | A person is a vagrant. That is, he has no home and no visible means of support. |
| 25.8 | A man forcibly rapes a woman. No other physical injury occurs. | .2 | A youngster under sixteen is truant from school. |

**Table 2.1**

**How do people rank the severity of crime?**

Respondents to a survey were asked to rank 204 illegal events ranging from school truancy to planting a lethal bomb. Severity scores were developed through mathematical techniques from the survey responses. A severity score of forty indicates that people believe the crime is twice as bad as a severity score of twenty.

SOURCE: U.S. Department of Justice, Bureau of Justice Statistics, *Report to the Nation on Crime and Justice*, 2d ed. (Washington, D.C.: Government Printing Office, 1988), 16.

only shape the law to their own advantage but also may dictate the use of enforcement resources so that certain groups are labeled and processed by the criminal justice system. Since the power of groups ebbs and flows, the criminal law, its application, and its interpretation will reflect those tidal alternations.[8]

In the United States we can point to various periods when the behaviors of certain groups were defined as criminal. Prohibition of alcohol early in the twentieth century is probably the best example. Joseph Gusfield has analyzed this movement as stemming from the political power of native-born Protestants concerned about the increasing number of immigrants from Catholic countries where alcohol was part of the culture.[9] Likewise, in the 1940s young men in Los Angeles known as "zootsuiters," which referred to their distinctive dress, were labeled deviant and the object of police action because they were perceived as flaunting traditional values. Conflict theorists would point to the fact that drug use by African-Americans (cocaine), Hispanics (marijuana), and Asians (opium) have been the focus of law enforcement efforts at various times. Today's war on drugs, to the extent that it focuses on the poor and powerless, is consistent with the conflict approach.

## Consensus versus Conflict: Emerging Theories

Conflict theorists say that criminal law is shaped by the dominant social and economic groups in society. From this perspective, the enactment of Prohibition was not motivated simply by a concern with the effects of alcohol consumption.

**mala in se**
Offenses that are wrong by their very nature, irrespective of statutory prohibition.

**mala prohibita**
Offenses prohibited by statute but not inherently wrong.

Which model better explains the sources of criminal law? At this point reaching a conclusion about the theoretical value of the consensus and conflict models is impossible. Certainly with respect to some laws, especially those prohibiting acts that are *mala in se,* wrong in themselves (murder, rape, assault), consensus exists in most Western societies on the values expressed in the law. Yet conflict theorists point out that even with these defined crimes, individuals with certain characteristics—for example the poor, minorities and the young—are treated more severely than others. In contrast, acts that are *mala prohibita,* or crimes because they are prohibited and not because they are wrong in themselves (vagrancy, gambling, drug use), have their source in the political power of special interests. As most criminal violations are now of the latter type, attention logically focuses on the conflict model.

Debate among scholars about the sources of the criminal law continues. Consensus scholars argue that in writing the criminal law, we evaluate various acts (heroin possession, robbery, rape) on the basis of some standard of values. Conflict scholars say that the standards of what ought to be criminal reflect various group and class definitions of conduct. Yet is there at least a partial consensus across all ethnic, racial, and class groups as to what is criminal? As Jerome Skolnick notes: "Surely, there is far greater negative consensus on the 'quality' of the behavior involved in forcible rape and armed robbery than in gambling or marijuana use. Shared definitions of crime exist, albeit variably, depending on the behavior in question, and the fact of sharing is also part of the social reality of crime."[10]

# Types of Crimes

The acts defined as criminal can be categorized in various ways. Scholars interested in the development of societal reaction to crime often use the distinction between *mala in se* and *mala prohibita*. A second way to categorize crimes is in terms of the legal distinction between crimes labeled *felonies* and those labeled *misdemeanors* (a distinction developed in Chapter 3). Criminologists have developed a third scheme that categorizes crimes according to the nature of the behavior and the type of person most likely to commit specific offenses. This scheme distinguishes five categories of crime: occupational crime, organized crime, visible crime, victimless crime, and political crime. Each type has its own level of risk and profitability, each arouses varying degrees of public disapproval, and each has its own group of offenders with differing characteristics.

## Occupational Crime

**Occupational crimes** are violations of the law committed through opportunities created in the course of a legal business or profession. Often viewed as shrewd business practices rather than as illegal offenses, they are crimes that, if perpetrated "correctly," are never discovered.

The problem of crimes committed in the course of business was first brought to the attention of scholars by Edwin Sutherland in 1939. Sutherland developed the concept of "white-collar crime" in which he emphasized the respectability of the offender and the occupational opportunity for the offense.[11] This orientation forced criminologists to recognize that criminal behavior was not primarily confined to lower-class people (so-called blue-collar crime) but reached into the upper echelons of society.

As the white-collar, blue-collar distinction lost much of its clarity in our modern postindustrial society, scholars have attempted to redefine Sutherland's idea. After reviewing the literature Gary Green has described four categories of occupational crimes:[12]

**1** *Occupational crimes for the benefit of employing organizations.* These are crimes where employers rather than offenders benefit directly, such as price fixing, theft of trade secrets, and falsification of product tests. In these instances an individual employee may commit the offense but, other than perhaps through a bonus or promotion, does not individually benefit. These are the crimes that are "committed in the suites rather than in the streets." Well-known examples include charges that the Ford Motor Company in the 1960s knew that the Pinto's gas tank might explode and yet did nothing about it, a two

**occupational crime**
Conduct in violation of the law that is committed through opportunities created in the course of a legal occupation.

Former television evangelist Jim Bakker and his wife, Tammy, outside their Palm Springs, California, home. He served nearly five years in federal prison for bilking contributors to his ministries of $150,000,000.

billion dollar overbilling of customers by the Exxon Corporation, the nation's largest oil company, and the seemingly continuous overbilling of the U.S. armed services by military contractors.

**2** *Occupational crimes through the exercise of state-based authority.* In these crimes the offender has the legal authority to enforce laws or to command others. Examples are the police officer who takes confiscated drugs from the evidence room, the politician who takes a bribe in exchange for his or her vote, or the notary public who falsifies a document. The 1978 ABSCAM case involving several congressmen and a senator who accepted bribes in exchange for introducing a private immigration bill and for obtaining government contracts for "Abdul Enterprises," an FBI sting operation, fits this category.

**3** *Occupational crimes committed by professionals in their capacity as professionals.* Physicians, lawyers, and stockbrokers might violate their professional oaths or take advantage of clients by, for instance, sexually exploiting a patient, illegally dispensing drugs, personally using funds placed in escrow, or using confidential stock-market information for personal gain. The conviction of stockbroker Ivan Boesky in 1986 for using confidential information to profit in securities trade is a good example of this category. Likewise Michael Milken, the "junk-bond king," was sentenced in 1989 to ten years in prison for securities fraud and for filing false information with the Securities and Exchange Commission.

**4** *Occupational crimes committed by individuals as individuals where opportunities are not based on governmental power or professional position.* Examples of this type of crime include employee theft from the organization, filing false expense claims, and embezzlement. Jim Bakker of the "Praise the Lord" television evangelism ministry is a recent example of someone who was charged with committing fraud for personal benefit.

Although highly profitable, most categories of occupational crime do not come to public attention. Regulatory agencies, such as the Federal Trade Commission and the Securities and Exchange Commission, are often ineffective in their enforcement of the law. Many business and professional organizations "police" themselves, dropping employees or members who commit offenses. However, the low level of enforcement and prosecution of occupational crimes may result from the fact that the general public does not view these offenses as it views crimes of violence or offenses such as robbery, which involve threats to personal safety. Yet the costs to society of occupational crimes are tremendous.

## Organized Crime

The term **organized crime** describes a social framework for the perpetration of criminal acts rather than specific types of offenses. Organized criminals provide goods and services to millions of people. They will engage in any illegal activity that provides a minimum of risk and a maximum of profit. Thus organized crime involves a network of enterprises, usually cutting across state and national boundaries, that range from legitimate businesses to shady involvement with labor unions to activities that cater to desires for "goods," such as drugs, sex, and pornography, that cannot be obtained legally.

With minor exceptions, organized crime seldom provides inputs to the criminal justice process. Investigations of the crime "families," known as the Mafia and Cosa Nostra by congressional committees and other governmental bodies, have provided detailed accounts of the structure, membership, and activities of these groups, yet few arrests are made and even fewer convictions gained. The FBI has been especially vocal about the impact of organized crime on American society, but it, too, has failed to provide the evidence that would put this particular type of criminal behind bars.

Although the public often associates organized crime with Americans of Italian ancestry, other ethnic groups have dominated at various times. One scholar has noted America's "queer ladder of social mobility," in which each new immigrant group has used organized crime as the first few rungs of the climb. The Irish were the first group to organize criminal activity on a large scale in the United States, followed by Jews who dominated gambling and labor racketeering at the turn of the century. The Italians came next and did not get a commanding leg up the ladder until the late 1930s.[13]

Today there is increasing evidence that African-Americans, Hispanics, and Asians have begun to manage organized crime enterprises in some cities.[14] Drug trafficking has brought Colombian and Mexican crime groups to U.S. shores, and reports from California document the emergence of Vietnamese-, Chinese-, and Japanese-led organizations.[15] These new groups do not fit the Mafia pattern. Law enforcement agencies have had to alter their tactics in dealing with the organized crimes of these non-Italian groups.[16]

## Visible Crime

**Visible crime**, often referred to as "street crime" or "ordinary crime" and committed primarily by disadvantaged classes in society, runs the gamut from shoplifting to homicide. For offenders, these crimes are the least profitable violations and, because they are visible, the least protected. These are the acts that most of the public regard as criminal, and dealing with them consumes most law enforcement, judicial, and correctional resources. Included in this category are crimes of violence, such as homicide, rape, and assault, as well as crimes against property, such as theft, larceny, and burglary.

As illustrated by "Jones," the central character in the following Close-Up, perpetrators of visible crimes generally come from the more impoverished people in society. This correlation has led some theorists to argue that the decidedly lower-class characteristics of the inhabitants of American correctional institutions reflect the class bias of a society that has singled out only certain types of criminal activity. They note that we do not prosecute occupational crimes with the same intensity as we do street crimes.

**organized crime**
A social framework for the perpetration of criminal acts, usually in such fields as gambling, drugs, and prostitution, in which illegal services that are in great demand are provided.

**visible crimes**
Offenses against persons and property committed primarily by members of the lower class. Often referred to as "street crimes" or "ordinary crimes," these are the offenses most upsetting to the public.

CLOSE-UP

# Portrait of a Mugger

His world is small, a whirlpool of lower New York street corners, tense friendships, family problems, small-change business deals, people without last names— and sudden violence. It is an insular world where "uptown" means a girl friend's apartment north of Houston Street and "the Bronx" is your brother's apartment on 287th Street. When it suited him, Jones stayed at his parents' home, a tiny shelter in "the projects," and when it didn't he stayed with one of his women.

One day we decided to play a rather serious game: we would pretend to be muggers.

"I don't know all the rules and answers, but the ones I know I'm sure of," Jones is saying as we begin my guided tour of victimland. "Rule number one is that everything's okay as long as you don't get caught." He is pointing out areas of interest along the way—you and your wallet, for example.

I see a jowly, middle-aged man with wavy hair carrying a grocery bag toward a car. We are about fifty yards from him.

Jones sees the man but does not turn. His eyes seem to be aimed at the pavement.

"Yeah, he'd be good. He's got his hands full. You let him get in the car, and you get in with him before he can close the door. You are right on top of him, and you show him the knife. He'll slide over and go along with it."

"After that?"

"If you think he's gonna chase you, you can put him in the trunk."

We turn toward a cluster of buildings. I see a man in a black suburban coat. He is taller and younger.

"Not him," Jones says, again without looking directly at him. "He looks hard. You could take him off in a hallway, but he would give you trouble in the street." . . .

We walk to Second Avenue, moving among crowds of shoppers—sad faces, tired arms filled with packages, coats, purses, flat hip-pocket wallets in the sunny afternoon . . . so much *money* in this speckled fool's gold afternoon. . . .

He looks across the street.

"There's a precinct house on that block. The check-cashing place near it is a good place to pull rips. Nobody thinks a dude would have the heart to do it so close to a cop station; so nobody watches it very closely."

We walk into a grimy side street between First and Second Avenues and stop across from a storefront. The red-and-blue sign—Checks Cashed/ Money Orders Filled—is ringed with light bulbs.

Jones looks at my watch and sees that it is two-fifteen.

"It's a little early now. Pretty soon, this place will be doin' business." We lean against a store window and wait.

Jones nudges me. "That dude's got cash. Watch him."

Across the street, I see a tall man with snow-white hair. He walks confidently, head erect, wearing a black cashmere coat.

Jones's street sense is astounding. The man hasn't moved directly toward the store, only stepped off the curb. He could be headed anywhere on the block.

Jones says he will cash a check.

He passes the storefront, then stops, steps backward, and disappears into the doorway.

"He is being careful. So he's got cash."

"A good victim?"

"Yeah."

Three minutes later, the man emerges and continues walking down the block.

"From the way he walks, I think he lives on this block."

"Why?"

"The way he moves. He looks like he knows where he's going. He's afraid to move too fast, but he looks like he knows where he wants to get to."

As Jones finishes the sentence, the tall old man turns on one foot and walks into a brownstone apartment building.

"When would you move?"

"I'd wait until he gets through the door. The building is old, so the second door won't lock fast. If you time it right, the lock won't stop you."

Jones drags on the cigarette he is holding.

"I'd be in there now. I'd let him start climbing the stairs. Then I'd take him."

And the old man, who looks like a statesman but lives on a bad block, would lose something. His Social Security check? A stock dividend? His life? . . .

SOURCE: From James Willwerth, *JONES: Portrait of a Mugger.* Copyright ©1974 by James Willwerth. Reprinted by permission of the publisher M. Evans and Co., Inc., New York, NY 10017.

On what grounds should this male prostitute be treated as a criminal under the law? Are there really crimes without victims?

## Crimes without Victims

**Crimes without victims** can be defined as offenses involving a willing and private exchange of goods or services that are in strong demand but are illegal. These are the offenses against morality: examples include prostitution, gambling, and drug use and sales. These are victimless since the participants in the exchange do not feel that they are being harmed. Prosecutions for these offenses are justified on the grounds that society as a whole is being injured because the moral fabric of the community is endangered. The use of the criminal law to enforce standards of morality is costly. These cases flood the courts, and enforcement of them necessitates the use of police informers.

Some people feel that classifying goods as prohibited only encourages organized crime to develop an apparatus to supply the desired products. If the sale and possession of heroin, for example, were to be legalized, its price would probably drop immediately, underworld elements would move to more profitable business opportunities, and the crimes perpetrated by users to obtain the money for their costly habit would be reduced. It can also be argued that purveyors of illicit goods and services depend on law enforcement activities to keep profits high. On the other hand, can crime truly be victimless? Although some may argue that individual adults should have the freedom to harm their bodies with drug use or their financial situation through gambling, but this position seems to ignore the impact of these activities on family members and others. But are the costs of the crimes and violence associated with the prohibition worth their impact on the values emphasized?

**crimes without victims**
Offenses involving a willing and private exchange of illegal goods or services for which there is a strong demand. Participants do not feel that they are being harmed. Prosecution is justified on the ground that society as a whole is being injured by the act.

## Political Crime

**political crimes**

Acts that constitute a threat against the state (such as treason, sedition, espionage).

**Political crime** includes activities, such as treason, sedition (rebellion), and espionage, that are viewed as threats to the government. Political freedom is always qualified, and American history has seen many laws enacted in response to apparent threats to the established order. The Sedition Act of 1789 provided for the punishment of those uttering or publishing statements against the government. The Smith Act of 1940 forbade advocating overthrow of the government by force or violence. During the turmoil surrounding the Vietnam War in the late 1960s, the government used charges of criminal conspiracy as a means to deter activities of those opposing the administration's policies.

In authoritarian countries the mere making of statements critical of the government is a crime that may result in prosecution and imprisonment. In Western democratic countries, some criminologists would aver, there is virtually no political crime except for a rare offense like treason. As noted by Francis Allen, "laws to proscribe political behavior are enacted in periods of strong public feeling, sometimes bordering on hysteria."[17] That is not to say illegal acts, such as the 1992 bombing of New York's World Trade Center, are not perpetrated for political purposes. Such crimes are punished because of the nature of the act, not because of its intended impact. A terrorist who kills a government official is prosecuted for homicide, as is a woman who kills her spouse.

An examination of the five categories of crime shows that there is considerable variation not only in the types of criminal behavior but also in the public's reaction to it. The public is most upset by visible crimes. To better understand the crime problem in America it is important to know how the amount and types of crimes are measured.

## How Much Crime Is There?

A recent newspaper headline proclaimed, "'Explosion' in Crime Powerful—but False." The accompanying article stressed that crime stories fill the evening news, setting the political agenda across the country. But is all the concern about rampant crime justified? As the author noted, "It is as though the country were confronting a devastating new wave of theft and violence. It isn't. There is no new national crime wave."[18]

Whatever the impressions left by tourist killings in Miami, carjacking deaths in Washington, drive-by murders in Los Angeles, and gang warfare in Wichita, the most reliable national crime figures available indicate that serious crime across the country has occurred much less frequently since the record-setting years of the early 1980s.[19]

That serious crime across the country occurs less frequently than it did during the early 1980s is now accepted as fact by researchers. Nevertheless, the media attention given to crime stories has made citizens fearful. The crime problem is listed near the top of American concerns (Figure 2.1), and presidents annually ask Congress to toughen efforts against

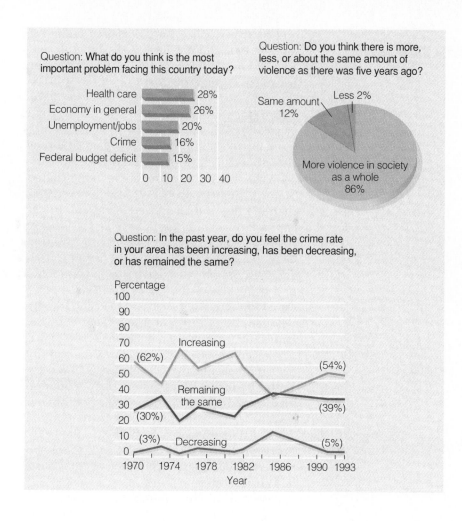

Question: What do you think is the most important problem facing this country today?

| | |
|---|---|
| Health care | 28% |
| Economy in general | 26% |
| Unemployment/jobs | 20% |
| Crime | 16% |
| Federal budget deficit | 15% |

0  10  20  30  40

Question: Do you think there is more, less, or about the same amount of violence as there was five years ago?

Same amount 12%
Less 2%
More violence in society as a whole 86%

Question: In the past year, do you feel the crime rate in your area has been increasing, has been decreasing, or has remained the same?

Percentage

Increasing (62%) ... (54%)
Remaining the same (30%) ... (39%)
Decreasing (3%) ... (5%)

1970  1974  1978  1982  1986  1990  1993
Year

**Figure 2.1**
**Crime: In the nation, in our neighborhood**
Crime remains one of the most important problems facing Americans. Over eight in ten people surveyed believe society is more violent than five years ago. A plurality say there is more crime in their neighborhood than a year ago.

SOURCE: "Public Opinion and Demographic Report," *The Public Perspective* 5 (November/December 1993):78.

crime. To gain a perspective on the amount of crime today, we need to look at America's past and at the experiences of other developed countries. We will then examine how the incidence of crime is measured and some of the problems involved in determining the extent and direction of criminal activity.

## Crime in Historical and Comparative Perspective

In view of the capacity of other eras to produce criminals, ours is neither the best nor the worst of times. There has always been too much crime, and virtually every generation since the founding of the Republic has felt threatened by it. References abound to serious outbreaks of violence following the Civil War, after World War I, during Prohibition, and in the midst of the Great Depression.

That there has always been a great deal of crime does not mean that the amount and types of crime have been the same. During the labor unrest of the 1880s and 1930s, pitched battles took place between strikers

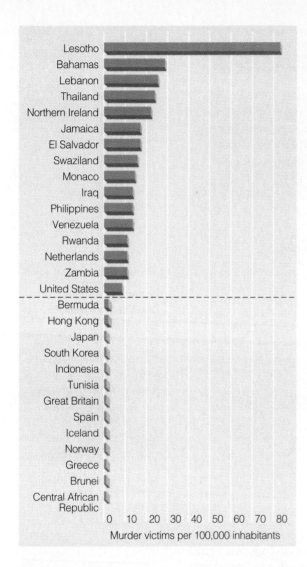

**Figure 2.2**
**Comparing homicide rates in different countries**

Why is the murder rate in the United States so much higher than in other developed and some less developed countries? (Note: Only countries with the highest and lowest rates are included. The dashed line indicates where countries have been left out.)

SOURCE: Interpol and United Nations Statistics, 1980–1986. Adapted from G. Deane, "Cross-National Comparison of Homicide: Age/sex-adjusted Rates Using the 1980 U.S. Homicide Experience as a Standard," *Journal of Quantitative Criminology* 3 (1987), 215–227.

and company police. Race riots occurred in Atlanta in 1907 and in Chicago, Washington, and East St. Louis, Illinois, in 1991. Organized crime became a special focus during the 1930s. The murder and non-negligent homicide rate, which reached a high in 1933 and a low during World War II, has actually decreased since 1980, even though the rate in some cities has risen dramatically during the last several years.

What is striking about crime in the United States is that the problem is so much greater than in other industrialized countries. In per capita terms, about ten American men die by criminal violence for every Japanese, Austrian, German, or Swedish man; about fifteen American men die for every Swiss or English man; and over twenty die for every Dane.[20] More than 150 countries, both developed and less developed, have lower murder rates than the United States, as shown in Figure 2.2.

When we look at robbery rates, the data are even more dismaying. The robbery rate in New York City is five times greater than in London and, incredibly, 125 times higher than that of Tokyo.[21] The 1980s saw crime in the United States stabilize at a very high level; in the 1990s, however, arrests for drug sales and possession skyrocketed, causing dislocations in the courts and corrections.

We can gain further insight into the nature and extent of crime in the United States by looking at countries, such as Iceland, where there is little crime. Some might say that because Iceland is small, homogeneous, and somewhat isolated, the crime problem in the United States is not comparable. But as suggested by the Comparative Perspective on Iceland (pages 56–57), there may be other factors that help to explain the differences in the amount and type of criminal activity in various countries.

Determining how much crime of various types actually takes place, however, is not as straightforward as it may seem. Let's examine more closely the sources of data about crime in the United States and what the data tell us about current trends in crime.

## Sources of Crime Data

One of the frustrations in studying criminal justice is the lack of accurate means of knowing the amount of crime. Surveys of the public indicate that much more crime occurs than is reported to the police. This phenomenon is referred to as the **dark figure of crime**.

Homicide and auto theft are the two offenses whose reported and estimated occurrences correspond most closely. In the case of homicide, this correspondence can be explained by the fact that a body must be accounted for; in the case of motor vehicle theft, by the fact that insurance payments require a police report be made. Of most serious concern is that about 45 percent of rape victims do not report their attacks to the police; almost half of robbery victims and 55 percent of those experiencing simple assault do not do so. Figure 2.3 shows the percentage of victimizations not reported to the police.

Many reasons have been advanced to account for nonreporting of crime. Some victims of rape and assault fear the embarrassment of public disclosure and interrogation by the police. Another reason is that the value of property lost by larceny, robbery, or burglary may not be worth the effort of a police investigation. Many citizens are also deterred from reporting a crime by an unwillingness to become "involved," to fill out papers at the station house, perhaps go to court, or appear at a police lineup. As these examples suggest, many feel it is rational not to report criminal incidents because the costs outweigh the gains.

Until the 1970s, the only criminal activities that were counted by government were those that were known to the police and that made their way into the Federal Bureau of Investigation's *Uniform Crime Reports* (*UCR*). Since 1972, however, the Department of Justice has sponsored the National Crime Victimization Surveys (NCVS). These are surveys of the public to determine the amount of victimization. One might say the data from these two sources should give us a clear picture of the amount of crime, crime trends, and the characteristics of offenders. However, the picture is blurred, some might say distorted, because of differences in the way crime is measured by the *UCR* and the NCVS.

**Uniform Crime Reports**  The *Uniform Crime Reports* are published annually by the FBI. At the urging of the International Association of Chiefs of Police, in 1930 Congress authorized this national and uniform system of compiling crime data. The *UCR* is the product of a voluntary national network through which about 16,000 local, state, and federal law enforcement agencies, policing 95 percent of the U.S. population, transmit information to Washington concerning the twenty-nine types of offenses listed in Table 2.2 (page 58). For eight major crimes—"index offenses"—the collected data show factors such as age, race, and number of reported crimes solved, while for the twenty-one other offense categories the data are not so complete.

**dark figure of crime**
A metaphor that emphasizes the dangerous dimension of crime that is never reported to the police.

Although the overall crime problem is sometimes exaggerated, this scene in Houston, Texas, is all too familiar. Why is there so much more violent crime in the United States than in other developed countries?

## Iceland: A Country with Little Crime

Iceland is a country where crime is not perceived as a problem. Why is it that Iceland should differ so much from its neighbors and from other developed countries? Is it the size of the population? The homogeneity of the people? The physical isolation from the major centers of Europe? What is it like to live in a country where there have been only twenty-one robberies over a twenty-year period, two homicides per year, and where the first bank robbery with a firearm occurred in 1984?

Iceland, with a population of 253,000, is an island republic the size of Virginia. It has strong cultural ties to Denmark, which ruled it from 1380 until World War II, and to the other countries of Scandinavia. The Icelandic population is ethnically homogeneous, there are relatively small differences along class lines, literacy is very high, and the Evangelical Lutheran Church is the church for about 95 percent of the population. The people enjoy a high standard of living, an extensive health and welfare system, and a 1 percent unemployment rate. To preserve the "purity" of the culture, governmental policies have been instituted to restrict immigration.

Even though 90 percent of the Icelandic people live in urban areas, the society is one where extended families, strong community ties, and a homogeneous culture seem to act as effective agents of social control. A principal reason for these features of Icelandic society is that there has been a cultural lag in the shift to industrialization and urbanization that began at the turn of the century. Iceland has retained many aspects of a stagnant agrarian society.

### Figure 2.3
### Percentage of victimizations not reported to the police

Why do some people not report their victimizations to the police? What can be done to encourage reporting?

SOURCE: U.S. Department of Justice, Bureau of Justice Statistics, *Report to the Nation on Crime and Justice*, 2d ed. (Washington, D.C.: Government Printing Office, 1988), 34.

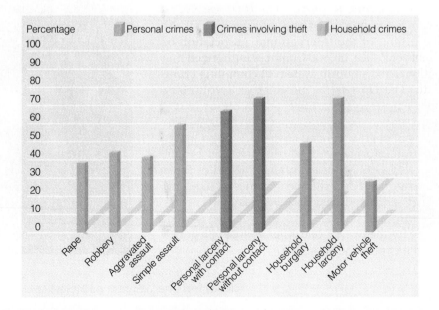

When compared to the United States, Icelandic crime rates are extremely low. For example, the assault rate per 100,000 people is 24, in the United States it is 383; the rate for homicide is .8 in Iceland, and 4 in the United States; the rate for rape is 10 in Iceland and 75 in the United States. The homogeneous population, geographic isolation from other countries, and prohibition of handgun ownership all may contribute to the low level of violence in Iceland.

There has been an increase in drug use in Iceland during the past decade but it is still minuscule compared to other Western countries. Marijuana use increased during the 1970s but has declined since then. In 1984 about 4 percent of Icelanders aged sixteen to thirty-six said they had consumed amphetamines. It was not until 1983 that police found cocaine for the first time; they first seized a significant amount (one kilo) in 1987.

Undoubtedly the size of Iceland's population and its isolation from the major drug supply routes account for the low level of drug abuse. Also it is easy to "seal" the country, since import routes are few, and it is difficult for drug users to hide their habit in such a tightly knit community. There seem to be no organized drug rings in Iceland.

Whereas most Western countries are preoccupied with the war on drugs, this social problem is overshadowed in Iceland by concern over the abuse of alcohol. Alcohol abuse has a high correlation with the crime rate, particularly in the form of drunken driving. Total consumption of alcohol has increased during recent decades and public drunkenness is the most common violation of the criminal law. With the number of automobiles per capita the highest in the world, Ice-

land's drunk-driving rules are strictly enforced with a resulting high arrest rate (1,400 per 100,000 people vs. 386 per 100,000 in the United States). Most arrests occur as a result of intensive routine highway checks. When blood tests reveal a level of .5 to 1.2 per milliliter alcohol, drivers lose their licenses for one month. When tests show a level of more than 1.2 per milliliter, drivers lose their licenses for a year. A third offense means a prison sentence. With low levels of serious crime and a policy of treating alcohol offenses severely, 20 percent of prisoners in Iceland have been committed for drunk driving.

The number of crimes reported to the Icelandic police has reflected the rapid transformation of the society during the past thirty years. As in other countries the crime rate increased after World War II but has leveled off during the past decade. The increases in crime compared to a generation ago can be accounted for by several factors. For example, the growth in economic crime seems to be a consequence of more complex business activities. Concern over the abuse of alcohol has resulted in proactive law enforcement policies that have contributed to the amount of crime as measured by arrests. But these "increases" must be viewed in the context of the very low levels of criminality in Iceland as compared to other developed countries. As with other Scandinavian countries, as well as such low-crime countries as Switzerland, there appear to be cultural, geographic, economic, and public policy factors that explain the relative absence of crime in Iceland.

SOURCE: From Omar H. Kristmundsson, "Crime and the Crime Control System of Iceland" (University of Connecticut, unpublished paper, 1990). Reprinted by permission.

Crime data are expressed three ways in the *UCR*: (1) as aggregates (a total of 672,478 robberies were reported to the police in 1992), (2) as percentage changes over different time periods (1992 represented a 2.2 percent decrease in crime from 1991), and (3) as a rate per 100,000 people in the U.S. (the robbery rate in 1992 was 263.6).

The value of the *UCR* has been questioned by scholars. They point out that the data concern only crimes reported to the police, that submission of the data is voluntary, that the reports are not truly uniform because events are defined according to differing criteria in various regions of the country, and that many occupational crimes are not included.[22] In response to some of the criticisms of the *UCR*, the FBI has made revisions in the program, which will be implemented nationwide during the late 1990s. Some offenses are being redefined, and police agencies are being asked to report more details about crime events. Using the **National**

**Uniform Crime Reports**

An annually published statistical summary of crimes reported to the police, which is based on voluntary reports to the FBI by local, state, and federal law enforcement agencies.

| Part I (Index Offenses) | Part II (Other Offenses) |
|---|---|
| 1. Criminal homicide | 9. Simple assaults |
| 2. Forcible rape | 10. Forgery and counterfeiting |
| 3. Robbery | 11. Fraud |
| 4. Aggravated assault | 12. Embezzlement |
| 5. Burglary | 13. Buying, receiving, or possessing stolen property |
| 6. Larceny-theft | 14. Vandalism |
| 7. Auto theft | 15. Weapons (carrying, possession, etc.) |
| 8. Arson | 16. Prostitution and commercialized vice |
| | 17. Sex offenses |
| | 18. Violation of narcotic drug laws |
| | 19. Gambling |
| | 20. Offenses against the family and children |
| | 21. Driving under the influence |
| | 22. Violation of liquor laws |
| | 23. Drunkenness |
| | 24. Disorderly conduct |
| | 25. Vagrancy |
| | 26. All other offenses (excluding traffic) |
| | 27. Suspicion |
| | 28. Curfew and loitering (juvenile) |
| | 29. Runaway (juvenile) |

**Table 2.2
Uniform Crime
Reports Offenses**

The *UCR* presents extensive data on eight index offenses and twenty-one other offenses for which there is less information. An important limitation of the *UCR* is that only crimes reported to the police are tabulated.

SOURCE: U.S. Department of Justice, Federal Bureau of Investigation, *Crime in the United States* (Washington, D.C.: Government Printing Office, 1993).

**National Incident-Based Reporting System**

A reporting system in which the police describe each offense in a crime incident together with data describing the offender, victim, and property.

**National Crime Victimization Surveys**

Interviews of samples of the U.S. population conducted by the Bureau of Justice Statistics to determine the number and types of criminal victimizations and thus the extent of unreported as well as reported crime.

**Incident-Based Reporting System** (NIBRS), police agencies in the future are to report all crimes committed during an incident, not just the most serious one as is currently the case. Whereas the *UCR* counts incidents and arrests for the eight index offenses and counts arrests for other offenses, NIBRS will provide detailed incident information on forty-six offenses in twenty-two crime categories. NIBRS, unlike the *UCR*, will distinguish between attempted and completed crimes. Other innovations include collection of data about the victim, offender, and the environments in which they interact.[23]

**National Crime Victimization Surveys** In 1972 the U.S. Bureau of the Census began the largest series of interview programs ever conducted to determine the extent and nature of crime victimization. These surveys, sponsored by the Department of Justice, are designed to generate estimates of quarterly and yearly victimization rates for all index offenses except homicide and arson. The **National Crime Victimization Surveys** (NCVS) are based on data collected through interviews with a national probability sample of 101,000 people representing 49,000 households. The same people are interviewed twice a year for three years about their experiences with crime in the previous six months. In addition, specialized surveys of twenty-six communities produce rates for many of the nation's largest cities. Separate studies of businesses are made. The results show that for the crimes measured (rape, robbery, assault, burglary, theft), 36 million victimizations affecting 22 million households (about 25 percent of all U.S. households) occur each year, a level much higher than that indicated by the number of crimes reported to the police.[24]

Each person interviewed in the national sample is asked a series of questions (for instance: Did anyone beat you up, attack you, or hit you with something such as a rock or a bottle?) to determine whether he or she has been victimized. For each affirmative response to these "incident screen" questions, detailed questions then elicit specific facts about the event, characteristics of the offender, and resulting financial losses or physical disabilities. The collection of such data permits the number of crimes that have occurred nationwide to be estimated, yields trend information on the offenders, and indicates emerging demographic patterns.

Although the victimization studies have added to our scientific knowledge about crime, there are a number of difficulties with these data. For example, it is obvious that the surveys are unlikely to gather information about offenses in which the persons being interviewed participated. NCVS representatives are undoubtedly seen as official representatives of government, and thus respondents may be reluctant to report crimes initiated by family or friends. Moreover, the surveys are organized to document the *victim's* perception of an incident, and it can be argued that laypersons do not have the legal background that would help them differentiate criminal from noncriminal behavior. The high number of incidents reported by the young, for example, is thought to be produced by defining schoolyard shakedowns or fights as criminal. Property thought to have been stolen may have been lost. Memories may grow hazy on dates and carry last year's crime into this year's data. The Bureau of Justice Statistics has recently redesigned certain aspects of the NCVS to improve accuracy and detail. Table 2.3 compares the *Uniform Crime Reports* and the National Crime Victimization Survey.

## Crime Trends

Despite some skepticism about the accuracy of the data concerning crime, there is general agreement that the amount of crime rose from its level in the mid-1960s. What remains in dispute is when the increase peaked and the direction of crime trends since that point. The National Crime Victimization Surveys show that the victimization rate peaked in 1981 and has since fallen 21 percent for personal thefts and 17 percent for household crimes. Only with violent crimes has the victimization rate not differed significantly, declining (2.4 percent) from the 1981 high.[25] The *Uniform Crime Reports* tell a somewhat different story: a dramatic rise in crime rates beginning in 1964 and continuing increases for most categories until 1980, when the rates began to stabilize or decline. Only the rates for violent crimes have continued to rise.[26] Crime trends for violent crimes are revealed in Figure 2.4.

| | Uniform Crime Reports | National Crime Victimization Surveys |
|---|---|---|
| **Offenses measured** | Homicide | |
| | Rape | Rape |
| | Robbery (personal and commercial | Robbery (Personal) |
| | Assault (aggravated) | Assault (aggravated and simple) |
| | Burglary (commercial and household) | Household burglary |
| | Larceny (commercial and household) | Larceny (personal and household) |
| | Motor vehicle theft | Motor vehicle theft |
| | Arson | |
| **Scope** | Crimes reported to the police in most jurisdictions; considerable flexibility in developing small-area data | Crimes both reported and not reported to police; all data are for the nation as a whole; some data are available for a few large geographic areas |
| **Collection method** | Police department reports to FBI | Survey interviews: periodically measures the total number of crimes committed by asking a national sample of 49,000 households representing 101,000 people over the age of twelve about their experiences as victims of crime during a specific period |
| **Kinds of information** | In addition to offense counts, provides information on crime clearances, persons arrested, persons charged, law enforcement officers killed and assaulted, and characteristics of homicide victims | Provides details about victims (such as age, race, sex, education, income, and whether the victim and offender were related) and about crimes (such as time and place of occurrence, whether or not reported to police, use of weapons, occurrence of injury, and economic consequences) |
| **Sponsor** | Department of Justice Federal Bureau of Investigation | Department of Justice Bureau of Justice Statistics |

**Table 2.3
The *UCR* and NCVS**

Compare the data sources. Remember that the *UCR* tabulates only crimes reported to the police, whereas the NCVS is based on interviews with victims.

SOURCE: U.S. Department of Justice, Bureau of Justice Statistics, *Report to the Nation on Crime and Justice*, 2d ed. (Washington, D.C.: Government Printing Office, 1988), 11.

The differences in the trends indicated by the NCVS and *UCR* are explained in part by the different data sources and different population bases on which their computations of crime rates are based. Remember, the *UCR* is based on crimes reported to the police, and the NCVS records crimes experienced by victims. Over time the gap between the *UCR* and the NCVS data has lessened. The Bureau of Justice Statistics found that in 1986, for the first time, more than half of all violent crimes were reported to the police and significant gains in reporting were found in other categories.[27] This trend undoubtedly reflects an increase in citizen willingness to report criminal behavior. The introduction of 911 phone numbers, the

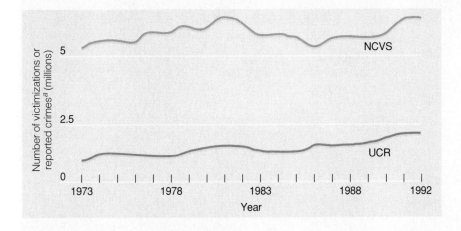

**Figure 2.4**
**Violent crime trends measured by *UCR* and NCVS**
Note that these data are for the *number* of violent victimizations reported, not for the victimization rate from 1973–1992.

SOURCE: U.S. Department of Justice, Bureau of Justice Statistics, *Highlights from Twenty Years of Surveying Crime Victims* (August, 1993), 4.

[a] Includes NCVS violent crimes of rape, robbery, aggravated assault, and simple assault, and *UCR* violent crimes of murder and nonnegligent manslaughter, forcible rape, robbery, and aggravated assault.

augmented presence of police in many communities, and neighborhood watch programs have helped this effort.

**Demographic Influences on Crime Trends**   The changing demographic characteristics of the American people, particularly with regard to age and urbanization, constitute a major ingredient in the analysis of crime trends. Criminologists have long shown that crime, especially those the public fear most, is largely a function of youth and young adulthood. Persons aged fourteen to twenty-four have been the most crime-prone group in the country. In 1993, for example, the *UCR* disclosed that 29 percent of those arrested for serious crimes were under the age of eighteen. Almost half of those arrested for violent crimes and 60 percent of those arrested for property crimes were under twenty-five.[28]

The rise in crime during the 1970s has been attributed by some criminologists to the post-World War II baby boom. By the mid-1970s, the high-risk crime group of fourteen-to-twenty-four-year-olds constituted a much larger portion than usual of the U.S. population. It was thus predicted that between 40 to 50 percent of the total arrests during that period could have been expected as the result of the overall population increase and the size of the crime-prone age group. Likewise, the decline in most crime rates during the 1980s has been attributed to the maturing of the post-World War II generation.

The impact of demographic factors such as age on the extent of crime has been disputed by other researchers, who argue that arrest and sentencing practices play a more important role than age in reducing crime. These researchers claim that the government's tougher response to crime in the 1980s should be given greater credit for the decline in crime rates. They assert that the lenient policies of the 1960s contributed to the rise of crime: crime went up as the probability of being arrested and being sent to prison for a serious crime went down. As crime-control policies were made more punitive in the late 1970s and 1980s, the probability of arrest and incarceration increased. In this view, the tougher stance has paralleled the fall of crime rates. However, the rise of violent crime since 1988 remains a puzzle for most criminologists.

Males aged 14–24 are the most crime-prone group. What factors might account for this?

**Rethinking Crime Trends**   Research has suggested that it is extremely difficult to point to specific factors that cause a rise or decrease in crime rates. It is also vexing to try to determine why the crime rate in the United States should be so much higher than the rates in other industrialized democracies. It was once thought that with the proper tools the crime problem could be analyzed and solved. Social scientists have discovered, however, that crime is an extremely complex phenomenon involving a number of basic influences on human behavior. Key questions remain: Do changes in crime trends occur because of demography, unemployment rates, housing conditions, and changes in family structure, or are they a result of the multiple interaction of these, and other, factors? Until we have a better understanding of the causes of change in criminal behavior patterns, it is premature to assign either blame or credit to governmental policies for shifts in crime rates.

## Crime Victimization

Much has been written about the characteristics of offenders, their modes of operation, and how the criminal justice system deals with them. Until the past few decades, however, researchers paid little note to crime victims. The criminological subfield of **victimology** emerged in the 1950s and began to focus attention on the following four questions: (1) who is victimized, (2) what is the impact of crime, (3) what is the experience of victims at the hands of the criminal justice system, and (4) what is the role of victims in precipitating the acts against them? We now turn to recent research on crime victimization.

## Who Is Victimized?

The probability of being victimized is not evenly spread across society. Michael Hindelang, Michael Gottfredson, and James Garofalo have developed a lifestyle-exposure theory to account for the fact that some people are more likely than others to be victimized.[29] They argue that demographic factors influence personal lifestyle—one's routine activities such as work, home life, and recreation. Lifestyles are related to different levels of exposure to dangerous places, times, and other people—situations where there is a high risk of victimization.[30] From the lifestyle-exposure perspective one can imagine the high probability of being robbed if one walks alone through a high crime area late at night to a parked luxury car. Figure 2.5 shows the links among the major factors used in the lifestyle-exposure model to determine the probability of personal victimization.

Data from twenty years of National Crime Victimization Surveys lend credence to the lifestyle-exposure model by giving us an understanding of the characteristics of crime victims. As shown in Table 2.4, the surveys shed light on the connections between gender, age, and race, and the probability of being a victim of the violent crimes of rape, robbery, and assault.

With the exception of rape and personal robbery with contact (purse snatching), males are more likely than females to be victims of crime. In any given year, the victimization rate is about 40 per 1,000 for males and 23 per 1,000 for females. Over a lifetime, of course, the chance of victimization is much higher, and the figures do not include such forms of victimization as murder, kidnapping, or harm from drunken drivers.[31]

**Figure 2.5**
**Lifestyle-exposure model of victimization**
Demographic characteristics provide the basis for individual and subcultural adaptations to a particular lifestyle and a resulting level of exposure to the probability of personal victimization.

SOURCE: Adapted from Robert F. Meier and Terance D. Miethe, "Understanding Theories of Criminal Victimization," *Crime and Justice: A Review of Research*, ed. Michael Tonry (Chicago: University of Chicago Press, 1993), 467.

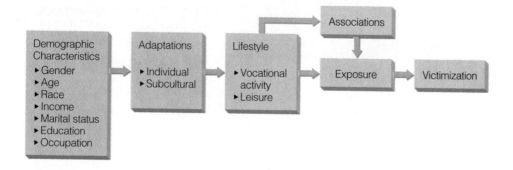

With respect to age, a majority of reported victimizations occur within the lower age group of twelve to twenty-four years. Youths between twelve and fifteen are most likely to be the victims of such crimes as personal larceny without contact, robbery, and simple assault. In light of concern about crimes against the elderly, a notable finding is that they are less likely than the young to be victimized.

Race is also an important factor, with blacks and other minorities being more likely than whites to be raped, robbed, and assaulted. Although white Americans are fearful of being victimized by black strangers, most violent crime is intraracial: three of every four victims are of the same race as the attacker (see Figure 2.6). The case is similar with property crimes: most victims and offenders are of the same racial and economic status.

Income also strongly determines exposure to crime. Economic factors largely determine where people live, work, and seek recreation. For people with low incomes these choices are limited. Some may have to live in

**Table 2.4**
**Who are the victims of personal crime?**
NCVS data helps clarify the characteristics of crime victims.

SOURCE: U.S. Department of Justice, Bureau of Justice Statistics, *Highlights from Twenty Years of Surveying Crime Victims* (Washington, D.C.: Government Printing Office, 1993), 18.

a Based on 10 or fewer cases.

| | Victims | Rate per 1,000 persons age 12 or over | | | Victims | Rate per 1,000 persons age 12 or over | |
|---|---|---|---|---|---|---|---|
| | | Violence | Theft | | | Violence | Theft |
| **Sex** | Male | 40 | 65 | **Family income** | Less than $7,500 | 59 | 62 |
| | Female | 23 | 58 | | $7,500–$9,999 | 42 | 61 |
| **Age** | 12–15 | 63 | 101 | | $10,000–$14,999 | 43 | 60 |
| | 16–19 | 91 | 94 | | $15,000–$24,999 | 31 | 57 |
| | 20–24 | 75 | 115 | | $25,000–$29,999 | 32 | 57 |
| | 25–34 | 35 | 71 | | $30,000–$49,999 | 25 | 60 |
| | 35–49 | 20 | 56 | | $50,000 or more | 20 | 66 |
| | 50–64 | 10 | 35 | **Education** | 0–4 years | 18 | 16 |
| | 65 and older | 4 | 20 | | 5–7 years | 45 | 67 |
| **Race** | White | 30 | 61 | | 8 years | 28 | 49 |
| | Black | 44 | 61 | | 9–11 years | 49 | 62 |
| | Other | 28 | 52 | | High school graduate | 28 | 49 |
| **Ethnicity** | Hispanic | 36 | 59 | | 1–3 years college | 36 | 83 |
| | Non-Hispanic | 31 | 61 | | College graduate | 18 | 68 |
| **Marital status by sex** | Males | | | **Residence** | Central city | 44 | 75 |
| | Never married | 80 | 97 | | 1,000,000 or more | 39 | 76 |
| | Divorced/separated | 44 | 95 | | 500,000–999,999 | 50 | 80 |
| | Married | 19 | 43 | | 250,000–499,999 | 54 | 70 |
| | Widowed | a | 23 | | 50,000–249,999 | 38 | 74 |
| | Females | | | | Suburban | 26 | 61 |
| | Never married | 43 | 90 | | Rural | 25 | 44 |
| | Divorced/separated | 45 | 74 | | | | |
| | Married | 11 | 44 | | | | |
| | Widowed | 6 | 22 | | | | |

crime-prone neighborhoods, lack security devices to protect their apartments or homes, are unable to avoid contact with potential offenders, or cannot partake of leisure activities in safe areas. Members of minority groups and the poor thus bear a disproportionate risk of being victimized, for most are likely to live in the inner-city zones where street crime is greatest. As one moves up the economic ladder there is greater flexibility in lifestyle-exposure choices and so more opportunities to avoid risky and vulnerable situations.[32]

Living in a city is, in fact, a significant element with regard to victimization. Violent crime is primarily a phenomenon of large cities. Of the 14 million index offenses known to the police in 1992, more than 13 million occurred in cities. Overall, studies have shown that crime rates invariably rise in proportion to proximity to the center of an urban area.

It is in the inner-cities with attendant high drug use that murder rates have skyrocketed. Most of those slain, like their killers, tend to be young and black. The homicide rate among black males aged twenty to twenty-nine is 100 per 100,000 population, about six times that for the same age bracket in the general population. A social time bomb exists in America's cities that unless changed can only lead to further crime and violence.

But it is not just because the residents of urban ghettos are poor that crime is so prevalent in their neighborhoods. Some poor neighborhoods are more crime-ridden than others. To understand why, it is important to acknowledge a variety of other factors, including the physical condition of the neighborhoods, the level of moral cynicism of the residents, and the extent of the opportunities for crime and of social control by families and government agencies.[33]

The lifestyle-exposure model helps us better understand some of the factors increasing or decreasing one's risk of being victimized, but what is the impact of crime on the nation and on individuals?

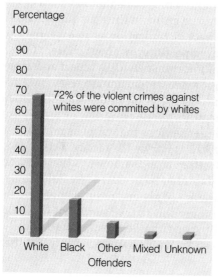

a  White victims

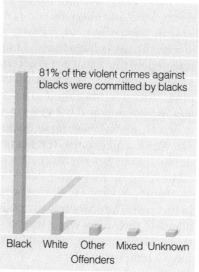

b  Black victims

**Figure 2.6**

**Victims and offenders are of the same race in three out of four violent crimes**

Although whites seem most fearful of being victimized by blacks, the fact is that most violent crime is intraracial. Why are there such misperceptions?

SOURCE: U.S. Department of Justice, Bureau of Justice Statistics, *Report to the Nation on Crime and Justice*, 2d ed. (Washington, D.C.: Government Printing Office, 1988), 21.

## What Is the Impact of Crime?

The fiscal impact of crime is difficult to estimate. One group of researchers, for example, calculated that the annual total receipts from criminal activity were between $26.9 billion and $136.9 billion.[34] The Bureau of Justice Statistics has estimated that American households lost over $19 billion in stolen property, cash losses, and medical expenses to crime in 1991.[35] The cost of operating the criminal justice system alone is over $50 billion per year. But such monetary costs do not measure the costs to consumers of organized crime activity, the pain and suffering of victims and their families, and the costs to citizens who seek to protect themselves by installing locks and alarms or by employing guards and security patrols.

**Fear as an Impact of Criminality**   One impact the crime problem has on the general population is the fear of crime. Fear limits freedom. Because they are fearful, many people confine their activities to "safe" areas at "safe" times. Fear also creates unmeasurable anxieties that affect human physiological and psychological well-being. Perhaps most unsettling, the very persons who have the least chance of being victimized by crime are often the most fearful.

Since 1965, public opinion organizations—Gallup, Harris, and others—have been asking Americans about their reactions to crime to determine whether they "feel more uneasy" or "fear to walk the streets at night." More than 40 percent of the public say that the fear of crime limits their freedom. In large cities more than 60 percent of residents say that they are afraid to walk through their neighborhoods at night; in small towns and rural areas, fewer than 30 percent express this concern. High levels of fear are also found, not surprisingly, among nonwhites and people of low income, the groups most likely to be victimized. Women, the elderly, and upper-income suburbanites, groups that generally have low rates of victimization, are also more frightened than the average citizen.

How do we account for the fearfulness of groups that have not experienced victimization and do not observe crime in their neighborhoods? Researchers point to vicarious or indirect victimization as an explanation. Some scholars believe that the media shape attitudes about crime.[36] Other researchers think that personal communication networks report and magnify the apparent volume of local violence. In particular, television reports and neighborhood conversations focus on and amplify crimes against women and the elderly. Accounts about old, frail, or otherwise defenseless victims seem to heighten perceptions that crime is rampant.

Among all groups, the fear of crime outstrips the reality. People evidently do not assess criminal victimization in the same ways that they do other risks, such as those caused by nature or by accident (see Table 2.5).

Most responses to the fear of crime are costly and require adjustments in lifestyle. The economically better off are able to take steps that will help alleviate their fears while the poor must endure their fears. Paradoxically, those who are most vulnerable are also least able to respond in ways that have a tempering effect.

## What Is the Experience of Victims within the Criminal Justice System?

In the concern about crime, victims are often forgotten. After crimes have been committed, victims often suffer loss, injury, and emotional trauma and are poorly treated by the agencies of criminal justice. Some say that they have been doubly victimized: by the criminal and by the system.

Once a crime has been reported to the police, victims frequently say they are interrogated as if they themselves were responsible for the offense. Officials are rude to them; they are called to appear in court repeatedly, only to be told that the case has been postponed, or, alternatively, they never hear another word about the incident and do not know if the criminal is still at large and ready to strike again. In addition, victims usually incur economic costs because of wages lost during court appearances, transportation expenses, and denied access to recovered property during a pending trial.

In the past two decades justice agencies have become increasingly sensitive to the interests of crime victims. This sensitivity has resulted in part from the recognition that victims are often the only witnesses to the event in question, and their help is necessary if a conviction is to result. If economic and emotional costs are involved in assisting law enforcement and judicial officials, then many citizens will not cooperate.

This awakened concern about the victims of crime is evident in the report of the President's Task Force on Victims of Crime.[37] The task force stressed the importance of achieving a balance between the needs and rights of the victim and those of the defendant. It urged that both be protected against intimidation, that restitution be required by the courts, and that the Sixth Amendment to the Constitution be changed so that the victim would have a right to participate in all of the critical judicial proceedings. In 1982 California voters passed Proposition 8, known as the "Victim's Bill of Rights" (Table 2.6). As a result, California law now places greater emphasis on restitution, involves the victim more closely in the criminal justice process, and gives correspondingly less weight to the rights of the accused. Other states have followed this lead. In 1984 Congress passed the Federal Victims of Crime Act, which establishes a fund supported by fines; the states are to receive half for victim compensation programs and half for victim assistance programs.

Programs of information, assistance in time of crisis, and compensation have been inaugurated in many states to help meet the needs of crime victims. Information programs are designed to

### Table 2.5
### How do crime rates compare with the rates of other events?

Crime is a major concern to many Americans, but what are the risks of victimization compared to other hazards of life?

SOURCE: U.S. Department of Justice, Bureau of Justice Statistics, *Highlights from Twenty Years of Surveying Crime Victims* (Washington, D.C.: Government Printing Office, 1993), 4.

| Events | Rate per 1,000 adults per year |
|---|---|
| Accidental injury, all circumstances | 220 |
| Accidental injury at home | 66 |
| **Personal theft** | 61 |
| Accidental injury at work | 47 |
| **Violent victimization** | 31 |
| **Assault** (aggravated and simple) | 25 |
| Injury in motor vehicle accident | 22 |
| Death, all causes | 11 |
| **Victimization with injury** | 11 |
| **Serious (aggravated) assault** | 8 |
| **Robbery** | 6 |
| Heart disease death | 5 |
| Cancer death | 3 |
| **Rape** (women only) | 1 |
| Accidental death, all circumstances | 0.4 |
| Pneumonia/influenza death | 0.4 |
| Motor vehicle accident death | 0.2 |
| Suicide | 0.2 |
| HIV infection death | 0.1 |
| **Homicide**/legal intervention | 0.1 |

**Victims of crimes have the right:**

1  to protection from criminal violence

2  to be kept informed by law enforcement agencies of their investigation of a crime

3  to be kept informed by the district attorney as to the progress of a criminal case

4  to be notified of any discretionary disposition of a case

5  to be notified of any release of the defendant after conviction

6  to be notified of any change in the defendant's status

7  to be informed of financial and social services available to crime victims

8  to be provided with appropriate employer intercession services

9  to be provided with adequate witness compensation

10  to be provided with a secure waiting area during court proceedings

11  to receive adequate protection from threats of harm arising out of cooperation with law enforcement personnel

12  to have any stolen or other personal property held by law enforcement offices returned as soon as possible

13  to be represented by an attorney for certain types of cases

14  to be made whole through restitution and/or civil law recovery

15  to have perpetrators prevented from being enriched by their crimes at the victim's expense

accomplish two goals: first, to sensitize justice officials to the need to treat crime victims courteously in order to secure their effective cooperation; second, to develop ways to let victims know what is happening at each stage of a case. In some states the investigating officer at the scene gives the crime victim a booklet containing information about the steps that will be taken and telephone numbers that can be called should questions arise. Assistance in time of crisis is most important when the victim faces medical, emotional, or financial problems as a result of a crime; rape crisis centers, prosecutors' victim assistance programs, and family shelters are among the programs that have been adopted. Compensation programs in most states now supplement the assistance offered by crisis centers to victims of violent crime and provide for payment of the medical expenses of those who cannot meet them. When property has been stolen or destroyed, compensation programs serve to encourage judges to order restitution.

## How Do Victims Precipitate Crime?

Criminologists have become concerned with the role victims may play in the criminal incident. By analyzing the characteristics of a variety of victims, researchers have advanced the idea that many victims voluntarily act in ways that invite the acts committed against them. The victim may bring about commission of a crime through consent, provocation, enticement, unnecessary risk taking, or carelessness with property.

To illustrate, Morton Hunt has listed six elements that may predispose a person to attack by a mugger.[38]

1　People on sidewalks late at night are three times as likely to be victimized as those who stay indoors after dark.

2　Age and physical disabilities make the elderly more vulnerable to attack than the young and strong.

3　Some people are more vulnerable because they are hampered by things they are carrying, by the attention they are giving to something, or by clothing that may block their view or make defense difficult.

4　The kinds of clothing people wear can be a clue to the likely amounts of cash or jewelry on their person.

5　Although most street crime is intraracial, more than half the robberies on American city streets are interracial—white victims of nonwhite strangers.

6　A person walking alone is more likely to be a target for a mugger than is someone with a companion.

Only during the past two decades have justice agencies become sensitive to the interests of crime victims. In many cases victims have felt that they were the ones on trial.

What do studies tell us about victim precipitation? First, there are instances when citizens do not take proper precautions to protect themselves. Using common sense and regulating behavior to prevent criminal attack may be part of the price of living in contemporary society. Second, under some circumstances, the victim, by some action, may provoke or entice another to commit a criminal act. Third, the victims in certain types of nonstranger crimes are unwilling to assist official agencies in investigation and prosecution activities. These considerations do not excuse criminal behavior, but they do force us to think about other dimensions of how the criminal act is perpetrated.

By studying the characteristics of victims, the impact of crime on society, the experience of victims at the hands of the criminal justice system, and the role of victims in precipitating crime, victimologists have shifted attention so that it is not solely on the offender. Now it is recognized that victims play a crucial role in dealing with the problem of crime. But this new attention does not mean that criminologists have lessened their interest in understanding the causes of crime. Let us now turn to examine the major theories of criminality.

# Theories of the Causes of Crime

Whenever news of a crime hits the headlines, whether the crime is a grisly murder or a complex bank fraud, the immediate question in the minds of most people is, "Why did he or she do it?" Do people commit crimes because of economic deprivation, greed, insanity, or just stupidity?

The causes of criminal behavior have been the subject of much speculation, theorizing, and research among scholars and the general public. Theories help scholars give meaning to their observations. By linking empirical data to concepts, explanatory theories can be constructed.

The development of one criminological theory can be seen by examining the work of the nineteenth-century Italian criminologist Cesare Lombroso. He developed a theory that criminality was biologically determined and supported his theory with data gathered by measuring the physical characteristics of convicts. Lombroso believed that criminals have "stigmata": asymmetrical faces, ponderous jaws, eye defects, prominent cheekbones, and other such characteristics. He claimed these features do not actually cause criminal behavior but do indicate that persons with such stigmata are primitives and have not evolved to the level of a cultured person. Although Lombroso's ideas have long been disproven, modern theory building follows the same method. Social scientists place empirical observations in a theoretical framework that helps explain reality.

Modern criminology is primarily concerned with understanding criminal behavior, the characteristics of offenders, and how the consequences of crime can be prevented or repaired. Notice that the focus is on the individual offender. Few criminologists ask questions about the influence on crime rates of factors such as the economy, policy, family, and education.[39] In the following section we look at the two major schools of thought in criminology—classical and positivist. We then examine biological, psychological, and sociological theories of the causes of criminal behavior.

## Classical and Positivist Criminology

Speculation about the causes of crime does not take place in a vacuum. Historically, criminological thought can be divided into the classical and positivist schools. Each approach was pioneered by scholars influenced by intellectual trends and forces preeminent in their times, such as religion, philosophy, and science.

**classical criminology**
A school of criminology that views behavior as stemming from free will, demands responsibility and accountability of all perpetrators, and stresses the need for punishments sufficiently severe to deter others.

**Classical Criminology**   Until the eighteenth century most Europeans explained criminal behavior in religious terms. They saw crime as a product of the devil's work; persons who did wrong were in the devil's possession. One orthodox Christian view was that all humanity had fallen with Adam and had thereafter been in a state of total depravity. Even up to the nineteenth century, indictments in both the United States and Europe often began, "[John Doe], not having the fear of God before his eyes but being moved and seduced by the instigation of the devil, did commit [a certain crime]." Not only did religious ideas guide thinking about crime, but also the concept of procedural rights had not yet been developed. Criminal law was thus administered arbitrarily. The accused had little opportunity to put forth a defense, confessions were extracted through torture, and corporal punishment or death was inflicted for a multitude of offenses.

In 1764 Cesare Beccaria's *Essay on Crimes and Punishments* was published in Italy.[40] It was the first attempt to explain crime in secular, or worldly, terms as opposed to religious terms. The book also pointed to injustices in the administration of criminal laws. Beccaria's ideas prompted reformers to apply principles of rationality to criminal law and procedures. From this movement came **classical criminology**, the major principles of which can be summarized as follows:

1   Criminal behavior is rational and most people have the potential to engage in illegal activity.

2   People may *choose* to commit a crime after weighing the benefits and consequences of their actions.

3   It is the fear of punishment that keeps most people in check, and thus the severity, certainty, and speed of the criminal sanction is the controlling factor.

4   The punishment should fit the crime, not the person who committed it.

5   The criminal justice system must be predictable, with laws and punishments known to the public.

Today there has been renewed interest in some aspects of classical theory. In particular, some scholars have argued that crimes may result from the rational choice of individuals who have weighed the benefits to be gained from the crime against the costs of being caught and punished. Generally, however, it has been the positivist school that has dominated American criminology.

**Positivist Criminology**   By the middle of the nineteenth century the ideas of the classical school seemed old-fashioned. Many scholars declared that Beccaria and his followers had been too concerned with law. Instead of emphasizing the legal and philosophical ramifications of the deviant act, as had been the classical tradition, it was argued that a **positivist criminology**, a scientific approach, should be used to understand the causes of crime and its treatment.

The central question of positivist criminology is "Why do people commit criminal acts?" Positivists argue that human behavior, including criminal, is determined by physical, mental, and social factors beyond the control of individuals. These factors correspond to the three main positivist approaches to criminality that are influential today: the biological, the psychological, and the sociological. Theories that attempt to explain criminal behavior on the basis of characteristics inherent in the individual offender are based on biology and psychology. Theories that focus on crime-inducing conditions in the community that influence the offender (poverty, social disorganization, subculture norms) are based on sociological reasoning.

Cesare Beccaria was the first to explain crime in secular as opposed to religious terms. He fought to bring order and rationality to criminal laws and procedures.

**positivist criminology**
A school of criminology that views behavior as stemming from social, biological, and psychological factors. It argues that punishment should be tailored to the individual needs of the offender.

It is important to understand the leading explanations of crime causation because their assumptions significantly affect the ways in which laws are enforced, guilt or innocence is determined, and misconduct is punished. As we examine each of the theories of criminal behavior, consider the implications for crime policies should each theory prove valid. For example, if biological theories of criminality are accepted as sound, then governmental policies designed to identify potential offenders through genetic analysis and their segregation or surveillance might be adopted. On the other hand, the validation of sociological theories might lead to governmental policies designed to eradicate poverty, improve education, and provide job training.

## Biological Explanations

Cesare Lombroso's (1836–1909) training in medicine aroused his interest in the physical characteristics that he believed differentiated the criminal from the law-abiding citizen (see Biography). As discussed above, he believed that offenders are *born* criminal and have traits that mark them as more primitive and savage people. Individuals so disabled have difficulty adjusting to modern society because they are frustrated by their social incompetence and by the rejection arising from it. Given this rejection, the criminal is thrust into illegal activity.

With the development of psychology, however, interest shifted from physical characteristics to the importance of inherited traits that affect the intelligence level and mental health of criminals. Some criminologists believed that criminals commit crimes as a means of alleviating the pathological urges they inherited from mentally defective ancestors. Criminologists with this orientation studied family genealogies to determine the correspondence between these traits and the criminal records of family members.

Two studies published in 1875 and 1916, one of a family given the fictitious name of Jukes and the other one named Kallikak, presented evidence that genetic deficiencies reproduced in offspring could condemn succeeding generations to lives of crime.[41] Richard Dugdale located more than one thousand descendants of the woman he called Ada Jukes, whom he dubbed the "mother of criminals." Among the family were 280 paupers, 60 thieves, 7 murderers, 140 criminals, 40 persons with venereal diseases, 50 prostitutes, and other types of undesirables. Similar data collected by Henry H. Goddard supported the belief that the Kallikak family, a group of relatives linked to the illegitimate son of Martin Kallikak, contained more criminals than the descendants of Martin's later marriage into a "good" family.

These early studies have been greatly criticized, but they were taken seriously in their time. In many states crime-control policies were enacted to require that habitual offenders be sterilized, which was done under the assumption that crime could be controlled if hereditary factors were not transmitted. This practice was declared unconstitutional by the U.S. Supreme Court in *Skinner* v. *Oklahoma* (1942).[42]

Although **biological explanations** of criminal behavior were ignored or condemned as racist after World War II, they have attracted renewed interest in more recent years. Publication in 1975 of Edward O. Wilson's *Sociobiology: The New Synthesis* spurred interest in links between biological factors and behavior.[43] The 1985 book by James Q. Wilson and Richard J. Herrnstein, *Crime and Human Nature,* reviews the biocriminology literature.[44] Unlike the early positivists, Wilson and Herrnstein do not point to single-factor explanations of criminality. New research on nutrition, neurology, genetics, and endocrinology has indicated that these factors may be related to the violent behavior of some people.[45]

These new perspectives have given biological explanations a renewed influence and have provided a needed corrective to the sociological and psychological explanations that have dominated criminology in this century. Scientists continue to pursue efforts to discover biological indicators of a propensity to violence and criminality.[46]

**biological explanations**
Explanations of crime that emphasize physiological and neurological factors.

## Psychological Explanations

Criminality has frequently been viewed as a form of deviant and even insane behavior. Before the eighteenth century, madness was generally ascribed to possession by demons. Some scholars, however, eventually suggested that deficiencies of the body and mind caused a person to act "abnormally." One of the early advocates of this idea was Henry Maudsley (1835–1918), an English psychologist, who believed that criminals were "morally insane."[47] Moral insanity, he argued, is an inherent quality, and crime is a way in which the deviant can express pathological urges. Without crime as an outlet for their unsound tendencies, criminals would become insane.

Sigmund Freud (1856–1939) is today looked upon as one of the intellectual giants of the twentieth century. He developed a theory of the unconscious according to which behavior can be caused by mental activity that takes place outside our conscious awareness. Freud also stressed the role of early childhood experiences in later psychological and social development. His theories are also reflected in psychoanalysis, a technique Freud developed for treating psychological problems.

Psychiatrists have related criminal behavior to such concepts as innate impulses, psychic conflict, and the repression of personality. According to **psychological explanations**, crime is a form of substitute behavior that compensates for abnormal urges and desires. Although there are great divergences among the practitioners of this school, a main thesis is that personality is formed during early childhood and is a key determinant of later behavior.

Among the theories developed by psychiatrists is that of the person variously described as the "psychopath," "sociopath," and "antisocial personality": a person who is unable to control impulses, cannot learn from experience, and does not experience normal human emotions, such as love. This kind of person is viewed as psychologically abnormal and conforms to the popular image of the crazed killer or sex fiend.

**psychological explanations**
Explanations of crime that emphasize mental processes and behavior.

During the 1940s, with the rise of psychology and after a number of widely publicized sex crimes, state legislatures were pressured to pass "sexual psychopath laws" designed to place these "homicidal sex fiends" into institutions for treatment of their disorders. It was subsequently shown, however, that such legislation was based on false assumptions. The passage of such laws reveals the political context within which the criminal law is fashioned.[48]

Psychological theories have been widely and variously criticized. Some critics talk about the difficulty of measuring emotional factors and of isolating persons thought to be **criminogenic**. Others point to the variety of theories, some conflicting, that have at their base a psychological approach to crime.

Despite these criticisms, psychological explanations of criminality have, however, played a major role in criminal justice policy during the twentieth century. Correctional policies emphasizing rehabilitation have been largely based on the belief that modifying personality can alter the offender's subsequent behavior. Psychotherapy, group therapy, behavioral modification and moral development programs were common in correctional institutions from the end of World War II to the mid-1970s. Only during the past two decades has there been a deemphasis of the psychological approach.

**criminogenic**
Thought to bring about criminal behavior in an individual.

## Sociological Explanations

A complementary perspective to psychological approaches to behavior is provided by sociology. Sociologists emphasize that people do not live as isolated individuals but as members of social groups, and it is these social influences that shape behavior. Thus **sociological explanations** of crime assume that the offender's personality and actions are molded by contact with the social environment and such factors as race, age, gender, and income.

The sociological orientation developed through European social theorists such as Emile Durkheim. He argued that when a simple, rural society develops into a complex urbanized one, traditional standards decline and some people are unable to adjust to the new rules. A group of researchers at the University of Chicago in the 1920s furthered the development of sociological explanations of crime. Scholars looked closely at the ecological factors of urban life that gave rise to crime: poverty, inadequate housing, broken families, and the problems of new immigrants.

Sociological explanations of criminality emphasize that criminals are made, not born. Among the several theories that emphasize the role of societal forces in molding criminal behavior, three deserve special mention: social structure theory, social process theory, and social conflict theory.

**sociological explanations**
Explanations of crime that emphasize the social conditions that bear on the individual as causes of criminal behavior.

**Social Structure Theory**  **Social structure theories** ascribe criminal behavior to the stratified nature of Western societies. That is, different social classes control very different amounts of wealth, status, and power. Those in the lower class tend to suffer from economic deprivation, lack of education, poor housing, and an inability to influence government agencies. Research has shown that during the 1980s the number of people living in

**social structure theories**
Theories that blame crime on the creation of a lower-class culture based on poverty and deprivation, and on the response of the poor to this situation.

What criminological theories are addressed by this scene?

poverty in the United States doubled and that today there is a wider spread between the rich and the poor.[49] Theorists argue that the structure of society results in a lower-class lifestyle that tends to create crime.

Sociologist Robert Merton extended Durkheim's ideas of the influence of social change and urbanization on crime. He emphasized that the structure of society often permits a situation of anomie to develop.[50] By **anomie** he meant social conditions in which the rules or norms that regulate behavior have weakened or disappeared. Persons may become anomic or frustrated when the rules are unclear or when they are unable to achieve their expectations. When the balance between cultural aspirations and social opportunities is lost or damaged, antisocial or deviant behavior may result. It is said, for example, that American society emphasizes individual success but excludes some of its members from the possibility of achieving that goal. It follows that those caught in this trap choose crime as a way out. Theorists believe that the movement of some ethnic groups into organized crime has been one way of overcoming such anomic frustrations. Others argue that the social disorganization of urbanized and industrial society brings about conditions in which, among other things, family structure breaks down, alcohol or drug abuse becomes more common, and the incidence of criminal behavior rises. They assert that to reduce crime, poverty must be eradicated and the structures of society be reformed.

**anomie**
A state of normlessness caused by a breakdown in the rules of social behavior.

**social process theories**
Theories that see criminality as normal behavior. Everyone has the potential to become a criminal, depending on the influences that impel one toward or away from crime and how one is regarded by others.

**learning theories**
Theories postulating that criminal behavior, like legal and normative behavior, is learned.

**differential association theories**
A theory that people become criminals because they encounter a large number of influences that regard criminal behavior as normal and acceptable, and that these influences outnumber those hostile to criminal behavior.

**control theories**
Theories postulating that criminal behavior occurs when the bonds that tie an individual to society are broken or weakened.

**labeling theories**
Theories emphasizing that the causes of criminal behavior are not found in the individual but in the social process through which certain acts are labeled deviant or criminal.

**Social Process Theory**   Criminal justice statistics make clear that criminality is not a phenomenon exclusive to the poor. For many criminologists, therefore, a social structure approach to the explanation of crime is inadequate. **Social process theories**, although existing since the 1930s, gained recognition in the 1960s and 1970s. Unlike social structure theories, social process theories assume that everyone, regardless of education, class, or upbringing, has the potential to become a criminal. It is the circumstances encountered in life that influence some people to commit criminal acts. Thus these theories try to explain the processes by which individuals become criminals.

A number of concepts and theories are grouped under the social process rubric. All share certain assumptions, yet there are important differences among them. The three major groups are learning theories, control theories, and labeling theories.

**Learning theories** hold that criminal activity is normal learned behavior. It is through social relations that some people have the chance or opportunity to learn how to be a criminal and to acquire the associated values. An assumption is that people imitate and learn from one another. Thus family and peers are viewed as primary influences on an individual's development.

In 1939 Edwin Sutherland clarified the learning process and proposed a theory of **differential association**. This theory states that behavior is learned through interactions with other persons, especially family members and others with whom close associations are maintained.[51] In particular, criminal behavior occurs when an individual encounters strong prescriptions for behavior that are more favorable than opposed to law violations. If a boy grows up in an environment of violence, in which, say, an older brother is involved in crime, then the boy is likely to learn criminal behavior. If those in the family, neighborhood, and gang believe that illegal activity is nothing to be ashamed of, then there is a greater probability that the young person will engage in crime.

**Control theory**, as developed by Travis Hirschi and later redefined with Michael Gottfredson, holds that social links keep people in line with accepted norms.[52] In other words, all members of society have the potential to commit crime but most people are restrained by their ties to such conventional institutions and individuals as the family, church, school, and peer groups. Thus, a person's sensitivity to the opinion of others, commitment to a conventional lifestyle, involvement of time and energy in that status, and belief in the standards or values shared by friends are all factors that influence a law-abiding existence. Should a person's life be lacking in one or more of these behavior-controlling bonds, criminal behavior may result.

The third social process approach to criminality, **labeling theory**, stresses that to understand the causes of crime we should not look at individuals but at the social process through which certain acts are labeled deviant. As Howard Becker notes, society creates deviance "by making the rules whose infraction constitutes deviance, and by applying those rules to particular people and labeling them outsiders."[53] Social control agencies, such as the police, courts, and corrections departments, are created to designate certain individuals as outside the normal, law-abiding community. Having been labeled deviant or criminal, the stigmatized individual comes to believe that the label is true, assumes the identity, and enters into a criminal career.

Labeling theory suggests that criminals are not very different from other members of the community, except that the agencies of justice have labeled them as deviant. It argues that the criminal justice system *creates* criminals by labeling people in order to serve its own bureaucratic or political ends. Policies to decriminalize drug, gambling, and prostitution offenses have been advocated by persons holding these views.

**Social Conflict Theory**  In the mid-1960s a new orientation challenged the existing biological, psychological, and sociological explanations of criminal behavior. **Social conflict theories** emphasize that criminal law and the criminal justice system are mainly the means of controlling society's poor and have-nots. The rich and well educated commit as many crimes as the poor, it is argued, but the poor are more likely to be punished because they are powerless and unsophisticated. The rich use the law to impose their version of morality on the whole of society for the purpose of protecting their property and physical safety. By manipulating the law, elites change the definition of illegal behavior to encompass activities that they view as threatening to the status quo.

As with those who favor other approaches to criminal behavior, there are divisions among the social conflict theorists. One group, referred to as critical, radical, or Marxist criminologists, argues that it is the class structure of society that results in certain groups being labeled as deviant. According to this view, "deviance is a status imputed to groups who share certain structural characteristics (e.g., powerlessness)."[54] Thus the criminal law is designed to aim at the behavior of particular groups or classes. One result is a deep hostility among the poor toward the social order, and this hostility is one factor contributing to criminal behavior. Moreover, when the status quo is threatened, legal definitions of criminal behavior are altered so as to ensnare those who challenge the system. For example, vagrancy laws have been used to arrest persons such as labor union organizers, civil rights workers, and peace activists when governmental and economic elites have considered their own interests to be threatened.

Like other explanations of the causes of criminal behavior, the sociological theories have been thoroughly criticized. It has been argued that they are imprecise, not supported by empirical evidence, and ideologically based. Criticism notwithstanding, sociological theories have served as the basis for many attempts to prevent crime and to rehabilitate offenders. Operation Weed and Seed, a U.S. Department of Justice program to "weed out" drug dealers while improving ("seeding") neighborhood conditions, is an example of sociological theories put into practice.

## Female Criminality

The preceding theories of crime causation are almost exclusively based on observations of male offenders. Only in the past few decades has the study of female criminality emerged, to a great extent as a result of the

**social conflict theories**
Theories that assume criminal law and the criminal justice system are primarily a means of controlling the poor and have-nots.

women's movement. Although a focus on female criminality raises new questions, scholars working in this area base their research on several of the above concepts and theories.[55]

Until recently, with the exception of so-called female crimes such as prostitution and shoplifting, little research was done on the female half of the population, which accounted for fewer than 10 percent of arrests. Two assumptions appear to have been operating. First was the assumption that most women were incapable of serious criminal activity; it was held that women, by nature, were too gentle, nurturing, and dependent to commit most crimes. Second was the assumption that those who did commit crimes were "bad" women; women, more so than men, were viewed as moral offenders, as "fallen," when they committed crimes. Today criminologists are focusing more intently on female offenders. Moreover, although female arrest rates for offenses such as fraud, robbery, and larceny, traditionally viewed as the province of males, still lag far behind those for men, they have increased considerably during the past two decades.

Why the upsurge in arrest rates for women? As Freda Adler has noted, "When we did not permit women to swim at the beaches, the female drowning rate was quite low. When women were not permitted to work as bank tellers or presidents, the female embezzlement rate was low."[56] In other words, some scholars argue that as women take places of equality with men in American society, distinctions of criminality based on sex are diminished. According to Rita Simon, because of social changes that have taken place since the 1950s, women enjoy greater freedom, are less likely to be victimized and oppressed by men, and are less likely to be dependent on them.[57] As a consequence, women will be less likely to engage in crimes of violence but more likely to commit business-related and property crimes.

But has there really been a change in female criminality? Some scholars believe that the increased focus on female criminality is a product of the women's movement and that arrest data do not suggest major shifts.[58] Crime data show that there has been an increase of 30.4 percent in women arrested for larceny-theft offenses (mainly shoplifting) and that drug arrests of women continue to mount. For most other crimes women remain minor players. As shown in Figure 2.7, women constitute fewer than 14 percent of arrestees in all but the larceny-theft *UCR* crime categories.

As the status of women change and as they pursue careers in business and industry, some observers believe that there will be an increase in economic and occupational crimes such as embezzlement and fraud. However, current research continues to show that those arrested tend to come from dysfunctional families where poverty and physical and substance abuse were present.[59] These characteristics, however, do not seem much different than those experienced by male offenders. Other researchers believe that the increased crime rates among women is in part due to police and prosecutors being more willing to treat them like men. Thus far, research about gender differences in the amount and nature of crime is inconclusive.[60]

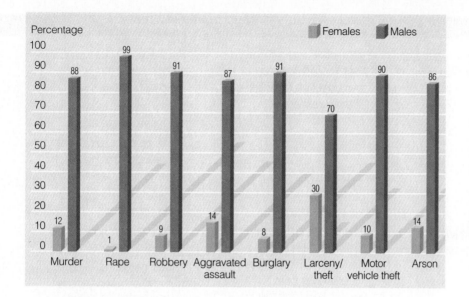

**Figure 2.7**
**How do the offense characteristics of men and women differ?**
While most arrests are of males, the share of arrests that are of females is highest for larceny-theft.

SOURCE: U.S. Department of Justice, *Crime in the United States* (Washington, D.C.: Government Printing Office, 1993), 16.

## Assessing Theories of Criminality

Undoubtedly all of the contemporary theories of crime that we have surveyed contain a kernel of truth. Unfortunately, none is powerful enough in itself to predict criminality or to establish a specific cause for an offender's behavior. The theories show other limitations as well. They tend to focus on visible crimes and the illegal activities of the poor. There seems to be little relationship between any of the theories and upper-class or organized crime. Most also focus on the behavior of males. What is missing and truly needed is a theory that integrates these disparate ideas about the causes of crime. Once we have a comprehensive and testable account of what causes crime we will be able to develop public policies to deal more effectively with the crime.

Table 2.7 summarizes the major theories of criminality and outlines some of the policy implications of each approach. These various policy options have serious advocates among both scholars and the general public. Perhaps we know far too little about the real causes of crime, but notice how many people think they hold the answers!

| Theory | Major Premise | Policy Implications | Policy Implementation |
|---|---|---|---|
| **Biological** | Genetic, biochemical, or neurological defects cause some people to commit crime. | Identification and treatment or control of persons with crime-producing biological factors. Selective incapacitation, intensive supervision. | 1  Use of drugs to inhibit biological urges of sex offenders.<br>2  Use of controlled diet to reduce levels of antisocial behavior caused by biochemical imbalances.<br>3  Identification of neurological defects through CAT scans. Use of drugs to suppress violent impulses.<br>4  Special education for those with learning disabilities. |
| **Psychological** | Personality and learning factors cause some people to commit crime. | Treatment of those with personality disorders to achieve mental health. Those whose illegal behavior stems from learning should have their behavior sanctioned so they will realize that crime is not rewarded. | 1  Psychotherapy and counseling to treat personality disorders.<br>2  Behavior modification strategies, such as electric shock and other negative impulses, to change learned behavior.<br>3  Counseling to enhance moral development.<br>4  Intensive individual and group therapies. |
| **Social Structure** | Crime is the result of underlying social conditions such as poverty, inequality, and unemployment. | Actions should be taken to reform social conditions that breed crime. | 1  Education and job training programs.<br>2  Urban redevelopment to improve housing, education, health care.<br>3  Community development to provide economic opportunities. |

**Table 2.7**
**Major theories of crime causation, their policy implications, and current examples of policy implementation**
If we accept a specific theory of crime causation we must be aware of its major premises, its policy implications, and the ways that the policies are implemented.

# Summary

Behavior that is defined as criminal varies from society to society and from one era to the next. Consensus theorists point to certain crimes that have consistently been part of the penal codes of Western civilization. Conflict theorists, however, argue that the criminal law is a product of pressures from political and economic elites. The definition of some behaviors as offensive, this very basic element of the criminal justice system, is thus a product of the social and political environment.

There are five broad categories of crime: occupational crime, organized crime, visible crime, crimes without victims, and political crime. Each type reflects characteristic behaviors and opportunities for illegal

| Theory | Major Premise | Policy Implications | Policy Implementation |
|--------|---------------|---------------------|------------------------|
| **Social Process** | Crime is normal learned behavior and is subject to either social control or labeling effects. | Individuals must be treated in groups, with emphasis on building conventional bonds and avoiding stigmatization. | 1 Youth programs that emphasize positive role models. <br> 2 Community organizing to establish neighborhood institutions and bonds that emphasize adherence to norms. <br> 3 Programs designed to promote family stability. |
| **Social Conflict** | Criminal definitions and sanctions are used by some groups to control other groups. | Fundamental changes in the political economy to reduce class conflict. | 1 Development of programs to remove injustice in society. <br> 2 Provision of resources to assist women, minorities, and the poor in dealing with the criminal justice system and other governmental agencies. <br> 3 Modification of criminal justice to deal similarly with crimes committed by upper-class members and crimes committed by lower-class members. |

acts and has the potential for the perpetrator to benefit from the act instead of being caught and convicted. The objectives and opportunities of different segments of society lead to their being associated with particular kinds of crimes.

The contemporary crime problem in the United States is not unique to our era. Throughout the history of the Republic there have been times when crime has reached high rates. What is difficult to understand is why crime rates in the United States are higher than rates in other developed countries.

The amount of crime is difficult to measure. The *Uniform Crime Reports* and the National Crime Victimization Surveys are the best sources of crime data. They are based on different reporting and collection methods, and they must be analyzed carefully.

Only in recent decades have researchers and policy makers directed their attention to the victims of crime. Research has focused on four issues: who is victimized, the impact of crime, the experiences of victims in the criminal justice system, and victim precipitation of crime.

Criminologists have developed a number of theories to explain the causes of criminal behavior. Members of the classical school emphasized reform of the criminal law, procedures, and punishments. They believed that individuals were free to choose legal or illegal means to achieve their goals. The rise of science led to the positivist school, whose adherents viewed behavior as stemming from social, biological, and psychological factors. Positivist criminology has dominated the study of criminal behavior in the twentieth century. Lacking is an integrated theory that can explain with confidence the causes of criminality.

## Questions for Review

1 What are the competing theories of the sources of the criminal law?
2 What are the five types of crimes?
3 What are the positive and negative attributes of the two major sources of crime data?
4 What are the four foci of victimization studies?
5 What are the major theories of criminality?

## Key Terms

anomie

biological explanations

classical criminology

conflict model

consensus model

control theories

crimes without victims

criminogenic

dark figure of crime

differential association theories

labeling theories

learning theories

*mala in se*

*mala prohibita*

National Crime Victimization Survey

National Incident-Based Reporting System

norms

occupational crime

organized crime

political crime

positivist criminology

psychological explanations

social conflict theories

social process theories

social structure theories

sociological explanations

*Uniform Crime Reports*

victimology

visible crime

## For Further Reading

Erikson, Kai T. *Wayward Puritans.* New York: Wiley, 1966. Analysis of three "crime waves" in Puritan New England.

Heidensohn, Frances M. *Women and Crime.* New York: New York University Press, 1985. An account and critique of criminological and sociological writings on women and criminality.

Katz, Jack. *Seductions of Crime: Moral and Sensual Attractions of Doing Evil.* New York: Basic Books, 1988. A challenge to positivist criminology that argues there is an emotional appeal to "being bad" and "being hard."

LaFree, Gary D. *Rape and Criminal Justice.* Belmont, Calif.: Wadsworth, 1989. Research on rape based on interviews with police officers, prosecutors, and judges in Indianapolis.

Messner, Steven F. and Richard Rosenfeld. *Crime and the American Dream.* Belmont, Calif.: Wadsworth, 1994. Argues that high levels of serious crime result from the normal functioning of the American social system.

Reinman, Jeffrey H. *The Rich Get Richer and the Poor Get Prison: Ideology, Class and Criminal Justice,* 2d ed. New York: Wiley, 1984. A radical perspective on crime and criminality. Well written, provocative.

Sutherland, Edwin H. *White Collar Crime.* New York: Holt, Rinehart, Winston, 1949. The classic statement of the concept of white-collar crime.

## Notes

1  Susan Estrich, *Real Rape* (Cambridge, Mass.: Harvard University Press, 1987), 92.

2  Robert A. Levine, "Gussi Sex Offenses: A Study in Social Control," *American Anthropologist* 61 (December 1959): 896–990. See also Edna Erez and Bankole Thompson, "Rape in Sierra Leone: Conflict between the Sexes and Conflict of Laws," *International Journal of Comparative and Applied Criminal Justice* 14 (1990): 201–210.

3  Cassia Spohn and Julie Horney, " 'The Law's the Law, But Fair Is Fair': Rape Shield Laws and Officials' Assessments of Sexual History Evidence," *Criminology* 29 (1991): 137–161.

4  Wolfgang Friedman, *Law in a Changing Society* (Berkeley: University of California Press, 1959), 165.

5  Emile Durkheim, *The Division of Labor in Society,* trans. George Simpson (Glencoe, Ill.: Free Press, 1960), 102.

6  U.S. Department of Justice, Bureau of Justice Statistics, *Report to the Nation on Crime and Justice,* 2d ed. (Washington, D.C.: Government Printing Office, 1988), 16.

7  Richard Quinney, *Crime and Justice in Society* (Boston: Little, Brown, 1969), 25.

8  *Ibid.*

9  Joseph R. Gusfield, *Symbolic Crusade: Status Politics and the American Temperance Movement* (Urbana: University of Illinois Press, 1967).

10  Jerome Skolnick, "Perspectives on Law and Order," in *Politics and Crime*, ed. Sawyer F. Sylvester, Jr., and Edward Sagarin (New York: Praeger, 1974), 13.

11  Edwin H. Sutherland, *White Collar Crime* (New York: Holt, Rinehart, Winston, 1949).

12  Gary S. Green, *Occupational Crime* (Chicago: Nelson-Hall, 1990), 10–15.

13  Francis S. J. Ianni, *Ethnic Succession in Organized Crime* (Washington, D.C.: Government Printing Office, 1973), 1–2.

14  Ko-lin Chin, *Chinese Subculture and Criminality: Non-traditional Crime Groups in America* (New York: Greenwood Press, 1990).

15  State of California, *Attorney General, Annual Report to the Legislature: Organized Crime in California* (Sacramento: California Department of Justice, 1986).

16  Chin, *Chinese Subculture and Criminality.*

17  Francis Allen, *The Crimes of Politics* (Cambridge, Mass.: Harvard University Press, 1974), 16–17.

18  Gary Blonston, " 'Explosion' in Crime Powerful—But False," *San Jose Mercury News*, 24 October 1993.

19  *Ibid.*

20  Eliot Currie, *Confronting Crime* (New York: Pantheon, 1985), 25.

21  Dane Archer and Rosemary Gartner, *Violence and Crime in Cross-National Perspective* (New Haven, Conn.: Yale University Press, 1984).

22  Albert D. Biderman and James P. Lynch, *Understanding Crime Incidence Statistics* (New York: Springer-Verlag, 1991).

23  U.S. Department of Justice, Bureau of Justice Statistics, *Bulletin* (October 1993).

24  *Ibid.*

25  U.S. Department of Justice, Bureau of Justice Statistics, *Bulletin* (October 1992).

26  U.S. Department of Justice, *Crime in the United States, 1992* (Washington, D.C.: Government Printing Office, 1993), 58.

27   U.S. Department of Justice, Bureau of Justice Statistics, *Bulletin* (October 1989), 5.

28   U.S. Department of Justice, *Crime in the United States* (Washington, D.C.: Government Printing Office, 1993), 216.

29   Michael Hindelang, Michael Gottfredson, and James Garafalo, *Victims of Personal Crime* (Cambridge, Mass.: Ballinger, 1978).

30   Robert F. Meier and Terance D. Miethe, "Understanding Theories of Criminal Victimization," *Crime and Justice: A Review of Research*, ed. Michael Tonry (Chicago: University of Chicago Press, 1993), 466.

31   U.S. Department of Justice, Bureau of Justice Statistics, *Highlights from Twenty Years of Surveying Crime Victims* (Washington, D.C.: Government Printing Office, 1993), 18.

32   Meier and Miethe, 468.

33   Rodney Stark, "Decent places: A Theory of the Ecology of Crime," *Criminology* 25 (1987): 893–909.

34   U.S. Department of Justice, Bureau of Justice Statistics, *Report to the Nation on Crime and Justice*, 2d ed. (Washington, D.C.: Government Printing Office, 1988), 114.

35   U.S. Department of Justice, *Highlights from Twenty Years of Surveying Crime Victims*.

36   Wesley G. Skogan and Michael G. Maxfield, *Coping with Crime* (Newbury Park, Calif.: Sage, 1981), 157.

37   President's Task Force on Victims of Crime, *Final Report* (Washington, D.C.: Government Printing Office, 1982).

38   Morton Hunt, *The Mugging* (New York: Atheneum, 1972), 135.

39   Steven F. Messner and Richard Rosenfeld, *Crime and the American Dream* (Belmont, Calif.: Wadsworth, 1994), 45–47.

40   Cesare Beccaria, *Essay on Crimes and Punishments* (Indianapolis, Ind.: Bobbs-Merrill, 1963).

41   Richard Dugdale, *The Jukes: Crime, Pauperism, Disease, and Heredity*, 4th ed. (New York: Putnam, 1910 [1875]); Arthur Estabrook, *The Jukes in 1915* (Washington, D.C.: Carnegie Institution, 1916); Henry H. Goddard, The Kallikak Family (New York: Macmillan, 1902).

42   *Skinner* v. *Oklahoma*, 316 U.S. 535 (1942).

43   Edward O. Wilson, *Sociobiology: The New Synthesis* (Cambridge, Mass.: Harvard University Press, 1975).

44 James Q. Wilson and Richard Herrnstein, *Crime and Human Nature* (New York: Simon and Schuster, 1985).

45 *San Francisco Chronicle*, 22 October 1993. The article was also published in *Science.*

46 Diana H. Fishbein, "Biological Perspectives in Criminology," *Criminology* 28 (February 1990): 27.

47 Henry Maudsley, *Responsibility in Mental Disease* (London: Macmillan, 1974).

48 Edwin H. Sutherland, "The Sexual Psychopath Laws," *Journal of Criminal Law and Criminology* 40 (January–February 1950): 543.

49 *The Forgotten Half* (Cambridge, Mass.: William F. Grand Foundation, 1988).

50 Robert K. Merton, "Social Structure and Anomie," *American Sociological Review* 2 (1938): 672–682.

51 Edwin H. Sutherland and Donald Cressey, *Criminology* (Philadelphia: Lippincott, 1970), 71–91.

52 Travis Hirschi, *Causes of Delinquency* (Berkeley: University of California Press, 1969); Michael Gottfredson and Travis Hirschi, *A General Theory of Crime* (Stanford, Calif.: Stanford University Press, 1990).

53  Howard S. Becker, *Outsiders: Studies in the Sociology of Deviance* (New York: Free Press, 1963).

54  Steven Spitzer, "Toward a Marxian Theory of Deviance," *Social Problems* 22 (1975): 639.

55  Sally S. Simpson, "Feminist Theory, Crime, and Justice," *Criminology* 27 (November 1989): 605. Simpson provides an excellent review of the literature.

56  Freda Adler, "Crime, an Equal Opportunity Employer," *Trial Magazine*, January 1977, 31.

57  Rita Simon, "Women and Crime Revisited," *Social Science Quarterly* 56 (March 1976): 658.

58  Joseph Weis, "Liberation and Crime: The Invention of the New Female Criminal," *Crime and Social Justice* 1 (1976): 17–26.

59  Jill Leslie Rosenbaum, "Family Dysfunction and Female Delinquency," *Crime and Delinquency* 35 (1989): 31–44.

60  Scott Decker, Richard Wright, Allison Redfern, and Dietrich Smith, "A Woman's Place Is in the Home: Females and Residential Burglary," *Justice Quarterly* 10 (March 1993): 142–162.

# Criminal Justice and the Rule of Law

The veteran Milwaukee police officers were understandably shocked when, in August 1991, they opened
the freezer in Jeffrey Dahmer's apartment and found
two human heads in a refrigerator, two in a freezer,
and seven others boiled clean. In the basement they found
an acid-filled blue barrel of body parts. Investigators soon learned
the full extent of Dahmer's crimes. The thirty-one-year-old laborer confessed to the police how he lured young men and boys from gay bars to
his apartment where he drugged and killed them, had sex with their
corpses, dissected and cannibalized the bodies.

Is there any question that Dahmer was insane when he committed
these crimes? If he does not meet the legal definition of insanity, who
does? As Richard Moran has noted, "All the defense really has to do is
describe the contents of his refrigerator and freezer. Normal murderers
do not mutilate their victims, nor do they display their heads or hearts.
Cannibalism is not an alternative lifestyle, nor is necrophilia just some
odd sexual preference."[1] However, the Wisconsin jury that convicted

Dahmer did not accept the defense that he was not guilty by reason of mental disease or defect. Dahmer will be incarcerated for the rest of his life.

How should society deal with people such as Jeffrey Dahmer? In recent years the names Charles Manson, "Son of Sam" David Berkowitz, John Wayne Gacy, and Henry Lee Lucas have come to public attention. All were serial killers whose behavior almost rivaled that of Hannibal (the Cannibal) Lecter in the movie *Silence of the Lambs*. Although the facts in these cases were not in doubt, the defendants' legal responsibility for their actions given the horrific aspects of their crimes became an issue. Were they sane when they committed their crimes? Were their rights protected as they proceeded from arrest to trial? What is an appropriate punishment for such individuals?

The case of Jeffrey Dahmer serves to remind us that even when someone is accused of such monstrous behavior, it is law that is at the base of the criminal justice system. Law governs the conduct of officials, and law structures the behavior of citizens. Law thus performs two functions: (1) it defines those behaviors that are labeled criminal, and (2) it describes the procedures to be followed under our adversarial system by those with the responsibility for law enforcement, adjudication, and corrections. Persons may not be convicted of committing an illegal act unless the state is able to prove that the conditions specified in the law were met and that the procedures required by the law were followed. Moreover it must be shown that the accused was **legally responsible** for the act as illustrated by the Dahmer case.

We have observed how criminal justice operates as an administrative system influenced by political and social forces; now the third necessary ingredient of our analysis—law—must be examined. This chapter explores the two aspects of criminal law: the substantive criminal law and the law of criminal procedure.

**legal responsibility**
The accountability of an individual for a crime because of the perpetrator's characteristics and the circumstances of the illegal act.

### Questions for Inquiry

- What are the foundations and sources of American criminal law?
- How does the substantive criminal law define crime and the legal responsibility of the accused?
- How does the procedural criminal law define the rights of the accused and processes that must be observed in dealing with a case?
- What are the major interpretations of the criminal justice amendments of the Constitution by the U.S. Supreme Court?

## Foundations of Criminal Law

In our system of justice, violators of society's rules are prosecuted and tried according to laws. Not all behavior that is offensive or considered deviant is criminal behavior. Only behaviors proscribed by the criminal code are illegal. We have seen that in different locations and times, different behaviors have been defined as criminal. What is basic to our system, however, is the assumption found in the Latin dictum *nullum crimen, nulla poena, sine lege*, "there can be no crime and no punishment except as the law prescribes." The criminal law, often referred to as the *penal code*, therefore embodies descriptions of both illegal behavior and the punishment to be administered and the ways in which justice officials must deal with defendants.

## Substantive Law and Procedural Law

Criminal law is thus divided into substantive law and procedural law. **Substantive law** stipulates the types of conduct that are criminal and the punishments to be imposed for such behavior. It embodies a view of the social order that the community desires to achieve. Substantive law answers the question, *What* is illegal? **Procedural law** sets forth the rules that govern enforcement of the substantive law. It stipulates the procedures that officials must follow in the enforcement, adjudication, and corrections portions of the criminal justice system. Procedural law limits the activities of police officers, judges, probation officers, and guards. It answers the question, *How* is the law enforced?

## Sources of Criminal Law

The earliest known codes of law appeared in ancient Mesopotamia's Sumerian Law (3100 B.C.) and the Code of Hammurabi (1750 B.C.). These were written codes, divided into sections to cover different types of offenses. Other significant ancestors of Western law include the Draconian Code, promulgated in the seventh century B.C. in classical Greece, and the Law of the Twelve Tables created by the Romans (450 B.C.). However, it is to England that the United States looks for the source of the greater part of its political and legal concepts. Of these concepts, the Anglo-American common law is probably the most important, for it is the major tie that binds the traditions of the two countries and differentiates them from the non-English-speaking world.

**Common Law**  **Common law** developed in England and was based on custom and tradition as interpreted by judges. In Continental Europe, a system of civil law developed in which the rules were formulated in codes or specially written stipulations. By contrast, the common law was not

The Draconian Code, promulgated in classical Greece in the seventh century B.C., is one of the earliest foundations of Western law.

**substantive criminal law**
Law defining the behaviors that are subject to punishment, and the sanctions for such offenses.

**procedural criminal law**
Law defining the procedures that officials must follow in the enforcement, adjudication, and correction portions of the criminal justice system.

**common law**
The Anglo-American system of uncodified law, in which judges follow precedents set by earlier decisions when they decide new but similar cases. The substantive and procedural criminal law was originally developed in this manner but was later codified by legislatures.

written down as a code that one could easily consult to learn what was proper. Rather, it took its form from the collected opinions of the English judges, who looked to custom in making decisions. The judges thus created law when they ruled on specific cases. These rulings then formed precedents to be followed in later rulings. Over time, as new situations arose and more opinions were written to resolve conflicts, the common law grew. This stability combined with flexibility in the face of new circumstances is the uniquely valuable characteristic of Anglo-American law.

Among the contributions of England to the American colonies was the common law system. Originally the English precedents and procedures were maintained in the New World, but changes in the structure of the common law of crime began to occur with the American Revolution and the ratification of a written constitution. Starting in the nineteenth century, state legislatures began to incorporate the common law into written penal codes and rules of criminal procedure. We continue to speak of the United States as having a common law system because the concept of precedent is maintained; yet in most states judges now consult legislatively enacted criminal codes to ascertain how wrongdoing is defined and the punishments that are to be exacted.

**Written Law**  One single document that clearly stated the criminal law, both substantive and procedural, would be helpful. It would allow citizens to know when they might be in danger of committing an illegal act and to be aware of their rights should official action be taken against them. If such a document could be written in simple language, society would probably need fewer attorneys. Compiling such a document would, of course, be impossible, and the criminal law must continue to be found in the four basic sources from which it is derived: constitutions, statutes, court decisions, or case law, and administrative regulations.

**constitutions**
The basic laws of a country defining the structure of government and the relationship of citizens to that government.

**Constitutions** provide the fundamental principles and procedural safeguards that serve as guides for the enactment of laws and the making of decisions. The Constitution of the United States was written in Philadelphia in 1787 and went into effect after it was ratified by the required number of states in 1788. The first ten amendments to the Constitution, the Bill of Rights, were added in 1791. Several of these amendments have a direct bearing on the criminal law since they include basic protections from governmental action, such as the right against unreasonable searches and seizures, the right to due process, the right to counsel, and the prohibition against cruel and unusual punishments. Most state constitutions also list these protections, and since the early 1960s the U.S. Supreme Court has required that criminal procedures in the states recognize the protections set forth in the U.S. Constitution.

**statutes**
Laws passed by legislatures. Statutory definitions of criminal offenses are embodied in penal codes.

**Statutes** are laws passed by legislative bodies; the substantive and procedural rules of most states are found in their statutes. Although the law of crime is primarily an activity of state legislatures, Congress and local governments also play a role in shaping criminal laws. As discussed in Chapter 1, federal criminal laws passed by Congress deal mainly with violations that occur on property of the U.S. government or with behavior that involves the national interest (treason) or the jurisdictions of more than one state (taking a kidnap victim across state lines). The states give cities and towns some authority to develop laws dealing with local problems. There is often an overlapping of jurisdictions among national, state, and local rules governing some criminal conduct. The possession or sale of narcotics, for example, may violate criminal laws at all three levels of government. In such situations, enforcement agencies may disagree as to which one will prosecute the offender.

If we want to know the definition of a crime covered by a statute, we consult a state's penal code. The behaviors that constitute each crime and the penalty to be imposed are clearly specified in each state's code. Although the laws of most of the states are similar, there are some differences. To encourage uniformity among the states in the substantive and procedural laws, the American Law Institute has developed a Model Penal Code that it urges legislatures to adopt.

Court decisions, often called **case law**, constitute a third source of criminal law. As noted, the major principle of the U.S. common law system is that judges look to earlier opinions to guide their determinations. Although much of the common law of crime has been replaced by statutes, reference to precedent is still very much an aid to lawyers and judges in the interpretation of these codified rules.

**case law**
Legal opinions having the status of law as enunciated by courts.

**Administrative regulations** are laws and rulings made by federal, state, and local agencies. Official bodies, such as the departments dealing with regulation of health, safety, and the environment, have been given power by the legislative or executive branch to develop rules to govern specific policy areas. Most such rules have been promulgated during the twentieth century to deal with modern problems: wages and hours, pollution, automobile traffic, industrial safety, pure food and drugs, and the like. Many of the rules are part of the criminal law, and violations are processed through the criminal justice system.

**administrative regulations**
Rules promulgated by governmental agencies to implement specific public policies.

When we talk of the criminal law, then, we refer to more than the penal code or some similar concise statement of rules. The criminal law, both substantive and procedural, is found in the four sources described here and is summarized in Figure 3.1.

## Felony and Misdemeanor

Another way of classifying crimes is according to their level of seriousness. The distinction between a felony and a misdemeanor is one of the oldest in the criminal law. Most laws define felonies and misdemeanors in regard to the punishment that may be exacted. Conviction on a felony charge usually means that a prison sentence of more than a year is authorized; even death might be authorized. Misdemeanants are dealt with more leniently; the sentence might be incarceration for less than a year, probation, or a fine. Some states use place of punishment as the defining criterion: prison for felonies, jail for misdemeanors.

Whether a defendant is charged with a felony or a misdemeanor is important not only in terms of potential punishment but also in terms of how the criminal justice system will process the defendant. Certain rights and penalties follow from this distinction. For example, the conditions under which the police may make an arrest, the right of indigents to have

**Figure 3.1**
**Sources of criminal law**
Although the codes of law existed in ancient times, it is to the common law of England that the concepts of American criminal law are primarily linked. The common law differentiates English-speaking systems from the civil law systems of the rest of the world.

### Constitutional Law

The Constitution of the United States and those of each state contain basic provisions defining the structure of government and the rights of citizens.

### Statutory Law

The substantive and procedural criminal laws are found in laws passed by legislative bodies such as the U.S. Congress and state legislatures.

### Case Law

Consistent with the common law heritage, legal opinions enunciated by judges in individual cases have the status of law.

### Administrative Law

Also having the status of law are some decisions of federal and state governmental agencies that have been given the power to regulate such areas as health, safety, and the environment in the public interest.

counsel provided by the state, and the trial level at which the charges will be heard are determined by whether a felony or misdemeanor is charged. Further, persons convicted of felonies may be barred from certain professions, such as law and medicine, and in many states are also barred from other occupations (bartender, police officer, barber). This type of sanction can be carried to ludicrous extremes. In some states former felons are prohibited from working where alcoholic beverages are sold or from refereeing professional wrestling matches.

## Criminal Law versus Civil Law

It is also important to clarify the distinctions between criminal law and **civil law**. A basic distinction is that a violation of criminal law is an offense against society as a whole; civil law regulates relationships between individuals (for example, property, damages, contracts). In addition, the focus of the criminal law is on the intent of the wrong-doer; the focus in civil law is on fixing the blame for the damage or injury. In the area of civil law known as *torts*, for example, the major concern is compensation to the individual wronged. If through your negligence your automobile collides with another, the owner of the other car may bring a civil suit against you to recover the amount of damages you have caused. In a separate action the state may charge you with a violation of the criminal law with regard to the operation of motor vehicles because your actions breached society's rules.

Although criminal and civil law are recognized as two distinct bodies, it should be understood that both attempt to control human behavior, steering people to act in a desired manner and imposing costs on those who violate social rules. The payment of monetary damages in a tort case may parallel payment of a fine in a criminal case. Civil actions are increasingly being taken against offenders who were previously the subject of only criminal laws. Some rape victims have instituted civil suits against their attackers and some department stores are suing shoplifters for substantial amounts. One rape victim won a judgment for more than $17 million against the company that managed the complex where she lived. The jury found that the company had not maintained secure conditions, with the result that the attacker easily gained entry to the woman's apartment.[2]

Another example of a link between criminal and civil law is found in the area of **civil forfeiture**. This concept, which is from English common law and which allows for the taking of property, has been resurrected in drug enforcement. U.S. courts have distinguished between forfeiture actions *in personam* (against a person) and those *in rem* (against a thing). Litigation against an owner of property is treated as criminal and forfeiture may result upon conviction of the offender. Actions *in rem* are civil, with courts maintaining the idea that the issue is over the guilt or innocence of the property itself. As Supreme Court Justice Field said in 1871, "The thing is the instrument of wrong, and is forfeited by reason of the unlawful use made of it.... [P]roceedings *in rem* [are] wholly independent of, and unaffected by, the criminal proceedings against the person."[3] Thus,

**civil law**
Laws regulating the relationships between or among individuals.

**civil forfeiture**
The relinquishing of assets to the state as the consequence of crime.

In recent years the police have used civil forfeiture to seize property that they believe was purchased with drug profits.

one finds court dockets that include cases titled *United States of America* vs. *667 Bottles of Wine* or *Florida* vs. *One 1986 Chevrolet Van*.

The foundations of the American criminal law are complex. The English common law and the laws found in such written sources as constitutions, statutes, case law, and administrative regulations all contribute to what most people call "the criminal law." But within this body of law is a major division between the substantive criminal law and the procedural criminal law.

## Substantive Criminal Law

As we have seen, the substantive criminal law defines the misbehavior that is subject to punishment and specifies the punishments for such offenses. Underlying the substantive criminal law is the basic doctrine that no one may be convicted of or punished for an offense unless the conduct constituting that offense has been authoritatively defined by the law. In short, the substantive criminal law defines what is illegal. It is a basic principle that people must know in advance what is required of them, but that is more easily said than done because language is often confusing and ambiguous. In such instances of ambiguity, the judiciary is responsible for interpreting the law so that the meaning intended by the legislature can be understood.

### Seven Principles of Criminal Law

The criteria used to decide whether a specific behavior is a crime are more complicated than might be imagined from the language of the penal code. Jerome Hall has developed a seven-point formalization of the major principles of Western law.[4] This system of interlocking legal propositions recognizes the existence of the same basic ingredients in every crime. For a behavior to be defined as criminal and subject to the penalties of the law, all seven of the following principles must be present:

1   *Legality*: the existence of a law defining the crime. Antisocial behavior is not a crime unless it has been prohibited by law *before* the act is committed. For example, the United States Constitution prohibits *ex post facto* laws—laws passed after the occurrence of a fact or an act.

2   *Actus reus*: behavior of either commission or omission by the accused that constitutes the violation. This principle emphasizes that behavior itself is required, not just bad intentions. In a modern case involving the principle of *actus reus*, the United States Supreme Court declared unconstitutional a California law making it a criminal offense for a person "to be addicted to the use of narcotics."[5] As Justice Potter Stewart, speaking for the Court, said, the California law did not deal with antisocial behavior but rather with a status, that of being addicted, and thus involved no criminal act.

3   *Causation*: a causal relationship between the act and the harm suffered. If one person shoots another and the victim dies in the hospital from pneumonia, it is difficult to show that the act (shooting) resulted in the harm (death).

4   *Harm*: damage inflicted on certain legally protected values (such as person, property, reputation) as a result of the act. This principle is often questioned by persons who feel that they are not committing a crime because they may be harming only themselves. Laws requiring motorcyclists to wear helmets have been challenged on this ground. Such laws, however, have been written with the recognition that accidental injury or death may have a harmful effect on others—dependents, for example.

The principle of harm also includes those acts where there is the potential for harm. Thus, behaviors involving attempt, conspiracy, and solicitation to commit a criminal act, the **inchoate offenses**, are justified. For example, if you plan with someone to kill your spouse, you and your fellow plotter can be charged with conspiracy to commit that murder, even if the murder does not occur.

**inchoate offenses**
Conduct made criminal even though it has not yet produced the harm that the law seeks to prevent.

5   *Concurrence*: the simultaneous occurrence of the intention and the act. For example, if you ask two electricians to enter your house to fix the wiring and while there they commit a burglary, they cannot also be accused of trespassing. The intent and the conduct are not fused. If, however, two people posing as electricians enter your house uninvited and commit a burglary, then they could also be accused of trespassing.

6   *Mens rea*: a guilty state of mind. The commission of the act is not in itself criminal unless it is accompanied by a guilty mind. This concept is related to *intent*—that is, the person's actions lead to the assumption that the crime was committed intentionally and on the basis of free will. Persons who commit an involuntary act or who are insane when they perform a legally forbidden act have not committed a crime because *mens rea* is not present. We will discuss the difficult concept of ***mens rea*** in more depth later in this section.

***mens rea***
"Guilty mind" or blameworthy state of mind, necessary for the imputation of responsibility for a criminal offense; criminal as distinguished from innocent intent.

**7** *Punishment*: the stipulation in the law of sanctions to be applied against persons found guilty of the forbidden behavior.

Criminal law theory is concerned largely with the elucidation of these seven principles, which are summarized in Figure 3.2. The seven principles provide the basis for authorities to define individual behavior as being against the law and to provide the accused with the basis for defense against the charges. From these principles flow the assumptions of the adversarial process. (For a contrasting view, see the Comparative Perspective on Islamic criminal law, pages 100–101.)

## Elements of a Crime

Legislatures define certain acts as crimes when they are committed in accordance with the seven principles just outlined, in the presence of certain "attendant circumstances," and while the offender is a certain state of mind. These three factors—the act (*actus reus*), the attendant circumstances, and the state of mind (*mens rea*)—are together called the *elements of a crime*. These elements can be seen in the section of one penal code dealing with burglary, which reads as follows:

### Section 3502. Burglary

**1** *Offense defined*: A person is guilty of burglary if he enters a building or occupied structure, or separately secured or occupied portion thereof, with intent to commit a crime therein, unless the premises are at the time open to the public or the actor is licensed or privileged to enter.

The elements of burglary are, therefore, entering a building or occupied structure (*actus reus*), with intent to commit a crime therein (*mens rea*), at a time when the premises are not open to the public and the actor is not licensed or privileged to enter (attendant circumstances). For an act to constitute burglary, all three elements must be present.

Even if it appears, according to the formal words of the applicable statute, that the accused has committed a crime, prosecution will be successful only if the elements correspond to the interpretations of the law made by the courts. The Pennsylvania judiciary has, for example, construed the *actus reus* of burglary to include entering a building, such as a store or tavern, open to the public, so long as the entry was "willful and malicious—that is, made with the intent to commit a felony therein." Thus one can be convicted of burglary for entering a store with the intent to steal even though entry was made during business hours and without force.

**Figure 3.2**
**The seven principles of criminal law**
These principles undergirding Western law provide the basis for defining behaviors that may be criminalized and the conditions that must be met for successful prosecution.

| A crime is | |
|---|---|
| **1** legally proscribed | (legality) |
| **2** human conduct | (*actus reus*) |
| **3** causative | (causation) |
| **4** of a given harm | (harm) |
| **5** which conduct coincides | (concurrence) |
| **6** with a blameworthy frame of mind | (*mens rea*) |
| **7** and is subject to punishment | (punishment) |

## Statutory Definitions of Crimes

The laws of the United States and of each of the states often define criminal acts somewhat differently. To find out how a state defines an offense, it is necessary to read its particular penal code; this document will give a general idea of which acts are illegal. But to fully understand the special interpretations of the code, it is important to analyze the judicial opinions that have sought to clarify the law.

To clarify the substantive criminal law, the following discussion focuses on two of the eight index crimes of the *Uniform Crime Reports*, homicide and rape. The elements of a crime may be interpreted somewhat differently in individual states.

**Murder and Nonnegligent Manslaughter**   A major problem in categorizing criminal behavior that has brought about death is that legislatures have subdivided the early common law definition of criminal homicide into degrees of murder and voluntary and involuntary manslaughter. In addition, some states have created new categories, such as reckless homicide, negligent homicide, and vehicular homicide. Each of these definitions involves slight variations in the *actus reus* and the *mens rea*. The *Uniform Crime Reports* (UCR) counts murder and nonnegligent manslaughter as index offenses. (Table 3.1, page 102, defines offenses according to the *UCR*.)

In legal terminology, the phrase *malice aforethought* is used to distinguish murder from manslaughter. This phrase indicates that the crime of murder is a deliberate, premeditated, and willful killing of another human being. In most states the definition of murder is also extended to circumstances either in which defendants knew that their behavior had a strong likelihood of causing death, showed indifference to life, and thus recklessly engaged in conduct that resulted in death, or in which their behavior resulted in death while they were engaged in committing a felony. Mitigating circumstances, such as "the heat of passion" or extreme provocation, would reduce the offense to manslaughter because the requirement of malice aforethought would be absent or diminished. Similarly, manslaughter would include a killing resulting from an attempt to defend oneself that was not fully excused as self-defense and a death resulting from a lesser degree of recklessness or negligence.

**Rape**   In recent years pressure has been brought to bear, especially by women's organizations, to ensure strict enforcement of the laws against rape. Successful prosecution for rape is difficult, however, because corroborating evidence is often lacking and the public humiliation to which victims are often subjected sometimes results in their withdrawal of charges. In an effort to encourage prosecution, some states have reformed their laws by removing the offending word *rape* and classifying the behavior as a sexual offense or an aggravated assault.

The statutory law traditionally has stipulated that the offense is committed if a male compels by force or threat a female who is not his wife to have sexual intercourse with him against her will. The charge may also be brought if the act is performed on a woman who is unconscious and

# Islamic Criminal Law

The 1979 revolution in Iran, the rise of fundamentalist Islamic thought throughout the world, and the 1991 Gulf War conflict with Iraq have made Americans aware of great cultural differences between Westerners and Middle Easterners. Islamic criminal law, in particular, appears to be at odds with justice as it is administered in Europe and the Americas. To the West, justice in Islamic states, such as Iran, Pakistan, and the Sudan, seems harsh and unforgiving. The practices of stoning for adultery and amputation for theft are often given as examples of the ferocity of Islamic law. What most Americans do not realize is that there are judicial and evidentiary safeguards within the *Shari'a*, the law of Islam.

Islamic criminal law is concerned with (1) the safety of the public from physical attack, insult, and humiliation, (2) the stability of the family, (3) the protection of property against theft, destruction, or unauthorized interference, and (4) the protection of the government and the Islamic faith against subversion.

Criminal acts are divided into three categories. *Hudud* offenses are crimes against God, and punishment is specified in the Koran and the Sunna, a compilation of Muhammad's statements. *Quesas* are crimes of physical assault and murder, which are punishable by retaliation—"the return of life for a life in case of murder." The victim or the surviving heirs may waive the punishment and ask for compensation (blood money) or may pardon the offender. *Ta'azir* offenses are those whose penalties are not fixed by the Koran or the Sunna but are within the discretion of the *qadi* (judge). As shown below for the seven *Hudud* offenses, the Koran defines the crime, specifies the elements of proof required, and sets the punishment.

## Theft

Theft is the taking of property belonging to another, the value of which is equal to or exceeds a prescribed amount, usually set at ten dirhams or about seventy-five cents. The property must be taken from the custody of another person in a secret manner, and the thief must obtain full possession of the property. "Custody" requires that the property should have been under guard or in a place of safekeeping.

## Extramarital Sexual Activity

Sexual relations outside marriage are believed to undermine marriage and lead to family conflict, jealousy, divorce, litigation, and the spread of disease.

**Islamic *Hudud* offenses, required proofs, and punishments**

| Crime | Proof | Punishment |
|---|---|---|
| Adultery | Four witnesses or confessions | Married persons: stoning to death. Convict is taken to a barren site. Stones are thrown first by witnesses, then by the *qadi*, and finally by the rest of the community.<br>For a woman, a grave is dug to receive the body.<br>Unmarried person: 100 lashes. *Maliki* school also punishes unmarried males with one year in prison or exile. |
| Defamation | Unsupported accusation of adultery | Free: 80 lashes.<br>Slave: 40 lashes.<br>Convict is lightly attired when whipped. |
| Apostasy | Two witnesses or confessions | Male: death by beheading.<br>Female: imprisonment until repentance. |
| Highway robbery | Two witnesses or confessions | With homicide: death by beheading. The body is then displayed in a crucifixion-like form.<br>Without homicide: amputation of right hand and left foot.<br>If arrested before commission: imprisonment until repentance. |
| Use of alcohol | Two witnesses or confessions | Free: 80 lashes (*Shafi'i*, 40).<br>Slave: 40 lashes.<br>Public whipping is applied with a stick, using moderate force without raising the hand above the head so as not to lacerate the skin. Blows are spread over the body and are not to be applied to the face and head. A male stands, and a female is seated. A doctor is present. Flogging is inflicted by scholars well versed in Islamic law, so that it is justly meted out. |
| Theft | Two witnesses or confessions | First offense: amputation of hand at wrist, by an authorized doctor.<br>Second offense: amputation of second hand at wrist, by an authorized doctor.<br>Third offense: amputation of foot at ankle, by an authorized doctor, or imprisonment until repentance. |
| Rebellion | Two witnesses or confessions | If captured: death.<br>If surrendered or arrested: *Ta'azir* punishment. |

## Defamation
In addition to false accusations of fornication, this offense includes impugning the legitimacy of a woman's child. Defamation by a husband of his wife leads to divorce and is not subject to punishment.

## Highway Robbery
This crime interferes with commerce and creates fear among travelers and is therefore subject to punishment.

## Use of Alcohol
Drinking wine and other intoxicating beverages is prohibited because it brings about indolence and inattention to religious duties.

## Apostasy
This is the voluntary renunciation of Islam. The offense is committed by any Muslim who converts to another faith, worships idols, or rejects any of the tenets of Islam.

## Rebellion
The intentional, forceful overthrow or attempted overthrow of the legitimate leader of the Islamic state.

SOURCE: From *Islamic Criminal Law and Procedure: An Introduction*, by M. Lippman, S. McConville, and M. Yerushalmi, 42–43. Copyright © 1988 by Praeger Publishers. Reprinted by permission of Greenwood Publishing Group, Inc., Westport, Conn. From "Hudud Crimes," by A. A. Mansour, in M. C. Bassiouni (ed.), *The Islamic Criminal Justice System*, 195. Copyright © 1982 by Oceana Publications. Reprinted by permission.

**Table 3.1**
**Definition of offenses in the**
*Uniform Crime Reports*
**(Part 1)**
States differ as to the exact
descriptions of offenses, but
these *UCR* definitions provide a
national standard that helps us
distinguish among various
criminal behaviors.

SOURCE: U.S. Department of Justice, Federal
Bureau of Investigation, *Uniform Crime Reports*,
1992 (Washington, D.C.: Government Printing
Office, 1993).

1  *Criminal homicide:*
   a. Murder and nonnegligent manslaughter: the willful (nonnegligent) killing of one human
   being by another. Deaths caused by negligence, attempts to kill, assaults to kill, suicides,
   accidental deaths and justifiable homicides are excluded. Justifiable homicides are limited to:
   (1) the killing of a felon by a law enforcement officer in the line of duty; and
   (2) the killing of a felon by a private citizen.
   b. Manslaughter by negligence: the killing of another person through gross negligence.
   Excludes traffic fatalities. While manslaughter by negligence is a Part I crime, it is not
   included in the Crime Index.

2  *Forcible rape:*
   The carnal knowledge of a female forcibly and against her will. Included are rapes by force
   and attempts or assaults to rape. Statutory offenses (no force used—victim under age of
   consent) are excluded.

3  *Robbery:*
   The taking or attempting to take anything of value from the care, custody, or control of a
   person or persons by force or threat of force of violence and/or by putting the victim in fear.

4  *Aggravated assault:*
   An unlawful attack by one person upon another for the purpose of inflicting severe or aggravated bodily injury. This type of assault usually is accompanied by the use of a weapon or
   by means likely to produce death or great bodily harm. Simple assaults are excluded.

5  *Burglary—breaking or entering:*
   The unlawful entry of a structure to commit a felony or a theft. Attempted forcible entry is
   included.

6  *Larceny-theft (except motor vehicle theft):*
   The unlawful taking, carrying, leading, or riding away of property from the possession or
   constructive possession of another. Examples are thefts of bicycles or automobile acces-
   sories, shoplifting, pocket-picking, or the stealing of any property or article which is not
   taken by force and violence or by fraud. Attempted larcenies are included. Embezzlement,
   "con" games, forgery, worthless checks, and so on, are excluded.

7  *Motor vehicle theft:*
   The theft or attempted theft of a motor vehicle. A motor vehicle is self-propelled and runs on
   the surface and not on rails. Specifically excluded from this category are motorboats, construction equipment, airplanes, and farming equipment.

8  *Arson:*
   Any willful or malicious burning or attempt to burn, with or without intent to defraud, a
   dwelling house, public building, motor vehicle or aircraft, personal property of another,
   and so on.

therefore unable to resist. If the female is under ten years of age, common
law regards her as unable to give consent. Note that this definition of the
law does not cover homosexual rape or forced sexual intercourse with
one's own wife, though statutory reforms and judicial opinions in some
states have dealt with these two situations in recent years.

The charge of rape raises difficult questions of both *actus reus* and
*mens rea*. Because the act usually takes place in private, prosecutors may

have difficulty showing that sexual intercourse took place without consent; some states require corroborating evidence from someone other than the victim. Force is a necessary element in the crime of rape. In some courts, the absence of injury to the victim's body has been taken to show that there was no resistance, which in some jurisdictions implies that consent was given.

Unlike murder, rape is not usually divided by statutes into degrees; but other offenses are often charged when elements of proof or mitigating circumstances warrant. In some states "deviate sexual intercourse," "sexual assault," "statutory rape," or "aggravated assault" are charges that may be used to designate sexual offenses that do not contain all the criminal elements necessary to prove rape.

In this examination of the crimes of murder and rape, we can see that the substantive criminal law contains the basic doctrines stipulating the conditions that must be met before a person can be convicted of an offense. The so-called seven principles of Western law categorize these doctrines, and the penal code of each of the states and the laws of the United States explicitly define offenses. But as illustrated in the following Close-Up (page 105), individual perceptions of what constitutes a crime also come into play. Does an acquaintance rape like the one described fit the legal definition of rape?

Women's organizations have brought pressure to bear to ensure the strict enforcement of the laws against rape. If you were prosecuting a charge of rape, what problems would you face in obtaining a conviction?

## Responsibility for Criminal Acts

Thus far we have examined the elements of crime and the statutory definition of offenses; we now need to look at the question of responsibility. Among the seven principles of criminal law, that of *mens rea* is crucial in establishing the perpetrator's responsibility for the act committed. To obtain a conviction, the prosecution must show that the individual not only committed the illegal act charged but also did so in a state of mind that makes it appropriate to hold the person responsible. This task is difficult because it requires that courts inquire into the mental state of the defendant at the time the act was committed.

Although many defendants in criminal cases openly admit that they committed the illegal behavior, they may still enter a plea of not guilty. They do so not only because they know the state must provide the evidence to prove them guilty but also, and more important, because they believe the necessary *mens rea* element was not present and they consequently are not criminally culpable. Perhaps accidents provide the clearest examples of such situations: the defendant argues that it was an accident that the gun went off and the neighbor was killed or that the car skidded into the pedestrian. As Justice Oliver Wendell Holmes once said, "Even a dog distinguishes between being stumbled over and being kicked."[6]

The courts label events *accidents* when responsibility is not fixed; *mens rea* is not present because the event was not intentional. But not everything that is claimed to be accidental is so judged by a court. In some situations the perpetrator is so negligent or reckless (the gun was kept loaded with the safety catch off) that the court may fix some degree of criminal responsibility.

Note that *mens rea*, or criminal responsibility, may be fixed without showing that the defendant was determined to do evil. In other words, it is not the quality of one's motives that establishes *mens rea* but the nature and the level of one's intention. The *Model Penal Code* lists four mental conditions that can be used to satisfy the requirement of *mens rea*: The act must have been performed intentionally, knowingly, recklessly, or negligently.[7] There are offenses that require a high degree of intent. For example, the crime of larceny requires a finding that the defendant intentionally took property to which she knew she was not entitled, *intending* to deprive the rightful owner of possession *permanently*.

One important exception to the *mens rea* principle concerns public welfare or **strict liability** offenses, acts that require no showing of intent to be adjudged criminal. The majority of such offenses are defined in legislation of a type first enacted in late-nineteenth century England and the United States to deal with issues connected with urban industrialization, such as sanitation, pure food, housing, and safety. Often the statutory language did not include a reference to *mens rea*. Some courts ruled that employers were not responsible for the carelessness of their workers because they had no knowledge of the criminal offenses being committed in their establishments. An employer who had not known that the food products being canned by his employees were contaminated, for example, was not held liable for a violation of pure food laws even if people who ate the food died as a result. Other courts, however, ruled that such owners had a special responsibility to the public to ensure the quality of their products and therefore could be found criminally liable if they failed to do so.

The concept of strict liability was best described by Justice Robert Jackson in *Morissette* v. *United States* (1952), in which he upheld the right of legislatures to make certain acts criminal even if *mens rea* was lacking.

## Acquaintance Rape

He was her friend. So the 26-year-old real estate agent agreed when he asked to come over after work one night. Around midnight, she unlocked the door to her one-room apartment overlooking Connecticut Avenue. She listened indulgently to her friend, a former lover, complain about his job managing a local restaurant. Finally, she asked him to leave. He seemed to ignore her, so she decided to lie on her bed, fully clothed. She dozed off as her friend droned on. At one point, she slipped under the comforter of her bed and wriggled out of her jeans. Sometime in the next hour, she was aware that he was sitting on the bed. Suddenly she awoke with a start, as she realized he had climbed on top of her.

She screamed and tried to push him off the bed. He shoved her back, wrenching her neck and pinning her down. She began to cry. He placed his hand tightly over her mouth and penetrated her. Sobbing and unable to breathe, she began to choke. Blood vessels around her eyes popped from lack of oxygen.

Then she stopped fighting and went limp, psychologically retreating to a place where he could not hurt her. His hand slipped off her mouth; she gasped "Just get it over with."

With that he stopped. He rolled off her. He apologized. He swore at himself. He said he had made a mistake and threatened to kill himself. Then he ran out of her apartment carrying his clothes.

SOURCE: Chris Spolar and Angela Walker, "Rape," *Washington Post* 4 September 1990, Health section, 4. © 1990, *The Washington Post*. Reprinted with permission.

---

Pointing to the need for health and welfare regulations, he stated that, although the offenses did not threaten the security of the state, they were offenses against its authority because their occurrence impaired the efficiency of the controls necessary for social order. "In this respect, whatever the intent of the violator, the injury is the same.... Hence, legislation applicable to such offenses does not specify intent as a necessary element."[8]

The reasoning employed by Justice Jackson to uphold the principle of strict liability, however, has not been followed in all circumstances. Some people believe that the principle should be applied only to regulatory offenses that require no incarceration and that carry no social stigma. In practice, the criminal penalty is usually imposed only after many attempts to induce an offender's compliance have failed. Some scholars believe that imprisonment would be unconstitutional for some strict liability crimes, but the incidence of such sentences has been so rare that the concept has not been tested.

In a technologically complex society, we may assume that the concept of strict liability will be expanded to a range of other acts in which a guilty mind is not present. It is also likely, however, that courts will restrict the application of the strict liability principle to situations in which recklessness or indifference is present.

The absence of *mens rea*, then, does not guarantee a verdict of not guilty in every circumstance. In most cases, however, it does relieve defendants of responsibility for acts that, if intentional, would be labeled criminal. In addition to the defense of accidents, eight defenses based on absence of criminal intent are recognized in appropriate circumstances: (1) entrapment, (2) self-defense, (3) necessity, (4) duress, (5) immaturity, (6) mistake of fact, (7) intoxication, and (8) insanity.

**Entrapment**   **Entrapment** is a defense that may be used to point to the absence of intent. The law excuses the actions of defendants from criminal responsibility when it is shown that government agents have induced an individual to commit the offense. That does not mean the police may not use undercover agents to set a trap for criminals, nor does it mean the police may not provide ordinary opportunities for the commission of a crime. But the entrapment defense may be used when the police have acted so as to encourage the criminal act.

The defense of entrapment has evolved through a series of court decisions in the twentieth century. In earlier eras judges were less concerned with whether the police had baited a citizen into committing an illegal act and were more concerned with whether or not the citizen took the bait. Now when the police investigate a crime or implant the idea for a crime in the mind of a person who then commits the offense, entrapment may have occurred. But as Damon Camp has pointed out, the problem of dealing with entrapment is arduous.[9]

The critical question concerns the predisposition of the defendant. In 1992 the Supreme Court emphasized that the prosecutor must show beyond a reasonable doubt that a defendant was predisposed to violate the law prior to first being approached by government agents. This case involved Keith Jacobson, a Nebraskan farmer, who, in 1984, ordered from a California bookstore magazines containing photographs of nude boys. The material did not violate the law at that time, but a few months later Congress passed the Child Protection Act and the U.S. Postal Service and the Customs Service began enforcement. These agencies set up five fictional organizations with names such as the American Hedonist Society and sent solicitations to Jacobson and others whose names were on the California bookstore mailing list. These solicitations urged Jacobson to fight the new law by ordering items which "we believe you will find to be both interesting and stimulating."[10] One postal inspector, using a pseudonym, even became Mr. Jacobson's "pen pal." When Jacobson ordered the material he was arrested by federal agents. No other pornographic material was found in his home.

For the majority, Justice Byron White wrote that government officials may not "originate a criminal design, implant in an innocent person's mind the disposition to commit a criminal act, and then induce commission of the crime so that the government may prosecute."[11]

**Self-defense**   A person who feels that he or she is in immediate danger of being harmed by another person's unlawful use of force may ward off the attack in self-defense. The laws of most states also recognize an individual's right to defend others from attack, to protect property, and to prevent the commission of a crime. The law also specifies the manner in which one may protect oneself; generally one must use only the level of force necessary.

One has the right to kill another person in self-defense if one believes that this amount of force is necessary to prevent one's own death, severe bodily harm, kidnapping, or rape. Under this standard courts would not uphold the shooting of an assailant armed with a broomstick unless, perhaps, it were shown that the accused thought that the weapon was a gun about to be fired. In most states self-defense is no justification for the use of force to resist arrest, even if it is later shown that the arrest was unlawful.

Bernhard Goetz, New York City's "subway vigilante," argued the self-defense justification when he was tried on attempted murder and assault charges for firing a .38 caliber pistol at four young men who threatened him with long screw drivers and demanded money as the subway rattled through the underground darkness. Goetz rushed from the scene, only to surrender nine days later to the police in Concord, New Hampshire, where he admitted the shooting, later saying he had done it in self-defense.

The incident sparked off one of America's most controversial criminal cases. Support for Goetz as someone who had stood up to lawlessness came from many quarters. He was charged with attempted murder, assault, and possession of an illegal weapon. A judge dismissed nine of the thirteen charges because of prosecution errors in the presentation of the case to the grand jury. Later the New York Court of Appeals reinstated the charges and clarified the state's standards for self-defense. It emphasized that Goetz had to *believe* deadly force was necessary and that the belief was reasonable. Goetz was retried and received a one-year sentence.

**Necessity**   Outlawed acts are often committed because the perpetrators believe that they are necessary for their own preservation or to avoid a greater evil. Necessity is sometimes confused with self-defense. The distinction between these defenses concerns the person who is injured by the act. When someone is acting in self-defense, he or she injures the creator of the criminal situation; when a person is acting from necessity, he or she harms a person who was in no way responsible for the imminent danger (although this party might have been imperiled by it). In short, necessity may be claimed as a defense in situations in which the accused was confronted with a choice of evils. The person speeding through traffic lights to get an injured child to the hospital or someone breaking and entering a building to seek refuge from a snowstorm could claim to be violating the law out of necessity.

Since 1884, legal students have been considering the English case *The Queen* v. *Dudley and Stephens*.[12] Thomas Dudley and Edwin Stephens were accused of the murder of Richard Parker after the ship on which they were employed sank 1,600 miles from the Cape of Good Hope. The three, together with another seaman named Brooks, managed to get into a lifeboat containing no drinking water and little food. After twenty days, Dudley and Stephens proposed to Brooks that Parker, the cabin boy, be killed and that they eat his remains as a necessity for survival. Brooks would not agree. With Stephens's assent, Dudley then killed the boy, and all three ate from his body for four days, at which time a passing vessel picked them up. Dudley and Stephens were committed for trial, but the jury had to inquire of a higher court whether the behavior was murder. It was agreed that

if the men had not fed upon the body of the boy they would … within the four days have died of famine. That the boy, being in a much weaker condition, was likely to have died before them. That at the time of the act there was no sail in sight, nor any reasonable prospect of relief. That under these circumstances there appeared to the prisoners that unless they then fed or very soon fed upon the boy or one of themselves they would die of starvation. That there was no appreciable chance of saving life except by killing some one for the others to eat.[13]

Given these arguments, one might think that the defense of necessity would have carried the day. But Lord Coleridge, the chief justice, argued that regardless of the temptation or the intensity of the suffering, standards had to be maintained and the law not weakened. Dudley and Stephens were given the death sentence, which the Crown later commuted to six months imprisonment.

**Duress (Coercion)**   Closely related to the defense of necessity is that of duress. The distinction is made on the basis of coercion: a person who has been forced or coerced by another into committing an act has acted under duress. Defendants who present this defense are arguing that they are actually the victims, not the criminals. Bank tellers who give deposited money to an armed robber are excused because the tellers were acting under duress and thus should not be held responsible. By contrast, the defense of necessity is used when the environmental situation (natural rather than human forces) was such that a choice was made to commit an illegal act (cannibalism on the high seas).

American courts normally uphold the defense of duress when it is shown that the defendant could not have done otherwise without the expectation of imminent bodily harm or death. Thus duress has not usually been allowed when it has been shown that defendants had opportunities to escape their plight or that there was a span of time between the threat and the act to find help. To illustrate, John Charles Green escaped from the Missouri Training Center, where he had been imprisoned for a three-year term, and was apprehended the next day by a state highway patrol officer some distance from the center. Green contended that his escape had been justified, because he had been subject to homosexual assaults in prison and the state had denied him access to the courts to mitigate his circumstances. This made it necessary that he escape in order to protect himself from submission to the threatened assault or the alternative of death or bodily harm.[14]

The Supreme Court of Missouri did not accept the defense; it said that the defendant was not being closely pursued by his assailants when he escaped and that he could have avoided the threatened consequences if he had reported to the authorities the names of those making the threats.

**Immaturity**   Anglo-American law traditionally has excused criminal behavior by children under the age of seven on the ground that they are immature and not responsible for their actions—*mens rea* was not present. Common law presumed that children seven to fourteen were not liable for their criminal acts; however, prosecutors could introduce evidence of a child's mental capacity to form *mens rea*. Juries could assume the existence of a guilty mind if, for example, it could be shown that the child had hidden evidence or had attempted to bribe a witness. As a child aged the assumption of immaturity weakened, and the assumption disappeared at age fourteen. Since the development of juvenile courts in the 1890s, children over the age of seven have not been tried by the rules and procedures governing adults. There are, however, various situations in which children may be tried as adults—if, for example, they are repeat offenders or are charged with having committed a particularly heinous offense. A major issue in the current death penalty debate is the justification for executing youths who murdered while underage.

**Mistake** The courts have generally upheld the view that ignorance of the law is no excuse for committing an illegal act. But what if there is a mistake of fact? Can mistake be used as a defense if a person knows the law but believes that it does not apply in the context of a given situation? Certainly defendants could not plead ignorance of the fact that stealing is against the law, but they could use the defense that they mistakenly thought the property was their own. Intent to steal would not be present in the latter situation. In many jurisdictions the crime of statutory rape may result in conviction if the man had intercourse with a female under the age of consent even if he believed—because she looked older or had told him so—that she was over that age. The *Model Penal Code* rejects this position.

**Intoxication** The law does not relieve an individual of responsibility for crimes committed while voluntarily intoxicated. There are, however, situations in which intoxication can be used as a defense, as when a person has been tricked into consuming a substance without knowing that it may result in intoxication. More complicated are situations in which the law requires it to be shown that a defendant had a specific, rather than a general, intent to commit a crime. For example, intoxication may be a defense against the charge of shoplifting on the ground that the defendant's condition was such that he simply forgot to pay and had not intended to steal. Drunkenness can also be used as a mitigating factor to reduce the seriousness of a charge.

**Insanity** The defense of insanity has been controversial. The general public may have the opinion that many criminals "escape" punishment through the skillful use of psychiatric testimony. Yet only about 1 percent of incarcerated individuals are held in mental hospitals because they had been adjudged "not guilty by reason of insanity."[15] The insanity defense is relatively rare and is generally advanced only in serious cases or where there is no other valid defense.

Over time American courts have followed five tests of criminal responsibility involving insanity: (1) the M'Naghten Rule, (2) the Irresistible Impulse Test, (3) the Durham Rule, (4) the *Model Penal Code*'s Substantial Capacity Test, and (5) the test as defined in the Comprehensive Control Act of 1984. For a comparison of these tests, see Table 3.2. The tests currently used in the various states are shown in Figure 3.3.

Before 1843 the defense of insanity could be used only by persons who were so deprived of understanding as to be incapable of knowing what they were doing. In that year Daniel M'Naghten was acquitted of killing Edward Drummond, whom he had thought to be Sir Robert Peel, the prime minister of Great Britain. M'Naghten claimed that he had been

| Test | Legal Standard Because of Mental Illness | Final Burden of Proof | Who Bears Burden of Proof |
|---|---|---|---|
| M'Naghten (1843) | "didn't know what he was doing or didn't know it was wrong" | Varies from proof by a balance of probabilities on the defense to proof beyond a reasonable doubt on the prosecutor | |
| Irresistible Impulse (1897) | "could not control his conduct" | | |
| Durham (1954) | "the criminal act was caused by his mental illness" | Beyond reasonable doubt | Prosecutor |
| Model Penal Code (1972) | "lacks substantial capacity to appreciate the wrongfulness of his conduct or to control it" | Beyond reasonable doubt | Prosecutor |
| Present Federal Law | "lacks capacity to appreciate the wrongfulness of his conduct" | Clear and convincing evidence | Defense |

**Table 3.2**
**Insanity defense standards**

The evolution of the standards for the insanity defense can be traced in this table.

SOURCE: U.S. Department of Justice, National Institute of Justice, *Crime File*, "Insanity Defense," by Norval Morris (Washington, D.C.: Government Printing Office, n.d.).

suffering from delusion at the time of the killing, but the public outcry against his acquittal caused the House of Lords to ask the court to define the law with regard to delusional persons. The judges of the Queen's Bench answered by saying that a finding of guilty cannot be made if, "at the time of the committing of the act, the party accused was laboring under such a defect of reason, from disease of the mind, as not to know the nature and quality of the act he was doing, or if he did know it that he did not know he was doing what was wrong."[16] This test, often referred to as the "right-from-wrong test," is today accepted by many states.

Over the years the M'Naghten Rule has often been criticized as not conforming with modern psychiatric concepts of mental disorder. It has been argued that individuals may be able to distinguish right from wrong and still be insane in the psychiatric sense, and that "disease of the mind," "know," and "nature and quality of the act" have not been adequately defined. Some states have supplemented the M'Naghten Rule by allowing defendants to plead that, although they knew what they were doing was wrong, they were unable to control an irresistible impulse to commit the crime. The *Irresistible Impulse Test* excuses defendants from responsibility when a mental disease was controlling their behavior even though they knew that what they were doing was wrong. Four states use this test in combination with the M'Naghten Rule.

The Durham Rule, originally developed in New Hampshire in 1871, was adopted by the Circuit Court of Appeals for the District of Columbia in 1954 in the case of *Durham* v. *United States*.[17] Monte Durham had a long history of criminal activity and of mental illness. At age twenty-six, he broke into a house with two companions. On appeal of his conviction,

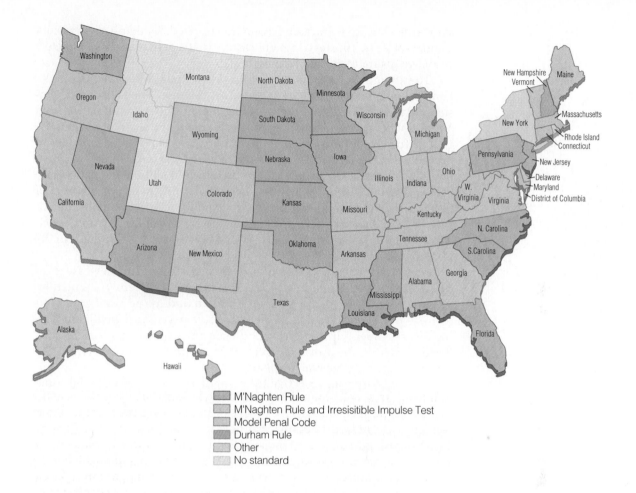

M'Naghten Rule
M'Naghten Rule and Irresisitible Impulse Test
Model Penal Code
Durham Rule
Other
No standard

Judge David Bazelon rejected the M'Naghten Rule, stating that an accused is not criminally responsible "if an unlawful act is the product of mental disease or mental defect." The Durham rule is based on the supposition that insanity is a product of many personality factors, not all of which may be present in every case.

The Durham Rule immediately aroused much controversy. In particular, it was argued that it offered no useful definition of "mental disease or defect." By 1972 (*United States* v. *Brawner*) the federal courts had overturned the Durham Rule in favor of a modified version of a test proposed in the *Model Penal Code*. By 1982 all federal courts and about half of the state courts had adopted the *Model Penal Code*'s Substantial Capacity Test. This rule states that a person is not responsible for criminal conduct "if at the time of such conduct as a result of mental disease or defect he lacks substantial capacity either to appreciate the criminality [wrongfulness] of his conduct or to conform his conduct to the requirements of law."[18] The Substantial Capacity Test is essentially a broadening and modifying of the M'Naghten and Irresistible Impulse rules. Key terms have been changed to conform better with modern psychological concepts, and the

**Figure 3.3**
**Standards for insanity used by the states**
State laws differ as to the standard to be applied in determining insanity.

SOURCE: Adapted from Ingo Keilitz and Junikus Fulton, *The Insanity Defense and Its Alternatives: A Guide for Policy Makers* (Williamsburg, Va.: National Center for State Courts, 1984),15, 88–89; U.S. Department of Justice, Bureau of Justice Statistics, *Report to the Nation on Crime and Justice*, 2d ed. (Washington, D.C.: Government Printing Office, 1988), 87.

standards lacking in Durham have been supplied. By emphasizing "substantial capacity," the test does not require that a defendant be completely unable to distinguish right from wrong.

The attempted assassination of President Ronald Reagan by John W. Hinckley reopened debate on the insanity defense. The facts that television pictures showed Hinckley shooting the president, that he came from a wealthy background and was thus able to enlist the aid of psychiatric experts to substantiate the claim of insanity, and that the federal rules of procedure in the District of Columbia required the government to prove him sane all fed widespread public outcries. In the immediate aftermath of his acquittal, several states abolished the insanity defense, members of Congress introduced bills to do likewise, and three major national organizations—the American Bar Association, the American Psychiatric Association, and the American Medical Association—proposed changes in the legal definition of insanity.

Among the changes that have occurred since the Hinckley case is introduction of the defense of "guilty but mentally ill," now adopted by twelve states.[19] This defense allows a jury to find the accused guilty but requires that correctional authorities provide psychiatric treatment during imprisonment. In fact, prison officials already have the authority to decide whether an inmate's psychiatric treatment will be within the prison walls or at a mental hospital.

Norval Morris suggests that the defendant's condition after the crime should be taken into account in the determination of the appropriate place of confinement—a hospital or a prison. Illness at the time of the crime should enter into the determination of the crime of which a defendant is found guilty; for example, a defendant found to be guilty of diminished capacity would be convicted of manslaughter rather than murder.[20]

The Comprehensive Crime Control Act of 1984 changed the federal rules on the insanity defense by limiting it to persons who are unable to appreciate the nature and quality or the wrongfulness of their acts as a result of severe mental disease or defect. This legislation seems to eliminate the Irresistible Impulse Test. It also shifts the burden of proof from the prosecutor, who in some federal courts had to prove beyond a reasonable doubt that the defendant was not insane, to the defendant, who has to prove his or her insanity. The act also creates a new commitment procedure whereby a person found not guilty only by reason of insanity is required to be committed to a mental hospital until it is determined that he or she no longer poses a danger to society. These provisions apply only to prosecutions in federal courts but are now spreading to a number of states.

The problem with these alternatives is that they do not fully acknowledge the concept of *mens rea*, which is deeply rooted in our legal system. In addition, although there is much public discussion of defendants who are found not guilty by reason of insanity, there are, in fact, few such cases. Persons who are ruled incompetent to stand trial because they are unable to assist in their own defense are committed to mental institutions until they are deemed healthy enough to answer the charges. Civil commitment is also the usual route for defendants who successfully plead insanity. Some observers believe that this defense should be abolished, arguing that

The public was outraged by the decision that John B. Hinckley was not guilty by reason of insanity of the attempted assassination of President Ronald Reagan. At the time, federal rules stipulated that once the insanity defense was offered, the prosecution must prove beyond a reasonable doubt that the accused was sane at the time of the action.

it is used to incarcerate legally innocent but dangerous people. Others emphasize that most criminals are somewhat unbalanced and that science cannot adequately measure the level of mental "disease" that allows borderline cases to use this defense. It is charged that the wealthy can pay for the testimony of psychiatrists in support of their defense, whereas the poor cannot. It is also erroneously believed that persons who use the insanity defense and are sent to mental hospitals somehow "beat the rap."

As can be seen in the case of Richard Hilliard Jackson, described in the following Close-Up, prosecutors, defense attorneys, and jurors confront many problematic issues when law and psychiatry are mixed with the question of criminal responsibility.

## Pitfalls Abundant in Insanity Plea

It was 3:30 A.M., Richard Hilliard Jackson had just taken three hours to explain his theory on the four states of "person" and his concept of death to a detective from the Metropolitan Police Department's homicide squad.

... Jackson claimed that the physical person is guided by a magnet-like uncontrollable power called The Force. The intellect remains after death, and the soul is the part of the intellect that lives forever. The After Death is a blessing, a state of freedom from pain, heartbreak, and defeat.

The Force could do anything, Jackson said, even kill.

The 37-year-old handyman ... was charged with the murder and robbery of an elderly Northeast Washington woman who had been found dead two weeks earlier. Jackson denied any involvement in her death.

... Defense attorneys argued that Jackson was insane when the woman was killed.

The jury ... did not accept [Jackson's] insanity defense and, after more than 24 hours of deliberation, determined that Jackson was sane at the time of the woman's death.

In the Jackson case there was a major difficulty in distilling the testimony from six psychiatrists down into terms the jury could understand. And there is a risk, experts say, that when psychiatric testimony is reduced to layman's terms the significance can be lost.

The psychiatrists "said [Jackson] had a mental problem; Okay, we all do," said one juror after the verdict was returned.

The psychiatrists testified that Jackson had symptoms consistent with paranoia and schizophrenia, but, said another juror, "there are other people walking around with these kinds of tendencies who don't commit any violent crime."

Jurors are inclined "to lock somebody up who was crazy for the rest of his life," according to former public defender Jeffrey Freund. He said jurors may be reluctant to vote for an insanity defense knowing a defendant could be swiftly released.

The jurors actually heard two separate trials, which took over a month to complete. The first proceeding was on the merits of the case—whether Jackson in fact murdered and robbed the woman, with the burden of proof being on the government. After the jury found Jackson guilty of second-degree murder and robbery, the same jury then heard a second trial on the issue of whether at the time the offense was committed Jackson was sane and thus responsible for his act.

Jackson, a chronic alcoholic who lived out of his car, went to 1044 Grant St. NE, ... to repair a fuse box for Dorothea J. King, a 69-year-old cleaning woman. The following day Mrs. King was found dead on her living room floor. She had been beaten and strangled.

Jackson claimed that at some point when he was with Mrs. King he blacked out and had no recollection of what happened.

The medical examiner said Mrs. King died between 3:30 P.M. and 11:00 P.M.... A neighbor testified that he saw Jackson's car outside Mrs. King's house at 11:00 P.M. that day. When he was arrested, Jackson had in his possession goods owned by Mrs. King.

"If he was insane at the time he committed the crime, why did he steal the property from this lady?" asked one juror. "This is what I think the majority [of the jurors] came around on."

"If he wasn't guilty, why didn't he get up [on the witness stand] and say something?" the juror asked.

Two days after Mrs. King's death, Jackson was arrested for disorderly conduct in a Maryland restaurant. According to police, he stood at the salad bar, waved his arms around, and screamed that someone was trying to steal his food. When his money was refunded in an attempt to calm him down, he began to rapidly shove lettuce into his mouth.

"He knew how to become insane at the right times," said one juror, who added that several members of the jury panel thought Jackson was feigning his illness. "I can't say he was faking," said another juror, "but I also thought [Jackson] knew what would be the best defense for him."

Beyond that skepticism, two other factors appeared to militate against the jury's acceptance of the insanity defense.

Jackson had pleaded guilty to manslaughter in connection with the death of his 9-year-old stepson [seven years previously]. The child was slain after Jackson, who had been drinking, had an argument with his wife. He spent about two years in prison for the offense.

The jury was told about the earlier killing because defense psychiatrists thought the [earlier] incident had some link to why Jackson killed the elderly Washington woman.

But perhaps the most damaging piece of evidence, and the key to the government's argument that Jackson had fabricated his mental illness, was a letter that Jackson wrote to a friend seven months after his arrest.

"... be sharp and go along with the insanity moves my attorney and I will make and say nothing about anything else," Jackson wrote.

"That did it," said one juror.

SOURCE: Laura A. Kiernan, "Pitfalls Abundant in Insanity Plea," *Washington Post,* 19 July 1977, A–1. Reprinted by permission.

# Procedural Criminal Law

In 1964 the U.S. Supreme Court overturned the Illinois conviction of Danny Escobedo for the killing of his brother-in-law on the ground that he had been denied the right to counsel as guaranteed by the Constitution.[21] The Chicago police had effectively prevented Escobedo's attorney from assisting him while he was being interrogated. The Court's decision was based on the procedural criminal law. Escobedo did not contend that the substantive elements of the case against him had not been met. His legal brief presented to the Supreme Court did not mention the absence of an *actus reus*, attendant circumstances, or *mens rea*, such that he should not have been charged with the murder of his brother-in-law. Rather, improper police procedures were the basis of his appeal. Escobedo argued that he had been denied due process because of a procedural violation.

Although the Supreme Court's opinion in *Escobedo* v. *Illinois* was issued in 1964, its foundation lies in the history of Anglo-American law, with precedent in the thirteenth-century Magna Carta. In that document, considered to be the first written guarantee of due process, King John of England promised that "no free man shall be arrested, or imprisoned, or disseized, or outlawed, or exiled, or in any way molested; nor will we proceed against him unless by the lawful judgment of his peers or by the law of the land." Thus was established a fundamental principle of procedural law: persons must be tried not through the use of arbitrary procedures but according to the process outlined in the law.

In the United States, **procedural due process** of law means that accused persons in criminal cases must be accorded certain rights as protections in keeping with the adversarial nature of the proceedings and that they will be tried according to legally established procedures. As Chapter 1 explained, the Due Process Model is based on the premise that freedom is so valuable that efforts must be made to prevent erroneous decisions that would result in an innocent person's being deprived of it. The state may act against accused persons only when it follows due process procedures, thus ensuring that the rights of all are maintained.

From childhood we have been taught that defendants are entitled to fair and speedy trials, to have counsel, to confront witnesses, and to know the charges brought against them. They are protected against having to serve as witnesses against themselves, being subjected to double jeopardy, and enduring cruel and unusual punishment. A key assumption underlying procedural criminal law is that there are limits to the government's powers to investigate and apprehend persons suspected of committing crimes.

Like substantive law, procedural criminal law is found in many places: in the U.S. and state constitutions, in statutes, and in judicial opinions. Among these, the Bill of Rights—the first ten amendments to the U.S. Constitution—holds a primary position. In most respects, the due process assumptions found there provide the basis for the procedures that have evolved and that constitute the rules implementing the daily practices of the criminal justice system. In particular, the Fourth, Fifth, Sixth, Eighth, and Fourteenth amendments are especially important and are outlined in the following sections. More detailed discussion of each right is presented in later chapters.

**procedural due process**
The constitutional requirement that all persons be treated fairly and justly by government officials. An accused person can be arrested, prosecuted, tried, and punished only in accordance with procedures prescribed by law.

## The Bill of Rights

Although the Bill of Rights was added to the U.S. Constitution soon after its ratification in 1789, the amendments had little impact on criminal justice until the mid-twentieth century. Under our system of federalism, most criminal acts are violations of state laws, but for most of our history the Bill of Rights was interpreted as protecting citizens only from acts of the national government. Hence important amendments—such as the Fourth, which guards against unreasonable searches and seizures, the Fifth, which outlines the basic due process rights in criminal cases, and the Sixth and Eighth, which cover procedures for fair trial and punishment—were viewed as having no bearing on cases that violated state law. When it was drafted, the Constitution delegated certain powers to the new federal

The Magna Carta, signed by England's King John in 1215, is the first written guarantee of due process. It established the principle that persons must be arrested and tried according to the processes outlined in the law.

government, but the power to safeguard the rights of individuals from unjust enforcement of state laws was not among them. Historians have shown that at the time of the addition of the Bill of Rights, it was the power of the new national government that citizens feared; the constitutions of many of the states already contained protections against illegal procedures at the local level. This position was clarified in 1833 when the U.S. Supreme Court ruled in the case of **Barron v. Baltimore** that the first ten amendments to the Constitution were limitations only on the federal government and were not binding on the states.[22] According to the ruling, when individual rights had been trampled, only the states, and not the Supreme Court, could interfere.

***Barron v. Baltimore*** (1833)
Bill of Rights applies only to actions of the federal government.

## The Fourteenth Amendment and Due Process

The ratification of the Fourteenth Amendment following the Civil War began a new period in the protection of citizens' rights. This amendment declares "No State shall make or enforce any law which shall abridge the privileges or immunities of citizens of the United States; nor shall any State deprive any person of life, liberty, or property, without due process of law; nor deny to any person within its jurisdiction the equal protection of the laws."

Ratification of the Fourteenth Amendment did not, however, guarantee that the Bill of Right's provisions would be applied to actions of the states. Although the Court used the Fourteenth Amendment to uphold property rights against state regulation, it was not until 1923, in the case of *Moore* v. *Dempsey*, that the Court began to require the states to uphold the rights of defendants in criminal cases under the Bill of Rights. Here the abuses of due process rights in Arkansas so shocked the justices that they reversed a decision of a state criminal court.[23] Five black men had been convicted of murder and sentenced to death in a forty-five-minute trial dominated by a howling lynch mob outside the courtroom. Nine years later the Court again invoked the due process clause in the famous Scottsboro case (***Powell v. Alabama***), in which nine illiterate young blacks were convicted of raping two white women in an open railroad freight car. Because the defendants had not been given effective counsel, the Court overturned their convictions.[24] In 1936 the justices threw out a confession for the first time (*Brown* v. *Mississippi*), because the statements had been beaten out of two defendants by sheriff's deputies wielding metal-studded belts.[25]

***Powell v. Alabama*** (1932)
Counsel must be provided defendants in a capital case.

In all these early cases, the barbaric nature of the offenses perpetrated by state authorities provided reason for moral outrage and demonstrated that due process had been denied. Until the 1960s, a majority of the Court held that the due process clause of the Fourteenth Amendment incorporated only those protections necessary to "fundamental fairness." In written Court opinions there is little legal analysis but rather an implication that the requirement of **fundamental fairness** had not been met. Only when state action "shocks the conscience" and offends the community's sense of fair play and decency would the Court rule that the Fourteenth Amendment's right to due process had been violated.[26]

**fundamental fairness**
A legal doctrine supporting the idea that so long as a state's conduct maintains the basic elements of fairness, the Constitution has not been violated.

## The Due Process Revolution

**incorporation**

The extension of the due process clause of the Fourteenth Amendment to make binding on state governments the rights guaranteed in the first ten amendments to the U.S. Constitution (Bill of Rights).

From the 1930s to the 1960s, when the fairness doctrine was supported by a majority on the Supreme Court, Justice Hugo Black had argued that all the provisions of the Bill of Rights should be applied to the states through the **incorporation** of the due process clause of the Fourteenth Amendment. Despite Black's arguments, it was not until 1953 that the due process revolution reached its full stride. In that year, Republican President Dwight D. Eisenhower named former California Governor Earl Warren chief justice of the United States and a new liberal majority began to form on the Court (see Biography).

The Warren Court's revolution refined the meaning of the due process requirements of the Constitution, moving from the dictum that the state must observe fundamental fairness to a demand for absolute compliance by state and local officials with most of the specific provisions of the Bill of Rights. Where the fairness test had permitted states to fashion their own procedures, voiding only those that failed the fairness test, the new approach imposed, in advance, detailed and objective procedural standards on the police and courts. The justices were firm in their determination to void convictions obtained in violation of these rules.

Warren and the associate justices on the Court were often criticized severely. Critics focused on Warren's abandonment of precedent in favor of what he regarded as fairness and on what some regarded as the Court's subordination of law to political preference. Others supported the Warren Court rulings, arguing that the Constitution must be used to uphold justice.

***Mapp v. Ohio* (1961)**

Fourth amendment protects citizens from unreasonable searches and seizures by the states.

In 1961, the Supreme Court ruled in the case of ***Mapp v. Ohio*** that the Fourth Amendment protections against unreasonable searches and seizures applied to the states. It was a milestone opinion because for the first time the Court insisted that it could supervise the nuts and bolts of state justice to ensure that due process was upheld. Beyond the Fourth Amendment lay the Fifth, with its protection against self-incrimination, the Sixth, which guarantees the right to counsel, and the Eighth, which prohibits excessive fines and cruel and unusual punishment. If these four amendments should be applied by the Court to the states, almost all the activities in the criminal justice system would come under the detailed control of the federal judiciary.

From 1962 to 1972, the Supreme Court, under the chief justiceships of both Earl Warren and Warren Burger, applied most criminal justice safeguards to the states. By the end of this period incorporation was virtually complete.

## The Fourth Amendment: Protection Against Unreasonable Searches and Seizures

The right of the people to be secure in their persons, houses, papers, and effects, against unreasonable searches and seizures, shall not be violated, and no Warrants shall issue, but upon probable cause, supported by Oath or affirmation, and particularly describing the place to be searched, and the persons or things to be seized.

The Fourth Amendment recognizes the right to privacy, but the application of this protection to the daily operations of the criminal justice system has caused problems. First, not all searches are prohibited, only those that are *unreasonable*. Second is the problem of what to do with evidence that is illegally obtained. Should murderers be set free because a vital piece of evidence was seized without a search warrant? The ambiguity of these portions of the amendment and the complexity of some arrest and investigation incidents have created difficulties.

**What Is Unreasonable?** Since 1968 the Court has tried in several rulings to define what is meant by "reasonable" in the context of the search-and-seizure provisions of the Fourth Amendment. Its conclusion seems to be that a personal search that is incident to a lawful arrest is legal. But even if it is not incident to an arrest, a search is sometimes legally justified when an officer believes a suspect is armed or when there is concern about the officer's or the public's safety. The extension of a search to the area surrounding an arrest has been ruled to be restricted to situations in which the suspect may reasonably be expected to obtain a weapon or destroy evidence. After an arrest has been made, but before the suspect has been removed from the premises, the police have more discretionary power to make a search because the defendant is in custody. But the legal and ethical complications of the Fourth Amendment pose many problems to the police (see A Question of Ethics, next page).

**Problems of the Exclusionary Rule** Paralleling the development of law in the search-and-seizure area are issues related to illegally obtained evidence. What remedy is available to a defendant who has been the subject of an unreasonable search and seizure? Since 1914 the Supreme Court has held to an **exclusionary rule**—illegally seized evidence must be excluded from trials in federal courts. The argument has been that the government must not soil its hands by profiting from illegally seized evidence and that without this rule the police would not be deterred from conducting raids in violation of the Fourth Amendment. In *Mapp* v. *Ohio* (1961) the exclusionary rule was extended to state courts, yet not all justices have agreed with this solution. Conservatives on the Court have argued that the rule has not been effective in deterring police misconduct and that it exacted a high price from society—that is, the release of countless guilty offenders. Liberals, on the other hand, have maintained that the exclusionary rule is a judgment that it is better for some guilty persons to go free than for the police to engage in forbidden conduct.

Of the amendments dealing with criminal justice, the Fourth appears to be the one most likely to undergo continuing interpretation. Not only are several of its provisions ambiguous, but also technological developments such as electronic surveillance lead to the need for new interpretations.

**exclusionary rule**
The principle that illegally obtained evidence must be excluded from a trial.

## A Question of Ethics

The short, muscular black man strode through the Los Angeles International Airport carrying an attache case and a small piece of luggage. He abruptly set down the bag and walked to a row of pay phones. His telephone conversation was interrupted by two Drug Enforcement Administration (DEA) agents, who grabbed the phone and started asking the man a series of questions. When the suspected "drug smuggler" did not respond, he fell or was thrown to the floor and was then handcuffed and led off for questioning. Only after his protestation that they had stopped the wrong person, was Joe Morgan—a broadcaster for ESPN, former Cincinnati Reds second baseman, and National Baseball Hall of Fame member—released.

Los Angeles narcotics detective Clayton Searle and DEA agent Bill Woessner claimed that they did nothing wrong; they merely responded to a DEA-developed profile of the characteristics of persons likely to be drug couriers. The fact that race is a major element of this profile has been justified as conforming to reality. Blacks and Hispanics, it is argued, are more likely to be involved as couriers in the drug trade. Others have claimed that this DEA profile is merely an expression of institutional racism—the darker your skin, the more likely that you will be stopped for questioning.

Is it ethical to base law enforcement actions on physical characteristics? Or should government agents stop and question only those whose behavior indicates they are committing or are about to commit a crime?

## The Fifth Amendment: Protection Against Self-Incrimination and Double Jeopardy

No person shall be held to answer for a capital, or otherwise infamous crime, unless on a presentment or indictment of a Grand Jury, except in cases arising in the land or naval forces, or in the Militia, when in actual service in time of war or public danger; nor shall any person be subject for the same offense to be twice put in jeopardy of life or limb; nor shall be compelled in any criminal case to be a witness against himself, nor be deprived of life, liberty, or property, without due process of law; nor shall private property be taken for public use, without just compensation.

Clearly, the Fifth Amendment provides a number of rights that speak to various portions of the criminal justice process. Here we examine the basic elements of two: self-incrimination and double jeopardy (concepts which are fully developed in Chapter 5).

**Self-Incrimination**   One of the most important of due process rights is the protection against **self-incrimination**, that is, persons shall not be compelled to be witnesses against themselves. This right is consistent with the assumption of the adversarial process that the state must prove the defendant's guilt. The right does not really stand alone but is integrated with other protections, especially the Fourth Amendment's prohibition of unreasonable search and seizure. The Sixth Amendment's right to counsel has also had an impact on the Fifth Amendment. The Fifth Amendment has its greatest force, however, with regard to interrogations and confessions.

Historically, the validity of confessions has hinged on their being voluntary, because a confession entails self-incrimination. Under the doctrine of fundamental fairness, which held sway until the 1960s, the Supreme Court was unwilling to allow confessions that were beaten out of suspects, that emerged after extended periods of questioning, or that resulted from other physical tactics for inducing admission of guilt. In the cases of *Escobedo* v. *Illinois* (1964) and *Miranda* v. *Arizona* (1966), the Court added that confessions made by suspects who had not been notified of their due process rights could not be admitted as evidence. To protect the rights of the accused, the Court emphasized the importance of allowing counsel to be present during the interrogation process. The police also had an obligation to inform suspects of their rights. These decisions shifted attention from due process rights in the courtroom to due process rights during the accused's initial contact with the police.

**self-incrimination**

The act of exposing oneself to prosecution by being forced to answer questions that may tend to incriminate oneself; it is protected against by the Fifth Amendment. In any criminal proceeding the prosecution must prove the charges by means of evidence other than the testimony of the accused.

**Escobedo** v. **Illinois** (1963)

Counsel must be provided when suspects are taken into police custody.

The exclusionary rule requires that evidence illegally seized not be used in a prosecution. Should the guilty go free if the police do not follow due process?

**Double Jeopardy**   Because of the limitations imposed by the Fifth Amendment, a person charged with a criminal act may be subjected to only one prosecution or punishment for that offense in the same jurisdiction. As previously noted, illegal acts often violate both state and federal laws, so the prohibition against **double jeopardy** does not necessarily rule out prosecution in successive jurisdictions as stated by the Supreme Court in *Bartkus* v. *Illinois* (1973).[27] Thus the Los Angeles police officers accused of using excessive force in the arrest of black motorist Rodney King were first acquitted by a California jury but were then prosecuted under federal civil rights laws by the U.S. government.

At what point in the criminal process does double jeopardy come into force? There have been a number of cases on this point, but the provision has generally been held to mean that if a case is dismissed before trial, a subsequent prosecution for the offense is permissible.

*Miranda* **v.** *Arizona* **(1966)**
Confessions made by suspects who were not notified of their due process rights cannot be admitted as evidence.

**double jeopardy**
The subjecting of a person to prosecution more than once for the same offense; prohibited by the Fifth Amendment.

## The Sixth Amendment: The Right to Counsel and to a Fair Trial

In all criminal prosecutions, the accused shall enjoy the right to a speedy and public trial, by an impartial jury of the State and district wherein the crime shall have been committed, which district shall have been previously ascertained by law, and to be informed of the nature and cause of the accusation; to be confronted with the witnesses against him; to have compulsory process for obtaining witnesses in his favor, and to have the assistance of counsel for his defense.

The Sixth Amendment includes a number of important provisions relating to fairness in a criminal prosecution, including the right to counsel, to a speedy and public trial, and to an impartial jury.

**Right to Counsel**   Although the accused's right to counsel in a criminal case had long prevailed in the federal courts, not until the landmark decision in *Gideon* v. *Wainwright* (1963) was this requirement made binding on the states. In previous cases, relying on the doctrine of fundamental fairness, the Supreme Court had ruled that states must provide indigents (poor people) with counsel only when the special circumstances of the case demanded such assistance. Thus, when conviction could result in death, when the issues were complex, or when the indigent defendant was either very young or mentally handicapped, counsel had to be provided.

At the time of the *Gideon* decision, only five states did not already provide attorneys for indigent defendants in felony cases, but the decision led to issues concerning the extension of this right. The next question concerned the point in the criminal justice process at which a lawyer had to be present. Beginning in 1963, the Supreme Court extended the right to counsel to preliminary hearings, to appeals, to a defendant out on bail after an indictment, to identification lineups, and to children in juvenile court proceedings. The effect of these cases was to ensure that poor defendants would have some of the protections that had always been available to defendants with money.

In sum, the rulings of the Court with regard to the right to counsel have been generally accepted throughout the nation with little criticism. Under most circumstances, counsel is made available, but the effectiveness of the counsel provided at public expense may still be open to question.

**Right to a Speedy and Public Trial** The founders of this country were aware that in other countries the accused often languished in jail awaiting trial and often was convicted in the seclusion of the judge's chambers. At the time of the American Revolution, the right to a speedy and public trial was recognized in the common law and had been incorporated into the constitutions of six of the original states. But the word *speedy* is vague, and the Supreme Court has recognized that the interest of quick processes may be in conflict with other interests of society (such as the need to collect evidence) as well as with interests of the defendant (such as the need for time to mount a defense).

The right to a public trial is intended to protect the accused against arbitrary conviction. The assumption is that if justice must be done in the open, judges and juries will act in accordance with the law. As with the matter of speed, the Supreme Court has recognized that there may be circumstances in which the need for a public trial has to be balanced against other interests. For example, the right to a public trial does not mean that all members of the public have the right to attend the trial. The seating capacity and the interests of a fair trial, free of outbursts from the audience, may weigh heavily. In trials concerning sex crimes when the victim or witness is a minor, courts have temporarily barred the public to spare the child embarrassment. Permitting the televising of trials has been an issue in many states.

The case of Clarence Gideon resulted in the requirement that states must provide defense counsel in felony cases for those who cannot pay for it.

**Right to an Impartial Jury**   The right to a jury trial was as well established in the American colonies at the time of the Revolution as it had been in England for centuries. In their charters, most of the colonies specifically guaranteed trial by jury, and references to this essential process are found in the debates of the First Continental Congress in 1774, the Declaration of Independence, the constitutions of the thirteen original states, and the Sixth Amendment to the U.S. Constitution. Because the crucial decisions in criminal—and civil—trials are made by an impartial jury of one's peers, a safeguard is erected against corrupt or overzealous officialdom.

The question of how to create juries that are representative of the community has not been answered with the unanimity expressed in regard to the principle itself. The Magna Carta stipulated that juries should be drawn from "peers" of the accused, and members were selected from the immediate vicinity of the crime. Because *peer* and *community* in medieval England may have had different meaning than they do today, scholars and the Supreme Court have advanced a number of definitions to clarify the nature and composition of impartial juries. Most scholars believe that impartiality can best be achieved when jurors are drawn at random from the broadest possible base, thereby balancing the different biases in the community against one another. The jury is expected to perform a representative function, and representativeness thus becomes the crucial concept permeating jury administration. Because courts have prohibited the systematic exclusion of any identifiable group of prospective jurors, random selection is the basis on which most trial juries in the United States are chosen. Rules governing the composition and functions of juries are fully discussed in Chapter 11.

## The Eighth Amendment: Protection Against Excessive Bail, Excessive Fines, and Cruel and Unusual Punishment

Excessive bail shall not be required, nor excessive fines imposed, nor cruel and unusual punishment inflicted.

Although it is the briefest of the amendments, the Eighth includes protections that concern the rights of defendants during the pretrial (bail) and corrections (fines, cruel and unusual punishment) phases of the criminal justice system.

**Release on Bail**   The purpose of bail is to allow for the release of the accused while he or she is awaiting trial. The Eighth Amendment does not require that release on bail be granted to all defendants, only that the amount of bail shall not be excessive. Despite the provisions, many states do not allow bail to persons charged with some offenses, such as murder, and there appear to be few restrictions on the amount that can be demanded. In 1987 the Supreme Court, in the case *United States* v. *Salerno and Cafaro*, upheld provisions of the Bail Reform Act of 1984 allowing federal judges to detain without bail suspects considered dangerous to the public.[28]

**Excessive Fines**   The prohibition against excessive fines received little contemporary attention by the Supreme Court until the 1993 case of *Austin* v. *United States*.[29] Here, the justices unanimously returned to the lower court for rehearing a case involving the forfeiture of an estimated $40 million worth of real estate and businesses as a result of a crackdown on a drug-trafficking operation. The court ruled that the sanctions were subject to the excessive fines clause, and therefore there had to be a relationship between the seriousness of the offense and the value of the property taken. The issue of fines and forfeiture as a criminal punishment is further discussed in Chapter 12.

**Cruel and Unusual Punishment**   The Founding Fathers were concerned about the barbaric punishments that had been inflicted in seventeenth- and eighteenth-century Europe when it was not unusual for offenders to be burned alive or stoned to death. In recent decades, attention has focused on the issue of capital punishment. In the case of *Furman* v. *Georgia* (1972), the Supreme Court ruled that the death penalty, as administered, constituted cruel and unusual punishment. Only two justices argued that the death penalty was, by its nature, cruel and unusual punishment, but a five-member majority agreed that the death sentences being considered were cruel and unusual, "in the same way that being struck by lightning is cruel and unusual. For, of all the people convicted of rapes and murders in 1967 and 1968, many just as reprehensible as these, the petitioners are among a capriciously selected random handful upon whom the sentence of death has in fact been imposed."[30] It seemed to the majority of the justices that it was not possible to determine why some offenders were executed while others were given life imprisonment.

Following this decision, many states passed laws designed to maintain the death penalty by removal of the arbitrary aspects of the proceedings. These new laws were tested in the 1976 case of *Gregg* v. *Georgia*; the Court upheld those statutes that permitted a sentencing judge or jury to take into account specific aggravating or mitigating circumstances in deciding whether a convicted murderer should be put to death.[31]

Since the reinstitution of capital punishment following *Gregg* v. *Georgia*, the death row population in the United States has soared to over 2,500, yet relatively few people have been executed. Each year approximately 250 people are given the death sentence, but no more than 34 are executed. The courts and society will be confronting the issue of capital punishment for years to come.

In the last three decades, the protections afforded to defendants in state criminal trials have greatly expanded. The Supreme Court has incorporated most portions of the Fourth, Fifth, Sixth, and Eighth Amendments as shown in Figure 3.4. As shown in Figure 3.5, these amendments protect defendants at various stages of the criminal justice process.

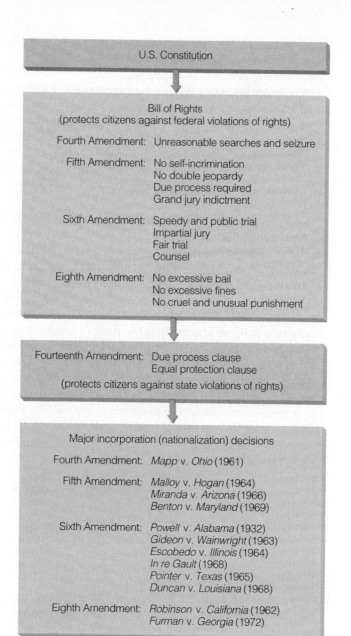

**Figure 3.4**
**Relationship of the Bill of Rights and the Fourteenth Amendment to the constitutional rights of the accused**

For most of U.S. history, the Bill of Rights protected citizens only against violations by the federal government. The Warren Court began the process of interpreting portions of the Fourteenth Amendment (incorporation) to protect citizens from unlawful actions by state officials.

## The Supreme Court Today

With the elevation of William Rehnquist to chief justice in 1986, a new conservative majority began to consider issues such as preventive detention, unreasonable searches and seizures, and administration of the death penalty. The appointment of Anthony Kennedy in 1988, of David Souter in 1989, and of Clarence Thomas in 1991 seemingly consolidated conservative power. Even with the replacement of Byron White by Ruth Bader Ginsburg in 1993 and the replacement of Harry Blackmun by Stephen Breyer in 1994, it will be some time before the conservative direction of the Court on criminal justice issues will be changed.

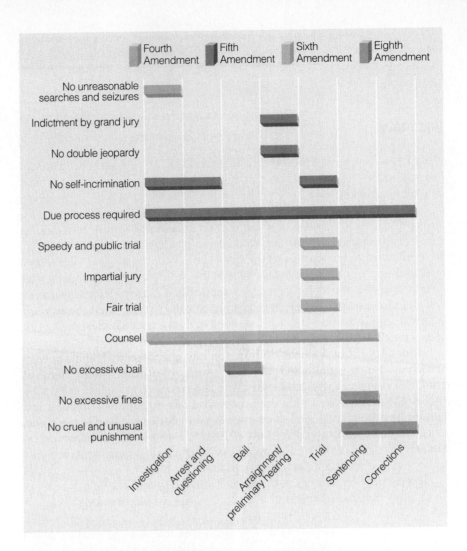

**Figure 3.5**
**Protections of the Bill of Rights**
The Bill of Rights protects defendants during various phases of the criminal justice process.

What can be said about the decisions of the Supreme Court since the due process revolution began under Warren? Will there be a retrenchment from the rights gained during the 1960s and 1970s? In seeking answers to these questions, we must remember that even the newly reconstituted Court has upheld the basic thrust of rights dealing with counsel, fair trials, and juveniles. Although the court has eroded the rights of defendants and given greater flexibility to police and correctional personnel, it has kept basic rights in place such as those specified in the Miranda decision. It is with regard to unreasonable searches and seizures, the exclusionary rule, and issues surrounding the death penalty that the Rehnquist Court can be expected to continue to retreat from some of the positions of the Warren and Burger years.

Civil libertarians, however, have taken heart by the actions of some state courts. Law professor Ronald Collins has pointed to about six hundred cases where state courts have interpreted their state constitutions to protect civil liberties more broadly than has the U.S. Supreme Court.[32] States cannot provide *less* protection on rights than those granted by the

U.S. Constitution but they can provide *more*. It may be that during the new era of conservativism on the Supreme Court, state courts will continue the civil liberties revolution begun by Chief Justice Warren.

## Summary

Only behaviors proscribed by the criminal law are illegal. The criminal law embodies descriptions not only of the forbidden behavior and the punishments to be administered but also of the ways in which justice officials must deal with defendants. The criminal law is thus divided into substantive law and procedural law. The criminal law may be found in constitutions, statutes, case law, and administrative regulations.

Substantive law concerns the question, "What is illegal?" For every criminal charge, it must be shown that the behavior of the accused was consistent with the seven principles that define crime. Defenses such as self-defense, necessity, and insanity may be used to show that the accused was not legally responsible for the offense. Every crime is classified as either a misdemeanor or a felony.

Procedural law focuses on how the law is enforced. The manner in which evidence is collected, the admission of witnesses' statements at trial, the judge's charge to the jury, and the rights of prisoners are only a few of the matters in which the procedural law stipulates what can and cannot be done. Since 1961, we have seen a major expansion of the rights of defendants through decisions by the U.S. Supreme Court. Interpretations by the justices of the Fourth, Fifth, Sixth, and Eighth Amendments have required the states to conform to these protections.

Many people believe that the substantive law and the rules of procedure have become so intricate that criminals escape punishment, court proceedings are unnecessarily drawn out, and the police are unable to do their job. Others contend that law and due process are essential for a just society. These positions remind us of the values summarized in the Due Process and Crime Control models and of the tensions existing between the rule of law and the administration of justice.

## Questions for Review

1   What two functions does law perform? What are the two major divisions of the law?

2   What are the sources of the criminal law? Where would you find it?

3   List the seven principles of criminal law theory.

4   What is meant by *mens rea*? Give examples of defenses that may be used by defendants in which they deny that *mens rea* existed when the crime was committed.

5   What is meant by the "incorporation" of the Fourteenth Amendment to the U.S. Constitution?

## Key Terms and Cases

administrative regulations

case law

civil forfeiture

civil law

common law

constitution

double jeopardy

entrapment

exclusionary rule

fundamental fairness

inchoate crimes

incorporation

legal responsibility

*mens rea*

procedural criminal law

procedural due process

self-incrimination

statutes

strict liability

substantive criminal law

*Barron* v. *Baltimore*

*Escobedo* v. *Illinois*

*Gideon* v. *Wainwright*

*Mapp* v. *Ohio*

*Miranda* v. *Arizona*

*Powell* v. *Alabama*

## For Further Reading

Fletcher, George P. *A Crime of Self Defense: Bernhard Goetz and the Law on Trial*. New York: Free Press, 1988. An insightful examination of the legal issues involved in the Goetz case.

Katz, Leo. *Bad Acts and Guilty Minds*. Chicago: University of Chicago Press, 1987. Exploration of questions raised by the insanity defense.

Lewis, Anthony. *Gideon's Trumpet*. New York: Vintage Books, 1964. A classic examination of the case of *Gideon* v. *Wainwright* showing the process by which the issues came to the U.S. Supreme Court.

Morris, Norval. *Madness and the Criminal Law*. Chicago: University of Chicago Press, 1982. A stimulating and controversial examination of the insanity defense by a leading criminal justice scholar.

Simpson, Alfred W. Bain. *Cannibalism and the Common Law*. Chicago: University of Chicago Press, 1984. Exciting study of the case of *The Queen* v. *Dudley and Stephens* showing that there were many such incidents during the age of sail where punishment did not follow.

Wolfe, Linda. *Wasted: The Preppie Murder Case*. New York: Simon and Schuster, 1989. An in-depth examination of the arrest and trial of Robert Chambers for the murder of Jennifer Levin.

## Notes

1  Richard Moran, "His Insanity Plea Can't Free Dahmer," *Boston Globe*, 2 February 1992, 60.

2  *New York Times*, 20 September 1991, A–1.

3  *Miller* v. *United States*, 78 U.S. 268 (1871).

4  Jerome Hall, *General Principles of Criminal Law*, 2d ed. (Indianapolis: Bobbs-Merrill, 1947), 18.

5  *Robinson v. California*, 370 U.S. 660 (1962).

6  Oliver Wendell Holmes, Jr., *Common Law* (Boston: Little, Brown, 1881), 3.

7  American Law Institute, *Model Penal Code* (Philadelphia: 1962), 32.

8  *Morissette v. United States*, 142 U.S. 246 (1952).

9  Damon D. Camp, "Out of the Quagmire: After *Jacobson v. United States*: Toward a More Balanced Entrapment Standard," *Journal of Criminal Law and Criminology* 83 (Winter 1993): 1055–1097.

10  *New York Times*, 7 April 1992, A–25.

11  *Jacobson v. United States*, 112 S.Ct. (1992).

12  *The Queen v. Dudley and Stephens*, 14 Q.B.D. 273 (1884).

13  Ibid.

14  *Missouri v. Green*, 470 S.W.2d 565 (1971).

15  U.S. Department of Justice, National Institute of Justice, *Crime File*, "Insanity Defense," prepared by Norval Morris (Washington, D.C.: Government Printing Office, n.d.)

16  M'Naghten's Case, 8 Eng. Rep. 718 (H.I. 1843).

17  *Durham v. United States*, 94 U.S. App. D.C. 228, 214 F. 2d 862 (1954).

18  *United States v. Brawner*, 471 F 2d 969 (1972).

19  John Klofas and Janette Yandrasits, " 'Guilty But Mentally Ill' and the Jury Trial: A Case Study," *Criminal Law Bulletin* 24 (1989): 424; Lisa A. Callahan, Margaret A. McGreevy, Carmen Cirincione, and Henry J. Steadman, "Measuring the Effects of the Guilty but Mentally Ill (GBMI) Verdict," *Law and Human Behavior* 16 (1992), 447–462.

20  Norval Morris, *Madness and the Criminal Law* (Chicago: University of Chicago Press, 1982), esp. chap. 2.

21  *Escobedo v. Illinois*, 364 U.S. 478 (1964).

22  *Barron v. Baltimore*, 32 U.S. 243 (1833).

23  *Moore v. Dempsey*, 261 U.S. 86 (1923).

24  *Powell v. Alabama*, 287 U.S. 45 (1932).

25  *Brown v. Mississippi*, 297 U.S. 278 (1936).

26  *Rochin v. California*, 342 U.S. 172 (1953).

27  *Bartkus v. Illinois*, 411 U.S. 423 (1973).

28  *United States v. Salerno and Cafaro*, 55 L.W. 463 (1987).

29  *Austin v. United States*, 61 L.W. 4811 (1993).

30  *Furman v. Georgia*, 408 U.S. 238 (1972).

31  *Gregg v. Georgia*, 96 S.Ct. 2909 (1976).

32  *Newsweek*, 8 October 1990, 76.

# Police

**Most of** us have gained an image of the police from movies and television, but the reality of law enforcement differs greatly from the dramatic exploits of the cops in the movie *The Fugitive* or on "Miami Vice." In some ways, it is curious that—although the police are the most visible agents of the criminal justice system in American society—our images of them mainly come from fictionalized accounts.

In Part 2 we deal with the police as the critical subunit of the system that confronts crime at the community level. Chapter 4 traces the history of policing and looks at its function and organization. Chapter 5 examines the daily operations of the police, and Chapter 6 analyzes current issues and trends in law enforcement. As we will see, police work often occurs in a hostile environment with crucial questions of life and death, honor and dishonor at stake. Officers are given discretion to deal with many situations; how they use that discretion has an important effect on the way society views policing.

PART TWO

# Police

In the early morning hours of 28 February 1993, nearly one hundred agents of the U.S. Bureau of Alcohol, Tobacco, and Firearms (ATF) approached the compound of the Branch Davidian religious cult outside Waco, Texas. Officers were attempting to serve search and arrest warrants, alleging that the compound contained illegal weapons. A burst of gunfire suddenly emanated from the buildings, which housed more than one hundred cult members. The federal agents returned fire. A ferocious forty-five-minute gun battle ensued during which four ATF officers were killed, sixteen others injured, and at least three members of the cult perished. For the next fifty-one days Americans watched the standoff between the government and the cult. On April 19 agents of the FBI and AFT, using tanks and tear gas and supported by a U.S. Army medical team, members of the McLennan County Sheriff's Office, and the Texas Rangers, battered the fortified walls of the compound. As the tear gas entered the buildings, they suddenly exploded in flames. Within an hour only the charred ruins of the complex remained. The death toll was an estimated eighty Davidian members, including seventeen children.

The events at Waco gave Americans an elementary education in the complexity of law enforcement functions and agencies in the United States. Before the confrontation, few had ever heard of the Bureau of Alcohol, Tobacco, and Firearms of the U.S. Treasury Department—or had known that it might take action in such circumstances. The fact that the final assault involved not only the ATF but also the FBI and Texas law enforcement agencies further illustrated the complex relationships among national, state, and local police forces. This complexity may have surprised and confused those Americans who think of criminal justice in terms of their local police.

The men and women in blue are the most visible presence of government in our society. Be they members of the local or state police, sheriff's departments, or federal agencies, the more than six hundred thousand sworn officers play crucial roles in American society. Citizens look to the police to perform a wide range of functions: prevention of crime, law enforcement, maintenance of order, and community services. However, public expectations about the responsibilities of the police are not always clear. Further, citizens necessarily form judgments about the police, and those judgments have a strong impact on the way order is maintained under law.

In a free society criticism of public agencies is to be expected. That is particularly true with respect to police as "by the very nature of their functions, [police] are an anomaly in a free society."[1] They are given a great deal of authority, including to arrest, search, detain, and use force, and all these actions are potentially disruptive of personal freedom. Democracy requires them to maintain order so that the free society may be possible. In fact, it has been said that the "strength of a democracy and the quality of life enjoyed by its citizens are determined in large measure by the ability of the police to discharge their duties."[2] If we are to depend on the "thin blue line" to protect democratic society, however, then the police and the public should clearly understand the duties and functions of policing.

This chapter focuses on the historical development, the policies, and the functions of the police and on the nature of decision making within the context of police work.

## Questions for Inquiry

- How have the police evolved in the United States?
- What are the agencies of policing and how are they organized in our federal system?
- What influences police policy and styles of policing?
- What are the functions of the police?
- How do police balance action, decision making, and discretion?

# A Historical Perspective

Law and order is not a new concept; it has been a focus of discussion since the first police force was formed in metropolitan London in 1829. Looking back even further to the Magna Carta, we see that limitations were placed on the constables and bailiffs of thirteenth-century England. We can read between the lines of this historic document to surmise that problems of police abuse, the maintenance of order, and the rule of law were similar to those encountered today. It is interesting that the same remedies—recruiting better police, stiffening the penalties for official malfeasance, creating a civilian board of control—were suggested even then to ensure that order was kept in accordance with the rule of law.

## The English Origins of the American Police

It is from the English tradition that the three major characteristics of American policing have evolved: (1) limited authority, (2) local control, and (3) organizational fragmentation. Like the British police, but unlike those in continental Europe, the police in the United States have limited authority; their powers and responsibilities are closely circumscribed by law. England, like the United States, has no nationwide police force; each unit is under local control. However, in contemporary England there are greater links between the central government and the local constabularies.[3] In the United States policing is fragmented: there are many types of agencies, each with its own special jurisdiction and responsibilities—constable, sheriff, urban police, the FBI, and so on.

Historians have shown that organizations to protect local citizens and property existed before the thirteenth century. The **frankpledge** system required that groups of ten families, called *tithings*, agree to uphold the law, maintain order, and commit to a court those who had violated the law. It was customary for every male above the age of twelve to be a part of the system. When a member became aware that a crime had occurred, he was obliged to raise a "hue and cry" and to join others in his tithing to track down the offender. The tithing was fined if members did not perform the obligatory duties.

The Statute of Winchester, enacted in 1285, established a parish constable system. It required all citizens, under the direction of the local constable, to pursue criminals. The position of constable was filled by selecting a man from the parish to be the law enforcement officer for one year on an unpaid basis. Watchmen were appointed to assist the constable. If a serious disturbance arose, the constable could press all members of the parish into police service.

This traditional system of community law enforcement was maintained well into the eighteenth century. The Industrial Revolution, however, hastened the growth of cities, changes in traditional patterns of life, and, as a result, social disorder. As a consequence, there was an almost complete breakdown of law and order in London.

**frankpledge**
A system in old English law whereby members of a tithing, a group of ten families, pledged to be responsible for the good conduct of all members over twelve years old.

**Sir Robert Peel**

**O**ne of the outstanding British states-men and politicians of the nineteenth century, Sir Robert Peel tremendously influenced the development of professional policing in England. Appointed secretary of state for the Home Department in 1822, Peel reformed the criminal law through the consolidation and rewriting of all offenses. His work with the criminal law and the rise in crime led him to believe that legal reform must be accompanied by improved methods of crime prevention. In 1829, he persuaded Parliament to pass the Metropolitan Police Act, which replaced the patchwork of private law enforcement systems then in use with the first disciplined and regular police force in the Greater London area.

Peel sought to reduce the costs of administering justice by establishing an efficient, full-time civil service that would serve the state, not local interests. He advocated full-time careers for the police and urged enhancement of the deterrent capacity of law enforcement. According to Peel, the core activity of the police should be preventive patrol by officers who were part of a civilian force, who did not carry arms, and who had been trained to prevent crime by being present in the community. He believed that effective prevention and law enforcement could be substituted for harsh penalties. England's "bobbies," or "Peelers," are the legacy of Sir Robert Peel.

In the 1750s, Henry Fielding and his brother, Sir John Fielding, led efforts to improve the police in England. Through the pages of the *Covent Garden Journal* they sought to educate the public on the problem of increased crime. They also published the *Weekly Pursuit*, a one-page flyer with descriptions of known offenders. Henry Fielding became a magistrate of London in 1748 and organized a small group of "thief-takers," men with previous service as constables, which became a roving band dedicated to breaking up criminal gangs, pursuing lawbreakers, and making arrests. So impressed was the government by this Bow Street Amateur Volunteer Force (known as the "Bow Street Runners") that money was provided each member and an attempt was made to extend the concept to other areas of London. But Henry Fielding died in 1754, and Sir John was unable to maintain the high level of integrity of the original group. Effectiveness waned. Riots broke out in the summer of 1780, and for nearly a week mobs ruled much of the city. That a new approach to law enforcement was necessary had become obvious.[4]

During the early eighteenth century, attempts were made to create a centralized police force for London. Opposition came from people who believed that police of any kind were synonymous with tyranny and the destruction of liberty.[5] It was not until 1829 that, under the prodding of Sir Robert Peel (see Biography), Parliament established the Metropolitan Constabulary for London. Structured along the lines of a military unit, the force of one thousand was commanded by two magistrates, later called *commissioners*, who were given administrative, but not judicial, duties. The ultimate responsibility for maintaining and, to a certain degree, supervising "bobbies" (named after Robert Peel) was vested in the home secretary. Because the home secretary was a member of the government, this first regular police force was in essence controlled by the democratically elected legislature.

The police in England during the early nineteenth century had a four-part mandate:

1 to prevent crime without the use of repressive force and to avoid intervention by the military in community disturbances;

2 to manage public order nonviolently, using force to obtain compliance only as a last resort;

3 to minimize and reduce conflict between the police and the public; and

4 to demonstrate efficiency by means of the absence of crime and disorder rather than by visible evidence of police actions in dealing with problems.[6]

The mandate was to keep a low profile while maintaining order. Lest a national force emerge that would threaten civil liberties, political leaders made every effort to keep supervision of the police at a local level. These concerns and precautions were also transported to the United States.

# The Development of the Police in the United States

Before the Revolution, Americans shared the English belief that community members had a basic responsibility to help maintain order; as a consequence, they readily adopted the offices of constable, sheriff, and night watchman. With the establishment of a federal governmental structure in 1789, police power remained with the states, again in response to the fear of centralized law enforcement activity. However, the police and their mandate in the United States developed in response to conditions that were unlike those in England. The United States peacekeeping forces also had to deal with ethnic diversity, local political control, regional differences, the exploration and settling of the West, and the more violent tradition of American society.

American policing is often described in terms of three historical periods: the Political Era (1840–1920), the Professional Model Era (1920–1970), and the Community Model Era (1970–present).[7] This division of history has been criticized as describing policing only in the urban areas of the Northeast without taking into account the very different development of the police in rural areas of the South and West. Even so, it is useful as a framework through which we can note differences in the organization of the police, the focus of police work, and the particular strategies employed.[8]

**The Political Era: 1840–1920**   The period from 1840–1920 is characterized as the Political Era because of the close ties developed between police and local political leaders.[9] In many cities the police appeared to be adjuncts of the local party machine. This relationship served both groups in that the political machines recruited and maintained the police while the police helped ward leaders get out the vote for favored candidates. Ranks in the force were often for sale to the highest bidder and many police officers were "on the take."

In the United States as in England, the growth of cities led to pressures for modernization of law enforcement. Social relations in nineteenth-century cities were quite different from those in the towns and countryside. In fact, from 1830 to 1870 there was unprecedented civil disorder in the major cities. Ethnic conflict stemming from massive immigration, hostility toward nonslave blacks and abolitionists, mob actions against banks and other institutions of property during economic declines, and violence in settling questions of morality created fears that democratic institutions would not survive.

During this period the large cities began to create constabularies. Boston and Philadelphia became the first to add a daytime police force to supplement the night watchmen; other cities quickly followed their lead. People soon recognized the inefficiency of separate day and night forces, and in 1844 the New York Legislature passed a law to create a unified force for cities under the command of a chief appointed by the mayor and council. By mid-century, most major American cities had adopted this pattern.

Aside from these political changes, the police continued to perform the watchman and reactive patrol functions of their predecessors and focused on crime prevention and order maintenance by foot patrol. The officer on the beat dealt with crime, disorder, and other problems as they arose. In addition, the police carried out service functions such as caring for derelicts, operating soup kitchens, regulating public health, and handling medical and social emergencies.[10] Equipped with "a communications organization and street presence," the urban police were virtually forced to become both city servants and crime control officers.[11] Because of their closeness to the community, the police enjoyed citizen support.

Police in the South developed differently because of slavery and the agrarian nature of that region. Historians have argued that the first organized police agencies with full-time officers developed in those cities with large slave populations (Charleston, New Orleans, Savannah, and Richmond) where the white masters lived in fear of possible uprisings.[12] "Slave patrols" were organized by the white owners as a means of dealing with runaways. The patrols had full power to break into the homes of blacks suspected of keeping arms, to execute corporal punishments on those who did not obey their orders, and to arrest runaways to return them to their masters.

The nineteenth-century westward expansion of the United States presented circumstances that were quite dissimilar to those in the urbanizing East and the agricultural South. Settlement preceded an ordered society, and individuals with a vested interest in "law and order" often had to take the law into their own hands through vigilante groups.[13]

One of the first official positions created in rural areas was that of sheriff. Although the sheriff had responsibilities similar to those of his counterpart in seventeenth-century England, the American officer was chosen by popular election and had broad powers to enforce the law. Sheriffs depended on the men of the community for assistance, and the *posse comitatus*, a concept borrowed from fifteenth-century Europe, came into being. This institution required local men to respond to the sheriff's call for assistance. As governments were formed in the western territories of the United States, marshals appointed by federal authority helped enforce the law. Some of the best-known folk heroes of American policing were U.S. Marshals Wyatt Earp, Bat Masterson, and Wild Bill Hickok, who attempted to bring law to the "Wild West."[14] While some federal marshals carried out extensive law enforcement activities, most had duties that were primarily judicial, including maintaining order in the courtroom and holding prisoners for trial.

Over time, criticisms of political influence on police actions in the Northeastern cities and the spread of urbanism to other parts of the country led to efforts to promote a new type of police organization with an orientation toward professionalism.

**The Professional Model Era: 1920–1970**   Policing was greatly influenced by the Progressive reform movement that marked the turn of the twentieth century. The Progressives were primarily upper-middle-class, educated Americans interested in two goals: the efficient operation of government and the provision of governmental services to improve the conditions of the less fortunate. They also hoped to rid government of undesirable influences, such as party politics and patronage. In regard to the crime problem the Progressives called for the creation of professional police forces.

The key to understanding the Progressives' concept of professionalism within law enforcement is found in their slogan "The police have to get out of politics, and politics has to get out of the police." August Vollmer, chief of police of Berkeley, California, was one of the leading advocates of professionalism; his contributions are outlined in the accompanying Biography. He and other police reformers, such as Leonhard Fuld, Raymond Fosdic, Bruce Smith, and O. W. Wilson, argued that the police be a professional force, a nonpartisan agency of government committed to the highest ideals of public service. This model of professional policing comprises six essential elements:

1   the force should stay out of politics,
2   members should be well trained and disciplined and tightly organized,
3   laws should be equally enforced,
4   the force should take advantage of technological developments,
5   merit should be the basis of personnel procedures,
6   the crime-fighting role should be prominent.

Of these six elements, the redirection of the police away from a primary focus on order maintenance to an emphasis on crime fighting did more to change the nature of American policing than any of the other five elements. This narrow focus on crime fighting removed the police from many of the ties they had developed within the communities they served. By the end of World War I, police departments had significantly reduced their involvement in public service functions. Instead, for the most part, cops became crime fighters.[15]

O. W. Wilson, a student of Vollmer, was a leading advocate of professionalism and a proponent of the use of motorized patrols, efficient radio communication, and rapid response to facilitate effective crime fighting. He felt that one-officer patrols were the best way to use personnel and that the two-way radio, which allowed for supervision by commanders, helped officers to be especially efficient.[16] Wilson emphasized the importance of rotating beat assignments so that officers on patrol would not become too familiar with individuals in the community and thus prone to police corruption. Advocates of professionalism urged that the police be made aware of the need to act lawfully and to protect the rights of all citizens, including those suspected of criminal acts. They sought to instill in officers a strong—some would even argue too rigid ("just the facts, ma'am")—commitment to the supremacy of the law and the importance of equal treatment.[17]

By the 1930s the police emphasized their concern with serious crimes, such as murder, assault, robbery, and rape. Fighting these crimes was important for gaining citizen support, as efforts to control victimless offenses and disorderliness and to provide social services aroused citizen opposition. As emphasized by Mark Moore and George Kelling, "The

clean, bureaucratic model of policing put forth by the reformers could be sustained only if the scope of police responsibility was narrowed to 'crime fighting.'"[18] Technology also helped emphasize discipline, equal enforcement of the law, and centralized decision making, which are so characteristic of professionals working in a bureaucracy.

The civil rights and antiwar movements, the urban riots, and the rise of crime in the 1960s challenged many assumptions of the professional model. In their attempts to maintain public order, the police in many cities appeared to be concerned primarily with maintaining the status quo. With American cities increasingly comprised of poor members of racial minorities, the professional style isolated officers from the communities they served. To many inner-city residents the police resembled more an occupying force than public servants who could be looked to for help. Although police continued to present themselves as crime fighters, citizens became increasingly aware that the police were often ineffective in this role.

**The Community Policing Era: 1970–Present**   Beginning in the 1970s there were calls for movement away from the crime-fighting focus and toward a greater emphasis on maintaining order and providing services to the community. Major research studies had been published since the 1960s that showed the complexities of police work and the extent to which day-to-day practices deviated from the ideals of the professional model. The research also questioned the effectiveness of the police in catching and deterring criminals. Three findings require emphasis:

1   Increasing the number of patrol officers in a neighborhood was found to have little effect on the crime rate.

2   Rapid response to calls for service does not greatly increase the arrest of criminals.

3   It is difficult, if not impossible, to improve rates of solving crimes.

These findings disputed major elements of the professional crime-fighter model and therefore undermined its acceptance.[19]

Critics have argued that the professional style isolated the police from the community and seemed not to be accountable to it. This isolation was especially true because of the heavy emphasis upon motorized patrol. The patrol car encapsulates the officer so that personal contacts with most citizens are lost. It is argued that the police should get out of their cars and spend more time directly confronting and assisting citizens with problems and interceding in potential situations. It may be mundane, prosaic work, but the result could well be that citizens would feel safer and might even be safer.[20]

In a provocative article, "Broken Windows: The Police and Neighborhood Safety," James Wilson and George Kelling argue for a reorientation of policing that emphasizes "little problems," such as the maintenance of order, provision of services to those in need, and adoption of strategies to reduce the fear of crime. They base their approach on three assumptions:

1   Neighborhood disorder creates fear. Areas with street people, youth gangs, prostitution, and drunks are high-crime areas.

2   Just as unrepaired broken windows are a signal that nobody cares and can lead to more serious vandalism, untended disorderly behavior is also a signal that the community does not care. That leads to more serious disorder and crime.

3   If the police are to deal with disorder to reduce fear and crime, they must rely on citizens for legitimacy and assistance.[21]

Advocates of the community policing approach urge a greater emphasis on foot patrols so that officers will become known to the citizens they serve, who in turn will cooperate with and assist the police. They believe that through attention to little problems, the police may not only reduce disorder and citizen fear but also improve public attitudes toward policing. When citizens respond positively to police order-maintenance efforts, police will have "improved bases of community and political support, which in turn can be exploited to gain further cooperation from citizens in a wide variety of activities."[22]

A call for a shift in policing to a problem-oriented approach recommends that the police be prepared to handle the broad range of troublesome situations—for example, battered wives, runaway children, noisy teenagers, accidents and persons in distress—that prompt citizens to turn to them.[23] Under this approach to citizen needs, the police should define the problem and look for its underlying causes.[24]

During the Professional Era, the police saw themselves as crime fighters, yet many inner-city residents saw them as an occupying force rather than as public servants who might be looked to for help.

**Figure 4.1**
**The organization of police in the United States**
Policing is found at all levels of government and involves many types of work.

**Federal**

The fifty police agencies of the federal government are primarily concerned with violations of federal law, especially those criminal acts that cross state boundaries.

**State**

All states except Hawaii have a law enforcement agency with statewide jurisdiction, yet only two-thirds of state forces have general police powers.

Although the contemporary reformers have argued for a greater focus on the order-maintenance and service functions of the police, they do not advocate dropping the crime-fighter role. Rather they have called for a reorientation of police priorities, with greater attention given to community needs and to a better understanding of the problems underlying crime, disorder, and incivility. Their proposals have been adopted by police executives in many cities and by such influential bodies as the Police Foundation and the Police Executive Research Forum. However, there are some American cities, especially in the Southwest and West, where, because of the dispersion of the population, it is unlikely that there will be a significant shift in resources to foot patrol. Time will tell if this new orientation will become as influential and widespread as was the focus on professionalism during the first half of the twentieth century.

The call for a new orientation of the police has not gone unchallenged.[25] Critics contend that those advocating the community focus have misread the history of the police in the United States. Samuel Walker, for example, maintains that the depersonalization of American policing by the professional crime-fighting model has been greatly exaggerated. He asserts, however, that a revitalized concept of police patrol, in light of the lessons of recent research, has merit.[26] Taking another view, Carl Klockars doubts that the police will actually give priority to maintaining order. As he says, "Although the police are miscast in the crime-fighting role, we in the audience insist that they play the part. In the face of nearly a century of false hopes and false promises the need and desire of the public and its press to believe that police can fight crime remain strong."[27] But it has also been noted that the police shaped these expectations to begin with and, therefore, can shape them in a different direction in the future.

**County**

In rural areas the county sheriff is responsible for law enforcement.

**Local**

Most police officers work for local governments and are responsible for order maintenance, law enforcement, and service.

Whichever policy direction the police take—professional crime fighting or community policing—it must be implemented through a bureaucratic structure. We now turn to an examination of police organization in the federal system of the United States.

## Organization of the Police in a Federal System

As discussed in Chapter 1, the federal system of government in the United States means that law enforcement, adjudication, and correctional agencies are found at both the national and the state level. Consistent with the ideas of Sir Robert Peel, police in the United States are decentralized with the greatest number of agencies and employees at the local level. The structure of police organization is shown in Figure 4.1. There are an estimated 17,500 police agencies in the United States at the national, state, county, and municipal levels.[28] Some of these agencies have limited jurisdictions, but most are general purpose agencies. A total of more than 800,000 people, both sworn and unsworn, are employed by police agencies. Law enforcement agencies include:

- 12,502 municipal departments
- 3,086 sheriff departments
- 1,721 special police agencies (limited jurisdictions for transit systems, parks, schools, and so on)
- 49 state police (every state except Hawaii)
- 50 federal law enforcement agencies[29]

**B**orn in Washington, D.C., J. Edgar Hoover served as special assistant to the U.S. attorney general from 1919 to 1921 before being appointed director of the FBI in 1924. With the agency racked by dissension and rife with politics, Hoover set out to eliminate politics from the FBI appointment process and to establish better training programs for new agents. He recognized the importance of improved technical methods and instituted such aids as a national fingerprint filing system and coordinated development of the Uniform Crime Reporting System. In his early career, Hoover's pursuit of such notorious criminals as Ma Barker, Machine Gun Kelly, Bonnie and Clyde, and John Dillinger helped to create an image of the FBI agent ("G-man") as the ultimate crime fighter. During the 1940s and 1950s, his anticommunist views, and the FBI's subversive-control functions, became prominent.

Hoover's long career sustained many criticisms of his management of the FBI, including accusations that the Bureau exceeded its jurisdiction, manipulated crime data, exaggerated reports of subversive activities, and hindered the civil rights movement. Nevertheless, his contributions to improved management of police work and to the FBI's effectiveness are widely recognized.

The local nature of law enforcement is further illustrated by the fact that 12 percent of the costs for police protection are expended by the national government, 15 percent by the state governments, and 73 percent by municipal and county governments. As we examine each type of police agency, note the focus of its work and its links to the criminal justice system.

## Federal Agencies

Entrusted with the enforcement of a list of specific federal laws, police organizations of the national government are part of the executive branch. Although few in number compared to state and local police agencies, federal law enforcement agencies have assumed a more dominant role in the mind of the public and the media. Recent campaigns by federal agencies against drugs, organized crime, insider trading, and environmental pollution are much in the public eye.

Among the law enforcement agencies at the federal level, the FBI has the broadest range of control, which encompasses investigation of all federal crimes not the responsibility of other agencies. Established as the Bureau of Investigation in 1908, it was not until J. Edgar Hoover (highlighted in accompanying Biography) became director in 1924 that the Bureau (renamed the Federal Bureau of Investigation in 1935) came into prominence. Hoover instituted major changes to increase the professionalism of the agency and to dispel its somewhat unsavory reputation for corruption and abuse of civil liberties. Within the FBI is the semiautonomous Drug Enforcement Agency (DEA).

The Treasury Department has branches concerned with violations of laws related to the collection of income taxes (Internal Revenue Service), alcohol and tobacco taxes and gun control (Bureau of Alcohol, Tobacco, and Firearms), and customs (Customs Service). Other federal agencies concerned with specific areas of law enforcement include the Secret Service Division of the Treasury (concerned with counterfeiting, forgery, and protection of the president), the Bureau of Postal Inspection of the Postal Service (concerned with mail offenses), and the Border Patrol of the Department of Justice Immigration and Naturalization Service. Other departments of the executive branch, such as the U.S. Coast Guard and the National Parks Service, are among the many federal agencies that have police powers related to their specific duties.[30]

Agencies of the federal government also cooperate with Interpol, the International Criminal Police Organization, headquartered in St. Cloud, France. Interpol has 146 member countries.[31] Its function is to foster cooperation among the police forces of the world with regard to crimes that are international in scope: drugs, terrorism, espionage, and those fleeing apprehension. Interpol maintains an intelligence databank on criminals and serves as a clearinghouse for information gathered by member agencies. The FBI, DEA, Treasury Department, Central Intelligence Agency, and the Internal Revenue Service all have strong ties to Interpol. Increasingly, Interpol has developed links with state and local police forces in the United States.[32]

## State Agencies

Each state except Hawaii has its own police force with statewide jurisdiction; even so, we can see the traditional emphasis on the local nature of policing. The American reluctance to centralize police power has kept state forces generally from replacing local officials. State police forces were not established until the early twentieth century and then primarily as a wing of the executive branch of state government that would enforce the law when local officials did not. The Pennsylvania State Constabulary, established in 1905, was the first such organization. By 1925 almost all states had an agency with some level of enforcement power.

The state forces are all charged with the regulation of traffic on major highways, and in two-thirds of the states they have been given general police powers.[33] In only about a dozen populous states, however, are they adequate to the task of general law enforcement outside the cities. Where the state police are well developed—as in Pennsylvania, New York, New Jersey, Massachusetts, and Michigan—they tend to fill a void in rural law enforcement. For the most part, however, they operate only in areas where no other form of police protection exists or where local officers request their expertise or the use of their facilities. For example, in many states the crime laboratory is operated by the state police as a means of assisting all local law enforcement agencies.

## County Agencies

Sheriffs are found in almost every one of the 3,100 counties in the United States.[34] They have the responsibility for policing rural areas, but over time many of their functions have been assumed by the state or local police. This is particularly true in portions of the Northeast. In parts of the South and West, however, the sheriff's office remains a well-organized force. In thirty-three of the states, sheriffs have broad authority, are elected, and occupy the position of chief law enforcement officer in the county. Even when the sheriff's office is well organized, though, it may lack jurisdiction over cities and towns. In addition to law enforcement duties, the sheriff is often an officer of the court and is charged with holding prisoners, serving court orders, and providing the bailiffs who are responsible for maintaining order in court. In many counties, appointments to the sheriff's office are governed by local politics, while in other places, such as Los Angeles County (California) and Multnomah County (Oregon), departments are staffed by professional, trained personnel.

## Local Agencies

Established by local government, the police of the cities and towns are vested by state law with general authority. The size of city police forces range from the more than 35,000 employees of the New York Police Department to the 1,602 localities with only one sworn officer. On a national

## Organization of the Police in France

France has a population of about 52 million and a unitary form of government. Political power and decision making are highly centralized in bureaucracies located in Paris. There is a single criminal code and standardized criminal justice procedures for the entire country. The country is divided into ninety-six territories known as departments and is further divided into districts and municipalities. In each district there is a commissaire of the republic who represents the central government and exercises supervision over the local mayors.

Police functions are divided between two separate forces under the direction of two ministries of the central government. With over 200,000 personnel employed in police duties, France has a ratio of law enforcement officers to the general population that is greater than that of the United States or England.

The older police force, the Gendarmerie Nationale, with over 80,000 officers, is under the military and is responsible for policing about 95 percent of the country's territory. The gendarmerie patrols the highways, rural areas, and those communities with populations of less than 10,000. Members are organized into brigades or squads. These brigades are collectively known as the Departmental Gen-

basis nearly 90 percent of the local police agencies serve populations of 25,000 or less; half of all sworn officers are employed in cities of at least 100,000.[35] The resulting ratio of officers to residents in cities of over 100,000 is 2.7 per 1,000, which is almost twice the average ratio for cities of fewer than 100,000.

In a metropolitan area composed of a central city and a number of independent suburbs, the policing function is usually divided among agencies at all governmental levels, and jurisdictional conflict may inhibit the efficient use of resources. In many large population areas, agreements allow for cross-jurisdiction cooperation. America is essentially a nation of small police forces, each of which operates independently within the limits of its jurisdiction. This system is in direct contrast to the centralized organization in France, where police are a national force divided between the Ministry of Interior and the Ministry of Defense (see Comparative Perspective).

darmerie. They operate from fixed points, reside in their duty area, and constitute the largest component of the force. A second agency, the Mobile Gendarmerie, may be deployed anywhere in the country. These are essentially riot police; their forces are motorized, have tanks, and even light aircraft. The Republican Guard, the third component of the Gendarmerie, is stationed in Paris, protects the president, and performs ceremonial functions.

The Police Nationale is under the Ministry of the Interior and operates mainly in urban centers with populations over 10,000. The Police Nationale is divided into the Directorate of Urban Police, which is responsible for policing the cities with patrol and investigative functions, and the Directorate of Criminal Investigation, which provides regional detective services and pursues cases beyond the scope of the city police or the gendarmerie. Another division, the Air and Frontier Police, is responsible for border protection. The Republican Security Companies are the urban version of the Mobile Gendarmerie but without the heavy armament....

In addition to traditional patrol and investigative functions, the Police Nationale also contains units responsible for the collection of intelligence information and for the countering of foreign subversion. The Directorate of General Intelligence and Gambling has 2,500 officers and has as its purpose the gathering of "intelligence of a political, social, and economic nature necessary for the information of government." This includes data from public opinion surveys, mass media, periodicals, and information gathered through the infiltration of various political, labor, and social groups. The Directorate of Counterespionage has the mission of countering the efforts of foreign agents on French soil intent on impairing the security of the country....

The police system of the central government of France is powerful; the number, armament, legal powers, and links to the military is most impressive. The turbulent history of France before and after the revolution of 1789 gave rise to the need for the government to be able to assert authority. Since the 1930s France has had to deal not only with crime but also with political instability—the Nazi invasion of 1940, weak governments following World War II, the Algerian crisis in 1958, and student rioting in 1968 all brought conditions that nearly toppled the existing regime. The need to maintain order in the streets would seem to be a major concern of the government.

SOURCE: Adapted from Philip John Stead, *The Police of France* (New York: Macmillan, 1983), 1–12. Copyright © 1983 by Macmillan Publishing Company, a division of Macmillan, Inc. Reprinted by permission of the publisher.

## Police Policy

Although the criminal law is written as if every infraction were expected to result in arrest and punishment, that is not the case. Limitations imposed by the law, legislatures, courts, and community greatly reduce the number of criminal acts that may become a focus of police activity. In addition, the police have wide discretion in determining how they deploy their resources, which types of behaviors are overlooked, and the particular circumstances in which officers do or do not make an arrest. Because criminal justice is a system with sequential tasks, the police are in a crucial position with regard to regulating the flow of cases to the prosecution and courts. Changes in enforcement policy—for example, increasing the size of the night patrol or tolerating certain types of vice—influence the amount of crime that comes to official attention and the system's ability to deal with offenders.

As previously discussed, the police have emphasized their crime-fighting role for most of the past half-century. As a result, in most communities

**Table 4.1**

**Styles of policing**

Wilson found three distinct styles of policing in the communities he studied. Each style emphasizes different police functions, and each is associated with the particular characteristics of the community.

SOURCE: Drawn from James Q. Wilson, *Varieties of Police Behavior* (Cambridge, Mass.: Harvard University Press, 1968).

| Style | Defining Characteristics | Community Type |
|---|---|---|
| Watchman | Emphasis on maintaining order | Declining industrial city, mixed racial/ethnic composition, "blue collar" |
| Legalistic | Emphasis on law enforcement | Reform-minded city government, mixed socioeconomic composition |
| Service | Emphasis on service with balance between law enforcement and order maintenance | Middle-class suburban communities |

police attention centers around the categories of crimes within the FBI's *Uniform Crime Reports*. These are the crimes that make headlines and that politicians point to when they ask for increases in the police budget. They are also the crimes generally committed by the poor.

Such a basic decision as how police resources will be deployed has an important effect on the types of persons arrested. Given the mixed social character of a metropolitan area, police administrators have to decide where to send their officers and what tactics to employ. Should a disproportionate number of officers be sent into high crime areas? Should the central business district be given an enhanced police presence during shopping hours? What should be the mix between traffic control and crime fighting?

American cities differ in their governmental, economic, racial/ethnic characteristics, and degree of urbanization. These factors can influence the style of policing expected by the community. In a classic study, James Q. Wilson pointed out that citizen expectations regarding police behavior are brought to bear through the political process in the choice of the top police executive. Chiefs who run departments that antagonize the community are likely to have their job for only a short time. Thus Wilson found that the political culture, reflecting the socioeconomic characteristics of a city and its organization of government, exerted a major influence on whether a city's police force operated in one of three different styles—the watchman, legalistic, or service style.[36] Each style is discussed below and in Table 4.1.

Departments with a *watchman* style emphasize order maintenance. Police administrators allow officers to ignore minor violations of the law, especially those involving traffic and juveniles, provided that order is maintained. The police thus exercise discretion to deal informally with many infractions, making arrests only when there are flagrant breaches of the law and when order cannot be maintained. Differential treatment of racial and ethnic groups is characteristic of this style.

In departments with a *legalistic* style police work is marked by professionalism and an emphasis on law enforcement. Officers are expected to detain a high proportion of juvenile offenders, act vigorously against illicit enterprises, issue traffic tickets, and make a large number of misdemeanor arrests. In legalistic departments officers act as if there were a single standard of community conduct—that which the law prescribes—rather than different standards for juveniles, minorities, drunks, and the like.

In suburban middle-class communities, a *service* style often predominates. Residents expect police work to be oriented toward providing service, thus burglaries and assaults are taken seriously, while arrests for minor infractions tend to be avoided when possible and replaced by informal, nonarrest sanctions. In these suburbs, citizens feel they should receive individualized treatment from their police.

Thus even before a crime is investigated or arrest made, a community's police have formulated policies and a style that will influence the level and type of enforcement. Since the police are the entry point to the criminal justice system, the total picture is shaped largely by the decisions made by officials concerning the allocation of resources and their perception of the style and level of law enforcement the community desires.

## Police Functions

The police are expected not only to maintain the peace and prevent crime, but also to direct traffic, handle accidents and illnesses, stop noisy gatherings, find missing persons, administer licensing regulations, provide ambulance services, take disturbed or inebriated people into protective custody, and so on. The list is long, it varies from place to place, and much police work has little to do with the penal code. Some researchers have even suggested that the police have more in common with agencies of municipal social service than with the criminal justice system.

The American Bar Association developed a list of the objectives and functions of the police as a first step in understanding that the police are concerned with more than maintaining order, enforcing the law, and serving the public. The breadth of police responsibility is impressive. Their duties include the following:

1   Prevent and control conduct widely recognized as threatening to life and property (serious crime).

2   Aid individuals in danger of physical harm, such as the victim of a criminal attack.

3   Protect constitutional guarantees, such as the right of free speech and assembly.

4   Facilitate the movement of people and vehicles.

5   Assist those who cannot care for themselves: the intoxicated, the addicted, the mentally ill, the physically disabled, the old, and the young.

6   Resolve conflict, whether it be between individuals, groups of individuals, or individuals and their government.

7   Identify problems that have the potential for becoming more serious problems for the individual citizen, for the police, or for government.

8   Create and maintain a feeling of security in the community.[37]

How did the police acquire such broad responsibilities? First, in many areas, the police belong to the only public agency that is available seven days a week, twenty-four hours a day, to respond to citizens' needs for help. Second, the police constitute the agency of government best able to perform the initial investigations required for the tasks just listed. Third, the capacity of the police to use force is a unifying theme of all their activity. The functions of the police can be categorized into three main groups: order maintenance, law enforcement, and service (see Figure 4.2).

## Order Maintenance

The **order-maintenance** function is a broad mandate to prevent behavior that either disturbs or threatens to disturb the public peace or that involves face-to-face conflict among two or more persons. A domestic quarrel, a noisy drunk, loud music in the night, a panhandler soliciting on the street, a tavern brawl—all are examples of disorder that may require the peacekeeping efforts of the police. Whereas most criminal laws specify acts that are illegal, laws regulating disorderly conduct deal with ambiguous situations that may be variously interpreted in accordance with the social environment and the perceptions and norms of the actors. Law enforcement comes into play when a law has been violated and only guilt must be assessed; order maintenance calls for intervention in situations in which the law may have been broken but which require the law to be interpreted and standards of right conduct and assignment of blame to be determined.

When we study the work of patrol officers, we can see that they are concerned primarily with behavior that either disturbs or threatens to disturb the peace. In these situations they confront the public in ambiguous circumstances and have wide discretion in matters of life and death, honor and dishonor. By walking the streets or driving in patrol cars, officers may be required to help persons in trouble, to manage crowds, to supervise a variety of services, and to assist people who are not fully accountable for what they do.

When responding to a domestic disturbance, officers may find themselves in the position of mediating a squabble among family members and deciding whether one member should be removed from the home (through arrest) to provide for the safety of the others. In all of these actions, patrol officers are not subject to direct external control. They have the power to arrest and also the freedom not to arrest. The order-maintenance function is further complicated by the fact that the patrol officer is normally expected to "handle" a situation rather than to enforce the law, and in such cases the atmosphere is likely to be emotionally charged.

As James Wilson says, "to the patrolman, 'enforcing the law' is what he does when there is no dispute—when making an arrest or issuing a summons exhausts his responsibilities."[38] When patrol officers in Miami were asked what their job consisted of, they answered in police academy

**Order Maintenance**

Preventing behavior that disturbs or threatens to disturb the peace. In these situations the police exercise discretion to determine if the law has been broken.

**Law Enforcement**

Controlling crime by intervening in situations where the law has been broken and identity of the guilty person must be established.

**Service**

Providing help to the public ranging from checking door locks to providing medical assistance to finding missing persons.

fashion, "protection of life and property and the preservation of peace," thus confirming what they believe to be their primary role—that of peace-keeper.[39] As we will see, studies of citizen complaints and requests for service justify this emphasis on the order-maintenance function.

## Law Enforcement

The **law enforcement** function of the police is concerned with situations in which the law has been violated and only the identity of the guilty needs to be determined. Police officers charged with major responsibilities in these areas are often in specialized branches, such as the vice squad and the burglary detail. Although the patrol officer may be the first officer on the scene of a crime, in serious cases the detective usually prepares the case for prosecution by bringing together all the evidence for the prosecuting attorney. When the offender is identified but not located, the detective conducts the search; if the offender is not identified, the detective has the responsibility of analyzing clues to determine who committed the crime.

Although the police emphasize their law enforcement function, their efficiency in this area has been questioned. Especially when crimes against property are committed, the perpetrator usually has a time advantage over the police. Police efficiency is further decreased when the crime is an offense against a person and the victim is unable to identify the offender or delays notifying the police beyond the time in which apprehension might reasonably be expected.

**Figure 4.2**
**Police Functions**

The police are given a wide range of responsibilities, from directing traffic to solving homicides, but the work can be divided into three functional categories: order maintenance, law enforcement, and service. Departments will emphasize one or more of these functions according to the community's government structure and socioeconomic characteristics.

**law enforcement**

The police function of controlling crime by intervening in situations in which it is clear that the law has been violated and only the identity of the guilty needs to be determined.

## Service

In modern society the police are increasingly called upon to perform services for the population, particularly to its lower-income citizens. This **service** function—providing first aid, rescuing animals, and extending social welfare—has become the dominant area of police activity, especially at night and on weekends. Analysis of more than 26,000 calls to twenty-one police departments confirms the long-held belief that about 80 percent of citizens' requests for police intervention involve matters unrelated to crime; in fact the largest percentage of calls, 21 percent, were requests for information.[40] Because the police department is accessible twenty-four hours every day, it is the agency to which people turn in times of trouble. Many departments provide information, operate ambulance services, locate missing persons, check locks on vacationers' homes, and stop would-be suicides.

Although it may appear that valuable resources are being expended for police work unrelated to crime, it has been claimed that such services do have ramifications that help in crime control. It is through the service function that officers gain knowledge of the community and that citizens in turn grow to rely on and trust the police. Checking the security of buildings is the service that most obviously helps prevent crime, but dealing with runaways, drunks, and public quarrels may help solve problems before they can lead to criminal behavior.

## Implementing the Mandate

Police agencies allocate their resources among law enforcement, order maintenance, service, and other activities according to community need, citizen requests, and departmental policy. The level of different police patrol activities can vary greatly according to community demands and expectations.

The findings of some studies demonstrate that although the public may depend on the order-maintenance and service functions of the police, citizens act as if law enforcement—the catching of lawbreakers—were the most important function. The preeminence of the crime-stopping image is shown by public opinion polls and the reasons given by recruits for joining the force. Police administrators have learned that public support for budget increases can be gained when the crime-fighter and law enforcement function is stressed. This emphasis is demonstrated by the internal organization of metropolitan departments, where high status is accorded the officers who perform law enforcement functions. This focus leads to the creation of specialized units within the detective division to deal with such crimes as homicide, burglary, and auto theft. The assumption seems to be that all other requirements of the citizenry will be handled by the patrol division. In some departments, this arrangement may create morale problems because a disproportionate measure of resources and prestige is allocated to the function that involves the minority of police actions. Police are occupied with peacekeeping but preoccupied with crime fighting.

Police work is sometimes exciting, often boring, and always stressful. Would you like this job?

## Police Actions and Decision Making

We have examined the organization of the police and the three functions of policing—law enforcement, order maintenance, and service. Now let us look at the daily actions of the police as they deal with citizens, exercise discretion, and make vital decisions. We will then examine domestic violence as an example of the response of the police to a serious problem.

### Citizen-Police Encounters

Encounters between citizens and the police in criminal situations are structured by the roles each participant plays, by the setting, and by the attitudes of the victim toward legal action. Although most citizens may believe that they have a civic obligation to assist the police by alerting them to criminal activity, an element of personal gain or loss exerts an important influence. Many people fail to call the police because they think it is not worth the effort and cost: filling out papers at the station, appearing as a witness, confronting a neighbor or relative. Clearly, then, citizens exercise control over the work of the police by their decisions to call or not to call them.

**clearance rate**
The percentage of crimes known to the police that they believe they have solved through an arrest; a statistic used as a measure of a police department's productivity.

**reactive**
Occurring in response to a stimulus, such as police activity in response to notification that a crime has been committed.

**proactive**
An active search for offenders on the part of the police in the absence of reports of violations of the law. Arrests for crimes without victims are usually proactive.

The **clearance rate**—the percentage of crimes known to the police that they believe they have solved through an arrest—is a basic measure of police performance as they deal with citizens. The clearance rate varies with each category of offense. In such **reactive** situations as burglary, the rate of apprehension is extremely low, only about 14 percent; much greater success is experienced with violent crimes (46 percent), in which the victims tend to know their assailants.[41] Arrests made through **proactive** police operations against prostitution, gambling, and drug traffic have a clearance rate, theoretically, of 100 percent.

The arrest of a person often results in the clearance of other reported offenses because the police make it a practice to connect arrested persons with similar, unsolved crimes when they can. Interrogation and lineups are standard procedures, as is the lesser-known operation of simply assigning unsolved crimes in the department's records to the defendant. Acknowledgment by offenders that they committed prior but unsolved crimes is often part of the bargain when guilty pleas are entered. Professional thieves know that they can gain favors from the police in exchange for "confessing" to unsolved crimes that they may not have committed.

## Police Discretion

Discretion is a characteristic of organizations. Whether in the corporate structure of General Motors or in the bureaucracy of a state welfare department, officials are given the authority to base decisions on their own judgment rather than on a formal set of rules. Thus executives and managers, but not workers on the assembly line, are given the power to make discretionary decisions. Within the police, however, discretion operates differently: discretion increases as one moves *down* the organizational hierarchy. Patrol officers, the most numerous, lowest-ranking, and recent officers, have the greatest amount of discretion. In addition, they deal with clients in isolation and are charged primarily with maintaining order and enforcing highly ambiguous laws concerning disorderly conduct, public drunkenness, breach of the peace, conflicts among citizens, and other situations in which the offensiveness of the participants' conduct is often open to dispute. James Wilson has caught the essence of the patrol officer's role when he describes it as one that "is unlike that of any other occupation ... one in which subprofessionals, working alone, exercise wide discretion in matters of utmost importance (life and death, honor and dishonor) in an environment that is apprehensive and perhaps hostile."[42]

In the final analysis, the individual officer decides whether and how the law should be applied. It is the officer on the scene who defines the situation and decides how it is to be handled. Four factors in particular affect the exercise of discretion by police officers:

**1**   *Characteristics of the crime*: Some crimes are considered trivial by the public, so, conversely, when the police become aware of a serious crime, they have less freedom to ignore it.

**2** *Relationship between the alleged criminal and the victim*: The closer the personal relationship, the more variable the exercise of discretion. Family squabbles may not be as grave as they appear, and police are wary of making arrests since a spouse may, on cool reflection, refuse to press charges.

**3** *Relationship between the police and the criminal or victim*: A respectful complainant will be taken more seriously than an antagonistic one. Likewise, a respectful alleged wrongdoer is less likely to be arrested.

**4** *Departmental policies*: The preferences of the chief and the city administration as reflected in the policy style will influence the exercise of discretion.[43]

In encounters between citizens and police, the matter of fairness is often intertwined with departmental policy. When should the patrol officer frisk? When should a deal be made with the addict-informer? Which disputes should be mediated on the spot and which left to adjudicatory personnel? Surprisingly, these conflicts between the demands of justice and policy are seldom decided by heads of departments but are left largely to the discretion of the officer on the scene. In fact, departmental control over police actions is lacking in certain types of activities.

Although some people advocate the development of detailed instructions to guide police officers, such an exercise would probably be fruitless. No matter how detailed the formal instructions, officers would still have to apply rules to cases. In the end, police administrators must decide what measures they will take to influence how their officers use discretion. The officers must have "a shared outlook or ethos that provides for them a common definition of the situations they are likely to encounter."[44]

## Domestic Violence: Encounters, Discretion, Action

By examining police actions with respect to the problem of domestic violence, we can discern the links between police-citizen encounters, the exercise of discretion, and actions taken (or not taken) by law enforcement officers. Domestic violence, also called "battering" and "spouse abuse," has been defined as assaultive behavior involving adults who are married or who have an ongoing or prior intimate relationship. In the overwhelming number of cases, domestic violence is perpetrated by men against women. Surveys have shown that domestic violence is not rare or limited to certain socioeconomic groups. In fact, a national survey of two thousand families led researchers to estimate that, during any one year, 1.7 million Americans had faced a spouse wielding a knife or gun and that well over two million had experienced a severe beating by their spouse.[45] Domestic violence in a household is not a single, isolated event. Rather, once a woman is victimized by domestic violence, she faces a high risk of being victimized again. Crime statistics support the belief that domestic violence may be lethal. *Uniform Crime Reports* data have shown that 30 percent of all female murder victims were killed by their husbands or boyfriends.[46]

## Battered Women, Reluctant Police

As Joanne Tremins was moving some belongings out of her ramshackle house on South Main Street [Torrington, Connecticut], her 350-pound husband ran over, grabbed the family cat and strangled it in front of Tremins and her children.

For more than three years, Tremins said, she had complained to Torrington police about beatings and threats from her husband. Instead of arresting him, she said, the police acted "like marriage counselors."

The cat attack finally prompted police to arrest Jeffrey Tremins on a minor charge of cruelty to animals. But four days later, outside a local cafe, he repeatedly punched his wife in the face and smashed her against a wall, fracturing her nose and causing lacerations and contusions to her face and left arm.

That Joanne Tremins is suing this New England town of 34,000 is not without historical irony. For it was here that Tracey Thurman ... won a $2 million judgment against the police department in a federal civil rights case that has revolutionized law enforcement attitudes toward domestic violence.

The Thurman case marked the first time that a battered woman was allowed to sue police in federal court for failing to protect her from her husband. The ruling held that such a failure amounts to sex discrimination and violates the Fourteenth Amendment.

The resulting spate of lawsuits has prompted police departments nationwide to reexamine their long-standing reluctance to make arrests in domestic assault cases, particularly when the wife refuses to press charges. State and local lawmakers, facing soaring municipal insurance costs, are also taking notice.

Here in hilly Torrington ... Police Chief Mahlon C. Sabo said [the Thurman case] had a "devastating" effect on the town and his seventy-member force. "The police somehow, over the years, became the mediators," said Sabo. "There was a feeling that it's between husband and wife. In most cases, after the officer left, the wife usually got battered around for calling the police in the first place."

Although the law now requires them to make arrests, police officers here said, the courts toss out many domestic cases for the same reason that long hampered police.

"Unfortunately, many women just want the case dropped and fail to recognize they're in a dangerous situation," said Anthony J. Salius, director of the family division of Connecticut Superior Court. "If she really doesn't want to prosecute, it's very difficult to have a trial because we don't have a witness."

Nearly five years after the attack by her estranged husband, Tracey Thurman remains scarred and partially paralyzed from multiple stab wounds to the chest, neck and face. Charles Thurman was sentenced to fourteen years in prison.

For eight months before the stabbing, Thurman repeatedly threatened his wife and their son, two. He worked at Skee's Diner, a few blocks from police headquarters, and repeatedly boasted to policemen he was serving that he intended to kill his wife, according to the lawsuit.

---

For too long, criminal justice agencies, and perhaps society as a whole, viewed domestic violence as a "private" affair best settled within the family (see the Close-Up "Battered Women, Reluctant Police"). Concern was often expressed that official involvement would only make the situation more difficult for the victim because she would have to face the possibility of reprisal.

From the viewpoint of most police departments, domestic violence was thought to be a "no-win" situation in which officers responding to calls for help were often set upon by one or both disputants. If an arrest was made, the police found that the victim often refused to cooperate with a prosecution arising from the incident. Further, entering a residence to handle such an emotion-laden incident was thought to be more dangerous than answering calls to investigate "real" criminal behavior. The belief was widespread that intervention in family disputes was a leading

Tracy Thurman won a landmark case against the Torrington, Connecticut, Police Department. It was the first time that a battered woman was able to sue police in federal court for failure to protect her from her husband.

In their defense, police said they arrested Thurman twice before the stabbing. The first charges were dropped, and a suspended sentence was imposed the second time. Tracey Thurman later obtained a court order barring her husband from harassing or assaulting her.

On June 10, 1983, Tracey Thurman called police and said her husband was menacing her. An officer did not arrive for twenty-five minutes and, although he found Charles Thurman holding a bloody knife, he delayed several minutes before making an arrest, giving Thurman enough time to kick his wife in the head repeatedly.

Less than a year after police were found liable in the attack on Thurman, Joanne Tremins also found that a restraining order obtained against her husband was worthless.... Tremins recounted how she made about sixty calls to police to complain about her husband, a cook. But she acknowledges that, on most of the occasions, when the police asked if she wanted him arrested, she said no.

"How could I say that?" she asked. "He's threatening to kill me if I have him arrested. He's threatening to kill my kids if I have him arrested. He'd stand behind the cops and pound his fist into the palm of his hand."

Hours before Tremins strangled the cat,... he beat and kicked his wife and her son, Stanley Andrews, fourteen. When an officer arrived, Joanne Tremins said, he told her that he could not make an arrest unless she filed a complaint at the police station.

"My son was all black and blue," Tremins said. "But [the officer] refused to come into my room and look at the blood all over the walls and the floor."

After Tremins was taken into custody for the cat incident, police did charge him with assaulting the son. He was released on bond, and his wife was issued a restraining order.

When her husband approached Tremins days later at a cafe in nearby Winsted, police refused to arrest him, despite the order. After the beating, Jeffrey Tremins was charged with assault and sentenced to two years in prison.

SOURCE: Howard Kurtz, "Battered Women, Reluctant Police," *Washington Post*, 28 February 1988, A–1. Copyright © 1988, The Washington Post. Reprinted with permission.

cause of officer death and injury. In those situations in which an arrest was made, the police have too often found that the victim refuses to co-operate with a prosecution.

The police response to domestic violence is a key example of a highly charged, uncertain, and potentially dangerous encounter with citizens in which officers must exercise discretion as they take action. Officers are expected to maintain order and, possibly, enforce the law in accordance with the criminal law, departmental policies, and the needs of the victim. Until very recently there were few formal directives to guide their actions.

A major issue facing officers who confront an incident of domestic violence is whether to arrest the assailant. In the past most police departments advised officers to try to calm the parties and to make referrals to social service agencies rather than to bring the attacker to the station for booking and eventual prosecution.

The first controlled experiment of the effectiveness of arrest in preventing recidivism in cases of domestic violence was conducted in Minneapolis.[47] During the eighteen-month study period of 330 cases, officers systematically selected one of three different tactics—arrest, advice or mediation, or ordering the offender to leave the house for an eight-hour period—as a means of handling misdemeanor-level incidents of domestic violence. It was found that offenders who had *not* been arrested had almost twice as much repeat violence during the six-month period following the incident as those who had been arrested. Since only 2 percent were subjected to further actions such as prosecution and trial by the criminal justice system, the study suggests that "arrest and initial incarceration alone may produce a deterrent effect, regardless of how the courts treat such cases, and that arrest makes an independent contribution to the deterrence potential of the criminal justice system."[48]

The Minneapolis experiment has been replicated in a number of jurisdictions to determine whether the results can be validated. A replication study in Omaha showed that arrest by itself did not appear to deter subsequent domestic conflict any more than did mediation or separation of those in the dispute.[49] The researchers suggest that additional strategies need to be developed to deal with the problem. Others have suggested that arrest followed by prosecution will have a greater impact on reducing domestic violence. However, a study of prosecutorial discretion in domestic violence cases in Milwaukee showed that factors such as the victim's injuries and the defendant's arrest record influenced the decision to charge, not just the fact of spouse abuse.[50]

Other policy changes have been enacted in many states that will force the police to confront the issue of domestic violence more directly (see the Close-Up "Battered Women, Reluctant Police"). Legislatures in some states have expanded officers' authority to arrest in these cases. In some places the law now mandates the arrest of suspects in misdemeanor incidents of domestic violence without obtaining a warrant even if the officer did not witness the crime but has probable cause to believe that one was committed by the person arrested. Police departments have also begun to enact policy guidelines. For example, the Seattle Police Department has listed a number of factors (gunshot wound, broken bones, intentionally inflicted burns) that should *always* be considered to involve a felony.[51] Other departments have developed procedures to assist victims and actions to be taken when protection orders are issued. Training programs on the dynamics of domestic violence have also been developed in most large departments and state academies to educate officers.

Even though we can identify several dramatic changes in the ways in which the police view the problem of domestic violence, the fact still remains that it is the officer in the field who must handle these situations. As with most law enforcement situations, laws, guidelines, and training help, but, as with so much other police work, reliance must be placed on the discretionary actions of the officer.

# Summary

The police in the United States owe their roots to the early nineteenth-century development of the police in England. Like their English counterparts, the American police have limited authority, are under local control, and are organizationally fragmented. There is no national police force in the United States as there is in continental Europe, yet there are law enforcement agencies in the federal government. Three eras of American policing can be discerned: the Political Era (1840–1920), the Professional Model Era (1920–1970), the Community Model Era (1970–present).

In the federal system of government of the United States, policing functions are carried out at the national, state, county, and local levels. At each level policing agencies have some responsibilities and must respond to the needs of different communities. Police executives develop policies as to how they will use their resources in their community. The watchman, legalistic, and service styles of policing have been documented.

The functions of the police are order maintenance, law enforcement, and service. Resources are allocated according to community needs, citizen requests, and departmental policies.

Discretion is a major factor in police actions and decisions. Unlike other occupations, discretion increases as officers move *down* the organizational hierarchy. That means the patrol officer, the person most in contact with citizens, exercises the greatest amount of discretion. The problem of domestic violence illustrates the links between police encounters with citizens, their exercise of discretion, and the actions they take.

# Questions for Review

1   What principles borrowed from England still underlie the police in the United States?

2   What are the three eras of policing in the United States and how are they characterized?

3   What are the functions of the police?

4   How do communities influence police policy and police styles?

5   How does the problem of domestic violence illustrate basic elements of police action?

# Key Terms

| | | |
|---|---|---|
| clearance rate | order maintenance | reactive |
| frankpledge | proactive | service |
| law enforcement | | |

# For Further Reading

Goldstein, Herman. *Problem-Oriented Policing*. New York: McGraw-Hill, 1990. Examination of the move toward problem-oriented, or community, policing. Argues for a shift to this focus.

Greene, Jack R., and Steven Mastrofski, eds. *Community Policing: Rhetoric or Reality?* New York: Praeger, 1988. An excellent collection of essays on community policing.

Muir, William K., Jr. *Police: Streetcorner Politicians*. Chicago: University of Chicago Press, 1979. A study of the different styles of police work as observed on the job.

Skolnick, Jerome H. *Justice without Trial: Law Enforcement in a Democratic Society*. New York: Wiley, 1966. One of the first books to examine the subculture of the police and the exercise of discretion.

Tonry, Michael, and Norval Morris, eds. *Modern Policing*. Chicago: University of Chicago Press, 1992. An outstanding collection of essays by leading scholars examining the history, organization, and operational tactics of the police.

Wilson, James Q. *Varieties of Police Behavior*. Cambridge, Mass.: Harvard University Press, 1968. A classic study of the styles of policing in different types of communities. Shows the impact of politics on the operations of the force.

# Notes

1 Herman Goldstein, *Policing a Free Society* (Cambridge, Mass.: Ballinger, 1977), 1.

2 Ibid.

3 David H. Bayley, "Comparative Organization of the Police in English-Speaking Countries," in *Modern Policing*, ed. Michael Tonry and Norval Morris (Chicago: University of Chicago Press, 1992), 509–545.

4 Thomas A. Critchley, *A History of Police in England and Wales* (London: T. A. Constable, 1967), 36.

5 Charles Reith, *The Blind Eye of History: A Study of the Origins of the Present Police Era* (London: Faber and Faber, 1952), 128.

6 Peter Manning, *Police Work* (Cambridge, Mass.: MIT Press, 1977), 82.

7 U.S. Department of Justice, National Institute of Justice, *Perspectives on Policing*, "The Evolving Strategy of Policing," by George L. Kelling and Mark H. Moore (November 1988).

8 Hubert Williams and Patrick V. Murphy, "The Evolving Strategy of Police: A Minority View," *Perspectives on Policing*, no. 13 (Washington, D.C.: National Institute of Justice, 1990).

9   Kelling and Moore, "The Evolving Strategy of Policing." For a study of the police in one city see Allen Steinberg, *The Transformation of Criminal Justice: Philadelphia 1800–1880* (Chapel Hill: University of North Carolina Press, 1989).

10  Eric H. Monkkonen, *Police in Urban America, 1860–1920* (Cambridge, England: Cambridge University Press, 1981), 127.

11  Eric Monkkonen, "History of Urban Police," in *Modern Policing*, 554.

12  J. F. Richardson, *Urban Police in the United States* (Port Washington, N.Y.: National University Publications, 1974), 19. Dennis C. Rousey, "Cops and Guns: Police Use of Deadly Force in Nineteenth-century New Orleans," *American Journal of Legal History* 28 (1984): 41–66.

13  Roger McGrath, *Gunfighters, Highwaymen, and Vigilantes: Violence on the California Frontier* (Berkeley: University of California Press, 1984).

14  Frederick Calhoun, *The Lawmen* (Washington, D.C.: Smithsonian Institution Press, 1990).

15  Monkkonen, *Police in Urban America*, 127.

16  For an examination of the impact of technology on police organization see Albert J. Reiss, Jr., "Police Organization in the Twentieth Century," in *Crime and Justice: A Review of Research*, vol. 15, ed. Michael Tonry and Norval Morris (Chicago: University of Chicago Press, 1992), 51–97.

17  Herman Goldstein, *Problem-Oriented Policing* (New York: McGraw-Hill, 1990), 7.

18  Mark H. Moore and George L. Kelling, " 'To Serve and to Protect': Learning from Police History," *Public Interest* (Winter 1983): 55.

19  Mark H. Moore, "Problem-solving and Community Policing," in *Modern Policing*, 99–158.

20  Ibid.

21  James Q. Wilson and George L. Kelling, "Broken Windows: The Police and Neighborhood Safety," *Atlantic Monthly*, March 1982, 29–38.

22  George L. Kelling, "Order Maintenance, the Quality of Urban Life, and Police: A Line of Argument," in *Police Leadership in America*, ed. William A. Geller (New York: Praeger, 1985), 299.

23  Herman Goldstein, "Improving Policing: A Problem-Oriented Approach," *Crime and Delinquency* 25 (1979): 236–257.

24  Malcolm K. Sparrow, Mark H. Moore, and David M. Kennedy, *Beyond 911: A New Era for Policing* (New York: Basic Books, 1990).

25  Lisa M. Reichers and Roy R. Roberg, "Community Policing: A Critical Review of Underlying Assumptions," *Journal of Police Science and Administration* 17 (1990): 105–114.

26  Samuel Walker, " 'Broken Windows' and Fractured History: The Use and Misuse of History in Recent Police Patrol Analysis," *Justice Quarterly* 1 (March 1984): 88.

27 Carl B. Klockars, "Order Maintenance, the Quality of Urban Life, and Police: A Different Line of Argument," in *Police Leadership in America*, ed. Geller, 300.

28 The problem of counting police agencies in the United States is discussed by David H. Bayley, "Comparative Organization of the Police," in *Modern Policing*, 512.

29 U.S. Department of Justice, Bureau of Justice Statistics, *Bulletin* (July 1993), 1.

30 William A. Geller and Norval Morris, "Relations between Federal and Local Police," in *Modern Policing*, 231–348.

31 Malcolm M. Anderson, *Policing the World: Interpol and the Politics of International Police Cooperation* (Oxford: Clarendon Press, 1989).

32 Geller and Morris, "Relations between Federal and Local Police," in *Modern Policing*, 297.

33 Donald A. Torres, *Handbook of State Police, Highway Patrols, and Investigative Agencies* (Westport, Conn.: Greenwood Press, 1987).

34 U.S. Department of Justice, Bureau of Justice Statistics, *Bulletin* (July 1993).

35 Ibid., 9.

36 James Q. Wilson, *Varieties of Police Behavior* (Cambridge, Mass.: Harvard University Press, 1968).

37 Goldstein, *Policing a Free Society*, 35.

38 Wilson, *Varieties of Police Behavior*, 16.

39 Jesse Rubin, "Police Identity and the Police Role," in *Police and the Community*, ed. Robert F. Steadman (Baltimore: Johns Hopkins University Press, 1972), 24.

40  Eric J. Scott, *Calls for Service: Citizen Demand and Initial Police Response*, U.S. Department of Justice (Washington, D.C.: Government Printing Office, 1981), 26–37.

41  U.S. Department of Justice, *Crime in the United States* (Washington, D.C.: Government Printing Office, 1990), 164.

42  Wilson, *Varieties of Police Behavior*, 30.

43  Herbert Jacob, *Urban Justice* (Boston: Little, Brown, 1973), 27.

44  Wilson, *Varieties of Police Behavior*, 33.

45  Murray A. Straus, Richard J. Gelle, and Suzanne K. Steinmetz, *Behind Closed Doors: Violence in the American Family* (Garden City, N.Y.: Anchor Press, 1980), 25–26, 32–36.

46  U.S. Department of Justice, *Crime in the United States* (1990), 39.

47  Lawrence W. Sherman and Richard A. Berk, "The Specific Deterrent Effect of Arrest for Domestic Assaults," *American Sociological Review* 49 (April 1984): 261–272.

48  Ibid. See also Kirk R. Williams and Richard Hawkins, "The Meaning of Arrest for Wife Assault," *Criminology* 27 (February 1989): 163.

49  Franklyn W. Dunford, David Huizinga, and Delbert S. Elliott, "The Role of Arrest in Domestic Assault: The Omaha Police Experiment," *Criminology* 28 (May 1990): 204.

50  Janell Schmidt and Ellen Hockstedler Steury, "Prosecutorial Discretion in Filing Charges in Domestic Violence Cases," *Criminology* 27 (August 1989): 487.

51  U.S. Department of Justice, National Institute of Justice, *Confronting Domestic Violence: A Guide for Criminal Justice Agencies* (Washington, D.C.: Government Printing Office, 1986), 34.

# Police Operations

**The story horrified racially tense Boston. A young white** couple was shot driving to their suburban home through a racially mixed neighborhood after attending a birthing class at Brigham and Women's Hospital. Carol Stuart died soon after the incident. An eight-week premature Christopher Stuart was taken from his mother's dying body but died seventeen days later. Chuck Stuart suffered a gunshot wound. Later he told police that while stopped at an intersection in the racially mixed Mission Hill district, a black man in a jogging suit shot him and his wife, suspecting that they were police undercover agents.

The mayor ordered every available cop into the hunt for the man Stuart had described. Hundreds of black men were stopped and frisked. The search continued for two months until William Bennett was arrested on the basis of information from three teenagers that his nephew had boasted that his uncle had shot the Stuarts. Bennett insisted that he was innocent, but his long rap sheet did not serve him well. Still, the police held off filing formal charges. Meanwhile the Boston news media were having a field day.

Bennett seemed to confirm for many Bostonians the link between African-Americans, drugs, and violence. It was not until Chuck Stuart's brother went to the Boston Police several months later that the story began to unravel. Matthew Stuart said that the night of the shooting he had driven to a prearranged spot in Mission Hill where his brother had given him a bag and told him to "Take this to Revere" (a town outside Boston). Matthew said he saw something on the front seat of Chuck's car but could not identify it. Upon opening the bag he discovered a gun and jewelry. He threw the gun and bag into a river. Chuck Stuart committed suicide the day after Matthew contacted the police. The police now believe Stuart killed his wife to collect insurance money.

The Stuart case describes the type of high-profile incident that gets attention. In much of America, law enforcement agencies are placed in difficult positions as they attempt to deal with crime, violence, racial tensions, and drugs. Chapter 5 focuses on police operations—the actual work of police agencies as they pursue offenders and prevent crimes. Because of the demands on them, the police must be organized so that patrol efforts can be coordinated, investigations conducted, arrests made, evidence assembled, and crimes solved. All of this must be accomplished within the rules laid down by the law.

## Questions for Inquiry

- How are the police organized?
- What three factors influence police response?
- What are the distinguishing functions of police patrol, investigation, and specialized operations units?
- What are the legal mandates that guide police actions?

## Organization of the Police

Because of the highly decentralized nature of policing in the United States, police departments vary in organization and service activities. While the majority of police officers are employed by departments with more than one thousand officers, a majority of departments have fewer than thirty officers each. One might think that population and crime levels would dictate the size of a police force, yet, as seen in Figure 5.1, these variables are not always related. For example, the Dallas police force is small relative to the population, but its index offenses are high; in contrast, Washington, D.C.'s index offenses rank in the middle range of the cities studied, but its police force is the largest. Such factors as the density of population, the number of nonresidents who spend part of their day working or visiting in a jurisdiction, local politics, and other pressures from the community influence the size of the force. In sum, there is really no one model or typical police agency with reference to functions, staffing, and resources.

Police departments have traditionally been organized in a military manner. A structure of ranks—from patrol officer to sergeant, lieutenant, captain, and up to chief—helps designate the authority and responsibility of each level within the organization. Like that of the military, this operations model is designed to emphasize superior-subordinate relationships so that discipline, control, and accountability are primary values. This emphasis is considered important both to mobilize police resources efficiently and to ensure that civil liberties are protected. The belief is that police objectives can be achieved most easily, effectively, and satisfactorily when the principles related to this framework are applied. A well-organized police department, shown in Figure 5.2, is structured to fulfill five functions:

1 Apportion the work load among members and units according to a logical plan.

2 Ensure that lines of authority and responsibility are as definite and direct as possible.

3 Specify a unity of command throughout so that there is no question as to which orders should be followed.

4 Place responsibility accompanied by commensurate authority with accountability.

5 Coordinate the efforts of members and units so that all will work harmoniously to accomplish the mission.

In large cities, not all policing activities can be physically carried out from a central office. As a result, districts or precincts are created so that most operations affecting particular geographical areas can function within them. The patrol and traffic divisions tend to be dispersed throughout the city, while specialized units work out of headquarters.

A major police department contains a separate functional division for each of the operational units: patrol, investigation, traffic, vice, and

**Figure 5.1**
**Sworn officers and index offenses per 1,000 population, in thirteen American cities**
These major cities have varying numbers of police officers and crimes per every 1,000 residents. As you can see, the amount of crime and numbers of police do not always correlate.

SOURCE: *Issues Paper, Metropolitan Police Department Resource Allocation* (Washington, D.C.: Police Executive Research Forum, 1990).

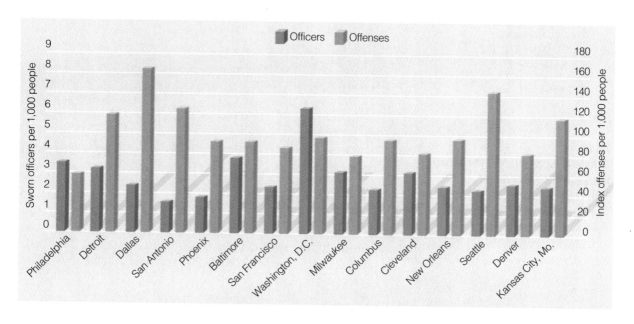

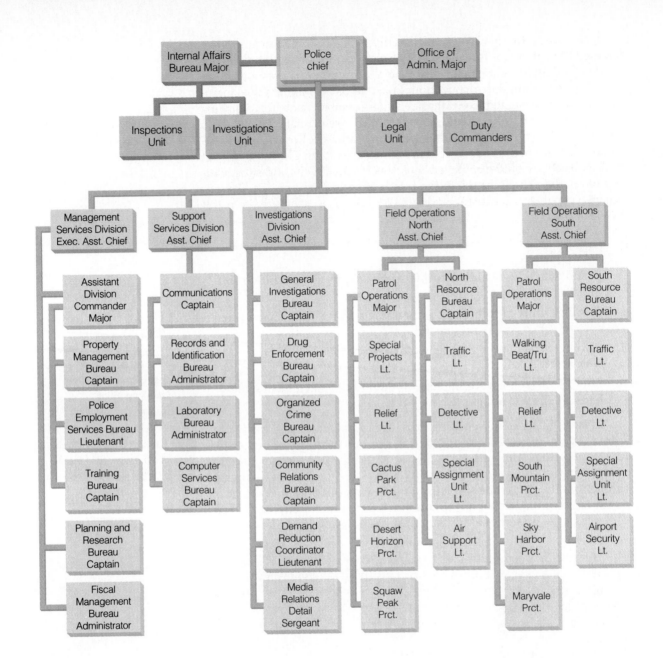

**Figure 5.2**
**Structural organization of the Phoenix,**
**Arizona, Police Department**
This is a typical police organization. Note the major divisions of
patrol, special operations, investigations, and management and
technical services. The administration of the internal affairs bureau
is closely tied to the chief.

SOURCE: City of Phoenix, Arizona, Police Department, *Annual Report, 1990.*

Police executives must set a style of law enforcement that fits the expectations of the community. What style of policing is desired in your community?

juvenile. These units perform the basic tasks of crime prevention and control. The patrol and investigation (detective) units are the core of the modern department. Patrol is traditionally the basic action arm of the police and deals with a wide range of functions, including preventing crime, apprehending offenders, arbitrating domestic quarrels, helping the ill, and assisting at the site of accidents. The investigation division is a specialized unit concerned primarily with apprehension and conviction of the perpetrators of more serious crimes. The separation of patrol and investigation sometimes complicates the definition of objectives, functions, and responsibilities of each unit. While the investigation unit usually concentrates on murder, rape, and major robberies, the patrol division has joint responsibility for investigating those crimes and also is responsible for investigation of lesser crimes, which of course are far more numerous.

Many departments have a traffic unit, but usually only police forces in middle-size to large cities maintain specialized vice and juvenile units. Vice is sometimes kept as part of the investigation unit, but because operations in this field present the risk of corruption, the specialized unit reports directly to the chief in some departments. Some cities have specialized units working only on drug enforcement. In large departments an internal affairs section, generally reporting directly to the chief, investigates charges of corruption and other disciplinary issues associated with the staff and officers. The juvenile unit is concerned primarily with crime prevention as it relates to young people. As with the other specialized units, the carrying out of its responsibilities depends upon close coordination with the patrol division.

## Police Response and Action

As we saw in Chapter 4, the police in a democracy are organized mainly to be *reactive* (citizen-invoked) to calls for service rather than *proactive* (police-invoked). Only in dealing with crimes without victims and traffic violations do law officers look for crime violations. Studies of mobilizations in urban areas substantiate the reactive nature of police work. They indicate that 81 percent of actions result from citizen telephone calls, 14 percent are initiated in the field by an officer, and 5 percent are initiated by people who request service in the field. Such a distribution not only influences the organization of a department but also, to a great extent, determines the way the police can respond to a case.

Because the police are primarily reactive they are usually able to arrive at the scene only after the crime has been committed and the perpetrator has fled. The job of finding the guilty party is thus hampered by the time lapse and the frequent unreliability of the information the victim supplies. In about one-third of calls no citizen is present when the police arrive to handle a complaint. To a large extent, then, reports by victims and observers define the boundaries of policing. Citizens have come to expect that the police will respond quickly to *every* call, not differentiating between those that require immediate attention and those that can be handled in a more routine manner. This has the effect of what is called "incident-driven policing."[1]

In some circumstances, however, the police do employ proactive strategies, relying on surveillance and undercover work to obtain the required information. Lacking complainants in traffic offenses and crimes without victims, the police must rely on informers, stakeouts, wiretapping, stings, and raids. Given the current focus on drug offenses, in many cities police resources have been reallocated so that a greater effort is being made to find and arrest those using or selling narcotics. Thus, proactively produced crime rates are nearly always rates of arrest rather than rates of known criminal acts. The result is a direct correlation between the crime rate for these proactive operations and the allocation of police personnel.

Three factors characterize the organizational context within which police actions and decisions are determined. First, the police stand as the essential gateway to the justice system, through which raw materials enter to be processed. They have the discretion not to arrest and to filter out cases they feel should not be forwarded. Those cases sent to the prosecutor for charging and then to the courts for adjudication begin with an individual officer's decision that probable cause exists to arrest. How the officer makes the arrest and collects supporting evidence to justify the action greatly influences the decisions of the prosecutor and judge.

Second, the administrative decision making of the police is structured by the fact that the ultimate fate of one group of clients (the accused) rests with other clients (prosecutor and judge). The police may introduce clients into the system, but the outcome of a case is largely in the hands of others. That the others are members of the legal profession and of higher social status than the police creates a potential for conflict.

Third, the police are in an odd situation because, although they are expected to act in accordance with a code of ethics, possess authority, and may decide the fate of clients, they must function within a chain of command. As part of a bureaucracy, they are expected to observe rules and follow the orders of superiors—all the while exercising professional discretion. They are duty-bound both to stay in line and to be responsible for independent decisions. To understand the impact of these organizational factors on the daily activities of the police, we will examine organizational response and productivity.

## Organizational Response

Although the police depend primarily on citizens for input into the criminal justice system, the nature of the police response is greatly influenced by the organizational character of the police bureaucracy. Through the functional structure of the operational divisions (patrol, vice, investigation, and so on), the quasi-military command system, and the various incentives used to induce the desired responses, the administrative environment influences how calls for actions are processed and how the police respond.

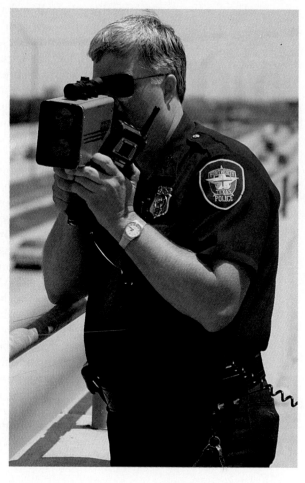

Technological advances, such as this laser radar gun, have brought dramatic changes to most police departments.

Police organizations are increasingly shaped by innovations in communications technology. These developments have led to a growing centralization both of command and control in departments and of decision making. The core of modern police departments is the communications center, where decisions are made to activate officers. Patrol officers are expected to be in constant contact with headquarters and are required to report each of their actions. Extensive use of the two-way radio has been a primary means for police administrators to limit the discretion of officers in the field. Whereas patrol officers might have once administered their own version of on-the-spot justice to a mischievous juvenile, now they may be expected to file a report, take the delinquent into custody, and initiate formal proceedings.

In most cities citizens can report crimes or call for information or assistance through the standardized 911 telephone number. The 911 system has resulted in many departments being inundated with calls, many of which are not directly related to police responsibilities. To improve efficiency, police departments use **differential response** strategies to calls for service. Such strategies are based on the premise that it is not always necessary to rush a patrol car to the scene when a call is received. A dispatcher

**differential response**
A patrol strategy that prioritizes calls for service and assigns various response options.

receives the call and asks for facts about the crime or need for service so that the most appropriate response can be made. The alternative response chosen depends on several factors, such as whether the incident is in progress, has just occurred, or occurred some time ago and whether anyone is or could be injured. The dispatcher may send an officer immediately to the scene, may assign a lower priority so that the response is delayed, may send nonsworn personnel to the scene, or may refer the caller to another agency. A delayed response is often just as effective as a very prompt one and callers are often satisfied as long as they know what to expect.

Studies have shown the effectiveness of differential police response. In Greensboro, North Carolina, 46.4 percent of all calls were categorized as eligible for a response other than the immediate dispatch of a patrol car; similar results were found in other test sites.[2] Differential police response permits resources to be saved because patrol units are not diverted to nonemergency situations.

The centralization of communications and decision making has not gone unchallenged. Many advocates of community policing believe that advancements in technology tend to isolate the police from the citizens they serve. In particular, the extensive use of motorized patrols has meant that residents have only a fleeting glimpse of officers as they cruise through their neighborhoods. In many urban areas the police are perceived as an outside force with little community contact and little knowledge or understanding of the problems peculiar to a neighborhood. In addition, it is argued, officers are not in a position to build a rapport with residents that would increase cooperation. The development of programs for community-oriented policing, discussed later in this chapter, are designed to overcome some of the negative aspects of the typical organizational response.

## Police Productivity

Like other public agencies, the police have difficulty measuring the quantity and quality of their work. How is "good" policing measured? Traditional measures such as the crime rate and the clearance rate do not really give the true picture, and thus nebulous descriptions are used. It is not uncommon to hear a weary patrol officer say when scanning the log at the end of a busy day, "Well, we worked tonight, but we didn't get any activity for the sergeant." What the officer means is that there were no arrests or other actions that show productivity.

Activity is one of the ways in which the police try to measure their work. It is the statistic used by sergeants to judge the productivity of their officers, by lieutenants to assure themselves that the sergeants are properly directing their officers, by captains to show their superiors that their districts are in capable hands, and by the chief to prove to the public that tax money is not being squandered. In most departments, effectiveness is based on actions such as the number of illegally parked cars ticketed, suspects stopped for questioning, arrests made, and the value of stolen goods that are recovered.

But should policing be measured only by such factual criteria as arrests made and cars ticketed? Should officers also be measured by crimes prevented, order maintained, and services rendered? For example, an officer observes from a distance a dispute between a Korean-American merchant and an African-American citizen. Only when the dispute turns violent does the officer move in to stop the violence and arrest both men. The violence leads to increased tensions in the racially mixed neighborhood, but the officer is able to chalk up two arrests. George Kelling asks, "Is this a success? Should the officer and the department be credited for this performance? Or were the arrests really indications of failure?"[3]

Police activity is more easily produced when it is police-invoked (proactive) than when it is citizen-invoked (reactive) because proactive responses allow police to choose their targets. Thus departmental policies concerning offenses such as traffic violations, public drunkenness, and crimes without victims greatly influence the record of police effectiveness. Proactive police work should theoretically show high levels of effectiveness since resources are deployed only when crime violators have been identified.

Productivity has traditionally reflected not only those police actions that were easily measured but also those actions expected by the public. Thus, the crime-fighter (law enforcement) function is more easily measured than the prevention of crime, the calming of community tensions, and the provision of services. To a great extent, crime-fighting statistics influence public support and drive police budgets.

## Delivery of Police Services

A distinction is often made between line and staff functions within police departments. **Line units**, or functions, are those that directly involve operational activities; staff functions supplement or support the line. Staff functions are found in the chief's office and the offices of administration and internal affairs (see Figure 5.2), as well as in the staff inspection bureau. The efficient police department must have a proper balance between line and staff duties so that they can be coordinated into an effective law enforcement, order-maintenance, and service force. The distribution of personnel in a department of the size and structure suggested by Figure 5.2 would probably be 7.5 percent administration, 84 percent operations, and 8.5 percent internal affairs. Within the operations area, the patrol bureau accounts for 55 percent of the personnel; the investigations division, 17 percent; the special operations division, 12 percent; and the specialized units of youth and vice, the remaining 16 percent.[4] Figure 5.3 shows the allocation of line personnel in the nation's six largest departments. The allocation of personnel should *not* be used as an index of importance, because within a department the number of persons required to fulfill a function varies.

We now examine the operations bureau, including the patrol, investigation, traffic, and vice units. As each operational unit is described, consider the work of the unit and its contribution to the overall effectiveness of policing.

**line units**
Police components that perform the direct operations and carry out the basic functions of patrol, investigation, traffic, vice, juvenile, and so on.

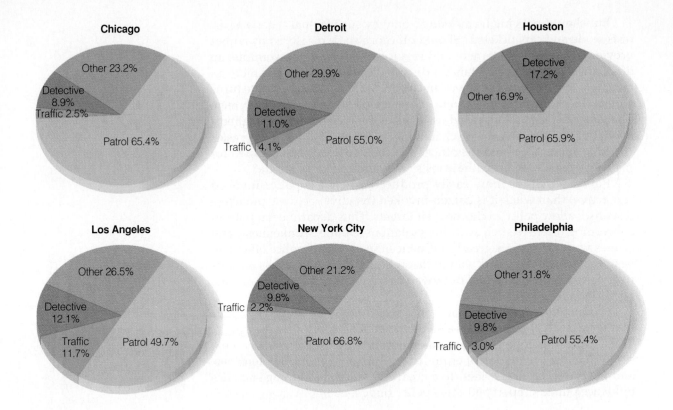

**Chicago**
Other 23.2%
Detective 8.9%
Traffic 2.5%
Patrol 65.4%

**Detroit**
Other 29.9%
Detective 11.0%
Traffic 4.1%
Patrol 55.0%

**Houston**
Detective 17.2%
Other 16.9%
Patrol 65.9%

**Los Angeles**
Other 26.5%
Detective 12.1%
Traffic 11.7%
Patrol 49.7%

**New York City**
Other 21.2%
Detective 9.8%
Traffic 2.2%
Patrol 66.8%

**Philadelphia**
Other 31.8%
Detective 9.8%
Traffic 3.0%
Patrol 55.4%

**Figure 5.3**

**Distribution of sworn police personnel in the nation's six largest departments (1986)**

What does the distribution of officers tell us about the role of the police in urban areas? How might smaller departments differ from these large, urban departments?

SOURCE: Adapted from Anthony Pate and Edwin Hamilton, *The Big Six, Policing America's Largest Departments* (Washington, D.C.: Police Foundation, 1990), 60.

NOTE: Other refers to specialized units such as communications, antiterrorism, administration, and personnel.

**sworn officers**

Police employees who have taken an oath and been given powers by the state to, for example, make arrests, use force, and transverse property, in accordance with their duties.

## Patrol Functions and Activities

Patrol is often called the backbone of police operations. The word *patrol* is thought to be derived from a French word, *patrouiller*, which originally meant "to tramp about in the mud." This translation clearly describes what one authority has called a function that is "arduous, tiring, difficult, and performed in conditions other than ideal."[5]

Every modern police department in the United States has a patrol unit; even in large specialized departments, patrol officers constitute up to two-thirds of all **sworn officers**. In small communities, police operations are not specialized, and the patrol force *is* the department. The patrol officer is the police generalist and must be prepared to assume a wide variety of responsibilities.

The patrol function has three components: answering calls for assistance, maintaining a police presence, and probing suspicious circumstances. Patrol officers are well suited to these activities because they are near the scene of most situations and can render timely help or move speedily to apprehend a suspect. When not responding to calls, they engage in preventive patrol—that is, making the police presence known—on the assumption that doing so will deter crime. Walking the streets of a neighborhood or cruising in a vehicle through the beat, the patrol officer is constantly on the lookout for suspicious people and behavior. As you read the Close-Up, "Saturday Night in a Squad Car" (pages 176–177), note the variety of actions by the officers in car 120 during their shift.

The object of the patrol function is to disperse the police in ways that eliminate or reduce opportunities for lawbreaking and that increase the likelihood a criminal will be caught while committing a crime or soon thereafter. Patrol officers also perform the important function of helping to maintain smooth relations between police and community. As the most visible members of the criminal justice system, they have a decisive effect on the willingness of citizens to cooperate in an investigation. In addition, their effective work can help to create a sense of security among citizens.

As the essential action arm of policing, patrol forces are engaged in a variety of activities, including preventing crime, maintaining order, arresting offenders, and aiding citizens. Performing these activities as part of their basic responsibility of responding to calls and making rounds on the streets may sound fairly straightforward, but it is complex in practice. There are many crucial actions an officer must perform at a crime scene, including the ways in which the officer confronts the situation, makes discretionary decisions, interacts with citizens, uses skill and imagination when conducting the investigation, questions suspects, interviews complainants and witnesses, and searches the crime scene and preserves physical evidence. How each patrol officer carries out these tasks is an indication of the quality of service rendered by the whole department.[6] (The division of patrol time in Wilmington, Delaware, is illustrated in Figure 5.4.)

One problem of modern police administration is that too often the patrol unit is taken for granted. Because the rank of patrol officer is close to the entry level for recruits, greater status is accorded detectives in the investigation unit. In addition, patrol work is viewed as cold, sometimes dirty, boring, and thankless. Yet patrol officers must carry the major burden of the criminal justice system. They must "confront the enraged husband, the crazed drug addict, the frightened runaway, the grieving mother, the desperate criminal, and the uninformed, apathetic, and often hostile citizen."[7] Because the patrol officer's job involves the most sensitive contact with the public, it is important that the most qualified officers do this work. Unfortunately, the low status of patrol assignments encourages officers to seek more prestigious work in their departments.

**Figure 5.4**
**Percentage of time allocated to various patrol activities by the police of Wilmington, Delaware**
The time spent on various activities was calculated by analyzing activity records for each police car unit. Note the range of activities and the time allocated for each.

SOURCE: Jack R. Greene and Carl B. Klockars, "What Police Do," in *Thinking about Police*, 2d ed., ed. Carl B. Klockars and Stephen D. Mastrofski (New York: McGraw-Hill, 1991), 279.

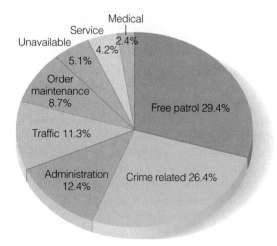

*Free Patrol:* park and walk

*Crime related:* officer in trouble, suspicious person/vehicle, crime in progress, alarm, investigate crime not in progress, service warrant/subpoena, assist other police

*Administration:* meal break, report writing, firearms training, police vehicle maintenance, at headquarters, court related

*Traffic:* accident investigation, parking problems, motor vehicle driving problems, traffic control, fire emergency

*Order maintenance:* order maintenance in progress, animal complaint, noise complaint

*Service:* service related

*Medical:* medical emergency, at local hospital

## Saturday Night in a Squad Car

Car 120 covers an area one-half mile wide by one mile long in the heart of downtown Minneapolis. Bisecting the district along its long axis is Hennepin Avenue, a street lined with bars, nightclubs, and movie theaters. South of Hennepin Avenue lie the shopping and business areas of Minneapolis; north of Hennepin are warehouses and older office buildings. At the east end of the district lies the Mississippi River, and along it, just north of Hennepin Avenue, is the Burlington Northern Railway Station. That portion of the district is heavily populated with derelict alcoholics.

**6:45** We saw some derelicts drinking wine, and the officers forced them to pour the wine out.

**7:00** 9 West Franklin, Apt., unwanted guest. The caretakers of the apartment building advised us that the ex-husband of one of their tenants was threatening harm to the tenant and abduction of the tenant's child. He had also threatened the babysitter. We determined the kind of car that the ex-husband was driving. The tenant then returned with a friend and asked us to keep out of the area so that her husband would not be afraid to find her. She then hoped to tell him that the divorce was final and that he ought not to bother her any more.

**7:50** Cassius Bar, fight. It had been settled by the time we arrived.

**7:58** Cafe, domestic. A twenty-year-old girl and her sister-in-law met us and advised us that the girl's stepfather, the proprietor of the cafe, had let the air out of the tires of the girl's car. He had also pulled loose some wires under the hood and then blocked their car with his. All of this had occurred in the cafe's parking lot. She also claimed that he had hit her. We talked to the stepfather and mother of the girl, and they said that they had taken this action in order to prevent the girl from driving to Wisconsin until she had cooled down. They claimed that she had had a fight with her husband, that she wanted to get away by driving to see her grandmother in Wisconsin, and that she was too emotionally upset to drive. This was apparently evidenced by the fact that she was willing to take her baby with her in only a short-sleeved shirt. The mother also told us that the girl was a bad driver with many arrests and that the car wasn't safe. The officers advised the girl that she call a tow truck and that, if she wished, she could sign a complaint against her parents in the morning. We then left.

**8:28** Cafe, "settle it this time." The sister-in-law claimed that she had been verbally abused by the stepfather. The officers decided to wait until the tow truck arrived. The stepfather moved the car that was blocking. The parents of the girl began to criticize the officer in sarcastic terms, saying such things as "Isn't it a shame that the police have nothing better to do than to spend hours helping to start a car." They also threatened not to give half-price food to police officers any more. The tow truck arrived and reinflated the tires of the car. However, the tow truck driver was unable to start the car. The stepfather, although advised by one of the officers not to do so, tried to move his car in a position to block his daughter's car. The officer at that point booked him for reckless driving and failure to obey a lawful police order. The officer had the stepfather's car towed away. Another squad

Television has given citizens an image of the patrol officer as rushing from one incident to another and making several arrests during the course of a tour. Research has shown, however, that most officers, on most duty tours, do not make even one arrest.[8] Taking formal measures against lawbreakers is clearly only a small part of patrol activity. Patrol officers are expected to be constantly "on guard," watching for suspicious persons and behaviors, providing information and assistance to the public. Because of their ability to exercise discretion, officers can handle situations without invoking formal processes. Patrol officers serve the public's need for security and assistance; their presence in a neighborhood or community, especially if they are on foot, is a major factor in reducing the fear of crime.

Historically, patrolling was done on foot, but with the development of the automobile, most patrol work is now carried out in squad cars. This

car came to sit on the situation until the tow truck had moved the girl's car to a service station. We took the stepfather to jail, where he immediately arranged to bail himself. The stepfather said that he was going right back. The officer replied, "We can book you more than you've got money." As soon as we left the police station, we went back to the parking lot and found that the girl's car had been started and that she had left town.

**9:55** Spruce, Apt., unwanted guest. The tenant told us that she had been ill and that she had not opened the door when her landlady knocked. The landlady then had opened the door and walked in. The officers [told] the landlady, "You can't just walk in. You are invading her privacy." The landlady replied, "The hell I can't, you damned hippie-lover. I'm going to call the mayor." "Go ahead," the officer said. He then added, "The next time this happens, we will advise the tenant to use a citizen's arrest on you."

**10:35** We saw a woman crying outside a downtown bar and a man with his hands on her. We stopped but were told by both that this was merely a domestic situation.

**10:50** The officers saw a drunk in an alley, awakened him, and sent him on his way.

**10:55** We saw a door open in a downtown automobile dealership. When we checked, we learned that all the employees were there to carry out an inventory.

**11:15** We noticed an elderly man in a car talking to a number of rather rough-looking motorcycle types. We stopped and learned from the motorcyclists that the man was very intoxicated. They offered to drive the car for him to a parking spot, and the officers allowed them to do this. The man was told by the officers to sleep off his drunk condition, and the officers took the keys from the car and threw them into the trunk so that he would be unable to drive further that evening.

**11:45** 15th and Hawthorne, gang fight. When we arrived, the officers from two other squad cars were busy booking some young men. The officers believed that occupants of the top floor of the building adjoining this corner had been throwing things at them. When the landlord refused admittance to that building, the officers broke the door down. The apartment from which the objects had been thrown was locked, and the tenants refused admittance. Again, the officers broke down the door and booked the occupants.

**12:25** Nicollet Hotel, blocked alley. By the time we arrived, the car which had blocked the alley had been driven away.

**12:55** 11th and LaSalle, take a stolen [police radio slang]. We made a report of a stolen automobile.

**1:22** We saw one woman and two men standing outside an apartment building. The men appeared to be fighting. One man and the woman said that the other man was bothering them. We sent him away. The couple then went into an apartment building. As we drove away, we saw the man who had been sent returning and trying to obtain entrance to the apartment building. We returned and booked him as a public drunk.

**1:45** Continental Hotel, see a robbery victim. We took a report from a young man who had been robbed at knife point. We drove around the neighborhood looking, without success, for his assailant.

SOURCE: Joseph M. Livermore, "Policing," *Minnesota Law Review* 55 (1971): 672–674. Reprinted by permission.

change has created a problem of supervision and accountability. Even with modern communications and departmental policies requiring officers to check with superiors concerning their actions, it is not possible to know everything that takes place.

Methods of allocating patrol officers and arriving at decisions about various means of transportation and communications have been a subject of research during the past decade. Though the results of these studies are not definitive, they have caused police specialists to rethink some traditional aspects of patrolling.

Attempts to change police practices have not always been successful because patrol methods that may appear to researchers to be the most effective often run counter to the desires of departmental personnel. We next examine some of the issues now affecting police administrators as they use their patrol forces both to control crime and to meet community needs: (1) allocation of patrol personnel, (2) preventive patrol, (3) response time, (4) foot patrol versus motorized patrol, (5) one-person versus two-person patrol units, (6) aggressive patrol, (7) community-oriented policing, and (8) special populations.

**Allocation of Patrol Personnel**   It has traditionally been assumed that patrol officers should be assigned where and when they will be most effective in preventing crime, maintaining order, and serving the public. This assumption poses a basic question for the police administrator: Where should I send the troops, and in what numbers? There are no precise guidelines to answer this question, and most allocation decisions seem to be based on the assumption that patrols should be concentrated in areas where the crime is occurring or in "problem" neighborhoods. Thus, crime statistics, the degree of industrialization, pressures from business people and community groups, ethnic composition, and socioeconomic characteristics are the major factors determining the distribution of police resources.

Many citizens victimized by crime near their homes believe that crime is distributed randomly and that there are no safe places—that danger lurks everywhere. Research, however, has challenged this assumption by pointing to the fact that crime "hot spots" may be identified in various cities. The research indicates that direct-contact predatory violations will occur when three elements converge: (1) motivated offenders, (2) suitable targets, and (3) the absence of capable guardians against the violation.[9] In a study of Minneapolis, researchers found that a relatively few "hot spots"—identified as corresponding to a place, defined as a street address or a street intersection—produced most calls to the police. By analyzing the location of these calls it was possible to identify the places that produced the most crime.[10] With this knowledge, officers can be assigned to **directed patrol** to give special proactive attention to the hot spot area. It remains to be seen if such increased police pressure reduces crime or merely shifts it to another neighborhood.[11]

**Preventive Patrol**   It has long been held that **preventive patrol** is an important deterrent to crime. Since the days of Peel it has been argued that a patrol officer moving through an area prevents criminals from committing illegal acts. The visible presence of officers on foot and in patrol cars and the rapid arrival of police at crime scenes are thought to be part of effective law enforcement techniques.

These assumptions were tested in Kansas City, Missouri, with surprising results. A fifteen-beat area was divided into three sections, with careful consideration given to ensuring similarity in crime rates, population characteristics, income levels, and calls for police service. In one section, designated "reactive," all preventive patrol was withdrawn, and the police entered only in response to citizens' calls for service. In another section, labeled "proactive," preventive patrol was raised as much as four times the normal level, and all other services were provided at the pre-experimental levels. The third section was used as a control, and the department maintained the usual level of services, including preventive

**directed patrol**
A patrol strategy designed to direct resources in a proactive manner against known high-crime areas.

**preventive patrol**
Providing regular protection to an area while maintaining a mobile police presence to deter potential criminals from committing crimes.

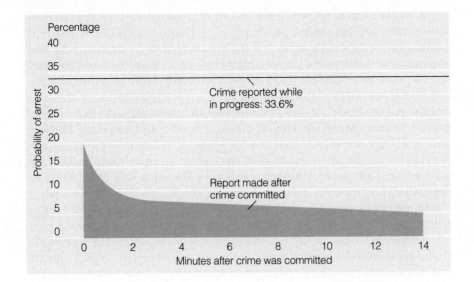

**Figure 5.5**
**Probability of arrest as a function of elapsed time after crime**
The probability of arrest declines sharply when the incident is not reported to the police within seconds. What does this mean with regard to patrol policies?

SOURCE: William Spelman and Dale Brown, "Calling the Police: Citizen Reports of Serious Crime" (Washington, D.C.: Police Executive Research Forum, 1981), 64. Reprinted by permission.

patrol. The researchers concluded that there were no significant differences in the amount of crime reported, the amount of crime measured by citizen surveys, or the extent to which citizens feared criminal attack.[12] The authors of the study also found that although 60 percent of officer time in all three sections was available for active patrolling, only 14.2 percent was actually spent in this manner. The officers were primarily engaged in administrative chores such as report writing and in other matters unrelated to patrolling.

Those who support the professional crime-fighting model of policing have criticized this and other studies of preventive patrol, claiming they attack the heart of police work. But the research simply called into question the inflexibility of traditional preventive patrol. The findings have been integral in leading many departments to shift their focus to greater attention on maintaining order and serving the community.

**Response Time**   With most officers in squad cars and with most citizens having ready access to a telephone, modern patrol tactics are based on the assumption that calls for assistance arrive at a central dispatching section of the department and from there officers will be directed to the site of the incident. It has been argued that because motorized officers are patrolling an area, they can respond rapidly to a call for help.

Several studies have measured the impact of police response time on the ability of officers to intercept a crime in progress and arrest the criminal. In what is now regarded as a classic study, William G. Spelman and Dale K. Brown found that the police were successful in only 29 of 1,000 cases, and it made little difference whether they arrived in two minutes or twenty. As Figure 5.5 indicates, the crucial factor was the speed with which citizens called the police.[13] Detractors of motorized patrols say that the value of the automobile's range, flexibility, and speed is lost when citizens are the delaying factor.

If the problem of response time is one of citizen delay, it might be possible to develop education programs or technological innovations that would reduce reporting time, but it appears that such strategies would not appreciably improve crime control through arrest. As Spelman and Brown point out, there are three major reasons for delay in calling the police. Some people find the situation *ambiguous*; they want to make sure that the police should be called. Others are so busily engaged in *coping activities*—taking care of the victim, directing traffic, and generally helping out—that they are unable to leave the scene. Still others experience *conflict* that they must first resolve; they may avoid an immediate decision or may seek the advice of someone else before placing a call. In addition to these decision-making delays, there are communication problems: a phone may not be readily available, the person may not know the correct number to call, and the police dispatcher may not be cooperative.

Although citizen delay is a major problem, as Figure 5.6 shows, its elimination would only marginally increase police ability to make an arrest. In about three-quarters of crime calls the police are reactive, in that the offenses (burglary, larceny, and the like) are "discovered" long after they have occurred. A much smaller portion are "involvement" crimes (robbery, rape, assault), which the victims know about immediately and can call the police.[14]

**Foot Patrol Versus Motorized Patrol**   One of the most frequent requests of citizens is that the officer be put back on the beat. Citizens and some researchers claim that patrol officers in squad cars have become remote from the people they protect and less attentive to the beat. It has been argued that the officer in the patrol car leads to ineffective policing since there is not an opportunity to know the neighborhood well. As Lawrence W. Sherman says, the rise of motorized patrols and telephone dispatching has changed the older strategy of "watching to prevent crime" to "waiting to respond to crime."[15] Because the officer rarely leaves the patrol car, citizens have few chances to tell the officer what is going on in the community: "who is angry at whom about what, whose children are running wild, what threats have been made, and who is suddenly living above his apparent means."[16] Without this information, the patrol officer cannot truly know the "neighborhood's citizens: being distant, the public seems both unreliable and uncontrollable."[17] As Mark Moore points out, "The price is that citizens, and particularly those who are afraid, do not call the police and, instead, absorb their losses and live with their fears."[18]

By contrast, an officer on foot is at home in the neighborhood and can more readily spot circumstances and people that warrant investigation. When patrol officers are close to the daily life of the beat, they are better positioned to detect criminal activity and to apprehend those who have violated the law. Furthermore, when patrol officers are familiar faces, they are less likely to be perceived as symbols of oppression by minority residents; this factor may help to lessen the intensity of any racial upheavals.

Until the 1930s, foot patrol was the dominant focus for police activity. As part of the professional crime-fighting model promoted by O. W. Wilson and others, motorized patrol came to be viewed as more effective. Officers on foot are seen as limited in their ability to respond, especially

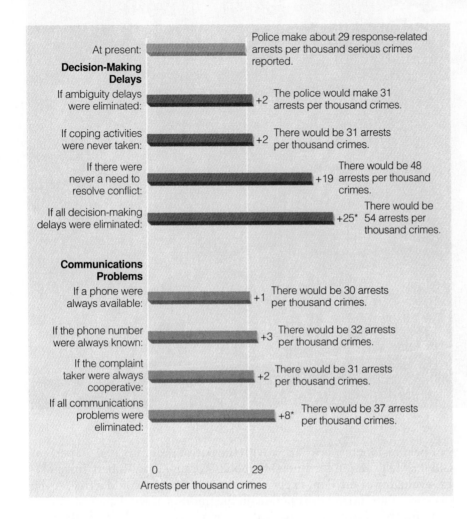

At present:

**Decision-Making Delays**

If ambiguity delays were eliminated: +2

If coping activities were never taken: +2

If there were never a need to resolve conflict: +19

If all decision-making delays were eliminated: +25*

**Communications Problems**

If a phone were always available: +1

If the phone number were always known: +3

If the complaint taker were always cooperative: +2

If all communications problems were eliminated: +8*

Police make about 29 response-related arrests per thousand serious crimes reported.

The police would make 31 arrests per thousand crimes.

There would be 31 arrests per thousand crimes.

There would be 48 arrests per thousand crimes.

There would be 54 arrests per thousand crimes.

There would be 30 arrests per thousand crimes.

There would be 32 arrests per thousand crimes.

There would be 31 arrests per thousand crimes.

There would be 37 arrests per thousand crimes.

0          29

Arrests per thousand crimes

**Figure 5.6**
**Potential increases in response-related arrests by eliminating key causes of delay**
Although emphasis has been on creating opportunities for citizens to call the police quickly (through 911 numbers), research has shown that a major factor in police response time is the observer's delay in recognizing that a crime has been committed and that the police should be called.

SOURCE: William G. Spelman and Dale K. Brown, *Calling the Police: Citizen Reporting of Serious Crime* (Washington, D.C.: Police Executive Research Forum, 1984), xxix.

NOTE: Even if all reporting delays could be eliminated, no more than 70 crimes per thousand could result in response-related arrests.

*a*The total is more than the sum of the individual savings because of the nonlinear nature of the relationship between reporting time and arrest.

where weather and other conditions impede their actions. Squad cars increase the territory that officers can patrol, and with two-way radios officers can be quickly deployed to the sites where their assistance is needed. Wilson believed that motorized officers would still observe, talk to, and constantly interact with citizens. He thought that patrol officers would use their cars to get to a location and then walk on foot throughout their beat. He did not see them as remaining in their vehicles for most of their tour, isolated from the community. A recent study of large cities shows that almost 94 percent of patrol time is taken up by motorized patrol.[19]

The past decade has seen a revival of interest in foot patrol, mainly in response to citizens' demands for a familiar figure walking their neighborhoods. Experiments have been carried out in several cities to test the cost and impact of foot patrol.[20] In general, these studies have shown that foot patrols do not greatly reduce crime but that citizens are pleased with it and fear crime less.[21]

The best evidence that citizens want foot patrols is probably seen in the experience of Flint, Michigan, where citizens voted to increase taxes in order to extend foot patrol to the entire city. Sixty-four percent of the

When officers become familiar faces in the neighborhood they can rely on citizen cooperation in helping to control crime.

foot-beat residents were happy with the patrol program, and 70 percent said they felt safer in their neighborhoods because of it. Robert Trojanowicz, evaluator of the Flint experiment on foot patrols would agree. As he has said, "Patrolmen who operate [in the traditional way] are just motorized officers without a car. Basically, they're doorshakers. But when the officer becomes actively involved in the community, that's when crime problems begin to be solved."[22]

**One- Versus Two-Person Patrol Units**   As in the controversy over beat patrol officers, the question of one- or two-person patrol units has raged in police circles. A 1991 study of large cities revealed that 70 percent of patrol cars are staffed by one officer, although there is much variation throughout the country. For example, Los Angeles uses one-person cars for about half of the units during the day, but only 9 percent at night. Philadelphia, however, uses only one-officer cars.[23]

Although the two-person squad car appears to be uneconomical, officers and their union leaders argue that safety requires the second person. On the other side, police administrators contend that the one-person squad car is much more cost-effective, enabling more cars to be deployed. Thus each car can cover a smaller geographic sector, more sectors of the city can be covered, and response time can be decreased. A further belief is that an officer operating alone is more alert, because he or she cannot be distracted by idle conversation with a fellow officer.

Research on this issue has been conducted in a number of cities.[24] What is clear is that with so many questions of organization and personnel, factors other than effectiveness and efficiency come into play. In specific cities, policies must be developed through negotiations among individual police chiefs, the leadership of the patrol officers union, and the political leaders of the funding agency. Even with these problems it seems that one-person cars are becoming more common.

**Aggressive Patrol**   **Aggressive patrol** is a proactive strategy that takes a wide variety of forms, from programs that encourage citizens to identify their valuables, to "sting" operations, to repeat offender programs. James Q. Wilson and Barbara Boland have shown that patrol tactics that increase the risk of arrest are associated with crime reduction. They argue that the effect of the police on crime depends less on how many officers are deployed in a particular area and more on what they do while they are there.[25]

An aggressive strategy allows officers to maximize the number of interventions and observations in the community. That does not mean they are encouraged to patrol in a hostile manner, for such tactics could have the effect of merely arousing the community.

In San Diego it was found that an aggressive patrol strategy of field interrogations and street stops was associated with a significant decrease in certain "suppressible" crimes: robbery, burglary, theft, auto theft, assault, sex crimes, malicious mischief, and disturbances. It was concluded that field interrogations deterred potential offenders, especially young, opportunistic ones.[26] Officers in an "anticrime patrol" in New York worked the streets of high-crime areas in civilian clothes. Although these officers represented only 5 percent of the men and women assigned to each precinct, during one year they made over 18 percent of the felony arrests, including more than half of the arrests for robbery and about 40 percent of the arrests for burglary and auto theft. The Kansas City force adopted procedures to distribute information about the most active burglars and robbers to officers before they went on patrol and created a specialized unit to stake out locations known to be likely targets of criminal activities (the back room of a liquor store, for example).

Repeat offender programs have proved successful in several cities in making conviction-successful arrests of career criminals. Using proactive tactics, the Washington, D.C. Repeat Offender Program targeted individuals with long records who were believed to be engaged in criminal activity. One squad of officers, the "Hunter" squad, focused on warrant targets, especially those sought for violent crimes; the "Trapper" squad initiated long-term investigations to close a large number of cases and to recover stolen property. "Fisherman" squads engaged in a variety of activities—buy/bust, follow-up on tips, warrant arrests, and "cruising" targeted areas for in-process crimes. The program proved to be effective in removing repeat offenders from the streets, but it was also costly because it moved officers away from former duties.[27]

Police antifencing operations, usually referred to as "stings," are a well-recognized and widely used law enforcement technique, particularly with regard to property offenses. Typically a storefront operation is set up, and the police pose as fences and engage in the purchase of stolen

**aggressive patrol**
A patrol strategy designed to maximize the number of police interventions and observations in the community.

property from thieves. As a result, large amounts of property are recovered and thieves are arrested and successfully prosecuted.

Questions regarding the impact of these operations have been raised. Robert Langworthy studied a police auto theft sting in Birmingham, and claims that, with respect to the department's goal of increased publicity and public support, the sting went well.[28] With respect to crime prevention, however, an apparent increase in auto theft may have been associated with the sting operation. He notes that sting operations have associated costs because the police engage in illegitimate behavior, a risk that is perhaps not worth taking.

The most cost-effective strategy for aggressive patrol seems to involve incentives that encourage officers to increase the number of field interrogations and traffic stops. To achieve an aggressive patrol strategy a police executive must recruit certain kinds of officers, train them appropriately, and devise requirements and reward systems (traffic ticket quotas, field interrogation obligations, promotional opportunities) to encourage these officers to follow the intended strategy.[29]

**Community-Oriented Policing**  As mentioned in Chapter 4, the new concept of community-oriented policing has taken hold in many cities. Although a somewhat general term, it is most often associated with attempts by the police to involve communities in making their neighborhoods safe. It recognizes that citizens may be just as concerned about disorder as about crime in their neighborhood. It emphasizes collaboration between police and citizens to determine community needs and the best ways to achieve them.[30] Community-oriented policing has emerged mainly because of perceived deficiencies in the crime-fighter focus of most urban forces that developed in the Professional Era.[31]

Community-oriented policing may be carried out, for example, by the permanent assignment of patrol officers to walk a neighborhood beat so that better relationships with residents can be cultivated, by the creation of police stations within the communities, by police-sponsored youth and elderly activities, and by surveying citizens to ascertain problems and needs. It can also mean that set priorities focus on certain problems affecting particular communities. Likewise, resources may be allocated to increase officers' responsiveness to those they serve.

Associated with community-oriented policing, **problem-oriented policing** tries to ascertain what is causing citizen calls for help.[32] Knowledge of an underlying problem can then be used to enlist community agencies and citizens to resolve the situation. One result is the police consider and respond to a wide variety of problems that affect the quality of life, not just to crime.[33]

Regardless of whether the police focus their resources on order maintenance, law enforcement, or service, they tend to respond to specific incidents. Typically, a citizen call or an officer's field observation triggers a police response to that event. The police are often asked to respond to a rash of similar crime-related incidents in the same location. Because the police traditionally focus on incidents, they do not seek to determine the underlying causes of these incidents. By contrast, those engaged in problem-oriented policing seek to address the underlying causes.

**problem-oriented policing**

An approach to policing in which officers seek to identify, analyze, and respond, on a routine basis, to the underlying circumstances that create the incidents that prompt citizens to call the police.

Two police departments, in Newport News, Virginia, and Baltimore County, Maryland, have gained national recognition for their implementation of problem-oriented policing.[34] Although differing in some respects in their procedures and organization, both departments involve police officers and the community in finding solutions that will reduce crime, disorder, and fear. (The approach is described in the Close-Up "The Problem-Oriented Approach," page 186.) With a problem-oriented approach, supervisors encourage officers to look beyond the department for information in analyzing problems. They urge personnel to talk to residents, business people, offenders, and public officials—anyone who might offer information. They may find that the incidents will cease if street lighting is more intensive, aggressive measures are taken against streetwalkers, or closing hours of a local bar are enforced. Whatever the solution, it usually means enlisting the help of agencies other than those of criminal justice.

Although community-oriented policing has been embraced by the police executives of major cities, the Police Foundation, the Police Executive Research Forum, and nationally known researchers, there have been difficulties with implementing it. As with any reform, traditional methods are difficult to change. Police managers are accustomed to dealing with problems according to established procedures and may believe that their authority is diminished through the decentralization of responsibility to precinct commanders.[35] Community policing does not reduce costs; it requires either the infusion of new money or the redistribution of existing budgets. It is difficult to measure efforts to reduce the fear of crime, solve underlying problems, maintain order, and serve the community. There are questions about the meaning and definition of community.[36] A clear definition of a community's interests may be lacking, especially in racially mixed neighborhoods. Finally, there are questions about the extent to which the police should extend their role beyond crime to deal with social problems.

**Special Populations**   In addition to the problems of crime, urban police forces must deal with a very complex population. On city streets there are an increasing number of people who are mentally ill, homeless, runaways, public inebriates, drug addicts, or infected with HIV. Jail crowding, the deinstitutionalization of mental health facilities, decriminalization of public drunkenness statutes, economic dislocations, and reductions in public assistance programs have all contributed to an increase in the number of "problem" people on the street. Most of these people are not involved in criminal activities, but their presence in the community is disturbing to residents.

Patrol officers must deal with a variety of social service agencies to assist individuals and to respond to order-maintenance requests of the public. The police must walk a very fine line regarding their authority to require individuals to enter a homeless shelter, to obtain medical assistance, or to be taken to a mental health unit.[37] Police departments have developed various organizational approaches to deal with the problem of special populations. In New York City, Los Angeles, and Philadelphia, special mobile units are equipped with restraining devices, mace, and medical equipment to handle disturbed people. Madison, Wisconsin has

## The Problem-Oriented Approach

At 1:32 A.M. a man we will call Fred Snyder dials 911 from a downtown corner phone booth. Officer Knox arrives four minutes later. Snyder says he was beaten and robbed twenty minutes before but didn't see the robber. Under persistent questioning Snyder admits he was with a prostitute, picked up in a bar. Later, in a hotel room, he discovered the prostitute was actually a man, who then beat Snyder and took his wallet.

Snyder wants to let the whole matter drop. He refuses medical treatment for his injuries. Knox finishes his report and lets Snyder go home. Later that day Knox's report reaches Detective Alexander's desk. She knows from experience the case will go nowhere, but she calls Snyder at work.

Snyder confirms the report but refuses to cooperate further. Knox and Alexander go on to other cases. Months later, reviewing crime statistics, the city council deplores the difficulty of attracting businesses or people downtown.

Midnight-watch patrol officers are tired of taking calls like Snyder's [a hypothetical example]. They and their sergeant, James Hogan, decide to reduce prostitution-related robberies, and Officer James Boswell volunteers to lead the effort.

First, Boswell interviews the twenty-eight prostitutes who work the downtown area to learn how they solicit, what happens when they get caught, and why they are not deterred. They work downtown bars, they tell him, because customers are easy to find and police patrols don't spot them soliciting. Arrests, the prostitutes tell Boswell, are just an inconvenience: Judges routinely sentence them to probation, and probation conditions are not enforced.

Boswell works with the Alcoholic Beverage Control Board and local bar owners to move the prostitutes into the street. At police request, the commonwealth's attorney agrees to ask the judges to put stiffer conditions on probation: Convicted prostitutes would be given a map of the city and told to stay out of the downtown area or go to jail for three months.

Boswell then works with the vice unit to make sure that downtown prostitutes are arrested and convicted and that patrol officers know which prostitutes are on probation. Probation violators *are* sent to jail, and within weeks all but a few of the prostitutes have left downtown.

Then Boswell talks to the prostitutes' customers, most of whom don't know that almost half the prostitutes working the street are actually men, posing as women. He intervenes in street transactions, formally introducing the customers to their male dates. The Navy sets up talks for him with incoming sailors to tell them about the male prostitutes and the associated safety and health risks.

In three months, the number of prostitutes working downtown drops from twenty-eight to six and robbery rates are cut in half. After eighteen months neither robbery nor prostitution show signs of returning to their earlier levels.

SOURCE: Adapted from William Spelman and John Eck, National Institute of Justice, "Problem-Oriented Policing," in *Research in Brief* (Washington, D.C.: Government Printing Office, 1987).

educated all officers about special populations and methods of dealing with them. Birmingham, Alabama uses civilian social workers to deal with the mentally ill, freeing the police to respond to other problems.[38]

It is clear that the handling of special populations is a major problem now confronting police in most cities. Each community must develop policies so that police will know when and how they are to intervene in situations where an individual may not have violated the criminal law but is upsetting residents.

To what extent law enforcement should engage in community policing without appearing to be mainly clearing the streets remains a key issue.

**The Future of Patrol**    Preventive patrol and a rapid response to calls for assistance have been hallmarks of policing in the United States for the past half century. Because of this orientation, most patrol officers are in squad cars linked to a dispatcher at the station house. A great deal of contemporary study is focused on patrol, the essential element of American policing.

A heavy orientation toward dispatch and prevention control may have narrowed the roles of the police in the community. But regardless of the type of patrol used—foot or vehicle—the police still depend highly on the community to report crimes, to cooperate with police investigations, and to appear in court as witnesses. Without the public's voluntary participation, the police may patrol indefinitely and have little impact on crime.

The research conducted during the past twenty-five years has perhaps raised as many questions as it has answered. Yet it is apparent that police forces in large cities need to consider a mix of patrol tactics that reflect the demographic and criminogenic characteristics of various neighborhoods. Many researchers believe that patrol operations have focused too narrowly on crime control, to the neglect of the order-maintenance activities for which police departments were originally formed. There is also a new focus on strategies to reduce the fear of crime, which is often out of proportion to the objective risk of a citizen's being victimized. Critics have urged that the police become more community oriented and return to the first principle of policing: "to remain in close and frequent contact with citizens."[39] To see this policy in action, we look to Japan where patrolling is done on foot as described in the Comparative Perspective on the next two pages.

## Investigation

The fictional Sherlock Holmes has long epitomized the detective for the public. With a minimum of clues, an intuitive mind, and a careful application of logic, he and his counterparts in thousands of dramas stalk the criminal until an arrest is made in the final moments. The Holmes model of investigation has been widely copied by scriptwriters for television and the movies. As a result, citizens believe that these fictive accounts portray how the police usually solve crimes.

In the real world, however, the investigative function is not the sole responsibility of one bureau in a police department, let alone of one detective. Patrol, traffic, vice, and sometimes juvenile units contribute. In small town and rural areas, patrol officers perform investigative duties.[40] In urban areas, the patrol unit, because it is normally represented at the scene of the crime, accomplishes much of the preliminary investigative work. The patrol unit's investigation can be crucial; as Figure 5.7 (page 190) indicates, successful prosecution in cases of robbery, larceny, and burglary is closely linked with the speed with which a suspect is arrested. In many incidents, however, the criminal is not immediately apprehended, and an investigation must determine who committed the crime and where that person is. This section looks at the investigative function and at the special police units that are set up to achieve two objectives: the identification and apprehension of offenders and the collection of evidence with which to prosecute them.

Detectives traditionally have enjoyed a prestigious position in police departments. The pay is higher, the hours are more flexible, and the

## Patrol in Japan

Japanese policemen are addressed by the public as *Omawari-san*—Mr. Walkabout. This is an accurate reflection of what the public sees the police doing most of the time. Foot-patrolling is done out of *kobans* [mini police stations in urban neighborhoods], usually for periods of an hour. Patrols are more common at night, when officers work in pairs.... Patrolmen amble at a ruminative pace that allows thorough observation.... Patrolling by automobile, which is much less common than foot patrolling, can be frustrating too. Due to the narrow congested streets of Japanese cities ... patrol cars are forced to move at a snail's pace....

Patrolling is by no means a matter of high adventure. For the most part it consists of watching and occasionally answering questions. Patrolmen rarely discover genuine emergencies; the chance of coincidence between patrolmen and sudden need are simply too great. Patrolling does not reduce reaction time or particularly enhance availability. What patrolling does is to demonstrate the existence of authority, correct minor inconveniences—such as illegally parked cars—and generate trust through the establishment of familiar personal relations with a neighborhood's inhabitants. On patrol, policemen are alert for different kinds of problems in different places. In a residential area they watch for people who appear out of place or furtive. In public parks they give attention to loitering males. Around major railroad stations they look for runaway adolescents, lured by the glamour of a big city, who could be victimized by criminal elements. They also watch for *teyhaishi*—labor contractors—who pick up and sell unskilled laborers to construction companies. In a neighborhood of bars and cabarets, patrolmen stare suspiciously at stylishly dressed women standing unescorted on street corners. They determine whether wheeled carts piled with food or cheap souvenirs are blocking pedestrian thoroughfares. Throughout every city they pay particular attention to illegally parked cars and cars that have been left with their doors unlocked....

When a Japanese policeman is out on patrol he makes a special point of talking to people about themselves, their purposes, and their behavior. These conversations may be innocent or investigatory. The law provides that policemen may stop and question people only if there is reasonable ground for suspecting they have committed or are about to commit a crime or have information about a crime. Nevertheless, standard procedure on patrol is to stop and question anyone whenever the policeman thinks it may be useful. One reason for doing so is to discover wanted persons. And the tactic has proved very effective; 40 percent of criminals wanted by the police have been

Referred to as "Mr. Walkabout," Japanese policemen patrol primarily on foot. In this busy shopping area officers are available to answer questions and deal with emergencies.

discovered by patrolmen on the street. Not only do officers learn to question people adroitly on the street, they become adept at getting people to agree to come to the *koban* so that more extended, less public inquiries can be made. People are under no obligation to do so, any more than they are to stop and answer questions. The key to success with these tactics is to be compelling without being coercive. This in turn depends on two factors: the manner of the police officer and a thorough knowledge of minor laws. The first reduces hostility, the second provides pretexts for opening conversations justifiably. People who park illegally, ride bicycles without a light, or fail to wear helmets when riding a motorcycle are inviting officers to stop them and ask probing questions. The importance with which the police view on-street interrogation is indicated by the fact that prefectural and national contests are held each year to give recognition to officers who are best at it.... Senior officers continually impress upon new recruits the importance of learning to ask questions in inoffensive ways so that innocent people are not affronted and unpleasant scenes can be avoided....

The most striking aspect of the variety of situations confronted by policemen is their compelling, unforced naturalness. The police see masses of utterly ordinary people who have been enmeshed in situations that are tediously complex and meaningful only to the persons immediately involved. The outcomes are of no interest to the community at large; the newspapers will not notice if matters are sorted out or not; superior officers have no way of recording the effort patrolmen expend in trying to be helpful; and the people themselves are incapable by and large of permanently escaping their predicaments. Policemen are responsible for tending these individuals, for showing that they appreciate—even when they are tired, hurried, bored, and preoccupied—the minute ways in which each person is unique. It is perhaps, the greatest service they render.

SOURCE: David H. Bayley, *Forces of Order: Police Behavior in Japan and the United States* (Berkeley: University of California Press, 1979), 33–34, 37, 41, 51–52. Copyright © 1976 The Regents of the University of California. Reprinted by permission.

supervision is more permissive than those of patrol officers. Detectives do not wear uniforms, and their work is considered more interesting than the patrol officer's. In addition to these incentives, they are engaged solely in law enforcement rather than in order maintenance or service work; hence their activities correspond more closely to the image of the police as crime fighters.

**Detective Responsibilities**   Every city with a population over 250,000 and 90 percent of the smaller cities have officers assigned to special investigative duties.[41] Within the investigative unit, detectives are frequently organized by the type of crime they investigate—homicide, robbery, forgery—or by a given geographical area. Reported crimes are automatically referred to the appropriate investigator. Investigative units are normally separated from the patrol chain of command. Many argue that this separation creates duplication of effort and lack of continuity in the handling of cases. It often means that vital pieces of information held by one branch are not known to the other.

Detectives are concerned primarily with law enforcement activities after a crime has been reported and a preliminary investigation held. Their investigative activities depend on the circumstances of the case:

1   When a serious crime occurs and the offender is immediately identified and apprehended, the detective prepares the case for presentation to the prosecuting attorney.

2   When the offender is identified but not apprehended, the detective tries to locate the individual.

3   When the offender is not identified but there are several suspects, the detective conducts investigations aimed at either confirming or disproving her or his suspicions.

4   When there is no suspect, the detective starts from scratch to determine who committed the crime.[42]

In performing the investigative function, detectives depend not only on their own experience but also on the technical expertise in their department or in a cooperating police force. They require information and must therefore rely on criminal files, laboratory technicians, and forensic scientists. Many small departments turn to the state crime laboratory or the FBI for such information when serious crimes have been committed. Detectives are often pictured as working alone, but in fact they are members of a departmental team.

**The Apprehension Process**   Discovery that a crime has been committed is likely to trigger events leading to the capture of a suspect and the gathering of evidence required for the suspect's conviction. Unfortunately, it may also lead to a number of dead ends, ranging from a decision by the victim not to report the crime, to an absence

**Figure 5.7**
**Percentage of convictions from offense to arrest measured by elapsed time**
Note that for each of the offenses the amount of time from the incident to the arrest is a major factor on successful conviction.

SOURCE: U.S. Department of Justice, Bureau of Justice Statistics, *Report to the Nation on Crime and Justice* (Washington, D.C.: Government Printing Office, 1983), 51.

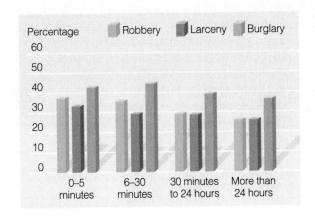

Much of the work of detectives involves the careful collection and documentation of evidence.

of clues pointing to a suspect, or to a lack of evidence linking the suspect to the crime.

As Figure 5.8 shows, the felony apprehension process can be viewed as a sequence of actions in response to the commission of a crime. The actions are designed to mount the resources of criminal justice to bring about the arrest of a suspect and to assemble enough supporting evidence to substantiate a charge, as follows:

**1** *Crime detected*: Information that a crime has been committed usually is in the form of a telephone call by the victim or complainant to the police. The beat patrol officer may also encounter a crime, but usually the police are alerted by others. Police may, for example, be alerted to crime in business premises by automatic security alarms connected to police headquarters; these help shorten response time and increase the likelihood of apprehending the perpetrator.

**2** *Preliminary investigation*: The first law enforcement official on the scene is usually a patrol officer who has been dispatched by radio. The officer is thus responsible for providing aid to the victim, for securing the crime scene for later investigation, and for documenting the initial facts of the crime. If a suspect is present or in the vicinity, the officer conducts a "hot" search and possibly apprehends a suspect. This work is crucial because the information gathered initially is essential. It addresses the basic facts of the crime, including identity of the victim, description of the suspect, and names of the witnesses. After the information is collected, it is transmitted to the investigation unit.

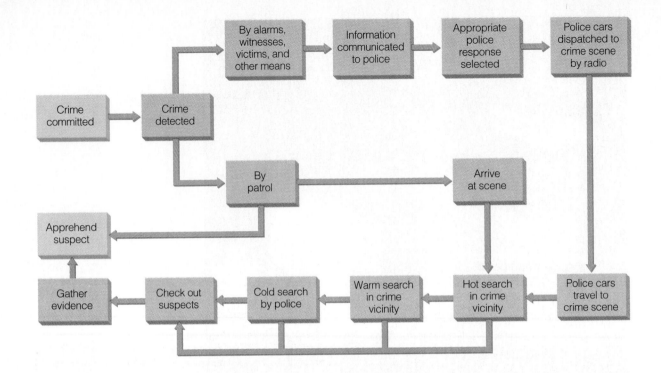

**Figure 5.8**
**The felony apprehension process**

Apprehension of a felony suspect may result from a sequence of actions taken in response to the crime by patrol officers and detectives. Coordination of police response is important in solving major crimes.

**3**  *Follow-up investigation*: After a crime has been detected and a preliminary investigation has been made, a detective determines further action. In a typical big-city department, incident reports from the previous day are analyzed immediately the next morning. Assignments are distributed to individual investigators according to their specialties. These investigators study the information, weigh each informational factor, and determine whether the factors are sufficient to indicate that the crime can be solved.

A study of the Kansas City (Missouri) Police Department showed that although homicide, rape, and suicide received considerable attention, fewer than 50 percent of all reported crimes received more than a minimal half-hour investigation by detectives. In many of these cases, detectives merely reported the facts discovered by the patrol officers during the preliminary investigations.[43]

Detectives must make several discretionary decisions concerning any investigation. As already noted, a decision must be made about whether the preliminary investigation has produced enough information to warrant a follow-up investigation. Decisions also must be made about the crime categories that should receive special attention and whether an investigation should be discontinued. Steven Brandl found that in burglary and robbery follow-up investigations the value of the lost property and the detective's expectation that the case would be resolved through an arrest were the primary factors influencing the amount of time and effort spent in solving the crime.[44]

When a full-scale investigation is thought warranted, a wider search—referred to as a "cold" search—for evidence or weapons is undertaken: witnesses may be reinterviewed, contact made with informants, and evidence assembled for analysis. The pressure of new cases, however, often requires an investigation in progress to be shelved so that resources may be directed at "warmer" incidents.

**4**  *Clearance and arrest*: The decision to arrest is a key part of the apprehension process. In some cases, additional evidence or links between suspects and their associates are not discovered if arrests are premature. A crime is cleared when evidence supports the arrest of a suspect or when a suspect admits having committed other unsolved offenses in department files. Clearance, however, does not mean that the suspect will eventually be found guilty.

**Forensic Techniques**  The use of science to aid investigations in the gathering, identification, and analysis of evidence has long been a part of American police practices. The scientific analysis of fingerprints, blood, semen, hair, textiles, and weapons has helped police in identifying perpetrators of crimes and has aided prosecutors in convincing jurors. Forensic laboratories exist in all states, and many large cities have their own scientists to provide technical assistance.

The development of DNA "fingerprinting" techniques is the latest addition to the detective's tool kit. These techniques are being used to identify people through their distinctive genotypic features. DNA, or deoxyribonucleic acid, is the basic building code for all chromosomes and is the same for all cells in a person's body—skin, blood, organs, and semen. The characteristics of certain segments of DNA vary from person to person, forming an individual genetic "fingerprint" for each. It is thus possible to analyze, for example, hair samples and compare them to those of suspects. Developed in the mid-1980s, DNA typing for law enforcement use has gained much attention. Some researchers, however, believe there is not yet a sound scientific foundation for the approach and claim the method is being used prematurely.[45] Courts in a number of states have accepted DNA results as evidence, although in a New York double-murder case a challenge to its introduction was successful.[46]

The full use of DNA typing has been hampered by too few laboratories equipped to undertake the analysis and general underutilization of forensic techniques. Several earlier studies showed that crime laboratories played a minor role in criminal investigation even though they potentially had great value.[47] The introduction of DNA fingerprinting may have an important impact on future investigations.

While DNA fingerprinting holds great promise, a case in Connecticut illustrates that what may appear to be conclusive evidence to the prosecution might not be so evaluated by a jury. In a rape trial an FBI specialist testified that DNA analysis revealed that the accused had not committed the crime. Rather than rely upon this statement, the jury chose to believe the victim because she seemed so certain in her identification of her assailant and gave a detailed description of the car within which the rape occurred.

**Evaluating the Investigation Function**  Research from a number of studies has raised important questions about the value of investigations and the role of detectives in the apprehension process. This research suggests that the police have overrated the importance of investigation as a means

Forensic science has become a valuable tool in the fight against crime.

of solving crimes and shows that most crimes are cleared because of arrests made by the patrol force at or near the scene. As long ago as 1967, a president's commission noted, "If a suspect is neither known to the victim nor arrested at the scene of the crime, the chances of ever arresting him are very slim."[48] Although detectives investigate most serious crimes, many crimes against persons and a great majority of crimes against property are never cleared, as Figure 5.9 indicates. Response time—the time between commission of the crime and the arrival of the police—becomes an important factor in the apprehension process, as is the information given by the victim or witnesses to the responding patrol officer.

A Rand Corporation study of 153 large police departments found that the major determinant of success in solving crimes was information identifying the perpetrator supplied by the victim or witnesses at the scene. Of those cases not immediately solved but ultimately cleared, most were cleared by such routine procedures as fingerprint searches, receipt of tips from informants, and mug-shot "show-ups." The report emphasizes that special actions by the investigating staff were important in only a very few cases. In summary, the study indicates that about 30 percent of the crimes were cleared by on-scene arrest and another 50 percent by the identification of victims or witnesses when the police arrived. Thus only about 20 percent could have been solved by detective work. But even among this group, the study found that most "were also solved by patrol officers, members of the public who spontaneously provide further information, or routine investigative practices."[49] That the solution to most crimes does not require detective work was substantiated by a study of a suburban department,[50] yet a study of burglaries and robberies in DeKalb County, Georgia, St. Petersburg, Florida, and Wichita, Kansas found that initial investigation by patrol officers followed by detective work was necessary to solve crimes.[51]

If the accumulating evidence should force a reassessment of the role of investigation, what policies might law enforcement officials adopt? The Rand research team suggests a number of reforms, including the following:

1 Reduce follow-up investigation on all cases except those involving the most serious offenses.

2 Assign generalist investigators (who would handle the obvious leads in routine cases) to the local operations commander.

3 Establish a major-offenders unit to investigate serious crimes.

4 Assign serious-offense investigations to closely supervised teams rather than to individual investigators.

5 Employ strike forces selectively and judiciously.

6 Initiate programs designed to impress on the citizen the crucial role he or she plays in solving crimes.[52]

Whether or not such changes are made, of what importance is the detective to police operations? The detective's role is important in at least two respects (apart from the ability to solve crimes). First, the prestigious rank of detective provides a goal to which the patrol officer may aspire. Second, citizens expect investigations to be carried out. As Herman Goldstein says: "One cannot dismiss lightly the public-relations value of detective work. It may fully justify the police resources that are invested. Persons treated sympathetically may offer greater assistance to the police in the future."[53]

It is clear that the realities of detective work do not match the myth, and to a large extent the belief that the investigator is the most important member of a police agency can have damaging repercussions. As a result

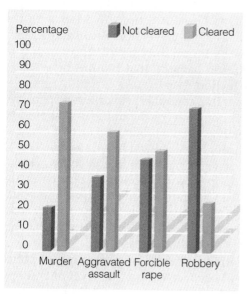
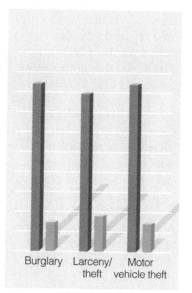

**a** Crimes of violence

**b** Crimes against property

**Figure 5.9**
**Crimes cleared by arrest**
The probability that a reported crime will be cleared by an arrest varies greatly by the type of offense.

SOURCE: U.S. Department of Justice, *Uniform Crime Reports* (Washington, D.C.: Government Printing Office, 1990), 24.

of this myth, patrol officers may feel their only job is to take reports, improper practices may be used to satisfy public expectations, and the citizenry may be lulled into believing that they need do nothing more after detectives take over. The realities of the crime problem, however, demand new responses to the traditional roles of law enforcement personnel.

## Specialized Operations

Patrol and investigation are the two largest and functionally most important units within a police department. In metropolitan areas, however, specialized units deal with particular types of problems; traffic, vice, and juvenile units are the most common, and in some cities separate units are created to deal with organized crime and narcotics. The work of the specialized units should not overshadow the fact that patrol and investigation also have a responsibility to deal with the same problems.

**Traffic**  Because almost everyone in the community is a pedestrian, passenger, or driver, almost everyone is affected by the problems associated with the automobile. The police are required to regulate the flow of vehicles, to investigate accidents, and to enforce traffic laws. This work may not seem to fall within the objectives of crime fighting or maintenance of order, but certain tasks of traffic control further these objectives. Enforcement of traffic laws contributes to the maintenance of order, educates the public in safe driving habits, and provides a visible community service. As an enforcer of traffic laws, the patrol officer has an opportunity to stop vehicles and interrogate drivers, with the result that stolen property and suspects connected with other criminal acts are often discovered. Most departments can now check automobile and operator license numbers against lists of wanted vehicles and suspects.

The traffic-control function basically includes accident investigation, traffic direction, and enforcement. These functions overlap with the broader goal of public safety and accident prevention. For example, accident data and observations made by the on-duty patrol officer may contribute to the pinpointing of traffic hazards that require new safety devices or even highway reconstruction.

Most authorities suggest that traffic control is primarily a responsibility of the patrol division and that personnel of the traffic unit should be limited to educational and preventive functions. Some argue that overemphasis on traffic-control work through specialized line units can lead to morale problems owing to the privileged nature of motorcycle work and can drain resources from more important patrol duties. In some cities, the police have hired civilians to deal with nonmoving and parking violations in order to make better use of resources. Nevertheless, in many cities police units that are assigned primarily to traffic-control duties concurrently perform patrol functions.

Enforcement of traffic regulations provides a key example of police discretion. This work is essentially proactive, and the level of enforcement can be considered a direct result of departmental policies and norms. Selective enforcement is the general policy, since the police have neither the desire nor the resources to enforce all traffic laws. As a consequence, many departments target particular intersections or highways for stiff enforcement, maintaining a visible presence as a deterrent to speeding motorists. The number of tickets for moving violations issued by various departments depends, in part, on the resources allocated to traffic control and on the importance that a police chief places on it, both of which reflect community and political values.

Traffic law enforcement is one of the areas in which police departments employ measures of productivity. Although few administrators will admit that they employ quota systems, officers seem to understand what is expected of them; that is one reason why traffic work is preferred to patrol. Further, the traffic officer need not get involved in situations such as family fights and need not "make hard-to-defend judgments about what people deserve."[54]

**Vice**   Enforcement of laws against vice—prostitution, gambling, drugs, and so forth—depends upon proactive police work that, in itself, often depends upon the use of undercover agents and informers. A specialized vice-control unit is part of most large city departments. Vigorous enforcement of the laws against vice requires that individual police officers be given wide latitude in the exercise of discretion. Police officers are often obliged "to engage in illegal and often degrading practices that must be concealed from the public."[55] The special nature of vice work requires the members of the unit to be well trained in the legal procedures that must be followed if arrests are to lead to convictions. The potential for corruption in vice work presents a number of administrative dilemmas. In addition, personnel are subject to transfer when their identities become known and their effectiveness is lost. As a further complication, political influence may sometimes dampen law enforcement efforts in this area.

Increasingly the police are using electronic surveillance technologies and undercover work to deal with vice crime.[56] Intelligence gathering that facilitates proactive police work is important for targeting individuals and organizations where drug or other crimes may be committed. The expansion of undercover work has caused concern among many who believe that it is a departure from the more traditional style of open policing. There are also concerns that the use of certain tactics violates civil liberties and will result in a greater intrusion of government into private affairs, be they criminal or not.[57]

Officers engaged in vice-control operations depend heavily on informants. Thus one of the major problems with these operations is that a mutually satisfactory relationship may develop between the law enforcer and the law violator. In the field of narcotics control, addicts may provide information on sellers. They are also used frequently as decoys to help trap sellers, a practice of questionable legality. In exchange for cooperating with the police, addicts are sometimes rewarded by being given small amounts of drugs, freedom from prosecution for possession, or police recommendations for leniency should they be sentenced. These practices result in a paradox: the police tolerate certain levels of vice in exchange for information that enables them to arrest other people for engaging in the same behavior they tolerate in the informant.

**Drug Enforcement**   Many large cities now have a separate bureau that deals only with drug enforcement. Within these agencies there may also be task forces dedicated to dealing with organized crime or gangs involved in drug dealing. Other sections may use sting operations to buy/arrest drug sellers on the street. Community drug education may also be a responsibility of another section.

Police drug enforcement policies may be guided by the goal of "aggressive law enforcement," allocating resources to attain a maximum number of arrests and to stop brazen street dealing. Police executives believe that it is important to demonstrate to dealers and to the community that enforcement actions will be taken.[58] Some communities such as Charleston, South Carolina have developed imaginative strategies in the drug war. A "flying-squad" of officers unexpectedly converges on high crime/drug use areas and makes arrest in a proactive, aggressive manner. In San Diego, California, and Fort Lauderdale, Florida, teams of police officers and building inspectors focus on buildings and housing projects known to contain drug sellers. Through safety inspections, enforcement of health and zoning codes, evictions, and the boarding up of structures, drug dealers can be routed from the neighborhood. As with other aspects of drug enforcement, the police depend upon community cooperation and support.

One tactic has been to disrupt the marketplace for drugs by applying a variety of law enforcement pressures. In Phoenix, Arizona and several other cities, police placed signs warning motorists driving into certain "drug neighborhoods" that they may be stopped and questioned. "Operation Pressure Point" was launched in New York City in 1983. One thousand police officers were moved into the Lower East Side, an area where a "drug supermarket" operated openly on the streets, impeding the activities of law-abiding citizens, intimidating residents, and flaunting law enforcement. The police made thousands of arrests, bulldozers leveled abandoned buildings, and storefronts rented to dealers were padlocked.[59] The drug supermarket was effectively shut down. In 1983 upwards of one hundred dealers could be observed on the streets of the Lower East Side, and by 1989 the streets had been cleared and uniformed officers were very apparent. The Operation Pressure Point approach has been used in other parts of New York, in Los Angeles, and in other cities. There are, however, questions regarding the overall effectiveness of the approach: Do the efforts simply shift the location of the drug market or do they diminish the demand for drugs?[60]

In cities throughout the country the police have shifted substantial portions of their resources to pursue drug offenders. The evidence shows that police efforts have been successful in disrupting drug markets, but often that means other law enforcement responsibilities have been neglected. As Francis C. Hall, retired commander of the New York Police Department's narcotics division, has said, "There comes a point when you have to say, what is the optimum number of people we should have directly involved in narcotics enforcement?"[61]

Although arrests for drug sale or possession have increased dramatically in response to the latest war on drugs, some observers believe that the law enforcement approach will not be successful. Clearly there are or-

Proactive police work, including work by undercover officers such as this one, is necessary for the enforcement of laws against vice. What are some of the problems associated with this approach?

ganizational and informational limitations on police narcotic enforcement work. We should ask whether there is a contradiction between the goal of drug control/eradication and the due process or justice model that emphasizes procedural guarantees. Can police drug work be seen as ritual? Might enforcement activities do "little but inflate police power, suggest to an ignorant public that something is being done, and perpetuate aspects of the police myth," as some suggest?[62] How should we evaluate this perspective given the current emphasis upon drug enforcement? Can the police make an impact?

## Police Actions and the Rule of Law

In a democratic society the police are expected to control crime within the framework of the law. Within the law enforcement processes of detection, apprehension, and arrest, police officers are required to perform their tasks in ways that conform to the law as specified in the U.S. Constitution, individual state constitutions, legislative statutes, and court interpretations. As Chapter 3 explained, the ideals of the rule of law and of due process aim to ensure that justice is accorded to all citizens and that officials of the state do not use their power to thwart the law. Three police practices—search and seizure, arrest, and interrogation—are specially structured to ensure that the rule of law is upheld and that the rights of citizens are protected. Although many police officers complain that they have been handcuffed by the due process decisions of the courts, that may be a price of maintaining freedom in a democratic society.

The Fourth, Fifth, and Sixth Amendments of the Bill of Rights bear directly on police activities. The Fourth protects citizens from unreasonable searches and seizures, the Fifth protects them from being compelled to testify against themselves, and the Sixth upholds the right to counsel. To make certain that the police would observe the provisions of the Bill of Rights, the Supreme Court has emphasized two devices: the exclusionary rule and the Sixth Amendment's right to counsel. The exclusionary rule, first developed by the Court in 1914 (*Weeks* v. *United States*), stipulates that illegally seized evidence or improperly given confessions shall be excluded from trials. The argument is made that the government must not soil its hands by profiting from police abuses of the law. It is further stated that, because of the rule, the police will be deterred from acting improperly. As an additional protection, the Sixth Amendment's provision of the right to counsel has been interpreted to mean that the defendant may have a lawyer present not only in the courtroom but also during earlier proceedings—even during interrogation in the station house. Through their training and policies the police are aware that their actions in the field or station house may jeopardize the building of a case strong enough to be prosecuted successfully.

## Search and Seizure

**search warrant**

An order of a court officer that allows a police officer to search a designated place for specific persons or items to be seized.

The application of the Fourth Amendment to the states was accomplished by the Supreme Court in *Mapp* v. *Ohio*, 1961. In that case, the Court ruled that evidence collected by the police in the course of an investigation must be gathered in accordance with the Fourth Amendment's strictures against *unreasonable* searches and seizures. The courts have said that there are circumstances which are reasonable when the police may indeed invade the privacy of a home or person. One such circumstance is the issuance of a **search warrant**.

**Search Warrant Criteria**   A search warrant is an order from a court official allowing a police officer to search a designated place. The officer must go to the court, give reasons for the search, and describe the particular place to be searched and the persons or things to be seized. Before a judge may grant the warrant authority, two conditions concerning probable cause and particularity must be met. First, the officer must provide reliable information indicating that there is *probable cause* to believe that a crime has been or is being committed. Second, the *particular* premises and pieces of property to be seized must be identified, and the officer must swear under oath that the facts given are correct. The police cannot obtain a search warrant that vaguely describes the evidence sought or the property to be searched.

**Warrantless Searches**   In some circumstances, the interests of crime control dictate that the police conduct a search without a warrant, and it is here that the courts have been most active in defining the term *unreasonable*. Searches of five kinds may be conducted without a warrant and still be in accord with the Constitution: (1) searches incident to a lawful arrest,

(2) searches during field interrogation, (3) searches of automobiles under special conditions, (4) seizures of evidence that is in "plain view," and (5) searches when consent is given. As we see in A Question of Ethics, warrantless searches raise a number of ethical concerns in police work.

*Incident to a Lawful Arrest*   When an officer has observed a crime or believes that one has been committed, an arrest may be made and a search conducted without a warrant. It is the fact of the lawful arrest that justifies the exception to the Fourth Amendment.[63] In part, the rationale for this exception is the possibility that the suspect will destroy evidence unless swift action is taken. But in *Chimel v. California* (1969), the Supreme Court also said that such a search is limited to the person of the arrestee and the area within the arrestee's "immediate control," defined as that area "from within which he might [obtain] a weapon or something that could have been used as evidence against him" in order to destroy it.[64] Thus, if the police are holding a person in one room of a house, they are not authorized to search and seize property in another part of the house, away from the suspect's physical presence.

*Field Interrogation*   The police often stop and interrogate persons without knowing any facts to justify an arrest. Clearly, much police activity involves interrogating people who are acting suspiciously or who are disturbing the public order. These street encounters, often called "threshold inquiries," allow for brief questioning and frisking: patting down the outside of the suspect's clothing to ascertain whether there is a concealed weapon.

In the case of *Terry v. Ohio* (1968), the Supreme Court upheld the stop-and-frisk procedure.[65] Here, a police officer noticed two men taking turns looking into a store window and then conferring. A third man joined them. Suspecting that a crime was about to be committed, the officer confronted them, removed pistols from two of the men, and charged them with carrying concealed weapons. The court ruled that it was a constitutional search since the officer had stopped them for the purpose of detention or interrogation and that, because he believed he was dealing with armed and dangerous individuals, the frisk could be conducted for his own safety or that of others.

On the basis of *Terry* and subsequent decisions, it is now accepted that a police officer is justified in stopping and questioning an individual

---

## A Question of Ethics

**O**fficer Mike Groton knocked on the apartment door. He and fellow officer Howard Reece had gone to this rundown part of town to arrest Richard Watson on the basis of evidence from an informer that Watson was a major drug seller. "Police officers, open up," said Groton. The door opened slowly, and a small, tense woman peered into the hallway.

"Ma'am, we have a warrant for the arrest of Richard Watson. Is he here?"

"No. I don't know any Watson," was the answer.

"Well, let us in so that we can see for ourselves."

Groton and Reece entered the apartment. Reece quickly proceeded to a back bedroom. The window leading to a fire escape was open and the bed looked as though someone had left it in a rush. Reece started to poke around the room, opening bureau drawers and searching the closet. In the back of the closet he noticed a woman's pocketbook hanging on a hook. He opened it and found three glassine packages of a white powder.

"Hey Mike, look what I found," he called. Groton came into the bedroom. "Looks like heroin to me," said Reece. "Too bad we can't use it."

"Why can't we use it? This is the place."

"But the warrant only specified the arrest of Watson. It didn't say anything about searching his closet."

"Let's just keep those packets. When we catch him we can 'find' it in his pocket."

What are the issues here? Can the officers keep the heroin packets? Is bending the rules acceptable in some circumstances? If so, do these circumstances warrant it? What should the officers do?

---

*Terry v. Ohio* (1968)
A police officer may stop and frisk an individual if it is reasonable to suspect that a crime has been committed.

if it is reasonable to assume that a crime has been committed. The individual may be frisked for a weapon if the officer fears for his or her life, and the officer is justified in going through the individual's clothing and person if the frisk has indicated something that might be a weapon. The courts have concluded that an officer may conduct this form of field interrogation in order to investigate suspicious persons without first showing probable cause. James Q. Wilson has advocated that police be more proactive in stopping and frisking persons thought to be carrying a gun without a license. Arrest and confiscation would follow. He argues that this would be more effective in reducing crime than legal restraints on gun possession.[66]

**Carroll v. United States** (1925)
An automobile may be searched if the police have probable cause to believe it contains criminal evidence.

*Automobiles*   A third special circumstance in which a search can be made without a warrant is when there is probable cause to believe that an automobile contains criminal evidence. The Supreme Court has distinguished automobiles from houses and persons on the grounds that a car that has been involved in a crime can be moved and evidence lost. First developed by the Supreme Court in 1925 (***Carroll v. United States***), this doctrine emphasizing the mobile nature of motor vehicles has been accepted, though the police must have reason to believe that the particular car is linked to a crime.[67]

Questions about the search of automobiles have plagued the court. If a car may be searched, then does that also include the trunk? Can the police also look inside articles kept in the trunk—a suitcase for example? These questions were addressed by the Court in *United States* v. *Ross* (1982).[68] Here the Court said that a warrantless search of an automobile and its contents is permitted if there is probable cause to believe that it contains evidence of a crime. The right to search the containers follows from the right to search the vehicle.

In recent years two new questions have confronted the justices: whether impounded automobiles are subject to warrantless search and whether searches may be made of automobiles stopped in routine traffic inspections. A 1968 case upheld the right of the police to enter an impounded vehicle subsequent to an arrest in order to inventory its contents.[69] This position was advanced when the Court said that a validly impounded car may be searched without probable cause or warrant on the ground that it is reasonable for an inventory of the contents to be taken as a protection against theft or charges of theft while the car is in police custody.[70]

With regard to the stopping of motorists at police roadblocks for the purpose of checking licenses and to determine the health or mental state of drivers, the Court said that random stops were illegal unless the police had some reasonable suspicion that a motor vehicle law was being violated.[71] This ruling eliminated police discretion to be selective in their stops but it upheld roadblocks set up to check drivers in a systematic manner.

The warrantless search of a car's occupants is still a cloudy legal area. Currently it appears that automobiles are seen as different from other areas considered private. Because of the importance of the automobile in American society, there will undoubtedly be additional interpretations of the Fourth Amendment with regard to unreasonable search and seizure.

The frisking of individuals and the searching of automobiles must be carried out according to the law. Officers must ensure that they do not lose a conviction because they acted improperly.

*"Plain View"*    Another exception to the requirement of a warrant occurs when officers seize items that are in "plain view" when they have reason to believe that the items are connected with a crime. If an officer has a warrant to search a house for cocaine, for example, and during the course of the search comes upon drug paraphernalia, the paraphernalia may also be seized. But for the plain-view doctrine to apply, the item must be plainly visible to a law enforcement officer who is in a lawful position when he inadvertently comes across an item, the evidentiary value of which is immediately apparent. Issues of probable cause and the place where items are found may be raised to invalidate the seizure. Whether the finding of the item was inadvertent may be the basis of a challenge as well.

Two decisions have further defined constitutionally allowable actions by police officers under the plain-view doctrine. In *New York* v. *Class* (1986) the Court said that a gun protruding from under a seat, seen by an officer when he entered a car to look for the vehicle identification number, was within the bounds of the doctrine.[72] However, in *Arizona* v. *Hicks* (1987) the Court ruled that an officer who moved a stereo system to find its identification number during a legal search for weapons had violated the Fourth Amendment ban against unreasonable search and seizure.[73] The serial number was not in plain view, and the police did not have probable cause to believe that the stereo had been stolen.

*Consent*    A citizen may waive the rights granted by the Fourth Amendment and allow the police to conduct a search or to seize items without a warrant and in the absence of special circumstances. The prosecution must be able to prove, however, that the consent was given voluntarily by the correct person. In some circumstances, as when passengers' belongings are searched by security employees before they board a plane and by customs agents at international borders, consent is implied. In the absence of such circumstances, however, consent must be clearly voluntary and not given as a consequence of duress or coercion.[74] Moreover, the consenting person must understand his or her right to deny the search. Questions about who may give consent center on permission given by persons other than the defendant—for example, landlords, cohabitants, or relatives.

## Arrest

**arrest**

The physical taking of a person into custody on the ground that there is probable cause to believe that he or she has committed a criminal offense. Police may use only reasonable physical force in making an arrest. The purpose of arrest is to hold the accused for a court proceeding.

**Arrest** is the seizure of an individual by a governmental official with authority to take the person into custody. It is more than a field interrogation or threshold inquiry, since the normal consequence of arrest is that the suspect is taken to the station house, and there proceedings begin that will eventually lead to prosecution and trial. The law of arrest combines the Fourth Amendment's protections and the local rules regarding procedure. Generally the arresting officer must be able to show there is probable cause to believe (1) a crime has been committed and (2) the person taken into custody has committed the crime.

Although the courts have not specifically *required* arrest only upon presentation of a warrant, they have implied that for felony arrests it is the preferred method. It is routine to make arrests without a warrant even though there may be adequate opportunity to obtain a warrant. In general, courts have upheld an arrest without a warrant when the officer can establish probable cause that a crime has been committed and that the defendant is the person who committed it and where the law of the particular jurisdiction allows for arrests without a warrant.[75]

## Interrogation

Among the rights guaranteed by the Fifth Amendment, one of the most important is the protection against self-incrimination, which means that persons shall not be compelled to be witnesses against themselves. This right is consistent with the assumption on which the adversarial process is based: the state must prove the defendant's guilt. The right has most force with regard to interrogations and confessions. The court will exclude from the evidence presented to the jurors any confession illegally obtained; furthermore, because of the Sixth Amendment, the suspect has the right to counsel during the interrogation process.

The Supreme Court ruled in *Escobedo* v. *Illinois* (1964) and *Miranda* v. *Arizona* (1966) that confessions made by suspects who have not been notified of their constitutional rights cannot be admitted as evidence.[76] To protect the rights of the accused, the Court emphasized the importance of allowing counsel to be present during the interrogation process. In addition, the Court said in effect that as soon as the investigation of an unsolved crime begins to focus on a particular suspect and when the suspect has been taken into custody, the so-called *Miranda* warnings have to be read aloud before interrogation can begin. Suspects must be told the following:

1   They have the right to remain silent.
2   If they decide to make a statement, it can and will be used against them in court.
3   They have the right to have an attorney present during interrogation or have an opportunity to consult with an attorney.
4   If they cannot afford an attorney, the state will provide one.

No sooner was the *Miranda* opinion announced than a hue and cry arose over the propriety of the new rules. Criticism of the Supreme Court came from a number of sources but especially from the law enforcement community. It was argued (1) that confessions are essential for the apprehension and conviction of law violators, (2) that informing suspects of their rights would greatly reduce the ability of the police to secure confessions, and (3) that few police would actually give the required warnings.

All of these assumptions have been challenged both by law enforcement officials and by social scientists studying the impact of the rulings. The most extensive of these studies focused on felony cases and found that fewer than 1 percent of the cases that reached the courts had been dismissed because of the exclusionary rule.[77] Similar findings were reported in a study of the rule's impact on the federal courts.[78] With some exceptions, it appears that the rule is an issue only in drug cases. In 7,500 felony cases in nine counties in three states, only 46 cases (0.6 percent) were lost because of the exclusionary rule. Most of these involved offenses that might have resulted in incarceration for less than six months. Indeed it can be argued that the exclusionary rule has had only a marginal impact on the criminal court system.[79]

In most cities the police depend on either catching the accused in the act or locating witnesses who will testify. Because most departments have limited resources for scientific investigation, suspects are not usually arrested until the crime is solved and conviction assured. Under these circumstances, interrogation becomes unnecessary.

Although police officials, politicians, and others felt that the *Miranda* rules would stifle efforts to control a rising crime rate, no such impact occurred. Neither was *Miranda* the boon that the Supreme Court and its defenders suggested it might be. Because of noncompliance during field and station house interrogation, the difficulties of developing schemes to provide effective counsel for indigent suspects, and distrust and misunderstanding on the part of suspects, the new protections had much less effect than had been anticipated. What seems to have occurred is that the police became more conscious of their requirements under the law. *Miranda* may have improved the professional atmosphere of the police environment.

## Modifications of the Exclusionary Rule

In the years since the cases of Daniel Escobedo and Ernesto Miranda were heard, a flow of cases to the Supreme Court has raised further questions about the exclusionary rule. As the number of conservative justices increased, some people expected the Court to overturn these landmark decisions. Though it has not done so, the conservative majority seems intent on halting the liberal thrust of previous decisions and shaping them to meet the complex demands of law enforcement. Decisions in recent cases have modified those of the Warren Court to such an extent that civil libertarians have complained that the exclusionary provisions are all but dead. They are not dead, but they have been modified by rulings in regard to particular circumstances in which searches and interrogations have been conducted.

There have been several key cases modifying the exclusionary rule as pronounced in *Miranda*. In *Harris* v. *New York* (1971), the Court ruled that statements that are trustworthy (not coerced) may be used to attack the credibility of a defendant who takes the stand even though the statements have been obtained in violation of the rule.[80] The prosecution charged that Harris had lied during his trial, and the Court ruled that his statements to the police before the trial could be introduced as evidence to prove the contention. In *Michigan* v. *Mosley* (1975), the Court ruled that a second interrogation session held after the suspect had initially refused to make a statement did not violate *Miranda*.[81] In *Rhode Island* v. *Innis* (1980), however, the Court actually broadened the application of *Miranda* by ruling that the safeguards against self-incrimination must be observed "whenever a person in custody is subjected to either express questioning or its equivalent."[82] In that case the suspect, riding with police officers in a squad car after being picked up in a murder investigation, heard one officer worry aloud to the other that because the murder had occurred near a school for handicapped children, some child might find the gun and be injured by it. At that the suspect told the officers where the gun could be found.

Three doctrines modifying the exclusionary rule have been enunciated. In the case of *New York* v. *Quarles* (1984), Justice William H. Rehnquist established a "public safety" exception to the suspect-warning doctrine.[83] Benjamin Quarles was charged with criminal possession of a weapon after a rape victim described him to the police. The officers located him in a supermarket. After frisking Quarles and discovering that he was wearing an empty shoulder holster, an officer asked where the gun was. Quarles nodded in the direction of some empty cartons: "The gun is over there." The officer retrieved a loaded .38 caliber revolver from one of the cartons, formally placed Quarles under arrest, and read him his *Miranda* rights from a printed card. Rehnquist said that the case presented a situation in which concern for public safety must take precedence over adherence to the literal language of the rules. The police were justified in asking the question by "immediate necessity."

A second doctrine, called the "inevitability of discovery exception," was stated by the Court in *Nix* v. *Williams* (1984).[84] This decision followed *Brewer* v. *Williams* (1977).[85] Robert Williams had been convicted of the murder of a ten-year-old girl. During the investigation, detectives searching for the body had given Williams what became known as the "Christian burial speech." Though they had promised his lawyer not to ask questions during a drive across the state with the suspect, they asked Williams to think about the fact that the parents of the girl were entitled to have an opportunity to provide a Christian burial for their child. Williams then told them where to find the body. In 1977 the Supreme

Court ruled that the detectives had violated the suspect's rights by inducing him to incriminate himself outside the presence of counsel. However, the Court left open the possibility that in a retrial the state could introduce the evidence of the body's discovery if it could be shown that it would have been found even without the defendant's testimony. Applying the inevitability of discovery exception, the Iowa courts found Williams guilty, and in 1984 the Supreme Court upheld the conviction. The chief justice said that the doctrine was designed to put the police "in the same, not a *worse*, position than they would have been in if no police error or misconduct had occurred."

A third doctrine, a "good-faith exception" to the exclusionary rule, has evolved. The Supreme Court has declared that evidence can be used even though it has been obtained under a search warrant that later is proved to be technically invalid. In *United States* v. *Leon* (1984), a 6–3 majority of the Court agreed that evidence obtained by law enforcement officers acting in reasonable reliance on a search warrant issued by a detached and neutral magistrate but ultimately found to be unsupported by probable cause could be used at trial. In dissent, Justice William Brennan, Jr., objected to the majority's effort to balance the costs and benefits of the exclusionary rule. The majority, he said, ignored the fundamental constitutional importance that was at stake in the case, and "It now appears that the Court's victory over the Fourth Amendment is complete."[86]

The Court has yet to determine the applicability of a good-faith exception to evidence seized by police officers during a warrantless search. It remains to be seen whether the exclusionary rule applies to evidence obtained by officers who reasonably but incorrectly believe they have a proper basis for a search.

Given the conservative majority on the Rehnquist Court, many observers expect that as more cases linked to the rights of defendants with regard to searches and interrogation come before the justices, the standard first enunciated by Chief Justice Warren in 1966 will be further eroded. It must be remembered, however, that although conservative justices may be concerned about crime control, they also respect legal precedent. That was illustrated in the 1990 case of *Minnick* v. *Mississippi*, where by a 6–2 vote the justices ruled that suspects have the right to have their lawyer present throughout police interrogation.[87] It is thus doubtful that the major thrust of the Warren and Burger courts will be completely overturned.

*United States* v. *Leon* (1984)
Evidence seized using a warrant later found defective is valid if the officer was acting in good faith.

## Law and Law Enforcement

As we have seen in this examination of the three major elements of the law enforcement process—detection, apprehension, and arrest—the law stipulates the actions that may be taken at each stage. Many people believe that the Supreme Court has gone too far and that criminals have gone free on technicalities as a result. Others emphasize that the Constitution protects all Americans against the unbridled exercise of power by the government and that the benefits of freedom are worth the price of releasing some criminals. It seems likely that this debate will continue and that the relationship between police actions and the rule of law will always be a subject of contention.

## Summary

Police operations not only are shaped by the formal organizational structures created to allocate law enforcement resources in an efficient manner but also are influenced by social and political processes both within and outside the department. The police are organized along military lines so that authority and responsibility can be located at appropriate levels. In the modern police department, operational divisions are responsible for law enforcement, order maintenance, and service. Although organization charts appear to show that police operations run like a well-adjusted machine, administrative leadership, recruitment, socialization of recruits to norms and values of the system, and the perspectives of the general public all shape how these activities are conducted.

Police services are delivered through the operations of the patrol, investigation, and specialized operations units. Patrol makes up two-thirds of sworn officers in most departments. The patrol function has three components: answering calls for assistance, maintaining a police presence, and probing suspicious circumstances. Issues concerning the allocation of personnel, response time, foot versus motorized patrol, and community-oriented policing dominate discussions of the future of policing. The investigation function is the responsibility of detectives in close coordination with patrol officers. The felony apprehension process is a sequence of actions that includes crime detection, preliminary investigation, follow-up investigation, clearance, and arrest. Specialized units dealing with traffic and vice are found in large departments.

The police must work within the law so as not to violate the rights of citizens. Decisions by the Supreme Court over the past quarter century have interpreted the Bill of Rights with regard to search and seizure, arrest, and interrogation. The exclusionary rule requires that evidence illegally obtained must not be used in the prosecution of a suspect. In recent years under the leadership of Chief Justice William Rehnquist and a conservative court, interpretations of key elements in the Bill of Rights have been narrowed.

## Questions for Review

1  What are some of the issues that influence police administrators in their allocation of resources?

2  What is the purpose of patrol? How is it carried out?

3  What has research shown about the effectiveness of patrol?

4  Why do detectives have so much prestige on the force?

5  How do various amendments to the Bill of Rights affect police operations?

## Key Terms and Cases

aggressive patrol

arrest

differential response

directed patrol

line units

preventive patrol

problem-oriented policing

search warrant

sworn officers

*Carroll* v. *U.S.* (1925)

*Terry* v. *Ohio* (1968)

*U.S.* v. *Leon* (1984)


## For Further Reading

Brown, Michael K. *Working the Street*. New York: Russell Sage Foundation, 1981. A study of patrol work by officers of the San Diego Police Force.

Geller, William A., ed. *Police Leadership in America*. New York: Praeger, 1985. A collection of essays written by some of the most progressive police executives.

Goldstein, Herman. *Problem-Oriented Policing*. New York: McGraw-Hill, 1990. Examination of the move toward problem-oriented, or community, policing with examples of its successful use.

Manning, Peter K. *Police Work*. Cambridge, Mass.: MIT Press, 1977. A look at police work. Manning argues that the police have an "impossible mandate." They have emphasized their crime-fighting stance, a role that they do not play successfully.

Skogan, Wesley G. *Disorder and Decline: Crime and the Spiral of Decay in American Neighborhoods*. New York: The Free Press, 1990. Support for community policing on the basis of studies spawned by the Wilson-Kelling thesis.

Skolnick, Jerome H., and David H. Bayley. *The New Blue Line*. New York: Free Press, 1986. A look at modern policing by two major criminal justice scholars.

## Notes

1  John Eck, William Spelman, Diane Hill, Darrel W. Stephens, John Stedman, and Gerald R. Murphy, *Problem Solving: Problem-Oriented Policing in Newport News* (Washington, D.C.: Police Executive Research Forum, 1987), 1–2.

2  Marcia Cohen and J. Thomas McEwen, "Handling Calls for Service: Alternatives to Traditional Policing," *National Institute of Justice Reports*, September 1984, 4.

3  George Kelling, "Measuring What Matters: A New Way of Thinking about Crime and Public Order," *The City Journal* (Spring 1992): 23.

4   *Survey of Police Operational and Administrative Practices* (Washington, D.C.: Police Executive Research Forum and Police Foundation, 1981), 22–24.

5   Samuel G. Chapman, *Police Patrol Readings*, 2d ed. (Springfield, Ill.: Charles C. Thomas, 1970), IX.

6   Samuel G. Chapman, "Police Patrol Administration," in *Municipal Police Administration*, 7th ed., ed. George D. Eastman and Esther Eastman (Washington, D.C.: International City Management Association, 1971), 77.

7   Charles D. Hale, *Fundamentals of Police Administration* (Boston: Holbrook Press, 1977), 105–106.

8   Albert Reiss, *The Police and the Public* (New Haven, Conn.: Yale University Press, 1971), 19; Egon Bittner, *The Functions of Police in Modern Society* (Cambridge, Mass.: Oelgeschlager, Gunn & Hain, 1980), 127.

9   Lawrence E. Cohen and Marcus Felson, "Social Change and Crime Rate Trends: A Routine Activity Approach," *American Sociological Review* 44 (1979): 589.

10  The results of this analysis were that 50 percent of calls to police were concentrated in 3 percent of all Minneapolis places and calls reporting all predatory crimes were found for robberies at 2.2 percent of places, all rapes at 1.2 percent of places, and all auto thefts at 2.7 percent of places. Lawrence W. Sherman, Patrick R. Gartin, and Michael E. Buerger, "Hot Spots of Predatory Crime: Routine Activities and the Criminology of Place," *Criminology* 27 (February 1989): 27.

11  Gary W. Cordner and Robert C. Trojanowicz, "Patrol," in *What Works in Policing? Operations and Administration Examined*, ed. Gary W. Cordner and Donna C. Hale (Cincinnati: Anderson, 1992), 11.

12  George Kelling, Tony Pate, Duane Dieckman, and Charles E. Brown, *The Kansas City Preventive Patrol Experiments: A Summary Report* (Washington, D.C.: Police Foundation, 1974).

13  William G. Spelman and Dale K. Brown, *Calling the Police: Citizen Reporting of Serious Crime* (Washington, D.C.: Police Executive Research Forum, 1984), XXIX.

14  Spelman and Brown, *Calling the Police*, 4.

15  Lawrence W. Sherman, "Patrol Strategies for Police," in *Crime and Public Policy*, ed. James Q. Wilson (San Francisco: ICS Press, 1983), 149.

16  Ibid.

17  Mark Harrison Moore, "Problem-Solving and Community Policing," in *Modern Policing*, ed. Michael Tonry and Norval Morris (Chicago: University of Chicago Press, 1992), 113.

18  Ibid.

19  Brian A. Reaves, *Police Departments in Large Cities* (Washington, D.C.: Bureau of Justice Statistics, 1989).

20  Lee A. Brown and Mary Ann Wycoff, "Policing Houston: Reducing Fear and Improving Service," *Crime and Delinquency* 33 (January 1987): 71; *The Newark Foot Patrol Experiment* (Washington, D.C.: Police Foundation, 1981); Robert C. Trojanowicz, *An Evaluation of the Neighborhood Foot Patrol Program in Flint, Michigan* (East Lansing: Michigan State University, n.d.)

21  Mark A. Cohen, Ted R. Miller, and Shelli B. Rossman, "The Costs and Consequences of Violent Behavior in the United States" (Paper prepared for the Panel on the Understanding and Control of Violent Behavior, National Research Council, National Academy of Science, Washington, D.C., 1990), 64–79.

22  Ben Davis, "Foot Patrol," *Police Centurian* (June 1984): 41.

23  Anthony Pate and Edwin H. Hamilton, *The Big Six: Policing America's Large Cities* (Washington, D.C.: Police Foundation, 1991).

24  In San Diego, one-officer cars were substituted for two-officer cars on a unit-for-unit basis. On the basis of calls handled, arrests, response time, monetary costs, and other measures, it was concluded that one-officer patrol was clearly as effective and more efficient than two-officer patrol. J. Boydstun, M. Sherry, and M. Moelter, *Patrol Staffing in San Diego: One- or Two-Officer Units* (Washington, D.C.: Police Foundation, 1977). On the question of officer safety, researchers in Kansas City and San Diego examined the frequency of injury for one-officer and two-officer units. Although the injury rate per officer was higher for one-officer patrols, the difference was not great, and evaluators believe that the question is still not fully answered. U.S. Department of Justice, National Institute of Justice, *Synthesizing and Extending the Results of Police Patrol Studies* (Washington, D.C.: Government Printing Office, 1985), 94.

25  James Q. Wilson and Barbara Boland, *The Effect of the Police on Crime*, U.S. Department of Justice (Washington, D.C.: Government Printing Office, 1979).

26  James Q. Wilson, *Thinking About Crime*, 2d rev. ed. (New York: Basic Books, 1983), 71.

27  Susan E. Martin and Lawrence W. Sherman, "Selective Apprehension: A Police Strategy for Repeat Offenders," *Criminology* 24 (February 1986): 155–173; Susan E. Martin, "Policing Career Criminals: An Examination of an Innovative Crime Control Program," *Journal of Criminal Law and Criminology* 77 (Winter 1986): 1159–1182.

28  Robert H. Langworthy, "Do Stings Control Crime? An Evaluation of a Police Fencing Operation," *Justice Quarterly* 6 (March 1989): 27.

29 Wilson and Boland, *Effect of the Police*, 4.

30 Mark Harrison Moore, "Problem-Solving and Community Policing," 99–158.

31 Patrick V. Murphy, "Organizing for Community Policing," in *Issues in Policing: New Perspectives*, ed. John W. Bizzack (Lexington, Ky.: Autumn Press, 1992), 113–128.

32 Herman Goldstein, *Problem-Oriented Policing* (New York: McGraw-Hill, 1990).

33 John E. Eck and William Spelman, "Who Ya Gonna Call? The Police as Problem Busters," *Crime and Delinquency* 33 (January 1987): 6.

34 Gary Cordner, "A Problem-Oriented Approach to Community-Oriented Policing," in *Community Policing: Rhetoric or Reality*, ed. Jack Greene and Stephen Matrofski (New York: Praeger, 1988), 135–152.

35 George L. Kelling and William J. Bratton, "Implementing Community Policing: The Administrative Problem," *Perspectives on Policing*, no. 17 (Washington, D.C.: National Institute of Justice, 1993).

36 Roger G. Dunham and Geoffrey P. Alpert, "Neighborhood Differences in Attitudes toward Policing: Evidence for a Mixed-Strategy Model of Policing in a Multi-Ethnic Setting," *Journal of Criminal Law and Criminology* 79 (1988): 504–523.

37 Candace McCoy, "Policing the Homeless," *Criminal Law Bulletin* 22 (May/June 1986): 263; Barney Melekian, "Police and the Homeless," *FBI Law Enforcement Bulletin* 59 (1990): 1–7.

38 U.S. Department of Justice, National Institute of Justice, *Research in Action* (January 1988); U.S. Department of Justice, National Institute of Justice, *Police Response to Special Populations*, by Peter Finn and Monique Sullivan (Washington, D.C.: Government Printing Office, 1987).

39 Hubert Williams and Antony M. Pate, "Returning to First Principles: Reducing the Fear of Crime in Newark," *Crime and Delinquency* 33 (January 1987): 53.

40 Vic Sims, "Criminal Investigation from a Small Town or Rural Perspective," in *Criminal Investigation: Essays and Cases*, ed. James N. Gilbert (Columbus, Ohio: Merrill, 1990), 1.

41 Peter Greenwood and Joan Petersilia, *The Criminal Investigation Process*, vol. 1, *Summary and Policy Implications* (Santa Monica, Calif.: Rand Corporation, 1975).

42 Herman Goldstein, *Policing a Free Society* (Cambridge, Mass.: Ballinger, 1977), 55. See also James Q. Wilson, *The Investigators: Managing FBI and Narcotics Agents* (New York: Basic Books, 1978).

43 Greenwood and Petersilia, *Summary and Policy Implications*, 19.

44  Steven G. Brandl, "The Impact of Case Characteristics on Detectives' Decision Making," *Justice Quarterly* 10 (September 1993): 141–142.

45  Peter J. Neufeld and Neville Colman, "When Science Takes the Witness Stand," *Scientific American* 262 (May 1990): 46.

46  Ibid.

47  B. Parker and J. L. Peterson, *Physical Evidence Utilization in the Administration of Criminal Justice* (Washington, D.C.: Government Printing Office, 1972).

48  President's Commission on Law Enforcement and Administration of Justice, *Task Force Report: The Police* (Washington, D.C.: Government Printing Office, 1967), 58.

49  Peter W. Greenwood, Jan M. Chaiken, and Joan Petersilia, *Criminal Investigation Process* (Lexington, Mass.: Lexington Books, 1977), 227.

50  Mark T. Willman and John R. Snortum, "Detective Work: The Criminal Investigation Process in a Medium-Sized Police Department," *Criminal Justice Review* 9 (1984): 33–39.

51  John E. Eck, *Solving Crimes: The Investigation of Burglary and Robbery* (Washington, D.C.: Police Executive Research Forum, 1983).

52  Greenwood and Petersilia, *Summary and Policy Implications*, X–XIII.

53  Goldstein, *Policing a Free Society*, 57.

54  James Q. Wilson, *Varieties of Police Behavior* (Cambridge, Mass.: Harvard University Press, 1967), 53.

55  Jonathan Rubinstein, *City Police* (New York: Farrar, Straus, and Giroux, 1973), 375.

56  For an account of undercover police work, see James J. Ness and Ellyn K. Ness, "Reflections on Undercover Street Experiences," in *Criminal Investigations: Essays and Cases*, ed. James M. Gilbert (Columbus, Ohio: Merrill, 1990), 105.

57  Gary T. Marx, *Undercover: Police Surveillance in America* (Berkeley: University of California Press, 1988).

58  U.S. Department of Justice, National Institute of Justice, Mark H. Moore and Mark A. R. Kleiman, "The Police and Drugs," in *Perspectives on Policing* (September 1989).

59  Lynn Zimmer, "Operation Pressure Point: The Disruption of Street-Level Trade on New York's Lower East Side" (Occasional papers from the Center for Research in Crime and Justice, New York University School of Law, 1987).

60  Bruce D. Johnson, Terry Williams, Kojo A. Dei, and Harry Sanabria, "Drug Abuse in the Inner City: Impact on Hard-Drug Users and the Community," *Drugs and Crime*, vol. 13, *Crime and Justice*, ed. Michael Tonry and James Q. Wilson (Chicago: University of Chicago Press, 1990), 32.

61  David E. Pitt, "Report from the Field on an Endless War," *New York Times*, 12 March 1989, 14.

62  Ibid.

63  *United States* v. *Robinson*, 414 U.S. 218 (1973).

64  *Chimel* v. *California*, 395 U.S. 752 (1969).

65  *Terry* v. *Ohio*, 392 U.S. 1 (1968).

66  James Q. Wilson, "Just Take Away Their Guns," *The New York Times Sunday Magazine*, 20 March 1994, 47.

67  *Carroll* v. *United States*, 267 U.S. 132 (1925).

68  *United States* v. *Ross*, 102 S.Ct. 2157 (1982).

69  *Harris* v. *United States*, 390 U.S. 234 (1968).

70  *South Dakota* v. *Opperman*, 428 U.S. 364 (1976).

71  *Delaware* v. *Prouse*, 440 U.S. 213 (1979).

72  *New York* v. *Class*, 54 L.W. 4178 (1986).

73  *Arizona* v. *Hicks*, 55 L.W. 4258 (1987). See also Kimberly Kingston, "Look But Don't Touch: The Plain View Doctrine," *FBI Law Enforcement Bulletin* (December 1987): 17.

74  *Wren* v. *United States*, 352 F.2d. 617 (1965).

75  *Carroll* v. *United States*, 267 U.S. 132 (1925).

76  *Escobedo* v. *Illinois*, 378 U.S. 478 (1964); *Miranda* v. *Arizona*, 384 U.S. 436 (1966).

77  U.S. Department of Justice, National Institute of Justice, *The Effects of the Exclusionary Rule: A Study in California* (Washington, D.C.: Government Printing Office, 1982).

78  U.S. Controller General of the United States, *Impact of the Exclusionary Rule on Federal Criminal Prosecutions*, Report GGD–79–45 (19 April 1979).

79  Peter Nardulli, "The Societal Cost of the Exclusionary Rule: An Empirical Assessment," *ABF Research Journal* (Summer 1983): 585–609.

80  *Harris* v. *New York*, 401 U.S. 222 (1971).

81  *Michigan* v. *Mosley*, 423 U.S. 93 (1975).

82  *Rhode Island* v. *Innis*, 446 U.S. 291 (1980).

83  *New York* v. *Quarles*, 467 U.S. 649 (1984).

84  *Nix* v. *Williams*, 52 L.W. 4732 (1984).

85  *Brewer* v. *Williams*, 430 U.S. 387 (1977).

86  *United States* v. *Leon*, 82 L.ed. 677 (1984).

87  *Minnick* v. *Mississippi*, 59 L.W. 4037 (1990).

# Policing: Issues and Trends

**A Sony camcorder owned by Los Angeles resident George** Holliday may have been the instrument that had the most dramatic impact on the American police in the 1990s. Awakened late at night by sirens on 3 March 1991, Holliday looked out his apartment window to see a helicopter spotlight shining on a white Hyundai surrounded by police cars. Holliday grabbed his new camcorder and directed it at the scene. The videotape showed a large black man on his hands and knees being repeatedly beaten by two police officers using their two-foot metal truncheons, while a third officer stomped on him as others watched.[1] The officers were seen striking the man on the ground, who attempted to rise, was beaten back down, and then beaten again.

Two days later, the ninety-second tape was shown on Los Angeles television and CNN broadcast it worldwide. The savage beating of Rodney King dominated the media for days, giving Americans "the most explicit and shocking news footage of police brutality ever to be seen on television."[2] The videotape provided dramatic evidence of police actions that many had previously dismissed as unlikely to happen in America.

The arrest and trial of the LAPD officers set in motion an additional series of events that raised further questions about American justice. After a long trial, the four officers were acquitted by an all-white jury in suburban Simi Valley. News of that decision astounded most Americans.[3] Many thought the evidence on the videotape was enough to convict the officers. The jury's decision confirmed the belief among African-Americans that the criminal justice system was racist. It led to massive rioting in the black and Hispanic area of South Central Los Angeles, resulting in fifty-three persons dead, over a billion dollars in damage, and a city seething with racial fury. Only after a second, federal trial and the conviction of two of the officers on civil rights charges would many Americans believe that justice had finally been done.

The Rodney King case highlights the fact that the legitimacy of the police is at stake when they take the law into their own hands. The relationship between the police and the community is often fragile, especially when racial, gender, and class bias are believed to influence their behavior. As the National Advisory Commission on Criminal Justice Standards and Goals pointed out, the police are not separate from the people because law enforcement draws its strength and authority from the citizenry.[4]

The police serve the people and must be responsive to them. Because of this relationship the police are being forced to face several key issues and trends, which are discussed in this chapter. We first look at the recruitment and training of the men and women who are members of the police profession. We then examine the subculture of the police, and by analyzing their norms and values we can develop a better understanding of police behavior. Third, the important link between the police and the community is described. Fourth, we examine the enduring problem of the abuse of power by the police and what is being done to enhance police accountability. Finally, we look at two trends—unionism and private policing—that greatly influence the present and future operations of the police.

## Questions for Inquiry

- Who are the police and why do they choose their profession?
- How does the subculture of the police influence officer behavior?
- What is the importance of the police-community link for crime prevention?
- What is the problem of the police abuse of power and how can it be controlled?
- What methods are there to increase police accountability to citizens?
- What role do labor unions play in policing?
- What is the future of private policing?

# Who Are the Police?

Although a job description identifies the formal duties and legal mandate of police officers, such a definition tells little about how individual officers actually do their work. To better understand police work, we need to look at the recruitment and training of officers and the changing profile of police in the United States.

## Recruitment

The policies determining the types of persons recruited and retained greatly dictate the behavior of those who serve in the nation's police departments. Police work requires persons who are sensitive to the complex social problems of contemporary society. If pay scales are low, educational requirements minimal, and physical standards unrealistic, police work will attract only those who are unable to enter more attractive occupations.

A majority of departments now offer entrance salaries of over $20,000 and require of new members only a high school education, good physical condition, and the absence of a criminal record. To widen the pool of recruits, more inclusive physical standards have been established so as not to discriminate against women and some ethnic groups, and many departments even overlook a minor criminal record if it was acquired in an applicant's youth. Qualifying standards vary greatly and depend to a large extent on a community's level of urbanization.

The reasons people offer for choosing police work as a career are shown in Table 6.1; they include the nature of the work as well as the remuneration. When John Van Maanen interviewed recruits in Union City, he found that "virtually all recruits alluded to the opportunity afforded by a police career to perform in a role which was perceived as consequential or important to society."[5] Working outside in a nonroutine job was

| Reason | Male | Female | Total |
|---|---|---|---|
| Variety | 62.2% | 92.1% | 69.4% |
| Responsibility | 50.4% | 55.3% | 51.6% |
| Serve public | 48.7% | 50% | 49% |
| Adventure | 49.6% | 39.5% | 47.1% |
| Security | 46.2% | 34.2% | 43.3% |
| Pay | 43.7% | 42.1% | 43.3% |
| Benefits | 36.1% | 31.6% | 35% |
| Advancement | 31.9% | 34.2% | 32.5% |
| Retirement | 27.7% | 5.3% | 22.3% |
| Prestige | 16% | 13.2% | 15.3% |

**Table 6.1**
**Reasons for choosing police work as a career**
To what extent do the reasons for choosing police work differ from the reasons that might be given for choosing other careers? What is indicated by the different responses given by men and women?

SOURCE: Harold P. Slater and Martin Reiser, "A Comparative Study of Factors Influencing Police Recruitment," *Journal of Police Science and Administration* 16 (1988): 170.

another important factor. Knowledge of police work through contact with family members or friends who are officers was also instrumental in people's decisions.

Departments are increasingly attracting recruits with a college education, although officers in rural areas and small cities are more likely to have lower education levels. In the past twenty years the educational level of American police officers has risen significantly. This rise is partly due to the Law Enforcement Education Program (LEEP), which, between 1969 and 1980, gave police officers and preservice students financial assistance to earn a college degree. About 60 percent of sworn officers now have more than two years of college education (see Figure 6.1).[6]

While recruiting efforts and entry requirements influence the types of people entering the pool of potential officers, their training affects their attitudes.

## Training

Upon joining a police department, the new recruit immediately faces the reality of the organization. He or she may have a citizen's understanding of the work but little knowledge of the procedures and tactics it entails. Throughout a probationary period, the recruit learns aspects of the work and is tested. Most states now require preservice training for all recruits, which often involves formal courses at a police academy. Large departments generally run their own programs, and a state police academy trains recruits from rural and small-town units. The courses range from two-week sessions, in which weapons handling and target practice are emphasized, to more academic four-month programs followed by fieldwork, such as those developed by the Los Angeles police and sheriff's departments. In the latter courses, recruits hear lectures on social relations, receive foreign language training, and learn emergency medical treatment.

Even with the increased amount of formal training that is given to the police, law enforcement is an art, not a science. There is no body of generalized, written knowledge, theory, or rules that can chart the police officer's way. The fact that police work is learned on the job rather than in the classroom is often impressed on recent academy graduates the first day on the job. They are typically supervised by an experienced officer whose opening remark may be, "Now I want you to forget all that stuff you learned at the academy."

The process of **socialization**, or "learning the ropes," includes learning the informal ways, rather than the rule-book ways, in which law enforcement operates. It involves learning

## Figure 6.1
## College education of sworn officers

During the past two decades advances have been made in increasing the number of police officers with at least some college education. However, about a quarter of all sworn officers have only high school.

SOURCE: David L. Carter, Allen D. Sapp, and Darrel W. Stephens, *The State of Police Education: Policy Direction for the Twenty-first Century* (Washington, D.C.: Police Executive Research Forum, 1989), 45.

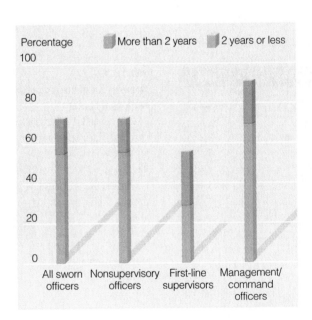

Although most new officers are formally trained, it is on the job that they really "learn the ropes."

about shortcuts, how to be "productive," what to avoid, and a host of other bits of wisdom, norms, and folklore that defines the subculture of a particular department. Recruits learn that loyalty to fellow officers, professional esprit de corps, and respect for police authority are esteemed values. New officers become socialized by fellow officers to the "real" way the job should be performed.

Like soldiers, patrol officers work in an organizational framework in which rank carries responsibilities and privileges; yet the success of the group depends on the cooperation of its members. All patrol officers are under direct supervision and must recognize that their performance is measured by the contribution they make to the group's work. They are also directly influenced by the pressure exerted from colleagues who work alongside them.

Patrol officers are expected to "handle" the multitude of different situations they confront. They find themselves dependent on their own personal skills and judgment. They move onto a social stage with an unknown cast of characters and are expected to perform in a setting and plot that can never be accurately predicted. They must be ever ready to act and to do so according to law. From arresting a fleeing assailant to protecting a fearful wife from her drunken husband to assisting in the search for a lost child, the patrol officer meets the public alone. That is a tall order.

**socialization**
The process by which the rules, symbols, and values of a group or subculture are learned by its members.

### The Changing Profile of the Police

There has been a major change in the composition of the police in the United States, moving away from the all-male, all-white police force that existed in most parts of the country until the 1970s. This shift was spurred

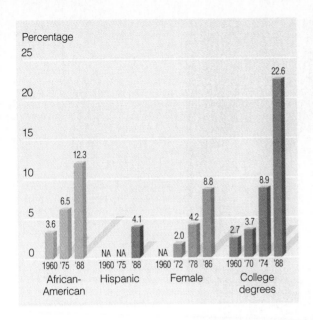

Percentage

25

20

15

10

5

0

22.6

12.3

6.5

3.6

4.1

NA NA

8.8

4.2

2.0

NA

8.9

2.7

3.7

| 1960 '75 '88 | 1960 '75 '88 | 1960 '72 '78 '86 | 1960 '70 '74 '88 |
| African-American | Hispanic | Female | College degrees |

**Figure 6.2**
**The changing profile of the American police officer**
Since 1970 there have been efforts to increase the percentage of minorities, women, and persons with college degrees on the force.

SOURCE: Samuel Walker, *The Police in America*, 2d ed. (New York: McGraw-Hill, 1992), 303.

by several factors. In 1968, the National Advisory Commission on Civil Disorders identified police-minority relations as a major contribution to the ghetto riots of the 1960s. The issue of homogeneous police forces received renewed emphasis with passage of equal opportunity legislation and with court decisions promoting affirmative action. The Equal Employment Opportunity Act of 1972 prohibits state and local governments from discriminating in their hiring. Affirmative action programs, designed to reduce or eliminate patterns of underemployment of women and minorities, have been created nationwide.

At the prodding of state and federal equal opportunity commissions, most city police forces have undertaken extensive campaigns to recruit more minority and female officers. As seen in Figure 6.2, there have been major changes in the profile of the American police officer.

**Minority Police Officers**   Changes in the racial composition of the police can be seen on a national basis, but what is the situation in America's cities where major portions of the African-American and Hispanic population reside? Samuel Walker conducted surveys of the country's fifty largest cities to measure the number of minority officers in the police forces compared to the racial divisions of the population.[7] He found progress, with 28 percent of the departments reporting an increase of 50 percent or more in the number of black officers and 23 percent reporting a similar increase in the number of Hispanic officers (see Figure 6.3).

As political power shifts toward minorities in some American cities, the composition of their police forces can be expected to reflect the change. But the election of an African-American or Hispanic mayor does not necessarily signal an immediate change in the composition of the police force. As public organizations face limited resources in the 1990s, there may be further reductions in the number of officers serving many financially strapped cities. Because of the important role played by seniority in layoff procedures, minority officers may be the first to go, and the gains of the past decade thus may be lost.

**Women on the Force**   Traditionally defined as "man's work," policing is increasingly attracting women. Although Lola Baldwin, the first policewoman in the United States, was made an officer in Portland, Oregon in 1905, the number of women officers remained minute—about 1.5 percent of all officers—until 1970. Even now, however, only 8.8 percent of sworn officers are women, although in some cities their proportion exceeds 10 percent.[8] Moreover, about half of the police agencies in the United States employ no women. Sexual and racial integration of police departments has progressed the furthest in cities with large black populations (such as Atlanta, Detroit, and Washington). In contrast, in cities where ethnic groups have long dominated (such as Buffalo, Boston, Philadelphia, and Minneapolis), the hiring of policewomen has been limited due to "the forces of traditionalism and resistance to change."[9] Also discouraging is the fact that few women achieve supervisory positions. Since the rate of promotion is slow, it could be "well into the twenty-first century before a significant number of women move into supervisory positions."[10]

Most policewomen have easily met the performance expectations of their superiors. Indeed, studies conducted by the Police Foundation and by other researchers point to a positive reception for women in law enforcement work. Research in Washington, D.C., in which a group of female recruits was compared to a group of male recruits, found that gender "is not a bona fide occupational qualification for doing police patrol work."[11] This study, corroborated in other cities, found that most citizens had generally positive reactions to the work of policewomen.

Despite positive reviews and increases in their numbers, women still have difficulty breaking into the traditionally male stronghold of police work. Cultural expectations of women often conflict with ideas about behavior appropriate for officers. As newcomers to the force, women have often found their upward mobility blocked and have had to contend with prejudice against their pioneering activities. Especially with regard to the assignment of women to patrol duty, questions such as the following are frequently raised:

- Can women handle situations involving force and violence?
- What changes in training and equipment must be made?

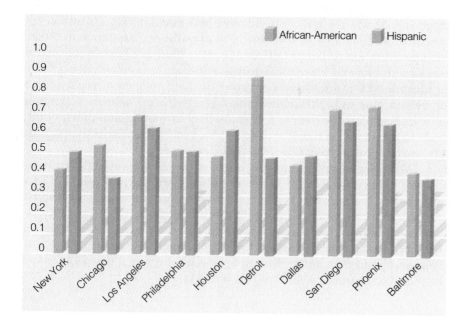

**Figure 6.3**
**Index of African-American and Hispanic police officers compared to size of minority population in ten largest U.S. cities**
The index was constructed by comparing the percentage of minorities employed in the police force to the percentage of minorities in the local population. An index of 1.00 shows that a department has achieved a theoretical ideal level of minority employment.

SOURCE: Samuel Walker, "Employment of Black and Hispanic Police Officers, 1983–1988: A Follow-up Study" (Occasional paper 89–1, Center for Applied Urban Research, University of Nebraska at Omaha, February 1989).

An increasing number of women have become officers. What are some of the problems they face? With the public? With their colleagues?

- Do women resent the loss of the "specialist" role they previously played in police work?
- Should women and men be treated equally in regard to promotion?
- Does assigning men and women as patrol partners tend to break up their families?

As these questions reveal, women have to overcome resistance from their fellow officers and some citizens. In particular, they encounter unpredictable resistance to their exercise of authority, as shown in the accompanying Close-Up of Officer Murphy. They are often subjected to sexist remarks and more overt forms of sexual harassment designed to undermine their authority. For many of their male counterparts, a female's entrance into this male domain is upsetting. These men complain that if their patrol partner is a woman, they cannot be sure of her ability to lend assistance in times of danger—that she simply lacks the physical stature to act effectively when the going gets rough.[12]

The future role of women in police work will undoubtedly evolve in concert with changes in the nature of policing, the cultural values of society, and the organization of law enforcement. As citizens become used to women on patrol and in other nontraditional roles, it will probably become less difficult for women officers to gain the compliance required in law enforcement work. Finally, there are signs that more and more citizens and policemen are beginning to take it for granted that women will be found on patrol as sworn officers of the law.

## Patrol Officer Cristina Murphy

Jim Dyer was drunk out of his mind when he called the Rochester Police Department on a recent Saturday night. He wanted to make a harassment complaint; a neighbor, he claimed, was trying to kill him with a chair. Officer Cristina Murphy, 27, a petite, dark-haired, soft-spoken three-year veteran of the Rochester P.D., took the call.

"What's the problem here?" she asked when she arrived at the scene. A crowd had gathered. Dyer's rage was good local fun.

"You're a *woman*!" Dyer complained as Murphy stepped from her squad car. "All they send me is *women*. I called earlier and they sent me a Puerto Rican and *she* didn't do nothing either."

"Mr. Dyer, what exactly is the problem?"

"Dickie Burroughs is the problem. He tried to kill me." Through a drunken haze, Dyer made certain things clear: He wanted Dickie Burroughs locked up. He wanted him sent to Attica for life. He wanted it done that night. Short of all that, Dyer hoped that the police might oblige him by roughing up his foe, just a little.

"We don't do that sort of thing," Murphy explained in the voice she uses with drunks and children. "Mr. Dyer, I can do one of two things for you. I can go find Mr. Burroughs and get his side of the story; I can talk to him. The other thing I can do is take a report from you and advise you how to take out a warrant. You'll have to go downtown for that."

Later, in her squad car, Murphy would say that she isn't usually so curt to complaining citizens. "But it's important not to take crap about being a female. Most of the stuff I get, I just let slip by. This guy, though, he really did not want service on his complaint, he wanted retribution. When he saw a woman taking his call, he figured that I wouldn't give it to him; it never struck him that no male officer would either. You know, *everyone* has an opinion about women being police officers—even drunks. Some people are very threatened by it. They just can't stand getting orders from a woman. White males, I think, are the most threatened. Black males seem the least—they look at me and they just see blue. Now women, they sometimes just can't stand the idea that a woman exists who can have power over them. They feel powerless and expect all women to feel that way too. As I said, everyone has an opinion."

SOURCE: Claudia Driefus, "People Are Always Asking Me What I'm Trying to Prove," *Police Magazine* (March 1980). Reprinted by permission of the Edna McConnell Clark Foundation.

## Subculture of the Police

A **subculture** is composed of the symbols, beliefs, values, and attitudes shared by the members of a particular group. The subculture of the police helps to define the "cop's world" and each officer's role in it. Like the subculture of any occupational group that sees itself as distinctive, the subculture of the police is based on a set of value premises stemming from their view of the nature of human behavior, their occupational environment, and their relationship to that environment. There are three key issues in our understanding of the police subculture: the concept of the "working personality," the social isolation of the police, and the stressful nature of much police work.

**subculture**
The aggregate of symbols, beliefs, and values shared by members of a subgroup within the larger society.

### Working Personality

Social scientists have demonstrated that there is a decided relationship between one's occupational environment and the way one interprets events. An occupation can be seen as a major badge of identity that a person protects as a representation of his or her self-esteem and person. Like doctors, teachers, janitors, and lawyers, the police as a group develop their own particular ways of perceiving and responding to their work environment. The police **working personality** thus influences the way officers view and interpret their occupational world. The elements of danger and authority define the police working personality.[13]

**Danger**    Because they operate in dangerous situations, officers are especially attentive to signs of potential violence and lawbreaking. They thus become suspicious persons, constantly on the lookout for indications that a crime is about to be committed or that they may be targets for lawbreakers.

Throughout the socialization process the recruit is warned to be suspicious and cautious and is told about fellow officers who were shot and killed while settling a family squabble or writing a ticket for speeding.[14] The folklore of the corps emphasizes that officers must always be on their guard. They must look for the unusual, including everything from persons who do not "belong" where they are observed to businesses opened at odd hours. They must watch for and interrogate persons, including those known to the officer from previous arrests, those who attempt to avoid or evade the officer, and those who loiter around playgrounds or public restrooms.[15] Given the variety of examples, it is not hard to understand how police officers become suspicious of everyone and all situations.

The element of unexpected danger creates such tension in police officers that they are constantly on edge and worried about the possibility of attack. People stopped for questioning may sense this tension. A suspect may not intend to attack an officer, but may see the officer's gruffness as uncalled-for hostility. If the suspect shows resentment, the officer may in turn interpret it as animosity and be even more on guard. Because the work demands continual preoccupation with potential violence, the police develop a perceptual shorthand to identify certain kinds of people as possible assailants—for example, persons whose gestures, language, or attire an officer has come to recognize as a prelude to violence.

**Authority**    The police represent authority, but unlike workers whose clients have learned to recognize their professional prerogatives (such as doctors, psychiatrists, lawyers), a police officer must *establish* authority—even when arrival at the scene itself may generate hostility. Certainly the symbols of police authority—the uniform, badge, gun, and nightstick—help, but more important is how police officers act within the social setting of each encounter. The officer must gain control of a situation by intervening, but the right to intervene may be challenged especially with order-maintenance situations. The order-maintenance function requires that the police stop fights, arrest drunks, and settle domestic quarrels—situations in which the laws are inexact and the presence of an officer may be unwelcomed by the offender or onlookers. The emphasis on authority may lead to use of excessive force or violence by officers who feel that their status has been placed in question by a person who represents a danger to them and to the community. Cries of police brutality often spring from such a circular chain of events.

In law enforcement situations, however, the officer can usually expect the victim's support; the shopkeeper will be pleased by the officer's arrival and will assist by describing the burglar. But when officers are dispatched to investigate a report of juveniles causing trouble in a public place, a neighborhood disturbance, or a victimless crime, they usually do not find a cooperative complainant and must contend not only with the perpetrators but also with others who may gather and expand the conflict. These circumstances require police to "handle the situation" rather than to enforce the law—that is, to assert authority without becoming emotionally involved. Even when verbally challenged by citizens on their personal conduct and right to enforce the law, they are expected to react in a detached or neutral manner.

The police officer, a symbol of authority which the public often gives low occupational status, must at times give orders to people with high status. Professionals, business people, and others of the middle class may respond to the officer not as a person working for the community interest but as a public servant whom they do not respect. Given the blue-collar background of many cops, maintaining self-respect and refusing to accept disrespectful attitudes may be important ways of resolving this problem.

In sum, working personality and occupational environment are so interlocked that they greatly influence the daily work of the police. Procedural requirements and the organizational structure of policing are overshadowed by the perceived need to establish authority in the face of danger.

*The occupational environment and working personality of officers are so interlocked that they greatly influence the daily experience of the police. How would you handle this situation?*

## Police Isolation

National studies of occupational status have shown that the public now ascribes more prestige to the police than it did in earlier decades. Public opinion polls indicate that most Americans have a fairly high opinion of the work of the police, although attitudes differ significantly by race (see Figure 6.4). Even in economically depressed inner-city areas where the police may be viewed as the tools of an unjust society, most inhabitants see them as protectors of their persons and property. Indeed, "the single most striking fact about the attitudes of citizens, black and white, toward the police is that in general these attitudes are positive, not negative."[16] Despite these findings, the police themselves do not believe that the public regards their vocation as honorable or their work as just. They feel that they are looked upon with suspicion, in part because they have been given the authority to use force to ensure compliance. Some scholars have argued that police cynicism increases their desire to use force on citizens.[17]

Throughout the publications of police organizations runs the theme that the public is extremely critical of law enforcement agents. But the general public is not the only group that is unappreciative of the police; other actors in the criminal justice system are often cited. Lawyers, prosecutors, and judges demean the officer's status by failing to treat the police with professional respect and by not dealing seriously with offenders whose behavior may have endangered the patrol officer. Part of the burden of being a police officer is that one is beset by self-doubt about professional status and worth in the public mind. This burden heightens the pressures on individual officers to isolate themselves within the police community.

Because they believe that the public is hostile to them and that the nature of law work aggravates the hostility, the police tend to separate themselves from the public, developing strong in-group ties. The police culture also encourages the strong bonding that commonly occurs among people who deal with violence. This solidarity "permits fallible men to perform an arduous and difficult task, and … places the highest value upon the obligation to back up and support a fellow officer."[18]

**Figure 6.4**
**Public opinion on the police**

Citizens were asked to rate the honesty and ethical standards of police and their ability to solve crimes. Note how opinion varies according to the race of the respondent

SOURCE: U.S. Department of Justice, Bureau of Justice Statistics, *Sourcebook of Criminal Justice* (Washington, D.C.: Government Printing Office, 1993), 169.

NOTE: Graph does not include "don't know" and "not sure/refused" responses.

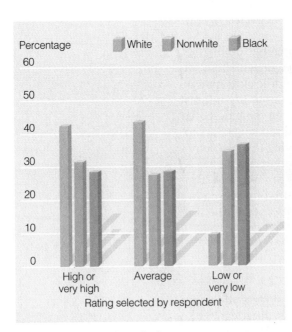

**a** Honesty and ethical standards

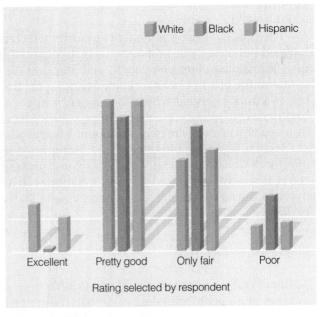

**b** Solving crime

Few other occupational groups have a world so circumscribed by a job's all-encompassing demands as that of the police. The uniqueness of their position limits their freedom to separate their vocational role from other aspects of their lives. From the time they are first given badges and guns, they must always carry these reminders of the position—the tools of the trade—and be prepared to use them. The requirements that they maintain vigilance against crime even when off duty and that they work at odd hours reinforce subculture values. These values are further supported as officers tend to interact primarily with their families and with other officers; indeed, there are limited opportunities for social contact with persons other than fellow officers.

When he gets off duty on the swing shift, there is little to do but go drinking and few people to do it with but other cops. He finds himself going bowling with them, going fishing, helping them paint their house or fix their cars. His family gets to know their families, and a kind of mutual protection society develops which turns out to be the only group in which the policeman is automatically entitled to respect.[19]

Even more important is that the police uniform and membership in the force are social liabilities. Wherever they go, the police are recognized by citizens who want to talk shop; others harangue them about the inadequacies of police service. The stress and isolation are continuous.

## Job Stress

The working environment and subculture of the police expose them to situations that affect their physical and mental health. This hazard has been fully recognized by law enforcement officials only since the late 1970s. One study of 2,300 officers in twenty departments found that 37 percent had serious marital problems, 36 percent had health problems, 23 percent had alcohol problems, 20 percent had problems with their children, and 10 percent had drug problems.[20] Newspaper and magazine articles with such titles as "Time Bombs in Blue" discuss the effects of the pent-up emotions and physical demands of the job.

Psychologists and other behavioral scientists have identified many of the factors that produce stress in police officers and have noted four general categories of stress to which police officers are subject:

1   *External stress*, produced by real threats and dangers, such as the necessity of entering a dark and unfamiliar building, responding to a "man with a gun" alarm, and pursuit of lawbreakers at high speeds.

2   *Organizational stress*, produced by elements that are inherent in the paramilitary character of police forces: constant adjustment to changing schedules, working at odd hours, complying with detailed rules and required procedures.

3   *Personal stress*, which may be generated by an officer's racial or gender status among peers and consequent difficulty in getting along with individual fellow officers and in adjusting to group-held values not compatible with one's own, perceptions of bias, and social isolation.

The threat of violence is one element contributing to the high degree of stress that police officers experience. The common experience among officers creates strong bonds, as evidenced by those attending a memorial service for a slain Dallas officer.

**4** *Operational stress*, the total effect of the daily confrontation with the tragedies of urban life; the need to deal with thieves, derelicts, and the mentally deranged; being lied to so often that all citizens become suspect; being required to place oneself in dangerous situations to protect a public that appears to be unappreciative; and the constant awareness of the possibility of being held legally liable for one's actions.[21]

Police departments have been slow to deal with stress, but some of the larger departments now provide psychological and medical counseling for officers. As in industry, an individual is often referred to a counselor only after a problem has been identified as resulting from a work-related incident. Unfortunately, because stress is usually internalized, it may not be identified for a long time; in popular terminology, it gets "bottled up" until it is manifested in the person's health, habits, or behavior. Some departments have instituted programs of prevention, group counseling, liability insurance, and family involvement. The legislatures of many states have instituted more liberal disability and retirement rules for police than for other public employees because their jobs are recognized to be more stressful and potentially debilitating.[22]

To summarize, the influence of the police subculture on the behavior of the individual officer is stronger when situations develop that produce conflict between the police and society. To endure their work, the police find they must relate to the public in ways that protect their own self-esteem. If the police view the public as essentially hostile and police work as aggravating that hostility, they will segregate themselves from the public by developing strong attitudes and norms that ensure that all members of the police fraternity conform to the interests of the group.

## Police and the Community

Being a police officer in an American city in the 1990s can be a debilitating experience. Hours of boring, routine work can be interrupted by short spurts of dangerous crime fighting. Although police work has always been frustrating and dangerous, officers today must deal with situations ranging from assisting the homeless to dealing with domestic violence to confronting shoot-outs at drug deals gone sour. Yet, law enforcement actions are often mishandled or misinterpreted, with the result that some members of the community are critical of the police.

### Conflict with the Community

Carrying out the complicated tasks of policing—law enforcement, order maintenance, and service—with efficiency and discretion is a formidable assignment even when the police have the public's support and cooperation. In urban ghettos—the neighborhoods that need and want effective policing—there is much distrust of the police; accordingly, citizens fail to report crimes and refuse to cooperate with investigations. Encounters between individual police officers and members of these communities are often charged with animosity and periodically turn into large-scale disorders.

Studies of attitudes toward the police in neighborhoods characterized according to race and social class have found that African-Americans considered the police to be more corrupt, less fair, tougher, and more excitable than did whites. However, race is not the only factor that influenced attitudes toward the police. Rather, race and personal experience with the police interacted to produce different results in the several areas. Attitudes toward the police may be associated with dissatisfaction about the quality of life in particular neighborhoods. When residents were asked whether "people in this neighborhood are treated as well as people living in other sections of the city," 40 percent of the ghetto blacks, 15 percent of the white working-class respondents, and 7 percent of the white middle-class respondents answered no.[23] Thus law enforcement policies and police actions clearly have a significant effect on the attitudes of some citizens concerning the fairness of the political community.

Why do some residents of the urban community resent the police? Studies have shown that permissive law enforcement and brutality are the two basic reasons for this resentment. The police are charged with failure in giving adequate protection and services to minority-group neighborhoods and, as we discuss more fully in the next section, with abusing residents physically or verbally. The police are seen as permissive when an officer treats an offense committed against a person of the same ethnic group as the offender more lightly than a similar incident in which offender and victim are members of different groups. The police often explain such differential treatment as a result of working in a hostile environment. The white patrol officer may fear that breaking up a street fight among members of a minority group will provoke the wrath of onlookers, while community residents may in fact view such negligence as a further indication that the police do not care about their neighborhood. It is said that the police do not work effectively on crimes such as narcotics sales, gambling, petty theft, and in-group assault, although these are the crimes that are most prevalent in the urban neighborhoods and cause the greatest insecurity and apprehension among residents.

Practically all studies document the prejudices of the police toward the poor and members of racial minorities. These attitudes lead many police officers to see all African-Americans or Hispanics as slum dwellers and thus as potential criminals, and as a result police tend to exaggerate the extent of minority crime. If both police and citizens view each other with intense hostility, then personal encounters will be strained and the potential for explosions, great. In such circumstances it is little wonder that the ghetto resident thinks of the police as an army of occupation and that the police think of themselves as combat soldiers. As noted by Jerome Skolnick and James Fyfe, the military organization of the police and the "war on crime" mentality encourage police violence against citizens of the inner city who are viewed as the enemy.[24] Yet it is also recognized that the police depend on citizens to help with crime prevention.

## Community Crime Prevention

There is a new recognition that the control of crime and disorder cannot be addressed solely by the police. Social control requires the involvement of all members of the community. Community crime prevention can be enhanced if there is collaboration between government agencies and neighborhood organizations. As Wesley Skogan has said, "voluntary local efforts must support official action if order is to be preserved within realistic budgetary limits and without sacrificing our civil liberties."[25] Across the country there has been a great increase in community programs designed to assist the police. We will examine several community-based approaches.

Citizen crime-watch groups have proliferated in many communities. It has been estimated that more than six million Americans are now members of such organizations, which often have direct channels to police departments. In Detroit, Neighborhood Watch is organized on 4,000 of the city's 12,000 blocks; in New York, the Blockwatchers are 70,000 strong and are "trained at precinct houses to watch, listen, and report accurately"; and in Dade County, Florida, the 175,000-member Citizens Crime Watch has extended its operations into schools in an effort to reduce drug use.[26]

The Crime Stoppers Program is designed to enlist public help in solving crimes. Originating in Albuquerque, New Mexico in 1975, it has spread across the country so that an estimated six hundred programs assist the police.[27] Television and radio stations have been enlisted to publicize an "unsolved crime of the week" and cash rewards are given for information that results in conviction of the offender. Although these programs result in the solving of some crimes, the numbers are insignificant when compared to the total. Problems of false arrest, defamation of character, and invasion of privacy have plagued some local programs.[28]

One group that gained national publicity in the 1980s was the Guardian Angels, which originated in New York City and spawned chapters in other parts of the country. The Angels were young people in distinctive apparel—red berets and T-shirts—who patrolled buses, subways, and streets as self-appointed peacekeepers. The mere presence of the Guardian Angels had a reassuring effect on people who traveled in what they believed to be dangerous neighborhoods. After a peak in the mid-1980s, the number of Guardian Angel organizations declined, yet their impact has been felt and their tactics have demonstrated the need for all citizens to be involved in crime prevention.[29]

How much can community organizations be relied upon to reduce crime and to ensure social order? The results are mixed. Research on forty neighborhoods in six cities shows that although crime prevention strategies and the development of voluntary community organizations are successful in more affluent neighborhoods, they are less likely to be found in neighborhoods where residents are poor and levels of disorder are high. In such areas, "residents typically are deeply suspicious of one another, report only a weak sense of community, perceive they have low levels of personal influence on neighborhood events, and feel that it is their neighbors, not 'outsiders,' whom they must watch with care."[30]

This attitude is especially detrimental because the police and the residents of a community must collaborate in maintaining standards of communal life, with the aim of reducing crime and—perhaps more important—the fear of crime. Law enforcement agencies require the support and assistance of the community for effective crime prevention and control. They must have support when they take actions that are consistent with neighborhood values and that help to maintain order. They must have assistance in the form of information about wrongdoing and cooperation with police investigation. As we will see in the next section, such community involvement and collaboration will not occur if the police abuse the power that society has bestowed on them.

## Police Abuse of Power

The beating of Rodney King, the New Orleans revenge killing by policemen of Adolph Archer who had shot an officer, and the seemingly endless police corruption scandals have brought the abuse of law enforcement power to the national agenda.[31] Although such incidents have occurred throughout American history, only during the past quarter century has an awakened citizenry focused attention on the illegal use of violence by police and the extent and potential of their corruption.

## Police Brutality and the Use of Force

In the racially heightened context of the contemporary city, conflicts between police and residents often result when it is alleged that law enforcement has been unprofessional. Citizens use the term *police brutality* to encompass a wide range of practices, from the use of profane or abusive language to physical force or violence. Stories of police incivility, physical abuse, and illegal actions are not new. In 1901, Frank Moss, a former police commissioner of New York, said:

For three years, there has been through the courts and the streets a dreary procession of citizens with broken heads and bruised bodies against few of whom was violence needed to effect an arrest. Many of them had done nothing to deserve an arrest. In a majority of such cases, no complaint was made. If the victim complains, his charge is generally dismissed. The police are practicing above the law.[32]

In Detroit, Los Angeles, Miami, and other cities a police-citizen confrontation has led to a riot. In some neighborhoods police may be perceived as an "occupying force."

More recently there have been published accounts of narcotics agents breaking into private homes and holding the residents at gunpoint while pulling apart the interiors in vain searches for drugs. That these have been cases of mistaken identity is no excuse. The physical violence against Rodney King and the killing of Adolph Archer are also inexcusable. No citizen should be placed in such circumstances. The following Close-Up raises issues of police misconduct and how it is handled.

Basic to the issue of police brutality is the question of the use of physical force. By law the police have the right to use force if necessary to make an arrest, to keep the peace, or to maintain public order. But just how much force is necessary and under what circumstances it may be used is a complex and arguable question. In particular, the use of deadly force in the apprehension of suspects has become a deeply emotional issue with a direct connection to community relations. A study by Jonathan Sorensen, James Marquart, and Deon Brock found support for the view that the greatest use of deadly force by the police is found in those communities with high levels of economic inequality and high proportions of minorities in the population.[33]

Surely no interaction between the police and the community causes more outrage and demoralization or precipitates more tension than the police shooting of a civilian.[34] Estimates of the number of citizens killed annually by the police range between 300 and 600, with about 1,500 more wounded.[35] That number has declined dramatically from the high level set in the 1970s.[36] The drop in police killings of civilians, however, should not obscure the fact that "the typical victim of deadly force employed in police-civilian contact has been a young black male."[37]

In March 1985 the Supreme Court for the first time ruled that police use of deadly force to apprehend an unarmed, nonviolent, fleeing felony

## Response to Police Misconduct

Two Minneapolis police officers were suspended for 30 days without pay for kicking and breaking the ribs of a man…[yet] both officers, Sgt. William Chaplin and Patrolman James Thernell, were acquitted of the same criminal charge by separate Hennepin County District Court juries. Minneapolis Police Chief Tony Bouza said the jury verdicts were wrong.

"The reality is the evidence was overwhelming," Bouza said. "As I read the transcripts of the criminal trials, I came to the inescapable conclusion that they should have been found guilty."

Bouza said he was persuaded by the testimony of two other Minneapolis policemen who said Chaplin and Thernell kicked 19-year-old Steve Goodwin when he was lying face down on the ground.…

The chief said the primary reason the juries voted for acquittal was that Goodwin "was a terrible witness. He's a street guy. He was hostile to the police. He made silly statements on the stand," Bouza said.

In addition, he said the acquittals reflected the reluctance of juries to convict police officers.

Bouza said that the criminal process, the civil process, and the internal disciplinary process "are distinct and separate. They might influence one another, but they are three separable events."

"This is an important symbolic case [because] it centers on one of the last holdouts of the old system, Bill Chaplin," Bouza said. "He is one of the leaders of this department. He has many admirable qualities and he has some qualities that make him a menace in the police world.

"He has been among the last to receive my message that brutality will not be condoned. He mistakes aggressive policing for doing anything you want on the streets."…

Chaplin, a 17-year veteran, previously was found guilty of "wanton and malicious" behavior in the beating of a suspect he arrested [and] was disciplined twice for incidents that occurred [earlier]. He was suspended for a few days following allegations of misuse of vice-squad funds. He was reprimanded after a fight in a northeast Minneapolis bar. Thernell, a 14-year veteran, had no disciplinary record.

Bouza said he expects the Minneapolis Police Federation to inform him that it will appeal the discipline. If the union appeals, the suspensions will be stayed until the appeals are resolved.

SOURCE: Adapted from Dennis J. McGrath, "Bouza Suspends Two Officers Whom Juries Acquitted," *Minneapolis Star and Tribune*, 27 April 1984, 38. Reprinted with permission from the *Minneapolis Star and Tribune*.

---

suspect violated the Fourth Amendment guarantee against unreasonable seizure. The case, *Tennessee v. Garner*, arose from the killing of Edward Garner, a fifteen-year-old eighth grader, by a member of the Memphis Police Department.[38]

Officer Elton Hymon and his fellow officer, Leslie Wright, were dispatched to answer a "prowler-inside" call. Arriving at the scene, they saw a woman standing on her porch and gesturing toward the adjacent house. She told them she had heard glass breaking and someone was inside next door. While Wright radioed for help, Hymon went to the back of the house, heard a door slam, and saw someone run across the backyard toward a six-foot chainlink fence. With his flashlight, Hymon was able to see that Garner was unarmed. The officer called out, "Police! Halt!" but Garner began to climb the fence. Convinced that if Garner made it over the fence he would escape, Hymon fired at him, hitting him in the back of the head. Garner died on the operating table, the ten dollars he had stolen in his pocket. Hymon was acting under Tennessee law and Memphis Police Department policy.

*Tennessee v. Garner* (1985)
Deadly force may not be used against an unarmed and fleeing suspect unless necessary to prevent the escape and the officer has probable cause to believe that the suspect poses a significant threat of death or serious injury to the officers or others.

Until the Supreme Court decision in *Tennessee* v. *Garner*, police in about half the states were guided by the common-law principle allowing the use of whatever force was necessary to arrest a fleeing felon. The justices set as a new standard that the police may not use deadly force in apprehending fleeing felons "unless it is necessary to prevent the escape and the officer has probable cause to believe that the suspect poses a significant threat of death or serious physical injury to the officer or others."[39] It is this element of dangerousness that the officer must evaluate before taking action. Thus, for example, an officer would be justified in using deadly force if the suspect "threatens the officer with a weapon or there is probable cause to believe that he has committed a crime involving the infliction or threatened infliction of serious physical harm."[40]

In the *Garner* decision the Supreme Court in effect invalidated state laws and local police policies that had allowed officers to shoot unarmed or otherwise nondangerous suspects if they resisted arrest or attempted to flee. However, many observers believe that this landmark decision will have little impact on the day-to-day actions of the police. Many states already have laws restricting the use of deadly force to the standard set by the Supreme Court. Other states may enact legislation that will meet the new criteria but perhaps not the spirit of the new standard. For example, new standards may allow the use of deadly force against suspects fleeing "violent" or "forcible" felonies whether or not an individual actually used force or violence. However, the threat of civil litigation against officers who shoot in situations like *Garner* may limit police actions. Departmental policies and the leadership of police executives in upholding the new standards can also make the difference between a city with few civilian killings by the police and a city with many killings.[41] Finally, it must be recognized that, even with court rulings, departmental policies, and state laws, as long as police officers carry weapons, some incidents will occur. Training, internal review of incidents, and disciplining or discharging of trigger-happy officers may help reduce the use of unnecessary force, but the problem will occasionally erupt as an issue separating the community from the police.

Mark Blumberg asserts that there has been tremendous progress over the past several decades with regard to the unrestrained use of firearms by police officers. He believes this progress has been made because firearms training has been improved, departments have instituted less permissive policies, social science has contributed to a better understanding of deadly force situations, and the Supreme Court has issued the *Garner* ruling.[42] Although progress has evidently been made regarding police brutality and use of deadly force, the issue of corruption remains an enduring problem. We look to this issue next.

## Corruption

Police corruption is not new to America. As Lawrence Sherman has noted, "virtually every urban police department in the United States has experienced both organized corruption and a major scandal over that corruption."[43] Earlier in the twentieth century, numerous city officials actively organized liquor and gambling businesses to provide personal income and to enhance political operations. In many cities a link was maintained between politicians and police officials so that favored clients would be protected and competitors harassed. Much of the Progressive-era movement to reform the police was designed to block such associations. Although political ties have been cut in most cities, corruption is still present.

Like the issue of police brutality, one of the difficulties of discussing police corruption is that of definition. Sometimes corruption is defined so broadly that it ranges from accepting a free cup of coffee (see A Question of Ethics) to robbing unlocked business establishments. Herman Goldstein suggests that corruption includes only those forms of behavior designed to produce personal gain for the officer or for others.[44] This definition, however, excludes the misuse of authority that may occur in a case of police brutality when personal gain is not involved. The distinction is often not easy to make. Criminal justice scholars make a distinction between corrupt officers who are "grass eaters" and those who are "meat eaters."

**Grass Eaters and Meat Eaters**   "Grass eaters" are officers who accept payoffs that the circumstances of police work bring their way. "Meat eaters" are officers who aggressively misuse their power for personal gain. Meat eaters are few, though their exploits make headlines; grass eaters are the heart of the problem. Because grass eaters are many, they make corruption respectable, and they encourage adherence to a code of secrecy that brands anyone who exposes corruption as a traitor.

In the past, poor salaries, politics, and recruitment practices have been cited as reasons that some police officers engage in corrupt practices. It has been said that a few "rotten apples" should not taint an entire police force, but corruption in some departments has been shown to be so rampant that the rotten-apple theory does not adequately explain the situation. The organization and structure of policing may also contribute to corruption. Much police work involves the enforcement of laws in situations where there is no complainant or where there may be doubt whether a law has actually been broken. Moreover, most police work is carried out at the officer's own discretion, without direct supervision.

The norms of a department and the code of the force may shield the corrupt cop from detection. As former police officer Kevin Hembury told New York City's Mollen Commission, which investigated police corruption in 1993, he learned at the police academy and in the locker room of

## A Question of Ethics

**B**ianco's Restaurant is a popular, noisy place in a tough section of town. Open from 6:30 A.M. until midnight, it is usually crowded with neighborhood regulars who like the low prices and ample portions, teenagers planning their next adventure, and people grabbing a quick bite to eat.

Officer Buchanan has just finished his late night "lunch" before returning to duty. As he proceeds toward the cash register, Cheryl Bianco, the manager, takes the bill from his hand and says, "This one's on me, John. It's nice to have you with us."

Officer Buchanan protests, "Thanks, but I'd better pay for my own meal."

"Why do you say that? The other cops don't object to getting a free meal now and then."

"Well, they may feel that way, but I don't want anyone to get the idea that I'm giving you special treatment," Buchanan replies.

"Come off it. Who's going to think that? I don't expect special treatment; we just want you to know we appreciate your work."

What are the issues involved here? If Buchanan refuses to accept Bianco's generosity, what is he saying about his role as a police officer? If he accepts the offer, what is he saying? Might citizens overhearing the conversation draw other meanings? Is turning down a $6.50 meal that important?

The enforcement of drug laws creates situations in which police corruption can occur.

the Seventy-third Precinct the "us against them" mentality and the "blue wall of silence"—that "cops never rat on other cops, that ratting on corrupt cops is worse than corruption itself." Exposed to the notorious drug trafficking and violence in his precinct, Hembury learned that "opportunities for money, drugs, power, and thrills were plentiful, and opportunities for friendly, productive contact with the thousands of good people who lived there were few." What startled the commission members was his statement that "no commanding officer ever asked how he and his colleagues were spending their days ... or how well they were serving the residents they were supposed to protect."[45]

Enforcement of vice laws, especially those regarding drugs, create formidable problems for police agencies. In many cities the financial rewards to the vice operators are so high that they can easily afford the expense of protecting themselves against enforcement. More importantly, police operations against victimless crimes are proactive; no one complains and no one requests enforcement of the law. In seeking out vice, police often depend on informants—persons who are willing to steer a member of the squad toward gamblers, prostitutes, or drug dealers in exchange for something of value, such as money, drugs, information, or tolerance. Once the exchange is made, the informant may gain the upper hand by threatening to expose the cop for offering a bribe.

Ellwyn Stoddard, who studied "blue-coat crime," contends that a measure of role ambivalence is inevitable among the police in a democratic society. Officers are responsible for protecting community members but are not given the powers necessary to carry out this mandate. As a result, conscientious police officers must often violate the law in order to perform their duties. Minor infractions by fellow officers are overlooked, but what may begin as a small departure from the rules can grow until it becomes routine. If over time illegal activity becomes routinized, then it can become part of an "identifiable informal 'code.' "[46] Stoddard notes that police officers become socialized to the code early in their careers. Those who deviate by "snitching" on their fellow officers may become objects of ridicule. If, however, corruption receives official attention, if it exceeds the limits of the code, other members of the force will distance themselves from the accused, in this way protecting the code. Terms of this blue-coat code are defined as follows:

- *Mooching*: Accepting free coffee, cigarettes, meals, liquor, groceries, or other items, justified as compensation either for being in an underpaid profession or for future acts of favoritism the donor may receive.

- *Bribery*: The receipt of cash or a "gift" in exchange for past or future assistance in avoidance of prosecution, such as a claim that the officer is unable to make a positive identification of a criminal, an officer's agreement to be in the wrong place at a time when a crime is to occur, or any other action that may be excused as carelessness but not offered as proof of deliberate miscarriage of justice. Distinguished from *mooching* by the higher value of the gift and by the mutual understanding in regard to services to be performed upon the acceptance of the gift.

- *Chiseling*: Demanding price discounts, free admission to places of entertainment whether in connection with police duty or not, and the like.

- *Extortion*: A demand for placement of an advertisement in a police magazine or purchase of tickets to a police function; the practice of holding a "street court" where minor traffic tickets can be avoided by the payment of cash "bail" to the arresting officer, with no receipt given.

- *Shopping*: Picking up small items such as candy bars, gum, and cigarettes at a store where the door has been accidentally left unlocked at the close of business hours.

- *Shakedown*: The practice of appropriating expensive items for personal use during an investigation of a break-in, burglary, or unlocked door and attributing their loss to criminal activity. Distinguished from *shopping* by the value of the items taken and the ease with which former ownership of items may be determined if the officer is caught in the act of procurement.

- *Premeditated theft*: Planned burglary, involving the use of tools, keys, or other devices to force entry, or any prearranged plan to acquire property unlawfully. Distinguished from *shakedown* only by the previous arrangements made in regard to the theft, not by the value of the items taken.

- *Favoritism*: The practice of issuing license tabs, window stickers, or courtesy cards that exempt users from arrest or citation for traffic offenses (sometimes extended to spouses, families, and friends of recipients).

- *Perjury*: Lying to provide an alibi for fellow officers apprehended in unlawful activity approved by the "code."

- *Prejudice*: Treatment of minority groups in a manner less than impartial, neutral, and objective, especially members of groups who are unlikely to have "influence" in city hall that might cause the arresting officer trouble.[47]

One of the most highly publicized investigations into police corruption was launched by New York City's Knapp Commission. In its 1972 report, the commission said that it had found corruption to be widespread in the New York City Police Department. In gambling, narcotics, prostitution, and the construction industry payments to police officers occurred regularly. Patrol officers on the beat not only received these "scores" but also shared them with superior officers. The amounts ranged from a few dollars in minor shakedowns to a narcotics payoff of $80,000. What most concerned the commission was that although most police officers were not themselves corrupt, they tolerated the practices and took no steps to prevent what they knew or suspected was happening. Corruption in the NYPD seems to follow twenty-year cycles, as evidenced by the 1993 Mollen Commission investigation.

Corruption scandals in the 1980s rocked the Philadelphia and Miami police departments.[48] In Philadelphia the officer appointed to lead the department's corruption investigation was himself given an eighteen-year prison sentence on evidence that he short-circuited the investigation and was netting $50,000 a month from operators of illegal electronic poker machines. In addition, twenty-six Philadelphia officers were charged with extortion to protect illegal gambling and prostitution operations. In 1988 more than one hundred Miami officers were implicated in corrupt practices with regard to drug dealers. Ten were indicted by a federal grand jury for participation in a $13 million theft of cocaine from a boat anchored in the Miami River. Three drug smugglers drowned when they jumped into the water as the officers approached. The officers later sold the cocaine they had confiscated. They pleaded guilty to murder-conspiracy or drug-trafficking charges and received reduced sentences of up to thirty years in prison.[49]

**Impact of Corruption**    Police corruption has multiple effects on law enforcement: criminals are allowed to pursue their illegal activities, departmental morale and supervision drop, and the image of the police suffers. The credibility of a police agency is extremely important given the need for the citizenry's cooperation. When there is a generally prevalent belief that the police are not much different from the "crooks," effective crime control is impossible.

It is startling that many people do not equate police corruption with other forms of criminal activity. Some accept the fact that officers proceed forcefully against minor offenders yet look the other way if a payoff is forthcoming. Furthermore, some citizens believe that police corruption is tolerable as long as the streets are safe. This attitude is unreasonable because police officers "on the take" are pursuing personal rather than community goals.

**Controlling Corruption**    As with other problems in a free society, the power of public opinion is crucial in controlling police corruption. The public, however, knows only about the major police scandals that are publicized in the media. When corruption reaches this level of notoriety, government agencies other than the police—prosecutors, attorney generals, grand juries, special investigating bodies, and others—step in to solve the problem through indictments and organizational reforms. For the vast majority of corrupt actions, however, the American political and legal systems have charged the police with keeping their own house in order. The more pernicious daily acts of corruption must be exposed and corrected through the internal mechanisms of law enforcement organizations. Departments receive complaints about officer behavior, investigate, and make recommendations that either clear the officer's name or result in disciplinary action. Departments also have policy statements that outline permissible conduct concerning the temptations often visited upon officers.

It is well recognized within police leadership that the top administrators of a department must set the tone on corruption. Successful police officials in major cities, such as Patrick Murphy, O. W. Wilson, Clarence Kelley, and Wyman Vernon, all took much-publicized stands that informed the general public and law enforcement employees that they would not tolerate the slightest act of corruption and would take swift action when any such act came to their attention.

## Civic Accountability

Relations between citizens and the police depend greatly on the confidence people have that officers will behave in accordance with the law and with departmental guidelines. Rapport is enhanced when citizens feel secure that the police will protect their persons and property and the civil liberties guaranteed by the Constitution. The issue of holding police accountable to civilian control without thereby destroying their effectiveness has received increasing concern. As noted by Allen Wagner and Scott Decker, "When the police are subjects of complaints, the process of law enforcement begins to break down."[50] Here we will examine four approaches that promote police accountability to citizens: (1) internal affairs units, (2) civilian review boards, (3) standards and accreditation, and (4) civil liability suits.

### Internal Affairs Units

Policing the police is primarily an internal matter that must be given top priority by administrators. The community must be confident the department has developed effective procedures to ensure that personnel will act to preserve the rights of citizens. Unfortunately, many departments have no formal complaint machinery, and when such machinery does exist, it often seems designed to discourage civilian input (see Figure 6.5). Rumor has it, for example, that a few years ago a sign over a pile of one-inch-square scraps of paper in the Internal Affairs Bureau of the San Francisco Police Department said "Write your complaints here."[51] Internal investigators on the force may assume that a citizen's grievance is an attack on the police as a whole and reflexively move to shield individual officers. In such a situation, administrators may be deprived of valuable information and so may be unable to correct the problem. The public, in turn, may be led to believe that the questioned practices are condoned or even expected.

**internal affairs unit**
A branch of a police department designated to receive and investigate complaints against officers alleging violation of rules and policies.

Depending on the size of the department, a single officer or an entire section may be designated an **internal affairs unit** to investigate wrongdoing. An officer who is charged with misconduct may face criminal prosecution or departmental disciplinary action that may lead to resignation, dismissal, or temporary suspension. Officers assigned to the unit carry responsibilities similar to those of the inspector general's staff in the military. They have the unenviable task of investigating complaints against fellow officers. The work of such units is described in the 1990 film, "Internal Affairs," in which a team of investigators aggressively pursues and eventually catches a patrol sergeant who is involved in drug dealing and murder. As is typical with Hollywood, the film depicts a dramatic case rather than the more common investigations of sexual harassment, alcohol or drug problems, misuse of physical force, and violations of departmental operational policies.

Officers are normally assigned to internal affairs for a specific time period, such as eight years. Internal affairs investigators find the work stressful as their status prevents them from maintaining personal relationships with their fellow officers. A wall of silence exists between investigators and their fellow officers; they may be shunned and unable to join the social aspects of police work, especially in smaller departments where everyone knows each other and fraternal bonds are strong.

The internal affairs unit must be provided with sufficient investigative resources to conduct its mission and must have direct access to the chief. Even when the top administrator supports the rooting out of misconduct, however, it is often difficult to persuade officers to testify against fellow officers. But maintenance of a "clean" force is essential if the crime prevention and law enforcement goals are to be met. When the police department demonstrates to the community that it is professionally responsible for the actions of its members, demands for review by an external body, discussed next, fade away.

## Civilian Review Boards

One criticism about members of public bureaucracies is that they serve to protect themselves. Thus, police departments are often criticized as "white-washing" complaints brought against individual officers or policies. Civilian review boards—which vary greatly in structure and procedures—are organized so that complaints can be channeled through a public committee of persons who are not sworn police officers.[52] The boards review how police departments dispose of citizen complaints and recommend remedial action. They do not have power to investigate or to discipline.

Creation in the 1960s of the first civilian review boards in New York and Philadelphia led to major political battles. In New York the Patrolman's Benevolent Association opposed creation of a board, which was subsequently rejected in a referendum by the voters. The Philadelphia board was dismantled after former police chief Frank Rizzo was elected as mayor. With the growth of minority political power in the 1980s there

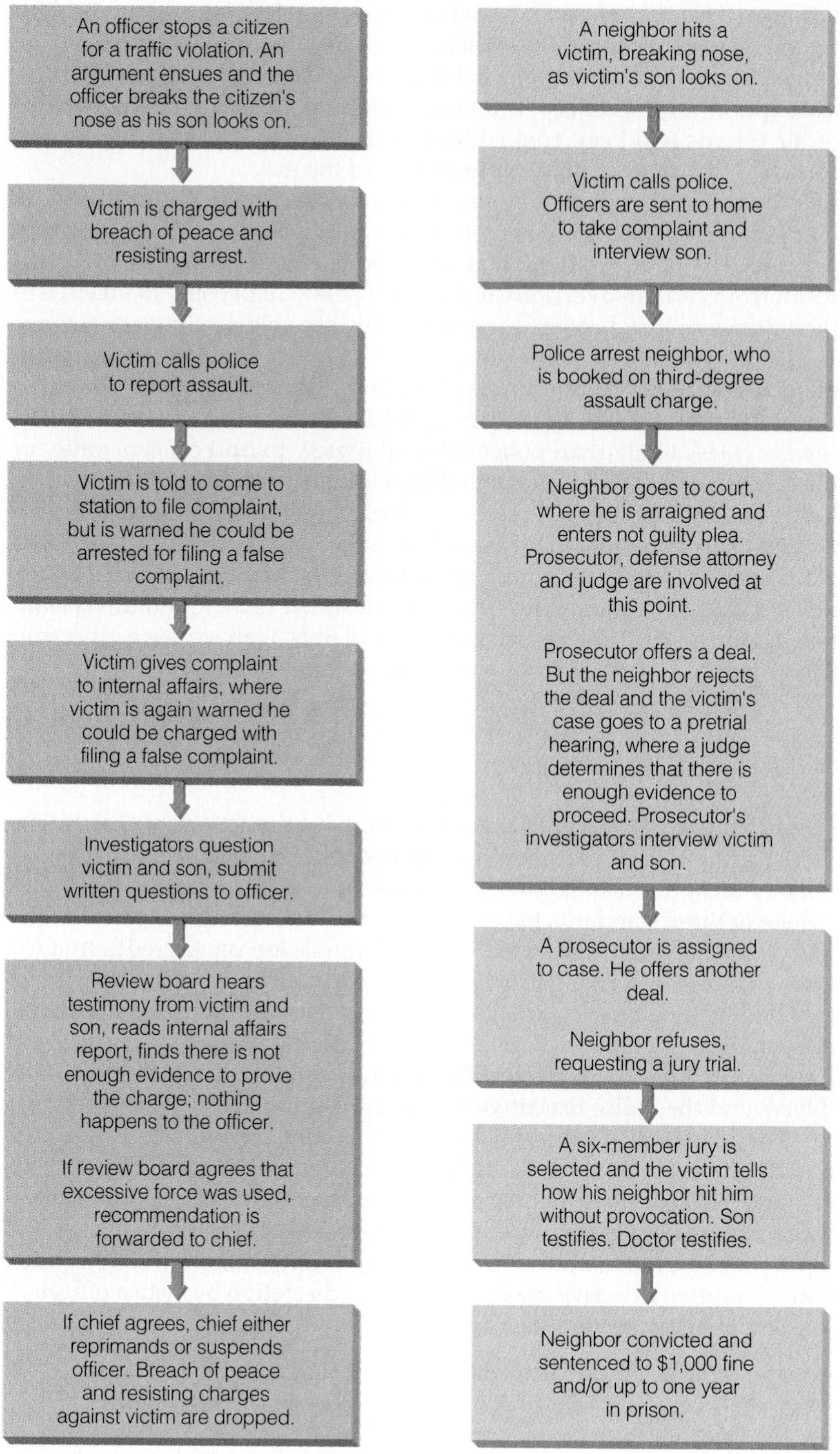

An officer stops a citizen for a traffic violation. An argument ensues and the officer breaks the citizen's nose as his son looks on.

↓

Victim is charged with breach of peace and resisting arrest.

↓

Victim calls police to report assault.

↓

Victim is told to come to station to file complaint, but is warned he could be arrested for filing a false complaint.

↓

Victim gives complaint to internal affairs, where victim is again warned he could be charged with filing a false complaint.

↓

Investigators question victim and son, submit written questions to officer.

↓

Review board hears testimony from victim and son, reads internal affairs report, finds there is not enough evidence to prove the charge; nothing happens to the officer.

If review board agrees that excessive force was used, recommendation is forwarded to chief.

↓

If chief agrees, chief either reprimands or suspends officer. Breach of peace and resisting charges against victim are dropped.

A neighbor hits a victim, breaking nose, as victim's son looks on.

↓

Victim calls police. Officers are sent to home to take complaint and interview son.

↓

Police arrest neighbor, who is booked on third-degree assault charge.

↓

Neighbor goes to court, where he is arraigned and enters not guilty plea. Prosecutor, defense attorney and judge are involved at this point.

Prosecutor offers a deal. But the neighbor rejects the deal and the victim's case goes to a pretrial hearing, where a judge determines that there is enough evidence to proceed. Prosecutor's investigators interview victim and son.

↓

A prosecutor is assigned to case. He offers another deal.

Neighbor refuses, requesting a jury trial.

↓

A six-member jury is selected and the victim tells how his neighbor hit him without provocation. Son testifies. Doctor testifies.

↓

Neighbor convicted and sentenced to $1,000 fine and/or up to one year in prison.

**Figure 6.5**
**Path of citizen complaints**
Compare the actions taken when a citizen is assaulted by a police officer in the course of dealing with a traffic violation and that of a citizen who is assaulted by a neighbor.

SOURCE: *Hartford Courant*, 30 September 1991.

has been a revival of civilian review boards. A 1991 survey of the fifty largest American cities found that thirty had some form of civilian review of the police.[53] The extent to which there has been a broader base of political support for the concept is demonstrated by the fact that twenty-three of the boards had been created by a local ordinance passed by the city council rather than by an executive order of the mayor.

The primary argument by the police against civilian review boards is that persons outside law enforcement do not understand the problems of policing. The police contend that low morale and performance problems result from civilian oversight and that officers will become ineffective in their duties as they become concerned over possible disciplinary actions. In fact, the civilian review agencies have not been harsh in their recommendations on police conduct. As noted by Wayne Kerstetter, "The experience in New York, Philadelphia, and Berkeley suggests that civilian review is less likely than police internal review to find officers guilty of misconduct and is more lenient in its disciplinary recommendations when it does find them guilty."[54] The review of police actions occurs after the incident has taken place and usually results in a question of the officer's word against that of the complainant. Given the low visibility of the incidents that lead to complaints, many are destined to be found unsubstantiated. During 1990, only 8 percent of complaints against police officers in San Francisco were upheld by the civilian review board.[55]

## Standards and Accreditation

Communities can gain greater accountability of the actions of their police by requiring that department operations be conducted according to nationally recognized standards. A movement to accredit departments that adhere to these standards has gained momentum during the past decade. This work has been supported by the Commission on Accreditation for Law Enforcement Agencies (CALEA), a private nonprofit corporation jointly developed by four major professional associations: International Association of Chiefs of Police (IACP), National Organization of Black Law Enforcement Executives (NOBLE), National Sheriffs Association (NSA), and the Police Executive Research Forum (PERF).

The *Standards*, first published in 1983, have been periodically updated. There are now nine hundred standards organized according to forty-eight topics. Each standard is a declarative statement, supplemented by an explanatory paragraph, that places clear-cut requirements on the agency. For example, under "Limits of Authority" standard 1.2.2. requires that "A written directive governs the use of discretion by sworn officers." The commentary section states:

In many agencies, the exercise of discretion is defined by a combination of written enforcement policies, training and supervision. The written directive should define the limits of individual discretion and provide guidelines for exercising discretion within those limits.[56]

Police departments have been almost completely silent on their use of discretion, so this requirement represents an enormous shift. However, the standard does not specifically define its coverage; for example, does it cover stop and frisk, handling of drunks, or the use of informants?

Police accreditation is voluntary. Organizations seeking accreditation contact CALEA and personnel from that organization work with the department to meet the standards. The process involves a self-evaluation by department executives, the development of management policies that meet the standards, and the training of officers with respect to those policies. CALEA personnel visit the department, examine the policies, and determine whether the standards are met in daily operations. Certification is given to departments that meet the criteria. The fact that a department is accredited by a national organization adds great local political value. Perhaps more importantly, the standards can be used as a key management tool. Officers are trained to understand the standards and can be held accountable for their actions.

## Civil Liability

Civil suits against departments for their misconduct have also helped to increase civic accountability.[57] Only recently has it been possible for citizens to sue public officials. In 1961 the U.S. Supreme Court ruled that Section 1983 of the Civil Rights Act of 1871 allows citizens to sue public officials for violations of their civil rights. This right was extended in 1978 when the Supreme Court said in *Monell* v. *Department of Social Services for the City of New York* that individual officials and the agency may be sued when an individual's civil rights are violated by the agency's "customs and usages." In other words, if an individual can show having been hurt by employees whose wrongful acts were the result of these "customs, practices, and policies, including poor training and supervision," then the individual can sue.[58] Suits from charges of brutality, false arrest, and negligence are increasingly being brought in both state and federal courts.

Damages in the millions of dollars have been awarded to plaintiffs by courts in a number of states, and individual police departments have settled civil suits out of court. For example, a Michigan court awarded $5.7 million to the heirs of a man mistakenly shot by a Detroit officer, and the city of Boston settled for $500,000 with the parents of a teenager shot to death. Los Angeles paid $8 million in monetary damages and Detroit paid $20 million in 1990.[59]

The courts have ruled that generally accepted professional practices and standards must be followed in police work. It is believed that the potential for civil suits has led to policy changes within departments. For example, the successful $2 million judgment won by Tracey Thurman against the Torrington, Connecticut, police undoubtedly had a profound impact on departments who suddenly became aware of their liability. (See the Close-Up in Chapter 4, "Battered Women, Reluctant Police.") Plaintiff's victories in civil suits have helped spur accreditation, as police executives believe that liability can be avoided or minimized if it can be demonstrated that officers are complying with the highest professional standards. In fact, insurance companies providing civil liability protection now offer discounts to departments that achieve accreditation.

We next examine one of the major organizations that deals with issues such as brutality, corruption, and civic accountability—the labor unions for police officers found in the departments of most cities.

## Unionism

During much of the twentieth century, police employee organizations were mainly fraternal associations designed to provide opportunities for fellowship, to serve the welfare needs (death benefits and insurance) of police families, and to promote charitable activities. In some cities, however, the police were organized for the purpose of collective bargaining, and by 1919, thirty-seven locals had been chartered by the American Federation of Labor (AFL). The Boston police strike of 1919 was in fact triggered by the refusal of the city to recognize one of these AFL affiliates. Not until the 1960s did the police, along with other public employees, begin to join labor unions in large numbers.[60] Today nearly three-fourths of all U.S. police officers are members of unions. About a third of the states do not have collective bargaining laws for public employees, however. In those jurisdictions a police "union" is not recognized by the law, even though such an organization may have informal powers to meet with management and discuss the concerns of its membership.[61]

The dramatic membership rise in police unions has been attributed to several factors: job dissatisfaction, especially with pay and working conditions; the perception that other public employees have been improving their positions through collective bargaining; the belief that the public is hostile to police needs; and an influx of young officers who hold less traditional views on relations between officer and police commissioner. Another factor is strong recruitment efforts by organized labor, which has sought to bolster membership through the enrollment of public employees as employment opportunities have shifted from the industrial to the service sectors of the economy.

The growth of police unionism has alarmed many law enforcement administrators and public officials.[62] Police chiefs fear they will be unable to manage their departments effectively because various aspects of personnel administration (such as transfers and promotions) will become mired in arbitration and grievance procedures. Thus many administrators view the union as interfering with their law enforcement leadership and with the officers in the ranks. Public officials have recognized the effectiveness of unions in gaining financial advantages for members and are thus wary of the demands placed on government resources, putting them in a position no politician likes: needing to raise taxes. Some commentators have also observed that the police, as the public embodiment of law enforcement, should not engage in actions such as strikes, slowdowns, and sickouts. They wonder about the impact on the practical and symbolic aspects of criminal justice should picket lines be formed around public buildings and the police refuse to work.

## Police Unions Today

Most officers are members of a labor union, but unlike the steelworkers and other trade unionists, they have no national organization representing all police. There are, in fact, different types of organizations at the local, state, and national levels. Police unions are locally based, in the main, because key law enforcement decisions are made at this level. There is also the sense among some officers that the organized police of a city can achieve their ends without the need to affiliate with and pay dues to a national labor union. The local character of the employment relationship helps to explain why the relatively centralized national police organizations have failed to enroll large numbers of officers as members.

The state level of police unionism is organized to pressure the state government for pensions, disability benefits, and the rights of public employees. Thus state federations of the local police organizations essentially function as lobbyists.

On the national level, the International Conference of Police Associations (ICPA) is the largest organization, with more than one hundred local and state units representing more than two hundred thousand officers. In 1978 this organization asked its members to approve application for entrance into the AFL-CIO, but the move was rejected by the rank and file. Subsequently, part of the membership broke away and formed the International Union of Police Associations (IUPA), to which the AFL-CIO then granted a charter. The Fraternal Order of Police (FOP) and the International Brotherhood of Police Officers (IBPO) are other major organizations representing law enforcement interests. Police officers are also members of national unions such as the American Federation of State, County, and Municipal Employees (AFSCME), a group with members in all sectors of public service, and the Teamsters.

## Impact of Police Unions

The police are little different from union members in other sectors of society: they are concerned primarily with wages, hours, and working conditions. Broader issues of changes in operating procedures have been raised only when they affect these three elements. Abuses of collective bargaining procedures have occurred, according to Hervey Juris and Peter Feuille, when union leaders have appealed directly to the public or a city council after failure to get police administrators to discuss contract terms in accordance with normal procedures.[63]

Some police administrators are concerned with union contracts which specify policies and procedures that they believe may interfere with their ability to run their departments. Restrictions on management's discretion in determining patrol officers' work shifts, criteria for promotion, and procedures for disciplining employees may worry administrators. Officers in some localities have succeeded in having a "police officer's bill of rights" written into their contracts, specifying the procedures that will be followed when an officer must submit to an investigation that could end in disciplinary action, demotion, or expulsion. These procedures may specify the right to counsel, the right to confront accusers, the keeping of verbatim transcripts of questioning, and the conditions under which interrogation may take place.

Police unions have often been antagonistic to changes in law enforcement organization and techniques when they have an effect on membership. For example, attempts to shift from two-person to one-person patrol cars were opposed by unions in at least two of the twenty-two cities studied by Juris and Feuille. In addition, police unions opposed efforts to employ civilians in clerical positions, on the ground that civilians constituted a potential security risk and that all police jobs required personnel who had street experience and the authority to arrest. Although the stated reasons may seem plausible, they are consistent "with the traditional trade union protectionist goal of safeguarding bargaining-unit work for incumbents."[64] In response to calls for increased recruitment of women and minorities, police unions have again tried to maintain the status quo. Affirmative action efforts, especially with regard to promotion, have been resisted by the unions because such practices threaten the prerogatives attached to seniority.

## Job Actions

Slowdowns, sickouts (the "blue flu"), and other disruptive tactics are common means that police unions use to exert pressure on employers. The strike has been used sparingly. It is illegal for most public employees to strike, and it was more than fifty years after the Boston Police Strike of 1919 before there was another such job action in a major American city. During the past several decades, however, New Orleans, San Francisco, Tucson, Oklahoma City, Las Cruces, New Mexico, and Youngstown, Ohio, have all experienced strikes by law enforcement officers.[65] In some of these actions the police returned to work within days; in others they stayed out as long as a month. In some cities strikers lost their jobs; in others they won pay raises. Aside from the legal prohibitions against strikes, individual members are ambivalent about deserting their responsibilities for a strike that would leave a city exposed to criminals.

In analyzing the causes of police strikes, researchers for the International Association of Chiefs of Police concluded that a combination of factors operated in each situation.[66] Among these the municipal financial crisis stands out. Beginning in the mid-1970s, American cities were faced with reduced federal allocations, local taxpayer revolts, and inflation. As personnel costs comprise as much as 85 percent of a city's operating budget, public employees usually bear the brunt of budget reductions. Many

Police unions have become an active force in some cities. Here, officers are shown protesting creation of an all-civilian review board.

police departments had been expanded earlier in the decade because of the public clamor for increased protection. In many parts of the country an upturn in the economy during the 1980s was reflected in higher police salaries, yet in the "rust belt" and the oil-producing states, allocations for public services did not keep pace. In the recession of the early 1990s, similar fiscal state and local crises have kept salaries down.

## Future of Police Unions

The increase in the use of collective bargaining by public employees since the 1970s has been phenomenal. Although most police officers have preferred to join local organizations rather than an affiliate of the AFL-CIO or some other national union, the strength of police unions has increased greatly in many cities. Clearly, police officials have to recognize this new influence on law enforcement administration. At the same time, in a public sector whose resources have diminished, state and local governments may not have the funds to increase salaries to keep pace with inflation. And there are still crucial questions about the role that unions should play in determining police department policies and the methods they can legitimately use to influence bargaining agreements.

As we will see in the next section, private policing has become a new and major player in the quest for security; a factor that has altered the law enforcement landscape.

## Private Policing

Private policing existed in Europe and the United States before the public organization of law enforcement, as witness Fielding's Bow Street Runners in England and the bounty hunters of the American West. During the late-nineteenth-century industrialization of the United States, the Pinkerton National Detective Agency provided industrial spies and strikebreakers to thwart labor union activities, and Wells, Fargo and Company was formed to provide security for banks and other businesses. In recent years businesses have felt an increasing need to employ private security forces to deal with shoplifting, employee pilfering, robbery, and airplane hijacking. Retail and industrial establishments today spend nearly as much for private protection as all localities spend for police protection. Many private groups—especially residents of upper-income suburbs—have also engaged private police to patrol their neighborhoods.

Private policing has become a $52 billion a year enterprise and is, as Figure 6.6 indicates, a growth industry. There are an estimated four thousand such agencies that in the aggregate have upward of a million and a half employees.[67] It has been estimated that by the year 2000 over $100 billion will be spent on private security in the United States. The private policing field is thus larger in both personnel and resources than the federal, state, and local public police forces combined.

The rise of private agencies demonstrates one aspect of the reformulation of the concept of policing. Policing is no longer simply the catching of criminals; it must "nowadays be understood more broadly as quintessentially about *order*."[68] The growth of private policing signifies not only the shifting of responsibility for policing public order, "but [also] the emergence of privately defined orders, policed by privately employed agents, that are in some cases inconsistent with, or even in conflict with, the public order proclaimed by the state."[69] Hence, we must recognize that such services are provided not only to stop lawbreakers and uphold order, as would the public police force, but also to regulate behaviors according to private policies that would not call for police action if done in a public space. For example, if you were to walk barefoot in Disney World, a behavior not permitted by the property's owner, you probably would be escorted off the premises.[70]

### Functions

The activities of private security personnel vary greatly: some employees merely act as watchmen and call the police at the first sign of trouble; others are deputized by public authority to carry out patrol and investigative duties similar to police officers; and still others rely on their presence and ability to make a "citizen's arrest" to deter lawbreakers. In most instances, private persons are authorized by law to make an arrest only when a felony has been committed in their presence. Thus private security agents or their companies face the possibility of being held civilly or even criminally liable for false arrest and the violation of an individual's

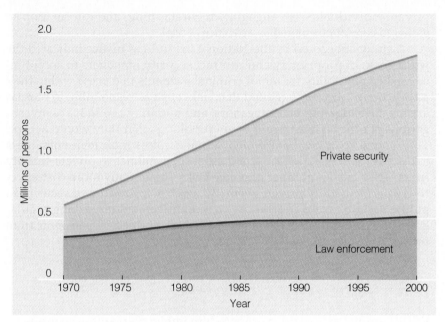

**a** Private security and law enforcement employment

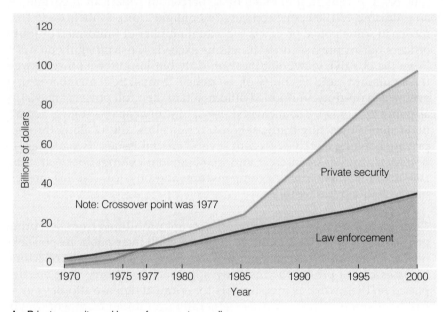

Note: Crossover point was 1977

**b** Private security and law enforcement spending

**Figure 6.6**
**Employment in private and public protection, 1970–2000 (projected)**

The number of people employed in the private security industry has surpassed the number employed by the public police and is growing. Such a large private force presents questions for the criminal justice system.

SOURCE: William Cunningham, John Strauchs, and Clifford Van Meter, *Private Security: Patterns and Trends* (Washington, D.C.: National Institute of Justice, 1991), 3.

civil rights. Some states have passed antishoplifting laws to give civil immunity to store personnel who reasonably but mistakenly detain people suspected of larceny. More ambiguous is the issue of a private guard's search of the person or property of a suspect. The suspect may resist and file a civil suit against the guard; if the search yields evidence of a crime, the evidence may not be admitted in court. Yet the Supreme Court has not applied the *Miranda* ruling to private police. Federal law prohibits private individuals from engaging in wiretapping, and information so gathered cannot be entered as evidence at trial.

A study sponsored by the National Institute of Justice indicated the willingness of proprietary and contract security managers to accept increased responsibility for minor criminal incidents that occur within their jurisdictions.[71] It was suggested that tasks such as responding to burglar alarms, investigating misdemeanors, and initiating preliminary investigations of other crimes could be undertakings that they would accept. Their counterpart law enforcement administrators indicated willingness to discuss the transfer of some of these responsibilities to private security firms. They cited a number of police tasks "potentially more cost-effectively performed by private security," such as provision of security in public buildings and courthouses and enforcement of parking regulations. Some of these tasks are already being performed by personnel from private firms in parts of the country.

## Private Employment of Public Police

Private employers are often eager to hire public police officers on a part-time basis. Although prohibited by 20 percent of American departments, an estimated 150,000 police officers "moonlight" for private firms.[72] That means in some police precincts the actual number of uniformed off-duty officers performing security functions exceeds those officially on duty. From the positive viewpoint these off-duty but in-uniform officers swell the availability and visibility of the police. It must be remembered that even when off-duty, uniformed officers retain their full powers and status as police personnel. The increased use of off-duty cops patrolling department stores, directing traffic at construction sites, and walking through private housing enclaves present several crucial issues. Two of these—potential conflict of interest and management prerogatives—are discussed here; others, such as compensation and physical stamina, are left for the reader to contemplate.

**Conflict of Interest**   Generally, officers are prohibited from accepting private jobs that involve conflicts of interest with their public responsibilities. For example, they may not work as process servers, bill collectors, repossessors, or pre-employment investigators for industry. Bans are also placed on their work as investigators for criminal defense attorneys or as bail bondsmen. Officers are also generally prohibited from working in places that profit from gambling operations, and many departments restrict employment in bars or other places where regulated goods or services are sold. However, there are no restrictions on their employment as private police outside these prohibited areas.

**Management Prerogatives**   What are the prerogatives of police managers with regard to officers who wish to supplement their salaries through off-duty work? Police executives have a responsibility to ensure that the public's interest in the presence of a ready force is supported, which means that the number of officers on a shift be maintained, that officers not appear for duty fatigued or physically weakened because of off-duty employment, and that selection for employment by private firms not result in conflict within the department.

Departments require that officers request permission for outside work. Permission may be denied for a number of reasons, including: work that lowers the dignity of the police, work that is physically dangerous and where unacceptable risks may result, work that is not in the "home" jurisdiction if approval is not granted by the "outside" police jurisdiction, work that requires more than eight hours of off-duty service, and work that interferes with the scheduled routine of the police department.

There are several management models designed to coordinate off-duty employment. The *department contract model* permits closer management control of off-duty work since employers must apply to the department to have officers assigned to them. Officers selected for off-duty work are compensated by the department, which is then reimbursed by the private employer. An overhead fee for the costs of this service is charged to the employer. Departments usually screen employers to ensure that the proposed use of officers will not conflict with departmental needs or the standards outlined above. When the private demand for police services exceeds the supply—and many departments find that is the case—the department contract model provides a way of rationally allocating staff to ensure that public needs are met.

The *officer contract model* allows each officer to independently find off-duty employment and to enter into a direct relationship with the private enterprise. Officers must apply to the department for permission, which is granted if the employment criteria are met. Problems develop with this model when an individual officer assumes a broker role, acting as an employment "agency" for fellow officers. This situation can lead to charges of favoritism and nepotism with disastrous consequences for discipline and morale.

With the *union brokerage model* the police union or association finds off-duty employment for its members. The union sets the conditions for the work and bargains with the department over pay, status, and conditions of the off-duty employment.

Each of these models has its backers. Albert Reiss notes that the more closely a department controls off-duty employment, the more liability it assumes for officers' actions when they work for private firms. Furthermore, there is an evolving case law about liability issues involving off-duty police officers.

What is not known is the impact of uniformed off-duty patrol on crime prevention and the public's perception of safety. It may be that public fears are reduced because of the visibility of officers whom they believe are acting in their official capacity.

## Public-Private Interface

The interface between public and private law enforcement is a matter of concern to professionals charged with crime control under law. Most private policing organizations have the prevention of crime as their goal;

others, however, adopt policelike methods and engage in investigation, apprehension, and prosecution. Private agents work for the people who employ them, and their goals may not always coincide with the public interest. Questions have been raised about the authority of private policing personnel to make arrests, to conduct searches, and to participate in undercover investigations. Of crucial importance is the issue of the boundary between the work of the police and that of private agencies. Lack of communication between public and private organizations has resulted in botched investigations, destruction of evidence, and overzealousness, all to the detriment of crime control. Yet most firms that offer private policing services stress that their chief concern is the prevention of crime and that their activities therefore do not conflict with the work of the public police.

These and other issues are seen to have impeded cooperation between public and private forces. Security managers do report some sharing of information and equipment. Cooperative efforts have been reported regarding tasks such as the transportation of hazardous materials, protection of dignitaries, crowd control, and investigation of economic crimes. Public and private police have worked together in undercover work. For example, a joint "sting" operation was conducted by the FBI and the security personnel of IBM in regard to the sale of computer secrets in Silicon Valley, the area around San Jose, California. Another public-private example is the National Auto Theft Bureau. This private, nonprofit organization acts as a clearinghouse for auto theft information. In many states, law enforcement officers and insurance agents are required by law to report auto theft information to the NATB.[73]

Security managers have said that they generally report *UCR* index crimes to the police. However, incidents of employee theft, insurance fraud, industrial espionage, commercial bribery, and computer crime tend *not* to be reported to public authorities. In such situations the chief concern of private companies is to prevent loss and protect assets. Although some such incidents are reported to the public prosecutor for action, the majority of them are resolved through internal procedures ("private justice") within the victimized company. Most businesses consider employee theft to be their greatest single crime problem. When such offenses are discovered, the offender may be "convicted" within the company and punished by forced restitution through payroll deductions, by loss of the job, or by dissemination of information about the incident throughout the industry. Thus an interesting question arises: to what extent does a parallel system of private justice exist with regard to some offenders and some crimes?[74]

Private organizations often bypass the public criminal justice system in an effort to avoid the need to cope with changing prosecution policies, administrative delays in prosecution, discovery rules that would open the internal affairs of the company to public scrutiny, and bad publicity. A survey by the United States Chamber of Commerce revealed that half of 446 business executives interviewed believed that law enforcement and the criminal justice system do a poor job of fighting property, organizational, and white-collar crimes against business.[75] But private policing is often criticized for employing people who are not properly trained, an issue that we next examine.

## Recruitment and Training

A major concern of law enforcement officials and civil libertarians is the recruitment and training of private security personnel. Studies have shown that such personnel are generally recruited from those with minimal education and training; because the pay is low, the work often attracts people who cannot find other jobs or who seek temporary work. Thus most of the work is done by the young and the retired. A study by the Rand Corporation found that fewer than half of the private security guards surveyed had a high school education and their average age was fifty-two. Perhaps more important, although "almost half of the respondents were armed, less than one-fifth reported having received any firearms training." Ninety-seven percent of the respondents failed to pass a "simple examination designed to test their knowledge of legal practice in typical job-related situations."[76] This portrait has been challenged by William Walsh, who argues that differences between private and public police are not that striking.[77]

As the private policing industry has grown, there have been calls for the examination and licensing of its personnel. Fewer than half of the states have such requirements. The National Council on Crime and Delinquency and the Private Security Advisory Council of the Law Enforcement Assistance Administration have offered model licensing statutes that specify periods of training and orientation, the wearing of uniforms that permit citizens to distinguish between public and private police, and the prohibition of employing any person who has a criminal record. In some states security firms are licensed, often by the attorney general, while in others the local police have this authority. In general, however, there is little regulation of such firms. The regulations that do exist tend to be focused on *contractual* as opposed to *proprietary* private policing services. Contractual security services are provided by private practitioners and agencies for a fee. Such practitioners include locksmiths, alarm specialists, and polygraph examiners and organizations such as Brink's, Burns, and Wackenhut, which provide guards and detectives. States and municipalities often require contract personnel to be licensed and bonded. Similar services are sometimes provided by proprietary security personnel, who are employed directly by the organization (retail stores, industrial plants, hospitals) they protect. With the exception of individuals required to carry weapons, proprietary security operations are not normally regulated by the state or municipality.

The private policing industry arose in response to a need; it grew because the product it offered was in demand. The need for the product may have resulted from the growth of crime, but it may also have developed

Private security is assuming an increasingly large role in American society. However, questions have been raised about the training, tactics, and jurisdiction of these "rent-a-cops."

because of the perception that the public police could not carry out a particular task. It is important that citizens distinguish between the actions of the public and private police. More importantly, private police must not hamper the work of law enforcement.

## Summary

United States policing faces a number of issues and trends as we move toward the twenty-first century. To meet current and future challenges, the police must recruit and train individuals who are committed to upholding the law and acting in ways that will gain the support of citizens. Improvements have been made during the past quarter century in recruiting officers who are well educated, from minority groups, and women. As a result the profile of the police has begun to change.

Like any profession the police work in an environment greatly influenced by their subculture, those norms and values that are specific to the job. The concept of the working personality helps us understand the influence of this subculture on how individual officers perceive their world. The isolation of police work not only strengthens bonds among officers but also may add to job stress.

For the police to be effective they must maintain their connection with the community. They must be attuned to changes in the community and adapt their tactics and approaches to new challenges. A public agency that resists change soon loses the very necessary element of public support. The problems of police brutality and corruption cause erosions of that support. Internal affairs units, civilian review boards, standards and accreditation, and civil liability suits are four approaches designed to increase police accountability to citizens.

Two trends in policing—unionism and private policing—have an impact on officers and departments. The unionization of officers has not only regularized but also challenged many practices of police executives. The expansion of private policing allows some officers to moonlight, but it adds a new dimension to how order is maintained and laws are enforced.

## Questions for Review

1　How do recruitment and training practices affect policing?

2　What is meant by the police subculture and how does it influence an officer's work?

3　What factors in the police officer's "working personality" influence an officer's work?

4　What are the pros and cons of the major approaches to making the police accountable to citizens?

5　What has the Supreme Court ruled regarding police use of deadly force?

6　How does the unionization of police officers affect the prerogatives of managers?

7　What are the problems associated with private policing?

## Key Terms and Cases

internal affairs unit
socialization

subculture
working personality

*Tennessee* v. *Garner* (1985)

## For Further Reading

Greene, Jack R., and Steven Mastrofski, eds. *Community Policing: Rhetoric or Reality?* New York: Praeger, 1988. An excellent collection of essays on community policing.

Juris, Hervey A., and Peter Feuille. *Police Unionism.* Lexington, Mass.: Lexington Books, 1973. Still the only major source of information on the development, actions, and issues of police unionism.

Maas, Peter. *Serpico.* New York: Bantam Books, 1973. The fascinating account of an undercover officer whose testimony was crucial to the Knapp Commission's investigation of police corruption.

Murano, Vincent. *Cop Hunter.* New York: Simon and Schuster, 1990. The story of an undercover cop who for ten years worked for the Internal Affairs Division of the New York City Police Department. Emphasizes the moral dilemmas of policing fellow officers.

Reiss, Albert J., Jr. *The Police and the Public.* New Haven, Conn.: Yale University Press, 1971. A classic study of the relationship of police officers to the public they serve.

Shearing, Clifford, and Philip C. Stenning, eds. *Private Policing.* Newbury Park, Calif.: Sage Publications, 1987. An excellent volume that explores various aspects of the private security industry.

Skolnick, Jerome H., and James J. Fyfe. *Above the Law: Police and the Excessive Use of Force*. New York: Free Press, 1993. Written in light of the Rodney King beating and the riots that followed. The authors believe that only by recruiting and supporting police chiefs who will uphold a policy of strict accountability can brutality be eliminated.

Westley, William. *Violence and the Police*. Cambridge, Mass.: MIT Press, 1970. Based on a 1951 study of the police, this book examines the fraternal bonds of officers and addresses the question of violence by officers.

## Notes

1   Jerome H. Skolnick and James J. Fyfe, *Above the Law: Police and the Excessive Use of Force* (New York: Free Press, 1993), chap. 1; see also Mike Sager, "Damn! They Gonna Lynch Us," *Gentlemen's Quarterly*, October 1991.

2   Skolnick and Fyfe, *Above the Law*.

3   Roger Parloff, "Maybe the Jury Was Right," *The American Lawyer* (June 1992): 7.

4   U.S. National Advisory Commission on Criminal Justice Standards and Goals, *A National Strategy to Reduce Crime* (Washington, D.C.: Government Printing Office, 1973), 44.

5   John Van Maanen, "Observations on the Making of Policemen," *Human Organization* 32 (1973): 407–418.

6   David L. Carter, Allen D. Sapp, and Darrel W. Stephens, *The State of Police Education: Policy Direction for the Twenty-first Century* (Washington, D.C.: Police Executive Research Forum, 1989), 43.

7   Samuel Walker, "Employment of Black and Hispanic Police Officers, 1983–1988: A Follow-up Study" (Occasional paper 89–1, Center for Applied Urban Research, University of Nebraska at Omaha, February 1989).

8   U.S. Department of Justice, *Crime in the United States* (Washington, D.C.: Government Printing Office, 1993), 217.

9   Susan Ehrlich Martin, *Breaking and Entering* (Berkeley: University of California Press, 1980), 27.

10   Susan E. Martin, "Women in Policing: The Eighties and Beyond," in *Police and Policing: Contemporary Issues*, ed. Dennis Jay Kenney (New York: Praeger, 1988), 6.

11   Peter Bloch and Deborah Anderson, *Policewomen on Patrol: First Report* (Washington, D.C.: Police Foundation, 1974), 1–7.

12   See Michael Charles, "Women in Policing: The Physical Aspects," *Journal of Police Science and Administration* 10 (1982): 10–19.

13   Jerome Skolnick, *Justice without Trial: Law Enforcement in a Democratic Society* (New York: Wiley, 1966), 44.

14   U.S. Department of Justice, National Institute of Justice, Joel Garner and Elizabeth Clemmer, "Danger to Police in Domestic Disturbances—A New Look," *Research in Brief* (Washington, D.C.: Government Printing Office, 1986).

15   Thomas F. Adams, "Field Interrogation," *Police* (March–April 1963): 28.

16   James W. Wilson, *Thinking about Crime*, 2d ed. (New York: Basic Books, 1983), 91.

17   Robert M. Regoli, John P. Crank, and Robert G. Culbertson, "Rejoinder-Police Cynicism: Theory Development and Reconstruction," *Justice Quarterly* 4 (1987): 281–286.

18   Michael K. Brown, *Working the Street* (New York: Russell Sage Foundation, 1981), 82.

19   James F. Ahern, *Police in Trouble* (New York: Hawthorne Books, 1972), 14.

20   John Blackmore, "Are Police Allowed to Have Problems of Their Own?" *Police Magazine* 1 (1978): 47–55.

21   Robert J. McGuire, "The Human Dimension in Urban Policing: Dealing with Stress in the 1980s," *Police Chief* 46 (November 1979): 27. See also Francis Cullen, Terrence Leming, Bruce Link, and John Wozniak, "The Impact of Social Supports in Police Stress," *Criminology* 23 (1985): 503–522.

22   Gail A. Goolkasian, Ronald W. Geddes, and William DeJong, "Coping with Police Stress," in *Critical Issues in Policing*, ed. Roger G. Dunham and Geoffrey P. Alpert (Prospect Heights, Ill.: Waveland Press, 1989), 498–507.

23   Herbert Jacob, "Black and White Perceptions of Justice in the City" (Paper presented at the Annual Meeting of the American Political Science Association, Chicago, 1970).

24   Skolnick and Fyfe, *Above the Law*, 160.

25   Wesley G. Skogan, *Disorder and Decline: Crime and the Spiral of Decay in American Neighborhoods* (New York: Free Press, 1990), 125.

26   *The Figgie Report Part Four: Reducing Crime in America—Successful Community Efforts* (Willowby, Ohio: Figgie International, 1983); James Garofalo and Maureen McLeod, "The Structure and Operation of Neighborhood Watch Programs in the United States," *Crime and Delinquency* 35 (1989): 326–344.

27   U.S. Department of Justice, National Institute of Justice, *Crime Stoppers: A National Evaluation*, by Dennis P. Rosenbaum, Arthur J. Lurigio, and Paul J. Lavrakas (Washington, D.C.: Government Printing Office, 1986).

28   Ibid.

29 Dennis Jay Kenney, "The Guardian Angels: The Related Social Issues," in *Police and Policing: Contemporary Issues*, ed. Dennis Jay Kenney (New York: Praeger, 1989), 225; Susan Pennell, Christine Curtis, Joel Henderson, and Jeff Tayman, "Guardian Angels: A Unique Approach to Crime Prevention," *Crime and Delinquency* 35 (1989): 378–400.

30 Skogan, *Disorder and Decline*, 130. See also Robert McGabey, "Economic Conditions: Neighborhood Organization and Urban Crime," in *Crime and Justice*, vol. 8, ed. Albert J. Reiss, Jr., and Michael Tonry (Chicago: University of Chicago Press, 1986), 230.

31 Skolnick and Fyfe, *Above the Law*, Chaps. 1, 2.

32 Frank Moss, "National Danger from Police Corruption," *North American Review* 173 (October 1901): 10–19.

33 Jonathan R. Sorensen, James W. Marquart, and Deon E. Brock, "Factors Related to Killings of Felons by Police Officers: A Test of the Community Violence and Conflict Hypotheses," *Justice Quarterly* 10 (September 1993): 439.

34 Amitai Schwartz, "A Role for Community Groups and Human Rights Agencies," in *Police Use of Deadly Force*, U.S. Department of Justice (Washington, D.C.: Government Printing Office, 1978), 54.

35 William Geller, "Deadly Force: What We Know," *Journal of Police Science and Administration* 10 (1982): 151–177; Lori Fridell, "Justifiable Use of Measures in Research on Deadly Force," *Journal of Criminal Justice* 17 (1989): 157–165.

36 Lawrence J. Sherman and Ellen G. Cohn, "Citizens Killed by Big City Police: 1970–84" (Unpublished manuscript, Crime Control Institute, Washington, D.C., October 1986).

37 James J. Fyfe, "Reducing the Use of Deadly Force: The New York Experience," in *Police Use of Deadly Force*, U.S. Department of Justice, 28.

38 *Tennessee* v. *Garner*, 53 L.W. 4410 (1985).

39 Ibid.

40 Ibid., 4412.

41 James J. Fyfe, "Police Use of Deadly Force: Research and Reform," in *Criminal Justice: Law and Politics*, 7th ed., ed. George F. Cole (Belmont, Calif.: Wadsworth, 1993), 128–142; James J. Fyfe and Jeffery T. Walker, "*Garner* Plus Five Years: An Examination of Supreme Court Intervention into Police Discretion and Legislative Prerogatives," *American Journal of Criminal Justice* 14 (1990): 167–188.

42 Mark Blumberg, "Controlling Police Use of Deadly Force: Assessing Two Decades of Progress," in *Critical Issues in Policing*, ed. Dunham and Alpert, 442–464.

43 Lawrence Sherman, *Scandal and Reform: Controlling Police Corruption* (Berkeley: University of California Press, 1978), XXIII.

44 Herman Goldstein, *Policing a Free Society* (Cambridge, Mass.: Ballinger, 1977), 190.

45  Joseph P. Armao and Leslie U. Cornfeld, "Why Good Cops Turn Rotten," *New York Times*, 1 November 1993, A–12. The authors are chief counsel and deputy chief counsel to the Mollen Commission.

46  Ellwyn R. Stoddard, "The Informal 'Code' of Police Deviancy: A Group Approach to Blue-Coat Crime," *Journal of Criminal Law, Criminology, and Police Science* 59 (1968): 204.

47  Ibid., 205.

48  *Crime Control Digest*, 25 November 1985, 30 June 1986, 3 August 1987.

49  John Dorshner, "The Dark Side of the Force," in *Critical Issues in Policing*, 250–270.

50  Allen E. Wagner and Scott H. Decker, "Evaluating Citizen Complaints Against the Police," in *Critical Issues in Policing*, 271.

51  Amitai Schwartz, "Reaching Systemic Police Abuses—The Need for Civilian Investigation of Misconduct: A Response to Wayne Kerstetter," in *Police Leadership in America*, ed. William A. Geller (New York: Praeger, 1985), 197.

52  Wayne A. Kerstetter, "Who Disciplines the Police? Who Should?" in *Police Leadership in America*, ed. Geller, 141–181.

53  Samuel Walker and Vic W. Bumphus, "Civilian Review of the Police: A National Survey of the Fifty Largest Cities, 1991," *Criminal Justice Policy Focus*, Criminal Justice Policy Research Group, Department of Criminal Justice, University of Nebraska at Omaha, 1991.

54  Kerstetter, "Who Disciplines the Police?", 162.

55  Skolnick and Fyfe, *Above the Law*, 229.

56  *Standards for Law Enforcement Agencies* (Fairfax, Va.: Commission on Accreditation for Law Enforcement Agencies, 1989), 1–2.

57  Victor E. Kappeler, *Critical Issues in Police Civil Liability* (Prospect Heights, Ill.: Waveland Press, 1993).

58  Skolnick and Fyfe, *Above the Law*, 202.

59  Rolando del Carmen, *Civil Liabilities in American Policing* (Englewood Cliffs, N.J.: Brady, 1991); Samuel Walker, *The Police in America*, 2d ed. (New York: McGraw-Hill, 1992); Skolnick and Fyfe, *Above the Law*, 202.

60  For a history of police unionism see Anthony V. Bouza, "Police Unions: Paper Tigers or Roaring Lions?" in *Police Leadership in America*, ed. Geller, 241.

61  James B. Jacobs, "Police Unions: How They Look from the Academic Side," in *Police Leadership in America*, ed. Geller, 287.

62  Robert B. Kleismet, "The Chief and the Union: May the Force Be With You," in *Police Leadership in America*, ed. Geller, 281.

63  Hervey A. Juris and Peter Feuille, "Employee Organizations," in *Police Personnel Administration*, ed. O. Glenn Stahl and Riach A. Steufenberger (Monterey, Calif.: Duxbury Press, 1974), 214.

64  Ibid.

65  William D. Gentel and Martha L. Handman, *Police Strikes: Causes and Prevention* (Washington, D.C.: Government Printing Office, 1980), 5; Richard M. Ayres, "Case Studies of Police Strikes in Two Cities— Albuquerque and Oklahoma City," *Journal of Police Science and Administration* 5 (1977): 19–30; L. Thomas Winfree and Frieda Gehlen, "Police Strikes: Public Support and Dissonance Education During a Strike by Police," *Journal of Police Science and Administration* 9 (1981): 451–452.

66  Gentel and Handman, *Police Strikes*.

67  William C. Cunningham, John H. Strauchs, and Clifford W. Van Meter, *Private Security Trends, 1970 to the Year 2000: The Hallcrest Report II* (Boston: Butterworth-Heinemann, 1990).

68  Clifford D. Shearing and Philip C. Stenning, "Reframing Policing," in *Private Policing*, ed. Shearing and Stenning (Newbury Park, Calif.: Sage, 1987), 13.

69  Ibid., 22.

70  Clifford D. Shearing and Philip C. Stenning, "Say 'Cheese!': The Disney Order That Is Not So Mickey Mouse," in *Private Policing*, 320.

71  U.S. Department of Justice, National Institute of Justice, William C. Cunningham and Todd H. Taylor, "The Growing Role of Private Security," *Research in Brief*, 1984.

72  U.S. Department of Justice, National Institute of Justice, *Private Employment of Public Police*, by Albert J. Reiss, Jr. (Washington, D.C.: Government Printing Office, 1988).

73  Gary T. Marx, "The Interweaving of Public and Private Police in Undercover Work," in *Private Policing*, 172–189.

74  See Melissa Davis, Richard Lundman, and Ramiro Martinez, Jr., "Private Corporate Justice: Store Police, Shoplifters, and Civil Recovery," *Social Problems* 38 (1991): 395–408.

75  Cited in Cunningham and Taylor, "The Growing Role of Private Security."

76  James S. Kakalik and Sorrell Wildhorn, *Private Police in the United States: Findings and Recommendations* (Washington, D.C.: Government Printing Office, 1972), 155.

77  William Walsh, "Private/Public Police Stereotypes: A Different Perspective," *Security Journal* 1 (1989): 21–27.

# Courts

**The arrest** of an individual in a democracy is only the first part of a complex process designed to separate the guilty from the innocent. Part 3 examines this process by which guilt is determined in accordance with the law's requirements. Here we shall look into the work of prosecutors, defense attorneys, bondsmen, and judges to understand the contribution each makes toward the ultimate decision. It is in the adjudicatory stage that the goals of an administrative system blunt the force of the adversarial process prescribed by law. Although we may focus on courtroom activities, most decisions relating to the disposition of a case are made in less public surroundings. After studying these chapters, we should ask ourselves whether justice is served by processes that are more akin to bargaining than to adversarial combat.

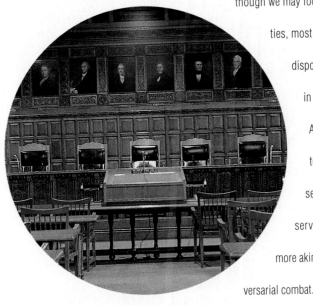

PART THREE

# Prosecuting Attorney

On 12 August 1983, Judy Johnson telephoned the Manhattan Beach, California police to report that her two-and-a-half-year-old son had been molested by Raymond Buckey, a teacher at the McMartin Preschool. This call precipitated the longest and costliest criminal trial in U.S. history.

Raymond Buckey was arrested soon after Judy Johnson's call to the police but was quickly released for lack of evidence. Johnson then wrote a letter to the district attorney saying that her son had gone with Peggy Buckey (shown in accompanying photo) to an armory behind her house, where "the goatman was" and where a ritual-like atmosphere prevailed. She wrote that her child was taken to a church where "Peggy drilled a child under the arms" and Ray "flew in the air." To gather evidence concerning these charges, the police sent a letter to two hundred parents asking for any information from their children about possible criminal acts at the McMartin school involving oral sex, handling of genitals, and sodomy. The letter set off a panic and hundreds of parents contacted the police.

The children initially denied being molested but through extensive taped interviews conducted by a therapist using anatomically correct dolls, the children were told that other children had divulged "yucky secrets" about the school and they were urged to do likewise. About 360 children eventually described abuse, including being molested by the teachers, being photographed while playing a "Naked Movie Star Game," and being raped and sodomized, and also described animal sacrifices and hidden tunnels under the school. These revelations were repeated in the press, shown on national television, and were the basis for countless radio talk shows. It was in this atmosphere that District Attorney Robert Philibosian instituted prosecution.[1]

Mr. Buckey, his mother, Peggy McMartin Buckey, his grandmother who had founded the school, his sister, and three other teachers were indicted by a grand jury on a total of 321 counts of sexual molestation of forty-eight children. While the gears of the criminal justice system ground to a conclusion, Buckey spent nearly five years and his mother two and a half years in jail awaiting trial, the Buckeys sold their preschool to pay legal fees, and taxpayers paid about $15 million for the prosecution and trial. Five and a half years later Mr. Buckey was acquitted on fifty-two counts of sexual molestation of children and a mistrial was declared on the remaining thirteen charges.

The McMartin case raises several key issues concerning the relationship among criminal justice policy, legal processes, and social concerns. Should a prosecution have been brought and a trial held on the basis of the evidence, considering, in particular, the way it was gathered? To what extent was District Attorney Robert Philibosian's decision to prosecute influenced by the police evidence, the media-generated public panic (at times reminiscent of the 1692 witchcraft trials in Salem, Massachusetts), or his own sagging campaign for reelection?

The McMartin Preschool case makes us aware of the most powerful figure in the administration of justice: the **prosecuting attorney**. These officials (also known in some states as district attorneys, county attorneys, commonwealth's attorneys, or state's attorneys) have been immortalized in novels and motion pictures, on radio and television, so that they have become almost folk heroes who secure conviction of the guilty while upholding justice for the innocent. In this chapter we examine the organization of prosecution in the United States and survey the influences that are brought to bear on the decision to prosecute.

**prosecuting attorney**
A legal representative of the state with sole responsibility for bringing criminal charges. In some states referred to as district attorney, state's attorney, or county attorney.

## Questions for Inquiry

- What is the structure of the prosecutorial system?
- What are the roles of the prosecuting attorney?
- What is the process by which criminal charges are filed against a person, and what role does the prosecutor's discretion play in that process?

- With whom does the prosecutor interact in decision making?
- How do prosecution policies influence staffing and decision making?
- What influences are brought to bear on the prosecutor's decision to charge?
- What are the advantages of community prosecution?

## The Prosecutorial System

As with other aspects of the American system of criminal justice, prosecution is primarily a responsibility of state and local governments. Violations of federal laws are prosecuted by **United States attorneys**, who are appointed by the president and who are members of the U.S. Department of Justice. The ninety-four U.S. attorneys and the two thousand assistant U.S. attorneys have offices in each federal district court jurisdiction. Federal prosecutors are heavily involved in the prosecution of drug, white-collar, and corruption cases.

Since most offenders have violated state laws, however, their cases are processed through the local criminal justice systems. Each state has an elected **attorney general**, and, in most states (one exception is Connecticut), these officials have the power to bring prosecutions under certain circumstances. In Alaska, Delaware, and Rhode Island the state attorney general also directs all local prosecutions. But it is in the 2,700 offices at the county level where most criminal cases are brought. In rural areas this office may be composed solely of the prosecuting attorney and a part-time assistant. In some urban jurisdictions, such as in Los Angeles with five hundred assistant prosecutors and additional numbers of legal assistants and investigators, the office is organized according to crime specialties. Most assistant prosecutors are young and seek to use the trial experience of the office as a means of moving on to more highly paid positions in a private law firm.[2]

The office of prosecutor at the county level of government typifies the decentralization of criminal justice. In all states except Connecticut and New Jersey prosecutors are elected, usually for a four-year term; the office is thus heavily involved in local politics. Traditionally, prosecutors have been responsible only to the voters. In most states, neither the governor nor the attorney general is authorized to investigate suspected illegal activity without the permission of the local prosecutor.

The prosecution of football legend O. J. Simpson for murder brought an unprecedented level of media attention to Los Angeles prosecutor Gil Garcetti and the members of his staff. Although most of a prosecutor's decisions are nearly invisible to the public, such high profile cases highlight the political aspect of a prosecutor's work.

**United States attorneys**
Officials responsible for the prosecution of crimes that violate the laws of the United States. Appointed by the president and assigned to a U.S. district court jurisdiction.

**state attorney general**
Chief legal officer of a state responsible for both civil and criminal matters.

Thomas E. Dewey

Thomas E. Dewey epitomized the "fighting prosecutor" who gains political prominence through crime-busting activities. In 1931, at the age of twenty-nine, Dewey was appointed chief assistant U.S. attorney for the southern district of New York. He soon gained a reputation as a "rackets buster" for his vigorous prosecution of gangster Irving "Waxey Gordon" Wexler for income tax evasion.

In 1935, Dewey began a campaign against organized crime as investigator for a New York City grand jury. He succeeded in convicting Lucky "King of Vice" Luciano and eight others on prostitution charges. The courtroom testimony of the prostitutes kept Dewey on the front pages of the newspapers for weeks.

In 1937 Dewey was elected district attorney for New York County (Manhattan). Several well-publicized prosecutions of gang leaders and political bosses enhanced his reputation as a crime fighter.

By 1940 Dewey's prominence led to two nominations for the U.S. presidency and three terms as governor of New York. After losing the presidential election to Harry S. Truman in 1948, Dewey returned to private practice and seemed to lose interest in the problem of crime, refusing to testify before the Kefauver Committee investigating organized crime in 1950. He continued his law practice until his death in 1971.

## Politics and Prosecution

The process of prosecution is inescapably political. The influence of prosecutors flows directly from their legal duties, but it must be understood within the context of the system's administrative and political environment. Prosecutors are often able to mesh their own ambitions with the needs of a political party. The appointment of deputies to the prosecutor's office, for example, may serve the party's desire for new blood and the prosecutor's need for young lawyers. Also, prosecutors may press charges in ways that enhance their own and the party's objectives. Cases may be processed so that only the few that are certain to be successful come to trial and hence help maintain the prosecutor's conviction record. Investigations may be initiated before an election to embarrass the opposition. Charges may be pressed against public officials for political gain. It is significant that certain groups and persons may receive less than impartial justice because of the prosecutor's determinations. American history is dotted with the names of people, such as Thomas E. Dewey (see Biography), who rose to political prominence on the basis of their performance as prosecuting attorney.

## Influence of the Prosecutor

The influence of the prosecutor also flows from the fact that, of the many positions in the legal system, the prosecuting attorney is concerned with all aspects of the system. From the time of arrest to the final disposition of a case, prosecutors can make decisions that will largely determine the cases to be prosecuted, the charges that are to be brought into the courtroom, the kinds of bargains that are to be made with the defendant, and the enthusiasm with which a case will be pursued. Throughout the justice process, prosecutors have links with the other actors in the system—police, defense attorneys, judges—and their decisions are usually affected not only by the types of relationships they maintain with these officials but also by the level of the public's awareness of their own actions.

The confidential nature of their decisions also enhances the prosecutor's power. For example, a prosecutor and a defense attorney may strike a bargain outside the courtroom whereby the prosecutor reduces a charge in exchange for a guilty plea or drops a charge altogether if the defendant agrees to seek psychiatric help. In such instances the "system" reaches a decision about a case in a way that is nearly invisible to the public.

Rarely is the scope of the prosecutor's discretionary power either publicly recognized or defined by statute. Generally, state laws are explicit in requiring the prosecution of offenders, yet nowhere in the laws are there specific descriptions of the elements that must be present before the prosecutor can take action. Most laws describe the prosecutor's responsibility in such vague terms as "prosecuting all crimes and civil actions to which state or county may be party." On occasions when the prosecutor's decisions have been challenged, they have been shielded from judicial inquiry

Although prosecutor and defense attorney are on opposing sides in the adversarial system, they often seek options that will work to their mutual benefit.

by an almost magical formula in the law: "within the prosecutor's discretion." In essence, the American people have placed prosecuting attorneys in a position in which they have to make choices but have not given them principles to guide their selection.

When prosecutors feel that the community no longer considers that an act proscribed by law constitutes criminal behavior, they will probably refuse to prosecute or will expend every effort to convince the complainant that prosecution should be avoided. Like other government officials, however, prosecutors are sensitive to the force of public opinion. Often they must take measures to protect themselves when they believe that a course of action is likely to arouse antipathy toward agencies of law enforcement rather than toward the accused. If they hold to an exaggerated notion of duty, they can arouse a storm of protest that may gain them reputations as "persecutors" and cost them the cooperation of the community. The fact that about three-fourths of American prosecutors serve counties with populations of fewer than 100,000 accentuates the potential influence of public opinion. Local pressures may bear heavily on the single prosecution official in a community. Without the backing of public opinion, law enforcement and prosecution officers are powerless. Prosecutors develop policies that reflect community attitudes, especially with regard to victimless crimes such as marijuana smoking, petty gambling, and prostitution. A New York prosecutor has remarked, "We are pledged to the enforcement of the law, but we have to use our heads in the process."

# Roles of the Prosecutor

References to the "prosecutor's dilemma" are often found in legal writings. As "lawyers for the state," prosecutors are expected to do everything in their power to win the public's case, yet as members of the legal profession, they are expected to engage in prosecution not to win convictions but to see that justice is done. As emphasized by the Canon of Ethics of the New York State Bar Association: "The primary duty of a lawyer engaged in public prosecution is not to convict, but to see that justice is done. The suppression of facts and the secreting of witnesses capable of establishing the innocence of the accused is highly reprehensible."[3] Nevertheless, the conditions under which prosecutors work are thought to create a "prosecutor's bias," sometimes called a "prosecution complex." Although they are theoretically supposed to represent all the people, including the accused, they consider themselves to be instruments of law enforcement.

We can understand the work of prosecutors and their place in an exchange system more clearly by examining the concept of *role*. A person may occupy a legally defined *position*, in this case that of prosecuting attorney, yet act out a conception of the role—that differs from those of other persons in the same position. A person's role, therefore, is a function not only of the formal aspects of the position but also of other important factors such as the individual player's personality, the environment within which he or she operates, and the individual's expectations concerning the attitudes of others with whom he or she interacts.

Prosecutors must define their roles by combining the professional dimensions of their work with the political context of their office. Role definition is complicated by the fact that prosecutors must maintain constant relationships with a variety of "others"—police officers, judges, defense attorneys, political party leaders, and so forth—and these actors may have competing ideas about what the prosecutor should do. The prosecutor's decisions will vitally affect the ability of the others to perform their duties and to achieve their objectives. Because the district attorneys are at the center of the adjudicative and enforcement functions, if they decide not to prosecute, then the judge and jury are helpless and the police officer's word is meaningless. If they decide to launch a campaign against drugs, pornography, or other social ills, then there are likely to be repercussions in both the political and the criminal justice arenas.

Four distinct role conceptions are commonly found among prosecutors.

1  *Trial counsel for the police.* Prosecutors who view their primary function in this light believe they should reflect law enforcement views in the courtroom and take a crime-fighter stance in public.

2  *House counsel for the police.* These prosecutors believe their primary function is to give legal advice so that arrests will stand up in court.

3  *Representative of the court.* Such prosecutors consider their primary responsibility to be enforcement of the rules of due process to ensure that the police act in accordance with the law and uphold the rights of defendants.

**4** *Elected official.* These prosecutors may be most responsive to community opinion. The possible political content of their decisions is one of their major concerns.

Each of these roles involves a different conception of the prosecutor's primary clients as well as his or her own responsibilities. In the first two roles described, prosecutors appear to believe that the police are the clients of their legal practice. Take a moment to consider who might be the clients of those prosecutors who view themselves as representatives of the court or as elected officials. As you read the Close-Up on pages 274–275, consider the work of the assistant district attorney depicted. How do his actions reflect his role orientation?

## Discretion of the Prosecutor

Their wide power of discretion makes it possible for prosecutors to structure their role to suit the political environment, their own personalities, and the interests of the others who are linked to the office. From the time the police turn a suspect's case over to the prosecutor, the prosecutor has almost undisputed control over major decisions such as which cases reach the courtroom and the charges a defendant will have to face. The discretion of American prosecutors contrasts sharply with their counterparts in European countries such as Germany (see the Comparative Perspective, pages 276–277).

That the police may arrest a person does not necessarily mean that the prosecutor will accept the charges against the suspect. Prosecutors can screen out cases they do not want to prosecute at their own discretion (see A Question of Ethics). While the proportion of such dismissals varies from place to place, estimates indicate that in most cities up to half of all arrests do not lead to the filing of formal charges. Prosecutors may decide not to press charges because of factors related to a particular case or because they have established policies dictating that charges will not be brought for certain offenses. For example, the U.S. Department of Justice provides its prosecutors with guidelines in determining whether a prosecution should be declined. The criteria include:

**1** federal law enforcement priorities

**2** the nature and seriousness of the offense

---

*A Question of Ethics*

**A**ssistant Prosecutor Debra McCoy looked at the case file. The police had arrested Leslie Wiggins, a prominent local businessman, for drunken driving. It seemed that Wiggins had been stopped after weaving on the highway at high speed. From the moment Officer Tompkins asked Wiggins to get out of the car, he knew he was very drunk. A Breathalyzer test revealed that Wiggins was well above the limit for sobriety. There was no question that this was an open-and-shut case. McCoy noted that Wiggins had been previously arrested, but the DWI (driving while intoxicated) charge had been dropped by her chief, Prosecutor Marc Gould.

"I don't know what happened last time," she thought, "but there is no question now." She recorded the charge of "driving while intoxicated" in the case file and forwarded it for review.

When the file had not yet returned for arraignment several days later, McCoy went to Gould's office.

"What happened to the Wiggins case?" she asked.

"Wiggins? Oh, that. Seems that the Breathalyzer wasn't reading right that night."

"Gee, I'm surprised. Tompkins didn't say anything about that when I talked with him yesterday. In fact, he was wondering when the case was coming up."

"Well, let's just not worry about this. I'm sure that Tompkins had other things to concern him. Don't think anything more about Wiggins."

McCoy left the office and wondered, "What's going on here?"

What *is* going on here? Will Gould's statement influence the case of other drivers who were tested on the Breathalyzer the evening that Wiggins was? How would dropping this case reflect on Gould or McCoy if the next time Wiggins is stopped it's at the scene of a fatal car accident? Is the fact that Wiggins is a prominent local businessman a factor?

## For the Assistant D.A., It's Nothing Like on TV

An eight-year-old boy, his voice soft but steady, told how he had seen robbers shoot his father to death in front of the family's Brooklyn grocery store.

"He had the key and was opening the car," the child said in a small interview room in state supreme court in downtown Brooklyn. "Then they came, the four men. They told him if he moved they would kill him. One man had a gun."

He looked down at his feet. His mother, a woman of about thirty, stared straight ahead in the chair next to him. "What was your father doing before he got shot?" asked Steven Samuel, a young assistant district attorney.

"He screamed."

There was a moment of silence. A detective who had arrested a suspect in the murder, which occurred several weeks before, pursed his lips. The widow shifted in her seat. Mr. Samuel gazed at the pen poised in his fingers, contemplating the latest of the many murder cases he has handled.

Mr. Samuel, who is thirty and five years out of law school, is typical of the 318 ADA's—assistant district attorneys—in the office of the District Attorney of Brooklyn, the largest local prosecutor's office in the country behind those of Chicago and Los Angeles.

"All right," said Mr. Samuel, breaking the stillness. "Now I'm going to take you into a room, and I want you to tell what you told me to the people in that room. They like to hear little boys tell stories."

As he strode down the corridor to where the child and other witnesses would repeat their accounts before a grand jury—which later would vote a murder indictment—Mr. Samuel described his own feelings in such a case. "It used to rattle me, the tragedy of it," he said. "But now I try to keep myself as emotionally detached as possible. When you're presenting a case, it helps to be as objective as possible."

Mr. Samuel, like many of his colleagues, views his job as a chance to pursue interesting work and gain valuable experience before moving on....

But perhaps the way in which Mr. Samuel most typifies his colleagues is that he and his routine often bear little resemblance to the portrayals of prosecutors on television and in the movies.

"My image of a prosecutor as a young kid was of Hamilton Burger, the district attorney in 'Perry Mason,'" said Mr. Samuel.

"He never had a guilty defendant."

Mr. Samuel, on the other hand, has won twenty-five convictions in the last three years, during which he has exclusively handled homicides. But he has also had three defendants who, the jury decided, were not guilty, despite his best efforts.

3　the deterrent effect of prosecution

4　the person's culpability in connection with the offense

5　the person's history with respect to criminal activity

6　the person's willingness to cooperate in the investigation or prosecution of others

7　the probable sentence or other consequences if the person is convicted[4]

Having decided that a crime should be prosecuted, the prosecutor has great freedom in determining the charges to be lodged. Incidents of criminal behavior often involve the breaking of a variety of laws, so the prosecutor can bring a single charge or multiple charges. Suppose that Smith, who is armed, breaks into a grocery store, assaults the proprietor, and robs the cash drawer. What charges may the prosecutor file? By virtue of having committed the robbery, the accused can be charged with at least

Then, too, in the television and movie scenarios, prosecutors generally spin their oratory in crowded, hushed courtrooms, unraveling plots complicated or clever, exciting or exotic....

"Murders committed during grocery and bar holdups, during disputes among acquaintances—two guys get into a fight over a dice game—these are typical of the cases I've had," Mr. Samuel said....

The day before, Mr. Samuel had won a conviction in the robbery-murder of a drug addict in East New York. But with his average workload of fifteen cases awaiting trial, this simply meant that Mr. Samuel could now focus on some of his other cases. So, at 10 A.M. in the Brooklyn branch of state supreme court, where the borough's felony crimes are prosecuted, he was scurrying from one courtroom to another, juggling appearances in several of his cases.

In one of the wood-paneled courtrooms, Mr. Samuel and a defense lawyer, Lewis Cohen, agreed to begin the next day to try the case of a man charged with killing an off-duty corrections officer. The officer had interrupted the defendant's attempt to hold up a Crown Heights bar, Mr. Samuel said as he scurried the single block back to his office, already calculating how he would prepare his evidence and line up his witnesses on such short notice.

Mr. Samuel had hardly begun reviewing the graphic police photographs of the murder scene and other evidence in the case when the phone rang. Detective Lambert Roessner had just arrived at supreme court with the witnesses in the case of the grocer whose son had seen him slain.

Shunted aside was the trial beginning tomorrow; Mr. Samuel would have to work on that at home at night. Now he had to hurry back to the court and prepare the witnesses in the case of the murdered grocer for their scheduled appearance before the grand jury that afternoon.

When the trial in the killing of the corrections officer was past the jury selection stage, Mr. Samuel rose to deliver his opening statement. "The people will prove," he declared in resonant, self-assured tones, "that Leon Taft killed Rudolph Smith during the holdup of the bar at 162A Utica Avenue."

As he presented the case against Mr. Taft, the young prosecutor rarely glanced at the defendant, a man hardly older than himself, with a shaved head, sitting at the defense table only a few feet away. All the witnesses were cooperative—the defense called none of its own—and Mr. Samuel, with detailed and systematic questioning, drew forth their moment-by-moment recollections of the fatal shooting.

Within a week, the verdict was in: guilty of murder.

"Justice was served," Mr. Samuel said, pausing only briefly before turning to the next case on his still-large agenda.

SOURCE: Joseph P. Fried, "For the Assistant D.A., It's Nothing Like on TV," *New York Times*, 18 October 1979, B–1. Copyright © 1979 by The New York Times Company. Reprinted by permission.

four violations: breaking and entering, assault, armed robbery, and carrying a dangerous weapon. Other charges may be added depending on the circumstances of the incident.

The concept of **necessarily included offense** helps us further understand the position of the prosecutor. We can ask: Could Smith have committed crime *A* without committing crime *B*? If the answer is yes, *B* is not a necessarily included offense. In the example of the armed robbery of a grocery store, Smith has committed the necessarily included offense of carrying a dangerous weapon in the course of the robbery. The prosecutor may charge Smith solely with the armed robbery or may include any number of other charges and combinations of charges based on the facts and discretion. By including as many charges as possible, the prosecutor increases his or her position in plea negotiations.

Selection of the charge or charges requires the prosecutor to decide also on the number of counts to be brought against the individual for the

**necessarily included offense**
An offense committed for the purpose of committing another offense, for example, trespass committed for the purpose of committing burglary.

**Chapter Seven:** Prosecuting Attorney    **275**

## Prosecution in Germany

Unlike their American counterparts, German prosecutors are required to prosecute all offenders. The concept of compulsory prosecution is based on the principle of legality in the German Code of Criminal Procedure, which states that the prosecutor is "obliged to take action in cases of all acts which are punishable by a court and capable of prosecution, so far as there is sufficient factual basis."

A significant difference between American and German prosecutors is that the latter are not elected. German prosecuting attorneys are civil servants who, like judges and other lawyers, have passed two comprehensive examinations after approximately seven or eight years of theoretical and practical training. They are subordinate to the head of the local office who is responsible to the state attorney general. The minister of justice of the state is at the top of the hierarchy. As in the United States, prosecution is primarily the responsibility of the state rather than of the federal government. Prosecutors are controlled by the hierarchical organization in which they are employed rather than by the public—at least to the extent that their personal careers are involved. Consequently, German prosecutors are basically immune from public opinion.

This fact is considered to be an important prerequisite for the legally required objectivity of the prosecutor. In the German system, a prosecutor is not a party in an adversarial system; rather, prosecutors are required to act not only against but also in favor of the suspect at any stage of the proceedings. For example, one-third of all fraud cases studied were dismissed because of lack of sufficient evidence even though the suspect had made a confession in the course of police investigation. Another consequence of the rule of objectivity is that prosecutors need not concern themselves with winning every case. In up to 20 percent of all cases studied, the accused was acquitted by the trial judge, usually at the request of the prosecutor.

### The Prosecutor's Office as an Investigating Agency

In Germany the prosecutor controls the police investigations of each reported criminal case. Therefore, the prosecutor is often called "head of the preliminary proceedings." However, except in a few sensational cases such as murder, big commercial crimes, and, recently, terrorism, prosecutors seldom are truly in a supervisory role. Instead, a typical investigatory situation progresses as follows.

An offense will usually be reported to the police, who will then open and register a file. The police lack any discretionary power in deciding whether or not to file a case. They must follow up every suspicion and present all registered offenses—however vague the evidence may be—to the prosecutor, who alone makes the final decision. The police carry out all necessary investigations. If the police feel a case has been thoroughly investigated, they will forward it to the prosecutor, who must decide whether further investigation is necessary. The prosecutor can take over the investigation or can return the case to the police for further inquiries. The law requires the prosecutor to do everything to solve the case—regardless of its seriousness. It does not permit him or her to "filter" out cases, as American prosecutors are authorized to do.

### The Prosecutor's Office as a Charging Agency

Calling the prosecutor's office a "charging agency" is something of a misnomer because on the average three out of four cases are dropped. The label refers to the main task of the prosecutor as it is the prosecutor's decision whether to charge or not. The charging decision involves two distinct considerations: evaluation of evidence and evaluation of guilt.

When prosecutors are *evaluating evidence*, they are more or less free in this decision. Some outside control is possible, however, since victims can file a formal complaint against the dismissal of a case. If the complaint is rejected by the attorney general (chief prosecutor of the state), the victim can file a motion for a judicial decision, which would, if successful, force the prosecutor to file a charge. Although this procedure is very seldom used, it is nonetheless feared by prosecutors. As a result, the status of victims may influence prosecutors' decisions. When the prosecutor is *evaluating guilt*, there are significant possibilities of hierarchical control over the decision. According to administrative rules issued by some of the ministries of justice of the states, deputy attorneys must present to their superiors for approval each case they want to dismiss based on minor guilt (mitigation). "In-house" instructions may also attempt to standardize the criteria by which "minor guilt" is defined.

The main task of prosecutors is to determine whether the evidence in a case is sufficient for conviction. As a result, they have large *practical* discretionary power when they describe whether "probable cause" exists in any given case. The prosecutor's "evaluation of evidence" was examined in two types of cases: petty and serious crimes.

It was found that if the damage (monetary value or physical injuries) was considerable or if the suspect had previously been convicted, the prosecutor was less inclined to drop the charge even if the evidence was weak. This situation might be explained by the possibility that the more serious the crime the more likely the accused is to retain defense counsel, which may hinder police investigation.

The relationship between the suspect and the victim also markedly affects the prosecutor's evaluation of the evidence. Cases involving acquaintances or relatives of the victim rather than stranger-to-stranger cases are more likely to be dismissed if they involve the crimes of theft, robbery, or rape. However, the opposite is true if the crime is fraud or embezzlement because of the special breach of trust connected with these types of acts.

In summary, then, it seems the prosecutor uses stricter evidentiary rules in *minor* offenses than in *serious* offenses. It may be that even though the evidence might not support a conviction in the more serious cases, the prosecutor still charges the case in order to use the charge itself as a sanction. The latter assumption is supported by the fact that prosecutors tend to regard prior criminal record as an element of proof and therefore charge recidivists more than first offenders. This tendency is in part counterbalanced by the judge, who—stressing the problem of proof more than the prosecutor—acquits more recidivists than first offenders.

Americans may wonder how the German system, with its compulsory prosecution, can be compatible with the efficient administration of justice in modern societies with substantial crime problems. They have come to believe that there is only one solution to the problem of overburdened criminal justice systems, namely that the prosecutor should serve as conservator of the system's resources through the practical use of plea bargaining and the discretion to discontinue prosecution. In Germany, the *entire* criminal justice system, including the legislative component, makes efforts to relieve the glut of cases and preserve the operation of the system. That is done through decriminalization, by making prosecution contingent upon the victim's formal motion, by turning felonies into misdemeanors, by extending the discretionary power of the prosecutor, and finally by simply increasing the staff of prosecutorial offices. This wide range of measures attempts to accomplish a balance between the requirements and the possibilities of effective law enforcement.

SOURCE: Adapted from Klaus Sessar, "Prosecutorial Discretion in Germany," in *The Prosecutor*, ed. William F. McDonald (Beverly Hills, Calif.: Sage, 1979), 255–273.

**count**
Each separate offense of which a person is accused in an indictment or an information.

**discovery**
A prosecutor's pretrial disclosure to the defense of facts and evidence to be introduced at trial.

**nolle prosequi**
An entry made by a prosecutor on the record of a case and announced in court to indicate that the charges specified will not be prosecuted. In effect, the charges are thereby dismissed.

same offense. Each **count** named in an indictment or an information deals with a specific criminal act, and under some conditions repeated acts result in multiple counts. A forger, for instance, may be charged with multiple counts, each carrying the potential for a similar penalty, for every act of forgery committed. It is because the prosecutor may charge multiple counts of the same criminal act that newspapers often announce that the accused may be liable for unrealistically long sentences—for example, five years for each of twenty counts. That is misleading, however, because judges may stipulate that the twenty terms of five years are to be served concurrently. In other words, the offender will serve only a total of five years, not the hundred years she or he would serve if the judge had stipulated consecutive terms.

The prosecutor's discretion may be limited by the procedure known as **discovery**, a legal requirement that some information in the case file be made available to the defense counsel. For example, the defense has the right to see any statements made by the accused while being interrogated by the police, and the results of any physical or psychological tests. Although the discovery procedure may suggest that the law unnecessarily limits the ability of the prosecution to win a case, the procedure is justified by the fact that the state has an obligation to act impartially and should not win a conviction through the use of deceit. The prosecutor has an obligation to secure justice, and knowledge of the evidence against the accused should help the accused to prepare an effective defense.

The prosecutor's discretion does not end with the decision to file a certain charge. After the charge has been made, the prosecutor may reduce it in exchange for a guilty plea or enter a notation of *nolle prosequi* (*nol. pros.*), indicating a freely made decision not to press the charge, either as a whole or as to one or more count. In our system of public prosecution there is no recourse to this decision. Finally, even when a conviction is obtained, the prosecutor can influence the sentence by submitting a recommendation concerning its nature.

## Exchange Relations

The formal rules of a bureaucracy do not completely account for the behavior of the actors within it; an informal structure arises from the social environment, personal relationships, and their interaction. In particular, although statutes define the formal relationships among the parts of the criminal justice system, research has shown that the actual ways in which the system operates are always in flux, often blurred, and usually open to negotiation. Thus the decisions made by the office of prosecuting attorney reflect those personal and organizational clients with whom it interacts.

The influence of a particular client group depends on such qualities as its role in the criminal justice process, the amount and type of contact it has with the office, and its ability to impede the work of the prosecutor if it should choose to do so. Prosecutors in some jurisdictions do control the charging decision; others are mere rubber stamps for the police. Some prosecutors wield extensive influence over the operations of the court by their ability to control the calendar, to appoint counsel for indigents, and to dominate the sentencing decisions; others are beholden to the judiciary and respond obediently to directions from the bench.

In short, the role conceptions of individual prosecutors and their clientele and the customs of particular criminal justice systems cause variations in the operation of the office. When a prosecution operation is described, it should be understood to reflect the exchange relations in one jurisdiction at one time. In this section we examine several such exchange relationships.

## Prosecutors and the Police

Although prosecuting attorneys have discretionary power to determine the disposition of cases, they depend upon the police to produce the raw materials with which they work. Most crimes occur before the police arrive at the scene and thus officers must reconstruct the situation on the basis of physical evidence and witness reports. There is considerable ambiguity in most sets of circumstances, so that the police, relying on their training, experience, and work routines, evaluate the crime as to its potential for an arrest and prosecution.

Because of their lack of investigative resources, prosecutors are unable to control the types of cases brought to them for disposition. The police may be under pressure to establish an impressive crime-clearance record and so may make many arrests without the substantiating evidence required to ensure conviction.

Nevertheless, prosecutors do have some means of exercising control in their relationships with the police. They have the ability to return cases for further investigation and to refuse to approve arrest warrants. Police requests for prosecution may be refused for several reasons unrelated to the facts of the case. First, prosecutors serve as the regulators of caseloads, not only for their own office but also for the rest of the judicial bureaucracy. Constitutional and statutory time limits prevent them and the courts from building a backlog of untried cases. Second, they may also reject police requests for prosecution because they do not want to take forward poorly developed cases that would place them in an embarrassing position in the courtroom. Finally, prosecutors may return cases in order to check on the quality of police work. Rather than expend the resources necessary to find additional evidence, the police may dispose of a case by sending it back to the prosecutor on a lesser charge so that it will lead to a guilty plea, or they may drop the case.

In most cases a deputy prosecutor and the assigned police officer occupy the boundary-spanning roles in this exchange relationship. After repeated contacts, deputies get to know the police officers they can trust, and these perceptions may be an important consideration in the decision to prosecute. Sometimes the police perform the ritual of "shopping around" for a deputy prosecutor who, past experience has led them to believe, is likely to be sympathetic to their view of a case. Some prosecution offices prevent this practice by stipulating that only the prosecutor, not deputies, can make primary decisions.

Police-prosecutor coordination has been a concern of criminal justice officials in recent decades.[5] It is argued that too often a lack of coordination between police investigators and prosecutors leads to case attrition. Part of the problem is that lawyers and police officers have different perspectives on crime and work for different criminal justice organizations. The police often take the position that they have made a valid arrest and that there should be no reason why a case should not be indicted and tried. Prosecutors look at cases to see if the evidence will result in a conviction. These different orientations often result in conflicts, with some cases "slipping through the cracks."

In response to the perceived need for greater coordination, police-prosecution teams have been created in many jurisdictions so that representatives of both departments work together on cases. This task-force approach is often used for drug or organized crime investigations and prosecutions where detailed information and evidence are required for a successful conviction. Cooperation between the police and prosecutors is necessary in drug cases since without a network of informers, peddlers cannot be caught with evidence that can bring about convictions. One pool of informers is comprised of people who have been arrested for drug violations. Through prosecutorial agreements to reduce charges or even to *nol. pros.*, the accused may return to the community to gather information for the police (see the accompanying Close-Up).

## Prosecutors and Victims

Until a very few years ago, the victim of a crime was the forgotten participant in the criminal justice process. One reason for this state of affairs lies in the nature of prosecution in the United States. In our system, a complainant depends on the prosecuting attorney to bring charges. If the prosecutor refuses, a private citizen cannot bring an indictment against a fellow citizen, as is possible in England.

Victims generally play a passive role in the criminal justice process, yet their cooperation is essential for successful prosecution. They must assist the police and prosecuting attorney by identifying the offender, and the basic evidence to be considered often depends on their testimony. In many types of cases, the nature of a victim's prior relations with the accused, the victim's actions at the time of the offense, and the victim's personal characteristics are deemed important if a case is to be successful before judge and jury.

The relationship of the accused to the victim has a strong bearing on a case involving violent crime and often presents a major problem to the prosecutor. In one study of crimes by persons who were not strangers to

## Drug Arrests:
## An Example of Exchange

Lt. Roger Cirella of the drug task force of the Seattle police force entered the office of Chief Deputy Prosecutor Michael Ryan. Cirella reported that during questioning a well-known drug dealer intimated that he could provide evidence against a pharmacist suspected of illegally selling drugs. The officer wanted to transfer the case to the friendlier hands of a certain deputy and to arrange for a reduction of charges and bail.

**Cirella**: Yesterday we got a break in the pharmacy case. We had arrested Sam Hanson after an undercover buy on First Avenue. He says that a druggist at the Green Cross Pharmacy is selling out the back door. We thought that something like that was happening since we had seen these bums standing around there but we've not been able to prove it. Hanson says he will cooperate if we'll go easy on him. Now, I'd like to get this case moved to Wadsworth, he's worked with us before and that new guy who's on it now just doesn't understand our problems.

**Ryan**: Okay, but what's that going to accomplish?

**Cirella**: We also need to be able to fix it so Hanson gets out on bail without letting the druggies out there know he has become an informer. If we can get Judge Griffin to reduce bail he can probably put up the bond. Now we also need to reduce the charges yet keep him on the string so that we can bring him right back if he doesn't play our game.

**Ryan**: I want to cooperate with you guys, but I can't let the boss get a lot of heat for letting a pusher out on the street. How are we going to know that he's not going to screw up?

**Cirella**: Believe me, we will keep tabs on him.

**Ryan**: Okay, but don't come here telling me we're going to get splashed with mud in the *Times*.

---

their victims, difficulties with the complainants accounted for 61 percent of the refusals to prosecute and 54 percent of the dismissals. Barbara Boland found in New Orleans that the conviction rate for crimes of violence committed by strangers was 48 percent, by friends or acquaintances it was 30 percent, and by family members it was 19 percent.[6] As the closeness of the accused's relationship to the victim increased, the likelihood of conviction decreased.

A study of the prosecution and disposition of felony arrests in New York City emphasized the crucial role of the victim and the exchange relationships that may exist in the prosecution process. By analyzing a sample of felony arrests, researchers learned that a high percentage of crimes in every category, from murder to burglary, involved victims with whom the accused had prior and often close relations. This finding was particularly true with respect to crimes of interpersonal violence: 83 percent of rape victims, 50 percent of manslaughter and attempted homicide victims, and 69 percent of assault victims knew their assailants.

Such findings are to be expected. Suspects known to their victims are more likely to be arrested than strangers, since they can be more easily identified by the complainants. The fact that the victim and the accused knew each other, however, led to the dropping of a large number of cases. Complainants were often reluctant to pursue prosecution. As the study noted, "Tempers had cooled, time had passed, informal efforts at mediation or restitution might have worked, or in some instances, the defendant had intimidated the complainant."[7]

Figure 7.1 shows the outcomes of stranger and nonstranger robberies and burglaries in New York City. Note that 88 percent of stranger robbery arrests resulted in conviction, with 68 percent on a felony charge. Of those arrested 65 percent were incarcerated, 32 percent for a year or more. In contrast, when the robbery victim knew the accused only 37 percent of those arrested were convicted, 23 percent incarcerated, and none served more than a year. The same pattern exists with burglaries, although the punishments were less severe. Most of the stranger burglars were convicted, but only 8 percent on a felony charge. Prosecutors probably bargained these cases down to misdemeanors because the evidence was not strong. As with acquaintance robberies, the burglars who knew their victims were treated more leniently by the prosecution.[8]

Research has thus substantiated that the relatively close defendant-victim relationship is by and large responsible for the dismissal of felony charges, their reduction to misdemeanors, or lenient sentences even when evidence of guilt is plentiful. Prosecutors are aware of such situations and are usually reluctant to press charges fully when there is a possibility that victims will have second thoughts as they realize that criminal law sanctions will be pressed on the offender. Many victims may not want to suf-

**Figure 7.1**
**Outcomes of stranger and nonstranger robberies and burglaries in New York City**
Victims of burglaries and robberies are less likely to pressure for conviction when the offender is known to them. If conviction is successful, the penalties tend to be less when a nonstranger is the offender.

SOURCE: Vera Institute of Justice, *Felony Arrests: Their Prosecution & Disposition in New York City's Courts* (New York: Longman, 1981), 58, 86. Copyright © 1981 by Longman Publishing Group. Reprinted by permission of Vera Institute of Justice.

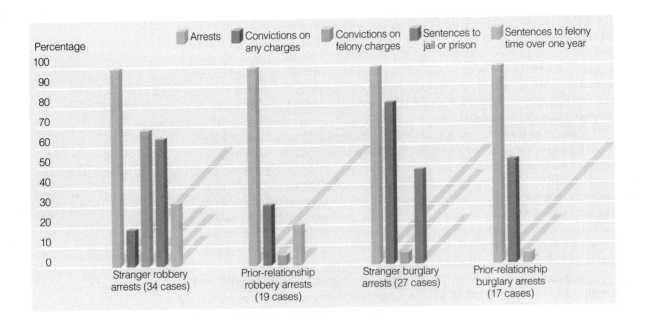

fer the consequences of cooperating with the prosecutor to convict a family member, friend, or neighbor.

In some cases involving strangers, the victim's personal characteristics and attitudes may influence the decision to prosecute. Prostitutes who claim rape, drug users who are assaulted by pushers, and children who may be unable to testify under pressure are viewed by prosecutors as victims whose characteristics make the securing of a conviction difficult. Prosecutors need the evidence provided by such victims but are also wary of the victim's effect on the jury.

## Prosecutors and the Courts

The influence of the courts on the decision to prosecute is very real. The sentencing history of each judge gives prosecutors, as well as other enforcement officials, an indication of the treatment a case may receive in the courtroom. Prosecutors' expectations of the court's action may affect their decision to prosecute or not. In the words of one prosecutor interviewed by the author: "There is great concern as to whose court a case will be assigned. After Judge Lewis threw out three cases in a row in which entrapment was involved, the police did not want to take any cases to him."

As lawyers for the state, prosecutors are expected to do everything it takes to win each case, yet they are also expected to see that justice is done.

Prosecutors depend on the plea-bargaining machinery to maintain their case flow. If guilty pleas are to be induced successfully, the sentencing actions of judges must be predictable. If the defendants and their lawyers are to be influenced to accept a lesser charge or a promise of a lighter sentence in exchange for a plea of guilty, there must be some basis to believe that the judges will fulfill their part of the arrangement. Since judges are unable to announce formally their agreement with the details of the bargain, their past performance influences the actors.

Within the limits imposed by law and by the demands of the system, prosecutors may regulate the flow of cases to the court. They can regulate the length of time between accusation and trial, holding cases until they have the evidence that will convict. They may also seek repeated adjournments and continuances until the public's interest dies down, witnesses become unavailable, or other difficulties more easily justify their requests for dismissal of prosecution. In many cities the prosecutor is able to determine the court that will receive a case and the judge who will hear it.

In most jurisdictions, persons arrested on felony charges must be given a preliminary hearing within ten days. For prosecutors, the preliminary hearing is an opportunity to evaluate the testimony of witnesses, to assess the strength of the evidence, and to try to predict the outcome of the case should it go to trial. Subsequently, prosecutors have several options: they may recommend that the case be held for trial, seek a reduction of the charges to those of a misdemeanor, or conclude that they have no case and drop the charges. These decisions are greatly influenced by the prosecutor's perception of the court's caseload and the attitudes of the judges.

## Prosecutors and the Community

As a part of the wider political system, the administration of criminal justice responds to its environment. As shown by the McMartin case described in the opening to this chapter, public opinion and the media can play a crucial role in creating an environment that is either supportive or critical of the prosecutor. Prosecuting attorneys, like police chiefs and school superintendents, will not be long in office if they are antagonistic to community values.

The influence of the public is particularly acute in those "gray areas" of the law where full enforcement is not expected. Legislatures may enact statutes that define the outer limits of criminal conduct, but that does not necessarily mean the laws will be fully enforced. Some statutes are passed as expressions of desirable morality and others are kept deliberately vague. Finally, some existing laws proscribe behavior that the community no longer considers criminal. Reflecting the public's attitude toward such laws, prosecutors usually disregard violations of laws regulating some forms of gambling, certain sexual practices, or obscenity.

Alternatively, the community may insist that charges be brought against people who flaunt its dominant values. Owners of adult bookstores and video rental shops may be harassed and their businesses closed if the prosecutor feels public pressure to wage a war on obscenity. The public is also prone to press for selective prosecution of persons who engage in some forms of "immoral" activity; for example, streetwalkers may be arrested, while call girls and "hostesses" are immune.

Studies have shown that the public's level of attention to the activities of the criminal justice system is low. Still, the community remains a potential source of pressure that leaders may activate against the prosecutor. The prosecutor's office always has the public in mind when it makes its decisions.

## The Impact of Exchange Relations

Although prosecutors are free from statutory checks on their power, they must make decisions within an organizational framework and are thus subject to the influence of other actors. The criminal justice system requires that a number of officials participate in the disposition of each case so bargaining occurs. Prosecutors, as the link between the police and the courts, hold a strategic bargaining position because all cases must pass through their office. Accordingly, they are able to regulate both the flow of cases and the conditions under which they will be processed. Given the caseload in metropolitan areas and the scarcity of resources to deal with it, officials are pressed to dispense justice efficiently. The prosecutors' influence over other actors is based on these stresses within the criminal justice environment. In addition, there is the dramatic aspect of their work, which can command public attention. This publicity, in turn, can be used as a weapon against the police, the courts, or other actors who do not cooperate with the efforts of their office. In all of these ways, exchange relations greatly influence prosecutors' decisions in the disposition of a case.

## Decision-Making Policies

In view of the differences in role conceptions, exchange relationships, and sociopolitical factors that influence the policies made by prosecutors, is it possible to generalize about how this vital sector of criminal justice operates? Prosecutors develop their own policies on how cases will be handled in their office. These policies structure the decisions that are made by the assistant prosecutors and thus have a decided impact on the administration of justice.

### The Pretrial Phase

Research indicates that throughout the pretrial phase the prosecutor and the prosecutor's assistants use a screening process to determine what action should be taken with regard to a particular case. Pretrial screening is designed to remove from the system cases that do not meet the legal test of probable cause, to divert cases that the prosecutor believes could be better handled by another agency, and to prepare appropriate charges. But the screening is influenced by the political and organizational incentives to maintain a high conviction rate, to allocate resources so that cases the community views as serious are prosecuted successfully, and to maintain open channels of communication and exchange with the other agencies of criminal justice.

Studies show great variation in the pretrial portion of the prosecutorial process. How prosecutors handle felony cases in two different jurisdictions is illustrated in Figure 7.2. Some offices make extensive use of screening and are less inclined to press charges. Pleas of guilty are the primary dispositional vehicle in some offices, while pleas of not guilty strain the courts' trial resources in other offices. Some offices remove cases soon after they are brought to the prosecutor's attention by the police; in others, disposition occurs as late as the first day of trial. The period from the receipt of the police report to the start of the trial is thus a time of review in which the prosecutor exercises discretion to determine what charging actions should be taken.

## Implementing Prosecution Policy

Joan Jacoby has analyzed the management policies that prosecutors use to achieve specific goals during the pretrial process and the ways in which they staff their offices toward those goals. On the basis of data from more than three thousand prosecutors, she has found three models: legal sufficiency, system efficiency, and trial sufficiency. She assumes that how a prosecutor handles a case is guided by the policy set forth in the model chosen. The choice of a policy model is shaped by personal considerations of the prosecutor (such as the role conception discussed earlier), by external factors such as crime levels, and by the relationship of prosecution to the other parts of the criminal justice system.[9]

The prosecution policy adopted by a particular office affects decisions regarding the screening and disposing of cases. As illustrated in Figure 7.3, the policy models dictate that prosecutors select certain points in the process for disposition of the vast majority of the cases presented to them by the police, thus strategies are adopted with regard to discovery, diversion, plea bargaining, and allocation of resources. Each model identifies the point in the process at which cases are filtered out of the system. These models are valuable management tools that the prosecutor can use to ensure implementation of a particular policy choice. They also aid our understanding of criminal justice.

**Figure 7.2**
**Differences in how prosecutors handle felony cases in two jurisdictions**
The discretion of the prosecutor is evident by the way in which felony cases are handled in two jurisdictions. Note that different screening policies seem to be in operation: cases are referred earlier in the process in Utah and later in Colorado.

SOURCE: U.S. Department of Justice, Bureau of Justice Statistics, *Report to the Nation on Crime and Justice*, 2d ed. (Washington, D.C.: Government Printing Office, 1988), 71.

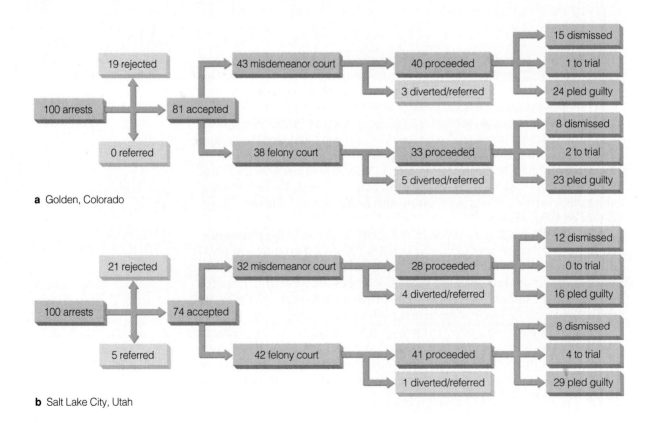

**a** Golden, Colorado

**b** Salt Lake City, Utah

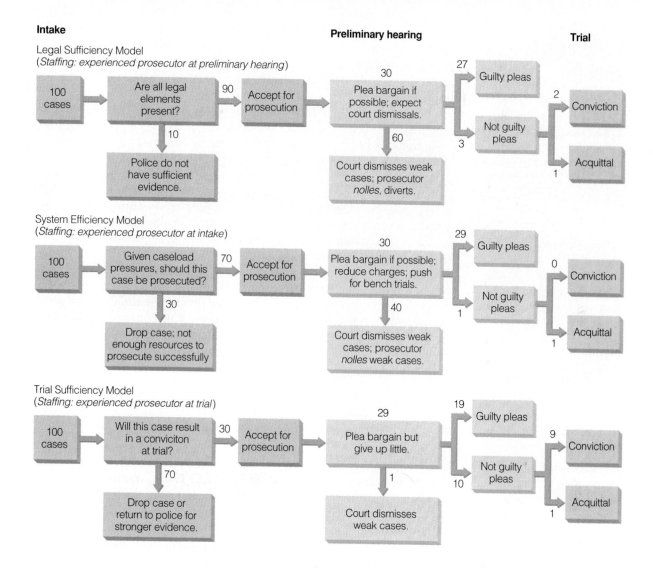

**Intake**

**Preliminary hearing**

**Trial**

Legal Sufficiency Model
(*Staffing: experienced prosecutor at preliminary hearing*)

100 cases → Are all legal elements present? —90→ Accept for prosecution → Plea bargain if possible; expect court dismissals. [30]

—10→ Police do not have sufficient evidence.

—60→ Court dismisses weak cases; prosecutor *nolles*, diverts.

—27→ Guilty pleas

—3→ Not guilty pleas —2→ Conviction / —1→ Acquittal

System Efficiency Model
(*Staffing: experienced prosecutor at intake*)

100 cases → Given caseload pressures, should this case be prosecuted? —70→ Accept for prosecution → Plea bargain if possible; reduce charges; push for bench trials. [30]

—30→ Drop case; not enough resources to prosecute successfully

—40→ Court dismisses weak cases; prosecutor *nolles* weak cases.

—29→ Guilty pleas

—1→ Not guilty pleas —0→ Conviction / —1→ Acquittal

Trial Sufficiency Model
(*Staffing: experienced prosecutor at trial*)

100 cases → Will this case result in a conviciton at trial? —30→ Accept for prosecution → Plea bargain but give up little. [29]

—70→ Drop case or return to police for stronger evidence.

—1→ Court dismisses weak cases.

—19→ Guilty pleas

—10→ Not guilty pleas —9→ Conviction / —1→ Acquittal

Under the **legal sufficiency** model, a case is initially screened merely for evidentiary defects before being given a preliminary court hearing. Some prosecutors believe that if a case is legally sufficient, they have a responsibility to accept it for prosecution. They ask, "Are the minimum legal elements present so that charges should be brought?" Thus a great many cases are accepted for prosecution, and various operational strategies are employed to prevent overload of the system. Under this model, assistant prosecutors (especially those assigned to misdemeanor courts) have little time to prepare individual cases, must use plea bargaining to the utmost, and expect many dismissals and acquittals.

The **system efficiency** model aims at a speedy and early disposition of a case. A prosecutor in an office that adheres to this policy asks, "What charges should be made in view of the caseload pressures on the system?" If the case did not appear defective, the prosecutor might charge

**Figure 7.3**
**Three policy models of prosecutorial case management and allocation of staff resources**
Prosecutors develop policies as to how their offices will manage cases. An assumption of these three models is that a portion of arrests will be dropped at some point in the system so that few cases reach trial.

the defendant with a felony but agree to reduce the charge to a misdemeanor—perhaps unlawful trespass or larceny—in exchange for a guilty plea. According to Jacoby's research, the system efficiency model is usually followed when the trial court is backlogged and the prosecutor has limited resources.

Under the **trial sufficiency** model, a case is accepted and charges made only at the level that can be sustained in court. The prosecutor asks, "Will this case result in a conviction?" That does not mean the prosecutor accepts only sure cases; it does mean that when the facts are present to sustain a conviction, every effort is made to secure that outcome. This model requires good police work, a prosecution staff experienced in trial work, and—because plea bargaining is minimized—court capacity. Rejected cases must be diverted from the system by alternative means.

Each policy requires the prosecutor to use strategies and deploy assistants in ways that are consistent with the overriding goal of the office. Accordingly, it is important for offices operating under the system efficiency model to have well-trained personnel at the intake point so that the critical decision to charge can be based on experience. Offices operating under the trial sufficiency model require skilled courtroom advocates. And offices operating under the legal sufficiency model may use less experienced personnel at the intake point but will need experienced plea negotiators later in the process.

## The Decision to Prosecute

Deciding whether to prosecute and what the charge will be is the focus of the formal job of the prosecuting attorney. These determinations can legally be made by them alone, and the consequences have a great impact not only on the defendants but also on the other agencies that participate in the administration of justice.

As the Due Process Model emphasizes, a decision to label a citizen a defendant in a criminal action should be undertaken only with full and serious understanding. There are negative aspects to being arrested, but there are even greater penalties attached to being charged with a crime. Once a suspect becomes a defendant, the entire weight of the criminal justice process is brought to bear on the individual. The state may restrain the person's liberty, and economic burdens are imposed by the requirement that bail be posted and a lawyer hired. There is also the nontangible penalty of damage to the person's reputation; though the public gives lip service to the idea of "innocent until proved guilty," it may also subscribe to the notion that where there's smoke, there's fire.

### The Accusatory Process

The **accusatory process** is the series of activities that take place from the moment a suspect is arrested and booked by the police to the moment the formal charging instrument—indictment or information—is filed with the court. During this process the activities of the police, grand jury, bail agency, and court are linked to those of the prosecuting attorney. Here the government must show only that there is a prima facie (that is, at first sight) case that a crime has been committed and that it was committed by the accused. Two questions are addressed by decision makers: Is there probable cause to restrict the liberty of the individual? and, Under the circumstances, would a reasonable person believe that the defendant committed the crime? If a grand jury or judge answers the questions affirmatively, a formal accusation instrument is presented, and the defendant is arraigned on the charges. These procedures are conducted within a relatively brief time, but the decisions made have an important effect on the accused: Personal liberty may be taken away, and the beginnings of a defense may have to be mounted. It is during the accusatory process that we can best observe how prosecutors in various parts of the United States conduct their formal duties.

As Chapter 1 explained, the legal instrument by which charges are brought against a person is either an *indictment* handed down by a grand jury or a prosecutor's *bill of information* ruled upon by a judge at a preliminary hearing. In some states the prosecutor must present the facts of the case to a grand jury; if the jurors agree that the facts warrant formal charges, they will vote a "true bill" authorizing an indictment. In other states there is no grand jury; the prosecutor files an information directly with the court at a preliminary hearing.

Although the formal description of these two charging processes (illustrated in Figure 7.4) seems clear-cut, there are operational variations that mix the roles of the city police, prosecutor, and court. The variations influence the "domain" of the prosecutor, that is, the decisions over which the prosecutor lays claim. In some places the prosecutor really controls the charging decision; in others, the police informally make the decision, which is then rubber stamped by the prosecutor; and in still others, the prosecutor not only controls the charging process but also is greatly involved in judicial functions such as determining the court calendar, appointing defense counsel for indigents, and sentencing.

The prosecutor's task is not simple. He or she must keep foremost in mind that behaviors must conform to the elements of a crime—the ingredients that must be present before a person can be convicted. The law defines robbery, for example, as an act in which there is (1) forcible taking, (2) of goods of another person, (3) by an individual who, (4) employs violence or puts victims in fear as a means to accomplish the theft. These elements also indicate what must be done to prove a case of robbery. The prosecutor must organize the evidence and witnesses so that each element can be proved to the satisfaction of judge and jury. If the prosecutor believes that cannot be done, lesser charges may be filed—for example, "assault with intent to rob" or "larceny from the person."

Case assessment is more than just a process of matching the police arrest report with the criminal code. As seen in the Close-Up on pages 292–293, it is an attempt by the prosecutor to determine whether the reported crime will appear credible and meet legal criteria in the eyes of judge and jury.

**accusatory process**
The series of events from the arrest of a suspect to the filing of a formal charging instrument (indictment or information) with the court.

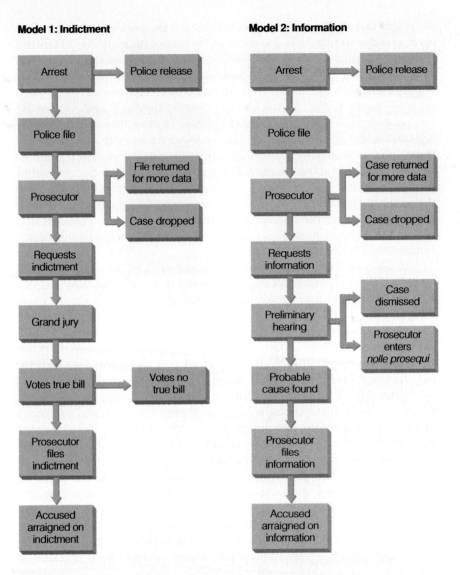

**Model 1: Indictment**

Arrest → Police release

Arrest ↓ Police file

Police file ↓ Prosecutor → File returned for more data

Prosecutor → Case dropped

Requests indictment

Grand jury

Votes true bill → Votes no true bill

Prosecutor files indictment

Accused arraigned on indictment

**Model 2: Information**

Arrest → Police release

Arrest ↓ Police file

Police file ↓ Prosecutor → Case returned for more data

Prosecutor → Case dropped

Requests information

Preliminary hearing → Case dismissed

Preliminary hearing → Prosecutor enters *nolle prosequi*

Probable cause found

Prosecutor files information

Accused arraigned on information

**Figure 7.4**
**Two models of the accusatory process**
Indictment and information are the two models used in the United States to accuse someone of having committed a crime. Note the role of the grand jury in the indictment model and the presence of a preliminary hearing in the information model. According to the ideal of due process, each model is designed to spare an innocent person the psychological, monetary, and other costs of prosecution.

## Considerations Influencing the Charging Decision

Determining the exact motivation of prosecutors when they select one charge over another is impossible. They can identify the factors that consciously entered into their choice, but they are seldom able to pinpoint the conversations they had or the words they read that were responsible for injecting these considerations, reinforcing them, and turning them into final decisions. In addition, there are elements of the personality and attitudes of each decision maker that are difficult to unravel. To what extent, for example, are prosecutors influenced by the race, ethnicity, and gender of the accused? A study of 70,000 cases filed in the Los Angeles County District Attorney's Office found that men were more likely than women to be prosecuted and that Hispanics were prosecuted more often than African-Americans, who were prosecuted more often than Anglos. The researchers believe that in marginal cases—those that could either be rejected or prosecuted—the scale is often tipped against minorities.[10]

Studies of the decision to prosecute do show a remarkable agreement on the objective elements that are considered, which can be classified as evidential, pragmatic, and organizational. We cannot tell whether one of these categories is more important than another, but we can note that at the initial stage, when a decision to file is made, the type and the amount of evidence reflected in the police report appear to be dominant factors. As a former deputy prosecutor told this author, "If you have the evidence, you file, then bring the other considerations in during the bargaining phase."

**Evidential Considerations**   Is there a case? Does the evidence warrant the arrest of an individual and the expense of a trial? These are major questions that prosecutors ask when they ponder whether to prosecute. Legally, a prosecution cannot hope to be successful without some proof that the required elements of a criminal act are present in the case, that the suspect has committed it, and that he or she formulated some intent to commit the act. Aside from the precise legal definition of the crime, prosecutors must decide whether the act is viewed as criminal within the local political context. Many offenses committed under borderline circumstances do not result in prosecution.

The nature of the crime may require the presentation of evidence that can prove a vague charge such as neglect. Prosecutors must be certain that the evidence will coincide with the court's interpretation of the term. In addition, evidence must be introduced that will connect the defendant with the criminal act: a confession, statements of witnesses, or physical evidence. All these requirements must be met within the context of the rules of evidence and the guarantees of due process. For some types of offenses, such as corporate crime, the investigative and legal resources necessary for a successful prosecution are extensive and just not available to the average district attorney's office.[11]

The nature of the complaint, the strength of the testimony of witnesses, and the attitude of the victim must also be evaluated. Whose interests are being served by prosecution must be considered. Often when complaints are based on marital or neighborhood quarrels or on quasi-civil offenses (for example, debt claims), the prosecutor must ensure that a violation of the criminal law has occurred and that the victim is not using the law for his or her own purposes. Evidence is weak when it is difficult to use in proving charges, when the value of a stolen article is questionable, when a case results from a brawl or other order-maintenance situation, or when corroboration (supporting testimony) is lacking. As noted in Figure 7.5 (page 294), problems with evidence and witnesses were the main reasons for rejecting cases in most of the prosecution offices studied.

**Pragmatic Considerations**   Prosecutors are able to individualize justice so that both the accused and society benefit. The character of accused persons, their status in the community, and the impact of prosecution on their families may influence the charges filed. Prosecutors may not invoke the full weight of the law when they believe that to do so would unduly punish

## Case Assessment

### Case 1: Robbery in the First Degree

The complainant is a professional man who works for the Better Business Bureau. He entered the Early Case Assessment Bureau with his Sunday *New York Times* tucked under his arm. His recall of the incident was clear, and he presented his story articulately. After the complainant had received instructions to appear before the grand jury the next morning and had then left the room, the assistant district attorney (ADA) remarked to the arresting officer (A/O):

> **ADA**: Do you think the defendants know the complainant is a homosexual?
> **A/O**: No.
> **ADA**: Would have been a great alibi. They could claim that they

had met and the complainant invited them up for a drink.

Being labeled a homosexual, prosecutors recognize, casts doubt upon the victim's credibility; stereotypes about homosexuals, and the kinds of encounters they are alleged to have, can jeopardize the chances of winning the case. Yet in this particular instance, other factors such as the clarity of the victim's recall and his professional status compensated for this vulnerability. The charge was not altered.

### Case 2: Robbery in the Second Degree

A young black complainant was accosted by two males. The defendants stopped the complainant and told him they wanted money. One put his hand on the complainant's chest and told him if he didn't produce "they would 'cap' him." The prosecutor asked the complainant what "cap" meant. The complainant replied that he didn't know. All he

---

**diversion**
An alternative to adjudication by which the defendant agrees to conditions set by the prosecutor (such as counseling or drug rehabilitation) in exchange for the withdrawal of charges.

the offender. Where the law is not flexible (mandatory sentences, for example), the prosecutor may believe that the gravity of the crime does not warrant such severe treatment. The rehabilitative potential, the seriousness of the offense, and the benefits to be gained by keeping a suspect's record clean weigh heavily in the decision to prosecute.

In many cases, prosecutors may seek alternatives that divert the offender from the criminal justice system. **Diversion** refers to acknowledged efforts to use alternatives to the formal processes of the justice system. Diversion by prosecutors usually occurs after a complaint has been made but before adjudication. It implies the halting or suspending of formal proceedings against a person who has violated the law in favor of a noncriminal disposition to the case.

In most systems, such efforts are directed at either diverting certain types of offenders to treatment programs for drug or alcohol abuse, to mental hospitals, or into voluntary public service, or persuading them to make restitution to their victims. In some states a case is screened from the system by the prosecutor with minimal or no restrictions. In other cases the prosecutor may place a charge "on hold" for a specified time (say, a year), at the end of which it is dropped if the individual has not been rearrested. In other states such informal dispositions are recommended in court by the prosecutor, and so-called accelerated rehabilitation is granted. As in the case of other discretionary practices, the fact of the arrest, prosecution, and disposition is expunged from the record at the expiration of an arrest-free period.

knew was that he didn't want to be hurt and he assumed that whatever capping was, he didn't want to find out. He gave them his money (included was one $10 bill torn in half, which was found in the possession of the defendant). One defendant reached inside the coat of the complainant. Then they left. The prosecutor reduced the charges from robbery in the second degree to grand larceny in the third degree. The prosecutor stated that if the grand jury asked (the complainant) what "cap" meant, he couldn't answer and therefore wouldn't be able to prove the threat of force in the robbery charge.

## Case 3: Robbery in the First Degree

**ADA**: How long have you known the defendant?

**Complainant**: I was a counselor in a drug program—Neighborhood Thing—and I met her there. I've seen her around since then. She was a Muslim and had a boyfriend and I didn't see her much then. But since she split I've seen her around.

ADA then asks the complainant to go out to the waiting room while he draws up the affidavit. The assessment officer says that this is the best complainant he's had in two years, but the ADA disagrees.

**ADA**: The people in the supreme court don't like prior-relationship cases. I think he was going out with her. The jury wouldn't like this. It's just a feel for the case. I don't like it.

This unknown but assumed prior relationship between the victim and the defendant somehow "normalizes" this encounter, relegating it to the range of typical everyday interactions that might occur between the victim and the defendant. The victim, in order to be seen as a "real" victim, must at least convince the prosecutor of the irregular character of the event.

SOURCE: Elizabeth A. Stanko, "The Impact of Victim Assessment on Prosecutors' Screening Decisions: The Case of the New York County District Attorney's Office," in *Law and Society Review* 16 (1981–1982): 225–238. Reprinted by permission of The Law and Society Association.

**Organizational Considerations** Organizational influences on the decision to prosecute are many. Certainly the exchange relationships between the police and the prosecutor, congestion within the system, and community pressures are considered at this juncture. Prosecutors must decide which charge is appropriate to the facts of the case, the needs of the defendant, and the needs of society. They may decide to throw the book at the defendant, only to have it boomerang when they are unable to prove the case in court. They may charge the defendant with serious or multiple offenses to increase their latitude in plea bargaining. These options are available to prosecutors from the time the police originally file a case with them until the judge pronounces sentence, as Figure 7.6 indicates.

In terms of exchange relationships, the prosecuting attorney is the one criminal justice actor who has significant interactions with every other major actor. Thus the personal relationships of the participants are more influential in decision making than are the written report of an incident. A prosecutor may be reluctant to reject a police officer's request for an arrest warrant even though the evidentiary aspects of the case may be weak. At the same time, prosecutors develop a sensitive awareness of the types of cases likely to lead to convictions in the local courts. They may refrain from filing a case that a judge might regard as a waste of time because the judge might doubt the prosecutor's judgment in future cases.

The expected public reaction is a factor in most decisions. Especially if the crime is of a heinous nature, such as child rape, if publicity has aroused the electorate, and if the victim is well known, the prosecutor's

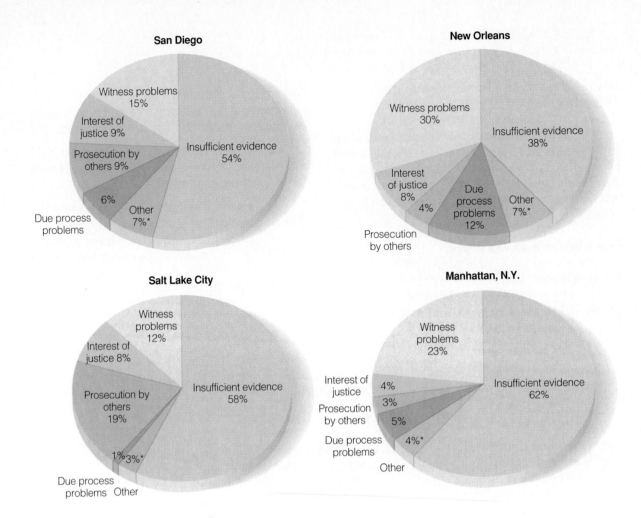

**San Diego**

Witness problems 15%
Interest of justice 9%
Prosecution by others 9%
Insufficient evidence 54%
6%
Due process problems
Other 7%*

**New Orleans**

Witness problems 30%
Insufficient evidence 38%
Interest of justice 8%
Due process problems 12%
4%
Other 7%*
Prosecution by others

**Salt Lake City**

Witness problems 12%
Interest of justice 8%
Prosecution by others 19%
Insufficient evidence 58%
1% 3%*
Due process problems   Other

**Manhattan, N.Y.**

Witness problems 23%
Interest of justice 4%
Prosecution by others 3%
Due process problems 5%
Insufficient evidence 62%
4%*
Other

**Figure 7.5**
**Reasons for declining to prosecute felony cases in four cities**

Insufficient evidence was the predominant reason for declining prosecution in the four cities studied, but note that the proportions vary.

SOURCE: Adapted from U.S. Department of Justice, Bureau of Justice Statistics, *Report to the Nation on Crime and Justice*, 2d ed. (Washington, D.C.: Government Printing Office, 1988), 73.

NOTE: Figures may not add up to 100 percent due to rounding.

*Includes plea to include another case and diversion.

discretion may be limited. In one instance, after newspapers publicized a rash of jailbreaks, a prosecutor abandoned the practice of charging escapees from the county jail with misdemeanors and brought in felony charges instead.

As has often been said, justice must "be seen publicly to be done." The public's respect for the criminal justice process is greatly affected by the behavior of prosecutors. Prosecutors must decide whether the community's regard for the law will be harmed if a person is brought to trial and is not convicted. Some people may feel that too many acquittals call into question the validity of the judicial process and undermine respect for law. Is it better to let a guilty person go free or to attempt a prosecution that is bound to fail?

The expenditure of organizational resources may be another reason for withholding prosecution. If the matter is trivial or if the accused must be extradited from another state, the costs may be too high to warrant action. If the accused is on parole or has a prior deferred or suspended sentence, a prosecutor may feel the best decision is to go before a judge and seek revocation of the parole.

As we have seen, evidential, pragmatic, and organizational factors influence the decision to prosecute. This discussion helps to clarify that the prosecuting attorney has a great deal of discretion to handle cases in ways that fit the requirements of the law, the prosecutorial organization, and justice.

## Toward Community Prosecution

One of the significant trends in criminal justice is the extent to which agencies are becoming more oriented toward the communities they serve. One of these trends is the development of community prosecution approaches that are based on the same assumptions that inspired community policing. Assistant prosecutors are assigned cases from a particular neighborhood or police precinct. These prosecutors get to know their assigned community, meet the residents, attend neighborhood events, and present information to community groups. By becoming a part of a community, they are able to better gauge the problems of neighborhood crime and disorder, coordinate efforts with the police, and encourage community assistance with criminal justice efforts.

Community prosecution recognizes that prosecutors are in a position to try to control crime in the local environment, to deal with the underlying problems that have caused crime and disorder, and to use the full range of their powers to deal with these problems. Unlike the traditional focus on felonies and other serious offenses, community prosecution acknowledges that citizens are equally concerned about lesser offenses that

**Figure 7.6**
**Typical actions of a prosecuting attorney in processing a felony case**
The prosecutor has certain responsibilities at various points in the criminal process. At each point the prosecutor is an advocate for the state's case against the accused.

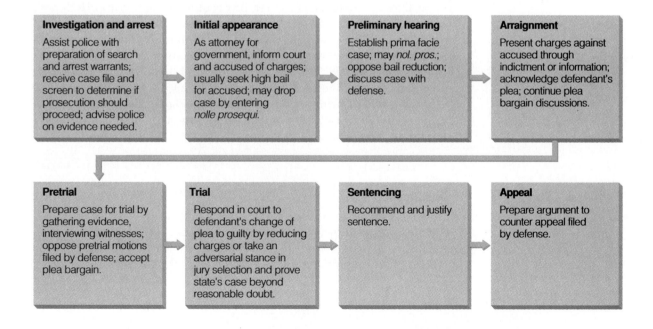

| Investigation and arrest | Initial appearance | Preliminary hearing | Arraignment |
|---|---|---|---|
| Assist police with preparation of search and arrest warrants; receive case file and screen to determine if prosecution should proceed; advise police on evidence needed. | As attorney for government, inform court and accused of charges; usually seek high bail for accused; may drop case by entering *nolle prosequi*. | Establish prima facie case; may *nol. pros.*; oppose bail reduction; discuss case with defense. | Present charges against accused through indictment or information; acknowledge defendant's plea; continue plea bargain discussions. |

| Pretrial | Trial | Sentencing | Appeal |
|---|---|---|---|
| Prepare case for trial by gathering evidence, interviewing witnesses; oppose pretrial motions filed by defense; accept plea bargain. | Respond in court to defendant's change of plea to guilty by reducing charges or take an adversarial stance in jury selection and prove state's case beyond reasonable doubt. | Recommend and justify sentence. | Prepare argument to counter appeal filed by defense. |

Prosecution policies are not made in isolation. They are created within the context of political and community pressures. Do you think prosecutors should be free of these pressures? Why or why not?

produce disorder or the perception of disorder in neighborhood life. Prostitution, drug sales, vandalism, and loitering are disruptive to residents of the community and are the types of offenses for which they demand prosecution. In cities where community policing has been established, prosecutors receive the fruits of law enforcement actions. One result is the reorienting of prosecution resources toward these less serious offenses.

Advocates of community prosecution argue that they can build cases against offenders more effectively because they know the residents, businesses, and social life of the neighborhood. When presenting a case before a judge the prosecutor is able to emphasize the impact of the offense on the lives of residents. However, prosecutors using this approach have learned that community prosecution requires additional resources. Having assistant prosecutors involved in the community and doing the in-depth research necessary to ascertain local needs is not cheap. Likewise, focusing on "low-level" crimes means that traditional ways of measuring effectiveness—convictions for serious offenses, for example—must be rethought. It is difficult to convince funding sources that money should be spent on the prosecution of prostitutes when the media emphasizes the chilling details of heinous crimes.

## Summary

The prosecuting attorney is justifiably called the central actor in the criminal justice system. Prosecutors not only are responsible for the decision to bring charges against defendants but also, in the vast majority of cases, participate in negotiations concerning the outcome. Prosecutors may conceive of their role in one of four ways: trial counsel for the police, house counsel for the police, representative of the court, and elected official. Thus the influence of prosecuting attorneys is extensive, but the fact remains that in the United States little public attention is given to their role. In many ways, a prosecutor's decisions have a potentially greater impact than those of a mayor or a city council. The level of law enforcement—and therefore a vital aspect of the quality of life—is directly related to the actions of the prosecutor.

Prosecutors enter into a series of exchange relationships with the police, victims, courts, and the community. The prosecutor's discretion is a major factor in the exchanges. These relationships influence the decision to prosecute and the other actions taken by the prosecution with regard to case disposition.

Prosecutors may develop policies for decision making that can be classified as legal sufficiency (many cases are accepted, but most are disposed of by plea bargaining or dismissal), system efficiency (cases are disposed of speedily and early in the process), or trial sufficiency (cases that seem certain to end in conviction are accepted for prosecution). These policies structure the organization of prosecution and the staffing of the office.

Because the decision to prosecute is the focus of their work, prosecutors are able to exercise discretion at various points in the justice process. The decision to file charges is made at the initial phase, but the charges may be altered, reduced, or dropped at different stages for reasons pertaining to evidence, for pragmatic considerations, or in the interests of the organizational needs of the system.

## Questions for Review

1    What are the formal powers of the prosecuting attorney?

2    How do prosecutors balance the professional dimension of their work with the political context of their office?

3    What are necessarily included offenses and how do they influence the listing of charges? What role does a prosecutor's discretion play in the charging process?

4    List the organizations and groups that influence the prosecutor's decision to prosecute.

5    What considerations influence the charging decision?

6    Why is the prosecuting attorney often cited as the most powerful office in the criminal justice system?

## Key Terms

accusatory process

count

discovery

diversion

legal sufficiency

necessarily included offense

*nolle prosequi*

prosecuting attorney

state attorney general

system efficiency

trial sufficiency

United States attorneys

## For Further Reading

Heilbroner, David. *Rough Justice: Days and Nights of a Young D.A.* New York: Pantheon Books. 1990. The experience of an assistant district attorney learning the ropes in New York's criminal courts.

Jacoby, Joan E. *The American Prosecutor: A Search for Identity*. Lexington, Mass.: Lexington Books, 1979. A history and survey of American prosecutors; their work and role conflicts.

McDonald, William F., ed. *The Prosecutor*. Beverly Hills, Calif.: Sage, 1979. A collection of articles written by scholars about various aspects of prosecution.

Miller, Frank W. *Prosecution: The Decision to Charge a Suspect with a Crime*. Boston: Little, Brown, 1969. An early study of the legal ramifications of the prosecutor's discretionary powers.

Moley, Raymond. *Politics and Criminal Prosecution*. New York: Minton, Balch, 1929. A classic examination of prosecutors and their links to politics.

Naifeh, Steven, and Gregory Smith White. *The Mormon Murders*. New York: New American Library, 1989. Prosecution for murder in the context of a scandal within the Mormon Church and its political ramifications.

Rowland, Judith. *The Ultimate Violation*. New York: Doubleday, 1985. A former San Diego district attorney describes her pioneering legal strategy to prosecute rapists.

Turow, Scott. *Presumed Innocent*. New York: Farrar, Straus, and Giroux, 1987. Fictional account of the indictment and trial of an urban prosecutor for the murder of a colleague. Excellent description of an urban court system.

# Notes

1 See *New York Times*, 24 January 1990, 1, for a concise summary of the case and the issues surrounding it.

2 U.S. Department of Justice, Bureau of Justice Statistics, *Bulletin* (March 1992), 2.

3 Alexander B. Smith and Harriet Pollack, *Crimes and Justice in a Mass Society* (New York: Xerox Publishers, 1972), 165.

4 U.S. Department of Justice, *Principles of Federal Prosecution* (Washington, D.C.: Government Printing Office, 1980), 7.

5 John Buchanan, "Police-Prosecutor Teams: Innovations in Several Jurisdictions," *NIJ Reports* (May/June, 1989): 2.

6 Barbara Boland, Elizabeth Brady, Herbert Tyson, and John Bassler, *The Prosecution of Felony Arrests*, U.S. Department of Justice, Bureau of Justice Statistics (Washington, D.C.: Government Printing Office, 1983), 9.

7 Vera Institute of Justice, *Felony Arrests: Their Prosecution and Disposition in New York City's Courts* (New York: Vera Institute of Justice, 1977), 135.

8 Vera Institute of Justice, *Felony Arrests*, rev. ed. (New York: Longman, 1981), 68, 86.

9 Joan E. Jacoby, "The Charging Policies of Prosecutors," in *The Prosecutor*, ed. William F. McDonald (Beverly Hills, Calif.: Sage, 1979), 75.

10 Cassia Spohn, John Gruhl, and Susan Welch, "The Impact of the Ethnicity and Gender of Defendants on the Decision to Reject or Dismiss Felony Charges," *Criminology* 25 (February 1987): 175.

11 Michael L. Benson, William J. Maakestad, Francis T. Cullen, and Gilbert Geis, "District Attorneys and Corporate Crime: Surveying the Prosecutorial Gatekeepers," *Criminology* 26 (August 1988): 505.

# Defense Attorney

Standing before Judge Robert L. McCrary, Jr., in the Circuit

Court of Bay County, Florida, was Clarence Earl

Gideon, drifter and former convict, charged with

breaking and entering with intent to commit a felony

under Florida law. His case may sound like any of the

thousands of felony and misdemeanor cases that are heard daily in

America's courtrooms, yet on that summer day in 1961, Clarence Gideon

made a request that eventually produced a path-breaking opinion from

the U.S. Supreme Court. As the trial transcript shows, Gideon misun-

derstood the law, a misunderstanding that was to make history. "The

United States Supreme Court," he proclaimed, "says I am entitled to be

represented by counsel."[1] As the Close-Up on the *Gideon* case (pages

302–303) further explains, the Supreme Court had not said so, but it

shortly would remedy that oversight.

The 1963 opinion by the Supreme Court in *Gideon* v. *Wainwright*

began a great expansion of the right of counsel from its origins in English

common law over four hundred years ago.[2] Originally the right of the

## The Persistent Defendant: *Gideon* v. *Wainwright*, 372 U.S. 335 (1963)

Clarence Earl Gideon, fifty-one years old, petty thief, drifter, and gambler, had spent most of his adult life in jails serving time for burglary and larceny. On 4 June 1961, he was arrested in Panama City, Florida, for breaking into a poolroom to steal coins from a cigarette machine, plus beer and soft drinks. After arraignment on July 31 for "unlawfully and feloniously" breaking and entering with intent to commit a misdemeanor—petty larceny—Gideon was held for trial in what appeared to be a routine case.

Standing before Judge Robert L. McCrary on August 4, Gideon surprised the court by requesting that counsel be appointed to assist with his defense.

**The Court**: What says the Defendant? Are you ready to go to trial?

**The Defendant**: I am not ready, Your Honor.

**The Court**: Why aren't you ready?

**The Defendant**: I have no Counsel.

**The Court**: Why do you not have Counsel? Did you know that your case was set for trial today?

**The Defendant**: Yes, sir, I knew that it was set for trial today.

**The Court**: Why, then, did you not secure Counsel and be prepared to go to trial?

**The Defendant**: Your Honor, ... I request this Court to appoint Counsel to represent me in this trial.

**The Court**: Mr. Gideon, I am sorry, but I cannot appoint ... Counsel to represent you in this case. Under the laws of the State of Florida, the only time the Court can appoint Counsel to represent a Defendant is when that person is charged with a capital offense. I am sorry, but I will have to deny your request to appoint Counsel to defend you in this case.

**The Defendant**: The United States Supreme Court says I am entitled to be represented by Counsel.

accused to have the assistance of counsel in the English courts was allowed only in the least serious matters. Not until the end of the eighteenth century did Parliament extend this right to defendants in felony cases. In America, although the right to counsel varied among the colonies, by 1776 the right was widely accepted, and some, such as Pennsylvania and Connecticut, provided attorneys for indigents in certain cases. With ratification of the Sixth Amendment to the U.S. Constitution in 1791, the right was recognized, at least in the federal courts. Throughout the nineteenth and early twentieth centuries, implementation of the right to counsel varied among the states. Some provided counsel to indigents for cases involving the death penalty, others granted counsel for a range of felonies and misdemeanors. After *Gideon* v. *Wainwright*, the right to counsel was assured for persons accused of felonies. Then, with the case of *Argersinger* v. *Hamlin* (1972), it was extended to any defendant charged with commission of a crime punishable by a prison sentence. Since more than 60 percent of all persons charged with crimes are unable to pay for a lawyer (and in some jurisdictions the percentage is closer to 90), the requirement that counsel must be provided for indigents has dramatically changed the way defendants are legally represented and the role of the defense attorney.

In this chapter we examine the world of criminal lawyers, which has been largely shaped by the *Gideon* decision. We will see that the structure of the American bar influences the type of person who enters criminal practice. Since defense attorneys, both privately retained and publicly

Acting as his own counsel, Gideon was unable to interrogate witnesses and present his defense in the way required by the law. The jury found him guilty, and on August 25 he was sentenced to five years in the Florida State Prison.

From his prison cell Gideon prepared a handwritten petition of appeal to the Florida Supreme Court. On October 30 it was denied without hearing. Despite the setback, Gideon persisted and filed a petition for review with the U.S. Supreme Court. On 4 June 1962, the Court granted the petition and appointed Abe Fortas, later to become a Supreme Court justice, to represent Gideon.

Fortas argued that an accused person cannot effectively defend himself and thus cannot receive due process and a fair trial. Without counsel, the accused cannot evaluate the lawfulness of his arrest, the validity of the indictment, whether preliminary motions should be filed, whether a proper search was carried out, whether the confession is admissible as evidence, and so on. Fortas noted that the indigent defendant is almost always in jail and cannot prepare his defense and that the trial judge cannot adequately perform the function of counsel. As he said, "To convict the poor without counsel while we guarantee the right to counsel to those who can afford it is also a denial of equal protection of the laws."

On 18 March 1963, a unanimous Supreme Court said that Gideon was entitled to counsel and that the Sixth Amendment obligated the states to provide counsel to indigent defendants. Speaking for the Court, Justice Hugo Black said:

> In our adversary system of criminal justice, any person hauled into court, who is too poor to hire a lawyer, cannot be assured a fair trial unless counsel is provided for him. This seems to us to be an obvious truth.

paid, are encouraged to handle many cases in an impersonal, bureaucratic manner, the adversarial norm of a vigorous defense is often lacking. Counsel often seeks to move cases as quickly as possible by persuading clients to plea bargain so that the ongoing routine of the courthouse progresses smoothly.

## Questions for Inquiry

- What is the reality of criminal defense work in the United States?
- Who becomes a defense attorney?
- How is counsel provided for indigent defendants?
- What role does defense counsel play in the system and what is the nature of the attorney-client relationship?

## The Defense Attorney: Image and Reality

**defense attorney**
The lawyer who represents the accused and the convicted offender in their dealings with criminal justice officials.

Most Americans have seen a **defense attorney** in action on television. The much-rerun "Perry Mason" and "L.A. Law" programs have shown the investigative, challenging, probing defense attorneys at their best.

**Clarence Seward Darrow**

Born in Kinsman, Ohio, Clarence Darrow studied law for one year at the University of Michigan before being admitted to the Ohio bar. After practicing law in Ohio for nine years, he moved to Chicago and began the career that made him one of the nation's famous defense attorneys.

Darrow devoted much of his career to political and labor cases. Because of his political beliefs, he resigned his position as corporate counsel for the Chicago and Western Railway during the Pullman strike of 1894. He defended socialist Eugene V. Debs against a charge of contempt of court in connection with that strike, as well as other radical political leaders such as "Big Bill" Hayward.

Darrow's two most famous cases occurred within a year of each other. In 1924 he became defense counsel in the trial of Richard Leopold and Nathan Loeb for the "thrill" murder of Bobby Franks. By basing his defense on a plea of temporary insanity and emphasizing the two defendants' abnormal conduct and personality development, Darrow was able to save them from the death penalty. In 1925 he was pitted against William Jennings Bryan, a longtime adversary in the famous Scopes "monkey trial" in Tennessee. Although he lost the case, his defense refuted the fundamentalist assertions underlying Bryan's antievolution argument.

Through television, movies, and literature, images of the famous defense attorney—Clarence Darrow (highlighted in the Biography), Richard "Racehorse" Haynes, F. Lee Bailey, Melvin Belli, Gerry Spence—have become familiar.

## The Role of the Defense Attorney

Counsel is essential for the defense of a person accused of a crime. Criminal lawyers are advocates; that is, they are understood to support the defendant by their investigative ability before trial, by their verbal skills in the courtroom, by their knowledge of the law, and by their ability to knit these talents together in a constant creative questioning of decisions at every stage of the judicial process. As an adversary the aggressive defense attorney insists that the government prove its case according to law. The stakes are high not only because the defendant's freedom is at stake but also because the essence of the adversary system assumes that well-qualified and active defense counsel keeps the system honest. Pressure from defense attorneys keeps the other actors from relaxing into the lethargy often associated with bureaucracy.

Defense attorneys represent their clients and are generally assumed to be responsible for both defense strategy and tactics. The client-counselor relationship is crucial; the qualities of respect, openness, and trust between the two are indispensable. If the defendant refuses to follow the attorney's advice, the lawyer may feel obligated to withdraw from the case in order to protect his or her own reputation.

The defense attorney performs specific functions as an advocate or representative of the accused, and Figure 8.1 shows the actions of counsel in a typical felony case that may proceed to trial. (In addition to these formal activities, the defense attorney also provides psychological support to the defendant and the defendant's family.) It is important to realize that counsel normally begins discussion of a plea bargain soon after the facts are known and continues negotiations until an acceptable agreement has been reached. Even after the trial has begun, a plea of not guilty may be changed to guilty as a result of bargaining.

## The Realities of the Defense Attorney

The opinions of the Supreme Court and the values of the Due Process Model are based on a conception of the defense attorney as a combative element in an adversarial proceeding. How closely does this conception square with reality? The adversary system is fully effective only if the exchange process and the organizational setting enhance the role of the criminal lawyer. Merely to require the provision of counsel may not help if the attorney provided is ill-educated and poorly paid and if the principles that structure the role of the defense attorney have been compromised by the values of the system. Rather than acting as the adversary and challenging the decisions made at each step in the process, defense

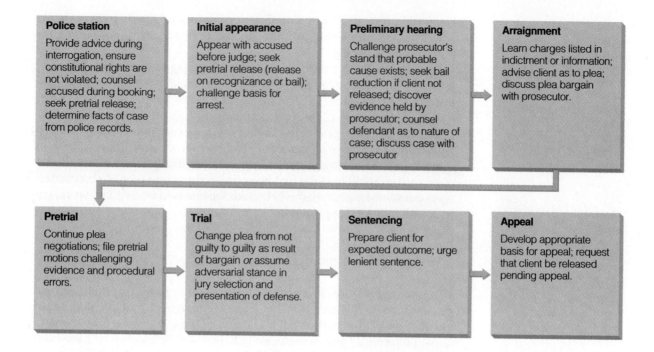

| Police station | Initial appearance | Preliminary hearing | Arraignment |
|---|---|---|---|
| Provide advice during interrogation, ensure constitutional rights are not violated; counsel accused during booking; seek pretrial release; determine facts of case from police records. | Appear with accused before judge; seek pretrial release (release on recognizance or bail); challenge basis for arrest. | Challenge prosecutor's stand that probable cause exists; seek bail reduction if client not released; discover evidence held by prosecutor; counsel defendant as to nature of case; discuss case with prosecutor | Learn charges listed in indictment or information; advise client as to plea; discuss plea bargain with prosecutor. |

| Pretrial | Trial | Sentencing | Appeal |
|---|---|---|---|
| Continue plea negotiations; file pretrial motions challenging evidence and procedural errors. | Change plea from not guilty to guilty as result of bargain *or* assume adversarial stance in jury selection and presentation of defense. | Prepare client for expected outcome; urge lenient sentence. | Develop appropriate basis for appeal; request that client be released pending appeal. |

counsel may, in fact, play the role of mediator between the defendant, prosecutor, and judge. The defense attorney may help the prosecutor and judge pull the loose ends together so that a bargain can be worked out. Whether that bargain is necessarily in the best interest of the defendant may, in certain instances, be open to question.

Defense attorneys have traditionally been caught between divergent concepts of their position. According to the Perry Mason image, they owe their client a full defense at every stage of the criminal process. Too often, however, the general public feels that defense lawyers are somehow soiled by their clients and are not so much engaged in freeing the innocent as in letting the guilty escape by exploiting technical loopholes in the law. Because most defense lawyers are continually on the losing side, they must also suffer the discontent of clients who feel that they did not work hard enough. The public defender is the special focus of such complaints. In some prisons, "P.D." is an abbreviation not for "public defender" but for "prison deliverer."

**Figure 8.1**
**Typical actions of a defense attorney processing a felony case**
Defense attorneys are advocates for the accused. They have an obligation to challenge within the law points made by the prosecution and to advise clients as to their rights.

## Private Counsel: An Endangered Species?

Of an estimated 800,000 practicing lawyers in the United States, only between 10,000 and 20,000 accept criminal cases on a "more than occasional" basis and of these only 14,000 are employed as public defenders. In the sole contemporary national study of the criminal bar, Paul Wice found that the number and quality of privately retained lawyers varied among cities, with legal, institutional, and political factors accounting for much of the variance.[3]

Given the small proportion of lawyers engaged in criminal practice, the questions arise: Who does take criminal cases? What are the qualifications of the practitioners? The average criminal lawyer practices alone, not as a member of a law firm; comes from a middle-class, nonprofessional background; graduated from a lesser law school; and entered private criminal practice after some experience as a public lawyer. Only an estimated 4 percent are women. Wice found that 38 percent of his sample of private criminal lawyers had been prosecutors and that 24 percent had been public defenders, had worked for legal services (civil law work), or had held civil service positions.[4]

## The Private Criminal Bar

When we survey the defense attorney scene it appears that three general groups of lawyers take criminal cases on a regular basis and that they might be called specialists in their field. The first group is composed of nationally known attorneys—for example, Belli, Bailey, and Spence—who have built their reputations by adhering to the Perry Mason pattern. But there are few of them; they are expensive; and they usually take only the dramatic, widely publicized cases; they do not frequent the county courthouse. A second group of lawyers practices in major metropolitan areas and is retained by professional criminals, such as drug dealers, gamblers, pornographers, and those in organized crime. In some cities—Miami, for one, with its large drug problem—lawyers in this category make a profitable living. But this group is fairly small because of its relatively limited clientele.

The largest group of attorneys in full-time criminal practice are courthouse regulars who accept many cases for small fees and who daily participate in the criminal justice system as either retained or assigned counsel. Rather than preparing their cases for disposition through the adversary process, these attorneys negotiate guilty pleas and try to convince their clients that they have received exceptional treatment. Such lawyers are valued for their negotiating rather than their adversarial skills. They operate in a relatively closed system where there are great pressures to process many cases for small fees, and they depend on the cooperation of judicial actors. These practitioners are less likely to be educated at top law schools; they must work harder and are financially less secure than lawyers who take the civil cases of business corporations.

In addition to these specialists in criminal practice are many private practitioners who are occasionally willing to take criminal cases. Often they are members of or connected with a law firm whose upper-class clients have run afoul of the law. Although this group of attorneys is fairly substantial, its members have little experience in trial work and do not

## Criminal Defenders: Law's Outcasts

The criminal lawyer's work goes far afield from what happens in court. It is the "getting around" that is important.

And getting around Richard Daly does.

By 8:30 A.M. on any given court day, his Thunderbird is parked on Market Street in front of the courthouse and he's soon into the flow.

A prostitute who had once been helped by Daly glad-eyes him in the corridor, tapping her lavender thick-soled shoes in a tattoo on the bare floor. "Stay cool, Mr. Richard," she says. Daly gives her his Jimmy Cagney smile; lots of teeth, briefly.

A clerk with a sheaf of traffic violations whispers something and Daly says thanks, which seems to please the clerk.

One after another, a variety of people move toward him like pieces of metal attracted to a magnet.

By 9 A.M., he's in the office of George Solomon, clerk of the Circuit Court of Criminal Causes. Solomon is a cousin of Sarkis Webbe, who shares Daly's office.

In Solomon's office, there is the special coterie gathered for morning coffee. The talk is easy. It's about cases. Solomon is there. And Daly. And Sidney Faber, the associate prosecuting attorney for the city of St. Louis, and Robert Wendt, an associate of Daly, and Norman London, and another lawyer, Gordan S. Benes.

Staying "tight" with Solomon's office is important to Daly because much of the processing flows through the clerk's hands. The better the relationship, the fewer the snarls and hassles.

He also is "tight" with Sidney Faber, the prosecutor. It is a mutual feeling. From Daly's point of view, he can pretty well talk out a case with Faber and get something favorable for his client. From Faber's point of view, it is profitable because by reaching an accord he doesn't have to fight Daly in court.

By 10 A.M., court opens and Daly is working the courthouse. This does not necessarily mean that he may be arguing a case. Mostly, it is filing of motions, seeing that certain things get done, seeing that he stays "tight" with the right people. James Lavin, for example. Lavin is clerk for two judges.

"Say I need a copy of all search warrants in cases I'm involved in," explains Daly. "It is proper that I get them, but getting them can be achieved efficiently and cooperatively, or can be full of hassles and delays. Of course, I want to get along with Lavin."

Which also means getting along reasonably well with the twenty or so others in the clerk's office.

At noon, the Daly coterie assembles near the chambers of Judge David Fitzgibbon. Lunch time. Cold cuts, coffee and Coke, and conversation.

The talk got around to fame and what it does to the lawyer and to his client ultimately, how it affects the performance of the criminal justice system.

"Frankly," Daly said, "becoming as well known as Morris Shenker or F. Lee Bailey or Percy Foreman could hurt my professional activity. I'd have to do something altogether different.

"Now, you might say that I have the courthouse wired. That is, I know how it works to the Nth degree. I have things functioning very smoothly. I'm not a big star, I don't draw outside attention. I'm able to accomplish a very good job as a defense lawyer."

SOURCE: Bernard Gavzer, "Criminal Defenders: Law's Outcasts," *Washington Post*, 18 February 1973. Copyright © 1973 by The Washington Post. Reprinted by permission.

have well-developed relationships with the actors in the criminal justice system. As the accompanying Close-Up reveals, insider know-how and relationships are critical in the system. Therefore, the reality is that these clients might be better served by a courthouse regular than by the private practitioner who only rarely handles a criminal case.

Thus far we have examined the practice of the private criminal bar in big cities. Studies have shown that in middle-size and small cities a greater portion of attorneys take defense work than in large metropolitan centers. But even in "middle America" criminal law is not important, either in terms of time spent or as a principal source of income.[5]

## The Environment of Criminal Practice

Various aspects of the criminal lawyers' practice help explain the difficulties of their work. Much of the service rendered by defense counsel involves preparing clients and their relatives for possible negative outcomes of their cases. Even a lawyer's exposure to "guilty knowledge" may be a psychological burden. Lawyers have explained that they may easily become emotionally entangled because they are the only judicial actors to view the defendant in the context of social environment and family ties.

Criminal lawyers must also interact continually with a lower class of clients and with police officials, social workers, and minor political appointees. They may be required to visit depressing places such as the local jail at all hours of the day and night. The work setting of most criminal lawyers is thus a far cry from the mahogany paneling, plush carpets, and stimulating conversation of the "inner-circle" law firm.

The fact that criminal practice does not pay well is probably the key variable of the defense attorney's environment and one that influences other aspects of criminal practice. For the most part, criminal defendants are poor, and losing a case is likely to reduce their earning capacity even further. Thus most attorneys must make every effort to get their fees in advance or somehow to tie defendants and their families to them financially. As one Washington, D.C., judge explained, "The lawyer goes out and tries to squeeze money from the defendant's mother or an aunt."[6] Even after winning a case, the defense attorney may be unable to collect the fee.

Such financial circumstances generally force most defense attorneys to handle a multitude of cases for modest fees. A fifteen-minute conference with the prosecutor and a five-minute appearance in court may earn the lawyer the same fee as a three-day trial. Criminal lawyers frequently say, "I make my money on the phone or in the prosecutor's office, not in the courtroom."

The fact of being on the losing side of most cases affects personal esteem. No one likes to lose, yet defense attorneys must quickly adjust to the fact that most of their clients are going to plead or be found guilty. Defense attorneys also face the possibility of "losing by winning." An attorney who mounts a zealous defense and thus secures the release of a defendant accused of a heinous crime may be censured by the community for using "technicalities" to defeat justice. In such cases, the defense attorney faces the additional risk of embarrassing the prosecution or the judge, thus reducing the possibility of future considerations from them. The environment of criminal practice, then, involves extensive physical, psychological, and social pressures. Many attorneys get "burned out" after only a few years of such practice; few criminal law specialists stay in the field past the age of fifty.

# Counsel for Indigents

A brief synopsis of the major Supreme Court rulings on the accused's right to counsel is set forth in Table 8.1. As we have seen, the Supreme Court's requirements that counsel be appointed early in the criminal justice process and that it be provided to all indigents accused of crimes punishable by prison sentences have drastically raised the percentage of defendants who become clients of publicly supported defender programs. Indigency is variously defined either by state law or by judicial discretion. Over time there has been a lessening of the requirements so that defendants in most of the country need not be truly indigent or completely without funds to be provided with publicly paid counsel. In many areas, federal poverty guidelines are used as the measure, while in other localities the fact of being unemployed, receiving welfare, or having a low income and dependents is enough to qualify for free counsel.

**Table 8.1**
**The right to counsel: major Supreme Court rulings**

| Case | Year | Ruling |
|------|------|--------|
| *Gideon* v. *Wainwright* | 1963 | The Fourteenth Amendment gives defendants in state noncapital felony cases the right to counsel. |
| *Escobedo* v. *Illinois* | 1964 | The accused has the right to counsel during interrogation by the police. |
| *Miranda* v. *Arizona* | 1966 | The right to counsel begins when investigation of a crime focuses on a suspect. The suspect must be informed of the right to remain silent and to have counsel and be informed that any statement made may be used against him or her. |
| *United States* v. *Wade* | 1967 | The defendant has the right to be assisted by counsel during a police lineup. (Extended to state defendants in *Gilbert* v. *California* [1967]). |
| *Coleman* v. *Alabama* | 1970 | Counsel must be present at a preliminary hearing. |
| *Argersinger* v. *Hamlin* | 1972 | Whenever a criminal charge may result in a prison sentence, the accused has the right to counsel. |
| *Ross* v. *Moffitt* | 1974 | States are not required to provide counsel for indigents beyond one appeal. |
| *Moore* v. *Illinois* | 1977 | The defendant has the right to counsel at a preliminary court hearing at which he or she appears to be identified by a witness. |
| *United States* v. *Henry* | 1980 | Government agents may not solicit a statement from a defendant covertly and then introduce the statement at trial. |
| *Strickland* v. *Washington* | 1984 | The defendant has the right to the *effective* assistance of counsel, whether privately retained or publicly provided. |

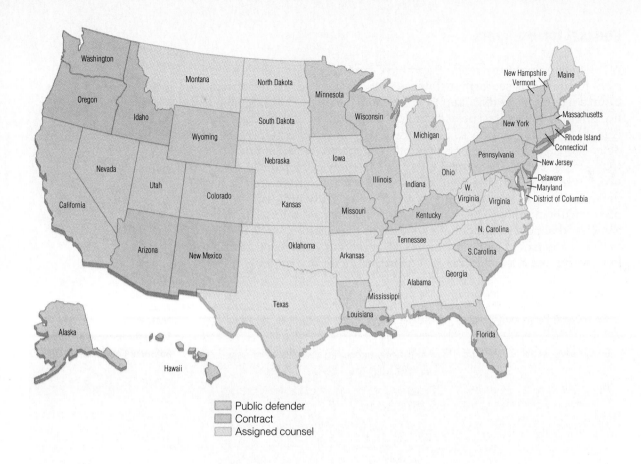

Washington
Oregon
Idaho
Montana
Wyoming
Nevada
Utah
California
Colorado
Arizona
New Mexico
North Dakota
South Dakota
Nebraska
Kansas
Oklahoma
Texas
Minnesota
Wisconsin
Iowa
Missouri
Arkansas
Louisiana
Illinois
Indiana
Michigan
Ohio
Kentucky
Tennessee
Mississippi
Alabama
Georgia
Florida
New Hampshire
Vermont
Maine
New York
Massachusetts
Rhode Island
Connecticut
Pennsylvania
New Jersey
Delaware
Maryland
District of Columbia
W. Virginia
Virginia
N. Carolina
S. Carolina
Alaska
Hawaii

☐ Public defender
☐ Contract
☐ Assigned counsel

**Figure 8.2**
**Indigent defense system used in each state by the majority of counties**

These aggregate descriptions often mask the fact that some states use a combination of approaches to indigent defense.

SOURCE: U.S. Department of Justice, Bureau of Justice Statistics, *Bulletin* (September 1988).

The quality of defense counsel available to the poor is a question for national debate. An unidentified prisoner in a Connecticut jail unwittingly contributed a zinger to the debate. When asked whether he had a lawyer when he went to court, he replied: "No, I had a public defender."[7]

Under ideal conditions, well-qualified counsel would be appointed early in the criminal justice process to pursue each case zealously in the best adversary tradition. Too often, however, the right to counsel is mocked by the assignment of a lawyer in the courtroom, a brief conference with the defendant, and a quick guilty plea. These factors—the quality of counsel, conditions of defense practice, and administrative pressures to move the caseload—are major concerns of those who are committed to the principle of due process. The adversary process can be realized only if an attorney has incentives to defend indigents with the same skill and vigor brought to bear for private clients.

# Methods of Providing Indigents with Counsel

In the United States there are three basic methods of providing counsel to indigent defendants: (1) the assigned counsel system, by which a court appoints a private attorney to represent a particular accused; (2) the contract system, by which an individual attorney, a nonprofit organization, or a private law firm contracts with a local government to provide legal services to indigent defendants for a specified dollar amount; and (3) public defender programs, established as public or private nonprofit organizations with full-time or part-time salaried staff. We look at each of these methods in turn. To determine the system in use in the majority of counties in each of the fifty states see Figure 8.2. Table 8.2 highlights the different methods used in nine jurisdictions.

**Assigned Counsel** Through the **assigned counsel** system, the court appoints a lawyer in private practice to represent an indigent defendant. This system is widely used in small cities and in rural areas, but even some urban areas with public defender systems follow the practice of assigning counsel in some circumstances, as when a case has multiple defendants and a conflict of interest might result if one were to be represented by a public lawyer. But there are also cities, such as Detroit, where the private bar has been able to insist that its members receive a major share of the cases (see Table 8.2).

Assigned counsel systems are organized on two bases: the ad hoc system and the coordinated system. In ad hoc assignment systems, private attorneys indicate to the judge that they are willing to take the cases of indigent defendants. When an indigent requires counsel the judge then either assigns lawyers in rotation from a prepared list or selects among attorneys who are known and present in the courtroom. The Question of Ethics on page 312 presents a telephone conversation in which a judge assigns a case to counsel. In coordinated assignment systems a court administrator oversees the appointment of counsel.[8]

Under both systems, the competence of attorneys who are willing to be assigned cases is sometimes questionable. In many urban areas where the assigned counsel system is used, such lawyers are largely recent law

**assigned counsel**
An attorney in private practice assigned by a court to represent an indigent and whose fee is paid by the government that has jurisdiction over the case.

**Table 8.2**
**Percentage of felony cases handled by different types of defense attorneys in nine jurisdictions**
Jurisdictions vary according to the percentage of cases handled by each form of counsel. Note the similarities and differences among these courts. To what extent do local traditions, politics, and judicial leadership influence the type of system?

SOURCE: Roger Hanson and Joy Chapper, *Indigent Defense Systems*, Report to the State Justice Institute. Copyright © 1991 by National Center for State Courts. (Williamsburg, Va.: National Center for State Courts, 1991).

| Types of Defense Attorneys | Detroit, Michigan | Seattle, Washington | Denver, Colorado | Norfolk, Virginia | Monterey, California | Globe, Arizona | Oxford, Maine | Island, Washington | San Juan, Washington |
|---|---|---|---|---|---|---|---|---|---|
| Public defender | 18.3% | 0.0% | 74.6% | 0.0% | 72.6% | 0.0% | 0.0% | 0.0% | 61.3% |
| Assigned counsel | 64.6 | 1.2 | 5.4 | 71.1 | 19.3 | 0.0 | 52.7 | 0.0 | 0.0 |
| Contract attorneys | 0.0 | 86.8 | 0.0 | 0.0 | 0.0 | 81.9 | 0.0 | 65.6 | 0.0 |
| Private counsel | 17.0 | 12.0 | 20.0 | 28.9 | 8.1 | 17.5 | 47.3 | 34.4 | 38.7 |
| | 99.9% | 100.0% | 100.0% | 100.0% | 100.0% | 99.4% | 100.0% | 100.0% | 100.0% |
| Total number of cases | 458 | 606 | 370 | 463 | 409 | 170 | 224 | 125 | 31 |
| Percentage indigent | 82.9% | 88.0% | 80.0% | 71.1% | 91.9% | 81.9% | 52.7% | 65.6% | 61.3% |

school graduates, younger, and rated by other members of the bar as less competent than retained counsel. In contrast, as the Comparative Perspective (pages 314–315) explains, the system in Denmark takes additional steps to ensure the competence and experience of attorneys assigned to defendants. Just as important as the quality of legal talent is the fact that a "courthouse regular" may become co-opted to serve the organizational needs of the system.

The fee schedule for assigned defenders of indigents is often low relative to what an attorney might otherwise charge (see Table 8.3, which shows the fees stipulated for the state of Colorado). Low fees may serve as an inducement for counsel to persuade the client to plead guilty to a lesser charge. Some assigned defenders find they can make more money by collecting a preparation fee of about fifty dollars, payable when an indigent client pleads guilty, rather than by going to trial. Handling many cases on this basis is more profitable for the attorney than spending an entire day in the courtroom at trial, for which the fee may be only two hundred dollars.

**Contract System**   In the newest method for providing defense services to poor people—currently used in a few, primarily western, counties—the government contracts with an individual attorney, a nonprofit association, or a private law firm. The majority of counties that have chosen this method are not heavily populated. Some jurisdictions use public defenders for most cases but contract for services in multiple-defendant situations that might present conflicts of interest, in cases considered to be extraordinarily complex, or in cases that require more time than the government's salaried lawyers can provide.

The terms of contracts vary.[9] The most common provision is for a block grant: a private law firm agrees to represent all cases for a fixed amount. Fixed-price contracts are the second most common type. Under such agreements lawyers agree to provide representation for a specified number of cases for a fixed amount per case. Some systems enter into a cost-plus arrangement: representation is provided at an estimated cost per case until the dollar amount of the contract is reached, at which point a new contract is negotiated.

**Public Defender**   The **public defender** is a twentieth-century response to the legal needs of the indigent. Started in Los Angeles County in 1914, when attorneys for the defense were first hired by the American government, the system has spread across the country. The most recent survey shows that public defender systems exist in 1,144 counties that comprise more than 70 percent of the U.S. population.[10] The public defender system is growing rapidly and is already the dominant form in forty-three of the fifty most populous counties; nationwide such programs serve 68 percent of the U.S. population. Public defender systems predominate in most large cities, in populous counties, and in about twenty statewide, state-funded jurisdictions. In other states they are organized and paid for by counties. Only two states, North Dakota and Maine, do not have public defenders.

Salaried public defenders represent a break with the hallowed tradition of the attorney as a private professional serving individual clients for a fee. The public defender system is often viewed as superior to the assigned counsel system because the attorneys are full-time specialists in criminal law. Although their actual efficiency has not been tested by researchers, public defenders are generally thought to be more efficient attorneys who do not create lengthy delays or make frivolous technical motions.

**public defender**
An attorney employed on a fulltime, salaried basis by the government to represent indigents.

| Standard Fees | Per Hour | |
|---|---|---|
| Attorney fees for trial court work: | | |
|   Out-of-court time | $25.00 | |
|   Pretrial, trial, posttrial time in court | $35.00 | |
| Attorney fees for appellate court work | $25.00 | |
| Guardian of estate or property | $25.00 | |
| Court-authorized investigative services | $25.00 | |

| Maximum Fee Payments | With Trial | Without Trial (Half Maximum) |
|---|---|---|
| Class 1 felonies and unclassified felonies where the maximum possible penalty is death, life, or more than 51 years | $5,000 | $2,500 |
| Class 2 felonies and unclassified felonies where the maximum possible penalty is 41 through 50 years | $2,500 | $1,250 |
| Class 3, 4, and 5 felonies and unclassified felonies where the maximum possible penalty is from 1 to 40 years | $2,000 | $1,000 |
| Class 1, 2, and 3 misdemeanors, unclassified misdemeanors, and petty offenses | $500 | $250 |
| Juvenile cases | $1,000 | $500 |
| Guardian *ad litem* | $1,000 | $ — |
| Mental health | None | None |

**Table 8.3**
**Compensation for assigned counsel in Colorado**
Colorado has a statewide fee schedule that stipulates the hourly rate that an attorney can charge for indigent defense. Note that maximum amounts for each case are stipulated.

SOURCE: Supreme Court of Colorado, Office of the Chief Justice, Directive 85–24, "Appointment of Attorneys to Represent Indigents."

## Public Defense in Denmark

Public defenders have been a part of the legal system in Denmark from as early as the sixteenth century. By the middle of the eighteenth century, laws regularizing the provision of counsel were developed. The Administration of Justice Act of 1919 as amended in 1978 set up the modern system. Although called a "public defender" system, it is similar to an "assigned counsel" system in the United States.

Attorneys who have been designated by the judiciary are assigned on a rotating basis to provide counsel for defendants charged with crimes. Defendants, however, are also permitted to request a particular individual from among this group to represent them if they do not want the attorney assigned by the court. More than 25,000 cases per year are handled by public defenders in Denmark.

Currently there are six hundred attorneys who have applied for and been selected by the judiciary to be defenders. Care is taken to ensure that very young lawyers, those with little experience, and

Public defense is often handled on a "zone" rather than on a person-to-person basis: public defenders are assigned to a particular courtroom and take all of its cases of indigent defendants. Thus the defendant has several attorneys, each of whom handles only a portion of the process: one the preliminary hearing, another the arraignment, and still another the trial, if there is a trial. No one attorney is solely responsible for defending the individual accused. In a study of Chicago felony cases, Janet Gilboy and John Schmidt found that 47 percent of defendants received such sequential representation by public defenders.[11] One effect of the dispersion of responsibility is that cases are handled routinely, and many of the special elements of an individual defense are lost. More critically, because the defendant is passed from one attorney to another, no relationship of trust is developed.

Whether or not the zone system is used, the style of defense in the typical public defender program is in marked contrast to the personalized relationship between client and privately retained attorney. Public defenders are street-level bureaucrats and thus there is a tendency to routinize decision making. Often confronted by overwhelming caseloads, they develop strategies to make decisions quickly and with a minimum expenditure of resources. Cases are standardized as much as possible, and the defense process is generally repetitive and routinized, with little

those who are in poor professional standing are not appointed. This means that those selected are reputed to belong to the better part of the profession. They carry on their public defender role along with their private civil and criminal practice. So concerned are the Danes with the quality of the representation that defenders may not substitute members of their firm when they are called upon to be in court, fines may be levied if the defender is negligent in a case, and ultimately the bar association may impose disciplinary sanctions for unethical conduct or poor work.

Counsel is provided to all indicted persons regardless of their financial condition. If an accused is found not guilty, he or she does not have to compensate the state for defense services. A convicted person may be required to repay the state defense in the form of restitution should their economic status warrant. Public defenders are paid on a per-case basis according to the amount of time spent in court and in preparing for the trial. The fees are calculated on a somewhat lower rate than the attorney could make if privately retained.

Recently there have been discussions about creating a centralized defender system with salaried civil service attorneys working within a public agency. This has been opposed on the grounds that the defender should have complete freedom to take those steps considered necessary to safeguard the interests of the client, a situation, it is argued, that can best be realized outside the bureaucratic environment of a public agency. In addition there is the feeling among some Danish lawyers that such a system would reduce the confidence that the accused should have in their attorneys. It is also thought that, as salaried employees, public defenders would be viewed as an integral part of the judicial system that the accused find overwhelming and hostile. It is agreed that a central public defense agency would be more cost effective, but thus far the Danes have placed a higher value on the independence of the criminal bar and the trust that their clients have in it.

SOURCE: Adapted from Hans Gammeltoft-Hansen, "Public Counsel for the Defense: The Danish System," in *The Defense Counsel*, ed. William F. McDonald (Beverly Hills, Calif.: Sage, 1983), 195–218. Copyright © 1983 by Sage Publications, Inc. Reprinted by permission.

individualized treatment of the special facts of each case. With experience, defenders develop mental images of typical clients so that the characteristics of the accused will help them to "place" the case in an established category and follow a standard procedure for disposition. Since the public defender has little time to interview clients and investigate each charge, negotiations with prosecutors and courtroom proceedings cover groups of

In urban areas, public defenders work under tremendous caseload pressure.

# Counsel for the Indigent in Four Locales

## Denver, Colorado

With a population of 505,000, the city and county of Denver is the largest urban area in the Rocky Mountain region. The population tends to be divided between a relatively affluent majority and an impoverished class (15 percent of the population live below the poverty line) made up primarily of the 17 percent of the population that is African-American or Hispanic.

Colorado has a statewide public defender system, which is responsible for all indigent cases except for those where there is a conflict (codefendants). The federal guidelines for determining indigency are used, but the information provided by defendants is not checked for accuracy. A ten dollar fee, waived for those in custody, is charged to those who apply for a public defender. An estimated 85 percent of felony defendants qualify for a public defender.

Twenty-six attorneys staff the Denver public defender's office. They are assisted by ten investigators and clerical staff. New defenders tend to be recent law school graduates who stay six to seven years. Public defenders are paid less than their counterparts in the district attorney's office.

## Detroit, Michigan

Wayne County has a population of 2,164,300. Half of the citizens live in the city of Detroit, making it the sixth largest city in the United States. Almost 40 percent of the population is nonwhite and about 15 percent live below the poverty level. Wayne County has a crime rate of almost 10,000 index crimes per 100,000 population.

Detroit provides attorneys to the indigent via assigned counsel and a nonprofit organization similar to a public defender agency. The assignments are distributed between two groups. Approximately 75 percent of the cases are assigned by judges to individual private attorneys; the remainder are allocated to the Legal Aid and Defenders Association, the nonprofit group. Attorneys are paid a fixed fee for their services based on the statutory punishment for the offense.

To be eligible for appointment as assigned counsel, attorneys must complete an application form listing professional experience, education, and criminal trial experience. Each applicant must be favorably reviewed by a committee of five judges. Once initially certified, an attorney can be assigned only those cases in which the penalty is twenty years or less imprisonment. With additional experience, assignment can be granted for the full range of cases.

Six hundred fifty attorneys are currently on the assigned counsel list. The pool is composed of about two hundred "hard-core" reg-

cases. Under these circumstances, and with a public defender who assumes that most of his or her clients are guilty of something, the atmosphere is different from the case of an attorney who believes clients to be innocent until the state proves them guilty. The accompanying Close-Up gives four views of how counsel is provided to indigents in different parts of the United States.

## Defendant and Attorney Perspectives on Indigent Counsel

Presentation of a defense to criminal charges requires an attorney-client relationship of trust and mutual respect. This relationship is especially difficult if the defendant is indigent and counsel is being provided by the state. If the client believes that the attorney is "only" a public defender who is not trying hard enough to build a defense, the client may not cooperate and even request that a new attorney be appointed. If the attorney sees the client as just one more case or if the client's story is not believed, the relationship may be strained and less effective. Each of the actors has a perspective on the other and on the criminal justice process.

ulars who depend upon assignments for a substantial portion of their caseload and income. The remainder are "irregulars" who look to assignments to supplement their private civil and criminal practice.

The perception that the defense bar was too cozy with the judiciary and that African-Americans were not receiving vigorous defense led to creation of the Legal Aid and Defenders Association (LADA) in the late 1960s. LADA is composed of twenty attorneys who by a Michigan Supreme Court order must receive 25 percent of felony case assignments. At any one time each LADA attorney carries between thirty and thirty-five cases. In many ways LADA may be best understood as providing services as would a public defender organization with staff attorneys.

### Oxford, Maine

With a population of only 50,200, Oxford County is located in the southwestern mountainous region of Maine. The per capita income averages $9,000 and about 13 percent of the population live below the federal poverty level. The crime rate is low by national standards, with a *UCR* index offense rate of 1,781 per 100,000 population. Less than one-half of 1 percent of the population are minorities.

Oxford County depends wholly on assigned counsel for indigent defense. By merely informing the court clerk, an attorney can receive assignments, which are given informally by the one visiting superior court judge who holds session for two or three weeks each month. At present only ten of the thirty-six attorneys practicing in the county receive indigent cases. Most of these attorneys also do private criminal and civil work.

Assigned counsel are paid by a voucher system and are allowed to charge forty dollars per hour for both in- and out-of-court work. Indigent defense is funded completely by the state.

### Gila County, Arizona

Gila County is a large geographic area half the size of the state of Rhode Island. Globe, the county seat, is located about ninety miles east of Phoenix in the state's copper-mining country. The population is about 40,000 with 16 percent being Hispanic and Native American, and 13 percent living below the poverty level. The violent crime rate is 2,500 per 100,000 population.

Gila County contracts with four local attorneys for the provision of defense services to the indigent. Compensation for each attorney averages $45,000 per year. The county provides additional support for investigators. All of the contract attorneys also maintain a private criminal and civil practice.

SOURCE: Roger Hanson and Joy Chapper, *Indigent Defense Systems*, Report to the State Justice Institute. Copyright © 1991 by National Center for State Courts. (Williamsburg, Va.: National Center for State Courts, 1991).

**The Defendant's Perspective** Defendants interviewed by Jonathan Casper saw the criminal justice process as not much different from life on the streets as they knew it—a harsh reality divorced from the abstract values of due process.[12] They perceived a gamelike quality to the system, with the police, prosecutors, defenders, and judges manipulating the defendants and one another for their own ends. From the perspective of the defendants, this was true even of their lawyers, the public defenders. As Casper comments, "most of those who were represented by public defenders thought their major adversary in the bargaining process to be not the prosecutor or the judge, but rather their own attorney, for he was the man with whom they had to bargain. They saw him as the surrogate of the prosecutor—a member of 'their little syndicate'—rather than as their own representative." In the view of one defendant, "a public defender is just like the prosecutor's assistant. Anything you tell this man, he's not gonna do anything but relay it back.... They'll come to some sort of agreement, and that's the best you're gonna get."[13]

**The Attorney's Perspective**   From the perspective of attorneys with public clients, criminal defendants give them little respect and trust. Attorneys who take the cases of indigents often believe that their clients have doubts about their status as legal practitioners, are skeptical about their skills as advocates, and worry about whose side they are on. These concerns make for a complicated relationship. When asked what makes their work unsatisfying, attorneys often point to their public clients. As one has said, "Sometimes we aren't treated the best by our clients....I had someone this morning whose father was yelling about how bad the public defender was right when I was appointed. That wasn't exactly thrilling."[14]

Much of an attorney's craft is based on an ability to persuade clients to follow advice. What is often referred to as "client control" requires client deference. In the absence of deference, the defendant may ignore the advice or suggestions of the attorney. "Without the client's trust, the attorney may not be believed; in turn, attorneys are not always sure if they can trust their clients. Once attorneys secure their client's confidence, they can exercise their judgment and satisfy a desire for professional autonomy."[15] The lawyer must engender in the defendant a sense that the attorney can be relied upon. Only then can the attorney feel assured that the defendant will not suddenly balk or unexpectedly reveal something that has been concealed.

## Private versus Public Defense

Do defendants who can afford their own counsel receive better legal services than those who cannot? At one time researchers thought that public defenders entered more guilty pleas than did lawyers who had been either privately retained or assigned to cases. But studies have cast doubt on this assumption. With publicly funded defense counsel now representing up to 85 percent of the cases in many localities, retained counsel may be viewed as an anomaly. Retained counsel may serve only upper-income defendants who are charged with white-collar crimes or drug dealers and organized crime figures who can pay the fees.

Recent studies indicate that little variation in ultimate case disposition can be associated with the type of defense.[16] This conclusion is supported by Peter Nardulli, who reports that the type of defense attorney made no difference in the plea packages negotiated in nine medium-sized court systems in Illinois, Michigan, and Pennsylvania.[17] In another study assigned counsel moved cases faster but the per-case cost was lower for public defenders.[18] A recent study by researchers from the National Center for State Courts greatly adds to our knowledge. In their analysis of felony cases in nine courts, little difference could be found among public defenders, assigned counsel, contracted counsel, and privately retained counsel regarding case disposition and length of sentences.[19] As Table 8.4 shows, there is little variation in case disposition among the indigent defense systems in each of the four jurisdictions.

| Type of Disposition | Detroit, Michigan | | | Denver, Colorado | | Norfolk, Virginia | | Monterey, California | | |
|---|---|---|---|---|---|---|---|---|---|---|
| | Public Defender | Assigned Counsel | Private Counsel | Public Defender | Private Counsel | Assigned Counsel | Private Counsel | Public Defender | Assigned Counsel | Private Counsel |
| Dismissals | 11.9% | 14.5% | 12.8% | 21.0% | 24.3% | 6.4% | 10.4% | 13.5% | 8.9% | 3.0% |
| Trial acquittals | 9.5 | 5.7 | 10.3 | 1.8 | 0.0 | 3.3 | 5.2 | 1.7 | 1.3 | 0.0 |
| Trial convictions | 22.6 | 14.5 | 24.4 | 5.1 | 9.5 | 5.2 | 2.2 | 7.1 | 11.4 | 18.2 |
| Guilty pleas | 54.8 | 64.9 | 52.6 | 72.1 | 66.2 | 85.1 | 81.3 | 76.8 | 78.5 | 78.8 |
| Diversion | 1.2 | .3 | 0.0 | 0.0 | 0.0 | 0.0 | .7 | 1.0 | 0.0 | 0.0 |
| | 100.0% | 99.9% | 100.1% | 100.0% | 100.0% | 100.0% | 99.8% | 101.1% | 101.1% | 100.0% |
| Total number of cases | 84 | 296 | 78 | 276 | 74 | 329 | 134 | 294 | 79 | 33 |

## Defense Counsel in the System

Most of the criminal lawyers in metropolitan courts work in a precarious professional environment. They work very hard for small fees in unpleasant surroundings and are not rewarded by professional or public acclaim. In a judicial system in which bargaining is a primary method of decision making, defense attorneys believe they must maintain close personal ties with the police, prosecutor, judges, and other court officials. Critics point out that the defender's independence is undermined by daily contact with the same prosecutors and judges. Private counsel has brief, businesslike encounters in the courtroom, but the public defender has a regular work site in the courtroom and thus presents himself or herself as one of its core personnel. He or she arrives at the defense table in the morning with case files for the day and only temporarily leaves this post when a private attorney's case is called. As the late, noted criminal lawyer Edward Bennett Williams has said:

The public defender and the prosecutor are trying cases against each other every day. They begin to look at their work like two wrestlers who wrestle with each other in a different city every night and in time get to be good friends. The biggest concern of the wrestlers is to be sure they do not hurt each other too much. They don't want to get hurt. They just want to make a living.[20]

An attorney's ability to establish and continue a pattern of informal exchange relations with these actors in the system is essential not only for professional survival but also for the opportunity to serve the needs of clients. An experienced attorney described his work as "getting along with people—salesmanship. That's what this young lawyer in my office right now doesn't know anything about. He's a moot court champion—great at research. But he doesn't know a damn thing about people."[21]

At every step of the criminal justice process, from the first contact with the accused until final disposition of the case, defense attorneys depend upon decisions made by other judicial actors. Even seemingly minor activities such as visiting the defendant in jail, learning the case against

**Table 8.4**

**Case disposition and types of defense attorneys**

Although the private versus public debate continues, the data show there are few variations in dispositon among the defense systems within each jurisdiction. Why are there differences among the cities with regard to case outcomes?

SOURCE: Roger Hanson and Joy Chapper, *Indigent Defense Systems*, Report to the State Justice Institute. Copyright © 1991 by National Center for State Courts. (Williamsburg, Va.: National Center for State Courts, 1991).

the defendant from the prosecutor, and setting bail can be difficult unless defense attorneys have the cooperation of others in the system. Thus their concern with preserving their relationships within that system may have greater weight than their short-term interest in particular clients.

We should not assume, however, that defense attorneys are at the complete mercy of other judicial actors. At any phase of the process, the defense can invoke the adversary model with its formal rules and public battles. The effective counsel can use this potential for a trial with its expensive, time-consuming, and disputatious features as a bargaining tool with the police, prosecutor, and judge. A well-known tactic of defense attorneys, certain to raise the ante in the bargaining process, is to ask for a trial and to proceed as if they meant it.

Some attorneys play the adversary role skillfully. They have developed a style that emphasizes the belligerence of a professional who is willing to fight the system for a client. Such lawyers are experienced in the courtroom and have built a practice around defending clients who can afford the expense of a trial. These lawyers must be willing to gamble that the trial results will benefit the accused and counsel more than any bargain arranged with the prosecutor. Having once broken the informal rules of the system, combative attorneys may find that they have jeopardized future cooperation from the police and prosecutor.

Some clients may expect their counsel to play the combatant role in the belief that they are not getting their money's worth unless verbal fireworks are involved. Yet even when fireworks do occur, one cannot be certain that the adversaries are engaged in a meaningful contest. Studies in some cities have shown that attorneys with clients who expect to get a vigorous defense may engage in the form of courtroom drama commonly known as the "slow plea of guilty," where negotiations have already determined the outcome of the case. One attorney described a slow plea as follows:

We had to put on one of these shows a few months ago. Well, we were all up there going through our orations, and the whole time the judge just sat there writing. Finally the DA reduced his charge, and the judge looked up long enough to say "Six months probation."[22]

In such cases, a defense attorney with a paying client who expects a return for the fee may arrange with the prosecutor and even the judge to stage a battle that is designed to culminate in a sentence agreed on previously.

For the criminal lawyer who depends on a large volume of petty cases from poor clients and assumes they are probably guilty of some offense, the incentives to bargain are strong. If the attorney is to secure cases, to serve clients' interests, and to maintain status as a practitioner, friendship and influence with judicial officials are essential. Specific benefits can be obtained from these sources: informal discovery of charges and plea bargaining from the prosecutor, fact finding and favorable testimony from the police, sentencing discretion and courtroom reception by the judge, and the influence of all three on the bail decision. For these courtesies, however, a price must be paid: information elicited from the client, a less than vigorous defense, the cultivation of active social relationships, political support, and a general attitude of cooperativeness.

Some clients may expect their counsel to play the combatant role in the belief that they are not getting their money's worth unless verbal fireworks are involved.

## Securing Cases

As do other professions in which a potential exists for client exploitation, the American bar has rigid strictures against the solicitation of clients. Lawyers with reputations as "ambulance chasers" soon find that colleagues hold their conduct in low regard. Unlike clients of the medical profession (which has similar rules of conduct), most citizens do not have a "family lawyer" and in exceptional circumstances must seek out legal services. To a great extent, persons in need of a lawyer depend on the recommendations of others; hence an attorney's reputation in the community is important. For both the lawyer trying to make a living and the accused who is in need of counsel, the difficulties of establishing contact may be severe.

Many criminal lawyers depend on a broker—whether a bondsman, police officer, fellow attorney, jail official—who is in a position to identify and channel business to the attorney. Criminal lawyers seeking clients must often make themselves known to a broker and must create a climate so that cases will be referred to them. A criminal lawyer may make contact with brokers through participation in social or political groups. Cooperative relations with the police, jail officials, and the prosecutor's office also help. For example, common sense tells us that a police officer is less likely to hand an attorney's business card to a prisoner if past experience has revealed that the lawyer is not cooperative.

## Relations with Clients

If criminal lawyers are not advocates using technical skills to win a case, then what service do they perform for the accused? One of the assets they sell is their influence within the judicial system: their ability to telephone the sheriff, enter the prosecutor's office, and bargain for their clients with judicial officials. On the basis of knowledge of the accused, the charge, the evidence, and the possible sanctions, defense attorneys may view their role as obtaining a penalty for a client that is at the lowest end of the range provided by statute. All these activities are played out so that clients believe they are getting their money's worth. Professional confidence, an aura of influence, and having the "inside dope" are essential.

Often the first arraignment is the greatest boon to the defense attorney. In this proceeding, the accused is told what the maximum penalty is for the charges made. When the lawyer negotiates a sentence of three to five years in prison, the client is grateful for having been spared the potential sixty-five years that the law prescribes for the multiple charges originally lodged. Thus, in one attorney's view, "the lawyer's fee is money charged for getting his client the normal penalty, which is substantially less than the maximum penalty under the law. Clients have no way of knowing what to expect from the system and one imagines attorneys do not go overboard in stressing 'I did what any attorney could do.'"[23]

A criminal lawyer is an agent-mediator for the client—that is, the lawyer is an adviser who explains the judicial process and informs the accused on what to expect.[24] This facet of the attorney's role may evolve into a confidence game in which the lawyer prepares the accused for defeat and then "cools him out" when it comes, as is likely. Defense attorneys help clients redefine their situation and restructure their perceptions, and thus prepare them to accept the consequences of a guilty plea. In the process of preparing a client, the lawyer is often assisted by the defendant's relatives, the probation officer, the prosecutor, and the judge. All try to emphasize that they want the accused to do the right things for his or her own good.

The interrelatedness of these services is evident: success in one venture depends on success in the other. If a client balks at the bargain that has been struck, the attorney's future influence with the prosecutor may be jeopardized. At the same time, the lawyer does not want to get a reputation for selling out clients; such a reputation may quickly end a career.

Public defenders have a special problem of client control. Defendants who have not selected their own counsel may not accept the bargain but insist that a trial be held. Because public defenders may fear a charge of misleading a client, they may have to invoke the "slow plea of guilty" drama. Thus the extent to which the defender *represents* the accused is open to question, for the trial may be used to impress on other defendants the fact that a cooperative attitude is important.

In their role as agent-mediators, criminal lawyers may in fact be viewed as double agents. With obligations to client and court, they are agents seeking to gain a satisfactory outcome for both. The position is filled with conflicts of interest that must all too often be resolved in favor of the organization that provides the attorney's means of professional existence.[25]

# Attorney Competence

The right to counsel is of little value when the counsel is not competent and effective. Questions about the adequacy of legal representation provided to both private and public clients have been of increasing concern to defense groups, bar associations, and the courts. There are, of course, many examples of incompetent representation. The training, the nature of the work itself, and the caseload all take their toll. In one case of note, trial counsel testified to not having conducted legal research concerning admissibility of certain physical and testimonial evidence and to making no objection to its introduction. A public defender's stamina must be enormous to handle caseloads of approximately two thousand cases a year (which works out to more than seven cases a day, five days a week, fifty-two weeks a year). One attorney so strained by workload resigned from the public defender's office, having decided that the presence of a live body as a defender was "actually doing the defendants more harm ... than if they had no representation at all."[26]

Other difficulties in providing effective representation can be cited as well. In jurisdictions where assigned counsel is provided for indigents, the lawyer chosen by the court may have little experience with the criminal law, may not know the key actors in the system, and may have little interest in the case. There may be a conflict of interest when the same attorney is appointed for codefendants.[27] Finally, caseload pressures may mean that there is little attorney-client contact before courtroom appearances; as a consequence, key information may not be communicated to the attorney.

The U.S. Supreme Court has only recently begun to examine the issue of attorney competence and the requirements that should be met if defendants are to receive effective counsel. In two 1984 cases, *United States* v. *Cronic* and *Strickland* v. *Washington*, the Court established a new standard of what constitutes the effective assistance of counsel.[28] Cronic had been charged with a complex mail fraud scheme, which had been investigated by the government for four and a half years. Just before trial, Cronic's retained lawyer withdrew and a young attorney with no trial experience, whose practice was primarily in real estate law, was appointed. The trial court allowed the new attorney only twenty-five days to prepare. The Supreme Court upheld Cronic's conviction on the grounds that, although the new trial counsel had made errors, there was no showing that the trial had not been a "meaningful" test of the prosecution's case or that the conviction had not been reliable.

The standard adopted in *Cronic* was applied in the capital case *Strickland* v. *Washington*, in which it was alleged that counsel had been incompetent. Washington was charged with three counts of capital murder, robbery, kidnapping, and other felonies. An experienced criminal lawyer was appointed as defense counsel. Against his attorney's advice, Washington confessed to two murders, waived a jury trial, and pleaded guilty to all charges. He then waived his right to be sentenced by an advisory capital sentencing jury and instead chose to be sentenced by the trial judge, who had a reputation for leniency. Feeling that the situation was hopeless, counsel did not adequately prepare for the sentencing hearing and sought neither character statements nor a psychiatric examination. Upon being sentenced to death, Washington appealed, asserting that counsel's failure to call witnesses, to seek a presentence investigation report, and to cross-examine medical experts constituted ineffective assistance. The Supreme Court rejected Washington's assertions, saying that his attorney was not unconstitutionally ineffective.

What emerges from the *Cronic* and *Strickland* cases is a standard of "reasonable competence" that the Supreme Court says should be applied when the issue of adequacy of representation is raised. That means a counsel's performance may be viewed as inadequate only if a reasonably competent attorney would not have acted as did the trial counsel. As noted by Justice Sandra Day O'Connor, the appellant must show "that there is a reasonable probability that, but for counsel's unprofessional errors, the result of the proceeding would have been different." Reviewing judges must thus determine only if the proceeding was fundamentally fair.

According to Gary Goodpaster, cases involving allegations of ineffective counsel present four major deficiencies of criminal defense attorneys:

1    failure to attempt to develop an effective working relationship with the client;
2    failure to conduct an adequate pretrial investigation;
3    failure to develop an "adversarial" or "fighting" attitude toward the prosecution and its case;
4    lack of knowledge or skill and failure to seek the advice of other counsel.[29]

Central here is the adequacy of defense counsel, given the nature of the criminal justice system, the constraints of resources on the system, and the work environment of legal practitioners.

## Summary

Television, movies, and literature provide an image of the criminal defense lawyer as a probing, investigative, and challenging attorney who works intently for her or his client. The defense attorney's role is to be an advocate—to use legal knowledge and verbal skills so that the government must prove its case according to the law. The reality of criminal defense work is, however, at odds with this image. There are relatively few attorneys in private practice who are criminal law specialists. Most defendants have attorneys who are either provided by the state or retained for the small fees that their clients can pay.

The right to counsel is enshrined in the Sixth Amendment of the Constitution, yet it has only been since 1961 that this right has been implemented in most state courts. Today indigent defendants who are charged with crimes that might lead to a prison term are provided with counsel by the state. This extension has brought about dramatic changes in the legal counsel received by almost three-quarters of criminal defendants.

Three systems are used to provide counsel to indigents: assigned counsel, where an attorney is assigned a case by a judge and a fee is paid by the government; contract system, where one or more law firms contracts with the local government to handle all indigent cases; and public defender, where a salaried government employee handles indigent cases. Choice of which system is used in a particular jurisdiction is influenced by factors such as the level of urbanism, the amount of public funding, and the participation of the bar.

Defense attorneys, either privately retained or those provided through public funds, must operate in an occupational environment greatly influenced by the need to secure cases, relations with clients, and financial considerations. Defense attorneys are agent-mediators in that they advise their clients and prepare defendants to plead guilty.

In recent years the issue of attorney competence has focused attention on defendants who have claimed that their lawyers were unprepared or unable to mount an effective defense. In *United States* v. *Cronic* and *Strickland* v. *Washington* the Supreme Court addressed this issue and enunciated the standard of "reasonable competence" as that which is required.

## Questions for Review

1   What are some of the problems faced by attorneys who engage in private defense practice?

2   What are the methods by which defense services are provided to indigents?

3   In what way is the defense attorney an agent-mediator?

4   Why might it be argued that publicly financed counsel better serves defendants than privately retained counsel?

5   What qualities would you want in an attorney if you were a defendant?

## Key Terms

assigned counsel          defense attorney          public defender

## For Further Reading

Bailey, F. Lee. *The Defense Never Rests*. New York: Stein and Day, 1971.
    Perspectives of one of America's best-known defense attorneys.
McDonald, William R., ed. *The Defense Counsel*. Beverly Hills, Calif.: Sage,
    1983. A collection of outstanding articles by social scientists and
    lawyers on defense counsel in criminal cases.

McIntyre, Lisa J. *The Public Defender: The Practice of Law in the Shadows of Repute*. Chicago: University of Chicago Press, 1987. A case study of the public defender's office in Cook County (Chicago), Illinois.

Moldovsky, Joel, and Rose DeWolf. *The Best Defense*. New York: Macmillan, 1975. As the authors note, the best defense is a good offense. Gives insights and flavor of private criminal practice.

Spence, Gerry. *With Justice for None*. New York: Penguin, 1989. A critique of how law is taught, practiced, and administered by a nationally known defense attorney.

Wice, Paul B. *Criminal Lawyers: An Endangered Species*. Beverly Hills, Calif.: Sage, 1978. National survey of the private defense bar.

Wishman, Seymour. *Confessions of a Criminal Lawyer*. New York: Penguin, 1982. Inside view of criminal practice in major cases.

## Notes

1   Anthony Lewis, *Gideon's Trumpet* (New York: Vintage, 1964), 10.

2   Francis A. Allen, "Right to Counsel," *Criminal Justice and the Supreme Court*, selections from the *American Encyclopedia of the American Constitution*, ed. Leonard W. Levy, Kenneth L. Karst, and Dennis J. Mahoney (New York: Macmillan, 1990), 227.

3   Paul B. Wice, *Criminal Lawyers: An Endangered Species* (Beverly Hills, Calif.: Sage, 1978), 29.

4   Wice, *Criminal Lawyers*, 75.

5   David W. Neubauer, *Criminal Justice in Middle America* (Morristown, N.J.: General Learning Press, 1974), 70.

6   Ibid., 173.

7   Jonathan D. Casper, "Did You Have a Lawyer When You Went to Court? No, I Had a Public Defender," *Yale Review of Law and Social Change* 1 (Spring 1971): 4–9.

8   Pauline Houlden and Steven Balkin, "Costs and Quality of Indigent Defense: Ad Hoc vs. Coordinated Assignment of the Private Bar within a Mixed System," *Justice System Journal* 10 (Summer 1985): 159.

9   Lawrence Spears, "Contract Counsel: A Different Way to Defend the Poor—How It's Working in North Dakota," *American Bar Association Journal on Criminal Justice* 6 (1991): 24–31.

10  U.S. Department of Justice, Bureau of Justice Statistics, *Bulletin* (September 1988).

11  Janet A. Gilboy and John R. Schmidt, "Replacing Lawyers: A Case Study of the Sequential Representation of Criminal Defendants," *Journal of Criminal Law and Criminology* 70 (1979): 2.

12  Casper, "Did You Have a Lawyer?" 5.

13  Ibid., 5, 6.

14 Roy B. Flemming, "Client Games: Defense Attorney Perspectives on Their Relations with Criminal Clients," *American Bar Foundation Research Journal* (Spring 1986): 258.

15 Ibid.

16 Paul Wice, "Private Criminal Defense: Reassessing an Endangered Species," in *The Defense Counsel*, ed. William F. McDonald (Beverly Hills, Calif.: Sage, 1983), 40.

17 Peter Nardulli, "Insider Justice: Defense Attorneys and the Handling of Felony Cases," *Journal of Criminal Law and Criminology* 79 (1986): 416.

18 Larry J. Cohen, Patricia P. Semple, and Robert E. Crew, Jr., "Assigned Counsel versus Public Defender Systems in Virginia," in *The Defense Counsel*, ed. William F. McDonald (Beverly Hills, Calif.: Sage, 1983), 143.

19 Roger Hanson and Joy Chapper, *Indigent Defense Systems*, Report to the State Justice Institute (Williamsburg, Va.: National Center for State Courts, 1991).

20 Edward Bennett Williams, *The Law*, interview by Donald MacDonald (New York: Center for the Study of Democratic Institutions, n.d.), 10.

21 Jackson B. Battle, "In Search of the Adversary System: The Cooperative Practices of Private Criminal Defense Attorneys," 50 *University of Texas Law Review* 66 (1971).

22 Ibid.

23 Neubauer, *Criminal Justice in Middle America*, 75.

24 Abraham Blumberg, "The Practice of Law As a Confidence Game," *Law and Society Review* 1 (1967): 11–39.

25 Ibid., 38.

26 *Cooper* v. *Fitzharris*, 551 F.2d 1162 (9th Cir. 1977).

27 *Burger* v. *Kemp*, 483 U.S. 776 (1987).

28 *United States* v. *Cronic*, 444 U.S. 654 (1984); *Strickland* v. *Washington*, 466 U.S. 686 (1984).

29 Gary Goodpaster, "The Adversary System, Advocacy, and Effective Assistance of Counsel in Criminal Cases," *New York University Review of Law and Social Change* 14 (1986): 90.

# Pretrial Processes

For several years "Arrest and Trial" was a popular television drama in which audiences were permitted to see an arrest, trial, and sentencing. Most viewers probably assumed that arrest and trial were linked and that all persons taken into custody ended up facing a judge and jury. But the reality is that few people arrested ever face trial—a major portion of cases are dropped through the discretionary action of the police, prosecutor, or judge. Up to 90 percent of people who are arraigned on an indictment plead guilty and thus do not have a trial. The filtering process operates so that only a small portion of those who are arrested by the police are eventually given a sentence.

Various kinds of cases are handled somewhat differently. Persons arrested and booked on a misdemeanor charge will usually be released on a promise to appear before a court at a later date. Persons arrested on a felony charge may be released on bail, but often not until they have appeared before a judge where the prosecutor must prove that there is **probable cause** to believe that a crime has been committed and that the accused should be tried for the matter. But these legal distinctions are only two of the many decisions that are made during the crucial pretrial period.

The interests of the public, the nature of the case, the character of the defendant, and the tactics of the opposing attorneys all help to determine whether a case is filtered out of the system before arraignment, is given routine treatment resulting in a plea bargain, becomes one of the few highly publicized trials that occur each year, or falls somewhere in between. The vast majority of cases are handled in ways that bear little resemblance to the adversarial processes described by the Due Process Model. In this chapter we focus on the pretrial period, when most major decisions are made concerning the fate of persons arrested. It is during these early stages of the criminal justice system that we can best see the links among the police, prosecution, defense, and court. Of particular importance are the practices and procedures of bail and plea bargaining.

**arraignment**

The act of calling an accused person before the court to hear the charges lodged against him or her and to enter a plea in response to those charges.

## Questions for Inquiry

- What are the methods for releasing the accused before trial?
- How does the bail system work and how is bail set?
- Why might the accused be held in pretrial detention?
- What is plea bargaining; how does it affect the criminal justice system?
- What are the constitutional implications of plea bargaining?

**Figure 9.1**
**Typical outcome of one hundred urban felony cases**
Crucial decisions are made by prosecutors and judges during the period before trial or plea. Once cases are bound over for disposition, guilty pleas are many, trials are few, and acquittals are rare.

SOURCE: Barbara Boland, Paul Mahanna, and Ronald Stones, *The Prosecution of Felony Arrests, 1988*, U.S. Department of Justice, Bureau of Justice Statistics (Washington, D.C.: Government Printing Office, 1992), 2.

## From Arrest to Trial or Plea

Following the arrest, booking, and initial appearance of a defendant, the pretrial processes begin. It is at this time that the prosecution and defense prepare their cases, an indictment or information is presented to the court, and a formal **arraignment** on the charges is held. More importantly, those cases that the prosecution believes will not pass judicial scrutiny are

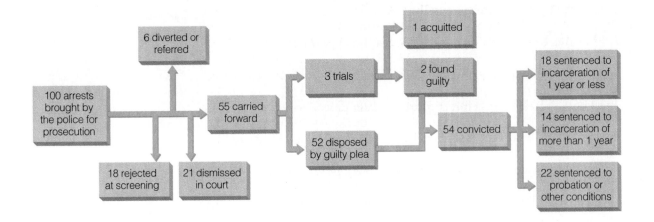

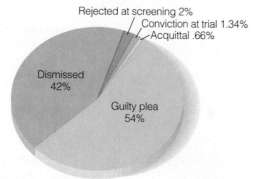

**Manhattan, N.Y.**

Rejected at screening 2%
Conviction at trial 1.34%
Acquittal .66%
Dismissed 42%
Guilty plea 54%

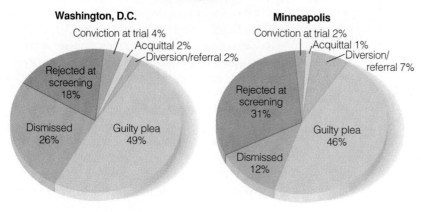

**Washington, D.C.**

Conviction at trial 4%
Acquittal 2%
Diversion/referral 2%
Rejected at screening 18%
Dismissed 26%
Guilty plea 49%

**Minneapolis**

Conviction at trial 2%
Acquittal 1%
Diversion/referral 7%
Rejected at screening 31%
Guilty plea 46%
Dismissed 12%

**Figure 9.2**
**Disposition of felony arrests in three American cities**
Note the differences in how cases are disposed in these cities. How might policy models account for these differences?

SOURCE: Barbara Boland, Paul Mahanna, and Ronald Stones, *The Prosecution of Felony Arrests, 1988,* U.S. Department of Justice, Bureau of Justice Statistics (Washington, D.C.: Government Printing Office, 1992), 6.

screened and filtered out of the system during this time. Prosecutors drop the cases of some defendants, return other cases to the police for further investigation, and recommend diversion for still others.

As shown in Figure 9.1, case attrition is a major factor in the criminal justice system.[1] The proportion of cases dropped at the various stages of the pretrial process varies from city to city. In some jurisdictions, most cases that do not result in conviction are rejected for prosecution before court charges are filed. In other jurisdictions, rates of postfiling dismissals may be as high as 40 percent or more. As shown in Figure 9.2, prosecutorial screening in Minneapolis is high, but the percentage of cases dropped after filing is low. By contrast, prosecutors in Manhattan reject a small percentage during the screening phase but drop 42 percent after filing.

During the pretrial process defendants are exposed to the informal and "assembly-line" atmosphere of the lower criminal courts. It is here that decisions are made about bail, arraignment, pleas, and the disposition of cases. Moving cases as quickly as possible seems to be the criteria of the judges and attorneys during the pretrial process. Courts throughout the

At each step of the pretrial process, from arrest to booking to initial hearing and arraignment, police and prosecutors must follow procedures specified by the law.

## Magistrates' Court in England

American visitors are usually impressed with the magistrates' court because its lay justices convey an air of dignified informality in their work. It is in England's five hundred magistrates' courts that most of the work of criminal justice is accomplished. Unlike the pomp and ceremony of trials in the Crown Court, the ambiance of the magistrates' court is that of a "people's court."

The room is usually without decoration; it contains only tables where the magistrates and solicitors sit and a few chairs for defendants, relatives, and onlookers. Sitting in panels of twos and threes, and with the assistance of a legally qualified clerk, the lay magistrates call the cases, receive evidence, listen to circumstances of mitigation, and make dispositions without the conveyor-belt atmosphere so typical of urban courts in the United States.

The 2,400 magistrates in England and Wales (Scotland has a separate criminal justice system) are unpaid volunteers who are expected to donate one day every two weeks to their judicial duties. Selection as a lay magistrate is an honor given to those who have exhibited a concern for civic activities. They are appointed on behalf

United States are under pressure to reduce the number of cases requiring formal trial by jury. Indeed, the maintenance of the system requires administrative decision making by prosecutors, defense attorneys, and judges to reduce the trial load. The lower courts of the American system contrast sharply with the informal, but more deliberative, magistrates court of England, as discussed in the Comparative Perspective above.

The defense uses the pretrial period to its own advantage. Through pretrial **motions** to the court, counsel may attempt to suppress evidence or to learn about the prosecutor's case. A motion is an application to a court requesting that an order be issued to bring about a specified action. A court hearing is held on the motion, and the presenting attorney must be able to support the contention made about procedures used in the arrest, the sufficiency of the evidence, or the exclusion of evidence. Typical pretrial motions by the defense include:

**motion**
An application to a court requesting that an order be issued to bring about a specified action.

1   motion to quash a search warrant

2   motion to exclude evidence, such as a confession

3   motion for severance (separate trials in cases with more than one defendant)

of the Crown by the lord chancellor upon the recommendation of local advisory committees after secret deliberations.

Critics argue that the appointment process results in a judiciary composed mainly of persons from the upper and professional classes, with the consequence that justice is biased against the poor. There have been recent efforts to ensure that the magistracy has a broader social base, yet the fact remains that it is those from the more privileged groups in the community who are able to give the time and who present themselves as being interested in performing this civic duty. As a result, the foreign visitor is immediately struck by the gulf in vocabulary and accent between those on the bench and the person in the dock.

The English divide offenses into three classes: indictable, and therefore triable by judge and jury at the Crown Court; summary, and therefore triable before the magistrates' court; or so-called either way, in which the defendant decides at which level he or she wishes to be tried. Magistrates' courts are the setting for summary trials and for committal proceedings for trials to be held in the Crown Court. Thus almost anyone charged with a crime appears before the lay justices.

One result is that even with indictable offenses, 87 percent of the dispositions result from sentences given by the magistrates' courts.

The penalties that the magistrates are authorized to impose for each offense reach a maximum of six months imprisonment and/or a one thousand pound fine. But magistrates may also use other correctional alternatives, such as community service, suspended sentences, and probation. A fine is the most frequent sanction, with 55 percent of all offenders receiving one.

The English magistrates' courts dispense an informal brand of justice quite different from lower courts in the United States, where prosecutors and defense attorneys argue over the introduction of evidence and due process rules. In England, police officers give their testimony and defendants present their cases with the assistance of counsel. There are usually questions from the bench, followed by a huddled conversation among the magistrates and then an announcement of guilt or innocence. Sentences are then imposed, more in the manner of a stern lecture than a swift recitation of the terms of the punishment. Sentencing is followed by the sound of the gavel and the call, "Next case."

4 motion to dismiss because of delay in bringing the case to trial

5 motion to suppress evidence illegally obtained

6 motion for pretrial discovery of the evidence held by the prosecutor

7 motion for a change of venue because a fair and impartial trial cannot be held in the original jurisdiction

Aggressive use of pretrial motions has strategic as well as substantive advantages. They can become part of the jockeying for position between the prosecution and defense. The following reasons have been given for filing numerous motions:

1 It forces a partial disclosure of the prosecutor's evidence at an early date.

2 It pressures the prosecutor to consider plea bargaining early in the proceeding.

3 It forces exposure of primary state witnesses at an inopportune time for the prosecution.

4 It raises matters the defense may want called to the trial judge's attention early in the proceedings.

5   It forces the prosecutor to make decisions before final preparation of the case.

6   It allows the defendant to see the defense counsel in action, which has a salutary effect on the client-attorney relationship.[2]

Although pretrial motions are entered in approximately 10 percent of felony cases and in less than 1 percent of misdemeanors, they can be used not only to secure the defendant's release but also to bargain, since the defense may want to give every indication that it is going to trial. A second, equally important function of the pretrial processes for the defense is to secure release of the defendant on bail. As the next section will explain, the defendant out on bail has enormous advantages over the defendant awaiting trial in jail.

## Bail: Pretrial Release

**bail**
An amount of money specified by a judge to be posted as a condition of pretrial release for the purpose of ensuring the appearance of the accused in court as required.

The practice of allowing defendants to be released from jail pending trial originated in Anglo-Saxon law. In a period when the time between arrest and trial was lengthy and the cost of detention burdensome, **bail** was used as a convenience to the sheriff, allowing him to release a prisoner from his responsibility and yet be fairly certain that he or she would be in court at the appointed time. As it is today, some form of surety was required, to be forfeited if the accused did not show up as promised. This concept, with modifications, was transferred across the Atlantic.

The Eighth Amendment prohibits excessive bail, and most state statutes are intended to ensure that the system is administered in a nondiscriminatory manner. Nonetheless, judicial personnel have a great deal of discretion in determining pretrial release. As early as 1835, the Supreme Court ruled that the purpose of bail was to ensure the presence of the accused in court to answer the indictment and to submit to trial.[3] This purpose is consistent with the belief that accused persons are innocent until proved otherwise and that they should not suffer hardship awaiting trial. Bail should not be used as punishment, for the accused has not been found guilty. The amount of bail should therefore be sufficient to ensure the defendant's presence for trial but no more than that amount. Yet concern persists about protection of the community while the defendant is on bail. As we discuss in more detail later in this chapter, Congress and some of the states have passed laws allowing the preventive detention of defendants who are believed by the judge to pose a threat to any other person or the community while awaiting trial.

### The Reality of the Bail System

The reality of the bail system is far from the ideal. The question of bail may arise at the police station, during the initial court appearance in a misdemeanor case, or at the arraignment in most felony cases. In almost all jurisdictions, the amount of bail is based primarily on the judge's per-

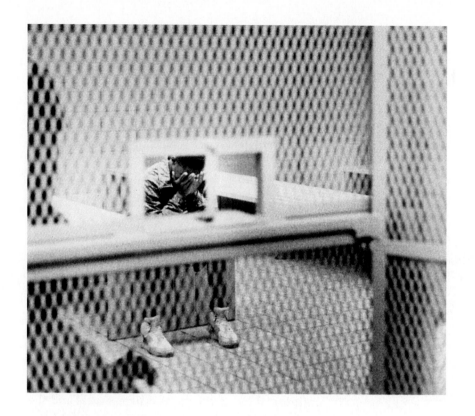

The period following arrest is the most stressful. Most jail suicides take place during the first few hours of confinement. What might be going through your mind as you waited for disposition of your case?

ception of the seriousness of the crime and the defendant's record. In part, this emphasis stems from a lack of information about the accused. Because bail must be allowed within twenty-four to forty-eight hours after an arrest, there is no time to seek background information on which to make a more just bail determination. The result is that judges have developed standard rates that are used in both courtroom and station house: so many dollars for such-and-such an offense. A judge may in certain instances set high bail in response to the police's wish to keep a defendant in custody. Defense attorneys have reported that bail of any amount has the effect of scaring the defendant but that a high bail implies that the judge believes the crime was vicious or that the defendant may not otherwise appear in court.

Critics of the bail system argue that the emphasis on monetary bail raises problems about the equality of the administration of justice. Imagine that you have been arrested and you have no money. Should you be denied a chance for freedom before trial simply because you are poor? What if you have little money and are forced to make a decision between bail and hiring a defense attorney? Professional criminals and the affluent have no difficulty making bail; for instance, established drug dealers can readily make bail and continue their criminal activities while awaiting trial. In contrast, a poor person arrested for a minor violation may spend the pretrial period in jail. Should the dangerous rich be allowed out on bail and the undangerous poor be kept in?

Figure 9.3
**Bail amounts for felony defendants, by type of offense**

The amount of bail varies according to the offense.

SOURCE: U.S. Department of Justice, Bureau of Justice Statistics, *National Update*, vol. 1 (July 1991), 5.

According to a study of felony defendants in the nation's most populous counties, nearly two-thirds were released before disposition of their cases, and almost half of the pretrial releases took place on the day of the arrest or the next day.[4] For most felony defendants bail is set at less than five thousand dollars. Figure 9.3 shows the amounts of bail set for various types of felony offenses. Those who cannot make bail (whether via cash, property, or a bond from a bonding company) must remain in jail awaiting trial. Given the length of delay between arraignment and trial in most courts and the hardships connected with pretrial detention, bondsmen are of critical import to many defendants.

## Bondsmen: Beneficiaries of Bail

The services of the professional bondsman are available twenty-four hours a day to those who need to produce sufficient cash to be released.[5] The supply of these services is determined by the number of bondsmen in the local surety market, the amount of credit available for bonding, the willingness of the agents to take risks, and the force with which the courts foreclose on defaulted bonds. The demand for bail bonds is influenced by such factors as arrest rates and the willingness of judges to release defendants on their own recognizance.

Using their own assets or those of an insurance company, bondsmen provide the surety required for a fee of between 5 and 10 percent. They are licensed by the state, choose their own clients, and may set their own collateral requirements. In addition, they may track down and return bail jumpers without extradition and by force if necessary. Bondsmen exert a strong influence on the court through their ability to cooperate with police officers, who may recommend their services rather than those of another bondsman. In return, they may refuse to provide bail for defendants whom the police do not wish to see released.

It is for this reason that reformers view bondsmen as a cardinal flaw in the bail system. Although bondsmen are private individuals with no formal ties to the judicial process, in effect they have the power to overrule a judge's decision. Bondsmen may withhold their services arbitrarily. Bondsmen, as the late Judge J. Skelly Wright succinctly said,

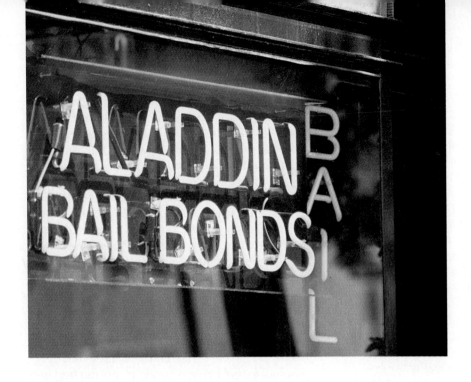

Providing bail bonds is a big business. Although practices are generally regulated by the state, bondsmen retain discretion as to whether to provide bail to an individual defendant.

hold the keys to the jail in their pockets. They determine for whom they will act as surety—who in their judgment is a good risk. The bad risks, in the bondsmen's judgment, and the ones who are unable to pay the bondsmen's fees, remain in jail. The court and the commissioner are relegated to the relatively unimportant chore of fixing the amount of bail.[6]

Although bonding professionals have an unsavory reputation, they do facilitate court operations. Their most important function is to maintain social control over the defendant during the pretrial period. Bondsmen stress to their clients the importance of appearing in court on the correct date, and they emphasize the penalties that may result if they fail to do so. Often pressure on friends and relatives, as well as telephone calls and mailed reminders, are used to ensure appearance. Like defense attorneys, bondsmen help prepare their clients for the probable fate in store for them, often encourage a plea of guilty, and usually forecast the sentence quite accurately. Bondsmen also share responsibility with judges for the defendant's release, thus providing a buffer should the defendant upset the public by committing further crimes before trial. In this era of crowded jails, bail bondsmen relieve some of the pressure.

## Bail Setting

Although the judiciary is responsible for the setting of bail, its powers are often delegated to other officials. When the offense is a misdemeanor, bail is generally set by a police officer according to a judicially prescribed schedule and, as the accompanying Question of Ethics (page 338) strongly demonstrates, with some discretion. In most jurisdictions, a judge sets bail for those charged with felonies by taking into account the severity of

Jim Rourke stood in front of Desk Sergeant Jack Sweeney at the Redwood City Police Station. Rourke was handcuffed and waiting to be booked. He had been caught by Officers Davis and Timulty outside a building in a prestigious neighborhood soon after the police had received a frantic 911 call from a resident who reported that someone had entered her apartment. Rourke was seen loitering in the alley with a flashlight in his back pocket. He was known to the police because of his prior arrests for entering at night. As Timulty held Rourke, Davis went around behind the desk and spoke to Sergeant Sweeney in a soft voice.

"I know we don't have much on this guy, but he's a bad egg and I bet he was the one who was in that apartment. The least we can do is set the bail high enough so that he'll know we are on to him."

"Davis, you know I can't do that. You've got nothing on him," said Sweeney.

"But how's it going to look in the press if we just let him go? You know the type of people who live in Littleton Manor. There will be hell to pay if it gets out that this guy just walks."

"Well, he did have the flashlight . . . I suppose that's enough to indicate that he's a suspect. Let's make the bail $1,000. I know he can't make that."

What is the purpose of bail? Was the amount set appropriate in this instance? Should Rourke be held merely because of the suspicion that he might have burglarized the apartment? Do you think the case would have been handled in the same way if the call had come from a poorer section of town?

the offense, the characteristics of the defendant, and community protection. With jails in many communities crowded, the availability of pretrial detention space has become an additional factor. Table 9.1 shows who sets bail in eleven large cities, where the process is carried out, and how the amount is determined.

When the judge or magistrate determines the amount of bail, he or she is influenced by the formal criteria and by the expectations of the prosecutor, defense counsel, police, and sometimes the bondsman. Exchanges among these actors affect the judge's decision. Inevitably, the prosecutor supports high bail, and the defense attorney asks that it be low, pointing out that the defendant must "take care of his family," "has a good job," or "is well liked in the neighborhood." The police may be particularly active in some settings in urging high bail, especially if they have expended extensive resources to apprehend the suspect or have had contact with the victims. It is not unknown for detectives to visit judge's chambers before an arraignment to tell the judge about aspects of the case that the police do not want raised in open court.

In studying bail settings in New York County Criminal Court, Frederic Suffet recorded the interactions of the prosecutor, defense attorney, and judge. He noted that the acknowledged standards, or "rules of the game"—seriousness of the charge, prior record, defendant's ties to the community—provided the accepted boundaries for interactions with respect to setting bail and enabling negotiations to proceed with a minimum of conflict.[7]

The study showed the prosecutor had more prestige than the defense attorney in the courtroom and was more likely to make the initial bail suggestion—and to get the judge to accept that suggestion. In fact, Suffet's analysis showed that judge and prosecutor hold similar conceptions as to the level of bail required and are reciprocally supportive.

Although the "manifest," or formal, purpose of setting bail is to stipulate an amount that will ensure the defendant's appearance in court, the latent purpose, or by-product, of this interaction is to spread responsibility for the defendant's release. By including the prosecutor and the defense counsel in the process, the judge can create a buffer between the court and the outraged public if an accused criminal released from custody pending a court appearance should commit a crime.

In addition to interpersonal influences, the local legal and political culture are important in the setting of bail. In a study of Detroit and Baltimore, Roy Flemming learned that the two cities approximated the extremes of pretrial treatment of felony defendants in larger American cities. In the Detroit Recorder's Court, nearly 48 percent of felony defendants arraigned were freed on their own recognizance, the median bail for the remainder was $2,000, and 32 percent were detained for the entire predisposition period. In the Baltimore District Court, only 12 percent of the accused were freed on their own recognizance, the median bail was $4,650, and 41 percent awaited disposition in jail.[8]

There were several influences contributing to these differences: the political climate in Detroit, described as "prodefendant" following reforms instituted after the riots in 1967, when thousands of black citizens were detained by means of exorbitant bail; a formal limit on the Wayne County Jail population; and bail-setting judges who held secure positions. In Baltimore, in contrast, bail was set by "low-status court officials or commissioners with insecure tenure who were more highly vulnerable" to criticisms of bail reform from the police and other public officials. Thus there was a high level of uncertainty among the people responsible for setting bail. And there were no population limits on detention facilities.

**Table 9.1**
**The bail process in eleven major cities**
Note that various actors make bail decisions. In most locales, the initial level for misdemeanors is set by a police officer who follows a schedule provided by the court.

SOURCE: Paul B. Wice, *Freedom for Sale* (Lexington, Mass.: D.C. Heath, 1974), 26.

| City | Who Sets Bail | | Where It Is Done | | How It Is Done | |
|------|---------------|--------|------------------|-------|----------------|--------|
| | Misdemeanor | Felony | Misdemeanor | Felony | Misdemeanor | Felony |
| Washington | Desk sergeant | Judge | Station house | Court of general sessions | Schedules | Discretion |
| San Francisco | Clerk of criminal court | Judge | Hall of justice | Hall of justice | Schedule | Discretion |
| Los Angeles | Police captain | Judge | Station house | Regional | Schedule | Discretion |
| Oakland | Police captain | Judge | Station house | Courthouse | | |
| Detroit | Desk sergeant Arresting magistrate | Arresting magistrate | Police station | Hall of justice | Schedule | Discretion |
| Chicago | Desk sergeant | Judge of bond court | Police station | Bond court or electronically | Schedule | Discretion |
| St. Louis | Desk sergeant | County circuit court judge | Police station | Police station or courthouse | Schedule | Flexible schedule |
| Baltimore | Desk sergeant | Judge | Police station | Police court | Schedule | Schedule |
| Indianapolis | Turnkey | Turnkey | City jail | City Jail | Schedule | Schedule |
| Atlanta | Police | Police | Police headquarters | Police headquarters | Discretion schedule | Discretion schedule |
| Philadelphia | Desk sergeant | Magistrate and district attorney | Station house | Police headquarters | Schedule | Discretion |

From a constitutional viewpoint, it has been argued that bail should be set in accordance with six presumptions:

1. The accused is entitled to release on his or her own recognizance.
2. Nonfinancial alternatives to bail will be used when possible.
3. The accused will receive a full and fair hearing.
4. Reasons will be stated for the decision.
5. Clear and convincing evidence will be offered to support a decision.
6. There will be a prompt and automatic review of all bail determinations.

Many people claim that requiring bail to be set in accordance with these presumptions greatly hampers the ability of the justice system to deal with offenders and to protect society. Others counter that personal freedom is so precious that failure to afford a person every opportunity to remain at large is a greater injustice.

## Reform of the System

Since the 1960s there has been a concerted effort to reform the bail system. Activated by early studies of pretrial detention in Philadelphia and New York, the reform movement has spread across the country. Criticisms of the pretrial release process have focused on judicial discretion in setting bail amounts, the poor being deprived of their freedom while the influential can afford bail, the perceived unsavory role of bondsmen, and jail conditions for those detained while awaiting trial.

As measured by the increased portion of defendants who are not detained, the bail reform movement can be judged a success. One study of twenty cities showed that the release rate in 1962 was 48 percent.[9] A recent survey of the nation's seventy-five most populous counties found that two-thirds of felony defendants were released before disposition of their cases. Of those detained, one in nine were held without bail.[10] These changes have occurred through several alternative methods developed to facilitate pretrial release. These methods are highlighted in Table 9.2, and some are discussed in the following sections.

**citation**

A written order issued by a law enforcement officer directing an alleged offender to appear in court at a specified time to answer a criminal charge; referred to as a *summons* in some jurisdictions.

**Citation**   The police have long been accustomed to issuing a **citation**, or summons, to appear in court—a "ticket"—to a person accused of committing a traffic offense or some other minor violation. By issuing the citation, the officer avoids taking the accused to the station house for booking and to court for arraignment and determination of bail. Such citations are being used with increasing frequency for more serious offenses, in part because the police want to reduce the amount of time they must spend booking minor offenders and waiting in arraignment court for their cases to come up for decision. In most jurisdictions, fewer than 5 percent of those given citations fail to appear. In some cities bail bondsmen have opposed this threat to their livelihood.

### Financial Bond

*Fully secured bail.* The defendant posts the full amount of bail with the court.

*Privately secured bail.* A bondsman signs a promissory note to the court for the bail amount and charges the defendant a fee for the service (usually 10 percent of the bail amount). If the defendant fails to appear, the bondsman must pay the court the full amount. The bondsman frequently requires the defendant to post collateral in addition to the fee.

*Percentage bail.* The courts allow the defendant to deposit a percentage (usually 10 percent) of the full bail with the court. The full amount of the bail is required if the defendant fails to appear. The percentage bail is returned after disposition of the case, although the court often retains 1 percent for administrative costs.

*Unsecured bail.* The defendant pays no money to the court but is liable for the full amount of bail should she or he fail to appear.

### Alternative Release Options

*Release on recognizance (ROR).* The court releases the defendant on her or his promise to appear in court as required.

*Conditional release.* The court releases the defendant subject to her or his following of specific conditions set by the court, such as attendance at drug treatment therapy or staying away from the complaining witness.

*Third-party custody.* The defendant is released into the custody of an individual or agency that promises to ensure her or his appearance in court. No monetary transactions are involved in this type of release.

**Table 9.2**
**Pretrial release methods**

SOURCE: U.S. Department of Justice, Bureau of Justice Statistics, *Report to the Nation on Crime and Justice*, 2d ed. (Washington, D.C.: Government Printing Office, 1988), 76.

**Release on Recognizance**    Pioneered in the 1960s by the Vera Institute of Justice in New York City, the **release on recognizance (ROR)** approach is based on the assumption that judges will grant releases if they are given verified information about defendants' reliability and roots in the community. Soon after arrest court personnel talk to defendants about their job, family, prior criminal record, and associations and then determine whether release should be recommended. In the first three years of the New York project, more than 10,000 defendants were interviewed, and approximately 3,500 were released. Only 1.5 percent failed to appear in court at the appointed time, an appearance rate almost three times better than the rate for those being released on bail.[11] Comparable programs in other cities have had similar results, although studies have shown that the percentage of those released on their own recognizance does not greatly increase with the creation of a formal pretrial release program.[12]

Today ROR programs exist in almost every major jurisdiction.[13] Often a pretrial release agency is a part of the court organization. In some places it is closely tied to the probation department and in some jurisdictions persons working to secure the release of individuals on their own recognizance are supported by private foundations.

**release on recognizance (ROR)**
Pretrial release granted on the defendant's promise to appear in court because the judge believes that the defendant's ties in the community are sufficient to guarantee the required appearance.

**Ten Percent Cash Bail**  Although ROR is an attractive alternative to money bail, judges are unwilling to release some defendants on their own recognizance. As yet another alternative, some states (Illinois, Kentucky, Nebraska, Oregon, Pennsylvania) have inaugurated bail programs in which the defendants deposit with the court cash equal to 10 percent of their bail. When they appear in court as required, 90 percent of this collateral is returned to them. Begun in Illinois in 1964, this plan is designed primarily to release as many defendants as possible without enriching the bondsmen.

**Bail Guidelines**  To deal with inequities caused by the unfettered exercise of judicial discretion, reformers have written guidelines for setting bail. The guidelines, designed to bring about consistency, specify the criteria that judges should use in setting bail and list appropriate amounts.

**Table 9.3**
**States with one or more provisions to ensure community safety in pretrial release**
Concern that some persons on bail are committing additional crimes while awaiting trial has caused some states to enact laws limiting pretrial release under certain circumstances.

SOURCE: U.S. Department of Justice, Bureau of Justice Statistics, *Report to the Nation on Crime and Justice*, 2d ed. (Washington, D.C.: Government Printing Office, 1988), 77.

| Type of Provision | States That Have Enacted the Provision |
|---|---|
| Exclusion of certain crimes from automatic bail eligibility | Colorado, District of Columbia, Florida, Georgia, Michigan, Nebraska, Wisconsin |
| Definition of the purpose of bail to ensure appearance and safety | Alaska, Arizona, California, Delaware, District of Columbia, Florida, Hawaii, Minnesota, South Carolina, South Dakota, Vermont, Virginia, Wisconsin |
| Inclusion of crime control factors in the release decision | Alabama, California, Florida, Georgia, Minnesota, South Dakota, Wisconsin |
| Inclusion of release conditions related to crime control | Alaska, Arkansas, Colorado, Delaware, District of Columbia, Florida, Hawaii, Illinois, Iowa, Minnesota, New Mexico, North Carolina, South Carolina, South Dakota, Vermont, Virginia, Washington, Wisconsin |
| Limitations on the right to bail for those previously convicted | Colorado, District of Columbia, Florida, Georgia, Hawaii, Indiana, Michigan, New Mexico, Texas, Utah, Wisconsin |
| Revocation of pretrial release when there is evidence that the accused committed a new crime | Arizona, Arkansas, Colorado, District of Columbia, Georgia, Hawaii, Illinois, Maryland, Massachusetts, Michigan, Nevada, New Mexico, New York, Rhode Island, Texas, Utah, Vermont, Wisconsin |
| Limitations on the right to bail for crimes alleged to have been committed while on release | Arizona, Arkansas, California, Colorado, District of Columbia, Florida, Georgia, Hawaii, Illinois, Indiana, Maryland, Massachusetts, Michigan, Nebraska, Nevada, New Mexico, New York, Rhode Island, South Dakota, Texas, Utah, Vermont, Virginia, Washington, Wisconsin |
| Provisions for pretrial detention to ensure safety | Arizona, Arkansas, California, Colorado, District of Columbia, Florida, Georgia, Hawaii, Illinois, Indiana, Maryland, Massachusetts, Michigan, Nebraska, Nevada, New Mexico, New York, Rhode Island, South Dakota, Texas, Utah, Vermont, Virginia, Washington, Wisconsin |

Judges are expected to follow the agreed-upon criteria but may deviate when they believe special circumstances are present. Guidelines aim at the rational setting of bail amounts in concert with concerns about the use of pretrial detention, the problem of fleeing, and the potential for additional crimes by the defendant awaiting trial. When guidelines were experimentally tested in the Philadelphia Municipal Court, a greater consistency among the judges was found.[14]

**Preventive Detention**   Reforms have been suggested not only by those concerned with inequities in the bail system but also by those concerned with crime.[15] Critics of the bail system point to a relationship between release on bail and the commission of crimes, arguing that the accused may commit other illegal acts while awaiting trial. As one more reflection of the debate over due process versus crime control, **preventive detention** was authorized by Congress in the Bail Reform Act of 1984.[16] Under the act, federal judges may consider whether the defendant poses a danger to the community when deciding whether (and under what conditions) to release him or her before trial. The legislation allows outright detention on the basis of presumed danger to particular persons or the community at large. This decision is made at a hearing to consider the prosecution's contention that: (1) there is a serious risk that the person will flee; (2) the person will obstruct justice or threaten, injure, or intimidate a prospective witness or juror; or (3) the offense is one of violence or one punishable by life imprisonment or death. As shown in Table 9.3, three-fourths of the states now have one or more provisions in the laws designed to ensure community safety in pretrial release.

Preventive detention would seem to be at odds with the Constitution's prohibition of excessive bail and the due process clause since the accused is held in custody until a verdict at trial is rendered. However, the Supreme Court has upheld its constitutionality. In *Schall* **v.** *Martin* (1984), the Court said that the detention of a juvenile was useful to protect both the welfare of the minor and the community as a whole.[17] The preventive detention provisions of the Bail Reform Act of 1984 were upheld in **U.S. v. Salerno** (1987).[18] The justices said that preventive detention was a legitimate use of governmental power since it was designed not to punish the accused but to deal with the problem of people committing crimes while on bail. Prevention of further damage to the community from these crimes was within the powers of Congress. By upholding the federal law, the Court also legitimized comparable state laws dealing with preventive detention.[19]

Proponents of preventive detention note that studies have shown that somewhere between 7 and 20 percent of persons under pretrial release commit crimes, and for some crimes the figure is as high as 34 to 70 percent. They claim preventive detention ensures that drug dealers, who often view bail as a business expense, cannot flee before trial. Martin Sorin argues that "pretrial criminals may account for as much as one-fifth of our nation's total crime problem."[20] Such findings have led researchers to argue that a small but identifiable group of defendants is not deterred by stringent release conditions and the prospect of revocation of bail. See the Close-Up on "Preventive Detention: Two Sides of an Issue" (page 344) for

**preventive detention**
The holding of a defendant for trial based on a judge's finding that, if released on bail, he or she would endanger the safety of any other person and the community.

*Schall* v. *Martin* **(1984)**
Pretrial detention of a juvenile is constitutional to protect welfare of the minor and the community.

*U.S.* v. *Salerno* **(1987)**
Preventive detention provisions of the Bail Reform Act of 1984 upheld; legitimate use of governmental power designed to prevent people from committing crimes while on bail.

## Preventive Detention:
## Two Sides of an Issue

For Ricardo Armstrong, there is the despair of trying to reunite his family after spending four months in a Cincinnati jail for bank robbery before being acquitted of the crime.

For friends and family of Linda Goldstone, there is the anguish of knowing that she would still be alive if there had been a way to keep Hernando Williams in jail while he was facing rape and assault charges in Chicago.

Ricardo Armstrong was one of the first defendants held under the Bail Reform Act of 1984. The twenty-eight-year-old janitor, who had a prior burglary conviction, was denied bail after being charged with robbing two Ohio banks.

From the start, Mr. Armstrong had insisted that bank robbery charges against him were part of some nightmarish mix-up.

A Cincinnati jury agreed. After viewing bank photographs of the robber, the jury acquitted Mr. Armstrong in what was apparently a case of mistaken identity.

Justice, it seemed, had been served—but not before Mr. Armstrong had spent four months in jail—and his wife left their home and moved with their children a thousand miles away.

"Who's going to get me back those four months?" he now asks bitterly. "Who's going to get me back my kids?" The Bail Reform Act makes no provision for compensating defendants who are jailed and later acquitted.

Proponents of the Bail Reform Act concede that some injustices inevitably occur. But they note that other cases, involving dangerous defendants set free on bond, ring just as tragically for victims of crimes that could have been prevented.

Prosecutors point to the release of Hernando Williams as the classic example of the need for preventive detention. Even as Mr. Williams, free on $25,000 bond, drove to court to face charges [of raping and beating a woman he abducted at a shopping mall], another woman lay trapped inside his car trunk. This victim, Linda Goldstone, a twenty-nine-year-old birthing instructor, was abducted by Mr. Williams as she walked to Northwestern Hospital and was forced at gunpoint to crawl into his trunk.

Over a four-day period, Mrs. Goldstone was removed from the trunk periodically to be raped and beaten until she was shot to death. Mr. Williams has been sentenced to death.

"Linda Goldstone might well be alive today if we'd had this law then," said Richard M. Daley, the Cook County state's attorney.

SOURCE: Adapted from Dirk Johnston, "Preventive Detention: Two Sides of an Issue," *New York Times*, 13 July 1987, A–13. Copyright © 1987 by The New York Times Company. Reprinted by permission.

---

a case in support of this argument. Research has shown that the nature and seriousness of the charge, a history of prior arrests, and the presence of drug addiction all have a strong bearing on the probability that a defendant will commit a pretrial criminal act.[21] Other scholars, however, contend that the criteria used to set bail are poor indicators of the probability a defendant will not appear in court as scheduled or will commit another crime while awaiting trial.[22]

What is the likely impact of preventive detention? One study by Stephen Kennedy and Kenneth Carlson suggested that, although preventive detention had influenced federal pretrial release practices, the percent of defendants released before trial remained relatively stable.[23] They believe this apparent contradiction results from the fact that before the Bail Reform Act judges set high bail for those accused whom they did not want to release. The new provisions mean this ruse is no longer necessary. The study showed that prevention detention was used mainly when the case involved violence, drugs, and immigration offenses.

Individuals who are unable to secure bail or to be released on their own recognizance are held in pretrial detention in the local jail to await their court appearance. As we will see, this experience has a major impact on these defendants in the criminal justice system.

## Pretrial Detention

American jails have been called the ultimate ghetto; in fact, most of the more than 444,000 people in jails on any one day are poor. About half are in pretrial detention, and the remainder are serving sentences (normally of less than one year) or awaiting transfer to state prison or to another jurisdiction. The function and the characteristics of jail are fully discussed in Chapter 13; here we address only that part of the incarcerated population that is being held awaiting trial.

For most suspects the period immediately after arrest is the most frightening. Imagine yourself in such circumstances. After being fingerprinted, photographed, and questioned, you are taken to the detention section of the jail. In some newer facilities you may be asked further questions about your background, physical condition, and mental health so that treatment may be provided if necessary. More than likely, there is no formal intake procedure, and you are simply put in a holding "tank." If you are a man, there are probably three or more strangers in the cell with you, men whose stories you do not know and whose behavior you cannot predict. If you are a woman, you are probably by yourself.[24] In either case, the guard leaves, and you are on your own. You now have time to think and to worry about your situation.

For most people this is a threatening scenario; they may experience panic. That is why the initial hours following arrest are often referred to as a period of crisis for the defendant. The vulnerability, the sense of hopelessness and fright, and the ominous threat of loss of freedom are never more stressful than in those first few hours of confinement. It is understandable that most jail suicides occur within the first six to ten hours of detention and that most psychotic episodes occur during or just after intake.

The crisis nature of arrest and detention can be exacerbated by other factors. Often the newly arrested person is intoxicated by alcohol or another drug; indeed, intoxication may have contributed to the very crime for which the person is being held. Sometimes the criminal behavior that has put the accused in jail stems from an emotional instability that may become more severe in detention. For young offenders, the oppressive threat and reality of personal violence can trigger debilitating depression.

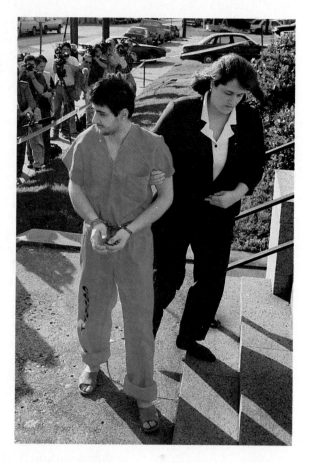

Suspects not able to make bail are held awaiting trial. What is the impact on the jury of an accused who rises from the audience when his case is called, compared to an accused who is escorted by the jailer to the defense table?

Without question, one of the most crucial times for the administrator and the offender comes immediately after arrest.

The fact that a defendant is being held in jail also seriously affects the ultimate disposition of his or her case. Consider the effect on a judge and jury of two hypothetical defendants: one steps neatly dressed from among the onlookers to the counsel's table; the other, in prison garb, is escorted by guards from a nearby cell to the counsel's table. Although it would be difficult to prove that these contrasting scenes affect the justice dispensed, various theories of human behavior suggest that the accused who has been detained is more likely to be labeled guilty. How we present ourselves to others influences their actions toward us.

Are those in pretrial detention more often convicted and given harsher sentences than those out on bail? The evidence is unclear. A study by Eric W. Single revealed that defendants held for trial in lieu of bail were more often convicted and, when convicted, went to prison more often and received longer sentences than those who posted bail.[25] John Goldkamp, however, found no such relationship in his study of the bail versus custody question in Philadelphia. What he did find was that those held in custody were more likely to get prison terms than those not detained.[26] One problem with this research is that it is difficult to isolate the detention factor from other variables such as the severity of the offense and the evidence supporting a guilty verdict.

One compelling fact about U.S. jails is that the conditions under which inmates (half of whom have not been convicted of the crimes for which they are being detained) are deplorable. Although half of those detained awaiting trial are released after forty days or less, there are many in some states who spend three or more months incarcerated while awaiting trial.[27] The hardship of detention before trial is serious because it creates pressure on defendants to waive their rights and to plead guilty.

## Plea Bargaining

The Supreme Court has ruled that plea bargaining is constitutional. Other courts, and prosecutors, claim it is absolutely necessary. Defense lawyers say it is often a boon to their clients. Former Chief Justice Warren Burger has said, "It is an elementary fact, historically and statistically, that the system of courts—the number of judges, prosecutors, and of court-rooms—has been based on the premise that approximately 90 percent of all defendants will plead guilty, leaving only 10 percent, more or less, to be tried."[28]

The process of **plea bargaining**—also referred to as negotiating a settlement, copping a plea, or copping out—was for many years one of the best-kept secrets of criminal justice practitioners because there were doubts about its constitutionality and it did not seem appropriate to a system based on adversary procedure. But Supreme Court decisions have clearly acknowledged the legitimacy of plea bargaining. In *Blackledge* v. *Allison* (1976), for example, the justices said: "Whatever might be the situ-

**plea bargaining**
Entering a plea of guilty to a criminal charge with the expectation of receiving some consideration for doing so. The defendant's goal is to receive a lighter penalty than the one formally warranted by the original offense.

ation in an ideal world, the fact is that the guilty plea and the often concomitant plea bargain are important components of this country's criminal justice system. Properly administered, they can benefit all concerned."[29] The Court has noted that plea bargaining flows from "the mutuality of advantage" to defendants and prosecutors, each with his or her own reasons for wanting to avoid trial.

In the broadest sense, plea bargaining is a defendant's agreement to plead guilty to a criminal charge with the reasonable expectation of receiving some consideration from the state for doing so. Some defendants plead guilty without entering into negotiations but expect to receive some benefit nevertheless, a practice called *implicit* plea bargaining. It is distinguished from *explicit* plea bargaining, an arrangement between the prosecutor and the defendant—sometimes with the participation of the judge—whereby a plea of guilty is exchanged for the prosecutor's agreement to press a charge less serious than that warranted by the facts and perhaps to recommend leniency to the judge.

The defendant's usual objective is to be charged with a crime carrying a lower potential maximum sentence, thus limiting the judge's discretion in sentencing. A plea may also be entered on one charge on agreement that the prosecutor will drop other charges in a multicount indictment. Another reason for seeking a lesser charge may be to avoid charges with legislatively mandated sentences or stipulations against probation or to escape a charge that carries an undesirable label, such as rapist or child molester. The prosecutor seeks to obtain a guilty plea to avoid combat in the courtroom. Although the imposition of the sentence remains a function of the court, the prosecutor draws up the indictment and usually has an important influence on the judge's sentencing decision. Clearly, plea bargaining is the most crucial stage in the criminal justice process and is the primary example of "bargain justice."

According to the traditional conception of adversarial justice, criminal cases are not "settled," as in civil law; the outcome is determined by the symbolic contest of the state versus the accused. Table 9.4 shows the percentages of guilty pleas in robbery and burglary cases in five jurisdictions. Note that the percentage varies little among the cities regardless of the number of trials, judges, and prosecutors. Table 9.5 shows the types of plea concessions made in these cases in the same jurisdictions. This study is consistent with others, and it is generally accepted that up to 90 percent of felony defendants in the United States plead guilty.

## Exchange Relationships in Plea Bargaining

Plea bargaining is essentially a series of exchange relationships in which the prosecutor, the defense attorney, the defendant, and, sometimes, the judge participate. All enter the contest with particular objectives; all attempt to structure the situation to their own advantage and come armed with tactics designed to improve their position; and all will see the exchange as a success from their own perspective. The exchange may be considered successful by the prosecutor who is able to convict the defendant without trial, by the defense attorney who is able to collect a fee with

| | New Orleans | Seattle (King County) | Norfolk | Tucson | Delaware County, Penn. |
|---|---|---|---|---|---|
| Population | 562,000 | 1,157,000 | 285,500 | 500,000 | 600,000 |
| Estimated annual indictments or informations filed | 5,063 | 4,500 | 2,800 | 2,309 | 3,000 |
| Number of felony judges | 10 | 8 | 3 | 7 | 4 |
| Number of prosecutors | 63 | 69 | 15 | 30 | 30 |
| Percentage of robbery and burglary defendants pleading guilty | 81% | 86% | 78% | 87% | 80% |
| Number of felony trials per year | 1,069 | 4,567 | 648 | 270 | 491 |
| Type of defense counsel and estimated percentage of defendants covered | Public 65% Assigned 10% Retained 25% | Public 64% Assigned 16% Retained 20% | Assigned 75% Retained 25% | Public 70% Assigned 3% Retained 27% | Public 65% Retained 35% |
| Prosecutorial restrictions on plea bargaining | Limited charge bargaining | For high-impact cases | Minimal | For career criminals | Minimal |

**Table 9.4**
**Plea bargaining in five jurisdictions: robbery and burglary**

The percentage of guilty pleas is about the same in all five jurisdictions regardless of the number of judges, number of felony trials, and number of indictments or informations.

SOURCE: William F. McDonald, *Plea Bargaining: Critical Issues and Common Practices* (Washington, D.C.: National Institute of Justice, 1985), 7.

a minimum of effort, and by the judge who is able to dispose of one more case from a crowded calendar.

**Tactics of Prosecutor and Defense**   Plea bargaining between defense counsel and prosecutor bears a striking resemblance to a formal ritual in which friendliness and joking mask the forceful advancement of antagonistic views. The pattern is familiar: initial humor, the stating of each viewpoint, resolution of conflict, and a final period of cementing the relationship. Throughout the session, each side tries to impress the other with its confidence in its own case while indicating weaknesses in the opponent's presentation. During the discussion, there appears to be a norm of openness and candor designed to maintain the relationship. Little effort seems to be made to conceal information that may later be useful to the adversary in the courtroom. As evidenced in the accompanying Question of Ethics, there seems to be a standing rule that confidences shared during negotiations will not be used in court.

Some attorneys, of course, do not conform to this norm. One prosecutor said: "There are some attorneys with whom we never bargain, because we can't. We don't like to penalize a defendant because he has an ass for an attorney, but when an attorney cannot be trusted, we have no alternative." Defense attorneys often feel that prosecutors are insulated from the human factors of a case and are thus unwilling to individualize justice. Since defense lawyers get to know the defendants, their problems, and their families, they may become emotionally attached to cases. As one defense lawyer told this author: "We have to impress the chief deputy prosecutor with the fact that he is dealing with humans, not with just a case. If the guy is guilty he should be imprisoned, but he should get only what is coming to him, no more."

A tactic that prosecutors commonly bring to plea-bargaining sessions is the multiple-offense indictment. One defense attorney commented: "Prosecutors throw everything into an indictment they can think of, down to and including spitting on the sidewalk. They then permit the defendant to plead guilty to one or two offenses, and he is supposed to think it's a victory."[30] Multiple-offense charges are especially important to prosecuting attorneys when they are faced with difficult cases—cases in which, for instance, the complainant is reluctant, the value of the stolen item is in question, and the reliability of the evidence is in doubt. Narcotics officers often file charges of selling a drug against defendants when they know they can convict only for possession. Since the accused persons know that the penalty for selling is much greater, they are tempted to plead guilty to the lesser charge.

Defense attorneys may approach these negotiations by threatening to ask for a jury trial if concessions are not made. Their hand is further strengthened if they have filed pretrial motions that require a formal response by the prosecutor. Another tactic is to seek rescheduling of pretrial activities, in the hope that, because of the delay, witnesses will become unavailable, public interest will die, and memories of the incident will be weakened by the time of the trial. Rather than resort to such legal maneuverings, some attorneys prefer to bargain on the basis of friendship. A defense attorney once commented:

I never use the Constitution. I bargain a case on the theory that it's a "cheap burglary" or a "cheap purse-snatching" or a "cheap whatever." Sure, I could suddenly start to negotiate by saying, "Ha,

## A Question of Ethics

Attorney Jonathan Bowman came bustling into the office of Assistant Prosecutor Wayne Charro with an armload of case files. Charro had been expecting the visit and knew what Bowman was likely to do.

"Wayne, I'd like to talk with you about these ten cases that I have for tomorrow. Most of them are just garbage, so I think we can get rid of them quickly. For example, here is the Buckley and Dickens case. They're codefendants and I've got them both. They're each charged with armed robbery, but Dickens says he did not have the gun. You've got to admit that the whole case is pretty flimsy, since the victim is confused as to what happened. How about a guilty plea on a reduced charge of Robbery 2 for Dickens? He's a young kid and deserves a break. He told me that Buckley actually planned this whole thing and held the gun to the woman's head. Buckley's not been very cooperative with me. I just don't like his attitude."

"Well Jon, I don't know. These guys have been in trouble before. If I go for the plea for Dickens, where does that place Buckley?"

How should Charro react to Bowman's statement? What are the ethical questions that would arise from this case should the offer of a guilty plea and charge reduction for Dickens be accepted? What should happen to Buckley? How might the resolution of this case affect future negotiations between Charro and Bowman?

| Type of concession | New Orleans | Seattle (King County) | Norfolk | Tucson | Delaware County, Penn. |
|---|---|---|---|---|---|
| Sentence recommendation only | 56% | 46% | 32% | 7% | 2% |
| Sentence recommendation plus charge reduction and/or dismissal | 4% | 42% | 37% | 3% | 31% |
| Charge reduction and/or dismissal only | 40% | 12% | 31% | 90% | 67% |

### Table 9.5

**Types of plea concessions in robbery and burglary cases in five jurisdictions**

Although the percentage of cases ending in a guilty plea is similar in all jurisdictions (see Table 9.4), the type of concession differs.

SOURCE: William F. McDonald, *Plea Bargaining: Critical Issues and Common Practices* (Washington, D.C.: National Institute of Justice, 1985), 7.

ha! You goofed. You should have given the defendant a warning." And I'd do just fine in that case, but my other clients would pay for this isolated success. The next time the district attorney had his foot on my throat, he'd push too.[31]

Often the bargain is struck in ways that might go unnoticed by the casual observer. To maintain some psychological distance between the adversaries, vague references are often made to disposition of the case. Such statements as "I think I can sell this to the boss" or "I'll see what can be done" signal the completion of a bargaining session and are interpreted by the actors as an agreement on the terms of the exchange. On other cases, negotiations are more specific, with a direct promise made that certain charges will be altered in exchange for a guilty plea.

Because negotiations are conducted primarily between the prosecutor and the defense attorney, the interests of the public and even of the defendant may become secondary considerations. Without the possibility of a trial, where evidence gathered in a legal manner must be presented, plea bargaining can shield unconstitutional practices by justice system actors from public view.

Neither the prosecutor nor the defense attorney is a free agent. Each must count on the cooperation of both defendants and judges. Attorneys often cite the difficulty they have convincing defendants that they should uphold their end of the bargain. Judges must cooperate in the agreement by sentencing the accused according to the prosecutor's recommendation. Although their role requires that they uphold the public interest, judges may be reluctant to interfere with a plea agreement in order to maintain future exchange relationships. Thus both the prosecutor and the defense attorney usually confer with the judge regarding the sentence to be imposed before agreeing on a plea. At the same time, however, the judicial role requires that judges hold in reserve their power to reject the agreement. Because uncertainty is one of the hazards of the organizational system, prosecutors and defense attorneys will evaluate each judicial decision as an indication of the judge's future behavior.

**Pleas without Bargaining**   Studies have indicated that in many courthouses the marketplace tactics of plea bargaining do not exist in certain types of cases, yet guilty pleas still remain as high as the national average.[32] The term *bargaining* may be misleading in that it implies haggling. Many scholars now argue that guilty pleas emerge after a consensus is reached to "settle the facts" by professionals—prosecutor, defense attorney, and sometimes the judge.[33] According to this perspective the parties first examine the facts of a case. What were the circumstances of the event? Is it *really* an assault or is it more of a pushing and shoving match? Did the victim first antagonize the accused? By settling on the facts, the defense and prosecution fit the behavior into "normal crime" categories— how charges are locally defined. Once the facts of the crime are settled and an agreement is reached on the appropriate charges, an agreement can be made on the sentence according to the locally defined **going rates** (the usual sentence for such an offense). The shared expectations on the

**going rate**
Local view of the appropriate sentence given the offense, the defendant's prior record, and other characteristics.

Plea bargaining has become such an integral part of the system that judges frequently take part in negotiations.

charge categories of the crime event, coupled with a sentence that is consistent with the going rate, can be referred to as *implicit bargaining.*

Douglas Maynard found that many cases are concluded when one party offers a disposition and the other simply agrees to it. Because courthouse actors are familiar with the definition and categorization of criminal acts, and know the going rate, bargaining is limited. In only a small number of cases did Maynard discover extensive, visible, and unambiguous bargaining. As he notes, the sharing of expectations

means simply that participants are able to read situations in like manner and infer what resolution will be mutually acceptable. Such a process in plea bargaining is surely aided by the participants' knowledge of the courtroom subculture. The establishment by legal practitioners of "going rates" for run-of-the-mill, "normal" crimes … in local jurisdictions and the administration of these rates as a matter of course … is a well-documented practice.[34]

We should expect to find implicit plea bargaining in courtrooms where the going rates are known to the participants. If there is much turnover among the actors, uncertainty would be likely to reduce the number of guilty pleas offered without negotiation. We should also expect bargaining to be more explicit over serious offenses, when the possible sentence would be incarceration. But underlying both the implicit and explicit models of plea bargaining is the assumption that there is a penalty for going to trial. The nature of that penalty may be an added factor that looms over all plea considerations.

It is also important to acknowledge that the local courtroom culture has a decided impact on the bargaining process; similar issues are not decided in the same manner from courthouse to courthouse. Particular ways of disposing of cases develop in each setting. In some courts a "slow plea" process will be the dominant method: defendants initially plead not guilty but change their pleas as the trials progress. In other courts, prosecutors may filter out various portions of the caseload through the dropping of cases or the diversion of offenders. The variety of routines, norms, and expectations may be much greater than was originally thought, and observers of any one courthouse may discover patterns that do not correspond exactly to the textbook description.

## Legal Issues in Plea Bargaining

The constitutionality of the guilty plea has evolved over the last several decades. Questions concerning the voluntariness of the plea and the sanctity of the agreement have forced the U.S. Supreme Court to confront these issues. In deciding these questions the justices have upheld the general constitutionality of the practice and have sought to ensure that due process rights have been upheld within the context of administrative decision making.

*Boykin* v. *Alabama* (1969)
Defendants must make an affirmative statement that they are voluntarily making a plea of guilty.

The voluntariness of the defendant to plea guilty is a central concern. In *Boykin* v. *Alabama* (1969) the Court ruled that defendants must make an affirmative statement that the plea was made voluntarily before a judge may accept the plea.[35] Courts have created standardized forms listing a series of questions for the defendant to affirm before the plea is accepted. Trial judges are also required to learn whether the defendant understands the implications of an agreement to plead guilty and to ensure that pressures were not brought by either the prosecutor or the defense attorney to coerce the plea.

*Alford* v. *North Carolina* (1970)
A plea of guilty may be accepted for the purpose of a lesser sentence by a defendant who maintains her or his innocence.

Can a trial court accept a guilty plea if the defendant's innocence is maintained? In *Alford* v. *North Carolina* (1970) the Court approved, in principle, a pleading of guilty by an innocent defendant for the purpose of obtaining a lesser sentence. Henry C. Alford was charged with first-degree murder, a capital offense. Although maintaining his innocence, Alford plea-bargained to second-degree murder, a charge for which the death penalty was not authorized. After receiving a thirty-year sentence, he complained to the Supreme Court that the plea had been coerced by the death penalty threat. He argued that he had never admitted his guilt throughout the proceedings. The Court disagreed, ruling that it was Alford's privilege to plead guilty to avoid a possible death penalty even though he continued to maintain his innocence. One result of this ruling is that courts in many parts of the country now routinely accept pleas based on the "Alford Doctrine," by which defendants plead guilty but say they are not guilty.[36]

*Santobello* v. *New York* (1971)
When a guilty plea rests on a promise of a prosecutor it must be fulfilled.

A second issue concerns fulfillment of the plea agreement. If the prosecutor has given a promise of leniency, it must be kept. In *Santobello* v. *New York* (1971), the Supreme Court ruled that "when a [guilty] plea rests in any significant degree on a promise or agreement of the prosecutor, so that it can be said to be part of the inducement or consideration, such promise must be fulfilled."[37] That defendants must also keep their side of the bargain was decided by the Court in *Ricketts v. Adamson* (1987). Ricketts agreed to plead guilty and testify against a codefendant in exchange for a reduction of the charges from first- to second-degree murder. He carried out the bargain but refused to testify a second time when the codefendant had his conviction reversed on appeal. The prosecutor then withdrew the offer to reduce the charge. The Supreme Court upheld the recharging and said that Ricketts had to suffer the consequences of his voluntary choice not to testify at the codefendant's second trial.[38]

*Ricketts* v. *Adamson* (1987)
Defendants must uphold plea agreement or suffer the consequences.

May prosecutors threaten to penalize defendants who insist upon their right to a jury trial? Paul Hayes was indicted in Kentucky for forging an $88.50 check. The prosecutor offered to recommend a sentence of five years imprisonment if a guilty plea was entered, but said that if Hayes pleaded not guilty, he would be indicted under the state's habitual criminal act. If Hayes was then found guilty, a mandatory life sentence would result because he had two prior convictions. Hayes rejected the guilty plea, went to trial, and was sentenced to life imprisonment. On appeal, the U.S. Supreme Court ruled in *Bordenkircher v. Hayes* (1978) that in the "give and take" of plea bargaining, the prosecutor's conduct did not violate constitutional protections.[39] Milwaukee judge Ralph Fine has charged that prosecutors around the country are now using this decision as a tool to extract guilty pleas from hesitant defendants.[40]

*Bordenkircher* v. *Hayes* (1978)
A defendant's rights were not violated by a prosecutor who warned that not to accept a guilty plea would result in a harsher sentence.

Plea bargaining, then, is no longer a secret of the courthouse. The Supreme Court has accepted the constitutionality of the practice and has emphasized the importance of protecting due process rights within this administrative context. As we see in the Close-Up "Plea Bargaining in Detroit Recorder's Court" (pages 354–355), when a plea is given, the judge is required to ask a series of questions to ensure that the method by which the bargain was struck adheres to these principles. At one time, this charade of the "copping-out ceremony" was one of the regular features of the courtroom day. But judges are increasingly discussing plea bargaining openly in their courts and admitting on the record that they are aware of plea negotiations. In many cases, judges have entered into plea discussions with respect to sentences in cases before them.

## Justification for Plea Bargaining

As early as the 1920s the legal profession was united in its opposition to plea bargaining. Roscoe Pound, Raymond Moley, and others associated with the crime surveys of the period stressed the opportunities for political influence as a factor in the administration of criminal justice. Today, under the pressures generated by crime in an urban society and the reality of bargaining, a shift has occurred so that professional groups are primarily interested in procedures that will allow for the review of guilty pleas and for other safeguards. Plea bargaining is now justified on the grounds that it individualizes justice and that it is administratively necessary.

## Plea Bargaining in Detroit Recorder's Court

The lawyer pushed through the swinging gate in the dark wood railing that separates court officials from the public and walked up and down past packed rows of spectators.

It was 10 o'clock on an August morning in Recorder's Court, which is the criminal court for the city of Detroit. In many ways, the scene could have been any criminal courtroom in the United States.

"Jackson," the lawyer called out. "Sam Jackson."

He was trying to find a client he had seen only once before, months ago, when he had been appointed to defend the man for a $100 fee paid by the state of Michigan. On the first day, he stood briefly beside his client as Jackson was arraigned and a date was set for his trial. Until this morning, when a courtroom clerk handed him a copy of the official court "paper" for the case, the lawyer had done nothing more.

"Jackson," he called again.

A slightly built black man in a polo shirt and work pants rose hesitantly a few rows back in the audience. Sam Jackson, a sometime laborer and truck driver, had, his record showed, been connected on and off with gambling and dope. He had been arrested nearly a year earlier for possession of a concealed pistol, which was found when a police detective stopped and searched his car,

and he had been free on bail since then, waiting for his trial.

"Jackson?" the lawyer asked, pushing down his glasses to peer at his client. "Okay, okay. Sit back down. I'll be with you in a minute."

Turning, he walked through the gate again toward a cluster of policemen, all in street clothes, standing and gossiping idly near the empty jury box. In the confusion and cacophony that characterize the criminal-courtroom scene, the policemen, numbering about thirty, were balanced by a swirling, changing mass of as many men opposite them. These are the criminal lawyers, most of whom work in Courtroom 8 every day. Their only clients, whose fees are usually paid by the state, are those assigned to them by the court. Some keep dingy offices in squat, grimy buildings across narrow Clinton Street from the courthouse; others have no offices at all and operate out of the courtroom itself. Known collectively as the "Clinton Street bar," they carry no briefcases and seldom consult lawbooks; their case preparation consists of marking trial dates in dog-eared date books and scanning court papers hurriedly on the day a case comes up.

"Detective Sanders," Jackson's lawyer said, "You got the Jackson case?" The policeman, recognizing the attorney, nodded. "Good," said the lawyer. Then, ignoring the judge nearby, the lawyer shouted the question that, in Recorder's Court, takes the place of trials, juries, legal rules, and the rest: "Hey, Sanders, what can you do for me today?"

**Individualized Justice**  Judges have traditionally individualized justice by fashioning sentences to the severity of the offense and the characteristics of the offender. Some have argued, however, that developments in the system have limited the discretion of the judge while increasing the opportunity for the prosecutor to allocate justice. This view suggests that if the criminal law is to be even minimally fair, the prosecutor's office must be able to determine case outcomes administratively.

The guilty plea is promoted in part by legislatures, which have dictated extreme sentence lengths. Legislatures respond to public pressures by fixing severe punishments. Criminal justice personnel individualize these punishments through the plea-bargaining process to serve the needs of the bureaucracy and to gain the acquiescence of the accused. In this way, courthouse practitioners develop shared norms as to the sentencing value attached to a particular offense. Courthouse regulars believe that those defendants who insist on a trial and are then found guilty and that

Coming together in the middle of the courtroom, the lawyer and policeman began to haggle amiably over what reduction the government might make in its charge against Jackson if he agreed to plead guilty rather than go to trial. If convicted of the felony charge by a jury, Jackson would be given a prison sentence of several years. The law required it. The policeman suggested that the charge might be reduced to "failure to present a gun for licensing," a misdemeanor carrying a penalty of only ninety days in jail, if Jackson pleaded guilty immediately. Together, the lawyer and Detective Sanders then joined a line of other attorneys and policemen that stretched to a back room occupied by the prosecutor—an official who is himself seldom seen in the courtroom.

In Sam Jackson's case, the prosecutor readily agreed to the bargain offered by the lawyer and policeman. The lawyer took Jackson into the bustling hallway outside the courtroom.

"I got you ninety days," he told Jackson enthusiastically. He did not refer at all to the crime itself or to his client's actual guilt or innocence. "It's a good deal. You have a record. You go to trial and get convicted on the felony and you're in trouble."

Jackson nodded in agreement.

"Remember," the lawyer cautioned as they returned to the courtroom, "don't hem and haw in front of the judge, or he might insist on a trial."

Jackson's turn came quickly. He stood mute, while the judge sorted through papers and read out the defendant's name and address and the charge originally placed against him. A court stenographer recorded everything.

"The prosecutor has signed a statement that he will accept your plea of guilty to a lesser charge," the judge announced. Then, like a clergyman reading a litany, with Jackson responding at appropriate pauses, he intoned, "You are pleading guilty because you are guilty?"

"Yes, sir."

"No one has threatened you or promised you anything?"

"No."

"No one has induced you to plead guilty?"

"No."

"You understand your constitutional right to a trial, and you are freely waiving that right?"

"Yes."

Turning sideways to stare out a window, the judge wearily recited, as he had again and again already that morning, "Let the record show that counsel was present, that the defendant was advised of his rights and that he understood them, and that the defendant waived his right to trial by jury or this court, and that he freely withdrew his plea of not guilty and entered a plea of guilty."

The court stenographer took down every word. The judge swiveled around again and sentenced Jackson to ninety days in jail.

SOURCE: Leonard Downie, Jr., *Justice Denied* (New York: Praeger, 1971), 18–22. Copyright © 1971 by Praeger Publishers. Reprinted by permission of the author.

those who refuse to cooperate should receive harsher sentences than defendants who "go along." It is often claimed that the acceptance of the guilty plea by the prosecutor and the judge may help to soften and individualize the occasional overharshness of the law.

**Administrative Necessity**   A second justification for plea bargaining is administrative necessity. As we have seen, a problem of criminal justice is that of mass production. The demands on the judicial process—including calendar congestion, the size of the prison population, and strains on judicial personnel—are overwhelming. A Manhattan prosecutor has said, "Our office keeps eight courtrooms extremely busy trying 5 percent of the cases. If even 10 percent of the cases ended in a trial, the system would break down. We can't afford to think very much about anything else."[41] Yet there are courts in large urban areas where guilty pleas are used much less frequently than the average.[42]

Studies have also cast doubt on the assumption that plea bargaining is a contemporary practice that developed as a response to increased caseloads. In fact, one study of case dispositions found that plea bargaining was practiced extensively in both high- and low-volume courts as early as 1880 and that trials have resulted from fewer than 10 percent of indictments since that time.[43] Others have shown that plea bargaining has been a major feature of American criminal justice since the Civil War.

Malcolm Feeley argues that the prevalence of plea bargaining has increased in direct proportion to the adversariness of the system. From a historical perspective, he says, the modern criminal justice system has expanded requirements of due process, has allocated increased resources to both the prosecution and the defense, has developed a substantive criminal law, and has increased the availability of defense counsel. If one examines conditions in the nineteenth century, a period often referred to nostalgically as the "golden era of trials," one finds

a process that is difficult for the contemporary observer to recognize; those accused of criminal offenses—misdemeanor or felony alike—were typically rushed through crowded and noisy courts either subject to a perfunctory trial lasting an hour or two or pressured to plead guilty by overbearing prosecutors whose practices were condoned by judges. All this took place without benefit of counsel.[44]

In the contemporary system, Feeley believes, the relationship between the state and the accused is more evenly balanced. It is this new relationship—"a relationship that did not hold in a great many criminal cases when trials were more prevalent but the accused more dependent"—that has increased the adversariness of the system, and thus the opportunity for negotiation.[45]

## Criticisms of Plea Bargaining

Although plea bargaining is pervasive in the American criminal justice system, its practice has been deplored by a number of scholars and by such prestigious groups as the American Bar Association. The criticisms are mainly of two kinds. The first emphasizes due process considerations and argues that plea bargaining does not provide procedural fairness to individual defendants because they forfeit the exercise of some of their constitutional rights, especially the right to trial by jury. The second criticism emphasizes sentencing policy and points out that society's interest in awarding appropriate sentences for criminal acts is diminished by plea bargaining. It is believed that in urban areas where caseloads are burdensome, harried prosecutors and judges make concessions based on administrative expediency, resulting in sentences lighter than those required by the penal code.

Plea bargaining also comes under fire because it is hidden from judicial scrutiny. Since the agreement is most often made at an early stage of the proceedings, the judge has little information about the crime or the defendant and cannot evaluate the prosecutor's appraisal of each. Nor can the judge make a knowledgeable review of the terms of the bargain—that is, a check on the amount of pressure applied to the defendant to plead guilty. The result of "bargain justice" is that the judge, the public, and sometimes even the defendant cannot know for certain who got what from whom in exchange for what.

Others claim plea bargaining is inconsistent with the espoused values of the adversarial system. Some critics believe that overuse of plea bargaining breeds disrespect and even contempt for the law. It is said that criminals look at the judicial process as a game or a sham, little different from other "deals" made in life.

Critics also contend that it is unjust to penalize persons who assert their right to a trial and are convicted by giving them stiffer sentences than they would have received if they had pleaded guilty. The evidence in this regard is unclear, although courthouse mythology upholds the view that a penalty is exacted from defendants who take up the court's time. In their analysis of robbery and burglary data from three California counties, David Brereton and Jonathan Casper found that a greater proportion of defendants who went to trial received prison sentences than of those who pleaded guilty.[46] Mark Cuniff's study of twenty-eight large jurisdictions also revealed that defendants pleading guilty were less likely to be sent to prison than those found guilty after a jury trial. Of interest is the fact that cases decided by the judge alone in a bench trial resulted in about the same proportion of offenders going to prison as cases in which the defendant pleaded guilty.[47]

Figure 9.4 presents the results of a Bureau of Justice Statistics study, which supports the view that offenders going to trial receive harsher punishments. It is important to view these results cautiously because it is difficult to determine the strength of the evidence against a defendant and the reason why a plea was not the method of disposition. When defendants view the stakes as high, however, they more likely will take a chance on a jury trial.

Finally, there is concern that innocent people will plead guilty to acts they did not commit. Although it is difficult to substantiate such suspicions, evidence exists that some defendants have indeed entered guilty pleas when they have committed no criminal offense. For example, the Colorado courts overturned a sentence on the ground that the defendant had been coerced by the judge's statement that he would "put him away forever if he did not accept the bargain."[48]

## Reforming Plea Bargaining

As we have seen, some believe that plea bargaining should be abolished. Others believe that as long as negotiations are in the open and that counsel for the defense is present, plea bargaining should be retained.

In a number of jurisdictions (Honolulu, New Orleans, El Paso, and Bronx), efforts have been made to ban plea bargaining.[49] The most noteworthy instance was in Alaska, where the state attorney general instructed district attorneys to stop the practice as of 15 August 1975.

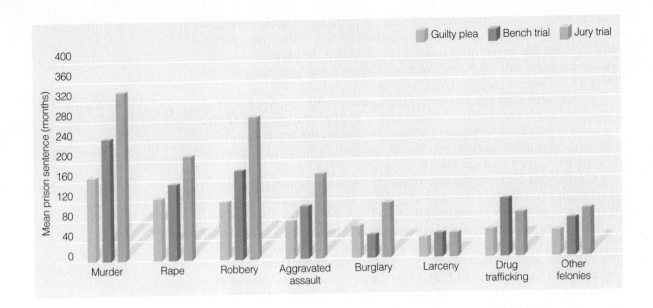

**Figure 9.4**

**Conviction by guilty plea, bench trial, or trial by jury: a comparison of prison sentences**

Although it appears it is in the offender's interest to plead guilty for most crimes, there is not enough information in this graph to support such a conclusion. What else would you need to know?

SOURCE: U.S. Department of Justice, Bureau of Justice Statistics, *Bulletin* (February 1990).

Criminal justice practitioners feared that the courts would be immediately flooded and that there would be a massive slowdown in moving the docket. Neither fear was realized. What happened was that direct bargaining was eliminated but the "implicit" form remained. There was also greater screening of cases by prosecutors so that only the strongest came to court. There was some increase in the punishment given minor cases, but there was little impact on the sentences received for serious cases.[50]

In 1982 California voters passed Proposition 8, a victims' bill of rights. Included in this new law was a stipulation that plea bargaining was not to occur in cases before the superior courts that involved serious crimes. However, the ban did not extend to cases decided in the municipal court. Candace McCoy has shown how Proposition 8 shifted plea bargaining to the lower courts, with only the most serious and disputatious felonies being bound over to the superior court.[51]

## Evaluating Plea Bargaining

Pleading guilty, either in the expectation of a lighter sentence or as part of a bargain, is a typical phenomenon of the American criminal justice system. The guilty plea occurs in up to 90 percent of felony cases before state and federal courts. Although often explained in terms of the heavy caseloads being processed through the system, plea bargaining can be in the interests of all the participants: the prosecutor secures a guilty plea and does not have to go to trial; the defense attorney is able to use time more efficiently; the judge moves the caseload; and the defendant receives a sentence that is less than the law could impose. With the decisions of the Supreme Court and the increased public awareness of plea bargaining, it can be expected that the practice will continue and will be increasingly legitimized.

# Summary

The period from arrest to acceptance of a guilty plea is the most crucial in our system of justice. Until the last twenty-five years, most criminal justice decisions by the Supreme Court focused on the trial in efforts to ensure an impartial jury and courtroom procedures in accordance with the Constitution. The pretrial processes, especially bail setting and plea bargaining, offer key insights into the making of administrative decisions that affect the future of criminal defendants within the context of law.

The Constitution preserves the right to bail, yet many defendants are held in pretrial detention because they are unable to make bail or because the judge believes that community safety would be jeopardized if they were released. A key actor in the bail system is the bondsman, an independent business person who will post bail for those who can pay the 10 percent fee. Not all defendants must make bail; many are released on their own recognizance because they have ties to the community and the judge believes that they will be in court when required.

Plea bargaining is a major feature of the criminal justice system. By pleading guilty, usually to a reduced charge, defendants may receive a lower sentence than if they went to trial. Often justified as permitting the individualization of the sentence and relieving heavy court caseloads, plea bargaining exists because it fits the needs of all concerned. Plea bargaining has been upheld as a constitutional practice by the Supreme Court provided that the defendant voluntarily makes the decision to plead guilty. Attempts to ban plea bargaining have generally failed, a fact that buttresses the belief that the practice is imbedded in the needs of the system.

## Questions for Review

1  What is the method of securing pretrial release for the accused?
2  What are the criteria used to set bail?
3  Is plea bargaining really necessary? Why does it exist?
4  What has the U.S. Supreme Court ruled about the constitutionality of plea bargaining? What safeguards has it imposed?

## Key Terms and Cases

arraignment

bail

citation

copping out

going rate

motion

preventive detention

probable cause

release on recognizance (ROR)

*Alford* v. *North Carolina* (1970)

*Bordenkircher* v. *Hayes* (1978)

*Boykin* v. *Alabama* (1969)

*Ricketts* v. *Adamson* (1987)

*Santobello* v. *New York* (1971)

*Schall* v. *Martin* (1984)

*U.S.* v. *Salerno* (1987)

## For Further Reading

Eskridge, Chris W. *Pretrial Release Programming*. New York: Clark Boardman, 1983. A survey of the history and trends of pretrial release programs.

Fine, Ralph A. *Escape of the Guilty*. New York: Dodd, Mead, 1986. A trial court judge's critical view of plea bargaining.

Flemming, Roy B. *Punishment Before Trial*. New York: Longman, 1982. Study of bail and pretrial release in Detroit and Baltimore. Shows the punishments imposed on defendants before trial.

Heumann, Milton. *Plea Bargaining*. Chicago: University of Chicago Press, 1978. How prosecutors, judges, and defense attorneys adapt to plea bargaining.

Maynard, Douglas W. *Inside Plea Bargaining*. New York: Plenum, 1984. Examination of the discourse surrounding plea bargaining as settlements are made by prosecutors and defense attorneys.

McCoy, Candace. *Politics and Plea Bargaining*. Philadelphia: University of Pennsylvania Press, 1993. A study of the 1982 California victim's rights legislation and its impact on plea bargaining.

Taubman, Bryna. *Preppy Murder Trial*. New York: St. Martins, 1988. A description of the events leading to the plea bargain of Robert Chambers in the death of Jennifer Levin.

Wice, Paul. *Freedom for Sale*. Lexington, Mass.: Lexington Books, 1974. A class survey of bail and its operation.

## Notes

1  Barbara Boland, Paul Mahanna, and Ronald Stones, *The Prosecution of Felony Arrests, 1988* (Washington, D.C.: Bureau of Justice Statistics, 1992).

2  Paul Wice, *Criminal Lawyers: An Endangered Species* (Beverly Hills, Calif.: Sage, 1978), 148.

3   *Ex Parte Milburn*, 34 U.S. 704 (1835).

4   U.S. Department of Justice, Bureau of Justice Statistics, *National Update*, vol. 1 (July 1991), 5.

5   D. Alan Henry and Bruce D. Beaudin, "Bail Bondsmen," *American Jail* 4 (1990): 8–16.

6   *Pannell v. U.S.*, 320 F. 2d 698 (D.C. Cir.) 1963.

7   Frederic Suffet, "Bail Setting: A Study of Courtroom Interaction," *Crime and Delinquency* 12 (October 1988): 318.

8   Roy B. Flemming, *Punishment Before Trial* (New York: Longman, 1982), 136–138.

9   Wayne H. Thomas, Jr., *Bail Reform in America* (Berkeley: University of California Press, 1976), 37–38, 65–66.

10  U.S. Department of Justice, Bureau of Justice Statistics, *National Update* 1 (July 1991): 5.

11  Ronald Goldfarb, *Ransom: A Critique of the American Bail System* (New York: Harper and Row, 1965), 137.

12  Malcolm Feeley, *Court Reform on Trial* (New York: Basic Books, 1983), 68–70.

13  Chris W. Eskridge, *Pretrial Release Programming* (New York: Clark Boardman, 1986), 27.

14  John Goldkamp and Michael E. Gottfriedson, *Policy Guidelines for Bail: An Experiment in Court Reform* (Philadelphia: Temple University Press, 1985), 198.

15  John S. Goldkamp, "Danger and Detention: A Second Generation of Bail Reform," *Journal of Criminal Law and Criminology* 76 (Spring 1985): 1–75.

16  Thomas Scott, "Pretrial Detention Under the Bail Reform Act of 1984," *American Criminal Law Review* 21 (1989): 19.

17  *Schall v. Martin*, 467 U.S. 253 (1984).

18  *U.S. v. Salerno*, 481 U.S. 739 (1987).

19  Marc Miller and Martin Gugenheim, "Pretrial Detention and Punishment," *Minnesota Law Review* 75 (1990): 335–426.

20  Martin D. Sorin, "How to Make Bail Safer," *Public Interest* 76 (Summer 1984): 102–110; Steven R. Schlesinger, "Criminal Procedure in the Courtroom," in *Crime and Public Policy*, ed. James Q. Wilson (San Francisco: Institute for Contemporary Studies, 1983), 188.

21  *Pretrial Release and Misconduct in the District of Columbia* (Washington, D.C.: Institute for Law and Social Research, 1980).

22  Goldkamp, "Danger and Detention."

23  Stephen Kennedy and Kenneth Carlson, *Pretrial Release and Detention: The Bail Reform Act of 1984* (Washington, D.C.: Bureau of Justice Statistics, 1988).

24  Ellen Hochstedler Stevry and Nancy Frank, "Gender Bias and Pretrial Release: More Pieces of the Puzzle," *Journal of Criminal Justice* 18 (1990): 417–432.

25 Eric W. Single, "The Consequence of Pretrial Detention" (Paper presented at the 1973 Annual Meeting of the American Sociological Association, New Orleans).

26 John Goldkamp, *Two Classes of Accused* (Cambridge, Mass.: Ballinger Press, 1979).

27 U.S. Department of Justice, Bureau of Justice Statistics, *Bulletin* (November 1992), 3.

28 Warren Burger, "Address at the American Bar Association Conference," *New York Times*, 11 August 1970, 1.

29 *Blackledge* v. *Allison*, 431 U.S. 63 (1976).

30 Albert Alschuler, "The Prosecutor's Role in Plea Bargaining," *University of Chicago Law Review* 35 (1968): 54.

31 Ibid., 79.

32 James Eisenstein, Roy B. Flemming, and Peter F. Nardulli, *The Contours of Justice: Communities and Their Courts* (Boston: Little, Brown, 1988), 118.

33 Pamela Utz, *Settling the Facts* (Lexington, Mass.: Lexington Books, 1978).

34 Douglas Maynard, "The Structure of Discourse in Misdemeanor Plea Bargaining," *Law and Society Review* 18 (1984): 81.

35 *Boykin* v. *Alabama*, 395 U.S. 238 (1969).

36 *Alford* v. *North Carolina*, 400 U.S. 25 (1970).

37 *Santobello* v. *New York*, 404 U.S. 257 (1971).

38 *Ricketts* v. *Adamson*, 481 U.S. 1 (1987).

39 *Bordenkircher* v. *Hayes*, 343 U.S. 357 (1978).

40 Ralph Adam Fine, *Escape of the Guilty* (New York: Dodd, Mead, 1986), 84.

41 Ibid., 55.

42 James Eisenstein and Herbert Jacob, *Felony Justice* (Boston: Little, Brown, 1977), 291. For example, Eisenstein and Jacob found that of Baltimore defendants who came to trial only 34.7 percent pled guilty, while in Chicago and Detroit this rate was 62 and 63 percent respectively.

43 Milton Heumann, *Plea Bargaining* (Chicago: University of Chicago Press, 1978).

44 Malcolm M. Feeley, "Plea Bargaining and the Structure of the Criminal Process," in *Criminal Justice: Law and Politics*, 7th ed., ed. George F. Cole (Belmont, Calif.: Wadsworth, 1993), 196.

45 Ibid.

46 David Brereton and Jonathan Casper, "Does It Pay to Plead Guilty? Differential Sentencing and the Function of Criminal Courts," *Law and Society Review* 16 (1981–82): 56–61.

47 Mark Cuniff, *Sentencing Outcomes in Twenty-Eight Felony Courts*, (Washington, D.C.: National Institute of Justice, 1987).

48 *People* v. *Clark*, 515 2d 1242 (Colorado, 1973).

49 *Wall Street Journal*, 10 December 1992.

50 Michael L. Rubenstein and Theresa J. White, "Alaska's Ban on Plea Bargaining," *Law and Society Review* 13 (1979): 367; Theresa White Carns and John Kruse, *Alaska's Plea Bargaining Ban: Re-evaluated* (Anchorage: Alaska Judicial Council, 1991).

51 Candace McCoy, *Politics and Plea Bargaining* (Philadelphia: University of Pennsylvania Press, 1993).

# Court

The traditional image of the courthouse is a building standing prominently on the central square of a town or city. It usually has a classic Greek architecture with a marble exterior. The courthouse's location and structure symbolize the prominence of the rule of law in the American social and governmental system. But not all judicial decisions are made in this idealized version of the courthouse. In some large cities, the courthouse is indistinguishable from the surrounding office buildings. In rural areas, "court" is often held in a small office or even in the converted living room of the justice of the peace.

Once in a courthouse you might be at a loss to find a particular court, for they are given a somewhat bewildering collection of names—municipal court, superior court, county court, district court, justice court, and so on. These names rarely tell us much about what the courts do. You might be further confused by signs that read "Clerk of Court," "Criminal Division, Part I," "Arraignment Court," "Juvenile Court." You might enter a crowded and noisy room in which groups of people appear before a judge and then move on in rapid succession, or you might watch a trial in progress that has all the dignity of an idealized image of the administration of justice—or you might see a circular table around which four or five adults and a fourteen-year-old girl are seated.

It is obvious that *court* refers to a variety of physical structures, names, functions, processes, and settings. Because of the fragmented and local nature of American governmental units, our courts have developed somewhat irregularly. Each court has been influenced by political and cultural aspects of its community's history. Although all of our courts are alike in that they follow the basic patterns of the Anglo-American legal tradition, each is distinctive in the way it is structured to perform particular functions and to deal with certain problems.

This chapter examines the structure of the American court system and looks at the conditions—from court congestion to the filtering process and exchange relationships—that influence decision making within it. It focuses on the key player—the judge—but it also shows that decisions on guilt or innocence, probation or prison essentially are made collectively by a small courtroom workgroup. As you read this chapter, put yourself in the position of each of the courtroom players discussed. Consider the issues from each perspective and ask yourself: Is justice being served?

## Questions for Inquiry

- What is the structure of the American system of courts?
- What are some of the management problems of the trial courts?
- What is meant by "courtroom workgroup" and how does this concept help explain court actions?
- What qualities are desired in a judge and how are they chosen in the United States?
- What is the problem of court delay and how can it be solved?

## The Structure of American Courts

Before we can analyze the problems of American criminal courts, we must understand their structure and management. The United States has a dual court system, federal and state. The U.S. Supreme Court oversees both systems and the Constitution protects the rights of defendants in criminal cases. The federal courts deal with those accused of violating the criminal laws of the national government, yet most criminal behavior violates state law and is processed in state systems, primarily in the trial courts of county and city government.

A major distinguishing factor of American trial courts is that they are strikingly decentralized. Throughout U.S. history it has been felt that courts should be close to the people and responsive to them. Only in a few relatively small states is the court system completely organized on a statewide basis, centrally administered, and funded by state government.

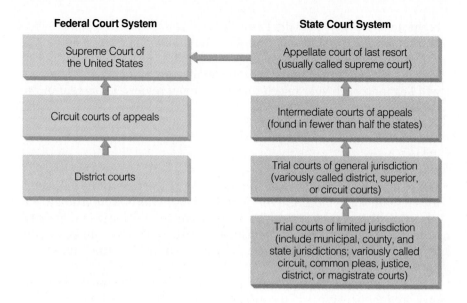

**Federal Court System**

Supreme Court of the United States

Circuit courts of appeals

District courts

**State Court System**

Appellate court of last resort (usually called supreme court)

Intermediate courts of appeals (found in fewer than half the states)

Trial courts of general jurisdiction (variously called district, superior, or circuit courts)

Trial courts of limited jurisdiction (include municipal, county, and state jurisdictions; variously called circuit, common pleas, justice, district, or magistrate courts)

**Figure 10.1**
**Dual court system of the United States and routes of appeal**
Whether a case is processed through the federal or the state court system depends on which law has been violated. The right of appeal to a higher court exists in either system.

In most of the country, the criminal courts operate under the state penal code but are staffed, managed, and financed by county or city government. Thus local political influences and community values are brought to bear on the courts: local officials determine their resources, residents comprise the staff, and justice operations are adjusted to fit community needs. Let us examine each of these systems in turn.

## Federal Courts

The left side of Figure 10.1 shows the federal court system arranged hierarchically, with the district courts at the base, the courts of appeals at the intermediate level, and the Supreme Court at the top. Ninety-four *United States district courts* are the courts of original jurisdiction (trial courts), where federal cases are first heard and decisions of fact are made. District courts are distributed throughout the country, with at least one in each state, one in the District of Columbia, and four in the U.S. territories. These courts hear the great majority of civil and criminal cases arising under federal law.

Above the federal district courts are twelve *United States Circuit Courts of Appeals*, each with jurisdiction over a geographic portion of the country, including one for the District of Columbia. Created in 1891 as a means of reducing the case burden of the Supreme Court, this intermediate level of the judiciary hears appeals from the district courts and from such administrative bodies as the U.S. Tax Court and the National Labor Relations Board. From three to nine judges are assigned to each court of appeals, and normally three jurists sit as a panel.

The Constitution gives original (trial) jurisdiction to the *United States Supreme Court* in only a few types of cases—suits between states, for example. The primary task of the high court is to hear appeals from the

**jurisdiction**
The territory or boundaries within which control may be exercised; hence, the legal and geographical range of a court's authority.

**appellate court**
A court that does not try criminal cases but hears appeals of decisions of lower courts.

**trial court of general jurisdiction**
A criminal court that has jurisdiction over all offenses, including felonies, and that in some states may also hear appeals.

**trial court of limited jurisdiction**
A criminal court of which the trial jurisdiction either includes no felonies or is limited to some category of felonies. Such courts have jurisdiction over misdemeanor cases, probable-cause hearings in felony cases, and, sometimes, felony trials that may result in penalties below a specified limit.

highest state courts and the lower federal courts. Its nine justices, appointed for life, review and attempt to maintain consistency in the law within the federal structure of the United States. As the highest court in the United States, the Supreme Court retains discretion over the cases it will hear and each year rejects as unworthy of review 90 percent of the two thousand cases that reach it.

## State Courts

The basic structure and organization of American state courts were borrowed, with some modification, from England. Efforts were made to ensure that the courts would be responsive to the local community. Legislatures created court systems that were decentralized, linked to the local political system, and dependent for resources on the nonjudicial branches of government.

The growth of commerce and population during the nineteenth century brought new types of disputes requiring judicial attention. Litigation increased, and there were more specialized cases. The states and localities responded to this challenge mainly by creating new courts with particular legal or geographical **jurisdictions**. Small claims courts, juvenile courts, and family relations courts were added in many states. In most states these changes produced a confusing structure of multiple courts with varying jurisdictions, overlapping responsibilities, and intercounty differences.

The courts of all fifty states are now organized into three tiers: **appellate courts** (courts of last resort and those with intermediate appellate jurisdiction), **trial courts of general jurisdiction**, and **trial courts of limited jurisdiction**. Although this basic structure is found throughout the United States, the number of courts, their names, and their specific functions vary widely. Figure 10.2 contrasts the court structure of Alaska, a reformed state, with that of Georgia, where the court structure has not been reformed. Both are organized according to the three-tier model, but Georgia has more courts and greater jurisdictional complexity, with multiple courts of limited jurisdiction.

**Figure 10.2**
**Court structures of Alaska (reformed) and Georgia (unreformed)**
Reformers have pushed for states to reduce the number of courts, to standardize court names, and to demarcate their jurisdictions clearly.
SOURCE: National Center for State Courts, *State Court Caseload Statistics: Annual Report* (Williamsburg, Va.: National Center for State Courts, 1989), 185, 194.

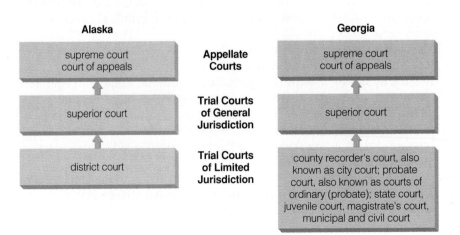

The powers of the approximately thirteen thousand *trial courts of limited jurisdiction*, often referred to as the "inferior" or "lower" trial courts, are limited to hearing the formal charges against accused persons in all cases, holding preliminary hearings of crimes that must be adjudicated at a higher level, and conducting summary trials (where a jury is not allowed) and, in some states, trials of persons accused of certain minor offenses. The law generally defines the court's jurisdiction according to the maximum jail sentence that may be imposed. A maximum fine of one thousand dollars and up to twelve months in jail is commonly the greatest penalty that these courts may impose. About 90 percent of all criminal cases pass through these lower courts. In most places they are organized and funded by county government.

These courts do not display the dignity and formal procedures of higher courts. They are not courts of record (no detailed account of the proceedings is kept), and the activities are conducted in an informal atmosphere. In most urban areas, endless numbers of people are serviced by these courts, and each defendant gets only a small portion of what should be his or her day in court.

The *trial courts of general jurisdiction* have the authority to try all cases, both civil and criminal. With regard to criminal cases, they are often referred to as felony courts. They are courts of record in that the proceedings are recorded and they follow formal procedures specified by law. In large metropolitan areas, they commonly have divisions that specialize in different kinds of cases. Most felony courts are funded by the state.

The *appellate courts* have no trial jurisdiction but hear only appeals from the lower courts. In some states only the state's supreme court—an appellate court of last resort—is found at this level; in others, an *intermediate court of appeals* exists in addition to the state's highest judicial body.

One of the reforms undertaken during the past quarter century has been the development of intermediate appellate courts (IACs). Today they are found in thirty-eight states, with plans being formulated in additional jurisdictions. These courts are designed to receive appeals from the trial courts so that the state supreme court (the court of last resort) can have the discretion to hear only those appeals that have widespread implications. Although the decisions of the IAC's may be reviewed by the state supreme court, they are in fact final for most cases.[1]

State supreme courts normally sit *en banc* (as a whole), with all justices participating in the case, while intermediate appellate courts are usually divided into panels of three judges who hear cases.

## Effective Management of the State Courts

Throughout most of this century, there have been serious efforts to reform the structure, administration, and financing of the state courts so that they can deal more effectively with their overwhelming caseloads. In 1906, Roscoe Pound, one of the nation's greatest judicial thinkers, delivered a speech that struck mainly at the organizational inadequacies of the judicial system.[2] Pound claimed that there were too many courts, which

resulted in duplication and inefficiency; furthermore, there was a great waste of judicial power because of rigid jurisdictional boundaries, poor use of resources, and the frequent granting of new trials. (For more on Pound and his memorable speech, see the accompanying Biography.)

Calls for reform of the organization and administration of the state courts have continued. Although various problems are usually identified, such as insufficient resources and the quality of politically appointed judges, the reform literature generally points to the fragmented and decentralized structure of state courts as impeding the effective administration of justice. Proposed solutions include the creation of a unified court system with four objectives:

1   The elimination of overlapping and conflicting jurisdictional boundaries (of both subject matter and geography).

2   A hierarchical and centralized court structure, with administrative responsibility vested in a chief justice and court of last resort.

3   The financing of the courts by state government.

4   A separate personnel system, centrally run by a state court administrator.

These themes—structure, centralization of administrative authority, funding, and a separate personnel system—have been at the forefront in the movement to reform the state courts so that they are more efficient and more effectively dispense justice.

## Structure

At the heart of reform efforts is the wish to consolidate and simplify court structures. A simple court structure is appealing because it creates an impression of clarity of purpose and efficiency. However, judicial decentralization and autonomy make it possible for local courts to become integral parts of the local political systems, thus providing community interest groups with access to judicial decision makers.

## Centralization of Administrative Authority

Who runs the courts? Who is in charge? These questions address not only the issue of authority within the court structure but also the autonomy of the judiciary. In decentralized court systems there is no overall authority to ensure continuity in procedures, to provide supervision, or to protect the judiciary from encroachment by the legislative and executive branches of government. The day-to-day administration of a state judiciary necessitates that some person or body handle matters such as assignment of judges, assignment of cases, record keeping, personnel, and financing. Contemporary proponents of a unified court system argue that either the supreme court of the state or its chief justice should be given the power to assign judges, set rules, and institute systemwide procedures.

## State Funding

State courts historically have been funded by county government. It is recognized that control of monetary resources is a crucial ingredient of power in any organization. Reformers have insisted that state government fund all courts and that the court administrator, under the direction of the chief justice, prepare for the legislature a budget for the entire system.

In a study of judicial funding, Marcia Lim found that while the state share of funding varied from 13 to 100 percent, the court systems of only twenty-one states received substantial or full support of their budget from the state.[3] Of costs for the judiciary, 62 percent is from county government and only 38 percent from state governments. A more striking fact is that the larger a state's population, the lower its percentage of court funding by state government.

During the past few years there has been a slow but significant move toward increased funding by a number of states. As court costs rise in an increasingly litigious society, local political leaders seem willing to allow the state to fund the judiciary.

## Separate Court Personnel System

Without a separate civil service system for judicial employees, a statewide unified court system cannot come into being and the courts remain beholden to local political powers. To remedy that situation, the 1974 American Bar Association (ABA) Standards Relating to Court Organization thus recommended a system of position classification, levels of compensation, and procedures for personnel evaluation.

## Toward Unified Court Systems

In recent years, deficiencies in the administration of justice have received much attention from state and federal governments. The rise in crime and the caseload problems of the courts have led to increased funding as a means of improving the administration of justice. Judicial expenditures in the states have more than doubled during the past decade. Several populous states have moved toward a unified court system, and employment in state and local courts has increased.

Although these facts may portend eventual realization of the reformers' objectives, questions are being raised about basic assumptions of the unified court system. It is now argued that the conventional wisdom of centralized management of state court systems does not conform to reality. It is said that a tidy organization chart does not reflect how the courts *really* work. We must look at the interactions of the major players—judge, prosecutor, defense attorney, clerk, and bailiff—to understand how the court functions.

## The Courtroom: How It Functions

With some variations justice is allocated in fairly similar ways throughout this large and diverse nation. There are some differences from state to state in the structure and organization of courts, in the methods used to select judges, and in the rules of criminal procedure, yet there are nationally shared values concerning how persons accused of crimes should be treated. These values are espoused in the laws and constitutions of the states and the United States. A person who grew up in New Jersey and is arrested in Idaho will find that guilt or innocence is determined approximately the same in both states.

Even with the overall similarity of the formal processes of adjudication, differences are discernible to anyone who has visited American courts. A study of criminal courts in nine communities in three states revealed it is not the laws and procedures that are different, but the way defendants are treated—the results of the judicial process.[4] Some courts sentence offenders to longer terms than do others. In some jurisdictions delays and tight release policies keep many of the accused in jail awaiting trial, while in other jurisdictions similar defendants are out on bail or have had their cases resolved expeditiously. Guilty pleas may make up 90 percent of dispositions in some communities but only 60 percent in others. How can we explain these differences among courts in various cities and even among different courtrooms in the same city?

**local legal culture**

Norms shared by members of a court community as to case handling and a participant's behavior in the judicial process.

Social scientists have long recognized that culture—the shared beliefs and attitudes of a community—has a great influence on how its members behave. Culture implies a consensus as to the definition of proper behavior. Researchers have identified a **local legal culture**—norms shared by members of a particular court community (judges, attorneys, clerks, bailiffs, and others)—as to case handling and a participant's behavior in the judicial process.[5] The local legal culture influences court operations in three ways:

1 Norms help participants distinguish between "our" court and other jurisdictions. Often a judge or prosecutor will expound upon how "we" do the job differently and better than in the neighboring county or central city.

2 Norms stipulate how members should treat one another. For example, mounting a strong adversarial defense may be viewed as not in keeping with the norms of one court while it is the expected behavior in another. In Montgomery County, Pennsylvania, a local attorney told researchers that "suits challenging the operation of the criminal system 'upset' the bar, and that 'upsetting the bar would be rocking the boat.'"[6]

**going rate**

Local view of the appropriate sentence given the offense and the defendant's prior record and other characteristics.

3 Norms describe how cases *should* be processed. The best example of this situation is the **going rate**, the local view of the appropriate sentence given the offense, the defendant's prior record, and other characteristics. The local legal culture also includes attitudes about issues such as the appropriateness of judicial participation in plea negotiations, when continuances should be given, and who is eligible for a public defender.

The differences among local legal cultures help to explain why court decisions are dissimilar even though the formal rules of criminal procedure are basically the same. Informal rules and practices arise within particular settings, and "the way things are done" differs from place to place. As one might expect, the local legal culture of Albuquerque differs from that of Tolland County or Baltimore. The customs and traditions of each jurisdiction vary because local practices are influenced by factors such as size, politics, and demographics. Among these, differences between urban and rural areas are a major factor.

In small town and rural settings, the local legal culture and the "going rate" have strong impacts on the allocation of justice.

## Urban and Rural Differences

It is well recognized that people treat each other differently in a city as compared to a rural area; as a consequence, these differences are reflected in the operation of criminal courts. In their nine-court study, James Eisenstein, Roy Flemming and Peter Nardulli found that community size was a major ingredient in determining local legal culture and thus the way justice was allocated.[7] In rural communities people know and interact with each other on personal terms. A small-town judge probably knows the accused and the victim and their family circumstances. In addition, the amount of crime is probably low and few officials are involved in the disposition process. By contrast, decisions in cities are made in a bureaucratic context—offenders are known only by their case record, multiple courtrooms are used, the courthouse has a large staff, and caseload pressures are great.

In a study of criminal courts in a rural Pennsylvania county, David Klingler found that there was little crime, a part-time judge, prosecutor, and public defender, and a desire to avoid trials. "Everyone was thoroughly familiar with the principals in each case—the arresting officer, the defendant and his or her family, the victim, witnesses, and the attorneys."[8] This familiarity made the actions of the judge, the opposing attorneys, and the defendant highly visible to the community. Given the extent of personal relationships in small communities, there is a strong desire to avoid conflict. One result is that the guilty plea is the predominant means of case disposition. In addition, going rates play a lesser role because precedents cannot be established since there are fewer cases. Third, with a low caseload, there is greater individualization, and less routine handling, of cases. These factors all increase the give-and-take among participants in small jurisdictions and thus raise the percentage of guilty pleas.

One problem with much of our knowledge of criminal justice is that it is based primarily on urban felony courts where the court community is large, where there are many cases, and where bureaucratic routines guide decisions. It is in crowded urban courts that scholars have noted the importance of the workgroup.

## The Courtroom Workgroup

The traditional picture of the courtroom highlights adversarial attitudes, but a more realistic depiction might emphasize the interactions among the major actors within the normative context of the local legal culture. Adjudication is also influenced by the fact that courtroom participants are organized in **workgroups**. From this perspective, the reciprocal relationships of the judge, prosecutor, and defense attorney, along with those of the support cast (clerk, reporter, and bailiff), are necessary to complete the group's basic task: the disposition of cases. The workgroup concept seems especially important in the analysis of urban courts—where there are many separate courtrooms in the same system, where the number of judicial actors is great, and where the caseload is heavy.

Merely placing the major actors in the courtroom does not instantly make them into a workgroup. A judge, prosecutor, defense attorney, defendant, and others together might be called a **grouping**, a conglomerate of persons. Only when the following conditions are met does a workgroup exist:

1   There must be *interaction* of the members.

2   The members share (that is, have the same attitudes about) one or more *motives* or *goals* that determine the direction in which the group will move.

3   The members develop a set of norms that determine the boundaries within which interpersonal relations may be established and actions may be performed.

4   If interaction continues, a set of roles becomes stabilized and the group differentiates itself from other groups.

5   A network of interpersonal relationships develops on the basis of the members' likes and dislikes for one another.[9]

**workgroup**
A collective of individuals who interact in the workplace on a continuing basis, share goals, develop norms regarding how activities should be carried out, and eventually establish a network of roles that differentiates the group from others.

**grouping**
A collective of individuals who interact in the workplace but, because of shifting membership, do not develop into a workgroup.

**Figure 10.3**
**The courtroom social system as a continuum**
How might the interactions of the actors of Courtroom A differ from those in Courtroom B?

Less interaction, lack of shared goals, group instability

More interaction, sharing of goals, group stability

Grouping                          Workgroup

Courtroom
A

Courtroom
B

The degree to which these conditions are met distinguishes a workgroup from a grouping. We might think of this system as a continuum, with the members in Courtroom A meeting only some conditions and thus acting closer to a grouping, and with the members of Courtroom B meeting all conditions and thus acting together as a closely knit workgroup, as noted in Figure 10.3.

Given this conceptual framework, research might place different sets of courtroom actors at different points on the continuum. For example, a rotation of judges among the courtrooms may limit the opportunity to develop workgroup norms and roles. Although the same prosecutors and defense attorneys may be present every day, bringing in a new judge, perhaps on a weekly basis, will require them to learn and accommodate to the various special ways that the judges on the circuit expect the proceedings to be run. In such a social network there is a basis for shared norms and role stability because some actors are regularly present, but there is enough interruption to keep strong relationships from developing. Cases proceed more formally, with less reliance on agreed-upon routines, than in a courtroom with a workgroup that has a well-developed pattern of interactions.

Alternatively, if the same actors are in the courtroom on a continuing basis, we may expect that the cooperative relationships among the judge, prosecutor, and defense attorney, along with those of the staff, will shape the manner in which decisions are made. Thus the defendant, a person from outside the workgroup, will confront "an organized network of relationships, in which each person who acts on his case is reacting to or anticipating the actions of others."[10] Through cooperation it is possible for each member to achieve individual goals as well as for the group to achieve its collective goals.

Even though our system is formally an adversarial one, courtroom participants form a workgroup that requires constant interaction, cooperation, and negotiation.

Although norms and goals are shared, each member of the courtroom workgroup occupies a specialized position and is expected to fit into the socially accepted definition of that status. Because the occupant of each position has specific rights and duties, there is no exchange of roles. When a lawyer moves from the public defender's office to the prosecutor's office and ultimately to the bench, each status mandates a different role in the courtroom workgroup. Because each actor is expected to perform a certain way, there can be a high degree of stability in the interpersonal relations among members: each member can become proficient at the work routines associated with his or her role, and the group can develop stable expectations concerning the actions of the members. Thus the business of the courtroom proceeds in a regularized, informal manner, with many established, but unrecorded, understandings among members that ease much of the work.

In addition to sharing norms with the other members of the courtroom workgroup, each actor represents a different sponsoring organization.[11] One organization, loosely called the *court*, sends judges; the prosecuting attorney's office sends assistant prosecutors; the public defender's office sends counsel for indigents. Sponsoring organizations determine and provide the resources for the courtroom workgroup and—perhaps more important—attempt to regulate the behavior of their representatives in the courtroom. Policies of a particular sponsoring organization may stipulate rules to be followed, may encourage or discourage plea bargaining, or may insist that police evidence conform strictly to formal requirements. Thus the judge, prosecutor, or public defender must meet the needs and goals of the workgroup while at the same time must satisfy superiors in their own sponsoring organization. The degree to which the chief judge, prosecuting attorney, or chief public defender oversees the work of the representative greatly influences the degree to which each courtroom member can adjust practices to meet the workgroup's goals.

Others play supporting roles in the courtroom drama. Members of the judge's staff, such as clerks and court reporters, have access to vast amounts of confidential information. This resource, as well as their access to the judge, may be used to enhance their own power within the group. Bailiffs, who maintain order in the courtroom and escort prisoners, are supplied by the sheriff. Probation officers, who provide presentence reports, are often present in the courtroom and work closely with the judge. Although not directly tied to the close interactions of the judge, prosecutor, and defense attorney, they provide information and perform duties in support of the major actors. Finally, all courtroom actors must keep in mind those others with whom they have ties. Prosecutors must not endanger their relationships with the police; defense attorneys know that the accused persons and their families expect a defense; judges must be alert to reactions to their decisions from the news media and from members of higher appellate courts. These pressures may have two effects. First, they may require that the actors give "performances" to satisfy their clients—dramatizations that must have the support of other members of the courtroom cast. Second, shielding the audience from the secrets of stage technique increases the group's cohesion.

Clerks and bailiffs, who provide support for the judge and attorneys, are also members of the courtroom workgroup.

The elements of the courtroom workgroup and the influences that bear on decision making are depicted in Figure 10.4. Note that the workgroup operates in an environment in which the local legal culture, recruitment and selection processes, cases, and the socioeconomic, political, and legal structures of the broader community all influence decision making.

**Physical Setting**   The work site of the courtroom group strengthens the interaction patterns of its members and separates them from their clientele groups. The physical surroundings separate the individual courtroom from other social spaces so that communications with those outside the group are limited.

The low visibility of courtroom activities to both the public and government officials is an additional characteristic of the judicial system. Judges enjoy a great deal of independence from supervision because few people are watching. The higher courts may supervise the administration of justice, but only a small percentage of criminal cases are appealed. Members of the general public may observe, but few citizens attend criminal court.

The bench is usually elevated to symbolize the judge's authority. Because it faces the lawyers' table, persons in the audience, and sometimes even the defendant, are unable to observe all the verbal and nonverbal exchanges. In some courts the attorneys for both sides sit toward either end of a long table; the furniture does not define them as adversaries. Throughout the proceedings, lawyers from both sides periodically engage in muffled conversations with the judge, out of the hearing range of the defendant and spectators. When judges call the attorneys into their chambers for private discussion, the defendants remain in the courtroom. In most settings, the defendants sit isolated either in the "dock" or in a

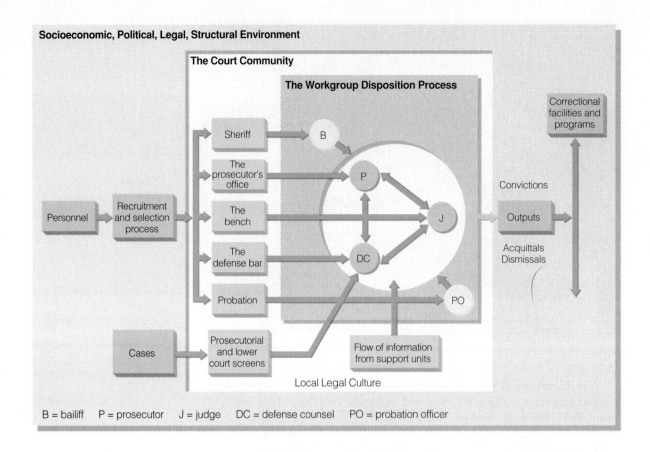

Socioeconomic, Political, Legal, Structural Environment

The Court Community

The Workgroup Disposition Process

Personnel → Recruitment and selection process

Sheriff → B

The prosecutor's office → P

The bench

The defense bar → DC

Probation → PO

J

Convictions

Outputs

Acquittals
Dismissals

Correctional facilities and programs

Cases → Prosecutorial and lower court screens

Flow of information from support units

Local Legal Culture

B = bailiff    P = prosecutor    J = judge    DC = defense counsel    PO = probation officer

**Figure 10.4**
**Model of criminal court decision making**

This model ties together the elements of the courtroom workgroup, sponsoring organizations, and local legal culture. Note the influences on decision making. Are there other factors that should be considered?

SOURCE: Adapted from: Peter Nardulli, James Eisenstein, and Roy Flemming, *Tenor of Justice: Criminal Courts and the Guilty Plea Process* (Urbana: University of Illinois Press, 1988). Copyright © 1988 by the Board of Trustees of the University of Illinois. Reprinted by permission of the University of Illinois Press.

chair behind their counsel to symbolize their status as silent observers with no power to negotiate their own fate.

Since public defenders often represent as many as 90 percent of the court's clients, they occupy a "permanent" place in the courtroom and only temporarily relinquish their desks to the few lawyers who have been privately retained. While the courtroom encounters of private attorneys are brief, businesslike, and temporary, public defenders view the courtroom as their regular workplace and thus give the impression that they are core members of the courtroom group.

**Role of the Judge**   In the view of some defendants, the judge is a peripheral figure who does not play an important part in determining the outcome of their case; the lawyer and prosecutor play much more significant roles in their eyes. From the perspective of these defendants, the judge's behavior shows the ultimate failure of the system and the complete submission of due process ideals to bureaucratic goals.

Yet judges are leaders of the courtroom team and are supposed to ensure that procedures are followed correctly. They are also administrators who are responsible for coordinating the process. Even so, there is latitude for each judge to play the role somewhat differently. Judges who run a loose administrative ship see themselves as somewhat above the battle.

They give other members of the team considerable freedom to discharge their responsibilities and will usually ratify group decisions. Although the task goals of the organization, in terms of the number of cases processed, might be low, the social relations within the courtroom group would probably be high.

Judges who run tighter ships see themselves as necessary leaders of the courtroom team. They anticipate problems, provide cues for other actors, threaten, cajole, and move the group toward an efficient accomplishment of goals. Such judges command respect and participate fully in the ongoing courtroom drama.

Because of their position within the process, judges possess the potential leadership resources to play their role according to these polar types or somewhere in between. How they define their role greatly influences the structure of interpersonal relations within the courtroom and the way the group performs its task, as measured by the output of its case decisions.

**Roles in the Workgroup**  The courtroom is a meeting place for professionals (lawyers, probation officers, and social workers) who proclaim that they work in the service of accused persons, supposedly to treat their needs and those of society. These are the agent-mediators who help the defendants redefine themselves in their interactions with others and prepare them for the next phase of what can be considered their "moral career."[12]

Dress may communicate the role each performer plays. Group members wear appropriate uniforms: the judge in robes, the attorneys in conservative suits. One may even observe differences between the clothing of the prosecutor and the defense attorney. Prosecutors dress in more somber colors (perhaps to identify their role with that of the judge), some defense attorneys tend toward more flamboyant outfits (perhaps to conform to their clients' expectations). Even the defendants may be dressed in uniforms—jail garb—if they are detained for lack of bail. Because most defendants are poor, their clothing tends to differentiate them from the group of court actors.

The role played by defendants in courtroom encounters greatly influences the perceptions of the agent-mediators and guides their decisions. Defendants are expected to present themselves according to the "ideal form" as conceived by the other persons along the moral career journey. If the defense attorney, social worker, family members, and other agent-mediators have been successful in getting defendants to redefine themselves during the pretrial phase, they should understand how they must perform their part. Ideally, they will act guilty, repentant, silent, and submissive. The guilty plea "ceremony" allows others in the courtroom to meet administrative needs within a legal context. For example, when the accused acknowledges guilt in public and testifies that he or she is entering the plea willingly and voluntarily, acceptance of the plea can be followed by a brief lecture from the judge about the seriousness of the wrongful act or the unhappiness the defendant has caused his or her family. Thus the defendant's contrite demeanor allows the judge to justify the lesser sentence negotiated by the prosecutor and the defense lawyer. The judge can "give a break" to the defendant for having cooperated.

The defendant who pleads not guilty or who otherwise gives an inappropriate performance may incur severe sanctions. In one study, Maureen Mileski observed that the judge's harsh manner in encounters was not related to the seriousness of the charge. Rather, a minor disruption in the courtroom or a show of disrespect for its personnel led to reprimands from the judge or to sentences that were more severe than usual. But she noted few cases in which the defendant's behavior was not according to form; only 5 percent elicited a harsh response from the judge. The vast majority conformed to the expectations of a routine bureaucratic encounter.[13]

## Felony Justice: The Impact of Courtroom Workgroups

The now classic research of James Eisenstein and Herbert Jacob on the felony disposition process in the courtrooms of Baltimore, Chicago, and Detroit offers important insights into the workgroup's influence on decisions in felony cases and provides comparative evidence showing differences in the criminal justice systems of three cities.[14] They found that the same type of felony case was handled very differently in each, yet the dispositions were remarkably similar for those defendants who reached the trial court. It was not the law, rules of procedure, or crime rate that produced the variation, but the structure of the courtroom workgroups, the influence of the sponsoring organizations, and the sociopolitical environment of each city.

As discussed in Chapter 9, many felony defendants never reach a trial court because their cases are dismissed or the charges against them are reduced to a misdemeanor at a preliminary hearing. Eisenstein and Jacob found that the preliminary hearings in the three cities had very different outcomes. In Chicago almost two-thirds of the cases presented were dismissed, whereas in Baltimore and Detroit about three-fifths and four-fifths, respectively, moved to the trial courtroom after probable cause was found. Although these differences are striking, they do not tell the entire story. Pretrial release determinations varied widely. About half of the Baltimore defendants remained in jail, compared with two-fifths in Chicago and Detroit. Baltimore released 21 percent on recognizance but levied high money bail for the remainder; practically no one was let out on recognizance in Chicago, but money bail was kept low; in Detroit, almost half were released on recognizance, and when money bail was required it was fairly low. Pretrial motions concerning the state's evidence were also treated variously. Since most Baltimore defendants went directly to a trial courtroom without a preliminary hearing, there was little opportunity to present pretrial motions to suppress evidence. The preliminary examination was conducted in an adversarial fashion in Detroit, less so in Chicago.

What influence did the courtroom workgroups have on these preliminary hearings? Eisenstein and Jacob found that the stable courtroom workgroups in Chicago developed informal procedures for screening cases. Because of the groups' close links to the trial courtrooms, they felt pressure to screen out many cases; hence the very high dismissal rate. In Detroit, also a city with stable workgroups, the prosecutors had already screened cases before they reached the courtroom; thus most of the defendants who appeared at preliminary hearings were sent to trial. Baltimore was characterized as having unstable workgroups, in part because members were frequently rotated and the sponsoring organizations exercised little supervisory control. As a result, fewer guilty pleas occurred and most defendants were forwarded to the grand jury and ultimately to the trial courts.[15]

Findings in regard to the trial court stage were similar. As shown in Table 10.1, the conviction rates of the cities were similar but the methods used to produce the dispositions differed substantially. It must be remembered, however, that Baltimore processed largely unscreened cases, whereas 40 percent of felony arrests in Detroit and 85 percent in Chicago had been dropped at the preliminary hearing. The data also show that each city arrived at the results differently. Detroit operated at a pace three times faster than that of Chicago and Baltimore. Chicago and Detroit relied primarily on guilty pleas, while Baltimore processed more cases through trials than through plea bargaining. But in all three cities the workgroups shunned the jury trial: fewer than 10 percent of the cases were disposed of in this manner.

Differential dispositions among the cities were reflections of, among other things, the organizational structure of the courtroom workgroups. How workgroups dealt with cases was also influenced by defendants' characteristics, the strength of the evidence, and the nature of the offense—factors that entered into the ongoing social system of the courtroom.

The disposition of felony cases results from the interaction of the courtroom members. The tasks that they perform require full participation, but they in turn are influenced by the policies of their sponsoring organizations. The degree to which the interdependence of these factors

| | Baltimore | Chicago | Detroit |
|---|---|---|---|
| Defendants whom court convicted sent to trial | 68.0% | 75.5% | 72.2% |
| Median number of days between grand jury indictment or information and trial courtroom disposition | 178 | 151.5 | 56 |
| Median number of days between arrest and trial courtroom disposition | 226 | 267.5 | 71.2 |
| Disposition methods | | | |
| Guilty pleas | 34.7% | 61.7% | 63.9% |
| Bench trials | 33.9% | 19.9% | 6.8% |
| Jury trials | 9.4% | 6.7% | 7.3% |
| Dismissals | 22.0% | 11.7% | 22.0% |
| | 100.0% | 100.0% | 100.0% |
| | (*N* = 549) | (*N* = 519) | (*N* = 1,208) |

**Table 10.1**
**Trial court dispositions of felony defendants in three cities**
With other factors being similar, the cities varied as to the method of case disposition. What might account for the lesser use of the guilty plea in Baltimore?

SOURCE: James Eisenstein and Herbert Jacob, *Felony Justice: An Organizational Analysis of Criminal Courts* (Boston: Little, Brown, 1977), 233. Copyright © 1977 by James Eisenstein and Herbert Jacob. Reprinted by permission of the authors.

affects the processes of felony justice varies between jurisdictions, over time in each jurisdiction, and from courtroom to courtroom. The stability of workgroup interactions can be upset by changes such as a new docket system, a shift by the public defender's office from a zone to a person-to-person strategy, or a decision by the prosecutor to institute policies where only cases expected to result in a conviction are brought to trial. When such shifts occur, new factors are brought to bear on the courtroom, and its members must adapt, with the result that an altered felony disposition configuration will evolve. But among the members of the courtroom workgroup it is the judge who is positioned to lead the group. Let us now look more closely at that position.

## To Be a Judge

Of the many actors in the criminal justice process, judges are perceived to hold the greatest amount of power. Their rulings and sentencing practices weigh heavily on the decisions of police, defense attorneys, and prosecutors. Although we tend to think of judges primarily in connection with trials, some of their work—signing warrants, fixing bail, arraigning defendants, accepting guilty pleas, scheduling cases—falls outside the formal trial process.

More than any other person in the system, the judge is expected to *embody* justice, thereby ensuring that the right to due process is respected and that the defendant is fairly treated. The black robe and gavel symbolize the impartiality we expect from our courts. The judge is supposed to act both in and outside the courthouse according to a well-defined role designed to prevent involvement in anything that could bring the judiciary into disrepute. (For a discussion of Italy's judiciary concerns, see the Comparative Perspective on pages 384–385.) Yet such are the pressures of today's justice system that the ideals of the judge's position have often been subordinated to the need to dispose of cases speedily.

The traditional image of the courtroom stresses the individuality, aloofness, and loneliness of the judge, sitting in robed splendor above the battle to control the actors before the bench. Courtroom activities are primarily concerned with fact finding, and judges function as lawgivers. They interpret legal precedents and apply them to the specific circumstances of the case. They are believed to be isolated from the social context of the courtroom participants and to base decisions on their own interpretation of the law after thoughtful consideration of the issues.

Lower court judges can exercise discretion in the disposition of summary offenses without the constant supervision of a higher court, and they have wide latitude in fixing sentences. Although judges are popularly portrayed as being forced to decide complex legal issues, in reality their courtroom tasks are routine. Because of the unending flow of cases, they operate with assembly-line precision; many judges, like many workers, soon tire of the repetition.

## Who Becomes a Judge?

In American society the position of judge, even if it is at the lowest level of the judicial hierarchy, has a significance that overshadows considerations of wealth. Public service, politics, and prestige in the community may be more important than dollars to the individuals who aspire to the judiciary. Compared to opportunities in the private practice of law, a seat on the bench may mean a significant drop in income for many attorneys.

Who, then, becomes a judge? One national survey of trial judges revealed that they were overwhelmingly white and male, were an average age of 53.4 years, and came from families connected to the local legal-political community. A majority (53.8 percent) had been in private legal practice; others had worked for government (many as prosecuting attorneys).[16] The average salaries for trial court judges of general jurisdiction range from about $62,000 in Indiana to $103,400 in Delaware; the national average is about $82,000.[17]

In many cities political factors dictate that judges be drawn from specific racial, religious, and ethnic groups. In Philadelphia, Paul Wice found that practically every judge he interviewed was either Jewish, Irish, or Italian.[18] Racial minorities, primarily African-American and Hispanic, are underrepresented on the bench. One study found only 1 percent of the nation's judges were black and half of that 1 percent were in six large cities.[19] When the racial and ethnic composition of the defendant population in urban courts is compared with the overwhelmingly white judiciary, it raises questions about the symbolic aspects of the allocation of justice.

In most cities, criminal court judges occupy the lowest rank in the judicial hierarchy. Lawyers and citizens alike fail to accord them the prestige that is part of the mystique usually surrounding members of the bench. Even their peers who hear civil cases may dismiss them. As in other professional relationships, the status of criminal trial judges may be linked to the status of the defendants. The judges are so close to the type of client they serve and they work under such unpleasant conditions that their reputation becomes tarnished and somewhat mundane, although they may retain some of the charisma of the judiciary. For many, the possibility of moving to civil or appellate courts sustains them while they deal with the heavy caseloads and tough working conditions of the criminal court.

The judge is expected to "embody justice," ensuring that the right to due process is respected and that the defendant is treated fairly.

## Erosion of Judicial Legitimacy in Italy

Independence and impartiality are cornerstones of the judicial role in Western cultures. Judges are expected to act in a professional manner, overcoming personal or political preferences in accordance with the requirement that decisions be made according to the law. Judges must act in ways that buttress their legitimacy so that citizens will accept judicial policies and decisions.

Judicial independence is usually secured through a system of separation of powers, but in the Italian case that works in only one direction. The judiciary is protected from the powers of other branches of government, but judges are allowed to hold posts in those agencies. Thus judges may also be employed full-time in the executive branch and in Parliament by taking temporary leave from their judicial tasks without losing either their place or seniority within the judiciary. About two hundred of the seven thousand magistrates are involved full-time in the activities of the legislative and executive branches of government, while ten times that number participate on a part-time basis. One result is a widely held perception that the agencies of government influence judicial decisions by playing on the ambitions and aspirations of the magistrates. Partisan politics are thought to have permeated the judicial ranks by the activities of its members; in fact, the National Magistrates Association is divided into three political factions pushing conservative, moderate, and leftist agendas. The press regularly makes innuendoes about political influences on judicial decisions by citing overzealous investigations of individuals later vindicated and investigations that are halted prematurely. Involvement of several judges in ... plotting a right-wing coup added to public skepticism of judicial impartiality.

Judicial objectivity was, until late 1989, complicated by the inquisitorial nature of the justice system, which placed both the judge

## Functions of the Judge

With so much public discussion about case backlogs in the criminal courts, you may be surprised to find the bench empty and the judge and staff absent if you visit a local courtroom. Where are the judges? What do they do? A study of the criminal courts in New York City revealed that, on the average, judges were on the bench only three hours and three minutes a day. Although this period is shorter than that prevailing in most

and the prosecutor on the same side of a criminal case. Sometimes these functions were merged into a single individual. Judges and prosecutors were jointly regarded as magistrates, shared the same training, were recruited in the same manner, were promoted by the same rules, and were able to shift from one position to another.

At the lowest level of the judiciary, the *perfectura*, where prison sentences of up to four years may be given, the same person served simultaneously as prosecutor and "impartial" third party. This role conflict was aggravated by the power of the prosecutor to direct the police, to manage the investigation, and even to initiate charges and arrests. The blurring of the prosecutor-judge was also found at higher court levels by participation of the judge in the pretrial phases of more than nine-tenths of all prosecutions that never come to trial.

Role confusion and work demands among Italian judges have also been heightened by the political terrorism and increased Mafia activity during the past two decades. These problems were perceived as threats to the state, which passed various internal security laws granting the police, prosecutors, and judges strong tools to deal with terrorism or the Mafia. Pretrial preventive detention of suspects for up to one year for each stage of the criminal process (a total of eight years for some crimes) was allowed. Use of *pentiti*, those who "repent" their crimes by implicating others (often after such inducements as cash, plastic surgery, and new identities), was authorized. Laws reinstated the fascist practice of allowing suspects to be interrogated without the presence of counsel and allowing electronic eavesdropping without prior approval of a judge.

The laws designed to counter political terrorism and Mafia activity pushed the Italian judges to use prosecution weapons that were inconsistent with notions of independence and objectivity. The role of judge became merged with that of the police and prosecution so that they were no longer impartial umpires. Some were so committed to the prosecution of terrorists and Mafioso that they became known as "assault judges," those who no longer separate politics and social issues from the law but try to make a name for themselves in the press by "attacking" the problem.

Use of these new laws [resulted in] a storm of protest among civil libertarians who criticized the unbridled discretion of judges, prosecutors, and the police. In November 1987, 80 percent of those casting ballots voted to remove the shield against civil liability of magistrates, a judicial protection found in most Western democracies. The Italian government then took additional actions to bolster the legitimacy of the judiciary. In 1988 it passed legislation for determining the civil liability of judges. These procedures allow courts to assess damages caused by the magistrate's alleged mistake. The state, not the jurist, pays the damages but the offending magistrate may be penalized through a reduction of annual salary.

More sweeping legislation was passed to replace the procedures of the civil code with those in line with American practices, labeled in the press "*Processo* Perry Mason." More in keeping with the adversarial system, the major elements of the new code separates prosecution from the arrest function, separates judicial from prosecutor functions, requires that investigations be completed in thirty days, shifts the burden of proof to the prosecution, and creates a new position of judge of first audience, who will determine, through an adversarial proceeding, if a prosecution should go forward. All of these procedures are designed to restore the independence, impartiality, and legitimacy of the Italian judiciary.

SOURCE: Adapted from Mary L. Volcansek, "The Judicial Role in Italy: Independence, Impartiality, and Legitimacy" *Judicature* 73 (April–May 1990): 322–327. Reprinted by permission of the author.

parts of the country, it does highlight questions about the work and function of the criminal court judge. If the judge is on the bench less than half a workday, then how does he or she spend the rest of it?

We tend to think that the judge's functions are primarily concerned with presiding at trials, but the work of most judges extends to all parts of the judicial process. Defendants see a judge whenever decisions about their future are being made: when bail is set, pretrial motions are made, pleas of guilty are accepted, a trial is conducted, a sentence is pronounced, and appeals are entered (see Figure 10.5). But in addition to responsibilities directly related to the processing of defendants, judges perform functions outside the courtroom that are related to the administration of the judicial system. Judges are adjudicators, negotiators, and administrators.

**Adjudicator** Judges must play a role of neutrality between the prosecution and the defense. They must apply the law to ensure that the rights of the accused are upheld as decisions are made concerning detention, plea, trial, and sentence. In discharging these responsibilities, judges are given a certain amount of discretion—for example, in setting the level of bail—but they must also conduct the proceedings according to law. Judges are the final arbiters of the law in the cases before them unless, on appeal, they are overruled by a higher court. If a nonjury trial is held, the judge not only rules on the issues of law but also decides issues of fact and ultimately determines the defendant's guilt or innocence. Judges may exercise discretion in the sentencing of convicted persons. In doing so, it is of great importance that they be fair and also give the appearance of fairness. They must avoid any conduct that may give the appearance or impression of being less than totally unbiased.

**Negotiator** Much of the criminal justice process is carried out through negotiation in the privacy of areas shielded from public view. Judges spend much of their time in their chambers talking with prosecutors and defense attorneys and often encourage the litigants to work out a guilty plea or to agree to conduct proceedings in a specific manner. In misde-

**Figure 10.5**
**Typical actions of a trial court judge in processing a felony case**
Throughout the entire process judges ensure that legal standards are upheld; they maintain courtroom decorum, protect rights of the accused, uphold speedy trial rules, and ensure proper maintenance of case records.

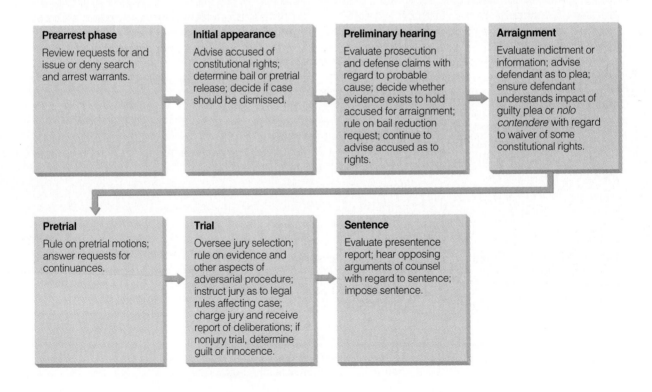

**Prearrest phase**
Review requests for and issue or deny search and arrest warrants.

**Initial appearance**
Advise accused of constitutional rights; determine bail or pretrial release; decide if case should be dismissed.

**Preliminary hearing**
Evaluate prosecution and defense claims with regard to probable cause; decide whether evidence exists to hold accused for arraignment; rule on bail reduction request; continue to advise accused as to rights.

**Arraignment**
Evaluate indictment or information; advise defendant as to plea; ensure defendant understands impact of guilty plea or *nolo contendere* with regard to waiver of some constitutional rights.

**Pretrial**
Rule on pretrial motions; answer requests for continuances.

**Trial**
Oversee jury selection; rule on evidence and other aspects of adversarial procedure; instruct jury as to legal rules affecting case; charge jury and receive report of deliberations; if nonjury trial, determine guilt or innocence.

**Sentence**
Evaluate presentence report; hear opposing arguments of counsel with regard to sentence; impose sentence.

Although we think of the judiciary primarily in terms of activities in the courtroom, much of a judge's work takes place in chambers and extends to the administration of the judicial system.

meanor courts, the remarks of the judge from the bench often take the form of advice to the disputants rather than formal points of law.

**Administrator**   A seldom-recognized function of most judges is the administration of the courthouse. In urban areas a professional court administrator may direct the personnel who are assigned to record keeping, case scheduling, and the many logistical operations that keep a system functioning. Even in cities, judges are responsible for the administration of their own courtroom and staff. In rural areas, the administrative responsibilities of judges may be more burdensome because professional court administrators are not usually employed. Therefore, budgeting, labor relations, and the maintenance of the physical plant may all come under a judge's supervision. As administrator, the judge is required to maintain contact with nonjudicial political actors such as county commissioners, legislators, and members of the state executive bureaucracy.

## How to Become a Judge

The quality of justice depends to a great extent on the quality of those who dispense it. As the American jurist Benjamin Cardozo once said, "in the long run, there is no guarantee of justice except the personality of the judge."[20] Because government has been given the power to deprive a citizen of his or her liberty and because society wants protection from wrongdoers, good judges are essential. Although the connection between these needs and the character and experience of those appointed to our highest courts has long been recognized, less interest has been focused on trial judges of the criminal courts. Yet it is in the lower courts where citizens most often have contact with the judiciary, and the public's impression of the criminal justice system is shaped to a great extent by the trial judge's behavior in the courtroom. When a judge is rude or inconsiderate or

## A Question of Ethics

Judge Harold Abrams of the Euclid District Court was angry. He had been sitting on the bench all Monday morning, arraigning, setting bail, and taking pleas from a steady stream of people who had been arrested over the weekend. Most of the people appearing before him were charged with offenses such as possession of a controlled substance, solicitation for prostitution, drunk and disorderly conduct—samples of the range of behaviors that had attracted police attention on Saturday night. He had seen many of the accused before, and a steady banter emanated from the bench as the judge took each case.

"So it's you again, Lucille. When are you girls going to learn that you can't walk up and down First Avenue? In that eight-inch skirt, you're a menace to traffic. We can't have every Tom, Dick, and Harry—and I mean mostly Dick—screwing his eyes on you and not on the road. Get what I mean?"

"But this time I was just going to the store to buy a loaf of bread."

"Sure. You mean you were walking to make some bread! In fact you don't do much walking, do you Lucille: you're mainly on your back! How do you plead?"

"Guilty, but I didn't do no soliciting."

"Fifty dollars and costs. Now, I suppose you'll be back on the Avenue to earn the fine. See you again Lucille."

Throughout this exchange the courtroom regulars grinned. You could really see quite a show in Judge Abrams's courtroom.

Is this the way justice should be allocated? Are Judge Abrams's banter and manner appropriate? What are the defendants learning about the administration of justice? Should the judge be removed from the bench?

allows the courtroom to become a noisy, crowded dispensary of rapid-fire justice, public confidence in the fairness and effectiveness of the criminal justice process is diminished. In A Question of Ethics, the behavior of Judge Abrams raises this issue.

All judges are addressed as "Your Honor," and we deferentially stand whenever they enter or leave the courtroom, yet too often they are chosen for reasons that have very little to do with either their legal qualifications or their judicial temperament. There is a strong reform movement to place men and women of quality on the bench. Reformers urge that judges be experts and believe that selection on a nonpolitical basis will produce higher quality, more efficient, more independent, and consequently more impartial and just members of the judiciary.

In opposition are those who argue that in a democracy the voters should elect the people charged with carrying out public policies, including judges. They contend that it is better to have a person on the trial court bench who can handle the steady stream of human problems confronting the judges of the nation.

**Methods of Selection**  Six methods are used to select state trial court judges: (1) gubernatorial selection, (2) legislative selection, (3) merit selection, (4) **nonpartisan election**, (5) **partisan election**, and (6) a hybrid of various methods. Table 10.2 shows the method used in each of the states. Throughout all the arguments in support of one method or another there is a persistent concern about the desired qualities in a judge and the assumption that the type of selection process will lead to a particular judicial style. On the one hand is the view that judges should be concerned only with the law; on the other, the view that they must feel the pulse of the people in order to render justice. Each selection method heightens opportunities for certain people and interests and diminishes them for others.

Selection by the electorate, as occurs in more than half the states, has long been part of this nation's tradition. One result is that judges must learn on the job after assuming office. This method seems to counter the notion that judges are especially trained to "find the law" and to exercise power in a manner worthy of Solomon—and is in direct contrast to Europe, where prospective judges are trained in law schools for careers as judges.

Campaigns for judgeships are generally low-key, low-visibility contests marked by little controversy: usually only a small portion of the

**nonpartisan election**
An election in which candidates who are not endorsed by political parties are presented to the voters for selection.

**partisan election**
An election in which candidates endorsed by political parties are presented to the voters for selection.

| Partisan Election | Nonpartisan Election | Gubernatorial Appointment | Legislative Election | Missouri Plan | Hybrid[a] |
|---|---|---|---|---|---|
| Alabama | Georgia | Delaware | South Carolina | Alaska | Arizona |
| Arkansas | Idaho | Maine | Virginia | Colorado | California |
| Illinois | Kentucky | Maryland | | Connecticut | Florida |
| Mississippi | Louisiana | Massachusetts | | Hawaii | Indiana |
| North Carolina | Michigan | New Hampshire | | Iowa | Kansas |
| Pennsylvania | Minnesota | New Jersey | | Nebraska | Missouri |
| Texas | Montana | | | New Mexico | New York |
| West Virginia | Nevada | | | Utah | Oklahoma |
| | North Dakota | | | Vermont | Rhode Island |
| | Ohio | | | Wyoming | South Dakota |
| | Oregon | | | | Tennessee |
| | Washington | | | | |
| | Wisconsin | | | | |

voters participate, judicial positions are not prominent on the ballot, candidates are constrained by ethical considerations from discussing issues, and public attention is centered on executive and legislative races. The situation was summarized well by Judge Samuel Rosenman of New York:

I learned at first hand what it meant for a judicial candidate to have to seek votes in political clubhouses, to ask for support of political district leaders, to receive financial contributions for his campaign from lawyers and others, and to make nonpolitical speeches about his own qualifications to audiences who could not care less—audiences who had little interest in any of the judicial candidates, of whom they had never heard, and whom they would never remember.[21]

Although popular election of judges may be an important part of our political heritage, these elections rarely capture the voters' notice.

In many cities judgeships provide much of the fuel for the party machine. Because of the honors and material rewards that may be gained from a place on the bench, parties are able to secure the energy and money of attorneys who seek a judgeship as the capstone of their career. In addition, a certain amount of courthouse patronage may be involved because clerks, bailiffs, and secretaries—all jobs that may be filled by active party workers—are appointed by the judge.

**Merit selection**, combining appointment and election, was first instituted in Missouri in 1940 and has now spread to other states. When a vacancy occurs, a nominating commission of citizens and attorneys for the empty bench sends the governor the names of three candidates from among whom the replacement is selected. After one year, a referendum is held to determine the judge's retention. The voter is asked, "Shall Judge X

**Table 10.2**

**Methods used by states for selection of trial judges**

States use different methods for the selection of judges. Many are initially appointed to fill a vacancy, however, thus having an advantage if they subsequently must run for election.

SOURCE: *The Book of the States, 1992–1993 Edition* (Lexington, Ky: Council of State Governments, 1992), 233–235.

[a]States using more than one method are classified as "Hybrid."

**merit selection**

A reform plan by which judges are nominated by a committee and appointed by the governor for a given period. When the term expires, the voters are asked to cast their approval or disapproval of the judge for a succeeding term. If the judge is disapproved, the committee nominates a successor for the governor's appointment.

remain in office?" With a majority vote, the judge serves out the term and can then come before the citizens on another ballot. Merit selection is designed to remove partisan politics from the judiciary and is also supposed to have the advantage of allowing the electorate to unseat judges. However, most judges selected under this procedure are in fact returned to the bench. Studies have shown that only a handful have been removed by the voters in merit selection states.[22]

Despite the impressive support of bar groups, merit selection has not gone unchallenged. It is said that although partisan politics may have been removed, it has merely been replaced by politics within the legal profession. Many lawyers regard it as a system favoring "blue bloods" (high-status attorneys with ties to corporations) to the detriment of the "little guy."[23]

**Results of Selection Methods**    What are the dynamics and consequences of using one selection method over another? Does each have class implications, as some believe, so that judges of only a certain social background reach the bench? Do some methods favor the choice of politically oriented judges as opposed to legally oriented judges? If each method has built-in biases, do these biases find their way into judges' decisions? Does one method favor judges who sentence lawbreakers more leniently and a different method favor judges who sentence lawbreakers more forcefully?

These questions have been hotly debated in the judicial reform and legal literature. It seems apparent that the selection method may influence the type of judge chosen. Some appointed judges would probably never have reached the bench if they had to win it through a partisan political campaign. Others who ran and won their election probably would not have been selected by a governor. In states where the legislature makes the decision the evidence shows that former legislators are preferred. But most research seems to indicate that although there is some difference in academic training and prior judicial experience among judges, these differences cannot be accounted for solely on the basis of the selection method.

The key point in this debate concerns the impact of selection methods on the actual behavior of judges. Here too the limited number of research studies are inconclusive. Martin Levin's early comparison of the criminal courts of Pittsburgh and Minneapolis is the major study of the relationship between selection methods and judicial decisions.[24] In Pittsburgh, judges were chosen through the highly politicized environment of a city controlled by the Democratic machine, which needs to maintain ethnic and religious balance even on a judicial ticket. Minneapolis has a system that is formally nonpartisan. The parties have almost no place in the selection of judges, but the bar association is influential. When vacancies occur, Minnesota governors have traditionally appointed judges according to the preference of the attorneys. From the Minneapolis system came judicial candidates who were usually members of large, business-oriented law firms and who had not been active in partisan politics. Levin believes that the differing selection methods and political settings of these two cities produced judges with opposing judicial philosophies and, as a result, contrasting sentencing decisions in the criminal courts. In general, Levin found that judges in Pittsburgh were more lenient than those in Minneapolis. Not only did white and black defendants receive more sentences of probation and shorter terms of incarceration in Pittsburgh, but also the pattern was maintained when the defendants' prior records, pleas, and ages were held constant.

The background of judges and the method of their selection seem to influence their decisions. An elimination process may operate, so that only certain types of persons who have had certain kinds of experiences are available for selection in each judicial system. But it would seem that any relationship between judges' backgrounds and their decisions is indirect. What is crucial is the variable of the city's political culture and its influence on judicial selection methods.

Trial court judges are central figures in every courthouse but even they must work within the local legal culture and the administrative demands of the criminal justice system. One of the major problems of American justice is court delay, a problem that we examine next.

## Delay in the Courts

One of the oldest concepts of the common law is that justice delayed is justice denied. In the United States a speedy trial is guaranteed by the Sixth Amendment to the Constitution, and the Supreme Court has characterized adherence to swift justice as an important safeguard to prevent undue incarceration before trial, to minimize anxiety accompanying public accusation, and to limit the possibilities that long delay will impair the abilities of accused persons to defend themselves.

Delay is usually described as an aberration and dysfunction of the system. Much of the research on delay has emphasized structural and resource problems associated with the organization of the courts. It has been suggested that the problems would go away if the numbers of judges and courtrooms were increased, if professional administrators were hired, and if sound management were instituted.

Studies by the National Center for State Courts question these assumptions.[25] When researchers examined the size, caseload, and management procedures of urban trial courts, they found major exceptions to the assumption that criminal cases are disposed of expeditiously only where there is a small volume of cases that are neither serious nor complex. As shown in Table 10.3, the researchers uncovered very little relationship between processing time and the number of felony filings per judge. The data show that the courts with the largest caseloads are not those with the slowest disposition times and that the comparatively underworked courts are not speedier.

The Pittsburgh court handles more cases per judge and is slower than the small-volume courts in Sacramento and Salinas; the Cleveland court is substantially slower than might be expected for its size; and the large

Detroit court processes criminal cases at a faster pace than others like it. The courts of Jersey City are not particularly distinguished by the numbers of their filings, or judges, yet they are the slowest of those examined.

Why, then, do some courts process cases much more quickly than others? The answer appears to concern the local legal culture and the social organization of the criminal justice system, not the formal, structural elements of courts. The participants become adapted to a certain pace of litigation, and these expectations are translated into others regarding how cases should proceed. What is viewed as the normal speed for the disposition of criminal cases in one system may be viewed as undue haste in another. As this book has emphasized, decisions are made in the context of an organization in which discretion is widely exercised. As the Close-Up on page 394 underscores, local norms, role relationships, and the incentives of the major actors determine the manner in which cases are processed. Unless the defendant is being held without bail while awaiting trial, there is little incentive for speed. In fact, as we will see, the defense may request a continuance—a postponement—to delay the making of key decisions, hoping that with time the outcome will benefit the accused.

## Continuances: Accommodations in the System

**continuance**
An adjournment of a scheduled case until a future date.

The **continuance** is a prime example of the type of accommodation that causes delay.[26] From a legal standpoint, the judge has the discretion to grant continuances so that the defense will have an opportunity to prepare its case. The need for time to obtain counsel, to prepare pretrial motions, to obtain evidence, or to find a witness can be used as a reason for postponement. The prosecution can also request continuances. Although they are less likely to have a request granted than the defense, especially if the defendant is being held for trial, prosecutors do receive a significant number of continuances in most courts.

Continuances have the effect of decreasing the number of guilty dispositions as the number of court appearances increases. Defendants are able to delay a trial in order to wear out witnesses, remain out on bail as long as possible, or wait for community interest to diminish. Even those defendants in pretrial detention may prefer a further stay in jail over a case decided quickly.[27]

## Rules for Speedy Trials

Congress and several states have tackled the problem of delay by enacting rules for speedy trials. These rules typically require that cases be moved from arrest to trial within certain strict time limits, and they provide for the dismissal of charges if the case is not brought to trial within the time specified. In 1974 Congress passed the Federal Speedy Trial Act that sets the maximum period from arrest to indictment at thirty days and from indictment to trial at seventy days. Cases that do not meet these requirements may be dismissed either with or without the option of rein-

| Jurisdiction | Number of FTE[a] Judges | Filings Per FTE Judge | Median Processing Time (Days) |
|---|---|---|---|
| Salinas, Calif. | 3.40 | 383 | 62 |
| Dayton, Ohio | 4.00 | 555 | 56 |
| St. Paul, Minn. | 5.00 | 495 | 77 |
| Jersey City, N.J. | 6.63 | 360 | 198 |
| Pittsburgh, Pa. | 7.00 | 843 | 153 |
| Sacramento, Calif. | 11.00 | 331 | 165 |
| Cleveland, Ohio | 16.50 | 574 | 135 |
| Detroit, Mich. | 34.00 | 480 | 71 |

**Table 10.3**
**Court structure and case delay**

As the data show, there is little relationship among the number of judges, the case filings per judge, and processing time. If these are not the variables that explain delay, what might be at work?

SOURCE: John Goerdt, et al., *Reexamining the Pace of Litigation in Thirty-nine Urban Trial Courts* (Williamsburg, Va.: National Center for State Courts, 1991), table 2.2, 2.5.

[a]FTE = Full-time equivalent.

statement of the charges, but it is expected that charges will not be reinstated without good reason. Although defendants may waive their right to a speedy trial under the rules, the prosecution can get an extension of the limits only if the "ends of justice" will thus be served or if there is a "judicial emergency."[28]

In assessing the results of the Speedy Trial Act, Malcolm Feeley found that it has not been taken seriously by most federal judges.[29] The legislation has had some indirect effects, however: the planning process has spurred administrative modernization of the courts, and procedures have been tightened in the interest of improved allocation of resources. The backlog of civil cases has grown as the courts have worked to bring criminal cases to trial before the charges have to be dismissed. In many courts it appears that only the formal requirements of the act have been met and that the problem of delay remains because the "ends of justice" exception is used extensively.

## Assessing Delay

Delay benefits not only defendants seeking lenient treatment but also defense attorneys, prosecutors, and judges. It helps attorneys maximize their fees, please their clients, and enhance their reputations for skill. Although a move to delay a case is usually initiated by the defense attorney, it cannot succeed without the cooperation of the prosecutor and judge. Prosecutors presumably understand the need to reach accommodations that will result in a bargained plea. Judges also realize that postponement usually helps prevent a full-length trial that would tie up the courtroom for an extended period. But the prosecutor and judge recognize that by assisting the defense attorney, they ensure the attorney's cooperation in turn.

Although formal changes have been proposed to reduce delay in the criminal courts, such changes will not be successful unless it is recognized that courtroom actors have individual and multiple goals. The personal needs of the defense attorney, prosecutor, and judge have been shown to be stronger than the broader goal of processing offenders quickly. Thus

## Making Things Happen: The Genius of Judge Harold Rothwax

Seated behind an elevated desk in the high-ceilinged courtroom, Judge Harold Rothwax does not look at all pleased. His broad face, an appealing face with something of the lumpy quality of an old prizefighter, is set and pale, and his head is pulled down between his shoulders. The two lawyers before him—a young assistant district attorney clutching a confusion of documents and a defense counsel whose brown toupee gleams in contrast to his own dull sideburns—place their hands on the massive desk and seem to brace themselves against his next words. A few spectators stare from the highbacked wooden benches, and in the well of the court the clerks and uniformed officers are still.

At a table perhaps twenty feet from the judge and behind the lawyers, the defendant stands waiting. He is a handsome white man in his early thirties, and his face above the light turtleneck projects a kind of distaste, as if his straight nose were picking up bad odors at this tawdry proceeding. But he has been in such surroundings many times before. As his record attests, he is a specialist in burglarizing the rooms of first-class hotels, and he often carries a gun to impress anyone unfortunate enough to discover him. He is, in short, a dangerous thief whose devotion to his work led most recently to his capture on one job while he was out on bail after another. He uses different names for different occasions, and he is in bad trouble this morning.

"Tell the defendant," says Judge Rothwax to the defense attorney, in a voice that cannot be heard beyond his desk, "that this is the last day for three and a half to seven. After this, it goes up. If he's going to take the offer, he has to decide now. If he doesn't take it, he's going to trial. We've had enough of this delay. Either he takes the plea, or we set a trial date *today*."

The lawyer looks at the judge for a moment without speaking and then turns and walks back to his client. It is clear that Rothwax is not going to tolerate further stalling. The defendant either must plead guilty to the reduced burglary charge offered by the district attorney—for which Rothwax had earlier indicated he would hand down a sentence of no more than three-and-a-half to seven years in prison—or must prepare to go to trial. Then if a jury convicts him on the original charge (and the prosecution's case seems very good), the trial judge will surely give him a much heavier sentence. And if the defendant wants to delay now and enter plea later, to avoid trial, the bargain offered today will be unavailable. This is the hard moment of truth in the plea-bargaining process for the handsome burglar, and his face, empty now of any disdain, is taut and angry. He speaks in a rapid whisper to his attorney, stares at Rothwax, shrugs and whispers to his lawyer again.

The lawyer comes back to the bench. "This guy is crazy," he says to Rothwax. "We'll go to trial."

"All right, gentlemen," the judge says briskly. "Let's settle on a date certain for trial."

"Judge, I'd like to be relieved of this case," says the defense lawyer. "This guy won't listen."

Rothwax shakes his head. "No," he replies. "You're the fourth lawyer he's had. That's enough. Let's pick a trial date." It is clear that there is no more room for discussion on this matter. A day two weeks later is selected. The defendant is taken out of the courtroom and back into detention. His case, of course, may still never go to trial, but it has been brought one step closer, largely because of pressure brought by Judge Rothwax. The calendar proceeds.

SOURCE: Loudon Wainwright, "Making Things Happen: The Genius of Judge Harold Rothwax," *Saturday Review*, 10 June 1978. Copyright © 1978 by *Saturday Review*. All rights reserved. Reprinted by permission.

system goals cannot be expected to dominate the criminal court until incentives are provided that are more rewarding to the actors than the fulfillment of their current needs.

The United States has a dual court system with separate federal and state courts. Most criminal justice cases are heard in state and local courts. Because of the decentralized nature of the judicial system, the trial courts operate under the state penal code but are staffed, managed, and financed by country or city government.

# Summary

Throughout this century reformers have attempted to change the structure of the state trial courts. These efforts have sought to consolidate the structure of the courts, centralize administrative authority, fund the courts by state government, and create a separate personnel system. Research, however, has shown that those states which have adopted these reforms are not necessarily better managed than unreformed states.

Research has emphasized that courtroom operations can be best explained by the concept of the workgroup. Although norms and goals are shared, each member of the courtroom group—judge, prosecutor, defense attorney, defendant, bailiff, and clerk—occupies a specialized position and is expected to fit into the socially accepted definition of that status. The cohesion of the workgroup is enhanced by the physical setting and by the delineation of roles. Exchange relationships characterize the interactions of the workgroup members in the processing of cases.

The judge is the most important figure in the criminal court. Decisions of the police, defense attorneys, and prosecutors are greatly affected by judicial rulings and sentencing practices. In more than half the states, judges are popularly elected, which usually means that candidates must be active in politics and are often nominated for a judgeship as a reward for party work. In other states judges are either appointed by the governor or legislature or selected by merit. Each method has its advocates, but the key issue concerns the decisions made by the judges once they are seated.

Delay is a major problem of the court, and it results from conflict between the goals of the system and the individual needs of the members of the courtroom team. Delay is often used to the advantage of the defense in order to lighten the expected sanction. Even in light of judicial requirements of a speedy trial, defense attorneys often request continuances so as to prolong the proceedings.

# Questions for Review

1   What is the courtroom workgroup? What is necessary for its formation?

2   Discuss the effects that partisan election of judges may have on the administration of justice. Which system of judicial selection do you think is most appropriate? Explain your reasons.

3   The judge plays several roles. What are they? In your opinion, do any of them conflict?

4   If you are being prosecuted on a drug charge, what tactics might your attorney use to get you a light sentence? How would these tactics influence court operations?

## Key Terms

appellate court

continuance

grouping

jurisdiction

local legal culture

merit selection

nonpartisan election

partisan election

trial court of general
jurisdiction

trial court of limited
jurisdiction

workgroup

## For Further Reading

Blumberg, Abraham S. *Criminal Justice*. Chicago: Quadrangle Books, 1967. A classic examination of the criminal courts as organizations.

Eisenstein, James, Roy Flemming, and Peter Nardulli. *The Contours of Justice: Communities and Their Courts*. Boston: Little, Brown, 1988. A study of nine felony courts in three states. Emphasizes the impact of the local legal culture on court operations.

Eisenstein, James, and Herbert Jacob. *Felony Justice: An Organizational Analysis of Criminal Courts*. Boston: Little, Brown, 1977. Felony courts in three cities. Develops the concept of the courtroom workgroup and its impact on decision making.

Feeley, Malcolm M. *Court Reform on Trial*. New York: Basic Books, 1983. Study of court reform efforts such as diversion, speedy trial, bail reform, and sentencing reform. Notes the difficulties of bringing about change.

Satter, Robert. *Doing Justice: A Trial Judge at Work*. (New York: Simon and Schuster, 1990). A judge's view of the cases that he faces daily and the factors that influence his decisions.

## Notes

1 Joy A. Chapper and Roger A. Hanson, *Intermediate Appellate Courts: Improving Case Processing* (Williamsburg, Va.: National Center for State Courts, 1990).

2 John H. Wigmore, "Roscoe Pound's St. Paul Address of 1906," *Journal of the American Judicature Society* 20 (1937): 136.

3 Marcia Lim, "A Status Report on State Court Financing," *State Court Journal* 11 (Summer 1987): 7.

4 James Eisenstein, Roy B. Flemming, and Peter F. Nardulli, *The Contours of Justice: Communities and Their Courts* (Boston: Little, Brown, 1988), 12.

5 Thomas W. Church, Jr., "Examining Local Legal Culture," *American Bar Foundation Research Journal* (Summer 1985): 449.

6 Eisenstein, Flemming, and Nardulli, *Contours of Justice*, 300.

7 Ibid., 261.

8 As cited in Eisenstein, Flemming, and Nardulli, *Contours of Justice*, 263.

9   A. Paul Hare, *Handbook of Small Group Research* (New York: Free Press, 1962), 9–10.

10  Edward J. Clynch and David W. Neubauer, "Trial Courts as Organizations," *Law and Policy Quarterly* 3 (1981): 59–94.

11  James Eisenstein and Herbert Jacob, *Felony Justice: An Organizational Analysis of Criminal Courts* (Boston: Little, Brown, 1977), 43.

12  Erving Goffman, *Asylums* (Garden City, N.J.: Doubleday, 1961), 169.

13  Maureen Mileski, "Courtroom Encounters," *Law and Society Review* 5 (1971): 524.

14  Eisenstein and Jacob, *Felony Justice*, 19–39.

15  Ibid.

16  John Paul Ryan, Allan Ashman, Bruce D. Sales, and Sandra Shane-DuBow, *American Trial Judges* (New York: Free Press, 1980), 182.

17  National Center for State Courts, *Survey of Judicial Salaries*, vol. 19 (January 1993).

18  Paul B. Wice, *Chaos in the Courthouse* (New York: Praeger, 1985), 96.

19  Ibid., 96.

20  Benjamin N. Cardozo, *The Nature of the Judicial Process* (New Haven, Conn.: Yale University Press, 1921), 149.

21  Samuel I. Rosenman, "A Better Way to Select Judges," *Journal of the American Judicature Society* 48 (1964): 86.

22  Lawrence Baum, "The Electoral Fates of Incumbent Judges in the Ohio Court of Common Pleas," *Judicature* 66 (1983): 420; William K. Hall and Larry T. Aspin, "What Twenty Years of Judicial Retention Elections Have Told Us," *Judicature* 70 (April–May 1987): 340.

23  Richard A. Watson and Ronald G. Downing, *The Politics of the Bench and the Bar: Judicial Selection under the Missouri Nonpartisan Court* Plan (New York: John Wiley, 1969).

24  Martin A. Levin, "Urban Politics and Policy Outcomes: The Criminal Courts," in *Criminal Justice: Law and Politics*, 5th ed., ed. George F. Cole (Pacific Grove, Calif.: Brooks/Cole, 1988), 330.

25  Thomas Church, Jr., Alan Carlson, Jo-Lynn Lee, and Teresa Tan, *Justice Delayed* (Williamsburg, Va.: National Center for State Courts, 1978); Barry Mahoney et al., *Implementing Delay Reduction and Delay Prevention Programs in Urban Trial Courts* (Williamsburg, Va.: National Center for State Courts, 1985).

26  "Too Many Continuances Number One Factor in Court Delay, Survey Finds," *Criminal Justice Newsletter*, 15 November 1988, 1.

27  Martin A. Levin, "Delay in Five Criminal Courts," *Journal of Legal Studies* 4 (1975): 83.

28  18 U.S.C. 3166. For an evaluation of the impact of this law see Joel Garner, "Delay Reduction in the Federal Courts: Rule 50(b) and the Federal Speedy Trial Act of 1974," *Journal of Quantitative Criminology* 3 (1987): 229–250.

29  Malcolm M. Feeley, *Court Reform on Trial* (New York: Basic Books, 1983), 173.

# Trial and Posttrial Processes

From the time Robert Chambers was indicted by a New York City grand jury on murder charges for the death of Jennifer Levin, until he plea-bargained as the jury deliberated his fate, the national media provided almost continuous attention to the activities surrounding the case. All the elements for a gripping drama were there in what became known as "The Preppie Murder Case." It had Robert Chambers and Jennifer Levin, two privileged young people; their preppie friends and the milieu of Manhattan's nightclubs, money, drugs, alcohol, and sex; and the defendant's claim that he had accidentally killed the victim during an incident of "rough sex" when he tried to stop Jennifer from squeezing his genitals. With the *New York Post* and the *Daily News* headlines screaming "Jenny Killed in Wild Sex" and "Sex Got Rough," the public was ready for the story to be played out in the courtroom.

At Chamber's trial Assistant District Attorney Linda Fairstein, chief of Manhattan's Sex Crimes Unit, entered into evidence blowups of the photographs of Jennifer's face and body as she lay dead in Central Park.

Robert's attorney, Jack Litman, objected to the use of the photos with their depiction of the gory details of the victim's death. When the judge allowed use of the photos, Litman shifted his tactics to emphasize Jennifer's promiscuity. When the prosecution entered a videotape of Robert's confession, Litman felt that the defendant came across to the jurors as a frightened, candid teenager, an impression that some felt rang true.

After a trial that lasted nearly three months, the jury took the case to determine the fate of Robert Chambers. On the ninth day of their deliberations—longer than any other case for a single defendant in New York's history—the tensions among the jurors became apparent not only to the media but also to the judge. With the possibility of a mistrial looming, the attorneys met with the judge in his chambers and began to work out the details of a plea bargain.

Late in the day Robert Chambers faced the judge and changed his plea to a reduced charge of guilty of first-degree manslaughter. The charge carried a sentence of five to fifteen years versus the possibility of life imprisonment for the charge of murder. As required, and to ensure that Chambers understood the plea, the judge questioned him. In response, Chambers initially said that he did not mean to hurt Jennifer. Assistant District Attorney Fairstein demanded that the question be phrased more directly. The judge asked, "Mr. Chambers, is it true that on August 26, 1986, you intended to cause serious physical injury to Jennifer Levin and thereby caused the death of Jennifer Levin?" Chambers answered, "Yes, Your Honor," yet he shook his head and his body language said no.[1]

Like other famous trials of the past—such as those of Bruno Hauptmann, kidnapper of the Lindbergh baby, Leopold and Loeb, teenagers indicted for the "thrill" murder of young Bobbie Franks, and Claus von Bulow, Danish-born socialite tried for the murder of his heiress wife with insulin injections—the trial of Robert Chambers contained all the ingredients of soap opera, and the public was eager for every tantalizing tidbit. The case is the type that occupies the top layer of Walker's criminal justice wedding cake—those celebrated cases that go to trial and command great public attention. Meanwhile, judges hand out hundreds of sentences to less publicized defendants whose crimes are perhaps no less heinous but who do not receive the trial by judge and jury guaranteed by the Bill of Rights. As we have seen, the vast majority of defendants plead guilty or are judged in a bench trial without jury. The number of full jury trials is small compared to the total number of cases processed by the judicial system. But the criminal trial and posttrial processes are important in communicating to the public the values and rules by which society lives.

## Questions for Inquiry

- What are the various stages of a criminal trial? How are juries chosen?
- What influences are brought to bear on judges as they determine a sentence?
- What is the basis for an appeal of a conviction?

## Trial: The Exceptional Case

According to the assumptions underlying the adversarial system, a trial by **jury** is a search for the truth. In reality, however, many other values, some of them in conflict, combine in a jury trial. The search must be conducted within the framework of the constitutionally guaranteed protections accorded the defendant. Thus the quest for truth must step aside when it conflicts with the individual's rights, which prohibit self-incrimination, unlawful searches and seizures, and other abuses of governmental authority. A trial by a jury composed of members of the community is one of the greatest safeguards against arbitrary and unlawful actions by criminal justice officials.

A trial is also a contest, a symbolic combat between the prosecution and the defense in which one party normally emerges the winner. The spirit of rivalry permeates the proceedings, and the determination to win may override the search for the truth.

Because trials are conducted in public, they are also a kind of stylized drama. As Steven Phillips has said, the trial

When the public thinks of defense attorneys, the image is often of such prominent lawyers as Melvin Belli, whose flamboyant tactics make national headlines. Most private defense attorneys show few of these colorful characteristics.

is also politics, in both the noblest and the basest senses of the word. A criminal trial is an almost primordial confrontation between the individual and society. At stake are values no less important than individual liberty on the one hand, and the need for social order on the other. It is also pragmatic, grass-roots clubhouse politics in its rawest form. Trial by jury is publicity, the news media, and the making and unmaking of reputations. Many a political career has begun or ended in a criminal courtroom.[2]

Who goes to trial? What are the characteristics of defendants who demand and receive the constitutionally stipulated trial by jury? Because data have not yet been accumulated to answer these questions, we must respond broadly that trials result when other forms of disposition (dismissal, diversion, plea negotiation) fail or are not sought. Often a dispute over the facts of a case is so irreconcilable that either the prosecutor or the defense attorney seeks a trial. The fact-finding function of the jury trial serves to resolve such a dispute. The defendant's prior record may also influence the state's decision to go to trial. If the evidence against a repeat offender is weak, the prosecutor may prefer to risk having a jury find the accused innocent rather than to strike a bargain that would yield only a minimal sanction. The state may lose the trial but still convey to the defendant the message that "we are after you."

**jury**
A panel consisting of a statutorily defined number of citizens selected according to law and sworn to determine matters of fact in a criminal action and to render a verdict of guilty or not guilty.

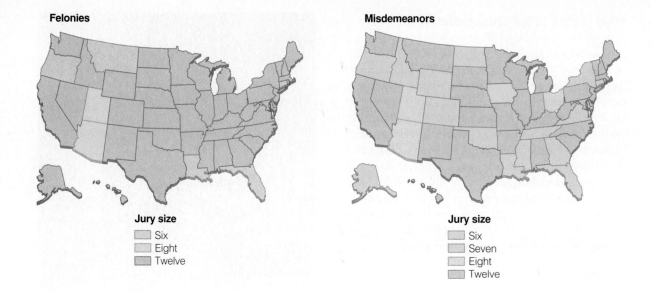

**Felonies**

**Misdemeanors**

Jury size
- Six
- Eight
- Twelve

Jury size
- Six
- Seven
- Eight
- Twelve

**Figure 11.1**

**Jury size for felony and misdemeanor trials**

All states require twelve-member juries in capital cases; six states permit juries of fewer than twelve members in felony cases. Does the smaller number of people on a jury have advantages or disadvantages? Would you rather have your case decided by a twelve- or six-person jury?

SOURCE: U.S. Department of Justice, Bureau of Justice Statistics, *Report to the Nation on Crime and Justice*, 2d ed. (Washington, D.C.: Government Printing Office, 1988), 86.

*Williams* v. *Florida* (1970)
Juries of fewer than twelve members are constitutional.

The seriousness of the charge is probably the most important factor influencing the decision to go to trial. A trial is rarely demanded by defendants charged with property crimes. Murder, armed robbery, or drug sales, all of which bring long prison terms, are more likely to require judge and jury. When the penalty is harsh, many defendants seem willing to take the risk inherent in a trial.

Since the adversarial process is designed to get to the truth, the rules of criminal law, procedure, and evidence govern the conduct of the trial. Trials are based on the idea that the prosecution and defense will compete before a judge and jury so that the truth will emerge. Above the battle, the judge sees to it that the rules are followed and that the jury impartially evaluates the evidence and reflects the community's interest. The jury is the sole evaluator of the facts in a case.

Eighty percent of all jury trials worldwide take place in the United States.[3] Among the legal systems of the world, it is only in common law countries such as Great Britain, Canada, Australia, and the United States that a group of laypersons determines guilt or innocence. In civil law countries, this function is usually performed by a judge or judges, often assisted by two or three lay assessors.

In the United States, a jury in a criminal trial is traditionally constituted of twelve citizens, but some states now allow as few as six. This reform was recommended to modernize court procedures and reduce expenses. It was upheld by the Supreme Court in **Williams v. Florida** (1970) and has been extended nationally, although twelve-person juries still are required in cases for which the sentence could be capital punishment.[4] In *Burch* v. *Louisiana* (1979), the Supreme Court ruled that in juries of six a unanimous vote for conviction is required, but with larger juries a majority verdict is enough for conviction.[5] (See Figure 11.1.) The change to six-person juries has its critics, who charge that the smaller group is less representative of the conflicting views in the community and too quick to bring in a verdict.

The right to trial by jury is ingrained in American ideology—it is mentioned in the Declaration of Independence, three amendments to the Constitution, and countless opinions of the Supreme Court. Yet only about 8 percent of criminal cases are decided by trial and fewer than half of all trials are conducted before a jury. Even so, jury trials have a decided impact on decisions made throughout the criminal justice system. The anticipated reactions of juries play a major role in plea bargaining, and even at the point of arrest, the question "Would a jury convict?" enters the decisional thinking of police officers. The decision to prosecute and the sentencing behavior of judges are influenced by the potential call for a jury.

Juries perform six vital functions in the criminal justice system:

1  Prevent government oppression by safeguarding citizens against arbitrary law enforcement.

2  Determine the guilt or innocence of the accused on the basis of the evidence presented.

3  Represent diverse community interests so that no one set of values or biases dominants decision making.

4  Serves as a buffer between the accused and the accuser.

5  Educates citizens selected for jury duty about the criminal justice system.

6  Symbolizes the rule of law and the community foundation that supports the criminal justice system.

Apart from legal stipulations, the choice of trial by jury is left to the accused, and the option becomes a major strategy of the defense. If the accused waives the right to trial by jury (in some states the prosecutor must agree), the case is decided by the judge, who serves as finder of fact and determines issues of law. Such trials are called **bench trials**. Nationally about 40 percent of felonies are decided by judges alone. As might be expected, the more serious the charge, the greater the likelihood of a case going to trial (see Table 11.1). But note the variation among the cities listed. What reasons might be given for these differences?

The decision to avoid a jury trial by having the case resolved solely by the bench varies considerably according to the offense and to regional customs. A principal consideration is whether a jury will believe the defendant's story. In addition, attorneys must estimate whether a harsher penalty will be incurred if a guilty verdict is returned by a jury rather than handed down by a judge.

**bench trial**
Trial conducted by a judge who acts as fact finder and determines issues of law. No jury participates.

**Table 11.1**
**Percent of indicted cases that went to trial, by offense**

There are differences in the percentage of cases that went to trial both by offense and by jurisdiction. It would seem that the stiffer the possible penalty, the greater the likelihood of a trial.

SOURCE: Adapted from U.S. Department of Justice, Bureau of Justice Statistics, *Report to the Nation on Crime and Justice*, 2d ed. (Washington, D.C.: Government Printing Office, 1988), 84.

| Jurisdiction | Homicide | Sexual Assault | Robbery | Larceny | Drug Offenses |
|---|---|---|---|---|---|
| Indianapolis, Ind. | 38% | 18% | 21% | 12% | 9% |
| Los Angeles, Calif. | 29 | 20 | 12 | 5 | 7 |
| Louisville, Ky. | 57 | 27 | 18 | 10 | 11 |
| New Orleans, La. | 22 | 18 | 16 | 7 | 7 |
| St. Louis, Mo. | 36 | 23 | 15 | 6 | 6 |
| San Diego, Calif. | 37 | 2 | 12 | 5 | 3 |
| Washington, D.C. | 43 | 32 | 22 | 12 | 10 |

## Trial Process

Although variations are found among the states, the trial process generally follows eight steps: (1) selection of the jury, (2) opening statements by prosecution and defense, (3) presentation of the prosecution's evidence and witnesses, (4) presentation of the defense's evidence and witnesses, (5) presentation of rebuttal witnesses, (6) closing arguments by each side, (7) instruction of the jury by the judge, and (8) decision by the jury. Although the proportion of trials may be small, it is essential to understand each step in the process and consider the broader societal impact of this institution. You may want to contrast trial processes in the United States with those in Russia as outlined in the Comparative Perspective on the following pages.

**Figure 11.2**
**Jury selection process, twelve-member jury**

Potential jurors are drawn at random from a source list. From this pool a panel is selected and presented for duty. The voir dire examination may remove some, while others will be seated.

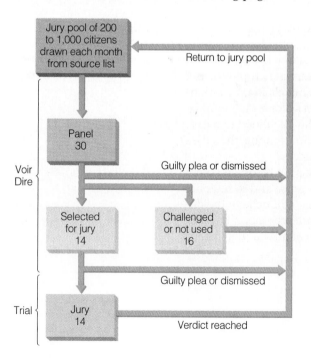

**Jury Selection**   Although history shows that juries were used in ancient Greece, the use of disinterested citizens to try the facts of a case is relatively new in Anglo-American law. Early English juries were composed of those most knowledgeable of and, on occasion, even those involved in a dispute. The idea that juries should comprise a cross section of the community evolved later.

A critical function of the jury is to represent diverse community interests. Even so, until the mid-twentieth century there were many states where women and members of minority groups were legally denied membership on juries. Yet a cross section of the community is necessary to ensure a counterbalancing of biases in order to minimize those who might convict on inadequate evidence. Unfortunately, the reality of jury selection processes often means that a cross section of the community is not in-

cluded and that class and racial bias influences decision making within the jury room. Furthermore, as demonstrated in the Question of Ethics on page 411, citizen enthusiasm for participation in the justice system can affect jury composition.

*Creation of the Pool*   Theoretically, every citizen of the community should have an equal chance of being chosen for jury duty in accordance with the process shown in Figure 11.2; but various stipulated qualifications have the effect of keeping certain citizens out of the jury pool. In most states, jurors are drawn from the list of registered voters, but research has shown that nonwhites, the poor, and the young register to vote at substantially lower rates than the remainder of the population. In addition, the Bureau of the Census has reported that only about 70 percent of those eligible actually register to vote and that in some areas the rate is as low as 40 percent. Over the past decade, the proportion of registered voters has continued to decrease. How can this issue be addressed?

Researchers agree that jury unrepresentativeness can best be attacked by the use of a comprehensive list from which citizens are randomly selected for duty.[6] Supplementary pools of citizens—for instance, licensed drivers, utility customers, taxpayers—would bring new names to the roster. Ideally, a cross section of the community could be found if the jury were randomly and scientifically selected from an up-to-date list of all adult citizens.

During jury selection, attorneys for each side may question prospective jurors to determine whether they are biased in ways that would make them incapable of rendering a fair verdict.

## A Murder Trial in Moscow

*Author's note: Although written in 1987 before the breakup of the Soviet Union, there has been little change in the essential elements of a criminal trial in Russia of the 1990s.*

Soviet justice: For Judge Natalia Nikolaevna Orlova, it was a stern and righteous concept. And here, in the People's Court of Moscow's Moskvaretskii district, she meted it out firmly and with unwavering faith....

[Defense Advocate Silva Abramovna Dubrovskaia] faced the usual order of things today. A judicial troika. And no jury. To begin with, there was Orlova.... She was flanked by two civilian jurists called *lay assessors*. The assessors, both women, were untrained in the law and served on the bench as representatives of local unions, shops, and factories. Although the assessors ostensibly were Orlova's equals, and judgments required a 2 to 1 majority vote, Silva knew that Orlova would call the shots. Her vote was the one that counted.

Silva faced another adversary.... Larisa Valentinovna Tolmachova was her name, and she was the prosecutor, or *prokuror*, who would try this case on behalf of the Soviet state.

Like other People's Judges,... Judge Orlova held broad procedural sway over the course and outcome of the trials that unfolded before her.... But Orlova's mandate extended even further. She was, in effect, the grand inquisitor of the courtroom proceedings. It was her job to pry facts from both friendly and hostile witnesses. The lawyers had their roles, to be sure,... But this was Orlova's show, and all others lined up behind her....

"Defendant! Please rise!" Orlova said. A man stood and faced the bench. He was young and quiet looking, with straight, sandy brown hair that swept in a wave over his forehead. He appeared tense and very much alone, lost in the unfamiliar territory of the dock....

All Soviet trials begin with a reading of [a report summarizing the state's case against the accused]. Orlova took the report and, somewhat wearily, began the tedious business of reading it aloud.

She began with an overview. On Saturday, August 22, 1987, at approximately 5:00 P.M. in a public square near Zhukov Way, house number 23, in central Moscow, A. I. Borzov, "who was in an inebriated condition," engaged one Evegenii I. Mosin in a brawl.... Borzov, she said, hit Mosin in the face at least five times with his fist. Borzov then threw a beer bottle as Mosin was backing away. The bottle landed, "in the vicinity of Mosin's forehead." After that Borzov went up to Mosin and "again gave him a fist to the face." Borzov then fled. "As a result of these blows, Borzov inflicted grave bodily injuries causing the victim's death."... If convicted, Borzov faced five to twelve years in a Soviet labor colony.

Orlova then read ... depositions that Borzov and others (the key eyewitnesses to the affair) had given to police during the pretrial investigation. According to Borzov,... [he] was minding his own business, passing the time with some drink and conversation. Sure, he and a neighbor, V. A. Ryzhkin, had downed a few vodkas.... That was the way it was until some man, a stranger named Mordvinov, came up to them. The comrade had booze on his breath and cuts on his face.... Mordvinov explained that he'd been in a fight with some relatives. Borzov offered him a beer. A short time later, two other men appeared. Mordvinov became agitated. They were his relatives, he said. One was called Bulantsov. The other was Mosin....

The relatives quarreled. Tempers grew hot. Bulantsov and Mosin came after Mordvinov. Borzov urged calm. A scuffle ensued and a metal rod appeared. Borzov said Mosin hit him across the face. The combatants parted. Bulantsov and Mosin, claiming victory, took some beer. Borzov asked them to put it back. When they didn't, Borzov grabbed a bottle and heaved it, hitting Mosin's head. Borzov then assaulted Mosin, striking him once across the face. Just once. Somebody shouted, "Police!" and Borzov and Ryzhkin fled. Mosin lay still on the ground, his head bloodied....

It took Orlova ten minutes to read the pretrial police report.... When she finished, Orlova told [Borzov] to stand.

"Do you understand the charges made against you?"

"Yes," he said.

"Do you recognize your guilt?"

"*Chastichno*," Borzov said. "In part."

Borzov had replied exactly as Silva had told him to. The young man was ready to take the blame for his part in the brawl—but only his part. Two wounds. No more. One, the result of the thrown bottle; the other caused by a fist to Mosin's face....

Once Orlova had completed the trial preliminaries, she moved briskly to the task at hand: the interrogation of the accused and of the other witnesses.

"Defendant!" Orlova said. "Tell the court what happened."

Borzov began to speak, at first haltingly, with head lowered and eyes averted, and then with greater speed and assurance he [repeated the statement he made during the pretrial investigation].

Orlova, who had studied the police report, offered a different account, one suggested by the pretrial deposition of an eyewitness other than Borzov. Isn't it true, she asked, that Mosin was actually *backing away* from Borzov when the bottle was thrown? If that was the case, Borzov's actions would have been offensive in nature and intent.

Borzov fell silent. He had been caught in a lie....

Silva winced. If that was in the police report, she had missed it. If it was true—and it must be, judging from Borzov's reaction—she had been misled. Borzov had told her that he threw the bottle because Mosin was on the attack. In his view, it was an act of self-defense. Now it appeared that the bottle toss was unprovoked and premeditated.

Orlova, with one question, had established to her own satisfaction the intent necessary to put Borzov away....

"Did you see any injuries on Mosin before you threw the bottle?" Orlova asked.

It was the key question, and it came to Borzov without warning.

"Yes," said Borzov. "I saw blood on him."

Silva was pleased. With that answer, Borzov had preserved a chance to salvage his defense.

Orlova paused. Then, unexpectedly, she exploded. "There is no reason for the events we are considering today!" she shouted. She gazed sternly at Borzov, who was still standing in the dock. "There is no reason for a man to have died! For what? An argument with relatives? A fight over beer?"

Orlova was finished for now. The formal judgment would come later. She turned to the state prosecutor. "Comrade *Prokuror*, do you have any questions?"

Larisa Tolmachova looked up from her desk, surveyed the accused and calmly opened fire.

"You're a candidate member of the Communist party, aren't you?" she asked.

"You should know about our party's campaign against alcohol abuse, shouldn't you? The campaign is of no concern to you, isn't that so?"

"What do you mean, it is of no concern to me?" Borzov asked.

"Your drunkenness caused Mosin's death," Tolmachova replied.

Pause. End of assault. Tolmachova had made her point, swiftly, and effectively....

As a party member, Silva shared the prosecutor's viewpoint of Borzov's breach of communist morality. But she was still a defense lawyer, Borzov's defense lawyer, and points had to be made on her client's behalf. Now that her turn to speak had come, she made them.

"Which of the men involved in the brawl did you know beforehand?" she asked Borzov.

"Only Ryzhkin," Borzov said.

"When you first saw Mosin, what did you notice?"

"He appeared to be beaten up. And he had blood on him."

"When you saw Mosin, did you have any desire to get into a fight?"

"None whatsoever."

"Who initiated the fight?"

"Mosin did."

"Besides throwing the bottle, you struck Mosin just once with your fist, correct?"

"Yes."

"But the police investigator said there were *five* blows on Mosin's face."

"I don't know who caused the other blows," Borzov said.

He had performed well. The possibility of complicity had been raised.

The next witness was Mordvinov....

It was good testimony, Silva thought, Mordvinov had corroborated Borzov's statement that Mosin was already injured before the fight in the square, and that Mosin had attacked Borzov before the bottle was thrown. Others were at fault, and Mordvinov had helped to spread the blame.

From [Prosecutor] Tolmachova's perspective, the testimony was damaging. It shifted attention away from the defendant, who was, after all, the culpable party. She moved to get things back on track.

"Did you see Borzov throw the bottle at Mosin?" she asked.

"Yes," said Mordvinov.

"Did you see the bottle hit Mosin?"

Affirmative ... Mordvinov said that to the best of his recollection, the bottle's impact caused Mosin to bleed even more than before.

Silva asked Orlova if she could question Borzov again, even though he had finished testifying. Orlova nodded. Soviet trials are freewheeling affairs, with few rigid procedural constraints. Lawyers and prosecutors can question at will as long as the judge gives permission.

"The bottle you threw at Mosin—did it break?" Silva asked.

"No," said Borzov.

"Are you certain?"

"Yes," he said.

Orlova interrupted. "But there was blood on Mosin's face?" she asked. "Where did it come from?"

"From his nose," Borzov said.

Good work, thought Silva. Borzov had turned the game around, attributing the blood on Mosin's face to the pre-existing injury Mordvinov had described. What impact the bottle had on Mosin remained unclear, which is exactly what Silva wanted.

Orlova then called Bulantsov to the stand. Bulantsov said that Mordvinov had already been drinking when he met him.... Bulantsov said he and Mordvinov traded barbs over some family affair, and before long bricks began flying. In the midst of this, Mosin appeared.

"Mordvinov beat him up," Bulantsov said.

Orlova looked up. "What kind of condition was Mosin in before the fight with Borzov?" she asked.

"I didn't see any blood on him," Bulantsov replied.

"How can you possibly remember that?" Silva interjected. "You were dead drunk. And two other people have said that Mosin was already bleeding. Are you lying?" Bulantsov didn't budge. Silva asked Orlova if she could question Mordvinov again. Orlova acquiesced. Mordvinov rose from his seat.

"Mordvinov," Silva said. "Is Bulantsov telling the truth?"

"No!" he said. "I didn't beat Mosin. Bulantsov did!" Mordvinov repeated that Mosin was already bloodied when he first saw him.

"Why would Bulantsov be lying?" Silva asked.

"Because he told me that *he* had beaten Mosin."

"Borzov," said Silva, turning to her client. "What do you think?"

"I agree with Mordvinov," Borzov said.

Bulantsov started to shout at Borzov, who replied in kind: "*You* were in an aggressive mood and *you* started the whole thing!" Bulantsov said Borzov was crazy. "It was Mordvinov," he shouted. The trial had become a verbal free-for-all. Borzov, Bulantsov, and Mordvinov all traded charges, each seeking to shade his guilt in the complicity of others. Orlova and Silva prodded them on, peppering them with questions. Only [Prosecutor] Tolmachova was silent.

It went on for the better part of ten minutes, until at 2:10 P.M., Orlova declared a recess until three o'clock.

[When the trial reconvened] Ryzhkin, an odd-looking figure in a tiger fur coat, took the stand. He testified that Mosin did indeed strike Borzov "on the face" during the quarrel at the park bench.

"Borzov told Mosin not to take any beer, and in response Mosin hit him," he said. That happened said Ryzhkin, before Borzov tossed the bottle. Ryzhkin also confirmed that Bulantsov was armed with a knife. And he said ... the bottle did not break.

"After the bottle was thrown," Orlova asked, "did you see Borzov hit Mosin?"

"Yes," Ryzhkin said.

"Did you hit Mosin as well?"

The question came out of nowhere, and Ryzhkin seemed stunned.

"No," he said.

Orlova asked Borzov to rise. "Defendant. Did Ryzhkin hit Mosin?" Borzov replied that Ryzhkin, in fact, did. Orlova to Ryzhkin: "What do you say? Is Borzov lying?" Ryzhkin hesitated, then muttered, "Yes." The judge seemed unconvinced. "Ryzhkin," she said firmly, "did you hit Mosin?"

"Well you could say that I fell on him," Ryzhkin said weakly.

Laughter erupted in the courtroom....

Silva Dubrovskaia was in a dour frame of mind as she entered the courthouse for the second day of Borzov's trial. The first day's proceedings had gone well. A scintilla of doubt had been raised about Borzov's culpability ... and that doubt had grown with each new witness. But the medical expert had yet to appear and his testimony would be critical.... And that was what Silva dreaded. Silva had read [Aleksandr Nikoaevich] Kuzin's pretrial reports and they gave her no cause for optimism....

Kuzin took his place next to Tolmachova at the *prokuror's* table. The seating arrangement suggested that the two were allies, and indeed, both worked for the state. But the alliance, to Tolmachova's dismay, crumbled as soon as the medical expert rose to speak.

Judge Orlova asked Kuzin to summarize his findings on the cause of Mosin's death.... There were five wounds on Mosin's head," Kuzin said. He described their locations. Orlova interrupted with the key question: "Which one of the wounds caused his death?"

"Any one of them could have caused the death," Kuzin said....

Tolmachova then spoke. "What caused the wounds?" she

In Russia, criminal justice is dispensed by a judge and two lay assessors. How would you compare this courtroom workgroup to one in the United States?

asked. "Can you tell us that?" Kuzin replied that he couldn't say for sure. "A fall on the asphalt. A bottle. A fist. A rock. Any or all of these could have produced the injuries."

Silva was now ready to play the hand she had hoped to play from the very beginning: she would seek conviction on a lesser charge—negligent rather than intentional homicide. Acquittal, she had said earlier, was not a possibility. "I can't hold Borzov faultless. In the end, it was he who threw the bottle."

At 10:37 A.M. Orlova ordered a half-hour recess.... The trial reconvened at 11:30 A.M. State Prosecutor Larisa Tolmachova rose and delivered her closing remarks.

"All the witnesses testified that Mosin was injured before the final disturbance with Borzov. But it was Borzov who threw the bottle, as Mosin was walking away from him. And it was Borzov who followed that up with a fist to Mosin's face.... It is equally apparent," she said, "that Borzov was not responsible for all five of the injuries inflicted on Mosin." And it is not clear, she added, that Borzov can be held liable for Mosin's death. "Consequently, I recommend that Borzov be found guilty of violating Criminal Code Article 108 Part One instead of Part Two as originally charged." Part One was a lesser offense ... [and] carried a maximum sentence of eight years, but Tolmachova sought a more lenient sentence. "In view of the fact that the defendant has no prior criminal record and keeping in mind his family,... five years deprivation of freedom at a strict regime labor camp," she said.

Five years instead of twelve. It was welcome news to Silva, who now rose to face the court....

"I urge you to compare Borzov's character and behavior with the other men, who are in fact responsible for triggering the whole unfortunate series of events," Silva said. "Do not forget—as the prosecutor did in her final speech—that Borzov had been attacked and struck even before he threw the bottle. And do not forget the testimony of Ryzhkin, who acknowledged that he, too, had hit Mosin."... "Why," Silva asked, "should one man take the blame for all?" ... Borzov, she

said, did not intend to cause Mosin serious harm. He threw the bottle in the heat of the moment and in the face of Mosin's aggressive behavior.... This was not a case of intentional homicide ... [but of] negligently inflicting grave bodily injuries, a charge carrying a maximum sentence of two years. With that she sat down.

"Comrade Defendant!" Orlova said. "Do you have a final word for the court?"

Borzov rose from the dock. He swayed, as if his legs would not hold him. "Respected court, I ask you ..." He paused and drew a deep breath ... "I threw the bottle because I was afraid," he cried. "I wanted to scare him. I was drinking.... I ask the court," he continued, "to keep in mind my long, honorable work record, to remember my family, to...."

Orlova and the two lay judges returned to the courtroom within thirty minutes. The judge held a multipage decision in her hands. The verdict had plainly been worked out the day before.... Orlova read the decision. Borzov, she said, was guilty of "intentional infliction of grave bodily injury as stated in Criminal Code Article 108 Part One." That was the lesser charge the prosecutor had requested. Silva's call for a conviction on the basis of negligence had been rejected.

Orlova said she could not accept the prosecutor's recommendation of five years punishment in a strict regime labor camp. Borzov, she said, would serve just four years in a labor colony of "reinforced" regime ... [a] less severe facility for first-timers like Borzov.

Silva knew that four years was an acceptable sentence. The trial had begun with the prospect of twelve. The confusion and ambiguity of the proceedings had caused Orlova to err on the side of caution.

At the very moment Orlova uttered the words "four years," two armed, uniformed policemen threw open the courtroom doors and walked up to Borzov ... and surrounded the defendant.

SOURCE: Adapted from Robert Rand, *Comrade Lawyer* (Boulder, Colo.: Westview Press, 1991). Used by permission of Westview Press, Boulder, Colorado.

Persons in some occupations—doctors, lawyers, teachers, police officers—are not called because their professional services are needed elsewhere; others are not called because of their connection with the criminal justice system. Some legislatures, particularly in states where jurors are required to serve thirty days, have added other categories because of pressures for exemption. In many localities, citizens may be excused if jury duty would cause economic or physical hardship. One result is that only about 15 percent of adult Americans have ever been placed in a jury pool. Because of this narrowing of the sources of potential jurors, there is a tendency for retirees, homemakers with grown children, and the unemployed—those who would not be inconvenienced by the time commitment—to be overrepresented on juries.

**Voir Dire**   As a protection against bias, prosecution and defense are allowed to challenge the seating of some jurors. This process of **voir dire** ("to speak the truth") examination is designed for the constitutional purpose of ensuring a fair trial. Attorneys for each side and the judge may question each potential juror about background, knowledge of the case, or acquaintance with the persons involved. If it appears that the juror will be unable to be fair, he or she may be **challenged for cause**. The challenge must be ruled on by the judge, and if it is sustained, the juror will be excused from participation in that specific case. There is usually no limit to the number of challenges for cause that both lawyers can make, and in some complex or controversial cases the voir dire is extremely time-consuming.

The **peremptory challenge** has a stronger influence on jury composition. It is used to exclude a person from service, and no reason need be given. An attorney may exercise this prerogative because of a hunch or because someone appears to be unsympathetic. Normally the defense is allowed eight to ten peremptory challenges and the prosecution six to eight.

Instances of "jury stacking" raise questions about voir dire.[7] In several highly publicized trials the assistance of social scientists has been sought—often with much success. Lawyers reason that if they can determine the social and attitudinal characteristics of persons most likely to sympathize with their side, then they can use such knowledge to select an agreeable jury. In fact, one consulting firm has boasted that where their advice has been used, their clients have succeeded in 95 percent of their cases.[8]

Even before such methods were used, the process of voir dire was attacked as too time-consuming. One proposed reform holds that only the judge should examine the jurors for bias; another calls for a sharp reduction in the number of challenges.

Any change would not come easily, however, for in addition to removing potential jurors who might be biased, voir dire also serves the important purpose of introducing the prosecutor and defense attorney to the panel. As nationally recognized lawyers F. Lee Bailey and Henry B. Rothblat have said,

As you interrogate the jurors you meet them personally for the first time. You are given a chance to start selling the defense. Your questions should educate each prospective juror to the legal principles of your defense.[9]

**voir dire**

An examination of prospective jurors through which the prosecution and defense screen out persons who might be biased or incapable of rendering a fair verdict.

**challenge for cause**

Removal of a prospective juror by showing bias or some other legal disability. The number of such challenges permitted is unlimited.

**peremptory challenge**

Removal of a prospective juror without assignment of any cause. The number of such challenges permitted is limited.

Indeed, in many ways, the voir dire examinations set the stage for the trial.

**Opening Statements**   After the jury has been selected, the trial begins. The clerk reads the complaint (indictment or information), and the prosecutor and the defense attorney may, if they desire, make opening statements to the jury to summarize the position that each side intends to take. The statements are not evidential, and judges normally keep tight control so that no prejudicial or inflammatory remarks are made. Lawyers use this phase of the trial to establish themselves with the jurors and emphasize points they intend to make later.

**Presentation of the Prosecution's Evidence**   One of the basic protections of the American criminal justice system is the assumption that the defendant is innocent until proved guilty. The prosecution has the burden of proving beyond a reasonable doubt, within the demands of the court procedures and rules of evidence, that the individual named in the indictment committed the crime. That does not mean absolute certainty is required, only that the evidence is such that there is no reasonable doubt.

By presenting evidence to the jury, the prosecution must establish a case showing that the defendant is guilty. Evidence is classified as real evidence, testimony, direct evidence, and circumstantial evidence. **Real evidence** might include such objects as a weapon, business records, fingerprints, or stolen property. Most evidence in a criminal trial, however, consists of the **testimony** of witnesses. Witnesses at a trial must be legally competent; thus the judge may be required to determine whether the witness whose testimony is challenged has the intelligence to tell the truth and the ability to recall what was seen. **Direct evidence** refers to eyewitness accounts—for example, "I saw John Smith fire the gun." **Circumstantial evidence** requires that the jury infer a fact from what the witness observed: "I saw John Smith walk behind his house with a gun. A few minutes later I heard a gun go off, and then Mr. Smith walked toward me holding a gun." The observation of the witness that Smith had a gun and that he heard a gun go off does not provide the direct evidence that Smith fired his gun; yet the jury may link the described facts and infer that Smith fired his gun. After a witness has given testimony, he or she may be cross-examined by counsel for the other side.

## A Question of Ethics

The return address on the official-looking envelope read "Jury Commissioner, District Court, Plainville, Massachusetts." Having a good idea of the contents, Donald Rotman tore open the envelope and pulled out a computer-generated form that read: "Donald A. Rotman, You are hereby summoned to be available for duty as a trial juror and are directed to report to the District Court of the Commonwealth of Massachusetts, 61 South Street, Plainville, at 9:00 A.M. on July 10. Failure to appear as instructed by law may subject you to a penalty as provided by law. Your juror number is 89367. The term of your jury duty will be one day or one trial."

"Hell! I can't do that, I want to go to Cape Cod that week. There must be some way out of this." Rotman looked at the bottom of the form and read, "You may apply to be excused from this duty if you are: an attorney; caring for a child under three; student or teacher during the school year,..." and about five other categories, none of which applied to him.

"This is no big deal. Everyone does it. I'll just tell them I'm going to summer school. They won't check."

Is getting out of jury duty no big deal? What are the implications of Donald's action? If Donald is required to serve on a jury, how might justice be affected by the fact that he had planned to spend that week on vacation? What exemptions to service should exist?

**real evidence**
Physical evidence such as a weapon, records, fingerprints, stolen property.

**testimony**
Oral evidence provided by a legally competent witness.

**direct evidence**
Eyewitness accounts.

**circumstantial evidence**
Evidence provided by a witness from which a jury must infer a fact.

The rules of evidence govern the facts that may be admitted into the case record. Real evidence that has been illegally seized, for example, may be excluded under the Fourth Amendment's protection against unreasonable searches and seizure. Likewise, statements by the defendant given outside the Supreme Court's requirements developed by the *Miranda* decision may also be excluded. Testimony that is hearsay or opinion cannot become a formal part of the trial record. The judge decides, with reference to these rules, what evidence may be heard. In making such decisions, the judge must weigh the importance of the evidence and balance it against the need for a fair trial. The attorney for each side contests the presentation of evidence with reference to the rules, to the trustworthiness of statements, and to the relevance of the information to the issues at hand.

Once the prosecution has presented all of the state's evidence against the defendant, the court is informed that the people's case rests. It is common for the defense then to ask the court to direct the jury to bring forth a verdict of not guilty. Such a motion is based on the defense contention that the state has not presented enough evidence to prove its case; it has not established all the elements of the crime charged. The judge rules on this motion, sustaining or overruling it. If the motion is sustained (it rarely is), the trial is ended; if it is overruled, the defense presents its evidence.

**Presentation of the Defense's Evidence**   There is no requirement that the defense answer the case presented by the prosecution. As it is the state's responsibility to prove the case beyond a reasonable doubt, it is theoretically possible—and in fact sometimes happens—that the defense rests its case immediately. Usually the accused's attorney employs one strategy or a combination of three strategies: (1) contrary evidence is introduced to rebut or cast doubt on the state's case, (2) an alibi is offered, or (3) an affirmative defense is presented. An affirmative defense is a legal excuse that permits the jury to find the defendant not responsible for the crime; defenses include self-defense, insanity, duress, and necessity (see Chapter 3).

A key issue for the defense is whether the accused will take the stand. The Fifth Amendment protection against self-incrimination means that the defendant does not have to testify. The Supreme Court has ruled that the prosecutor may not comment on, nor can the jury draw inferences from, the defendant's decision not to appear in his or her own defense.[10] The decision is not taken lightly, because if the defendant does testify, the prosecution may cross-examine. Cross-examination is broader than direct examination, and the prosecutor may question the defendant not only about the crime but also about his or her past and often is able to introduce testimony about prior convictions. Another consideration for many criminal lawyers is that juries may expect to hear both sides of what happened. Lawyers recognize that denying jurors this opportunity may prejudice some of them against the client, for jurors may wonder what is being hidden by the defendant who chooses not to testify.

**Presentation of Rebuttal Witnesses**   On completion of the defense's case, the prosecution may present witnesses whose testimony is designed to discredit that of preceding witnesses. Evidence previously introduced by the prosecution may not be rehashed, but new evidence may be presented. If the prosecution brings rebuttal witnesses, the defense has the opportunity to examine them and to present new witnesses in rebuttal.

**Closing Arguments by Each Side**   When each side has completed its presentation of the evidence, prosecution and defense make closing arguments to the jury. The attorneys present the facts of the case in a manner that is most favorable to their side. The prosecutor may use the summation to connect the evidential and legal elements and to try to show that isolated bits of evidence form a cohesive whole that proves the accused to be guilty. The defense, on the other hand, may set forth the applicable law and try to show that the prosecution has not proved its case, that the testimony raised questions instead of providing answers, and that the need to prove beyond a reasonable doubt is very demanding. Each side reminds the jury of its duty not to be swayed by emotion and to evaluate the evidence impartially.

Veteran attorneys feel that the closing argument is a major chance to appeal directly to the members of the jury. Some lawyers use the emotional and spellbinding techniques of experienced actors in their summations in order to sway the jury. But for many it is also an opportunity to show the defendant, the agent-mediators, or their supervisors that they have placed their full effort into the trial.

**Judge's Instructions to the Jury**   The jury decides the facts of the case, but the judge determines the law. Before the jurors retire to consider the defendant's fate, the judge instructs them about the manner in which the law bears on their decision. The judge may discuss basic legal principles such as proof beyond a reasonable doubt, the legal requirements necessary to show that all the elements have been proved by the prosecution, or the rights of the defendant. More specific aspects of the law bearing on the decision, such as complicated court rulings on the nature of the insanity defense or the manner in which certain types of evidence have been gathered, may be included in the judge's instructions. In some complicated trials the judge may spend an entire day instructing the jury.

The concept of **reasonable doubt** is at the heart of the jury system. The prosecution is not required to prove the guilt of the defendant beyond *all* doubt. Instead, if a juror is

> satisfied to a moral certainty that this defendant…is guilty of any one of the crimes charged here, you may safely say that you have been convinced beyond a reasonable doubt. If your mind is wavering, or if you are uncertain…you have not been convinced beyond a reasonable doubt and must render a verdict of not guilty.[11]

A vote for acquittal should not be based on sympathy or the reluctance of a jury to perform a disagreeable task.

The experience of listening to the judge may become an ordeal for the jurors, who must assimilate perhaps two or three hours of instruction on the law and the evidence. It is assumed that somehow they will absorb these details so that when they are in the jury room they will draw on their instant expertise.[12] Finally, the judge explains the charges and the

**reasonable doubt**
The standard used by a juror to decide if the prosecution has provided enough evidence for conviction. Jurors should vote for acquittal if they can give a reason to support this position.

*Twelve Angry Men* depicted the tensions that often emerge in a jury room. The 1957 film showed how jurors' values, biases, and life experiences affect their deliberations—and how one juror's belief in the innocence of the defendant could sway the other members.

possible verdicts. Trials usually involve multiple charges, and the judge must instruct the jurors in such a way that their decisions will be consistent with the law and the evidence.

**Decision by the Jury**  After they have heard the case and have been instructed by the judge, the jurors retire to a room where they have complete privacy. They elect a foreperson to run the meeting, and deliberations begin. Until now, the jurors have been passive observers of the trial, unable to question witnesses; now they can discuss the facts that have been presented. Throughout their deliberations the jurors may be sequestered; if they are allowed to spend nights at home, they are ordered not to discuss the case with anyone. The jury may request that the judge reread to them portions of the instructions, ask for additional instructions, or seek portions of the transcript.

In almost every state and in the federal courts, the verdict must be unanimous. Only Louisiana, Montana, Oregon, Oklahoma, and Texas permit majority decisions in a criminal case whose jury is composed of twelve people. If the jury becomes deadlocked and cannot reach a verdict, the trial ends with a hung jury. When a verdict is reached, the judge, prosecution, and defense reassemble in the courtroom to hear it. The prosecution or the defense may request that the jury be polled: each member tells his or her vote in open court. This procedure presumably ensures that there has been no pressure by other members. If the verdict is guilty, the judge may continue bail or may incarcerate the convicted person to await a presentence report. If the verdict is not guilty, the defendant is freed. Because the Fifth Amendment guarantees that a person shall not be "twice put in jeopardy of life or limb," prosecutors may not appeal a jury's finding or reinstitute the same charges.

## Evaluating the Jury System

The question of which factors in a trial lead to the jury's verdict is always intriguing. The 1957 film *Twelve Angry Men* depicts jury deliberations and the emotions that often rule decision making. The actor Henry Fonda, initially the lone holdout against conviction, gradually sways other members as doubts are raised about the evidence that the prosecution has presented. After hours of deliberation in a hot, cramped room a vote for acquittal is finally reached.

Social scientists have been hampered in studying the process of juror decision making because of the secrecy of actual juries. Simulated juries have been used with interesting results. Early research at the University of Chicago Law School found that, consistent with theories of group behavior, participation and influence in the process are related to social status. Men were found to be more active than women, whites more active than minority members, and the better educated more active than those less educated. Much of the discussion in the jury room was not directly concerned with the testimony but rather with trial procedures, opinions about the witnesses, and personal reminiscences.[13] In 30 percent of the cases, a vote taken soon after sequestration was the only one necessary to reach a verdict; in the rest of the cases, the majority on the first ballot eventually prevailed in 90 percent of the cases.[14] Because of group pressure, only rarely did a lone juror produce a hung jury. More recent findings have upheld the importance of group pressure on decision making.[15]

In evaluating the jury system, researchers have tried to discover whether juries and judges view cases differently. Harry Kalven and Hans Zeisel attempted to answer this question by examining more than thirty-five hundred criminal trials in which juries played a part. They found that the judge and jury agreed on the outcome in 75.4 percent of the trials but that a jury was more lenient than a judge. The total conviction rate by juries was 64.5 percent; by judges, 83.3 percent.[16] The very high rate of conviction supports the idea that the filtering process removes doubtful cases before trial. A study by Robert Roper and Victor Flango has challenged the earlier Kalven and Zeisel findings.[17] In examining data from all fifty states, Roper and Flango found that juries convicted felons at a higher rate than did judges and that judges were more conviction-prone in regard to nonfelons.

Kalven and Zeisel's analysis of the factors that caused disagreement between judge and jury revealed that 54 percent of disagreements were attributable to "issues of evidence," about 29 percent to "sentiments on the law," about 11 percent to "sentiments on the defendant," and about 6 percent to other factors. Juries clearly do more than merely deal with questions of fact. Much of the disagreement between judge and jury was favorable to the defendant, an indication that citizens recognize certain values that fall outside the official rules. In weighing the evidence, the jury was strongly impressed by a defendant who had no criminal record and took the stand, especially when the charge was serious. Juries tend to take a more liberal view of such issues as self-defense than judges and are likely to minimize the seriousness of an offense if they are impressed by some attribute of the victim. For example, if the victim of an assault is a prostitute, the jury may minimize the assault. Presumably because judges have more experience with the process, they are more likely to confer the guilty label on defendants who are sent to trial after the examination of the police and prosecutor.

## Jury Duty

The *Juror's Manual* of the United States District Court says that jury service is "perhaps the most vital duty next to fighting in the defense of one's country." Every year nearly two million Americans respond to the call to perform this civic duty even though doing so usually entails personal and financial hardship. Compensation is usually minimal, and not all employers pay for time lost from the job.

Most jurors experience great frustration with the system as they wait for endless hours in barren courthouse rooms to be called for actual service. Often they are placed on a jury only to have their function preempted by a sudden change of plea to guilty during the trial. The result is wasted juror time and wasted money. Unfortunately, what could be a valuable civic education often leaves jurors with an unnecessarily negative impression of the entire criminal justice system.

To deal with some of the more negative aspects of jury duty, some courts have introduced the "one-day-one-trial" system. Traditionally, citizens are asked to be jurors for a thirty-day term, and although only a few may be needed for a particular day, the entire pool may be present in the courthouse for the full thirty-day period. In the new system, jurors serve for either one day or the duration of one trial. Prospective jurors who are challenged at voir dire or who are not called to a courtroom are dismissed at the end of their first day and have thus fulfilled their jury duty for the year. Those who are accepted on a jury are required to serve for the duration of that trial, normally about three days. The consensus of jurors, judges, and court administrators is that the one-day-one-trial system is a great improvement.

# The Sentencing Process

Regardless of how and where the decision has been made—misdemeanor court or felony court, plea bargain or adversarial contest, bench or jury trial—judges have the responsibility for imposing sentence. As the distinguished jurist Irving A. Kaufman has said:

> If the hundreds of American judges who sit on criminal cases were polled as to what was the most trying facet of their jobs, the vast majority would almost certainly answer "sentencing." In no other judicial function is the judge more alone; no other act of his carries greater potentialities for good or evil than the determination of how society will treat its transgressors.[18]

Chapter 12 examines the goals of the criminal sanction and the forms that punishment may take, such as prison, fines, death, or probation. Here we look at several of the factors that social scientists believe influence the sentencing process: (1) the administrative context of the courts, (2) the attitudes and values of judges, (3) the presentence report, and (4) sentencing guidelines.

## The Administrative Context

Although legislatures enact penal codes as if the letter of the law were to be followed, judges are very much influenced by the administrative context within which they sentence. We can therefore see real differences between the assembly-line style of justice in the misdemeanor courts and the more formal style found in felony courts.

**Assembly-Line Justice: Misdemeanor Courts**   The lower courts are of limited jurisdiction because the law restricts the severity of the punishments they can allocate, usually to less than a year in prison. In a sense they are "people's courts." It is here that about 90 percent of criminal cases are heard, either for arraignment and preliminary hearing or for dismissal or trial and sentence. Only a minority of cases adjudicated in lower courts end in jail sentences; the preponderance of offenders are sanctioned through fines, probation, community service, and restitution.

Because most lower courts are overloaded, minimal time is allotted an individual case. Judicial decisions are mass-produced because actors in the system work on the basis of three assumptions. First, there is a high probability that any person brought before a court is guilty; doubtful cases will be filtered out of the system by the police and prosecution. Second, the vast majority of defendants will plead guilty. Third, those charged with minor offenses will be processed in volume. The citation will be read by the clerk, a guilty plea given, and sentence pronounced by the judge.

## Quiet, Efficient Justice in a Small City Court

City Court in this quiet upstate community [Saratoga Springs] sometimes looks very much like Criminal Court in New York City. The public defender meets his clients for the first time in the courtroom. Much of the judicial action takes place briskly before the bench. And the prosecutor is amenable to "down charging" for first offenders.

The process is efficient, the atmosphere is dignified, and case disposition is fairly predictable, with dismissals and adjournments granted on merit. And as Judge Lawrence J. LaBelle puts it, "Our 'don't shows' amount to only 1 percent."

The differences of scale, of course, are enormous. The one hundred cases that represent a month's work [here] are equal to a single day's calendar for many judges in Criminal Court in Manhattan. Misdemeanors are handled only twice a week, on Mondays and Thursdays.

The contrast between the court here and in New York City is well known to defendants. "They'll say that in the city they wouldn't bother with this," said the public defender, John P. Pastore.

Judge LaBelle, a practicing lawyer, works part-time in the $21,000-a-year post of City Court judge, as his father did from 1934 to 1950.

"When I began in 1970," he said, "there was less than an hour and a half's work a day. Today, it's 60 percent of my time. We're bordering on a full-time judgeship."

The judge described courtroom conditions as "horrendous," but they seemed orderly and efficient on a recent day, when the court handled more than two dozen cases.

The day began, as it often does in most courts, with informal discussions in chambers. Judge LaBelle's court assistant went over some of the cases as Frank B. Williams, an assistant district attorney, and the public defender discussed the scheduled trial of a woman charged with welfare fraud. It seemed that the charges might be dropped.

Although the lower criminal courts have been criticized because of their assembly-line characteristics, social scientists are now beginning to reassess this view. Susan Silbey argues, for example, that the informality, availability, and diversity of the lower courts are their most valuable qualities. As she points out, the lower courts have a unique capacity to resolve cases effectively because they are placed at the entry point of the system, are dispersed throughout the nation, and are embedded within local communities.[19] These courts are oriented toward an individualized justice that is responsive to the community. The judges appear to be more interested in responding to "problems" than to formally defined "crimes." Thus they seek to use their discretion to impose sentences that will fit the needs of the offender and the community rather than adhering strictly to the harshness of the sentences provided by law (see the Close-Up on justice in a small court).

In addition to the formal sanctions prescribed by law, other punishments are imposed on persons who get caught in the criminal justice system, even on those who ultimately are not convicted. If a person is arrested and released without having been charged, if the case is dismissed at a preliminary hearing, or if it is "nolled" at trial, various tangible and intangible costs are still to be borne. Time spent in jail awaiting trial, the cost of a bail bond, and lost days on the job have an immediate tangible impact.

The judge looked up. "Are you telling me it was a bad arrest?" he asked. Although the defendant "had not given notice that her husband had moved back in," [Mr. Williams] said, she had accurately reported the number of family members living with her, making it difficult to prove intentional fraud.

There were roughly thirty people in the courtroom, a few sitting inside the railing after being escorted from the local jail. The rest, in the rows of wooden benches, were other defendants, family members or friends, lawyers, and potential jurors.

In the first cases, the defendants were defended by Mr. Pastore. Then Judge LaBelle said, "Now we'll take cases where attorneys are ready." They included traffic violations, petty larceny, disorderly conduct, and aggravated harassment—with many offenses including intoxication.

Judge LaBelle was relatively tough on drunken drivers. One man who pleaded guilty to speeding and failing to keep to the right, but with no drinking charges, was fined $45. The next case, a man who was charged with driving while intoxicated, received a $250 fine, a civil surcharge of $10, and was required to attend a course for drunken drivers.

One by one, the defendants appeared before the bench, the majority pleading guilty to reduced charges, many paying fines ranging from $25 to $50, and none going to jail that day. Cases were put over, defendants were encouraged to settle civil disputes and, finally, the woman charged with wrongfully acquiring welfare funds was "dismissed in the interests of justice," as Judge LaBelle put it.

The potential jurors filed out, the judge returned to his chambers, and the accused left, passing a sign behind the bench that reads, "Not All Are Guilty."

SOURCE: Adapted from John Feron, "In an Upstate City Court, a Feeling of Quiet, Efficient Justice," *New York Times*, 30 June 1983, B–4. Copyright © 1983 by The New York Times Company. Reprinted by permission.

For most people, simply being arrested is a frightening and costly experience. It is impossible to measure the psychic and social price of being stigmatized, separated from family, and deprived of freedom. As the title of a book by Malcolm Feeley claims, *The Process Is the Punishment*.[20]

Feeley believes that the pretrial costs not only have an impact on the unconvicted but also encourage rapid and perfunctory practices in the courtroom and guilty pleas. As he notes, the costs of the pretrial process to the individual defendant may answer several puzzling questions: Why do so many waive their right to free appointed counsel? Why do so many people not show up for court at all? Why do people choose the available adversarial options so infrequently?[21] Let us now turn to examine felony court processes where the cases are serious and the punishments harsher than in misdemeanor court.

**Felony Courts**   Felony cases are processed and offenders are sentenced in courts of general jurisdiction. Because of the seriousness of the punishment the atmosphere is more formal and generally lacks the hurly-burly of misdemeanor court. But even here, where judges may send an individual to prison for a long term or even impose the death penalty, administrative pressures bear on judicial decision making.

Sentencing is the point at which the judge is able to impose punishments that implement the goals of the criminal sanction.

A study of sentencing practices in state felony courts provides data on the type of sanction imposed, as seen in Table 11.2. The figure relates the conviction offense to the type of sentence imposed. In deciding the punishment, the judge will have the presentence report, prepared by a probation officer, as a guide; organizational considerations and community norms will also influence the decision.

## Attitudes and Values of Judges

That judges exhibit different sentencing tendencies is taken as a fact of life by criminal lawyers and the court community. As early as 1933 one report noted that "some recidivists know the sentencing tendencies of judges so well that the accused will frequently attempt to choose which is to sentence them, and ... are frequently able to do this."[22]

The sentence differences among judges can be ascribed to several factors: the conflicting goals of criminal justice, the administrative pressures on the judge, and the influence of community values on the system. Each factor to some extent structures the judge's exercise of discretion in sentencing offenders. In addition, a judge's perception of these factors depends on his or her own attitudes toward the law, toward a particular crime, or toward a type of offender.

Sentencing disparities among judges may be further explained by the fact that judges are products of different backgrounds and have different social values. Martin Levin's study of the criminal courts of Pittsburgh and Minneapolis showed the influence of judges' values on sentencing behavior. He found that Pittsburgh judges, all of whom came from humble backgrounds, exhibited a greater empathy toward defendants than did judges in Minneapolis, who tended to come from upper-class backgrounds. Where the Pittsburgh judges tried to base their decisions on what they believed was best for the defendants, Minneapolis judges were more legally oriented and considered society's need for protection from criminal behavior more strongly.[23]

## Presentence Report

Although sentencing is the judge's responsibility, the **presentence report** has become an important ingredient in the judicial mix. Although the primary purpose of the presentence report is to help the judge select the appropriate sentence for the offender, it also assists in the classification of probationers, prisoners, and parolees with respect to treatment planning and risk assessment. Usually a probation officer investigates the convicted person's background, criminal record, job status, and mental condition in order to suggest a sentence that is in the interests of both the person and society. In some states, however, probation officers present only factual material to the judge and make no sentencing recommendation. The probation officer may weigh hearsay as well as firsthand information.

Given the crucial role of the presentence report and the manner in which its information is collected, one might expect that the offender would have a right to examine it and to challenge the contents. In 1949 the Supreme Court ruled in *Williams* v. *New York* that a convicted person did not have a Sixth Amendment right to cross-examine persons who supplied the information in the report.[24] Since then, however, the Court has ruled that a defendant is denied due process if a sentence is based on information that the defendant is not given the opportunity to deny or explain.[25]

The presentence report helps to ease the strain of decision making on judges by shifting partial responsibility to the probation department. Because many sentencing alternatives are open to them, they often rely on the report for guidance. After studying sentencing decisions in California, Robert Carter and Leslie Wilkins found a high correlation (96 percent) between the recommendation for probation in the presentence report and the court's disposition of individual cases.[26] When the probation officer recommended incarceration, there was a slight weakening of this relationship, an indication that the officers were more punitive than the judges.

In most jurisdictions the probation department is part of the judiciary and under the institutional supervision of the judges; hence it is not as independent as might be expected. A close relationship between the probation officers and the members of the court is often justified on the ground that judges will place greater trust in the information provided by staff members under their immediate supervision. Rather than presenting an independent and impartial report, probation officers may be more interested in second-guessing the judge. Yet it is also a concern that, because of the pressure of their duties, judges may rely totally on the presentence recommendations and merely ratify the suggestions of the probation officers without applying their own judicial perspective to the decisions.

The impression of the offender that the presentence report conveys is very important. The probation officer's language is crucial. Summary statements may be written in a completely noncommittal style or may convey the sense that the defendant is worth saving or is unruly. Judges read the report to gain an understanding of the

**presentence report**

A report that is prepared by a probation office after an investigation into the background of a convicted offender and that is designed to help the judge determine an appropriate sentence.

**Table 11.2**

**Types of felony sentences imposed by state courts, 1990**

Note that although we often equate a felony conviction with a sentence to prison, almost a third of felony offenders are given probation.

SOURCE: U.S. Department of Justice, Bureau of Justice Statistics, *Bulletin* (March 1993), 2.

NOTE: For persons receiving a combination of sentences, the sentence designation came from the most severe penalty imposed—prison being the most severe, followed by jail, then probation.

| Most Serious Conviction Offense | Percent of Felons Sentenced to | | |
|---|---|---|---|
| | Prison | Jail | Probation |
| All offenses | 46% | 25% | 29% |
| Violent offenses | 59% | 21% | 20% |
| Murder | 91 | 4 | 5 |
| Rape | 67 | 19 | 14 |
| Robbery | 73 | 17 | 10 |
| Aggravated assault | 45 | 27 | 28 |
| Other violent | 42 | 25 | 33 |
| Property offenses | 44% | 22% | 34% |
| Burglary | 54 | 21 | 25 |
| Larceny | 40 | 25 | 35 |
| Fraud | 33 | 20 | 47 |
| Drug offenses | 43% | 29% | 28% |
| Possession | 35 | 29 | 36 |
| Trafficking | 49 | 28 | 23 |
| Weapons offenses | 38% | 24% | 38% |
| Other offenses | 37% | 29% | 34% |

## Presentence Report

STATE OF NEW MEXICO

Corrections Department
Field Service Division
Santa Fe, New Mexico 87501

Date: January 4, 1994
To:     The Honorable Manuel Baca
From: Presentence Unit, Officer Brian Gaines
Re:     Richard Knight

### Evaluation

Appearing before Your Honor for sentencing is twenty-year-old Richard Knight who on November 10, 1993, pursuant to a Plea and

**CLOSE-UP**

Disposition Agreement, entered a plea of guilty to Aggravated Assault Upon a Peace Officer (Deadly Weapon) (Firearm Enhancement), as charged in Information Number 89–5736900. The terms of the agreement stipulate that the maximum period of incarceration be limited to one year, that restitution be made on all counts and charges whether dismissed or not, and that all remaining charges in the Indictment and DA Files 39780 be dismissed.

The defendant is an only child, born and raised in Albuquerque. He attended West Mesa High School until the eleventh grade, at which time he dropped out. Richard declared that he felt school was "too difficult" and that he decided that it would be more beneficial for him to obtain steady employment rather than to complete his education. The defendant further stated that he felt it was "too late for vocational training" because of the impending one-year prison sentence he faces, due to the Firearm Enhancement penalty for his offense.

---

defendant's attitude. A comment such as "the defendant appears unrepentant" can send a person to prison. (An example of a presentence report appears in the accompanying Close-Up.)

### Sentencing Guidelines

**sentencing guidelines**
An instrument developed for judges that indicates the usual sanctions given previously to particular offenses.

In recent years, **sentencing guidelines**, designed to constrain the discretion of judges, have been established in the federal courts, in several states, and in selected jurisdictions within other states. Guidelines have been advocated as one method of reducing the disparity among sentences given to offenders convicted of the same offense. Although statutes provide a variety of sentencing options for particular crimes, guidelines direct a judge to more specific actions that *should* be taken. The range of sentence options provided for most offenses are based on the seriousness of the crime and on the criminal history of an offender.

For sentencing guidelines, as for parole guidelines (discussed in Chapter 17), a grid is constructed on the basis of two scores, one related to the seriousness of the offense, the other to characteristics of the offender that indicate the likelihood of recidivism (see Table 11.3). The offender

The longest period of time the defendant has held a job has been for six months with Frank's Concrete Company. He has been employed with the Madrid Construction Company since August 1993 (verified). Richard lives with his parents who provide most of his financial support. Conflicts between his mother and himself, the defendant claimed, precipitated his recent lawless actions by causing him to "not care about anything." He stressed the fact that he is now once again "getting along" with his mother. Although the defendant contends that he doesn't abuse drugs, he later contradicted himself by declaring that he "gets drunk every weekend." He noted that he was inebriated when he committed the present offense.

In regard to the present offense, the defendant recalled that other individuals at the party attempted to stab his friend and that he and his companion left and returned with a gun in order to settle the score. Richard claimed remorse for his offense and stated that his past family problems led him to spend most of his time on the streets, where he became more prone to violent conduct. The defendant admitted being a member of the 18th Street Gang.

## Recommendation

It is respectfully recommended that the defendant be sentenced to three years incarceration, on Information Number 89–5736900, and that the sentence be suspended. It is further recommended that the defendant be incarcerated for one year as to the mandatory Firearm Enhancement and then placed on three years probation under the following special conditions:

1. That restitution be made to Juan Lopez in the amount of $622.40.

2. That the defendant either maintain full-time employment or obtain his GED, and

3. That the defendant discontinue fraternizing with the 18th Street Gang members and terminate his own membership in the gang.

score is arrived at by summing the points allocated to characteristics such as the number of juvenile, adult misdemeanor, and adult felony convictions; the number of times incarcerated; whether the accused was on probation or parole or had escaped from confinement at the time of the last offense; and employment status or educational achievement. Judges are expected to provide a written explanation when they depart from the guidelines.

Sentencing guidelines are expected to be reviewed and modified periodically so that recent decisions will be included. Some critics argue that because the guidelines reflect only what has happened they do not reform sentencing. Others question the choice of characteristics included in the offender scale and wonder whether some are used to mask racial criteria. However, as noted by Terance Miethe and Charles Moore, the Minnesota guidelines have resulted in sentences that are "more uniform, more predictable, and more socioeconomically neutral than before the guidelines."[27] Unlike some reforms designed to limit the discretion of judges, guidelines attempt to structure that discretion to reflect the collective experience of sentencing in a particular city. Some prefer the use of guidelines to the legislative enactment of a penal code based on mandatory or definite sentences.

| Severity Levels of Conviction Offense | Criminal History Score | | | | | | |
|---|---|---|---|---|---|---|---|
| | 0 | 1 | 2 | 3 | 4 | 5 | 6 or More |
| Unauthorized use of motor vehicle | 12 | 12 | 12 | 15 | 18 | 21 | 24 |
| Possession of marijuana | | | | | | | *23–25* |
| Theft-related crimes ($150–$2,500) | 12 | 12 | 14 | 17 | 20 | 23 | 27 |
| Sale of marijuana | | | | | | | *25–29* |
| Theft crimes ($150–$2,500) | 12 | 13 | 16 | 19 | 22 | 27 | 32 |
| | | | | | *21–23* | *25–29* | *30–34* |
| Burglary—felony intent | 12 | 15 | 18 | 21 | 25 | 32 | 41 |
| Receiving stolen goods ($150–$2,500) | | | | | *24–26* | *30–34* | *37–45* |
| Simple robbery | 18 | 23 | 27 | 30 | 38 | 36 | 54 |
| | | | | *29–31* | *36–40* | *43–49* | *50–58* |
| Assault, second degree | 21 | 26 | 30 | 34 | 44 | 54 | 65 |
| | | | | *33–35* | *42–46* | *50–58* | *60–70* |
| Aggravated robbery | 24 | 32 | 41 | 49 | 65 | 81 | 97 |
| | *23–25* | *30–34* | *38–44* | *45–53* | *60–70* | *75–87* | *90–104* |
| Assault, first degree | 43 | 54 | 65 | 76 | 95 | 113 | 132 |
| Criminal sexual conduct, first degree | *41–45* | *50–58* | *60–70* | *71–81* | *89–101* | *106–120* | *124–140* |
| Murder, third degree | 97 | 119 | 127 | 149 | 176 | 205 | 230 |
| | *91–100* | *116–122* | *124–130* | *143–155* | *168–184* | *195–215* | *218–242* |
| Murder, second degree | 116 | 140 | 162 | 203 | 243 | 284 | 324 |
| | *111–121* | *144–147* | *153–171* | *192–214* | *231–255* | *270–298* | *309–339* |

**Table 11.3**

**Minnesota sentencing guidelines grid (presumptive sentence length in months)**

The italicized numbers within the grid denote the range within which a judge may sentence without the sentence being deemed a departure. The criminal history score is computed by adding one point for each prior felony conviction, one-half point for each prior gross misdemeanor conviction, and one-quarter point for each prior misdemeanor conviction.

SOURCE: Minnesota Sentencing Guidelines Commission, *Report to the Legislature* (1983).

NOTE: First-degree murder is excluded from the guidelines by law and is punished by life imprisonment.

## Appeals

Imposition of a sentence does not mean that it must be served immediately; the defendant has the right to appeal the verdict to a higher court. An **appeal** is based on a contention that one or more errors of law were made during the criminal justice process. A defendant might base an appeal, for example, on the contention that evidence was improperly admitted, that the judge did not charge the jury correctly, or that a guilty plea was not made voluntarily. Appeals are based on questions of procedure, not on the defendant's guilt or innocence. It is for the government to prove, in the ways required by the law, that the individual is guilty. If mistakes were made by the prosecution or judge, then a conviction may be reversed. The conviction is then set aside, and the defendant may be retried. Many states provide for an automatic appeal in capital cases.

### Basis for Appeals

Unlike most other Western countries, the United States does not allow the terms of the sentence to be appealed in most circumstances. An appeal may be filed when it is contended that the judge selected penalties that did not accord with the law or that there were violations of either due process or equal protection. But if the law gave the judge the discretion to impose a sentence of, for example, ten years in a particular case and the defendant thought that his or her actions warranted only eight, it would be quite unusual for the sentence to be overturned on appeal unless some procedural defect were shown. It would be necessary to show that the decision was illegal, unreasonable, or unconstitutional.

A case originating in a state court is usually appealed through that state's judicial system. When a state case involves a constitutional question, however, it may be appealed to the U.S. Supreme Court. Almost four-fifths of all appeals are decided by state courts.

There has been an increase in the number of appeals in both the state and federal courts during the past decade. What is the nature of these cases? A five-state study by Joy Chapper and Roger Hanson showed: (1) although a majority of appeals occur after trial convictions, about a quarter result from nontrial proceedings such as guilty pleas and probation revocations; (2) homicides and other serious crimes against persons comprise over 50 percent of appeals; (3) most appeals arise from cases in which the sentence is five years or less; and (4) the issues raised at appeal tend to concern the introduction of evidence, the sufficiency of evidence, and jury instructions.[28]

Chapper and Hanson found that in almost 80 percent of the cases they examined, the appeals were not successful and the decisions of the trial courts were affirmed. Table 11.4 shows the percentage distribution of the outcomes from the appellate process.

## Habeas Corpus

Known as "the great writ," **habeas corpus** is a court command to a person holding a prisoner in custody that requires the prisoner be brought before a judge. This procedure permits a judge to decide whether the person is being legally held. Article III of the U.S. Constitution has been interpreted to extend the application of habeas corpus to federal prisoners, and over time the use of the writ led to a kind of appellate review of the conviction. The right was extended by Congress in 1867 to state prisoners, allowing review of their convictions in federal court after state remedies had been exhausted.

Although very few habeas corpus petitions are successful in federal court (about 3 percent), the number filed has increased by almost 700 percent since the 1870s. This increase has caused concern among federal judges, who find their criminal caseloads greatly expanded. Various tactics, such as allowing magistrates to review petitions and eliminate the frivolous, have been used to deal with the increase.

**appeal**
A request to a higher court that it review actions taken in a completed trial.

**habeas corpus**
A writ or judicial order requesting that a person holding another person produce the prisoner and give reasons to justify continued confinement.

**Table 11.4**
**Percentage distribution of alternative outcomes in five state appellate courts**
Although the public seems to believe that defendants exercising their right of appeal will be released, this study shows that while 20 percent have their convictions reversed, only a few are acquitted by the appellate court.

SOURCE: Joy Chapper and Roger Hanson, *Understanding Reversible Error in Criminal Appeals* (Williamsburg, Va.: National Center for State Court, 1989).

| Appeal Outcome | Percentage of Appeals | Percentage of Appeals Reversed |
|---|---|---|
| Conviction affirmed | 79.4 | — |
| Conviction reversed | 20.6 | 100.0 |
| Acquittal | 1.9 | 9.4 |
| New trial | 6.6 | 31.9 |
| Resentencing | 7.3 | 35.3 |
| Other | 4.8 | 23.4 |

## Evaluating the Appellate Process

The public seems to believe that many offenders are being "let off" through the appellate process. In addition, frustrated by the problems of crime, some conservatives have argued that opportunities for appeal should be limited. It is said that too many offenders delay imposition of their sentences and that others completely evade the sanctions by filing appeals endlessly. This practice not only increases the workload of the courts but also jeopardizes the concept of the finality of the justice process. It is important to note, however, that since 90 percent of accused persons plead guilty, the number of cases that might be appealed is greatly diminished.

A successful appeal for the defendant, one that results in reversal of the conviction, normally means that the case is remanded to the lower court for a new trial. At this point the state must consider whether the procedural errors in the original trial can be overcome and whether it is worth additional expenditure to bring the defendant into court again. Appeal performs the important function of righting wrongs. Beyond that, its presence is a constant influence on the daily operations of the criminal justice system.

## Summary

The public's assumptions about the criminal justice system are greatly influenced by newspapers and television. Most people are exposed to only the most noteworthy cases—the criminal trials that become public dramas. In this chapter, the final one in the part on adjudication, you have seen the eight steps of the trial process: jury selection, opening statements, presentation of the prosecution's evidence, presentation of the defense's evidence, presentation of rebuttal witnesses, closing arguments, judge's instructions to the jury, and the jury's decision.

The sanction imposed by the court heavily influences the actions of the judge, the prosecutor, the defense attorney, and the defendant. The sentencing process in misdemeanor courts is akin to an assembly line in which cases are dealt with in a speedy and routinized manner. In felony courts the processes are more formal, but even here guilty pleas predominate and there are few trials by juries. The judge is guided by a presentence report prepared by a probation officer. In many states, sentencing guidelines, designed to reduce sentence disparity, force the judge to choose a sanction that is similar to those imposed on other offenders convicted of the same offense.

Offenders may appeal their convictions on legal grounds, but in most jurisdictions in the United States it is not possible to appeal the sentence. Part 4 focuses on postconviction strategies. The sentencing process, introduced in this chapter, is explored more fully in Chapter 12.

## Questions for Review

1   Since there are so few jury trials, what types of cases would you expect to find adjudicated in this manner? Why?
2   Given that so few cases ever reach a jury, why are juries such an important part of the criminal justice system?
3   What influences the sentencing behavior of judges?
4   What are the major differences between misdemeanor and felony courts?
5   What is the impact of appeals on the criminal justice system?
6   What is a habeas corpus petition?

## Key Terms and Cases

| | | |
|---|---|---|
| appeal | *habeas corpus* | sentencing guidelines |
| bench trial | jury | testimony |
| challenge for cause | peremptory challenge | voir dire |
| circumstantial evidence | presentence report | *Williams* v. *Florida* (1970) |
| direct evidence | real evidence | |
| | reasonable doubt | |

## For Further Reading

Harris, Jean. *Stranger in Two Worlds*. New York: Macmillan, 1986. The autobiography of Jean Harris, whose trial and murder conviction occupied public attention. This book tells of her experience through the trial and while incarcerated.

Hastie, Reid, Steven Penrod, and Nancy Pennington. *Inside the Jury*. (Cambridge: Harvard University Press, 1983). A study of the jury process and the elements of decision making.

Levine, James P. *Juries and Politics*. Pacific Grove, Calif.: Brooks/Cole, 1992. An overview of the jury system in the United States with a special perspective on the influence of politics.

Wishman, Seymour. *Anatomy of a Jury*. New York: Times Books, 1986. Inside the jury room.

Wolfe, Linda. *Wasted: The Preppie Murder*. New York: Simon and Schuster, 1989. A full account of the case of *The People* v. *Robert Chambers* and the people involved.

# Notes

1  Linda Wolfe, *Wasted: The Preppie Murder* (New York: Simon and Schuster, 1989), 293.

2  Steven Phillips, *No Heroes, No Villains* (New York: Random House, 1977), 109.

3  Valerie P. Hans and Neil Vidmar, *Judging the Jury* (New York: Plenum, 1986), 109.

4  399 U.S. 78 (1970).

5  441 U.S. 130 (1979).

6  David Kairys, Joseph B. Kadane, and John P. Lehoczky, "Jury Representativeness: A Mandate for Multiple Source Lists," 65 *California Law Review* 776 (1977).

7  James J. Gobert, "In Search of the Impartial Jury," *Journal of Criminal Law and Criminology* 79 (1988): 269–327; Marvin B. Steinberg, "The Case for Eliminating Peremptory Challenges," *Criminal Law Bulletin* 27 (1991): 216–229.

8  Hans and Vidmar, *Judging the Jury*, 90.

9  F. Lee Bailey and Henry B. Rothblat, *Successful Techniques for Criminal Trials* (New York: Lawyers Cooperative, 1971), 83.

10  *Griffin* v. *California*, 380 U.S. 609 (1965).

11  Phillips, *No Heroes, No Villains*, 214.

12  Geoffrey P. Kramer and Dorean M. Koenig, "Do Jurors Understand Criminal Justice Instructions? Analyzing the Results of the Michigan Juror Comprehension Project, *University of Michigan Journal of Law Reform* 23 (1990): 401–437.

13  Fred Strodtbeck, Rita James, and Gordon Hawkins, "Social Status in Jury Deliberations," *American Sociological Review* 22 (1957): 713–719.

14  David W. Broeder, "The University of Chicago Jury Project," 38 *Nebraska Law Review* 774 (1959).

15  Reid Hastie, Steven Penrod, and Nancy Pennington, *Inside the Jury* (Cambridge, Mass.: Harvard University Press, 1983), 199.

16  Harry Kalven, Jr., and Hans Zeisel, *The American Jury* (Boston: Little, Brown, 1966), 62.

17  Robert Roper and Victor Flango, "Trials Before Judges and Juries," *Justice System Journal* 8 (Spring 1983): 186.

18  As quoted in Ronald L. Goldfarb and Linda R. Singer, *After Conviction* (New York: Simon and Schuster, 1973), 138.

19  Susan S. Silbey, "Making Sense of the Lower Courts," *Justice System Journal* 6 (Spring 1981): 20.

20  Malcolm Feeley, *The Process Is the Punishment* (New York: Russell Sage Foundation, 1979).

21  Feeley, *Process Is the Punishment*, 200.

22  Frederick J. Gaudet, G. S. Harris, and C. W. St. John, "Individual Differences in Sentencing Tendencies of Judges," *Journal of Criminal Law and Criminology* 23 (1933): 814.

23  Martin A. Levin, "Urban Politics and Policy Outcomes: The Criminal Courts," in *Criminal Justice: Law and Politics*, 6th ed., ed. George F. Cole (Belmont, Calif.: Wadsworth, 1993), 348.

24  337 U.S. 241 (1949).

25  430 U.S. 349 (1977).

26  Robert M. Carter and Leslie T. Wilkins, "Some Factors in Sentencing Policy," *Journal of Criminal Law, Criminology, and Police Science* 58 (1967): 503.

27  Terance D. Miethe and Charles A. Moore, "Sentencing Guidelines: Their Effect in Minnesota," *Research in Brief* (Washington, D.C.: National Institute of Justice, 1989).

28  Joy A. Chapper and Roger A. Hanson, *Understanding Reversible Error in Criminal Appeals* (Williamsburg, Va.: National Center for State Courts, 1989), 4.

# Corrections

**Throughout history** there has been no agreement about the best sanctions to use against lawbreakers. Unfortunately, over time the corrections system has risen to peaks of excited reform, only to drop to valleys of despairing failure. In Part 4 we look at how the American system of criminal justice now deals with offenders. As we will see, the processes of sentencing and corrections are intended to penalize the individual found guilty and to impress upon others that those who transgress the law will be punished. Chapters 12 through 17 will discuss how offenders are treated and how various influences have structured our correctional system. As these chapters unfold, recall the processes that have occurred before the imposition of a sentence and how these processes are linked to the ways offenders are punished in the correctional portion of the criminal justice system.

# Sentencing

**"All rise!"** The courtroom audience stands as Judge John G. Davies of the United States District Court of Los Angeles, robed in black, strides from his office and mounts the dais. On this day in August 1993 the courtroom is packed with attorneys, reporters, and members of the defendants' families. Judge Davies is about to sentence Sergeant Stacey C. Koon and Officer Laurence M. Powell, convicted in April 1993 of violating the civil rights of Rodney G. King when they beat him with their batons in March 1991 following a traffic stop. The beating, shown on television throughout the world, shocked the public. It was the acquittal of Koon, Powell, and two other officers of assault charges in a 1992 state trial that led to the Los Angeles riots in which more than fifty people died.

In the days before sentencing there had been much speculation in the media as to the judge's intentions. Under the federal sentencing guidelines the officers could receive punishments ranging from probation to ten years in prison and fines up to $250,000. Los Angeles officials had voiced concern about the possibility of further riots if the minority community viewed the sentences as lenient.

Rather than simply announcing the terms of the punishment, Judge Davies took pains to review the case and to explain the reasons for the sentence. He seemed to be sympathetic to the officers, who he described as "good family men and good police officers."[1] He accepted their argument that Mr. King, a paroled felon who had fled from the police and resisted arrest, bore much of the responsibility for the beating. But he found the blows inflicted that finally subdued King to be totally unjustified and criminal.

In sentencing officers Koon and Powell to prison terms of thirty to thirty-seven months, Judge Davies was required to employ the federal guidelines. As discussed in Chapter 11, guidelines are used by judges to calculate a sentence based on the offense and on aggravating and mitigating factors. The judge explained that he had adjusted the sentence downward because of the victim's conduct, because of the officers' public humiliation and job loss, and because the offenders did not present a danger to the community (see Figure 12.1). In August 1994 the U.S. Ninth Circuit Court of Appeals ruled that Judge Davies had improperly deviated from the guidelines when he made deductions from the offense score. The court ordered that the officers be resentenced and given more prison time.

Sentencing, or the specification of the sanction, can be viewed as both the beginning and the end of the criminal justice system. After guilt has been established, a decision must be made concerning what to do with the convicted person. Public interest seems to wane at this point; usually the convicted criminal is out of sight and thus out of mind as far as society is concerned. But for the offender, the passing of sentence is the beginning of corrections, with its restriction of freedom and its promise of rehabilitation.

**Figure 12.1**
**Sentencing according to the U.S. sentencing guidelines**
Here is how Judge John G. Davies computed the sentences of Sgt. Stacey Koon and Officer Laurence Powell, using federal guidelines that assign certain points for each offense and that deduct points for each mitigating circumstance.
SOURCE: *New York Times*, 6 August 1993.

| Offenses | |
|---|---|
| Aggravated assault | 15 |
| Use of dangerous weapon | 4 |
| Bodily injury | 2 |
| Civil rights violation | 6 |
| Subtotal | 27 |

**Sentence for 27 points = 70 to 87 months**

| Deductions | |
|---|---|
| Victim's conduct | −5 |
| Notoriety, double jeopardy, loss of job, lack of danger, atypical case | −3 |
| Subtotal | −8 |
| **Total** | 19 |

**Sentence for 19 points = 30 to 37 months**

The criminal justice system aims to solve the three basic problems in the law: What conduct should be designated as criminal? What must be determined before a person can be found to have committed a criminal offense? What should be done with persons who are found to have committed criminal offenses? Earlier chapters emphasized the first two problems, but, as we have seen, the assumptions a society makes about any of the three problems greatly influence its interpretation of the others. The answers given by the legal system to the first question constitute the basic norms of the society: do not murder, rob, sell drugs, commit treason. The process of determining guilt or innocence is stipulated by the law and is greatly influenced by the administrative and interpersonal considerations of criminal justice actors. In this chapter we will begin to examine the third problem: the sanctions or punishments specified by the law. We will consider the four goals of punishment: retribution, deterrence, incapacitation, and rehabilitation. We will then explore the forms (incarceration, inter-mediate sanctions, probation, and death) that the punishment takes to achieve the goals.

## Questions for Inquiry

- What are the goals of punishment?
- What is the reality of sentencing? Is it based on one objective?
- What are the various types of sentences that judges may impose?
- Does our criminal justice system treat all wrongdoers equally?

## The Goals of Punishment

Officer Laurence M. Powell (above) and Sergeant Stacey C. Koon (pictured on page 433) were originally sentenced to prison terms of thirty to thirty-seven months for violating the civil rights of Rodney G. King, but an August 1994 appeals court ruling ordered that they be given longer sentences.

Throughout the history of Western civilization, punishment for violations of the criminal law has been shaped by philosophical and moral orienta-tions. Although the ultimate goal of the criminal sanction is assumed to be the maintenance of social order, different justifications have emerged in different eras to legitimize the punishment imposed by the state. The ancient custom of severing a limb of a thief who stole was once justified as an act of retribution; in later periods, similar penalties were exacted—capital punishment, for example—on the grounds of incapacitation or deterrence. Over time, Western countries have moved away from the im-position of physical pain as a form of retribution and toward greater re-liance on restrictions of freedom and the use of social and psychological efforts to change behavior.

In the United States today the term *punishment* often has an ideologi-cal connotation that links it to retribution and not to the other justifica-tions for the criminal sanction. It is difficult for some people to reconcile the goal of rehabilitation with the fact of punishment. Are individuals being punished if they are in a correctional facility that emphasizes ther-apy? Is probation a punishment?

Herbert Packer argues that punishment is marked by these elements:

1 The presence of an offense.
2 The infliction of pain on account of the commission of the offense.
3 A dominant purpose that is neither to compensate someone injured by the offense nor to better the offender's condition but to prevent further offenses or to inflict what is thought to be deserved pain on the offender.[2]

Note that Packer emphasizes two major goals of criminal punishment: the deserved infliction of suffering on evildoers and the prevention of crime.

Jeremy Bentham was the foremost writer on jurisprudence and criminology of the late eighteenth century. Although he earned a master's degree in law at Oxford and was admitted to the bar in 1767 he actually spent little time practicing law. Instead, he is best known for promulgating the theory of *utilitarianism*. He believed that human beings decide how to act by calculating the relative amounts of pleasure and pain derived from various actions and that all laws should therefore be guided by a principle of rational utility. When applied to punishment, this principle demands that the "pleasure" value of committing a crime be outweighed by the pain associated with punishment. People would not rationally choose to commit crimes if they were deterred by the likelihood of a quick, certain, and commensurate penalty.

Bentham applied utilitarian principles to prison management as well. He advocated many prison reforms, including reform of prisoners' morals, health care, and education. His planned "panopticon" prison was of circular design to reduce the number of guards required (they could view all prisoners from the center of the circle) and was to be operated by a manager who would employ the convicts in contract labor. The prison in Stateville, Illinois, built between 1916 and 1924, was modeled on his design.

In the twentieth century four goals of the criminal sanction are acknowledged in the United States: retribution (deserved punishment), deterrence, incapacitation, and rehabilitation. Although no one goal is the sole reason for a particular sentence, from the 1940s until the 1970s most legislatures stipulated that rehabilitation was to be given priority. That judges often acknowledged the importance of other goals and that legislatures failed to appropriate more resources to implement the rehabilitative goal did not strike many citizens as odd.

## Retribution, or Deserved Punishment

"An eye for an eye, a tooth for a tooth" has been a purpose of the criminal sanction since biblical times. Although the ancient saying may sound barbaric today, it can be thought of as a definition of **retribution**: Those who do a wrong should be punished alike, in proportion to the gravity of the offense or to the extent to which others have been made to suffer. Retribution is punishment that is deserved.

Some scholars claim that the desire for retribution is a basic human emotion. They maintain that if the state does not provide criminal sanctions—through which the community may express its revulsion of offensive acts—citizens will take the law into their own hands. Retribution is thus an expression of the community's disapproval of crime. According to this view, if retribution is not exacted, the disapproval may also disappear. A community that is too ready to forgive a wrongdoer may end up approving the crime.

A recent development in criminal justice has been the resurgence of interest in retribution as a justification for the criminal sanction. Using the concept of "just deserts or deserved punishment," some theorists have advanced the idea that one who infringes on the rights of others does wrong and deserves blame for that conduct.[3] Andrew von Hirsch, a leading contemporary writer on punishment, has said that in such instances "the sanctioning authority is entitled to choose a response that expresses moral disapproval: namely, punishment."[4] The argument is made by von Hirsch and others that punishment should be applied only for the wrong inflicted and not for utilitarian benefits (deterrence, incapacitation, rehabilitation). Offenders should be penalized for their wrongful acts because fairness and justice demand punishment.

## Deterrence

In the eighteenth and nineteenth centuries, followers of Jeremy Bentham, called Benthamites or utilitarians, were struck by what seemed to be the pointlessness of retribution. These reformers held to Bentham's theory of utilitarianism (described in the Biography), which claimed that human behavior was governed by an individual's calculation of whether an action will ultimately result in more pleasure or pain. They argued that punishment by itself is unjustifiable unless it can be shown that more "good" results if it is inflicted than if it is withheld. The presumed good was the prevention of the greater evil, crime. The basic objective of punishment, they said, was to deter potential criminals by the example of the sanctions laid on the guilty.

Contemporary ideas of deterrence have incorporated two subsidiary concepts: **general deterrence**, which is probably most directly linked to Bentham's ideas, and **special deterrence**. The premise of general deterrence is that the general population will be dissuaded from criminal behavior by observing that punishment will necessarily follow commission of a crime and that the pain of punishment will be greater than the benefits which may stem from the illegal act. For general deterrence to be effective, the public must be informed of the equation and continually reminded of it by the punishments of the convicted. The punishment must be severe enough so that all will be impressed by the consequences. Public hanging was once considered to be important for its effect as a general deterrent.

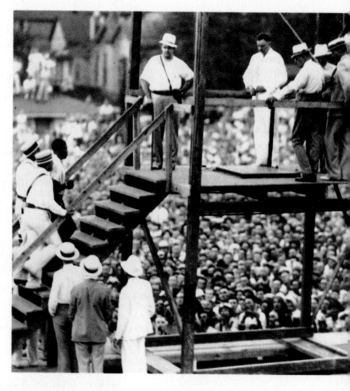

Public executions are thought to strengthen general deterrence. The hanging of Rainey Bethea in Owensboro, Kentucky, in 1936 was the last such execution in the United States. Why have we moved executions out of public view?

Special deterrence (often called *specific* or *individual deterrence*) is concerned with changes in the behavior of the convicted. It is individualized in that the amount and the type of punishment are calculated to deter the criminal from repeating the offense. Under special deterrence, the most important question becomes, "What does the criminal need?"

There are some obvious difficulties with the concept of deterrence. In many cases, for example, the goals of general and special deterrence are incompatible. The level of punishment necessary to impress the populace may be inconsistent with the needs of an individual offender. For example, the public disgrace and disbarment of a wrongdoing attorney may be effective in preventing her or him from committing further criminal acts, but to some observers the sanction may seem inconsequential.

A larger problem with the goal of deterrence is obtaining proof of its effectiveness. Social science is unable to measure the effects of general deterrence; only those who are *not* deterred come to the attention of criminal justice researchers, while a valid study of the deterrent effects of punishment would have to examine the impact of different forms of the criminal sanction on various *potential* lawbreakers. An additional consideration is how the criminal justice system influences the effect of deterrence through the speed, certainty, and severity of the allocated punishment. While deterrence is believed to be a prominent goal of the criminal sanction, the exact nature of deterrence and the extent to which sentencing policies may be altered to fulfill its purpose rest on a shaky scientific foundation.

**retribution**
Punishment inflicted on a person who has infringed on the rights of others and so deserves to be penalized. The severity of the sanction should fit the seriousness of the crime.

**general deterrence**
Punishment of criminals that is intended to serve as an example to the general public and to discourage the commission of offenses.

## Incapacitation

**special deterrence**
Punishment that is inflicted on criminals with the intent to discourage them from committing any future crimes.

**incapacitation**
Deprivation of the ability to commit crimes against society, usually by detention in prison.

"Lock them up and throw away the key!" Such sentiments are heard often from citizens outraged by some illegal act. The assumption of **incapacitation** is that a crime may be prevented if criminals are physically restrained. In primitive societies, banishment from the community was the usual method of preventing a recurrence of forbidden behavior. In early America, offenders often agreed to move away or to join the army as an alternative to some other form of punishment. Prison is the typical mode of incapacitation, since offenders can be kept under control so that they cannot violate the rules of society. Capital punishment is the ultimate method of incapacitation.

Any policy that incarcerates or physically restricts the offender has some incapacitative effect, even when retribution, deterrence, or rehabilitation is the espoused goal. But the incapacitative sanction is different from these other goals in that it is future oriented (unlike retribution); it is based on personal characteristics of the offender, not on characteristics of the crime (unlike general deterrence); and it is not intended to reform the criminal (unlike rehabilitation). Incapacitation is thus imposed because a person of a certain personality has committed a particular type of crime and is believed to be likely to repeat the offense.

One problem of incapacitation is that of undue severity. If its objective is prevention, imprisonment may be justified for both a trivial and a serious offense. A more important issue is the length of incarceration. Presumably, offenders are not released until the state is reasonably sure that they will no longer commit crimes. Not only is such a prediction difficult to make, but also it may be that these offenders can never be released.[5]

**selective incapacitation**
Making optimum use of expensive and limited prison space by targeting for incarceration those individuals whose incapacity will do the most to reduce crime.

In recent years greater attention has been paid to the concept of **selective incapacitation**. Research has suggested that a relatively small number of offenders are responsible for a large number of violent and property crimes. Burglars, for example, tend to commit many offenses before they are caught, so it is argued that they should receive long terms in prison. Sentencing policies, it is asserted, should be directed so that such career criminals will be imprisoned for long periods.[6] The costs of such a policy, however, are worth considering: correctional facilities would have to be expanded; it would be more difficult to obtain convictions because the accused would not plea bargain if aware that a long prison term would result; and policing activities would have to be upgraded to catch and convict these serious offenders.

## Rehabilitation

**rehabilitation**
The goal of restoring a convicted offender to a constructive place in society through some form of vocational, educational, or therapeutic treatment.

**Rehabilitation** is undoubtedly the most appealing modern justification for use of the criminal sanction. That the offender should be treated and resocialized while under the care of the state is not an entirely new idea and is even found in some of Bentham's writings. What is new is the belief that techniques are available to identify and treat the causes of the offender's behavior. If the criminal behavior is assumed to result from some social, psychological, or biological disorder, then the treatment of that disorder becomes the primary goal of corrections. Because rehabilitation is oriented solely toward the offender, no relationship can be maintained between the severity of the punishment and the gravity of the crime.

According to the concept of rehabilitation, offenders are not being punished, they are being treated and will return to society when they are well. The assumption that offenders are in need of treatment, not punishment, requires that they remain in custody only until they are "cured." Consequently, the judge should set not a fixed sentence but rather an **indeterminate sentence** with maximum and minimum terms so that correctional officials, through the parole board, may release inmates when they have been rehabilitated. The indeterminate sentence is also justified by the failures of fixed sentences: If prisoners know when they are going to be released, they may not engage in the treatment programs prescribed for their rehabilitation.

From the 1940s until the 1970s the rehabilitative ideal was so widely shared that matters of treatment and reform of the offender were generally the only issues given serious attention in the whole field of criminal justice and corrections. Since then, however, the rehabilitative model has come under closer scrutiny and has been partially discredited. Some social scientists have even wondered whether the causes of crime and individual disorders can be accurately diagnosed or treated.

The various goals of punishment are summarized in Table 12.1.

**indeterminate sentence**
A period set by a judge in which there is a spread between the minimum date for a decision on parole eligibility and a maximum date for completion of the sentence. In holding that the time necessary for treatment cannot be set, the indeterminate sentence is closely associated with rehabilitation.

| Goal | Judge's Statement |
|------|-------------------|
| Retribution | I am imposing this sentence because you deserve to be punished for violating the civil rights of Rodney King. Your criminal behavior in this case is the basis of the punishment. Justice requires that I impose a sanction at a level that illustrates the importance that the community places on upholding limitations on police use of force. |
| Deterrence | I am imposing this sentence so that your punishment for violation of Rodney King's civil rights will serve as an example and deter others who may contemplate similar actions. In addition, I hope that this sentence will deter you from ever again committing such an illegal act. |
| Incapacitation | I am imposing this sentence so that you will be incapacitated and hence unable to violate someone's civil rights during the length of this term. Since you have not committed prior offenses, selective incapacitation is not warranted. |
| Rehabilitation | The trial testimony and information contained in the presentence report makes me believe that there are aspects of your personality that led you to violate the civil rights of Rodney King. I am therefore imposing this sentence so that you can receive treatment that will rectify your behavior so that you will not commit another criminal act. With proper treatment you should be able to return to society and lead a crime-free life. |

**Table 12.1**
**The goals of punishment**
At sentencing the judge usually gives reasons for the punishments imposed. Here are possible statements that Judge John G. Davies might have given to Los Angeles police officers Stacey Koon and Laurence Powell depending upon the goal of the sanction that he wanted to promote.

## The Reality of Sentencing

Although the goals and justifications of criminal sanctions are often discussed as if they were distinct, most of the objectives overlap to a great extent. A sentence of life imprisonment can be philosophically justified in terms of its primary goal of incapacitation, but the secondary functions of retribution and deterrence are also present. Deterrence is such a broad concept that it mixes well with all the other purposes, with the possible exception of rehabilitation, where logically only specific deterrence applies. Bentham's notion that the pain of criminal punishment must be present as an example to others cannot be met if the prescribed treatment for the rehabilitation of offenders requires a therapeutic environment.

As the Close-Up on the following pages illustrates, the burden of determining a sentence that accommodates these values in a particular case is an extremely difficult task for the trial judge. In one case, a forger may be sentenced to prison as an example to others despite the fact that she is no threat to community safety and is probably not in need of rehabilitative corrections. In another case, the judge may impose a light sentence on a youthful offender who, although he has committed a serious crime, may be a good risk for rehabilitation if he can be moved quickly back into society.

That judges have wide powers of discretion with regard to sentencing is reflected in the combining of forms to tailor the punishment to the offender. The judge may stipulate, for example, that the prison terms for two charges are to run either concurrently or consecutively or that all or part of the period of imprisonment is to be suspended. In other situations, the offender may be given a combination of a suspended prison term, probation, and a fine. Execution of the sentence may be suspended as long as the offender stays out of trouble, makes restitution, or seeks medical treatment. The judge may delay imposing any sentence but retain power to set penalties at a later date if conditions warrant. The variety of choices emphasizes the fluidity of sentencing. Judges have wide discretion with regard to sentencing, which often results in disparity of sentences given to similar offenders convicted of the same crime.

## Forms of the Criminal Sanction

**intermediate sanctions**

A variety of punishments that are more restrictive than traditional probation but less stringent and less costly than incarceration.

Incarceration, **intermediate sanctions**, probation, and death are the basic forms that the criminal sanction takes in the United States. In the popular mind, incarceration is the expected fate for most felons and serious misdemeanants—and has been throughout American history. This image has been maintained over time through books, songs, and films. As a consequence, much of the public views alternatives to incarceration, such as probation, as sanctions that allow offenders to "get off." However, the form and the severity of criminal punishment vary across cultures, as seen in the Comparative Perspective on the use of corporal punishment in Singapore (pages 444–445).

Many scholars believe that sentencing structures in the United States are both too severe and too lenient—many offenders who do not warrant incarceration are sent to prison, and many who should be given more restrictive punishments receive little probation supervision. It is because there seems to be little use of sanctions more severe than probation but less severe than incarceration that Norval Morris and Michael Tonry have advocated the more widespread use of intermediate sanctions.[7] These punishments provide a variety of restrictions on freedom, such as fines, house arrest, intensive supervision probation, restitution, and community service. They can be used singly or in combination in order to exact a punishment equal to the severity of the offense and the characteristics of the offender. With prisons now overcrowded and overwhelming probation caseloads in many urban areas, intermediate punishments are attracting renewed attention.

Among the forms of the criminal sanction is capital punishment. Questions about the morality and usefulness of capital punishment have been argued throughout recent history. We will consider these questions in some detail later in this section and ask why there has been a revival of death sentences and so few executions during the past decade.

## Incarceration

Imprisonment is the most visible penalty imposed by U.S. courts. Though fewer than 30 percent of persons under correctional supervision are in prisons and jails, incarceration remains the almost exclusive means for punishing those who commit serious crimes, and it is also widely used against misdemeanants. Because of its severity, imprisonment is thought to have the greatest effect in deterring potential offenders, but it is expensive for the state to carry out and may prevent the offender's later reintegration into society.

Penal codes vary as to whether the permitted sentences are indeterminate, determinate, or mandatory. Each type of sentence makes certain assumptions about the goals of the criminal sanction, and each allocates discretionary authority. It is also from the types of sentences authorized by the legislature that the problems of disparity, unchecked discretion, and excessive lengths occur.

**Good Time**   Although not a type of sentence, "good time" and its impact on sentencing should be mentioned here. In all but four states, days are subtracted from prisoners' minimum or maximum term for good behavior or for participation in various types of vocational, educational, and treatment programs. Correctional officials consider these sentence-reduction policies necessary to maintain institutional order and to reduce overcrowding. Good time is also taken into consideration by prosecutors and defense attorneys during plea bargaining.

## A Trial Judge at Work:
## Judge Robert Satter

I am never more conscious of striving to balance the scales of justice than when I am sentencing the convicted. On one scale is society, violated by a crime, on the other is the defendant, fallible, but nonetheless human.

As a trial judge I am faced with the insistent task of sentencing a particular defendant who never fails to assert his own individuality. I hear each cry out, in the words of Thomas Wolfe, "Does not this wonderful and unique I, that never was before and never will be again; this I of tender favor, beloved of the gods, come before the Eye of Judgment and always plead exception?"

In my early years on the bench, I presided mainly over misdemeanors, which are crimes punishable by a sentence of less than one year in jail. Because they are not so serious, I could be more creative, or even experimental, in sentencing.

When sparing a defendant from going to jail, I often imposed conditions related to the crime or the underlying cause of the crime. Young boys charged with destroying public property might be required to spend several Saturdays weeding the flower beds in the town green. A man charged with exposing himself in public might be required to obtain psychiatric treatment. If a husband was accused of beating his wife for the first time, I would get the court family relations officer to counsel the couple. When a crime stemmed from alcoholism, I would order that the offender attend Alcoholics Anonymous.

Later in my career when I came to hear felony cases, I found to my surprise that sentencing for minor crimes is more difficult than sentencing for serious ones. The decision for misdemeanors is whether to incarcerate; that is the hard one. The decision for felonies is the number of years in the state prison; that is much easier. But sometimes even felony cases present the dilemma of whether to imprison or not to imprison.

George Edwards was tried before me for sexual assault, first degree. The victim, Barbara Babson, was a personable woman in her late twenties and a junior executive in an insurance company. She described on the stand what had happened to her:

> I was returning to my Hartford apartment with two armloads of groceries. As I entered the elevator, a man followed me. He seemed vaguely familiar but I couldn't quite place him. When I reached my floor and started to open my door, I noticed him behind me. He offered to hold my bags. God, I knew right then I was making a mistake. He pushed me into the apartment and slammed the door. He said, "Don't you know me? I work at Travelers with you." Then I remembered him in the cafeteria and I remembered him once staring at me. Now I could feel his eyes roving over my body, and I heard him say, "I want to screw you." He said it so calmly at first, I didn't believe him. I tried to talk him out of it. When he grabbed my neck, I began to cry and then to scream. His grip tightened, and that really scared me. He forced me into the bedroom, made me take off my clothes. "Then," she sobbed, "he pushed my legs apart and entered me."

"What happened next?" the state's attorney asked.

"He told me he was going to wait in the next room, and if I tried to leave he would kill me. I found some cardboards, wrote HELP! on them, and put them in my window. But nobody came. Eventually I got up the courage to open the door, and he had left. I immediately called the police."

Edwards's lawyer cross-examined her vigorously, dragging her through the intimate details of her sex life. Then he tried to get her to admit that she had willingly participated in sex with the defendant. Through it all, she maintained her poise. She left the stand with her version of the crime intact.

Edwards took the stand in his own defense. A tall man with bushy hair, he was wearing baggy trousers and a rumpled shirt. In a low voice he testified that the woman had always smiled at him at work. He had learned her name and address and gone to her apartment house that day. When he offered to help her with her bundles, she invited him into her apartment. She was very nice and very willing to have sex. He denied using force.

I did not believe him. I could not conceive that Miss Babson would have called the police, pressed the charges, and relived the horrors of the experience on the stand if the crime had not been committed as she testified. The jury did not believe him either. They readily returned a verdict of guilty.

First-degree sexual assault is a class B felony punishable by a maximum of twenty years in the state prison. If I had sentenced Edwards then, I would have sent him to prison for many years. But sentencing could take place only after a presentence report had been prepared by a probation officer.

The report was dropped off in my chambers a few days before the sentencing date. Unlike the trial, which had portrayed Edwards in the context of the crime, the presentence report portrayed the crime in the context of Edwards's life.

It revealed that Edwards was thirty-one years old, born of a black father and white mother. He had graduated from high school and had an associate's degree from a community college. He had served in Vietnam, where he had been decorated with the Purple Heart for wounds in action and the Bronze Star for bravery under fire. After the army, Edwards had worked successfully as a coordinator of youth programs in the inner city of Hartford. Simultaneously he had taken computer courses. At the time of the crime, he was a computer programmer at Travelers Insurance Company. Edwards was separated from his wife and child, and fellow employees had recently noticed a personality change in him; he seemed withdrawn, depressed, and sometimes confused. His only criminal offense was a disorderly conduct charge three months before the crime, which had not been prosecuted.

I gazed out the window of my chambers and reflected. What should be my sentence?

Before the rescheduled date, I had weighed the factors, made up my mind, and lived with my decision for several days. In serious criminal cases I do not like to make snap judgment from the bench. I may sometimes allow myself to be persuaded by the lawyers' arguments to reduce a preconceived sentence, but never to raise it.

I nod to the state's attorney to begin. He asks to have Miss Babson speak first. She comes forward to the counsel table. "That man," she says, pointing to Edwards, "did a horrible thing. He should be severely punished not only for what he did to me, but for what he could do to other women. I am furious at him. As far as I am concerned, Judge, I hope you lock him up and throw away the key."

She abruptly stops and sits down. The state's attorney deliberately pauses to let her words sink in before he stands up. Speaking with less emotion but equal determination, he says,

*This was a vicious crime. There are not many more serious than rape. The defendant cynically tried to put the blame on the victim. But it didn't wash. She has been damaged in the most fundamental way. And the defendant doesn't show the slightest remorse. I urge the maximum punishment of twenty years in prison.*

Edwards's lawyer starts off by mentioning his client's splendid Vietnam war record and his lack of a criminal record. Then he goes on, "George and his wife have begun living together again with their child, and they are trying to pick up the pieces of their lives. More important," the lawyer continues, "George started seeing a psychiatrist six weeks ago."

The lawyer concludes, "If you will give George a suspended sentence, Your Honor, and make a condition of probation that he stay in treatment, he won't be before this court again. George Edwards is a good risk."

I look at Edwards. "Do you have anything you want to say, Mr. Edwards?"

The question takes him by surprise. Gathering his thoughts, he says with emotion, "I'm sorry for what I did, Judge. I'm sorry for Barbara, and I understand how she feels. I'm sorry for my wife. I'm…" His voice trails off.

I gaze out the courtroom window struggling for the words to express my sentence. I am always conscious that the same sentence can be given in a way that arouses grudging acceptance or deep hostility.

*Mr. Edwards, you have committed a serious crime. I am not going to punish you to set an example for others, because you should not be held responsible for the incidence of crime in our society. I am going to punish you because, as a mature person, you must pay a price for your offense. The state's attorney asks for twenty years because of the gravity of the crime. Your attorney asks for a suspended sentence because you are attempting to deal with whatever within you caused you to commit the crime. Both make valid arguments. I am partially adopting both recommendations. I herewith sentence you to state prison for six years.*

Edwards wilts. His wife gasps. I continue.

*However, I am suspending execution after four years. I am placing you on probation for the two-year balance of your term on the condition that you continue in psychiatric treatment until discharged by your doctor. The state is entitled to punish you for the crime that you have committed and the harm you have done. You are entitled to leniency for what I discern to be the sincere effort you are making to help yourself.*

Edwards turns to his wife, who rushes up to embrace him. Miss Babson nods to me, not angrily, I think. She walks out of the courtroom and back into her life. As I rise at the bench, a sheriff is leading Edwards down the stairwell to the lockup.

SOURCE: Robert Satter, *Doing Justice: A Trial Judge at Work* (New York: Simon and Schuster, 1990), 170–181. Copyright © 1990 by Robert Satter. Reprinted by permission of the author.

## Corporal Punishment in Singapore

A Singapore court's decision to sentence an American teenager, Michael Fay, to receive a flogging for vandalizing cars with spray paint produced a predictable nod of approval from many Singaporeans, long accustomed to their government's firm hand. For many Americans the punishment seemed unduly harsh, yet others expressed the view that this might be the answer to our crime problem.

Fay was sentenced to six strokes of the cane; four months in prison; and a $2,230 fine after pleading guilty to two counts of vandalism, two counts of mischief, and one count of possessing stolen property. Canings, the term for floggings, in Singapore are carried out by a jailer trained in martial arts who uses a moistened, four-foot rattan cane. The offender is stripped, bound by the hands and feet to a wooden trestle. Pads covering his kidneys and groin are the only protection from the cane. Should he pass out, a doctor will revive him before the caning continues. The wounds generally take two weeks to heal; scarring is permanent.

The amount of good time that can be earned varies among the states—usually from five to ten days a month. The amounts are written into the penal codes of some states and stipulated in department of corrections policy directives in others. In some states, when ninety days of good time are earned, they are vested; that is, they cannot be taken away because of future misbehavior. Prisoners who then violate the rules risk losing only days not vested.

**Indeterminate Sentences** In accord with the goal of rehabilitation, which dominated corrections for much of the past half century, state legislatures also adopted indeterminate (often termed *indefinite*) sentences. On the basis of the notion that correctional personnel must be given the discretion to make a release decision on the grounds of successful treatment, penal codes with indeterminate sentences stipulate a minimum and a maximum amount of time to be served in prison: one to five years, three to ten years, ten to twenty years, one year to life, and so on. At the time of sentencing, the offender knows only the range and that he or she will probably be eligible for parole at some point after the minimum term (minus good time) has been served.

After Singapore gained independence from Britain, the government imposed increasingly harsh penalties for a range of crimes, culminating in laws against such offenses as armed robbery and drug trafficking carrying a mandatory death penalty. Singapore has dropped some traditional safeguards, such as jury trials, on grounds that guilty criminals were manipulating the system to walk free.

Statistics comparing the small city-state of Singapore with Los Angeles, with its roughly equal population of about 3.5 million, provide a dramatic contrast. In 1993, 58 murders, 80 rapes, 1,008 robberies, and 3,162 car thefts were reported in Singapore. Los Angeles Police Department statistics for the same period show 1,100 homicides, 1,855 rapes, 39, 227 robberies, and 65,541 car thefts. There are fewer than 3,800 full-time police officers in Singapore; all guns are outlawed, except those belonging to the police and armed forces. Gun possession carries a stiff prison term, and those who fire one during a crime face a mandatory death sentence.

Another difference with Los Angeles is the makeup of the society itself: 77 percent ethnic Chinese and 14 percent conservative Muslim Malays living in relative isolation on a small island. There is virtually no poverty—80 percent of the people own their homes—and the family remains the backbone of society. There are few divorces, and children live at home until marriage. As in many Asian societies, public shame, for the criminal and for his family, is a potent deterrent.

According to Singapore officials, sentences are intended not just as punishment but as a deterrent. For example, when an 18-year-old man who was called "educationally subnormal" repeatedly kissed a woman in an elevator, he was charged with molestation. A court sentenced him to six months in prison. When the man's lawyer appealed, Chief Justice Yong Pung How, saying "sentences have been too light; they are not having a deterrent effect," increased the punishment to include three whacks of the rattan cane.

SOURCE: Adapted from Charles P. Wallace, "Singapore's Justice System: Harsh, Temptingly Effective," *The Hartford Courant*, 4 April 1994, 1.

Incarceration is the greatest restriction on freedom. Since 1980 the number of people in prison has more than doubled.

**determinate sentence**

A sentence that fixes the term of imprisonment at a specified period of time.

State penal codes vary in the degree of sentencing discretion they permit judges. (For an illustration of discretion in action, see A Question of Ethics.) Court discretion can be described as narrow if the range of sentencing options available to the judge is restricted by law to a third of the statutory maximum sentence for each offense. Thus for a person convicted of a crime carrying a twelve-year statutory maximum, judges with narrow discretion must select a sentence from within, at most, a four-year range (six to ten years, say, or eight to twelve). Even so, the sentences imposed may bear little relation to the amount of time actually served, because parole boards in most of these states have broad discretion in making release decisions.

**Determinate Sentences**  Growing dissatisfaction with the rehabilitative goal led to efforts in support of determinate sentences based on the assumption of deserved punishment. With a **determinate sentence**, a convicted offender is given a specific length of time to be served (two years, five years, ten years). At the end of this term, again minus credited good time, the prisoner is automatically freed, without need for a review by a parole board. Hence release is not tied to participation in a treatment program or to judgment by a parole board on the offender's likelihood of returning to criminal activities.

As states have moved toward determinate structures, some have adopted penal codes that stipulate a specific term for each crime category; others still allow the judge to choose a range of time to be served. Some states emphasize a determinate presumptive sentence; the legislature or often a commission specifies a term based on a time range (for example, fourteen to twenty months) into which most cases should fall. Only in special circumstances should judges veer from the presumptive sentence. Whichever variant is used, however, the offender theoretically knows at sentencing the amount of time to be served. One result of determinate sentencing is that legislatures have tended to reduce judicial discretion as a means of limiting sentencing disparities and ensuring that terms will correspond to those deemed appropriate by the elected body.

**Mandatory Sentences**  Recent years have brought allegations that many offenders are being set free by lenient judges and that the objective of crime control requires greater certainty that criminals will be incapacitated. As a response to these sentencing practices, in 1994 many citizens and politicians advocated life imprisonment without parole for three felony convictions—nicknamed "three strikes you're out." Legislatures have responded to the public outcry and now all but two states require **mandatory sentences**, which stipulate some minimum period of incarceration that must be served by persons convicted of selected crimes. No regard may be given to the circumstances of the offense or the background of the individual; the judge has no discretion and is not allowed to suspend the sentence.

As indicated by Figure 12.2, mandatory prison terms are most often specified for violent crimes, drug violations, habitual offenders, or crimes in which a firearm was used. For example, the Massachusetts gun law decrees that anyone convicted of possessing an unregistered firearm *must* spend one year in jail. But like the 1973 Rockefeller drug law of New York, the Massachusetts law has had no deterrent or incapacitative effects.[8] In the New York case, the draconian sentences prescribed by the law merely raised the stakes for the defendant so high that the prosecution had to bargain to move cases. Studies of the Michigan Felony Firearms Statute found that, although the law was intended to reduce judicial discretion in sentencing, the result was to transfer wide discretion to the prosecuting attorney.[9] As seen in the Close-Up on page 448, the new three strikes law in Washington State has had several unintended consequences.

**mandatory sentence**
A type of sentence determined by statutes, which require that a certain penalty shall be imposed and executed upon certain convicted offenders.

**Figure 12.2**
**Jurisdictions requiring mandatory prison terms in four crime categories**
Although researchers have questioned the effectiveness of mandatory sentences, they are part of the penal code in most states. Why do you suppose this is so?

SOURCE: U.S. Department of Justice, Bureau of Justice Statistics, *Bulletin* (Washington, D.C.: Government Printing Office, 1983), 3.

**a** States with mandatory prison terms for violent crimes

**b** States with mandatory prison terms for habitual offenders

**c** States with mandatory prison terms for narcotic/drug law violations

**d** States with mandatory prison terms for crimes with handguns or other firearms

## A Three-Strike Penal Law Shows It's Not As Simple As It Seems

In the fight against violent crime, perhaps no idea is more popular than "three strikes and you're out"—locking up repeat offenders for life without parole.... But only one state, Washington, has any experience with it. Two months after a law went on the books requiring criminals to spend life in prison without parole if they are convicted of three felonies, the first faces of "three strikes" are emerging. And they present a picture that is more complicated than the baseball slogan that inspired 76 percent of Washington State voters to back the measure last fall.

Prosecutors and police officers say the law has had some unintended side effects. With nothing to lose, some criminals are showing a tendency to be more violent or desperate when officers try to arrest them. And prosecutors say first- and second-time offenders are less willing to plea bargain, which would mean pleading to a felony—the first or second "strike." These offenders are instead forcing full trials in a court system that has neither the manpower nor the space to take on the extra load.

Among the first candidates for life in prison under the three-strikes law, several seem to fit the profile of violent predators with long criminal histories. But other cases may not be what voters here had in mind....

The case most troubling to the law's critics is that of Larry Lee Fisher, thirty-five, who has been in and out of jail since he was a teenager. His first strike was in 1986 when he was convicted of robbery in the second degree—pushing his grandfather down and taking $390 from him. Mr. Fisher served four months in jail. Two years later came his second strike, a $100 robbery of a pizza parlor in which he concealed his finger and said it was a gun. He served seventeen months on a work farm.

Last month Mr. Fisher was arrested for holding up a sandwich shop in Everett, again without a gun but pretending he had one, pointing his finger inside his coat pocket. The police found him an hour after the holdup drinking beer in a nearby tavern. Normally, he would face about twenty-two months in jail. But now, if convicted, he will spend the rest of his life in prison....

Dave LaCourse, a leader of the three-strikes initiative said Mr. Fisher's case was unusual but not unintended. "Here's a guy with ten misdemeanors on his record, he's thirty-five years old and he hasn't learned his lesson yet," Mr. LaCourse said. "What's it going to take? He seems to be one of those people who's making crime a career."...

Washington prosecutors said states now considering three-strikes laws would do well not to put too many crimes in the mix of what qualifies. Because of cases like Larry Lee Fisher's, Washington's law may have to be refined, they said.

"Don't assume this will have a dramatic effect on crime," said John Ladenburg, Pierce County prosecutor. "This is not a cure-all. This is not going to fix crime. What it will do is get some of the worst offenders off of the street forever."

SOURCE: Adapted from Timothy Egan, "A Three-Strike Penal Law Shows It's Not As Simple As It Seems," *New York Times*, 15 February 1994, 1. Copyright © 1994 by The New York Times Company. Reprinted by permission.

After surveying the history of mandatory sentences, Michael Tonry claims they "do not work."[10] What appears to happen is that courtroom workgroups view the mandatory penalties as too harsh, given the circumstances of many cases. They therefore avoid the mandatory provisions by exacting a guilty plea to a lesser charge or by interpreting the record so that the requirements do not apply.

Although many criminal justice scholars believe that mandatory sentences do not achieve their purpose, research conducted on Florida's mandatory minimum sentences does support their effectiveness.[11] The Florida law is designed to ensure that certain categories of offenders are not released early (through good time and other provisions) before a certain portion of their sentence has been served. Eleven categories of offenders—for example, those convicted of capital offenses and of certain drug and firearms offenses and those designated habitual offenders—come under the mandatory provisions. The impact of these laws has been cited as a major cause for increased incarceration lengths with a resulting growth in the prison population.

**The Sentence Versus Actual Time Served**  Judges in the United States often prescribe long periods of incarceration for serious crimes. But there is a great difference between the length of the sentence announced in the courtroom and the amount of time actually served by offenders. Credit for time spent in jail awaiting the sentence, the application of good time, and, in most states, release to the community on parole all greatly reduce the period of incarceration. Figure 12.3 gives credibility to the recognition that the average felony offender spends about two years in prison.

Because of the variation in sentencing and releasing laws, it is difficult to compare the amount of time actually served with the length of sentence imposed throughout the United States. It is possible, however, to compare different offenses in the same state. The Bureau of Justice Statistics has brought to light an interesting phenomenon: the more serious the offense, the smaller the proportion of the sentence served. An auto thief, say, may be sentenced to twenty-four months in prison but actually serve twenty months, or 83.3 percent of the sentence; a murderer may be sentenced to thirty years but actually serve fifteen years, or 50 percent of the sentence.[12] As we will see in Chapter 17, these examples are not atypical.

## Intermediate Sanctions

Prison crowding and low levels of probation supervision have renewed interest in the development and use of intermediate sanctions, those punishments less severe than incarceration and more restrictive than probation, including fines, home confinement, intensive probation supervision, restitution, community service, boot camp, and forfeiture. Joan Petersilia and Susan Turner estimate that if murderers and rapists, plus those who had been previously incarcerated, and those with a prior sentence for violence were excluded from consideration for intermediate punishments, 29 percent of those who are now prison bound would be sanctioned in the community.[13]

In advocating intermediate punishments, Morris and Tonry stipulate that these sanctions not be used in isolation but that they be combined to reflect the severity of the offense, the characteristics of the offender, and the needs of

**Figure 12.3**
**Average time served by state inmates, by offense**
The data indicate that the average felony offender spends about two years in prison. What would be the public's reaction to this fact?

SOURCE: Adapted from U.S. Department of Justice, Bureau of Justice Statistics, *Report to the Nation on Crime and Justice*, 2d ed. (Washington, D.C.: Government Printing Office, 1988), 100.

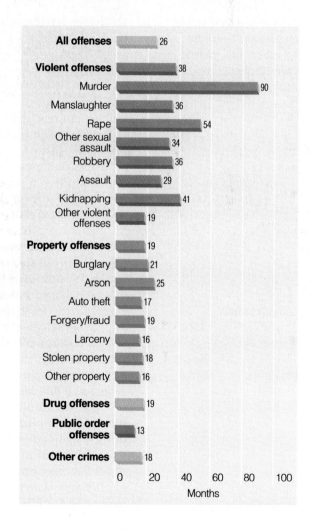

the community.[14] A second requirement for effective use of intermediate punishments is that they be supported and enforced by mechanisms that take seriously any breach of the conditions of the sentence. Too often criminal justice agencies have put few resources into the enforcement of nonincarcerative sentences. If the law does not fulfill its promises, offenders may feel that they have "beaten" the system, resulting in a meaningless punishment. Citizens viewing the ineffectiveness of the system may develop the attitude that nothing works and that there is a need for stiffer sentences. The various forms of intermediate sanctions and their implementation are discussed fully in Chapter 14.

## Probation

Community service is one form of intermediate punishment. Advocates of these sanctions stress that offenders need to recognize responsibility for their acts.

Nearly 65 percent of adults under correctional supervision are on **probation**. Probation is designed to simultaneously maintain control of and assist offenders while permitting them to live in the community under supervision. Because probation is a judicial act and is given by grace of the state—it is not extended as a right—conditions are imposed that specify how the offender will serve the term. If the conditions of probation are not met, the supervising officer may return the offender to court and recommend that the probation be revoked and that the sentence be served in prison.

**probation**
A sentence allowing the offender to serve the sentence imposed by the court in the community under supervision.

Probation gives hope for the rehabilitation of the offender who has not committed a serious crime or whose past record is clean. It is also viewed as a way of maintaining surveillance over offenders so that they do not continue criminal behavior.

Although probationers serve their sentences in the community and not in prison, the sanction is often tied to incarceration. Judges may set a prison term but suspend it upon successful completion of a period of probation. In some jurisdictions, after a portion of an offender's prison term is served, the court is authorized to modify it to probation. This sanction is often referred to as **shock probation** (called *split probation* in California), by which an offender sentenced to prison is released after a period of incarceration (the shock) and resentenced to probation. An offender on probation may be required to spend intermittent periods, such as weekends or nights, in jail. Whatever the specific terms of the probationary sentence, it emphasizes guidance and supervision in the community.

**shock probation**
A sentence in which the offender is released after a short incarceration and resentenced to probation.

The success of probation in preventing recidivism is difficult to document. Most studies of revocation either for commission of a new offense or for violation of the conditions of probation indicate that from one-fifth to one-third of probationers fail. A Rand Corporation study has cast doubt on more optimistic reports of probation effectiveness.[15] A sample of offenders from two urban California counties who had been placed on probation for FBI index crimes was studied after forty months. It was found that 65 percent of the total sample had been arrested for another felony or misdemeanor; 51 percent of the sample had been convicted of another crime; and 34 percent of the sample had been reincarcerated for technical violations of their probation or for new offenses. It should be noted, however, that the California study looked at offenders who had committed serious crimes; most probationers are first-time offenders who have been convicted of misdemeanors or lesser felonies. It is assumed that recidivism among first-time offenders would not be as great as with serious offenders.

## Death

Between 1930 and 1967, when the Supreme Court ordered a stay of executions pending a hearing on the issue, more than 3,800 men and women were executed in the United States for criminal offenses. In 1935, a particularly active year for use of this sanction, 199 persons were executed. During recent decades, however, public attention has focused on capital punishment and on the question of its consistency with the Eighth Amendment's prohibition against cruel and unusual punishment.

The number of persons under sentence of death has increased dramatically in the past decade. About 2,850 persons were awaiting execution in thirty-seven of the death penalty states and in the federal jurisdiction in 1994 (see Figure 12.4). Two-thirds of those on death row were in the South, with the greatest number in that area concentrated in Texas, Georgia, Alabama, and Florida (see Figure 12.5).

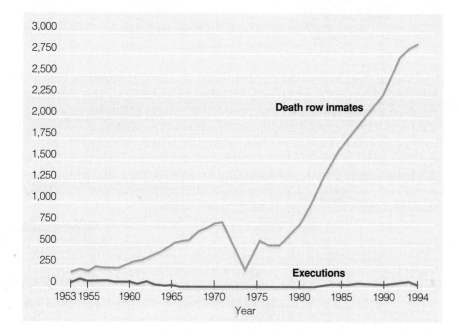

**Figure 12.4**
**Persons under sentence of death and persons executed, 1953–1994**

Since 1976 approximately two hundred fifty new offenders have been added to death row each year, yet the number of executions has never been greater than thirty-eight. What explains this situation?

SOURCE: NAACP Legal Defense and Education Fund, *Death Row, USA* (April 1994).

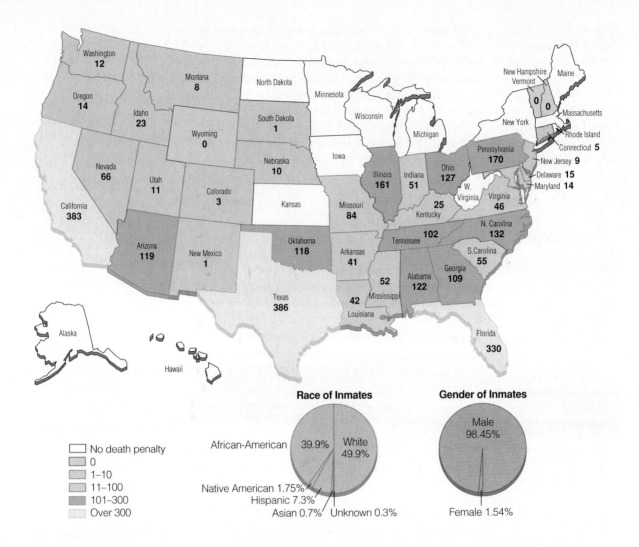

Race of Inmates

African-American 39.9% | White 49.9%
Native American 1.75%
Hispanic 7.3%
Asian 0.7% | Unknown 0.3%

Gender of Inmates

Male 98.45%
Female 1.54%

No death penalty
0
1–10
11–100
101–300
Over 300

**Figure 12.5
Death row census,
April 1994**

As can be seen, many of the inmates on death row are concentrated in certain states. Blacks make up about 13 percent of the U.S. population yet make up 39.9 percent of the death row population. How might you explain this higher percentage of death sentences?

SOURCE: NAACP Legal Defense and Education Fund, *Death Row, USA* (April 1994).

**The Death Penalty and the Constitution**  The fact that death is final and irreversible makes it different from other punishments. This difference has been invoked by courts in examining questions of due process in capital punishment cases. The issue of due process has led to constitutional rulings on every phase of the proceedings, from jury selection to sentencing instructions. Because life is in the balance, capital cases must be conducted according to higher standards of fairness. We will examine three major cases—*Furman* v. *Georgia*, *Gregg* v. *Georgia*, and *McCleskey* v. *Kemp*—that challenged the constitutionality of the sanction.

In the 1972 case of ***Furman* v. *Georgia***, the Supreme Court ruled for the first time that the death penalty, as administered, constituted cruel and unusual punishment, thereby voiding the laws of the thirty-nine states and the District of Columbia that provided for the death penalty at that time.[16] Every member of the Court wrote an opinion, for even among the majority, agreement could not be reached on the legal reasons to support the ban on the death penalty. Only two of the justices argued that capital punishment per se was cruel and unusual, in violation of the Eighth Amendment.

By 1976 thirty-five states had enacted new legislation designed to eliminate the faults cited in *Furman* v. *Georgia*. In many states the new laws also expanded the methods of execution. Many legislators thought that lethal injection would be a "cleaner" way to bring about death (see Figure 12.6).

The new laws were tested before the Supreme Court in June 1976 in the case of *Gregg* v. *Georgia*.[17] The Court upheld those laws that required the sentencing judge or jury to take into account specific aggravating and mitigating factors in deciding which convicted murderers should be sentenced to death.

The U.S. Supreme Court may have dispelled the hopes of death penalty opponents in April 1987. In the case of *McCleskey* v. *Kemp* the Court rejected a constitutional challenge to the administration of the death penalty in Georgia.[18] Warren McCleskey, a black man, had been convicted of two counts of armed robbery and one count of murder following the

*Furman* v. *Georgia* (1972)
Death penalty, as administered, constituted cruel and unusual treatment.

### Figure 12.6
### Methods of execution authorized by state

An increasing number of states authorize the use of lethal injections. What reasons might be given for the acceptance of this method?

SOURCE: U.S. Department of Justice, Bureau of Justice Statistics, *Bulletin* (Washington, D.C.: Government Printing Office, October 1992), 7.

No death penalty
Lethal injection
Electrocution
Lethal gas
Lethal injection/electrocution
Lethal injection/lethal gas
Lethal injection/hanging
Lethal injection/firing squad

Capital punishment is an enduring public issue that elicits strong emotions both pro and con.

**Gregg v. Georgia** (1976)
Upheld death penalty law in which judge and jury considered mitigating and aggravating circumstances in deciding which convicted murderers should be given death.

**McCleskey v. Kemp** (1987)
Rejected a challenge of Georgia's death penalty on grounds of racial discrimination.

robbery of an Atlanta furniture store and the killing of a white police officer during the incident. McCleskey appealed his sentence, arguing that the death penalty in Georgia was being unconstitutionally administered in a racially discriminatory manner.

After McCleskey lost two appeals in lower federal courts, his case was presented before the U.S. Supreme Court. McCleskey's attorneys cited research that showed a disparity in the imposition of the death sentence in Georgia based on the race of the murder victim and, to a lesser extent, the race of the defendant. Researchers had examined over two thousand Georgia murder cases and found that defendants charged with killing white persons had received the death penalty eleven times more often than had those charged with killing black victims. Even after compensating for 230 factors, such as the viciousness of the crime or the quality of the evidence, the research showed that the death sentence was four times more likely to be imposed when the victim was white. Although 60 percent of Georgia homicide victims are black, all seven people put to death in that state since 1976 had been convicted of killing white people; six of the seven murderers were black.

By a 5–4 vote the justices rejected McCleskey's assertion. Justice Lewis Powell, for the majority, said that the appeal challenged the discretionary aspects of the criminal justice system, especially with regard to prosecutors, judges, and juries. He wrote that discretion would certainly lead to disparities but that to show the Georgia law was being administered in an unconstitutional manner, McCleskey would have to prove that the decision makers in his case had acted with a discriminatory purpose by producing evidence specific to the case and not the generalized statistical study. McCleskey was executed in 1991.

**What Is the Future of the Death Penalty?**   Jurists and activists have focused on four legal issues related to the death penalty in recent years. The first three issues are put forth by opponents of capital punishment, who argue that it is cruel and unusual punishment per se to execute offenders who are insane, who committed their crimes as minors, and who are retarded. According to these arguments, it is unconstitutional and morally wrong to execute a person who does not have the mental capacity of an adult.[19] The fourth issue is taken up by Chief Justice Rehnquist, who has proposed that the lengthy appeals process be streamlined. We examine each of these issues in turn.

*Execution of the Insane*   Insanity is a recognized defense for commission of a crime because *mens rea*, criminal intent, is not present. But should people who become mentally disabled *after* they are sentenced to death be executed? The Supreme Court answered this question in 1986 in the case of *Ford* v. *Wainwright*.[20] Neither at Ford's trial nor when he was given the death sentence was there a suggestion that he was incompetent. Only after he was incarcerated did he begin to have delusions, believing that the Ku Klux Klan was part of an elaborate conspiracy to force him to commit suicide and that his women relatives were being tortured and sexually abused somewhere in the prison.

With evidence of these delusions, Ford's counsel invoked the procedures of the Florida law governing the determination of competency of a condemned inmate. Three psychiatrists examined the offender and each filed a separate and conflicting report with the governor, who subsequently signed Ford's death warrant.

Ford appealed to the U.S. Supreme Court, which concluded that the Eighth Amendment prohibited the state from inflicting the death penalty on the insane—the accused first must comprehend that he had been sentenced to death and, second, must be able to comprehend why. Justice Thurgood Marshall cited the common law that questioned the retributive and deterrent value of executing a mentally disabled person. In addition, he argued, the idea of executing the insane is offensive to humanity.

The issue of the accused's competency to be executed arose again in 1991, during Governor Bill Clinton's campaign for the Democratic nomination for president.[21] In Arkansas Rickey Ray Rector killed two men, one of whom was a police officer, and then put a pistol to his own head. He shot himself in the temple, lifting three inches off the front of his brain, essentially giving himself a frontal lobotomy and leaving him with the understanding of a small child. In prison he howled day and night, jumped around, and seemed to have no idea that he was to be executed.

The U.S. Supreme Court turned down his appeal. The Arkansas Parole and Community Rehabilitation Board held a clemency hearing but unanimously turned down a recommendation that Governor Clinton commute the death sentence to life imprisonment without parole. Clinton did not stop the execution and Rector died on 24 January 1991, through a lethal injection.

*Execution of Minors*   The laws of thirteen states do not specify an age below which offenders cannot be given capital punishment. Since 1642, when the Plymouth Colony in Massachusetts hanged a teenage boy for bestiality, 281 juveniles have been executed in the United States.[22] Opponents of the death penalty have focused their position on the long-held recognition that the adolescent psyche is in a kind of turmoiled and diminished capacity, thus exempting juveniles from execution.

Dalton Prejean, a minor when he killed a state trooper, was executed in the Louisiana electric chair in 1990.

The Supreme Court has been divided on the issue of the death penalty for juveniles. In *Thompson* v. *Oklahoma* (1988) the court narrowly decided that William Wayne Thompson, who was fifteen when he committed murder, should not be executed.[23] A plurality of four justices held that executing juveniles did not comport with the "evolving standards of decency that mark the progress of a maturing society." The dissenters said that Thompson had been correctly sentenced under Oklahoma law. Within a year the Court again considered the issue and this time upheld the death sentence. In both *Stanford* v. *Kentucky* (1989) and *Wilkins* v. *Missouri* (1989), the justices upheld the convictions of offenders who were sixteen and seventeen at the time of their crime.[24] All of the justices agreed that interpretation of the cruel and unusual punishment clause rests on the "evolving standards of decency that mark the progress of a maturing society." However, the justices disagreed as to the factors that should be used to make that determination.

With the Supreme Court evidently sanctioning executions of juveniles under some circumstances, Louisiana put to death Dalton Prejean, a juvenile at the time of the offense, on 18 May 1990. There are currently thirty-one males on death rows who were under the age of eighteen at the time their offenses occurred.[25]

*Execution of the Retarded*    An estimated two hundred fifty offenders on the nation's death rows are classified as retarded. It is argued that retarded people have difficulty defending themselves in court because they have problems remembering details, locating witnesses, and testifying credibly in their own behalf. It is also asserted that executing the retarded serves neither retributive nor deterrent purposes since the general public may believe that it was the fact of the mental disability that caused the offender to commit the crime.[26]

In 1989 the Supreme Court upheld the Texas death penalty statute and said that the Eighth Amendment does not prohibit execution of the mentally retarded. The case involved Johnny Paul Penry, a convicted killer with an I.Q. of about 70 and the mental capacity of a seven year old.[27] The court noted that only Georgia and Maryland prohibited execution of the mentally retarded. Now, years after the Supreme Court decision, Penry is still on death row in Texas, in part because of the appeals process.

*Appeals*    Another recent dilemma over capital punishment is the long appeals process. The average length of time between imposition of the sentence by a trial court to the date that the sentence is carried out is be-

Increasingly, lethal injection is replacing the electric chair as the most common means of execution. What ethical and political questions might be raised by the use of one method over the other?

tween seven and eight years. During this time sentences are reviewed by the state courts and through the writ of habeas corpus by the federal courts. Chief Justice Rehnquist has been particularly active in pushing to allow only one habeas corpus appeal to the federal courts in death penalty cases. This position was upheld by the Supreme Court in April 1991, when it said that only in exceptional circumstances should a prisoner be allowed to use the writ more than once.[28]

Appellate review is a time-consuming and expensive process, but it also has an impact. From 1977 (the year after *Gregg*) to 1988, there were 3,057 persons sentenced to death and 104 people executed; however, 1,249 were removed from death row as a result of appeal, commutation by a governor, or death while awaiting execution.[29] Had the expedited appeals process advocated by the chief justice been in effect, would these death sentences have been overturned?

**The Death Penalty: A Continuing Controversy**   The philosophical and legal arguments over capital punishment continue. More than two hundred fifty new death sentences are being given out each year yet the number of executions remain low. Is this situation the result of a complicated appeals process or a lack of certainty by both political leaders and society about the taking of human life? Why is public opinion in support of capital punishment growing? Maybe the death penalty has more significance as a political symbol than as a deterrent to crime. Is it possible that in the future the United States will stop executing criminal offenders, thereby joining the other industrial democracies that do not have the death penalty?

Offenders are punished in various ways with the forms of the criminal sanction designed to serve various purposes (see Table 12.2).

| Form of Sanction | Description | Purposes |
|---|---|---|
| **Incarceration** | Imprisonment | |
| Indeterminate sentence | Stipulates a maximum and minimum length of time to be served. | Incapacitation, deterrence, rehabilitation. |
| Determinate sentence | Stipulates a specific length of time to be served. | Retribution, deterrence, incapacitation. |
| Mandatory sentence | Stipulates a minimum amount of time for given crimes that must be served. | Incapacitation, deterrence. |
| Good time | Subtracts days from an inmate's sentence because of good behavior or participation in prison programs. | Rewards behavior, relieves prison crowding, helps maintain prison discipline. |
| **Intermediate sanctions** | Punishment for those requiring sanctions more restrictive than probation but less restrictive than prison. | Retribution, deterrence. |
| Administered by the Judiciary | | |
|   Fine | Money paid to state by offender. | Retribution, deterrence. |
|   Restitution | Money paid to victim by offender. | Retribution, deterrence. |
|   Forfeiture | Seizure by the state of property illegally obtained or acquired with resources illegally obtained. | Retribution, deterrence. |
| Administered in the Community | | |
|   Community service | Requires offender to perform work for the community. | Retribution, deterrence. |
|   Home confinement | Requires offender to stay in home during certain times. | Retribution, deterrence, incapacitation. |
|   Intensive probation supervision | Requires strict and frequent reporting to probation officer. | Retribution, deterrence, incapacitation. |
| Administered institutionally | | |
|   Boot camp/shock incarceration | Short term institutional sentence emphasizing physical development and discipline, followed by probation. | Retribution, deterrence, rehabilitation. |
| **Probation** | Allows offender to serve a sentence in the community under supervision. | Retribution, incapacitation, rehabilitation. |
| **Death** | Execution. | Incapacitation, deterrence, retribution. |

**Table 12.2**
**The punishment of offenders**
The goals of the criminal sanction are carried out in a variety of ways depending upon the provisions of the law, the characteristics of the offenders, and the discretion of the judge. Judges may impose sentences that combine several forms to achieve punishment objectives.

# Who Gets the Harshest Punishments?

An initial impression may be that minorities and the impoverished receive the longest prison terms and are placed on probation the fewest times. The prison populations of most states are more heavily comprised of African-Americans and Hispanics than is the general population. Does this situation reflect prejudicial attitudes of judges, police officers, and prosecutors? Are poor people more liable to commit violations that elicit a strong response from society? Are enforcement resources distributed so that certain groups are subject to closer scrutiny than other groups? The research evidence on these and similar questions is inconclusive. Although some studies have shown that members of racial minorities and the poor are treated more harshly by the system, other research has been unable to demonstrate a direct link between harshness of sentence and race or social class.

One study of sentencing in Texas found that African-Americans received longer prison terms than whites for most offenses but shorter terms than whites for others. Blacks received longer sentences than whites when they were convicted of burglary (largely an interracial offense). By contrast, blacks received shorter sentences than whites when they were convicted of murder (a predominantly intraracial offense) or of intraracial rape.[30]

Analysis of a sample of 2,366 sentencing files for blacks and whites drawn from fifty thousand felony convictions in "Metro City" indicated discrimination on the basis of race. When Cassia Spohn, John Gruhl, and Susan Welch took into account prior record, charge, legal representation, and severity of sentence, they found that black men received harsher sentences than white men; however, this disparity could primarily result from blacks having been charged with more serious offenses and having more serious prior criminal records. The researchers also found that defendants who had private attorneys or had been released pending trial received less severe sentences. Because of the racial link to social class, these factors were an indirect form of racial discrimination. But even after both legal and extralegal factors were taken into account, the researchers found that the incarceration rate for black men was 20 percent higher than that for white men. Whites were more likely to receive long periods of probation; blacks were more likely to receive short prison terms.[31] Thus we must consider how racial attitudes concerning property and morals influence enforcement of the law.

Another serious dilemma for the criminal justice system concerns those who are falsely convicted and sentenced. While much public concern is expressed over those who "beat the system" and go free, comparatively little attention is paid to those who are innocent, yet convicted. Each year several cases of persons convicted but innocent come to national attention. For example, Randall Dale Adams, whose story was portrayed in the movie "The Thin Blue Line," had his murder conviction overturned in 1989 after spending twelve years on death row. Likewise, James Richardson was freed after twenty-one years wrongfully spent in Florida prisons for the poisoning deaths of seven children. How prevalent are such miscarriages of justice? C. Ronald Huff and Arye Rattner estimate that about 1 percent of felony convictions are in error.[32] They cite eyewitness error, unethical conduct by police and prosecutors, community pressure, false accusations, inadequacy of counsel, and plea bargaining pressures as contributing to wrongful convictions. Beyond the fact that the real criminal is presumably still free in such cases, the standards of our society are damaged when an innocent person has been wrongfully convicted.

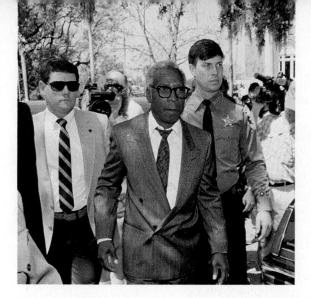

Opponents of capital punishment point to the possibility of error and the finality of death. Here James Richardson is released from Florida's death row after his murder conviction was overturned.

## Summary

Sentencing—the specification of the sanction—can be viewed as both the beginning and the end of the criminal justice system. With guilt established, a decision must be made concerning what to do with the person who has been convicted. Much of the effort of the defendant, prosecutor, and defense attorney during the presentencing phase is based on assumptions about the sanction that may follow conviction. Various justifications for the criminal sanctions have been given in succeeding eras to legitimize the punishment imposed by the state. Although the goals of retribution (punishment that is deserved), deterrence (punishment to serve as an example to the public and to the offender), incapacitation (punishment imposed to prevent the offender from committing future crimes), and rehabilitation (punishment imposed to restore and treat the offender) can be viewed as distinct, they overlap a great deal. Rehabilitation appears to be the one goal that, if carried out according to its model, does not overlap with the others.

When a judge sentences an offender in open court, the effect is felt not only by the individual facing the bench but also by the official actors in the criminal justice system and by the general public. Four forms of punishment are imposed in American courts: incarceration, intermediate sanctions, probation, and death. A sentence often reflects the values and culture of the criminal justice system and its impact is felt throughout the system.

As long as judges are given discretion in sentencing, as long as the corrections process is expected to serve the multiple goals of retribution, deterrence, incapacitation, and rehabilitation, and as long as the law permits judges to create punishments to fit the criminal, disparities will exist. The excesses in the sentencing process give many people cause for concern about the contemporary criminal justice system.

## Questions for Review

1 What are the major differences among deterrence, rehabilitation, retribution, and incapacitation?

2 What are the forms of the criminal sanction?

3 What purposes do intermediate sanctions serve?

4 What has been the Supreme Court's position on the constitutionality of the death penalty?

5 Is there a link between sentences and social class and race?


## Key Terms and Cases

| | | |
|---|---|---|
| determinate sentence | mandatory sentence | special deterrence |
| general deterrence | probation | *Furman* v. *Georgia* (1972) |
| incapacitation | rehabilitation | |
| indeterminate sentence | retribution | *Gregg* v. *Georgia* (1976) |
| | selective incapacitation | *McCleskey* v. *Kemp* (1987) |
| intermediate sanctions | shock probation | |


## For Further Reading

Gaylin, Willard. *The Killing of Bonnie Garland*. New York: Simon and Schuster, 1982. True story of the murder of a Yale student by her boyfriend and the reaction of the criminal justice system to the crime. Raises important questions about the goals of the criminal sanction and the role of the victim in the process.

Goodstein, Lynne, and John Hepburn. *Determinate Sentencing and Imprisonment: A Failure of Reform*. Cincinnati: W. H. Anderson, 1985. Analysis of the movement for determinate sentencing and its impact.

Haas, Kenneth C., and James A. Inciardi, eds. *Challenging Capital Punishment: Legal and Social Science Approaches*. Newbury Park, Calif.: Sage, 1988. An excellent collection of articles concerning the death penalty debate.

Hirsch, Andrew von. *Doing Justice*. New York: Hill and Wang, 1976. The modern restatement of retributive theory with its implications for sentencing.

Johnson, Robert. *Death Work*. Pacific Grove, Calif.: Brooks/Cole, 1989. A look at those on death row—prisoners and correctional officers—and the impact of capital punishment on their lives.

Morris, Norval, and Michael Tonry. *Between Prison and Probation: Intermediate Punishments in a Rational Sentencing System*. New York: Oxford University Press, 1990. Urges development of a range of intermediate punishments that can sanction offenders more severely than probation but less severely than incarceration.

Prejean, Helen. *Dead Man Walking*. New York: Random House, 1993. An account by a Roman Catholic nun of her association with Patrick Sonnier, a condemned prisoner in Louisiana, as he faces execution.

Wheeler, Stanton, Kenneth Mann, and Austin Sarat. *Sitting in Judgment: The Sentencing of White-Collar Criminals*. New Haven, Conn.: Yale University Press, 1988. Describes what federal district court judges consider as they sentence criminals, particularly white-collar criminals.

## Notes

1   *New York Times*, 6 August 1993, A–16.

2   Herbert L. Packer, *The Limits of the Criminal Sanction* (Stanford, Calif.: Stanford University Press, 1968), 33–34.

3   Twentieth Century Fund, Task Force on Criminal Sentencing, *Fair and Certain Punishment* (New York: McGraw-Hill, 1976).

4   Andrew von Hirsch, *Doing Justice* (New York: Hill and Wang, 1976), 49.

5   Packer, *Limits of the Criminal Sanction*, 51.

6   Peter Greenwood, "Controlling the Crime Rate through Imprisonment," in *Crime and Public Policy*, ed. James Q. Wilson (San Francisco: ICS Press, 1983), 258.

7   Norval Morris and Michael Tonry, *Between Prison and Probation: Intermediate Punishments in a Rational Sentencing System* (New York: Oxford University Press, 1990).

8   U.S. Department of Justice, "Mandatory Sentencing: The Experience of Two States," *Policy Briefs* (Washington, D.C.: Government Printing Office, 1982).

9   Milton Heumann and Colin Loftin, "Mandatory Sentencing and the Abolition of Plea Bargaining: The Michigan Felony Firearm Statute," *Law and Society Review* 13 (Winter 1979): 393–430.

10  Michael Tonry, "Mandatory Penalties," in *Crime and Justice: A Review of Research*, ed. Michael Tonry (Chicago: University of Chicago Press, 1992), 243–273.

11  Florida Department of Corrections, "Mandatory Minimum Sentences in Florida: Past Trends and Future Implications" (11 February 1991).

12  U.S. Department of Justice, Bureau of Justice Statistics, *Bulletin* (January 1988).

13  Joan Petersilia and Susan Turner, "The Potential of Intermediate Sanctions," *State Government* (March/April 1989), 65.

14  Morris and Tonry, *Between Prison and Probation*, 37.

15  Joan Petersilia, Susan Turner, James Kahan, and Joyce Peterson, *Granting Felons Probation: Public Risks and Alternatives* (Santa Monica, Calif.: Rand Corporation, 1985).

16  408 U.S. 238 (1972).

17  428 U.S. 153 (1976).

18  478 U.S. 1019 (1987).

19  Mark A. Small, "A Review of Death Penalty Caselaw: Future Directions for Program Evaluation," *Criminal Justice Policy Review* 5 (June 1991): 117; Candace McCoy, "The Death Penalty Continued," *Federal Probation* (March 1990): 77.

20  *Ford v. Wainwright*, 477 U.S. 399 (1985).

21  Marshall Frady, "Death in Arkansas," *New Yorker*, 23 February 1993, 105.

22  Ron Rosenbaum, "Too Young to Die?" *New York Times Magazine*, 12 March 1989, 60.

23  108 S.Ct. 2687 (1988).

24  45 Cr.L. Rptr. 3203 (1989).

25  NAACP Legal Defense and Educational Fund, *Death Row, USA* (Fall 1993).

26  Philip L. Fetzer, "Execution of the Mentally Retarded: A Punishment without Justification," *South Carolina Law Review* 40 (1989): 419.

27  *Penry v. Lynaugh*, 45 Cr.L. Rptr. 3188 (1989).

28  *McCleskey v. Zant*, 59 L.W. 4288 (1991).

29  U.S. Department of Justice, Bureau of Justice Statistics, *Bulletin* (July 1989).

30  Henry A. Bullock, "Significance of the Racial Factor in the Length of Prison Sentences," *Journal of Criminal Law, Criminology, and Police Science* 52 (1961): 411.

31  Cassia Spohn, John Gruhl, and Susan Welch, "The Effect of Race on Sentencing: A Reexamination of an Unsettled Question," *Law and Society Review* 16 (1981–82): 85.

32  C. Ronald Huff and Arye Rattner, "Convicted But Innocent: False Positives and the Criminal Justice Process," in *Controversial Issues in Crime and Justice*, ed. Joseph E. Scott and Travis Hirschi (Newbury Park, Calif.: Sage, 1988), 130.

# Corrections

For most citizens, prison comes to mind when they think of corrections. This perception is perhaps understandable, given the history of corrections in this country, the folklore, films, and songs about prison life, and the fact that incarceration is the most visible aspect of the process. Many have unexpectedly come across the looming walls, barbed-wire fences, and searchlights of the modern prison on a drive through the countryside. The prison is also brought to our attention by the media whenever there is inmate unrest or an escape. And it is the prison that legislators and politicians seem to consider when they debate changes in the penal code or the annual appropriation for corrections.

For students of criminal justice, it should be no surprise that the term *corrections* refers to the great number of programs, services, facilities, and organizations responsible for the management of people who have been accused or convicted of criminal offenses. In addition to prisons and jails, corrections also includes probation, halfway houses, education and work release programs, parole supervision, counseling, and community service.

Correctional programs operate in Salvation Army hostels, in forest camp sites, along roadsides, in medical clinics, and in urban storefronts. More than four million adults and juveniles are given correctional supervision by more than five hundred thousand administrators, psychologists, officers, counselors, social workers, and others. That means 1 out of every 43 adults (1 of every 24 men and 1 of every 162 women) in America either is being supervised in the community (on probation or parole) or is incarcerated. Corrections is a system authorized by all levels of government, administered by both public and private organizations, and with a total yearly cost of over $25 billion.[1] This chapter provides an overview of the corrections system, exploring its history, organization, and many characteristics.

### Questions for Inquiry

- How has the American system of corrections developed?
- What roles are played by federal, state, and local governments in corrections?
- What are the trends regarding the number and types of persons incarcerated?

## Development of Corrections

As we look at United States corrections today, we may wonder how we got here. Why are offenders now placed on probation or incarcerated rather than being whipped or burned as they were in colonial times? Why is corrections organized primarily on a state and local, rather than a national, basis? How do political and social attitudes influence the allocation and type of punishment? We can see that the great hopes of one period faltered and turned into the dismay of another. What, if anything, might be done to change this cycle?

The correctional system in use today did not just spring up full-blown: over time its goals and practices have shifted to reflect social and political trends. In analyzing corrections over the past two hundred years, we can discern swings in the pendulum as one approach and then another attempted to deal with the problem of the criminal offender (see Figure 13.1). As we examine the shifts from the Enlightenment to the Progressive Era to the present day, we should also reflect on our present situation and speculate about the future of criminal punishment.

### The Invention of the Penitentiary

The latter part of the eighteenth century stands out as a remarkable period, one in which scholars and social reformers in Europe and America engaged in an almost complete rethinking of the nature of society and the

**Figure 13.1**
**Development of corrections in the United States**
Correctional policies have evolved over time. Elements from each era can be found in corrections procedures today.

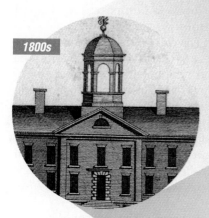

**1700s**

**Corporal Punishment**
During the colonial and early post-Revolutionary years, Americans used physical punishment, a legacy from Europe.

**1800s**

**Penitentiary Movement**
A major idea of the Enlightenment, which shook Europe and the United States in the early 1800s, was that criminals should be placed in institutions where they would have opportunities for work and penitence.

**1950s**

**Rehabilitation Model**
The rise of psychology shifted the emphasis of corrections to reform of offenders through treatment programs.

**1970s**

**Community Model**
Criticisms of correctional institutions led to the belief that most offenders should be supervised in the community so that they could be reintegrated into society.

**1980s**

**Incarceration Model**
Contemporary crime control policies place greater emphasis on the incarceration of offenders.

place of the individual in it. The Enlightenment, as the philosophical movement was called, challenged traditional assumptions by emphasizing the individual, the limitations on government, and rationalism. It was the major intellectual force behind the American Revolution and had a direct impact on the administration of criminal law and on the goals and practices of corrections. Questions were raised about matters such as the procedures used to determine guilt, the limits on government's power to punish, the nature of criminal behavior, and the appropriate means to correct offenders. At a time of overcrowded and unmanaged jails, brutal corporal punishment, and rising crime levels in Europe and the United States, the great period of correctional reform was launched.

The French scholar Michel Foucault has chronicled the spread of Enlightenment ideas during the late eighteenth century. In Europe, after the French Revolution torture was eliminated as a public spectacle and "modern" penal codes were adopted that emphasized selecting and modifying punishment to fit the individual offender. Most importantly, the late eighteenth century "saw the disappearance of the tortured, dismembered, amputated body, symbolically branded on face or shoulder, exposed alive or dead to public view." As punishment moved away from the infliction of pain, the offender's body was no longer the major target of penal policy. Instead, correctional intervention was to change the individual and set him or her on the right path.[2]

Of the many persons who actively promoted the reform of corrections, John Howard (1726–1790), sheriff of Bedfordshire, England, stands out. His book, *The State of Prisons in England and Wales* (1777), led to the development of the **penitentiary**.[3] Howard's book is an unsentimental, factual account of his observations of the prisons that he visited. He found the conditions to be horrible, and he was particularly concerned that the prisons were run without regard to discipline. Public response to the book resulted in the passage by Parliament of the Penitentiary Act of 1779. The act called for the creation of a house of hard labor in which people convicted of crimes would be imprisoned for up to two years. The institution would be based on four principles:

1 a secure and sanitary structure
2 systematic inspection
3 the abolition of fees
4 a reformatory regime

Prisoners were to be confined to solitary cells during the night and to silent labor in common rooms during the day. The regimen was to be strict and ordered. Perhaps influenced by his Quaker friends, Howard believed that the new institution should be not only a place of industry but also a place where criminals could have an opportunity for penitence (sorrow and shame for their wrongs) and repentance (willingness to change their ways); its purpose was to punish and to reform.

**penitentiary**

An institution intended to isolate prisoners from society and from one another so that they can reflect on their past misdeeds, repent, and thus undergo reformation.

John Howard's revelations about conditions in the prisons of England and Wales resulted in passage of the Penitentiary Act of 1779.

Howard saw the act approved but it was not implemented until 1842. Meanwhile, his conception of the penitentiary had traveled across the Atlantic and was planted in the more fertile soil of Pennsylvania and New York, where it blossomed.

During the colonial and early post-revolutionary years, Americans used physical punishment, a legacy from Europe, as the main criminal sanction. Stocks, flogging, branding, and maiming were the primary means used to control deviancy, and fines were also used to maintain public safety. For more serious crimes, gallows were used frequently. In the state of New York about 20 percent of all crimes on the books were capital offenses, and criminals were regularly sentenced to death for picking pockets, burglary, robbery, and horse stealing.[4] Jails existed throughout the country, but they served only the limited purpose of holding people awaiting trial or punishment or those unable to pay their debts. Jails were not then a part of the correctional scheme.

In the fifty years following the establishment of the American Republic in 1776, new and radical ideas evolved concerning criminal punishment. Part of the impetus for change came from the post-revolutionary patriotic fervor that blamed recidivism and criminal behavior on English laws. Still more, however, the new correctional philosophy coincided with the ideals of reform as found in the Declaration of Independence, with its optimistic view of human nature and its implied belief in each person's perfectibility. Accordingly, social progress was seen to be possible through reforms carried out according to the dictates of "pure reason." Emphasis shifted from the assumption that deviance was inherent in human nature to the belief that crime was a result of forces operating in the environment. If the humane and optimistic ideals of the new nation were to be realized, then it was necessary to reform the criminal element of society.

**Benjamin Rush**

Benjamin Rush (1745–1813), physician, patriot, signer of the Declaration of Independence, and social reformer, was born in Pennsylvania and began practicing medicine there in 1769. He was widely recognized for his work in medicine, particularly his insistence on the importance of personal hygiene, and served as surgeon general under Washington during the Revolutionary War. He also helped organize the Pennsylvania Society for the Abolition of Slavery.

Rush was active in various reform movements, especially those dealing with treatment of the mentally ill and with prisoners. His interest in methods then being used to punish criminals led him to protest laws assigning punishments such as shaved heads, whippings, and other public displays. In *An Enquiry into the Effects of Public Punishment upon Criminals* (1787), he maintained that such excesses served only to harden criminals. He was opposed to capital punishment and wrote *On Punishing Murder by Death* (1792), which condemned the practice as an offspring of monarchical divine right, a principle contrary to a republican form of government. He is probably best known for advocating the penitentiary as a replacement for capital and corporal punishment.

In the first decades of the nineteenth century the creation of penitentiaries in Pennsylvania and New York attracted the attention of legislators in other states and also investigators from Europe. In 1831, France sent Alexis de Tocqueville and Gustave Auguste de Beaumont, England sent William Crawford, and Prussia dispatched Nicholas Julius. Travelers from abroad with no special interest in penology made it a point to include a penitentiary on their itinerary, much as they planned visits to a southern plantation, a textile mill, or a frontier town. The U.S. penitentiary had indeed become world famous by the mid-1800s.

**The Pennsylvania System** Reform of the penal structure became the goal of several humanitarian groups in the United States. The first of these groups was the Philadelphia Society for Alleviating the Miseries of Public Prisons, formed in 1787. Under the leadership of Dr. Benjamin Rush (see Biography), this group, which included many Quakers, urged replacement of capital and corporal (bodily) punishment by incarceration. The Quakers believed that criminals could best be reformed if they were placed in solitary confinement so that, alone in their cells, they could consider their deviant acts, repent, and reform.

In a series of legislative acts in 1790, Pennsylvania provided for the solitary confinement of "hardened and atrocious offenders" in the existing three-story, stone Walnut Street Jail in Philadelphia. This plain building, forty by twenty-five feet, housed eight cells on each floor, and there was an attached yard. Each cell held one inmate and was small and dark (only six by eight feet, and nine feet high). From a small, grated window high on the outside wall prisoners "could perceive neither heaven nor earth." No communications of any kind were allowed. It was from this limited beginning that the Pennsylvania system of **separate confinement** evolved. In accordance with this approach, each inmate was isolated from other inmates. It was believed that only under such conditions could true rehabilitation occur.

The opening of the Eastern Penitentiary near Philadelphia in 1829 marked the culmination of forty-two years of reform activity by the Philadelphia Society. On 25 October 1829, the first prisoner arrived. Charles Williams, eighteen years old and sentenced to a two-year term for larceny, was assigned to a cell twelve by eight by ten feet that had an individual exercise yard some eighteen feet long. Designed according to the system, the prison isolated inmates not only from the community but also from one another. In each cell was a fold-up steel bedstead, a simple toilet, a wooden stool, a workbench, and eating utensils. Light came from an eight-inch window in the ceiling. Solitary labor, Bible reading, and reflection were the keys to the moral rehabilitation that was supposed to occur within the prison walls. Although the cell was larger than most in use today, it was the only world the prisoner would see for the duration of the sentence. The only other human voice the prisoner heard would be that of a clergyman who would visit on Sundays. Nothing was to distract the penitent prisoner from the path toward reform.

As described by Robert Vaux, one of the original Philadelphia reformers, the Pennsylvania system was based on the following principles:

1    Prisoners should be treated not vengefully but in ways to convince them that through hard and selective forms of suffering they could change their lives.

2    To prevent the prison from being a corruptive influence, solitary confinement of all inmates should be practiced.

3    In seclusion offenders have an opportunity to reflect on their transgressions so that they may repent.

4    Solitary confinement is a punishing discipline because humans are by nature social animals.

5    Solitary confinement is economical because prisoners do not need long periods of time to acquire the penitential experience, fewer keepers are needed, and the costs of clothing are reduced.[5]

**separate confinement**
A penitentiary system, developed in Pennsylvania, in which each inmate was held in isolation from other inmates. All activities, including craft work, took place in the cells.

Unfortunately for Vaux and the Quakers, the system soon proved unworkable. The Walnut Street Jail became overcrowded as more and more offenders were held for longer periods; it became a virtual warehouse of humanity. Politicians in Philadelphia took over operation of the jail. The Western Penitentiary (near Pittsburgh) also became overcrowded and was soon declared outmoded because isolation was not complete and the cells were too small for solitary labor. It was recommended for demolition in 1833.

**The New York System**    In 1819 New York opened a new state penitentiary in Auburn that evolved as a rival to Pennsylvania's concept of separate confinement. In New York the use of incarceration was not questioned, only the regimen to which the prisoners were to be exposed. Under the Auburn system, prisoners were kept in individual cells at night but congregated in workshops during the day. In this **congregate system**, however, inmates were forbidden to talk to one another or even to exchange glances while on the job or at meals. One of the advantages of the New York system was that it cost less because one guard could supervise an entire group of prisoners. In addition, Auburn reflected some of the growing emphases of the Industrial Revolution. The men were to have the benefits of labor as well as meditation. They were to live under tight control, on a simple diet, and according to an undeviating routine, but they would work to pay for a portion of their keep.

**congregate system**
A penitentiary system, developed in Auburn, New York, in which each inmate was held in isolation during the night but worked with fellow prisoners during the day under a rule of silence.

American reformers saw the New York approach as a great advance in penology, and it was copied throughout the land. At an 1826 meeting of prison reformers in Boston, the New York system was described in glowing terms:

At Auburn, we have a more beautiful example still, of what may be done by proper discipline, in a prison well constructed.... The unremitted industry, the entire subordination, and subdued feeling among the convicts has probably no parallel among any equal number of convicts. In their solitary cells, they spend the night with no other book than the Bible, and at sunrise they proceed in military order, under the eye of the turnkey in solid columns, with the lock march to the workshops.[6]

During this period of reform, advocates of both the Pennsylvania and New York plans debated on public platforms and in the nation's periodicals. Often the two systems have been contrasted by noting that the Pennsylvania (Quaker) method aimed to produce honest persons whereas the New York system sought to mold obedient citizens. Advocates of both systems agreed that the prisoner must be isolated from society and placed on a disciplined routine. They believed that deviancy was a result of corruption pervading the community and that institutions such as the family and the church were not providing a counterbalance. Only when offenders were removed from temptations and subjected to a steady and regular regimen could they become useful citizens. The convicts were not inherently depraved, rather, they were victims of a society that had not protected them from vice. The hope was while offenders were being punished, they would become penitent, see the error of their ways, and want to place themselves on the right path.

By the mid-nineteenth century, reformers had become disillusioned with the results of the penitentiary movement. Deterrence and rehabilitation had been achieved in neither the New York nor the Pennsylvania system nor in their copies. The failure of the penitentiaries, however, was seen as a problem of poor administration rather than as an indictment of the concept of incarcerative penalties. Within forty years of their advocates' optimistic proclamations, penitentiaries had become overcrowded, understaffed, and minimally financed. Discipline had become lax, administrators were viewed as corrupt, and the institutions had become places of brutality. At Sing Sing penitentiary in Ossining, New York, in 1870, for example, investigators discovered "that dealers were publicly supplying prisoners with almost anything they would pay for" and that convicts were "playing all sorts of games, reading, scheming, trafficking."[7]

## The Reformatory Movement

**penology**

A branch of criminology dealing with the management of prisons and the treatment of offenders.

In 1870 the newly formed National Prison Association (predecessor of today's American Correctional Association), met in Cincinnati and issued a Declaration of Principles, which signaled a new round of penal reform. Progressive penologists such as Franklin Sanborn, Enoch Wines, and Zebulon Brockway (see Biography) advocated a new design for **penology**. The goal should be the treatment of criminals through their moral regeneration: the reformation of criminals, "not the infliction of vindictive suffering."

The Declaration of Principles asserted that prisons should be operated according to a philosophy of inmate change that would reward reformation with release. Fixed sentences should be replaced by sentences of indeterminate length, and proof of reformation should replace the "mere lapse of time" in bringing about the prisoner's freedom. This reformation program should be encouraged through a progressive classification of prisoners based on character and improvement. But in this connection it should be remembered that, like the Quakers, these progressive reformers looked to institutional life as the way to rehabilitate. Inmates should be made into well-adjusted citizens, but the process should be done behind walls. The Cincinnati Declaration could thus in good faith insist: "Reformation is a work of time; and a benevolent regard to the good of the criminal himself, as well as to the protection of society, requires that his sentence be long enough for reformatory processes to take effect."[8]

**Elmira Reformatory**  The new progressive approach took shape at Elmira, New York, in 1876. According to Superintendent Zebulon Brockway, the key to reform and rehabilitation lay in education:

> The effect of education is reformatory, for it tends to dissipate poverty by imparting intelligence sufficient to conduct ordinary affairs, and puts into the mind, necessarily, habits of punctuality, method, and perseverance.... If culture, then, has a refining influence, it is only necessary to carry it far enough, in combination always with due religious agencies, to cultivate the criminal out of his criminality, and to constitute him a reformed man.[9]

Brockway's approach at Elmira Reformatory was supported by New York legislation that provided for indeterminate sentences, permitting the reformatory to release inmates on parole when their reform had been assured. At Elmira, attempts were made to create a school-like atmosphere with courses in both academic and moral subjects. Inmates who performed well in the courses and who lived according to the reformatory discipline were placed in separate categories so that they could progress to a point where they were eligible for parole. Poor grades and misconduct extended an inmate's tenure. Society could reform criminals, Enoch Wines said, only "by placing the prisoner's fate, as far as possible, in his own hands, by enabling him, through industry and good conduct, to raise himself, step by step, to a position of less restraint; while idleness and bad conduct, on the other hand, keep him in a state of coercion and restraint."[10]

By 1900 the reformatory movement had spread throughout the nation, but by the onset of World War I it was already in decline. In most institutions the architecture, the attitudes of the guards, and the emphasis on discipline differed little from previous penal orientations. The educational and rehabilitative efforts too often were subordinate to the traditional punitive emphasis. Even Brockway admitted difficulty in distinguishing between inmates whose attitudes had changed and those who superficially conformed to prison rules. Being a good prisoner, the traditional emphasis, became the way to win parole in most of these institutions.

## The Reforms of the Progressives

The first two decades of the twentieth century were also a period of reform as social and political ideas confronted modern developments such as industrialization, urbanization, and the advancement of science. This was the era of the Progressives, who attacked the excesses of urban society, in particular those of big business, and advocated state action to deal with the social problems of slums, vice, and crime. They believed that

civic-minded people could apply scientific findings to social problems in ways that would benefit all. They believed that social and behavioral concepts, rather than religious or moral precepts, could rehabilitate criminals. The new activists relied on the developments of modern criminology associated with a scientific approach to crime and human behavior known as the positivist school, which focused on the behavior of the offender.

Armed with this positivist view of criminal behavior and a faith in the efficacy of state action to reform offenders, the Progressives fought for changes in correctional methods. Their efforts centered on two strategies: one designed to improve conditions in the environments they believed to be breeding grounds of crime, the other emphasizing ways to rehabilitate the individual offender. They instituted the presentence report, with its extensive personal history, to enable judges and correctional officials to analyze an individual's problem and to take action toward rehabilitation. By the 1920s, probation, indeterminate sentence and parole, and treatment programs were being espoused by reform penologists as the instruments of this more scientific approach to criminality.

## The Rehabilitation Model

Although the Progressives were instrumental in advancing the new penology, it was not until the 1930s that attempts were made to implement fully what became known as the rehabilitation model of corrections. Penologists operating under the banner of the newly prestigious social and behavioral sciences helped shift the emphasis of the postconviction sanction to the treatment of criminals, whose social, intellectual, or biological deficiencies were seen as the causes of their illegal activities. The essential structural elements of parole, probation, and the indeterminate sentence were already in place in most states. Therefore, incorporating the rehabilitation model required only the addition of classification systems that would diagnose offenders and treatment programs that would rehabilitate them. Advocates of this approach held that the goal of rehabilitation could be achieved by using modern scientific theories of criminality. Because they likened the new correctional methods to those used by hospital physicians, this approach was often referred to as the *medical model*. Under this approach, correctional institutions were staffed with persons who could diagnose the causes of an individual's criminal behavior, prescribe a treatment program, and determine when a cure had been effected so that the offender could be released to the community.

Following World War II, rehabilitation won new adherents. Group therapy, behavior modification, counseling, and numerous other approaches all became part of the "new penology." Yet even during the 1950s, when the medical model was at its zenith, only a small proportion of state correctional budgets was allocated for rehabilitation. This dichotomy between the rhetoric of the rehabilitation model and the reality that institutions were still being run with custody as an overriding goal frustrated those who believed in the benefits of treatment. The failure of these new techniques to stem crime, the changes in the characteristics of the prison population, and the misuse of the discretion required by the model prompted another cycle of correctional reform, so that by 1970 rehabilitation as a goal had become discredited.

## The Community Model

As we have seen, correctional goals and methods have been greatly influenced by the social and political values of particular periods. During the 1960s and early 1970s, U.S. society experienced the civil rights movement, the war on poverty, and resistance to the war in Vietnam. It was a time in which the conventional ways of government were challenged. In 1967 the President's Commission on Law Enforcement and the Administration of Justice reported that

crime and delinquency are symptoms of failures and disorganization of the community.... The task of corrections, therefore, includes building or rebuilding social ties, obtaining employment and education, securing in the larger sense a place for the offender in the routine functioning of society.[11]

**Community corrections** was based on the assumption that the goal of the criminal justice system should be to reintegrate the offender into the community. As we see in the Comparative Perspective on pages 476–477, reintegration is a chief goal of corrections in Sweden. How it is achieved highlights some of the differences between the correctional systems in the United States and Sweden.

Proponents of the community model advocated rehabilitation of offenders within the community, not in prisons. Prisons were viewed as artificial institutions that interfered with the offender's ability to develop a crime-free life. It was argued that corrections should de-emphasize psychological treatment and emphasize programs that would increase opportunities for offenders to be successful citizens. Imprisonment was to be avoided, if possible, in favor of probation, so that offenders could engage in vocational and educational programs that would increase their chances of adjusting to community life. For the small proportion of offenders who had to be incarcerated, the amount of time in prison should be only a short interval until release on parole. To further the goal of reintegration, correctional workers were to serve as advocates for offenders as they dealt with governmental agencies providing employment counseling, medical treatment, and financial assistance. The community model, however, was shortlived. By the mid-1970s the reform movement seemed so dispirited that many penologists abandoned it in despair.

**community corrections**
A model of corrections based on the assumption that the reintegration of the offender into the community should be the goal of the criminal justice system.

## Corrections in the 1990s

As the political climate changed in the seventies and eighties, legislators, judges, and corrections officials responded with a renewed emphasis upon incarceration as a way to solve the crime problem. Certain structures of rehabilitation were attacked, including indeterminate sentences,

## Corrections in Sweden

The Swedish corrections system is run by an independent agency called *Kriminalvards-styrelsen*—literally the "criminal care administration." Inmates often make fun of this designation, "We are not prisoners, or inmates, or convicts," said one man mockingly, "We are consumers of criminal care." Swedish officials translate the title as the National Correctional Administration. This is the agency responsible for pretrial detention, probation supervision, prisons, and parole supervision.

On a given day, the Correctional Administration is responsible for about three thousand inmates serving sentences and about six hundred awaiting trial. In most countries, a half dozen institutions would be considered more than enough to hold the small number of inmates. But in Sweden they believe in small institutions, hence the inmates are housed in 103 different facilities. There are 20 national prisons, 57 local, and 26 remand institutions for pretrial detainees. The maximum capacity ranges from 10 to 435, most between 20 to 40, and thus appear to be more akin to halfway houses in the United States. The prisons have a total capacity for 1,700 inmates housed in "open" institutions—without walls or fences and 2,400 in closed facilities.

Sixty-five percent of Swedish prisoners serve sentences of three months or less, 13 percent three to six months, 9.5 percent six to

treatment programs, and discretionary release on parole. It was argued that treatment should be available only to those prisoners who chose it and that longer sentences, especially for career criminals and those who had committed violent crimes, should be imposed.

The doubling of the probation and prison populations during the 1980s put such great pressure on correctional approaches that most states could only provide minimal services. Probation departments began to emphasize risk assessment, a means of evaluating the supervision level needed by each offender. Thus those likely to recidivate could be given the most supervision, while those least likely could be allowed to live in the community with less contact with a probation officer. Officials supervising jammed correctional institutions had to de-emphasize treatment programs because of space and fiscal limitations. Prison crowding necessitated a greater emphasis upon custody goals and the provision of a secure environment.

twelve months, 8 percent twelve to twenty-four months, and only 4 percent more than two years. But these figures cannot be directly compared to data on time served in the United States. The Swedish data include drunk drivers, draft resisters, and other minor offenders who would not be incarcerated in the United States or who would serve time in the county jail. In Sweden there is no distinction between felons and misdemeanants: all enter the same correctional system.

The time served in Sweden by serious offenders, however, is indeed shorter than in the United States. Burglars, embezzlers, and others found guilty of "gross theft" serve between six months and three years in prison. The minimum sentence for most violent crimes is one or two years; the maximum up to ten. Most murderers get ten years. Some receive life imprisonment but are almost always pardoned after ten to twelve years.

Legislation passed in 1974 puts great emphasis upon the reintegration of prisoners into the community. It states that the "natural" form of correctional care is noninstitutional and that every effort should be made to keep offenders out of prison and to maximize contacts with the outside world for those who are incarcerated. To accomplish this goal judges were instructed to make greater use of probation; inmates in local institutions were given the right to leave the facility during the day to work, study, and participate in recreation; furlough programs were to be developed; and long-term prisoners not viewed as security risks were to be given short-term periods of release to study, secure treatment, or for other reasons that would facilitate the prisoner's adjustment to society.

These policies have served to place greater emphasis upon community corrections, particularly probation and parole. The Correctional Administration supervises thirteen thousand offenders on probation and four thousand on parole. There are 689 probation/ parole officers who carry an average caseload of twenty-six. They are assisted by ten thousand "private supervisors"—volunteers who supervise two or three probationers or parolees in their spare time for a nominal salary.

Since the 1930s Sweden has gained the reputation of taking social welfare policies further than any developed nation. The Swedish political ideology emphasizes the similarities among citizens rather than the differences and encourages a sense of collective responsibility which seeks to protect the rights and needs of its weakest members. Governmental policies have been developed to assist these citizens, even those who have broken the law. As Claes Amilon, deputy director of the Correctional Administration wrote in a United Nations report, "A society without slums cannot let its prisoners live under slum conditions; a society which has accepted collective responsibility for the physical and economic welfare of its citizens cannot abuse the rights even of those who transgress its laws."

SOURCE: Adapted from Michael S. Serrill, "Profile/Sweden," *Corrections Magazine*, 3 (June 1977): 11. Reprinted by permission of the author. Adapted from Alvar Nelson, "Sweden," in *Major Criminal Justice Systems*, 2d ed., ed. George F. Cole, Stanislaw J. Frankowski, and Marc G. Gertz (Newbury Park, Calif.: Sage, 1987), 134. Copyright © 1987 Sage Publications, Inc. Reprinted by permission.

To a great extent corrections in the 1990s are driven by the public's demand for crime control, the war on drugs, and the financial resources of states. Although the National Crime Victimization Survey has shown the level of crime to be fairly stable since the mid-1970s, the public continues to demand greater efforts by government to control crime. Legislators have responded by increasing the penalties for criminal violations, especially those involving drugs and violence. Increased police resources have been allocated to the arrest of drug dealers, and as the courts respond with stiffer penalties for those offenders, corrections has reaped a bumper harvest of probation and prison populations. During the 1980s there was a boom in new construction in an attempt to reduce prison crowding. State governments are now under severe fiscal pressure and are confronting the reality that both prison construction and operations are extremely expensive. Probation departments continue to face immense caseloads as more offenders are supervised in the community. The increased use of intermediate sanctions are creating both new problems and new opportunities for corrections in the 1990s.

Corrections is at a crossroads. In some states more money is allocated to corrections than to higher education. At some point the public may begin to question these expenditures, especially if there appears to be no reduction in criminality, and we may see a different swing of the correctional pendulum.

## Organization of Corrections in the United States

The administration of corrections is fragmented in that various levels of government are involved. Each level of government has some responsibility for corrections, and often one level exercises little supervision over another. The federal government, the fifty states, the District of Columbia, the 3,047 counties, and most cities each have at least one facility and many programs. State and local governments pay about 95 percent of the cost of all correctional activities in the nation.[12]

The scope of federal criminal laws is less broad than that of state laws; as a result, only about one hundred thousand adults out of more than four million adults and juveniles under correctional supervision are under federal supervision. In most areas, maintaining prisons and parole is the responsibility of the state, while counties have some misdemeanant jails but no authority over the short-term jails operated by towns and cities. Jails are operated mainly by local governments (usually sheriff's departments), but in six states they are integrated with the state prison system. Most correctional activities are part of the executive branch of government, but most probation offices are attached to the judiciary and are paid for by county government. In addition, juvenile and adult corrections are separate.

The fragmentation of corrections is illustrated in Table 13.1, which shows the distribution of correctional responsibilities in the Philadelphia metropolitan area. Note that all levels of government—federal, state, county, and municipal—operate correctional programs. Furthermore, various departments within these levels are responsible for implementing programs.

### The Federal Corrections System

The U.S. Bureau of Prisons was created by Congress in 1930, and it now operates an integrated system of prisons containing over eighty thousand inmates. Facilities and inmates are classified in a security-level system ranging from Level 1 (the least secure, camp-type settings such as the Federal Prison Camp in Tyndall, Florida) through Level 6 (the most secure, such as the U.S. Penitentiary in Marion, Illinois). Between these extremes are Levels 2 through 5 federal correctional institutions—other U.S. peni-

| | Correctional Function | Level and Branch of Government | Responsible Agency |
|---|---|---|---|
| **Adult Corrections** | Pretrial detention | Municipal/executive | Department of Human Services |
| | Probation supervision | County/courts | Court of Common Pleas |
| | Halfway houses | Municipal/executive | Department of Human Services |
| | Houses of corrections | Municipal/executive | Department of Human Services |
| | County prisons | Municipal/executive | Department of Human Services |
| | State prisons | State/executive | Department of Corrections |
| | County parole | County/executive | Court of Common Pleas |
| | State parole | State/executive | Board of Probation and Parole |
| **Juvenile Corrections** | Detention | Municipal/executive | Department of Public Welfare |
| | Probation supervision | County/courts | Court of Common Pleas |
| | Dependent/neglect | State/executive | Department of Human Services |
| | Training schools | State/executive | Department of Public Welfare |
| | Private placements | Private | Many |
| | Juvenile aftercare | State/executive | Department of Public Welfare |
| **Federal Corrections** | Probation/parole | Federal/courts | U.S. Courts |
| | Incarceration | Federal/executive | Bureau of Prisons |

tentiaries, administrative institutions, medical facilities, and specialized institutions for women and juveniles. Because of the nature of federal criminal law, prisoners in most federal facilities are quite different from those in state institutions. In general, the population contains more inmates who have been convicted of white-collar crimes, although drug offenders are increasing. There are fewer offenders who have committed crimes of violence than are found in most state institutions.

Probation and parole supervision for U.S. offenders are provided by the Division of Probation, a branch of the Administrative Office of the United States Courts. Officers are appointed by the federal judiciary and serve the court.

**Table 13.1**
**Distribution of correctional responsibilities in Philadelphia County, Pennsylvania**
Note the various correctional functions performed by different government agencies.

SOURCE: Taken from the annual reports of the responsible agencies.

## The State Corrections Systems

Every state has a centralized department of the executive branch that administers corrections, but the extent of their responsibility for programs varies. In some states, for example, probation and parole programs are operated by a department of corrections, while in other states probation is under the judiciary, and parole is handled separately. Wide variation also exists in the way correctional responsibilities are divided between state and local governments. The differences can be seen in the proportion of

California's Folsom Prison is a maximum security institution. Although these inmates seem to be free to roam the facility, discipline is strict and security is tight.

correctional employees who work for the state. In Connecticut, Rhode Island, and Vermont, for example, 100 percent are state employees as compared to 47 percent in California.

There is a wide range of state correctional institutions, facilities, and programs for adult felons, including prisons, reformatories, industrial institutions, prison farms, conservation campuses, forestry campuses, and halfway houses. Despite this variety, most state prisons are generally old and large. Over half of the nation's inmates are in institutions with average daily populations of more than one thousand, and about 35 percent are in prisons built more than fifty years ago. Some states have created small facilities that are designed to meet individual correctional needs, but most inmates are in very large, antiquated "megaprisons" that often need repair.

State correctional institutions are classified by the level of security they afford, and their type of population shifts according to the special needs of the offenders. The security level is easily recognized by the physical characteristics of the buildings: the massive stone walls of maximum security prisons are topped by barbed wire and strategically placed guard towers; minimum security institutions are often indistinguishable from college campuses or apartment complexes.

The maximum security prison (where 26 percent of state inmates are confined) is built like a fortress, surrounded by stone walls with guard towers and designed to prevent escape. Inmates live in cells that have plumbing and sanitary facilities. The barred doors may be operated electronically so that an officer can confine all prisoners to their cells with the flick of a switch. The purpose of the maximum security facility is custody and discipline; there is a military-style approach to order. Prisoners follow a strict routine. Some of the most famous prisons, such as Stateville, Attica, Yuma, and Sing Sing, are maximum security facilities.

The medium security prison (holding 49 percent of state inmates) resembles the maximum security prison in appearance. It is organized on a somewhat different basis, however, resulting in an atmosphere that is less rigid and tense. Prisoners have more privileges and contact with the outside world through visitors, mail, and freer access to radio and television. The medium security prison places a greater emphasis on rehabilitative programs because inmates are not perceived to be hardened criminals, although in most states they have probably committed serious crimes.

The minimum security prison (with 25 percent of state inmates) houses least violent offenders, principally white-collar criminals. The minimum security prison does not have the guard towers and stone walls usually associated with correctional institutions. Often the buildings are surrounded by chain-link fencing. Prisoners usually live in dormitories or even in small private rooms rather than in barred cells. There is a relatively high level of personal freedom: inmates may have television sets, choose their own clothes, and move about casually within the buildings. Particular reliance is placed on treatment programs, and there are opportunities for education and work release. Although outsiders may sometimes feel that little punishment is associated with the minimum security facility, it is still a prison; restrictions are placed on inmates, and they remain segregated from society.

## Jails: Local Correctional Facilities

The U.S. jail has been called the "poorhouse of the twentieth century."[13] Most Americans do not distinguish between jails and prisons, but there is an important distinction. The jail is a strange correctional hybrid: part detention center for people awaiting trial, part penal institution for sentenced misdemeanants, and part holding facility for social misfits of one kind or another taken off the street. Prisons usually hold only offenders sentenced to terms longer than one year. Although much emphasis has been placed upon the importance of correctional facilities and programs located in the community to serve those who do not require long-term incarceration, local jails and short-term institutions in the United States are generally considered to be poorly managed custodial institutions.

There are approximately 3,300 locally administered jails in the United States with the authority to detain individuals for more than forty-eight hours. The ten largest hold 20 percent of the nation's jailed inmates. The Los Angeles County Men's Central Jail holds more than eight thousand inmates. Most jails, however, are much smaller: 63 percent hold fewer than fifty persons. Small jails are becoming less numerous because of new construction and new regional, multicounty facilities.

The most recent one-day census of the jail population found 444,584 inmates (one of every 428 U.S. adult residents), a 61 percent increase in five years. The characteristics of these inmates are shown in Figure 13.2. But the *number* of persons held at any one time in jail does not tell the complete story. Many people are held for less than twenty-four hours; others may reside in jail as sentenced inmates for up to one year; a few may await their trial for more than a year. In fact, the turnover rate is so great that more than twenty million Americans are jailed in one year. More citizens see the insides of jails than see the insides of prisons, mental hospitals, and halfway houses combined.[14]

Jails are usually locally administered by elected officials (sheriffs or county administrators). Only in Alaska, Connecticut, Delaware, Hawaii, Rhode Island, and Vermont are they run by the state government. Jails have traditionally been run by law enforcement agencies. It seems reasonable that the agency that arrests and transports defendants to court should also administer the facility that holds them, but generally neither

**Figure 13.2**
**Characteristics of adult inmates, U.S. jails, 30 June 1992**

The multipurpose function of the jail is shown by the fact that more than half of the inmates are unconvicted and are being held for arraignment or trial.

SOURCE: U.S. Department of Justice, Bureau of Justice Statistics, *Bulletin* (August 1993).

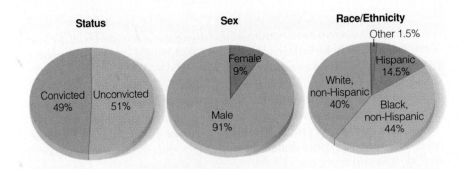

**Status**

Convicted 49%  Unconvicted 51%

**Sex**

Female 9%
Male 91%

**Race/Ethnicity**

Other 1.5%
Hispanic 14.5%
White, non-Hispanic 40%
Black, non-Hispanic 44%

sheriffs nor their deputies have much interest in corrections. They think of themselves as police officers and of the jail as merely an extension of law enforcement activities. It is important to remember, however, that almost half of the jail inmates are sentenced offenders under correctional authority.

The primary function of jails is to hold persons awaiting trial and persons who have been sentenced as misdemeanants to terms of no more than one year. This figure is deceptive, though, since on a national basis about 50 percent of jail inmates are pretrial detainees. In some states, convicted felons may serve terms of more than one year in jail rather than in prison. But for 87 percent of the sentenced population, stays in jail are less than one month.

Jails increasingly are housing sentenced felony offenders for whom space is lacking at the state prisons. Others held in jail are persons awaiting transportation to prison and persons convicted of parole or probation violations. This backup of inmates has caused difficulties for judges and jail administrators who must often put misdemeanants on probation because there is no jail space available.

Jails and police lockups shoulder responsibility for housing not only criminal defendants and offenders but also those persons viewed as problems by society. Here we can see how the criminal justice system is linked to other agencies of government. The deinstitutionalization of mental patients in particular has shifted a new population to criminal justice. Many such people are unable to cope with urban living and are often reported to the police when they act in a deviant manner that, although not illegal, is upsetting to the citizenry (urinating in public, appearing disoriented, shouting obscenities, and so on). The police must handle such situations, and temporary confinement in the lockup or jail may be necessary if no appropriate social service facilities are immediately available. In Denver, for example, the situation has been described as a revolving door that shifts these "street people" from the police station to the wing of the jail designated for psychiatric cases, often to court, and then back to the street.

The national concern about drunk driving has also placed an additional burden on jails. In response to groups such as Mothers Against Drunk Driving (MADD), legislators have passed mandatory jail sentences for persons convicted of driving while intoxicated. MADD instigated pressures on the criminal justice system that caused the police to devote additional resources to catching drunk drivers and the courts to impose tough sentences of incarceration, with the result that jails are inundated with offenders. Such campaigns can bring the local jail to the point of organizational breakdown.

Because of constant inmate turnover and because local control provides an incentive to keep costs down, correctional services are usually lacking. Recreational facilities and treatment programs are not found in most jails. Medical services are generally minimal. Such conditions add to the idleness and tensions of time spent in jail. Suicides and high levels of violence are hallmarks of many jails. In any one year almost half the people who die while in jail have committed suicide.

The mixture of offenders of widely diverse ages and criminal histories is another oft-cited problem in U.S. jails. Because most inmates are viewed as temporary residents, little attempt is made to classify them for either security or treatment purposes. Horror stories of the mistreatment of young offenders by older, stronger, and more violent inmates occasionally come to public attention. The physical condition of most jails aggravates this situation, because most are old, overcrowded, and lack in basic facilities. Many sentenced felons prefer to move on to state prison where the conditions are likely to be better.

As criminal justice policy has become more punitive, jails, like prisons, have become crowded. Surveys have documented increases averaging 6 percent during each of the past five years. Even with new construction, release on recognizance programs, diversion, intensive probation supervision, and house arrest with electronic monitoring, the jail population continues to rise. With the cost of building new facilities as high as $100,000 per cell and the cost of incarcerating an inmate about $15,000 per year, the $4.5 billion annual cost of operating jails places a great financial burden on local governments. As we will see later in this chapter, these costs for jails are low when compared to the cost of prisons.

## Institutions for Women

Because so few women are sent to prison, the number and adequacy of facilities for them are limited. Although the ratio of arrests is approximately six men to one woman, the ratio of admissions to state and federal correctional institutions is eighteen men to one woman. Of inmates in state and federal prisons, 6 percent are women.[15]

Until the beginning of the nineteenth century, female offenders in Europe and North America were treated no differently than male offenders and were not separated from males when they were incarcerated. Only with John Howard's 1777 expose of prison conditions in England and the development of the penitentiary in Philadelphia did attention begin to focus on the plight of the female offender. Among the English reformers, Elizabeth Gurney Fry, a middle-class Quaker, was the first person to press for changes (see Biography). When she and fellow Quakers visited London's Newgate Prison in 1813, they were shocked by the conditions in which the female prisoners and their children were living.

News of Fry's efforts spread to the United States, and the Women's Prison Association was formed in New York in 1844. Its goal was to improve the treatment of female prisoners and to separate them from males. It was not until 1873 that the first U.S. prison intended exclusively for women was built in Indiana. Within fifty years thirteen other states had followed this lead. There are now forty-five state and two federal institutions for women. In some states with no separate facilities for women, women offenders are assigned to a separate section of the state prison; other women offenders are housed in neighboring states by intergovernmental contract.

Conditions in correctional facilities for women are more pleasant than those of similar institutions for men. Usually the buildings have no gun towers and barbed wire. Because of the small population, however, most states have only one facility, which is often located in a rural setting far removed from urban centers. Thus women prisoners may be more isolated than men from their families and communities. Pressure from women's organizations and the apparent rise in the incidence of crime among women may bring about a greater equality in corrections for men and women. For more information on life in correctional institutions for women see Chapter 15.

## Private Prisons

One response to prison crowding has come from private entrepreneurs who argue that they can build and run prisons at least as effectively, safely, and humanely as any level of government. Their efficiency, they believe, can lower costs for taxpayers while allowing a profit for themselves. The contracting of correctional services on a piecemeal basis is not new and varies from jurisdiction to jurisdiction; services such as food, medical care, educational and vocational training, maintenance, security, and industrial programs are provided by private businesses. But the idea of running *entire* institutions for adult felons under private contract is new.

The first privately operated correctional institution was the Intensive Treatment Unit, a twenty-bed, high-security, dormitory-style training school for delinquents that opened in 1975 by the RCA Corporation in Weaversville, Pennsylvania. In January 1985 Kentucky's Marion Adjustment Center became the first privately owned and operated (by the U.S. Corrections Corporation) facility for the incarceration of adult felons sentenced at least to a level of minimum security. By mid-1989, Charles Logan counted about twelve companies running about twenty-four adult confinement institutions totaling some seven thousand beds in about twelve states. He notes that a precise count is difficult to cite because it is not always clear how to classify institutions and because contractual prisons and jails can spring rapidly in and out of existence.[16] Currently adult confinement institutions under private operation include jails, state and county prisons, prerelease facilities, lockups for parole violators being returned to custody, and detention centers for the U.S. Immigration and Naturalization Service (INS).

The major advantages cited by advocates are that privately operated prisons provide the same level of care as the states but they do it more cheaply and flexibly. Logan's study of private prisons points to the difficulties of measuring the costs and quality of these institutions.[17] One issue is that many of the "true costs" (fringe benefits, contracting supervision, federal grants) are not taken into consideration. The quoted rates of existing private facilities range greatly. A report for the National Institute for Corrections, for example, cites a cost of $30 a day at Okeechobee, Florida, and $110 a day at the Weaversville facility. The INS facilities for illegal aliens operate on average daily rates of twenty-three to twenty-eight dollars.[18] In regard to the issue of care, we have only the evaluation of juvenile justice expert James Finkenauer that the Weaversville facility is "better staffed, organized, and equipped than any program of its size that I know."[19] In regard to flexibility, it is argued that because correctional space requirements fluctuate, private entrepreneurs can provide additional space when it is needed and their contracts can go unrenewed when it is not.

A number of political, fiscal, and administrative issues must be considered and resolved before corrections can become heavily committed to the private ownership and operation of prisons. The political issues, including ethical questions of the propriety of delegating social-control functions to persons other than the state, may be the most difficult to overcome. Some experts believe that the administration of justice is a basic function of government and that it should not be delegated. There is also concern that correctional policy would be skewed. For example, contractors might use their political influence to continue programs not in the public interest; they would press for the maintenance of high occupancy levels, thus widening the net of social control; and they would be interested only in skimming off the "cream of the crop," leaving the most problematic inmates to the public correctional system. Though it is not yet possible to demonstrate the fiscal value of private corrections, labor unions have opposed these incursions into the public sector, pointing out that the salaries, benefits, and pensions of workers in other spheres such as private security are lower than those of their public counterparts. Finally, there are questions about quality of services, accountability of service providers to corrections officials, and problems related to contract supervision. Opponents cite the many instances in which privately contracted services in group homes, day-care centers, hospitals, and schools have been terminated upon reports of corruption, brutality, and provision of only minimal services.

The idea of privately run correctional facilities has stimulated much interest among the general public and within the criminal justice community. There may be further privatization of criminal justice services, or privatization may become only a limited venture that was initiated at a time of prison crowding, fiscal constraints on governments, and a revival of the free-enterprise ideology. The controversy about privatization has, however, forced corrections to rethink some strongly held beliefs. In this regard the possibility of competition from the private sector may be positive.

## Prison Populations: Trends and Characteristics

For most of the past fifty years the number of persons incarcerated in the United States remained fairly stable and the characteristics of those individuals changed little. During the 1940s and 1950s, the incarceration rate was maintained at about 120 per 100,000 population and the prisoners were overwhelmingly white, poor, and convicted for nonviolent crimes.

For a brief period in the late 1960s, when the trend in correctional circles was to stress deinstitutionalization and community corrections, the incarceration rate actually decreased. But by the mid-1970s, the prison population started its meteoric climb. The characteristics of inmates changed, with increased numbers of African-Americans, Hispanics, and persons sentenced for violent offenses. Today the American prison is a much-changed institution from just three decades before.

### Incarceration Trends

Every year on December 31 a census of the U.S. prison population is taken for the Bureau of Justice Statistics. Each year during the past decade the census has shown new record highs for the number of men and women incarcerated in state and federal prisons. As shown in Figure 13.3, this rise has been dramatic.

In many states the influx of new adult inmates have crowded already bulging institutions; some offenders are held in county jails and temporary quarters while others make do in corridors and basements. Faced

**Figure 13.3**
**Incarceration per 100,000 population, 1940–1993**
Between 1940 to 1970 the incarceration rate was steady. It has only been since 1975 that there has been a continuing increase. The rate today is about double what it was in 1980.

SOURCE: U.S. Department of Justice, Bureau of Justice Statistics, *Bulletin* (June 1994).

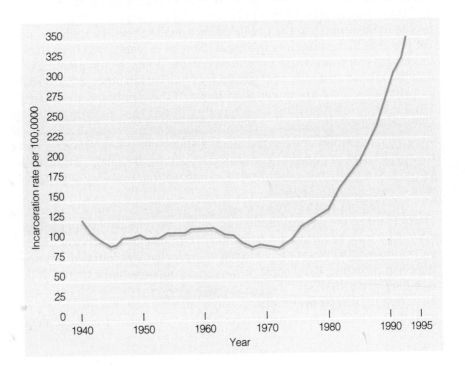

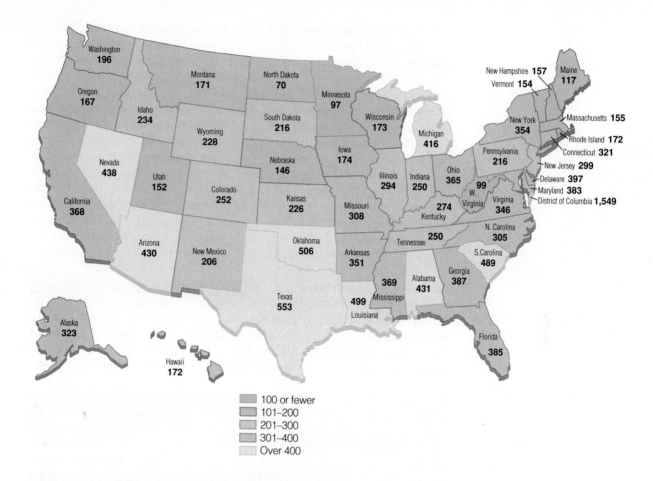

| | |
|---|---|
| Washington **196** | |
| Oregon **167** | |
| Montana **171** | |
| North Dakota **70** | |
| Idaho **234** | |
| Minnesota **97** | |
| New Hampshire **157** | Maine **117** |
| Vermont **154** | |
| South Dakota **216** | |
| Wisconsin **173** | |
| New York **354** | Massachusetts **155** |
| Wyoming **228** | |
| Michigan **416** | Rhode Island **172** |
| Nevada **438** | Connecticut **321** |
| Utah **152** | Iowa **174** |
| Pennsylvania **216** | New Jersey **299** |
| Nebraska **146** | Delaware **397** |
| Illinois **294** | Indiana **250** | Ohio **365** | Maryland **383** |
| California **368** | Colorado **252** | W. Virginia **99** | District of Columbia **1,549** |
| Kansas **226** | Missouri **308** | Virginia **346** | |
| Kentucky **274** | N. Carolina **305** | |
| Arizona **430** | New Mexico **206** | Oklahoma **506** | Tennessee **250** | |
| Arkansas **351** | S.Carolina **489** | |
| Texas **553** | Mississippi **369** | Alabama **431** | Georgia **387** |
| Louisiana **499** | |
| Alaska **323** | Florida **385** |
| Hawaii **172** | |

100 or fewer
101–200
201–300
301–400
Over 400

with such conditions, courts in some states have demanded that changes be made, because they view the overcrowding as a violation of the equal protection and cruel and unusual punishment portions of the Bill of Rights. In most states prison construction has become a growth industry, with massive public expenditures for new facilities that are immediately filled when they open.

Four hypotheses have been advanced to account for the growth of the American prison population: regional attitudes, public attitudes, improved police and prosecution, and prison construction. We discuss each in turn.

**Regional Attitudes**   As Figure 13.4 shows, some of the highest ratio of prisoners to the civilian population are found in the states of the "Old Confederacy." In 1993 that region incarcerated at the rate of 381 persons for each 100,000 inhabitants, a ratio higher than the national average of 351. Those favoring this regional perspective to explain the population increase point to the high levels of violence in the South, the long sentences dictated by the penal codes, and a history of racial conflict. It is suggested that African-American males are prime candidates for incarceration in these states. But, as the figure also reveals, there are exceptions to the

**Figure 13.4**
**Sentenced prisoners in state institutions per 100,000 civilian population, 1993**
What can be said about the differences in incarceration rates among the states? There are not only regional differences but also differences between contiguous states that would seem to have similar socioeconomic and crime characteristics.

SOURCE: U.S. Department of Justice, Bureau of Justice Statistics, *Bulletin* (June 1994).

regional hypothesis: Alaska, Arizona, Delaware, the District of Columbia, Michigan, and Nevada all have incarceration rates above the national average.

**Public Attitudes**   A second hypothesis is that a hardening of public attitudes toward criminals during the past decade has been reflected in longer sentences, in a smaller proportion of those convicted being granted probation, and in fewer being released at the time of the first parole hearing. As discussed in Chapter 12, some states have passed penal codes that greatly limit the discretion of judges in sentencing offenders who have committed certain types of crimes. In addition, the shift to determinate sentences has removed the safety valve of discretionary parole release, which in the past has been important to corrections administrators when prison populations have risen. Evidence from determinate sentencing states suggests that offenders are now spending more time incarcerated.

**Better Police and Prosecution**   A third hypothesis is that the billions of dollars spent on the crime problem, especially the war on drugs, may be paying off. Although crime rates overall have been fairly steady during the last decade, arrest and prosecution rates for drug-related offenses and the violence accompanying drugs have risen. Accordingly, the success of police and prosecution is affecting the corrections subsystem.

**Prison Construction**   Finally, the increased rate of incarceration may be related to the creation of additional space in the nation's prisons. Again, public attitudes in favor of more punitive sentencing policies may have influenced legislators to build more prisons. After new cells are constructed, judges may feel little hesitation in sentencing offenders to prison. When space was short, the same judges reserved incarceration for only the most violent convicts. The escalating incarceration rate may primarily reflect the impact of prison expansion programs in some states. For an alternative approach, see the accompanying Close-Up.

The contemporary rise in the incarceration rate has brought increased pressures to build more prisons. With courts sentencing more and more offenders to imprisonment, some people argue that space must be made available. For health and security reasons, the crowded conditions in existing facilities cannot be tolerated or permitted to worsen. But organization theorists contend that, once built, prisons will stay filled because of the organizational needs of the correctional bureaucracy. In other words, "beds will be filled." Society, it is argued, penalizes minor offenders when serious crime is not viewed as a problem and lets off those same offenders when serious crime has become endemic. Thus, if murder is relatively uncommon, criminal justice resources will be diverted to shoplifters, drug abusers, or prostitutes. Similarly, when violent offenses are more prevalent, there may be proposals to decriminalize the victimless crimes, such as drug use, prostitution, and gambling.

Building costs are perhaps one of the greatest deterrents to prison expansion. Legislatures typically discuss new construction in terms of $25,000 to $125,000 per cell, but recent economic analyses have shown that these estimates are low. One study computed the true cost of constructing and operating a hypothetical five hundred-bed medium secu-

CLOSE-UP

## The Price of Punishment in Delaware

John O'Connell's job is to try to make sense of Delaware's correctional system and to advise its elected officials on proposed policies and legislation. His work is a major reason that experts cite the state as a leader in the national effort to rein in the costs of dealing with criminals....

"What happens in Delaware and other states is that politicians come up with a lot of piecemeal legislation to deal with highly specific kinds of criminal behavior without knowing anything about the law's overall impact on the corrections system," Mr. O'Connell said. "Today, we can add analytical data to the mix of well-meaning intentions and emotional feelings."

The state Statistical Analysis Center, which Mr. O'Connell heads ... advises the legislature, which is free to ignore its advice. In 1989, for example, the center advised lawmakers that mandatory sentencing provisions of an antidrug bill would, among other things, increase the prison population by more than four hundred in five years.

The legislature passed the law anyway, prescribing a mandatory minimum sentence of three years in prison for anyone convicted of possessing 5 to 15 grams of cocaine or heroin. Last year, a study by the center found that courts had convicted 424 persons under the law and had imprisoned them at a cost to the state of $26.6 million. About 78 percent of the offenders had never been in prison before.

If these 424 had been placed in alternative programs,... taxpayers would have spent only $2.3 million, and the state would have achieved similar results.

As a result of this study the legislature passed a resolution that essentially asks the state attorney general, whose office also handles all local prosecutions, to ignore the law unless the offender is a drug trafficker.

Governor Michael N. Castle, a Republican who signed the law, said the legislature is now trying to save face by leaving it on the books. "Everyone is reluctant to seem soft on crime," he said....

In 1987, Delaware began restructuring its criminal justice system. A key change was sentencing guidelines that encouraged judges to send nonviolent offenders to the least expensive community-based program that would provide a combination of punishment and rehabilitation.

The state also began increasing its emphasis on alternative programs. While there are now 4,000 inmates in Delaware prisons, the state's alternative programs include a residential drug-treatment program for 16 offenders, home confinement with electronic monitoring for 135, two halfway houses for 250, probation with daily supervision for 1,100, and probation with weekly supervision for 7,000.

The efforts have begun to pay off. Delaware's crime rates now fall below national averages, even though the state has traditionally imprisoned a larger-than-average percentage of its population. But between 1987 and 1990, the latest years for which data is available, the state's incarceration rate increased only 3.3 percent compared with a national increase of 31.9 percent....

State studies also found that the number of offenders in alternative programs who had committed subsequent crimes or violated the rules of the programs was no higher than the number of offenders who had committed crimes after completing their prison terms.

SOURCE: Michael deCourcy Hinds, "The Price of Punishment in Delaware," *New York Times*, 7 August 1992, A–17. Copyright © 1992 by The New York Times Company. Reprinted by permission.

rity prison, using actual designs and construction estimates. In addition to the base cost of $61,015 per cell, or approximately $30 million for the facility, hidden (but expected) costs such as architects' fees, furnishings, and site preparation expenses pushed the estimate to $82,246 per cell ($41 million for the facility). At a conservative estimate of $14,000 per inmate per year, the operating cost would be $7 million a year. Thus the thirty-year bill to the taxpayers for construction and operation would be $350 million versus $30 million as originally proposed by the legislature.[20]

Given current public attitudes on crime and punishment, continued high crime rates, and the expansion of prison space, it is likely that incarceration rates will remain high. Perhaps only when the costs of this form of punishment have a direct impact on the taxpayers' pocketbooks will there be a shift in policies. It may also be that at some point the correctional pendulum will again swing, with a greater emphasis on intermediate punishments that do not require incarceration.

## Who Is in Prison?

The size of the inmate population directly affects correctional officials' ability to do their work. Crowding increases the potential for violence and greatly strains staff morale. Furthermore, when rehabilitative programs are filled, new offenders cannot be placed in them. In addition, the mix of the inmate community in terms of age, race, and criminal record affects the operation of correctional institutions.

What are the characteristics of the inmates in our nation's prisons? On the basis of a national survey of state prisons, the Bureau of Justice Statistics said in 1982, and later confirmed in 1991, that this population is predominantly comprised of

**Figure 13.5**
**Sociodemographic and offense characteristics of state prison inmates**
These data reflect the types of people found in state prisons. What do they indicate about the belief that many offenders do not "need" to be incarcerated?

SOURCE: U.S. Department of Justice, Bureau of Justice Statistics, *Survey of State Prison Inmates* (Washington, D.C.: Government Printing Office, 1993), 3.

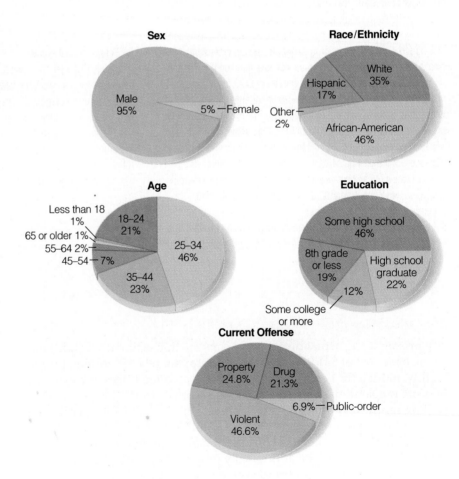

poor young adult males with less than a high school education. Prison is not a new experience for them; they have been incarcerated before, many first as juveniles. The offense that brought them to prison was a violent crime or burglary. On the average they already served 1½ years on a maximum sentence of 8½ years. Along with a criminal history, they have a history of drug abuse and are also likely to have a history of alcohol abuse.[21]

The summary characteristics described above are further illustrated in Figure 13.5. Note that most prisoners are in their late twenties to early thirties, have less than a high school education, and are disproportionately members of minority groups. In addition, more than half are incarcerated for violent crime.

It is clear from recent studies that inmates who are recidivists and who are convicted of violent crimes make up an overwhelming portion of the prison population. More than 60 percent of inmates have been either incarcerated or on probation at least twice; 45 percent of them, three or more times; and nearly 20 percent, six or more times. Two-thirds of the inmates were serving a sentence for a violent crime or had previously been convicted of a violent crime.[22] These are major shifts from the prison populations of earlier decades, when only about 40 percent of all inmates had committed such offenses. Today's prisoner has a history of persistent criminality. Beyond these shifts in the prison population, two additional factors affect correctional operations: Acquired Immune Deficiency Syndrome (AIDS) in the prison population and increased numbers of elderly prisoners.

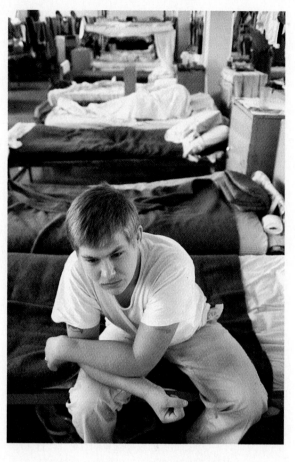

The prison population is composed predominantly of poor, young males. What might the future be like for this Georgia inmate?

## AIDS, Offenders, and Corrections

Almost eighteen thousand federal and state prison inmates have tested positive for the human immunodeficiency virus (HIV) that causes AIDS.[23] Statistical probabilities based on the demographic characteristics of the correctional population only partially reflect the impact of AIDS. The potential impact on corrections is further heightened by the fact that the probation, parole, jail, and prison populations contain a high concentration of individuals at particular risk for the disease—those with histories of intravenous drug use and, to a lesser extent, homosexual behavior. Not surprisingly, studies have shown that offenders with AIDS tend to be concentrated in those areas of the country where drug use is highest (the District of Columbia, New York, New Jersey). Among heterosexual males

## A Question of Ethics

The policy directive was precise:

*All inmates will be tested for HIV. All inmates found to be positive will be placed in Wing A, regardless of their physical condition, conviction offense, or time remaining in their sentence.*

Testing for the deadly virus began at Elmwood State Prison soon after Warden True's directive was posted. All 753 inmates were tested over a three-week period, and every new prisoner entering the institution first had blood drawn at the medical unit for testing.

Six weeks after the directive was posted, the test results were known. For most of the inmates there was relief in learning they had not contracted the virus. For a few, however, the notice that they were to report to the prison doctor was a prelude to knowledge that a medical death sentence had been issued. The news that they had tested positive was traumatic. Most responded with an expletive, others burst into tears, still others sat in stunned silence.

The new prison policy was leaked to the press. The state chapter of the American Civil Liberties Union and the Howard Association for Prisoners' Rights responded immediately by calling for a meeting with Warden True. In a press conference they protested the "state's invasion of privacy" and the "discriminatory act of segregating gay and drug users, most of the latter being African-American and Hispanic." They emphasized that it would be years before most of the infected would develop a "full" case of AIDS; corrections should respond with compassion, not stigmatization.

Warden True told reporters that he was responsible for the health of all inmates and that the policy had been developed to prevent transmission of the disease. He said that although the HIV inmates would be segregated, they would have access to all facilities available to the general inmate population but at separate times. He denied that he intended to stigmatize the twenty prisoners who had thus far tested positive.

What do you suppose Warden True considered in developing this policy? Is his policy likely to cause harm or good? Is it ethical to segregate the prison population? Is it ethical to add conditions to parole for prisoners who test HIV positive?

with AIDS, the ratio of African-Americans to whites is 12.0 to 1; for Hispanics 9.3 to 1.[24] Thus, there is a greater number of minority group members in the correctional population who are drug users and have AIDS.

Whether the offender has symptoms of AIDS or simply tests positive for the virus, probation and parole officials must confront several problems. These problems differ from those that jail and prison administrators face; they are most affected by questions and policy issues concerning the people under their supervision. Probation and parole officers can make their clients aware of community resources to deal with their health problems, but they lack the ability to force offenders to avail themselves of these services. Institutional administrators, on the other hand, are able to develop policies such as methods to prevent transmission of the disease, the housing of those infected, and medical care for inmates who have the full range of symptoms. In determining what actions should be taken, administrators have found that a host of legal, political, medical, budgetary, and attitudinal factors impinge on their ability to make what they believe are the best decisions.

At this time, AIDS is the leading cause of death among males between the ages of twenty-five and forty-four. This precise age group is heavily represented in prison, probation, and parole—nearly three-quarters of the adults under correctional supervision fall in this age range. Therefore, in addition to longstanding issues that corrections must address (violence, boredom, drug use, homosexual behavior in prison), it must now also address AIDS and related health issues (see A Question of Ethics).

### The Elderly Offender

Correctional officials have recently become aware of an increasing number of prison inmates who are older than fifty-five. Nationally that number is now more than 20,000, with about 400 over 85 years old. About half of these inmates are serving long sentences, the other half committed crimes late in life. While still a small portion of the total inmate population, these numbers are doubling every four years. Elderly prisoners have security needs that are different from the average inmate. In some state institutions older offenders are housed separately so they will not have to mix with the younger, tougher inmates. Elderly inmates often have costly medical needs that corrections must carry. The average yearly maintenance and medical costs for inmates over fifty-five is about $69,000—triple that of the norm. This higher cost is due, in part, to the treatment of chronic illnesses such as heart disease, strokes, and cancer.[25]

In the context of overcrowded facilities, the contemporary inmate population presents correctional workers with a challenge. Resources may not be available to provide rehabilitative programs for most inmates. Even if they are, the goal of maintaining a safe and healthy environment may tax the staff's abilities. These difficulties are multiplied still further in the face of AIDS. In addition, the corrections system is having to deal with a different type of inmate, one who is more prone to violence, and with a prison society where racial tensions are great. At the same time, corrections must manage the problems of elderly inmates, a growing segment of the prison population. Furthermore, there are the problems inherent in trying to deal with individuals in crowded, dated facilities. How well this correctional challenge is met will have an important impact on American society.

## Summary

From colonial days to the present, the methods of imposing criminal sanctions considered appropriate have varied. With the development of the penitentiary at the beginning of the nineteenth century, incarceration became the primary means of dealing with serious offenders. Although keeping offenders in custody has continued as a dominant goal, rehabilitation and reintegration into the community were alternative objectives from the end of World War II until the early 1970s. With the shift to an emphasis upon deserved punishment and crime control, corrections had to develop new policies and programs. Today corrections is faced with higher rates of incarceration and probation. We cannot now foresee when the number of offenders under correctional supervision will level off or decrease or what alternatives to traditional programs might emerge in the coming years.

There are three major instruments of incarceration in the United States: the Federal Bureau of Prisons, state prison systems, and local (mainly county-run) jails. Prisons hold offenders who have been sentenced to more than one year while jails house both pretrial detainees and offenders sentenced to less than one year of incarceration. There are also separate prison facilities for women. A small, but increasing, number of prisons are being built and operated by private corporations. The number and the type of inmates in an institution greatly influence the character of that facility and the problems faced by administrators.

Prison populations have more than doubled during the past ten years, and there has been a great increase in facilities and the staff to administer them. There also has been a change in inmate characteristics and the problems they bring to institutions. In particular, the two problems of HIV infection and elderly inmates are presenting correctional officials with new challenges.

## Questions for Review

1   What were the major differences between the New York and Pennsylvania systems in the nineteenth century?
2   What are some of the influences on administrators of local jails?
3   Who was Elizabeth Gurney Fry and what role did she play in correctional reform?
4   Why are private prisons attractive to some state legislators?
5   What are some of the management problems associated with offenders who have contacted HIV?

## Key Terms

community corrections          penitentiary          separate confinement
congregate system              penology

## For Further Reading

Clear, Todd R., and George F. Cole. *American Corrections*. 3d ed. Belmont, Calif.: Wadsworth, 1994. An overview of American corrections, designed for corrections courses.

DiIulio, John, Jr. *No Escape: The Future of American Corrections*. New York: Basic Books, 1991. Essays on the governing of prisons and other issues related to the future of corrections.

Foucault, Michel. *Discipline and Punish*. Translated by Alan Sheridan. New York: Pantheon, 1977. Describes the transition of the focus of correctional punishment from the body of the offender to the use of the penitentiary to reform the individual.

Irwin, John. *The Jail*. Berkeley, Calif.: University of California Press, 1985. A description of the multiple functions and problems of the American jail.

Logan, Charles. *Private Prisons: Cons and Pros*. New York: Oxford University Press, 1990. A definitive view of the issues surrounding the private prison question.

Rothman, David J. *Conscience and Convenience*. Boston: Little, Brown, 1980. Argues that conscience activated the Progressives to reform corrections yet the new structures for rehabilitation operated for the convenience of administrators.

———. *The Discovery of the Asylum: Social Order and Disorder in the New Republic*. Boston: Little, Brown, 1971. Rothman notes that before the nineteenth century deviants were cared for in the community. Urbanization and industrialization brought into being government institutions to handle this function.

## Notes

1   U.S. Department of Justice, Bureau of Justice Statistics, *Sourcebook of Criminal Justice Statistics* (Washington, D.C.: Government Printing Office, 1991), 19; U.S. Department of Justice, Bureau of Justice Statistics, *National Update* (Washington, D.C.: Government Printing Office, January 1992), 4.

2   Michel Foucault, *Discipline and Punish*, trans. Alan Sheridan (New York: Pantheon, 1977), 8, 16.

3   John Howard, *The State of Prisons in England and Wales* (London: J. M. Dent, 1929).

4   David J. Rothman, *The Discovery of Asylum: Social Order and Disorder in the New Republic* (Boston: Little, Brown, 1971), 49.

5   Thorsten Sellin, "The Origin of the Pennsylvania System of Prison Discipline," *Prison Journal* 50 (Spring-Summer 1970): 15–17.

6   Ronald L. Goldfarb and Linda R. Singer, *After Conviction* (New York: Simon and Schuster, 1973), 30.

7   David J. Rothman, *Conscience and Convenience* (Boston: Little, Brown, 1980), 18.

8   Ibid., 32.

9   Goldfarb and Singer, *After Conviction*, 40.

10  As quoted in Goldfarb and Singer, *After Conviction*, 41.

11  President's Commission on Law Enforcement and the Administration of Justice, *The Challenge of Crime in a Free Society* (Washington, D.C.: Government Printing Office, 1967), 7.

12  U.S. Department of Justice, Bureau of Justice Statistics, *Report to the Nation on Crime and Justice*, 2d ed. (Washington, D.C.: Government Printing Office, 1988), 117.

13  Ronald Goldfarb, *Jails: The Ultimate Ghetto* (Garden City, N.Y.: Doubleday, 1975), 29.

14  U.S. Department of Justice, Bureau of Justice Statistics, *Bulletin* (August 1993).

15  U.S. Department of Justice, Bureau of Justice Statistics, *Bulletin* (May 1994).

16  Charles Logan, *Private Prisons: Cons and Pros* (New York: Oxford University Press, 1990), 16.

17  Charles H. Logan, "Well Kept: Comparing Quality of Confinement in Private and Public Prisons, *The Journal of Criminal Law and Criminology* 83 (Fall 1992): 577–613.

18  Camille G. Camp and George M. Camp, *Private Sector Involvement in Prison Services and Operations*, Report to the National Institute of Corrections (Washington, D.C.: February 1984).

19  Cited in Kevin Krajick, "Punishment for Profit," *Across the Board* 21 (1984): 25.

20  *Time to Build?* (New York: Edna McConnell Clark Foundation, 1984), 18–19.

21  U.S. Department of Justice, Bureau of Justice Statistics, *Bulletin* (December 1982), 1; *Survey of State Prison Inmates* (Washington, D.C.: Government Printing Office, 1993), 3.

22  Ibid.

23  U.S. Department of Justice, Bureau of Justice Statistics, *Special Report* (September 1993), 1.

24  Mark Blumberg, "Issues and Controversies with Respect to the Management of AIDS in Corrections," in *AIDS: The Impact on the Criminal Justice System*, ed. Mark Blumberg (Columbus, Ohio: Merrill, 1990), 195.

25  *Newsweek*, 20 November 1989, 70.

# Community Corrections:
# Probation and Intermediate Sanctions

## 14

**Todd Harrison emptied the trash into the waiting truck as** his coworkers moved from can-to-can in the Bayside, Florida, recreation area. He wore his usual uniform—a baseball cap turned backwards, sunglasses, and a T-shirt emblazoned with the name "B.U.M." Harrison was one of ten probationers working under the watchful eye of Rich Clark, employed as a community service supervisor by the nonprofit organization, Upward Now, Inc. Two years before, Harrison had been sentenced to three years on probation and one hundred hours of community service for a larceny conviction. Since Todd was nineteen at the time of his arrest and had no prior record, the judge had given him a community sentence instead of sending him to prison, which was the usual sentence for more experienced criminals convicted of the same offense. Harrison lives with his mother, works the late shift at a convenience store, reports to his probation officer monthly, and spends five hours every Saturday under the supervision of Clark to complete his community service. Things are looking up for Todd Harrison as he moves toward completion of his punishment.

Scenes such as this one are becoming more common across the United States. During the past few years there has been a major shift in American corrections. After a decade that focused strongly on crime control through incarceration, experts in the field have shifted to a new (or renewed) emphasis on community corrections, adding a series of intermediate sanctions to the existing punishments of probation and parole. This swing in philosophy corresponds to increased public recognition that the crime problem is not being solved. In coming years community corrections can be expected to play a much greater role in the criminal justice system. With incarceration rates at record highs, probation and intermediate sanctions appear to many criminal justice experts to be less expensive and just as effective as prison.

## Questions for Inquiry

- What philosophical assumptions underlie community corrections?
- How did probation evolve, and in what ways are probation sentences implemented today?
- What are the types of intermediate sanctions and how are they administered?
- What are the concerns of community corrections as we move toward the twenty-first century?

## Community Corrections: Assumptions

During the 1980s many legislatures passed tough sentencing laws, mandated prison terms for certain offenses, and stipulated that new priorities stressing incarceration should guide corrections. Yet after a boom in the prison construction industry and a doubling of the incarceration rate, state governments are acknowledging that prisons are expensive. Many criminal justice scholars now argue that community corrections is a better response to criminal conduct for those offenders who do not require incarceration.

The American correctional system has not emphasized incarceration to the exclusion of other forms of the criminal sanction. Even during the nineteenth-century reform period it was recognized that supervision in the community was a more appropriate means to produce the desired change in some offenders. The development of probation in the 1840s and the transplantation of parole from England in the 1880s best exemplify this community approach. Until the 1950s, however, many states still relied more on incarceration than on probation and parole, and it was not until the 1960s that community alternatives were developed.

In the late 1980s, with prison crowding becoming a major national problem, there was new interest in creating a set of intermediate sanctions—intensive probation supervision, home confinement, and electronic monitoring—by which offenders, who might normally be sent to prison, could be supervised in the community. As Figure 14.1 shows, today almost three-quarters of all persons under correctional supervision are living in their communities.

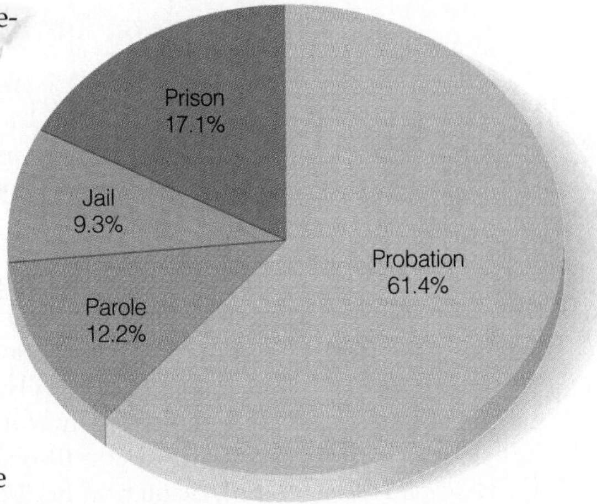

Release under supervision in the community allows judges, parole boards, and correctional officials to reduce the prison population. As a result, offenders who have committed more serious crimes, for which they would earlier have been sentenced to prison, are hitting the street under correctional supervision instead. Given the characteristics of these offenders, community corrections has taken a tougher stance. Surveillance now outweighs the rehabilitative and reintegrative functions emphasized in the past.

Community corrections aims at building ties that can reintegrate the offender to the community: help in restoring family links, obtaining employment and education, and developing a sense of place and pride in daily life. The community model of corrections assumes that the offender must change, but it also recognizes that factors within the community that might encourage criminal behavior (unemployment, for example) must also change.

Four factors are usually cited in support of community corrections. First, the background characteristics or crimes of some offenders are not serious enough to warrant incarceration. Second, community supervision is cheaper than incarceration. Third, if rehabilitation is measured by **recidivism** rates, prison is no more effective than community supervision. In fact, some studies show that just being in prison raises the offender's potential for recidivism. Fourth, incarceration is more destructive to both the offender and society. In addition to the pangs of imprisonment and the harmful effects of prison life, there is the suffering of family members, particularly the children of female offenders.

Central to the community corrections approach is a belief in the "least restrictive alternative," the notion that the criminal sanction should be applied only to the minimum extent necessary to meet the community's need for protection, the gravity of the offense, and society's need for deserved punishment. Supporters of community corrections urge the expansion of postincarceration programs such as halfway houses, work release and furlough programs, and parole services to assist and reintegrate the offender into the community. These community methods all reflect the belief that corrective actions should give offenders opportunities to succeed in law-abiding activities and to reduce their contact with the criminal world.

**Figure 14.1**
**Percentage of persons under correctional supervision in all categories**
Although most people think of corrections as prisons and jails, in fact almost three-quarters of offenders are supervised within the community.

SOURCE: U.S. Department of Justice, Bureau of Justice Statistics, *National Update* (January 1992), 4.

**recidivism**
A return to criminal behavior.

# Probation: Correction without Incarceration

**Probation** denotes the conditional release of the offender into the community under supervision. It imposes conditions and retains the authority of the sentencing court to modify the conditions of the sentence or to resentence the offender. Often the judge imposes a prison term but then suspends execution of that sentence and instead places the offender on probation. Increasingly, however, judges in some states are using the tactics of shock incarceration or split sentences in which a period in prison is followed by probation.

Judges normally stipulate conditions as to how the probationer is to live in the community. If the offense and background characteristics warrant, these conditions may require that the probationer obtain drug, alcohol, or mental health treatment. If the offense was a result of domestic violence or sexual abuse, then the order may stipulate that the probationer not have contact with the victim. Restitution, community service, or a fine may be ordered as part of the punishment. These orders are in addition to the standard conditions that the client cooperate with the probation officer and not commit another offense. The probationer who meets the conditions set by the court may remain in the community. The probationer who violates these terms or is arrested for another offense may have probation revoked and be sent to prison.

The number of probationers is at a record level and is still rising. While much has been written about overcrowded prisons, the adult probation population has also been increasing—over 7 percent a year, up 44 percent in 1990 since 1985. At the same time the political climate has supported harsher correctional policies, with the result that probation goals are now oriented more toward punishment of the offender and protection of the community rather than toward rehabilitation. Probation budgets in many states have been cut and caseloads increased as greater resources are diverted to prisons. However, the reality of overcrowded prisons undoubtedly means that judges will be forced to place more offenders convicted of serious crimes, especially drug crimes, on probation. That means probation will involve an increasing number of clients whose risk of recidivating is high.

## Origins and Evolution of Probation

Although historical antecedents for probation are found in the procedures of reprieves and pardons of early English courts, John Augustus, a prosperous Bostonian, has become known as the world's first probation officer (see Biography). By persuading a judge in the Boston Police Court to place a convicted offender in his custody, Augustus was able to assist his probationer so that the man appeared to be rehabilitated when he returned for sentencing.

Massachusetts developed the first statewide probation system in 1880, and by 1920 twenty-one other states had followed suit. The federal courts were authorized to hire probation officers in 1925, and by the beginning of World War II forty-four states had implemented the concept.

Probation originated as a humanitarian method of allowing first-time and minor offenders a second chance. To that end, probation officers were to use a casework model, which involved intervention in the client's life and guidance toward the "right" path. The offender was to refrain from criminal acts and to behave morally. Early officers were thus actively involved in all aspects of the offender's life: family, religion, employment, and free time. They were to provide a role model or moral leadership for those who had been in trouble.

With the rising influence of psychology in the 1920s, the probation officer continued as a caseworker, but the emphasis shifted to therapeutic counseling in the office rather than on assistance in the community. This shift produced several important changes. First, the officer was no longer primarily a community supervisor charged with enforcing a particular morality. Second, the officer became more of a clinical social worker whose goal was to help the offender solve psychological and social problems. In keeping with the goals of the rehabilitation model, the probation officer had extensive discretion to diagnose the problem and treat it. Third, the offender was expected to become actively involved in the treatment program.

During the 1960s, another shift occurred in the orientation of probation, perhaps reflecting the emphasis of the war on poverty. Rather than counseling offenders in their offices, probation officers provided them with concrete social services, such as assistance with employment, housing, finances, and education. Officers backed away from direct involvement in the lives of offenders, on the assumption that when offenders exercised more control over their own goals and activities, they improved their chances of adjustment to the community. Finally, instead of being a counselor or therapist, the probation officer was to be an advocate, dealing with the private and public institutions on the offender's behalf.

In the late 1970s the orientation of probation again changed. The goals of rehabilitation and reintegration gave way to an orientation widely referred to as "risk control." This approach, dominant today, tries to minimize the probability that an offender will commit a new offense. Risk control combines values of the just deserts model of the criminal sanction, which holds that punishment should be commensurate with the offense and that correctional intervention should neither raise nor lower the level of punishment, with the commonly accepted idea that the community deserves protection. Hence, the amount and the type of supervision provided are based on estimates of risk that the probationer will return to criminal behavior.

## Organization of Probation

Today over 60 percent of offenders in the United States are placed on probation. Estimates are that at any one time there are over two and a half million probationers. Some observers claim that placing an offender on probation today is to do almost nothing. Given the huge caseloads of probation officers, offenders receive very little guidance, supervision, or

**John Augustus**

John Augustus was a Boston bootmaker who became a self-appointed probation officer, thereby developing the concept of probation as an alternative to incarceration. His innovation began in 1841 when he posted bail for a man charged with being a common drunkard. His philanthropic activities had already made Augustus a frequent observer in the courts, so the judge was willing to defer sentencing for three weeks, and the man was released into Augustus' custody. At the end of this period, the man convinced the judge of his reform and received only a nominal fine. The concept of probation had been introduced.

Augustus often appeared in Boston courts, acting as counsel and furnishing bail. He found homes for juvenile offenders and frequently obtained lodging and employment for adults accused or convicted of violating vice or temperance laws. Between 1842 and 1858 he bailed out 1,946 people, making himself liable to the extent of $243,235. He reported great success with his charges and asserted that, with help, most of them eventually led upright lives. Augustus's primary sources of financial support were his own business and voluntary contributions. His efforts created a practice that became an established part of criminal justice.

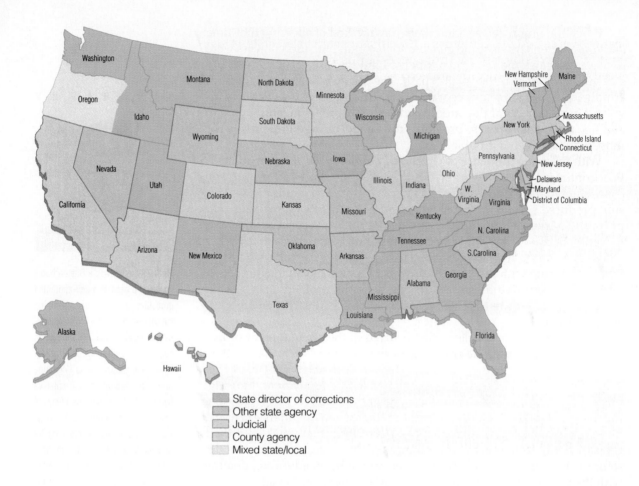

State director of corrections
Other state agency
Judicial
County agency
Mixed state/local

**Figure 14.2**
**Probation organizational structures**

Probation is primarily a local responsibility. Even when it operates under state jurisdiction, the county judge has the largest influence over probation decisions.

SOURCE: *Research in Action* (Washington, D.C.: National Institute of Justice, 1988), 2.

assistance. A Philadelphia criminal court judge, Lois Forer, has remarked: "Probation is not a penalty. The offender continues with his life-style.... If he is a wealthy doctor, he continues with his practice; if he is an unemployed youth, he continues to be unemployed. Probation is a meaningless rite; it is a sop to the conscience of the court."[1]

Probation may be viewed as a form of corrections, but in many states it is administered by the judiciary, and it is very much a local affair. As shown in Figure 14.2, in about 25 percent of the states, probation is a responsibility of county and local government. The state sets the standards and provides financial support and training courses. This locally based approach accounts for about two-thirds of all persons under probation supervision.[2] Although in many jurisdictions the state is formally responsible for all probation services, the locally elected county judges are really in charge. This system has its benefits—and its problems. On the positive side, keeping probationers under court supervision prevents them from being unduly stigmatized as they might be under corrections, as most citizens equate that department with prisons. On the negative side, some judges know little about corrections, and probation increases the administrative duties of the already overworked courts.

Perhaps the strongest argument in favor of judicial control is that probation works best when there is a close relationship between the judge and the supervising officer. Proponents of this system say that judges need to work with probation officers they can trust, whose presentence reports they can accurately evaluate, and whom they can rely on to report the success or failure of individual cases. In addition, judges are likely to appoint probation officers who are responsive to the local political system.

Probation officers need direct access to corrections and other human services agencies to use them most effectively and for the most benefit to their clients; yet these services are located within the executive branch of government. In some states this consideration has led to combining probation and parole services in the same agency, a move which proponents claim increases effectiveness and efficiency. Others point out, however, that probationers are quite different from parolees, for they have not developed criminal life-styles to the same degree and do not have the same problems of reintegration into the community.

## Probation Services

As we have seen, probation officers are often expected to act as both police personnel and social workers. In addition to assisting the judiciary with presentence investigations and reports, they supervise clients in order to keep them out of trouble and assist them in the community. Not surprisingly, individual officers may emphasize one role over the other, and the potential for conflict is great. But studies have shown that most probation officers have backgrounds in social service and are partial to that role.

One of the continuing issues related to probation services is the size of the caseload. Can a caseload that is efficient in the use of resources be effective in the guidance of offenders? The 50-unit caseload established in the 1930s by the National Probation Association was reduced to 35 by the President's Commission on Law Enforcement and the Administration of Justice in 1967; yet the national average is currently about 115, and in extreme cases it reaches more than 300. Although the sizable caseload is usually identified as a major obstacle to successful operation of probation, recent evidence indicates that the size of the caseload is less significant than the nature of the supervision experience, the classification of offenders, the professionalism of the officer, and the services available from the agencies of correction.

Probation officials have developed methods of classifying clients according to their service needs, the element of risk that they pose to the community, and the chance of recidivism. It is through this process that probationers may be granted less supervision as they continue to live without violation of the conditions of their sentence. Risk classification schemes are consistent with the deserved punishment model of the criminal sanction in that the most serious cases receive the greatest restrictions and supervision.[3] Whether these cases actually receive the intended level of supervision is influenced by several factors, including ease or risk of actual supervision. Consider the war on drugs. It has significantly increased probation levels in urban areas because large numbers of drug traffickers and people convicted of drug possession are placed on probation.[4] Many of these offenders have committed violent acts and live in inner-city areas marked by drug selling, turf battles, and attempts to control drug markets.

Under these conditions, direct supervision can be a dangerous task for the probation officer. In some urban areas, probationers are merely required to telephone or mail reports of their current residence and employment. In such cases, which justification for the criminal sanction—deserved punishment, rehabilitation, deterrence, or incapacitation—is being realized? If none is being realized, the offender is getting off.

## Revocation of Probation

Probationers who violate the provisions of their sentences may be taken back to court. Revocation of probation can result from a new arrest or conviction or from failure to comply with a condition of probation. Since probation is usually granted in conjunction with a suspended jail or prison sentence, incarceration may follow revocation. Probation officers and judges have widely varying notions of what constitutes grounds for revoking probation. Once the officer has decided to call a violation to the attention of the court, the probationer may be arrested or summoned for a revocation hearing. Since the contemporary emphasis is on avoiding incarceration except for flagrant and continual violation of the conditions of probation, most revocations today occur because of a new arrest or conviction.

*Mempa* v. *Rhay* (1967)
Probationers have the right to counsel at a hearing considering revocation of a suspended sentence.

*Gagnon* v. *Scarpelli* (1973)
Required that before probation may be revoked, a two-stage hearing must be held and the offender provided with specific elements of due process.

Not until 1967 did the United States Supreme Court give an opinion concerning the due process rights of probationers at a revocation hearing. In *Mempa* v. *Rhay* it determined that a state probationer had the right to counsel at a revocation proceeding, but nowhere in the opinion did the Court refer to any requirement for a hearing.[5] This issue was addressed by the Court in *Gagnon* v. *Scarpelli* (1973).[6] Here the justices ruled that revocation of probation and parole demands a preliminary and a final hearing. When a probationer is taken into custody for violating the conditions of probation, a preliminary hearing must be held to determine whether probable cause exists to believe that the incident occurred. If there is a finding of probable cause, a final hearing, where the revocation decision is made, becomes mandatory. At these hearings the probationer has the right to cross-examine witnesses and to be given notice of the alleged violations and a written report of the proceedings. The Court ruled, though, that there is no automatic right to counsel: this decision is to be made on a case-by-case basis. It is then that the judge decides upon incarceration and its length. If the violation has been minor, the judge may simply continue probation, but with greater restrictions.

Probation is at a crossroads. Does continuation of the service-provider orientation make sense today? Is it realistic to expect that the individual probation officer can possibly know all that is required to be effective in the specialized fields of human services? Some corrections experts have urged that the probation unit contract with community agencies for human services and return the probation officer to supervision. Others argue that, especially in urban areas, probation does nothing. Because of huge caseloads and indifferent officers, offenders can easily avoid supervision and check in perfunctorily with their probation officers. In such cases, probation has little effect on crime control.

Indeed, the effectiveness of probation is increasingly being questioned. Probation does produce less recidivism than incarceration, but researchers now wonder if this effect is a direct result of supervision or an indirect result of the maturation process. Most offenders placed on probation do not become career criminals, their criminal activity is short-lived, and they become stable citizens as they get jobs and marry. Even most of those who are arrested a second time do not repeat their mistake again. What rallies support for probation is its relatively low cost: keeping an offender on probation rather than behind bars costs roughly $700 a year, resulting in yearly savings to the criminal justice system of more than $17,000.

In recent years as prison space has become scarce and overcrowded institutions a problem, increasing numbers of felony offenders have been placed on probation. Over one-third of the nation's probationers have been convicted on felony charges. In addition, upward of 75 percent of probationers are addicted to drugs or alcohol. These factors present new challenges for probation, since officers can no longer assume that their clients pose little threat to society and that they are capable of living productive lives in the community.

If probation is to be a viable alternative to incarceration, the resources must be made available so that it can do its job of supervision and assistance. The new demands upon probation have given rise to calls for increased electronic monitoring and for risk management systems that provide different levels of supervision for different kinds of offenses.

## Intermediate Sanctions in the Community

Dissatisfaction with the traditional means of probation supervision and the crowding of American prisons has resulted in a call for intermediate sanctions that will allow serious offenders to be punished in the community. The case for intermediate sanctions can be made on several grounds, but Norval Morris and Michael Tonry have articulated it well: "Prison is used excessively; probation is used even more excessively; between the two is a near vacuum of purposive and enforced punishments."[7] As noted in Chapter 12, the emphasis is on creating sanctions that are more restrictive than probation, that are punishments equal to the offense and the characteristics of the offender, and that can be carried out while still protecting the community.

Intermediate sanctions may be viewed as a continuum—a range of punishments that vary in levels of intrusiveness and control. Probation plus a fine or community service may be appropriate for minor offenses while six weeks of boot camp followed by intensive probation supervision may be the deserved punishment for someone who has been convicted of a more serious crime. But some have argued that intermediate sanctions add to the number of persons under correctional authority and that the inclusion of sanctions with probation may mean that the offender is unable to comply with the conditions of the sentence.[8]

Across the country many different types of intermediate sanctions are being used. They can be divided into three categories: (1) those administered primarily by the judiciary (fines, restitution, forfeiture); (2) those administered primarily within the community, with a supervision component (home confinement, community service, day reporting centers, and intensive probation supervision); and (3) those administered institutionally, then followed by community supervision. It is important to emphasize that each individual intermediate sanction may be imposed singly or in tandem with others. Thus it is not surprising that a fine may be combined with probation, or that boot camp can be combined with community service and probation.

## Sanctions Administered Primarily by the Judiciary

A number of intermediate sanctions are administered primarily by the judiciary. We discuss three below—fines, restitution, and forfeiture. Since all three involve the transfer of money or property from the offender to the government, the judiciary is deemed the proper branch not only to impose the sanction but also to collect that which is due.

**fine**
A sum of money to be paid to the state by a convicted person as punishment for an offense.

**Fines** **Fines** are routinely imposed today for offenses ranging from traffic violations to felonies. Recent studies have shown that the fine is used widely as a criminal sanction and that probably well over one billion dollars in fines are collected annually by courts across the country.[9] Judges in the lower courts are more positively disposed to fines than are judges in higher courts, yet fines are extensively imposed by courts that handle only felonies. Perhaps most important, however, is the fact that fines are rarely used as the *sole* punishment for crimes more serious than motor vehicle violations. Typically, fines are used in conjunction with other sanctions, such as probation and incarceration. For example, a judge may impose two years probation and a five hundred dollar fine.

Many judges do not make greater use of fines because they are difficult to collect and enforce.[10] For most other sanctions, the judge can generally rely on another agency of government, usually in the executive branch, to carry out the sentence; monetary penalties are typically the only criminal sanction executed directly by the court. Perhaps the judiciary sees little incentive to expend its own resources in administering the collection of fines. Judges report that fine enforcement receives a low priority.

In addition, some judges are concerned that—since offenders tend to be poor—fines would be paid from the proceeds of additional illegal acts. Furthermore, reliance on fines as an alternative to incarceration might mean the affluent would be able to "buy" their way out of jail while the poor would have to serve time.

In contrast to the United States, fines are used extensively in Europe, where they are enforced. They are normally the sole sanction for a wide range of crimes. The amounts are geared to the severity of the offense and the resources of the offender. To deal with the concern that fines exact a heavier toll on the poor than on the wealthy, Sweden and Germany have developed the "day fine," described in the Comparative Perspective on pages 510–511. Under this system the fines levied are adjusted to the differing economic circumstances of offenders who have committed the same crime.

Experiments with the day-fine concept are now taking place in Arizona, Connecticut, Iowa, and Oregon. We should soon see whether the idea can work in the United States. Fines are gaining increased attention from judges and criminal justice planners as they struggle with overcrowded jails and prisons and overwhelming probation caseloads and as their dissatisfaction with present sentencing alternatives mounts.

**Restitution**   In its simplest form, **restitution** is repayment to a victim who has suffered some form of financial loss as a result of the offender's crime. In the Middle Ages restitution was a common way to settle a criminal case: the offender was ordered to do the victim's work or to give the victim money. The growth of the modern state meant that less attention was given to "private" arrangements between offender and victim and greater attention to the wrong done to the community by the offender.

Victim restitution has always been a part of the U.S. criminal justice system, but a largely unpublicized one, produced by informal agreements between enforcement officials and offenders, at the station house and during plea bargaining, and by sentence recommendations. It is only since the late 1970s that it has been institutionalized in many areas. It is usually carried out as a condition of probation.

**Forfeiture**   With passage of the Racketeer Influence and Corrupt Organizations Act (RICO) and the Continuing Criminal Enterprise Act (CCE) in 1970, Congress resurrected forfeiture, a criminal sanction that had been dormant since the American Revolution. Through amendments in 1984 and 1986 Congress improved procedures for implementing the forfeiture provisions of the law.[11] Similar laws are now found in most states, particularly with respect to controlled substances and organized crime.

**Forfeiture** is seizure by the government of property derived from or used in criminal activity. Forfeiture proceedings can be either civil or criminal. Using the civil law, property used in criminal activity (contraband, equipment to manufacture illegal drugs, automobiles) can be seized

**restitution**
Compensation for injury an offender has inflicted in the form of payment of money to the victim or the performance of service to the community.

**forfeiture**
Seizure by the government of property and other assets derived from or used in criminal activity.

## Day Fines in Germany: Could the Concept Work Here?

The idea that the amount of a fine should be related not only to the offense but also to the income of the offender is hardly new. In the twelfth century it was recognized that criminal punishments weigh more heavily on some offenders than on others. Thus by imposing different levels of fines on offenders who have committed the same offense but who have different levels of financial assets, it is believed that greater fairness can be achieved.

Modern implementation of relative fines began with creation of the day-fine system in Finland in 1921, followed by its development in Sweden (1931) and Denmark (1939). The Federal Republic of Germany instituted day fines in 1975. Since then, there has been a major change in the punishments of offenders so that now more than 80 percent of those convicted receive a fine-alone sentence.

Judges determine the amount of the day fine through a two-stage process. First, judges relate the crime to offense guidelines, which have established the minimum and maximum number of day-

without a finding of guilt (see Chapter 3). Criminal forfeiture is a punishment imposed as a result of conviction at the time of sentencing. It requires that the offender relinquish various assets related to the crime.

An estimated one billion dollars in assets were confiscated from drug dealers by state and federal officials from 1985 to 1990.[12] In recent years, concern about the excessive use of this sanction has been raised. In a 1993 opinion, the Supreme Court ruled that the Eighth Amendment's ban on excessive fines requires that there be a relationship between the seriousness of the offense and the property that is taken.[13]

## Sanctions Administered in the Community

Today there is much discussion of intermediate sanctions in the community, which are administered primarily by probation departments or by nonprofit organizations under government contract. Here we examine four: home confinement, community service, day reporting centers, and intensive probation supervision.

fine units for each offense. For example, according to the guidelines, theft may be punished by a day fine within the range of ten to fifty units. Judges choose the number of units by considering the culpability of the offender and by examining the offender's motivation and the circumstances surrounding the crime. Second, the value of these units is determined. The German day fine is essentially calculated as the cost of a day of freedom: the amount of income an offender would have forfeited if incarcerated for a day. One day-fine unit is equal to offender's average net daily income (considering salary, pensions, welfare benefits, interests, and so on), without deductions for family maintenance, so long as the offender and the offender's dependents have a minimal standard of living. Finally, the law calls for publication of the number of units and their value for each day fine set by the court so that the sentencing judgment is publicly known.

To illustrate the impact of the day-fine system, say a judge is faced with two defendants who have separately been convicted of theft. One defendant is a truck driver who earns an average of DM 100 per day and the other is a business manager whose earnings average DM 300 per day. The judge uses the guidelines and decides that the circumstances of the theft and the criminal record of each offender is the same. It is decided that forty day-fine units should be assessed to each. By multiplying these units by the average daily income for each, the truck driver's fine is DM 4,000 and the manager's fine is DM 12,000.

Since the day-fine system was introduced in Germany there has been an increase in the use of fines and a decrease in short-term incarceration. The size of fines have also increased, reflecting the fact that affluent offenders are being punished at levels corresponding to their worth. Likewise, fines for poor offenders have remained relatively low. These results have been accomplished without an increase in the default rate.

What factors would have a bearing on whether a day-fine system would work in the United States? How might the day fine for a truck driver and a cocaine dealer compare?

**Home Confinement** Given the increase in prison crowding and technological innovations that provide for electronic monitoring, **home confinement**, a sentence imposed by a court that requires convicted offenders to spend all or part of the time in their own residence, has gained new attention from criminal justice planners. Conditions are placed on permissible actions; some offenders are allowed to go to a place of employment, education, or treatment during the day but must return to their residence by a specific hour. Home confinement has the advantage of flexibility, since it can be used as a sole sanction or in combination with other penalties and can be imposed at almost any point in the criminal justice process: during the pretrial period, after a short term in jail or prison, or as a condition of probation or parole.[14]

The development of electronic monitoring equipment makes contemporary home confinement a viable sentencing alternative.[15] There are two basic types of electronic devices. A continuously signaling device has a transmitter that is attached to the probationer, and a receiver-dialer is attached to the probationer's home telephone. It reports to a central computer at the monitoring agency when the signal stops, indicating that the

**home confinement**
A sentence requiring the offender to remain inside his or her home during specified periods.

offender is not in the house and alerting correctional officials of the unauthorized absence. A second device uses a computer that is programmed to telephone the probationer randomly or at specific times. The offender must answer the phone within a certain amount of time and verify that he or she is indeed the person under supervision.[16]

Electronic monitoring has not been as widely adopted as might be expected. Probation departments have found that the devices are both expensive and not foolproof. Thirty-three states now have some type of permanent or experimental program using electronic monitoring, but offenders sentenced in those states still represent only about twelve thousand persons.[17] Of interest is the type of offender under electronic monitoring. As shown in Figure 14.3, many have committed major traffic offenses and property offenses, but a few probationers who have committed serious crimes are also being monitored. Presumably these offenders might otherwise have been incarcerated.

Some criminal justice planners are concerned that home confinement has merely widened the net of social control—that persons who formerly would have been placed on "regular" probation will now be given house arrest with its greater restrictions. Others, however, have noted that with increased numbers of high-risk offenders on probation, home confinement is a necessary shift in correctional policy.

This intermediate sanction has received much favorable publicity, yet there are legal, technical, and correctional issues that must be resolved before house arrest with electronic monitoring can become a standard form of the criminal sanction. Some criminal justice scholars have questioned its constitutionality, saying that monitoring may violate the Fourth Amendment's protection against unreasonable searches and seizures. Here the issue is privacy and the invasion of one's domicile by government. Technical problems with the monitoring devices have dogged many experiments. Failure rates among those under home confinement may prove to be high. Being one's own warden is a difficult task, and visits by friends and community enticements may become overwhelming distractions for many offenders.[18] Tolerance levels for home confinement have not yet been researched, but some observers believe that four months of full-time monitoring is about the limit before a violation will occur.

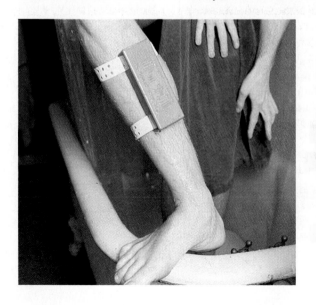

One type of electronic monitoring uses a transmitter attached to the offender. How might offenders "trick" this device?

**Community Service** **Community service** is unpaid service to the public to overcome or compensate society for some of the harm caused by a crime; it may take a variety of forms, including assisting in a social service agency or cleaning parks. The sentence specifies the number of hours to be worked and usually requires supervision by a probation officer. Community service can be tailored to the economic and ability levels of the offender. There is also symbolic value in the offender's effort to make reparations to the community offended by the crime.

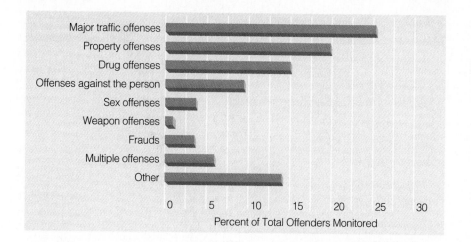

**Figure 14.3**
**Electronically monitored offenders categorized by offense**
Although most monitored offenders have committed offenses for which prison is not the normal disposition, there are a few who have committed crimes that might have resulted in their incarceration.

SOURCE: Annesley K. Schmidt, "Electronic Monitoring of Offenders Increases," *Research in Action* (Washington, D.C.: National Institute of Justice, 1989), 2.

Although community service has many supporters, some labor unions and workers criticize it, saying that offenders are taking jobs from crime-free citizens. Beyond this objection, some experts believe that if community service is imposed as the sole sanction, some offenders may receive relatively mild punishments. That may be particularly true when the sanction is applied to upper-class and white-collar criminals. Some experts note that while community service can be a useful criminal justice sanction for a property crime, it is of little value if violence figured in the offense. Others note that community service seems to have had mixed results with reducing the criminal behavior of participants.[19]

**community service**
A sentence requiring the offender to perform a certain amount of labor in the community.

**Day Reporting Centers**   To ensure that probationers with employment and treatment stipulations attached to their sentences comply with those requirements, **day reporting centers** have been created in some states.[20] Originally developed in Great Britain, day reporting centers have been expanded in the United States in recent years. They are designed to ensure that sentences are followed and that offenders and the general public will view probation supervision as credible.

Most day reporting centers incorporate multiple correctional methods. For example, in some centers offenders are required to be in the facility for eight hours or to report for urine checks (for drug abuse) before going to work. In others, the treatment is comparable to that of a halfway house—but without the offender living in a residential facility. Drug and alcohol treatment, literacy programs, and assistance in job searches may be available in some centers.

Thus far, the results of these programs have not been formally evaluated. One study of New York City's program found that its stiff eligibility requirements resulted in few cases entering the program. In Connecticut, however, more than six thousand offenders report daily to such centers.[21]

**day reporting center**
A community correctional center where an offender reports each day to comply with elements of a sentence.

**Intensive Probation Supervision**   In response to research findings indicating that a small core of high-risk offenders commits a disproportionate amount of crime and adds to overcrowded prison conditions, various localities have developed programs for the intensive supervision of

## Table 14.1
### Key features of selected IPS programs in thirty-one states

IPS entails more than daily contacts with a probation officer; twenty-three other restrictions are often imposed. Given a choice, would you prefer IPS or a short prison term?

SOURCE: James M. Byrne, Arther I. Lurigio, and Christopher Baird, "The Effectiveness of the New Intensive Supervision Programs," *Research in Corrections* 2 (September 1989): 16. Reprinted by permission.

| Program Feature | Number of States Using Feature | Percentage of IPS Programs with Feature |
|---|---|---|
| Curfew/house arrest | 25 | 80.6 |
| Electronic monitoring | 6 | 19.3 |
| Mandatory (high needs) referrals/special conditions | 22 | 70.9 |
| Team supervision | 18 | 58.1 |
| Drug monitoring | 27 | 87.1 |
| Alcohol monitoring | 27 | 87.1 |
| Community service | 21 | 67.7 |
| Probation fees | 13 | 41.9 |
| Split sentence/shock incarceration | 22 | 70.9 |
| Community sponsors | 4 | 12.9 |
| Restitution | 21 | 67.7 |
| Objective risk assessment | 30 | 96.7 |
| Objective needs assessment | 29 | 93.5 |

**intensive probation supervision**
Probation granted under conditions of strict reporting to a probation officer with a limited caseload.

certain offenders.[22] **Intensive probation supervision** (IPS) is a way of using probation as an intermediate punishment. It is thought that daily contact between the probationer and officer may cut rearrests and may permit offenders who might otherwise go to prison to be released into the community. As noted in Table 14.1, additional restrictions are often imposed on offenders who receive intensive probation supervision.

Programs of intensive supervision have been characterized as "old-style" probation, because each officer has only twenty clients and frequent face-to-face contacts are required. Because the intention is to place in the community those high-risk offenders who would normally be incarcerated, it is expected that resources will be saved. But questions have been raised about how effective constant surveillance is to probationers who also need help with securing employment and dealing with emotional and family situations and their own drug or alcohol problems.

A Georgia program requires probationers to meet with a probation officer or a surveillance officer five times a week, to provide 132 hours of community service work, and (except in unusual cases) to abide by a 10 P.M. curfew. The standards are enforced by teams of one probation officer and one surveillance officer, who together supervise twenty-five probationers. Evaluation of the Georgia program suggests that it has helped to significantly reduce the flow of offenders to prison and that the cost of IPS, although higher than regular probation, is much less than a prison term. Recidivism rates are lower for those under intensive supervision than for either regular probationers or those released from prison on parole.[23]

Intensive supervision is popular among probation administrators, judges, and prosecutors. Programs have been instituted in many states, with most requiring a specific number of monthly contacts with probation officers; performance of community service; curfews; drug and alcohol abuse testing; and referral to appropriate job training, education, or treatment programs. Intensive supervision programs have been evaluated in a number of states.[24]

Observers have warned that intensive supervision should not be viewed as a panacea, since evidence from earlier attempts at the approach showed that as caseloads were reduced, recidivism increased. Many probationers were sent to prison because officers had more time to detect violations.[25]

One interesting aspect of the intensive probation supervision experience is that, given the option of serving a prison term or participating in IPS, many offenders have chosen prison. In New Jersey, 15 percent of offenders withdrew their applications for IPS once they knew the conditions and requirements. When offenders in Marion County, Oregon, were asked if they would participate in IPS, one-third chose prison.[26] It would seem that these offenders would rather spend a short time in prison where conditions differ little from their accustomed life to a longer period under demanding conditions. IPS does not represent freedom to these offenders because it is so intrusive and the risk of revocation is perceived as high.

Intensive probation supervision does not necessarily fulfill the goals of corrections. There are problems associated with the "high-risk" target group, with the methods of supervision, and the operational context within which it operates. Yet IPS has rejuvenated probation; some of the most effective offender supervision is being carried out by these programs.[27]

## Sanctions Administered in Institutions and the Community

**Boot camps**, which are among the most publicized intermediate sanctions, now operate in thirty states (see Figure 14.4).[28] Although programs vary, they are all based on the belief that young offenders can be "shocked" out of criminal behavior if they undergo a physically rigorous, disciplined, and demanding regimen for a short period before being returned to the community for supervision. The boot camp concept, also called "shock incarceration," is drawn from the military and includes educational and job training programs as well as other rehabilitative services.

Offenders are typically sentenced to a short period (90 to 180 days) in a military-style boot camp where they receive physical training and perform hard labor under a regimen of strict discipline. Boot camp inmates are housed separately from regular prisoners and spend the day at work, in school or job training, in military drills, and in physical training. Like the Marine Corps, most programs emphasize a spit-and-polish environment and keep the offenders in a disciplined routine that helps build self-esteem.

Upon successful completion of the program, offenders are released to the community and remain under supervision. At this point probation officers take over, and the conditions of the sentence are imposed. Only now are evaluations of these programs being conducted, so it is too early to tell what impact shock incarceration will have on recidivism. Some advocates argue that boot camps build the self-esteem necessary to keep offenders out of future trouble. This view is supported by a study of shock

**boot camp/shock incarceration**
A short-term institutional sentence, usually followed by probation, that puts the offender through a physical regimen designed to develop discipline and respect for authority.

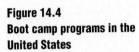

**Figure 14.4**
**Boot camp programs in the United States**

Boot camps for young offenders have rapidly spread across the correctional landscape. The concept has attracted much public and legislative support even though initial research has questioned many of its assumptions.

SOURCE: U.S. Department of Justice, *National Institute of Justice Journal* (November 1993), 21.

States with programs
States planning or considering programs
States with no programs

incarceration in Louisiana, which determined that those completing the course left the boot camp with more positive attitudes in regard to their experience and toward society in general, compared with those who were incarcerated in prison.[29] Critics believe that the emphasis on physical training does not focus on the real problems affecting young offenders. Others point out that like the military, shock incarceration builds esprit de corp and solidarity, characteristics that have the potential for improving the leadership qualities of the young offender and that, when taken back to the streets, may actually enhance a criminal career.[30] A study of offenders released from Louisiana boot camps found that "37 percent were arrested at least once during their first year of freedom, compared to 25.7 percent of parolees."[31]

## Implementing Intermediate Sanctions

Although the use of intermediate sanctions has spread rapidly across the country, there have been problems with their implementation. Three issues deserve special notice: (1) Which agencies should implement the sanctions? (2) What should be the characteristics of the offenders who are given intermediate sanctions? (3) Will the corrections net widen over offenders as a result of these sanctions?

Administrative politics is an ongoing factor in any public service organization and corrections is no exception. In many states there is competition as to which agency will receive additional funding to administer intermediate sanctions programs. For example, will the traditional agencies of community corrections, such as probation, receive the funding, or

will the programs be administered on contract by nonprofit organizations? Probation organizations argue that they know the field, have the experienced staff, and—given the additional resources—could do an excellent job. They correctly note that a great portion of offenders sentenced to intermediate sanctions are also on probation. Critics of probation argue that the traditional agencies are entrenched and not receptive to the innovations of intermediate sanctions. They say that probation agencies place a high priority on the traditional supervision function and will not become actively involved in helping clients solve their problems.

A second issue concerns the type of offender given an intermediate sanction. One school of thought emphasizes the seriousness of the offense, another concentrates on the problems of the offender. If offenders are categorized according to the seriousness of the offense, then they may be so closely supervised that they will not be able to take advantage of the community services provided—and thus be unable to abide by the terms of their sentence. For example, sanctions for serious offenders may accumulate so that a sentence includes probation, drug testing, addiction treatment, and home confinement.[32] It is argued that even the most willing probationer will find it impossible to fulfill the terms of such a sentence.

Offender characteristics are a concern in another way. Some agencies want to accept into their intermediate sanctions program only those offenders who *will* succeed. The agencies are concerned about their success

Boot camps for young offenders have received much publicity since they were first introduced in the 1980s. Advocates believe that boot camps build self-esteem and discipline. Skeptics wonder if this is another correctional panacea.

ratio, especially as it might jeopardize future funding. Critics note that this strategy leads to "creaming," taking the most promising offenders and leaving those with problems to traditional sanctions.

The third issue concerns **net widening**, a term used to describe a process in which the new sanction increases, rather than reduces, the control over an offender's life. This can occur when a judge imposes a *more* intrusive sanction than ordinary, rather than the *less* intrusive option. For example, rather than merely giving an offender probation, the judge might also require that the offender perform community service. Critics of intermediate sanctions argue that they have created:

- *Wider nets.* Reforms increase the proportion of individuals in society whose behavior is regulated or controlled by the state.

- *Stronger nets.* Reforms augment the state's capacity to control individuals through intensification of the state's intervention powers.

- *Different nets.* Reforms transfer or create jurisdictional authority from one agency or control system to another.[33]

As we have seen, a major development in corrections has been the creation of intermediate sanctions that can punish in the community those offenders who require greater supervision than is offered by probation and those who need not be incarcerated. Although the use of intermediate sanctions has many supporters, certain problems have hindered their implementation. With incarceration rates still at record highs and probation caseloads increasing, we can expect that intermediate sanctions will play a major role in corrections in the 1990s.

## Community Corrections in the 1990s

Between 1980 and 1990 there was tremendous growth in community corrections. In 1980 there were 1.4 million Americans under community supervision; by 1990 this figure had grown to 3.2 million, an increase of more than 130 percent. Yet, despite its wide usage, community corrections often lacks public support, in part because it suffers from an image of being soft on crime. As a result, in some localities community corrections has difficulties obtaining the resources it needs and cannot successfully compete with other criminal justice and human services agencies for support.

Community corrections also has to contend with the fact that—based on their crimes, criminal records, and drug problems—offenders today require closer supervision than those formerly placed on probation.[34] In New York, for example, 77 percent of probationers are convicted felons and about one-third have been found guilty of violent crimes. Yet, as Joan Petersilia points out, these people are supervised on caseloads of several hundred.[35]

We can expect that greater caseload pressures will be placed on community corrections in the next several years. To meet the demands of working with about three-fourths of offenders, community corrections needs an infusion of resources. Public support is essential but will be forthcoming only if citizens believe that offenders are being given the punishments they deserve. Citizens must recognize that policies designed to punish offenders within the community are not mere "slaps on the wrists," but are meaningful sanctions that allow law violators to retain and reforge their ties to their families and to society.

## Summary

Methods for dealing with criminal offenders have evolved since the reform activities of Philadelphia's Quakers, but uncertainty remains about which methods should be used. Community supervision through probation and intermediate sanctions has been a major element of U.S. corrections. During the 1960s and 1970s the concept of community corrections, a model that emphasized the reintegration of the offender and the provision of rehabilitative services in the community, drew the attention of penologists. In the more conservative environment of the 1980s, the reintegration focus waned. Today community corrections focuses less on the provision of services to offenders and more on surveillance of those offenders.

Probation is the sanction imposed on about two-thirds of offenders, who live in the community under the supervision and the rules set by a probation officer. If the rules are violated or if the offender is arrested for another offense, the probation may be revoked and a prison sentence imposed. Probation is commonly used in conjunction with intermediate sanctions.

Intermediate sanctions are designed to provide punishment alternatives that are more restrictive than probation and less restrictive than prison. The range of intermediate sanctions allows judges to design sentences that incorporate one or more of the punishments.

Some intermediate sanctions are implemented by the courts, others by probation and correctional agencies. The main forms are fines, restitution, community service, forfeiture, day reporting centers, home confinement, intensive probation supervision, and boot camps/shock incarceration. Electronic monitoring may be incorporated into some of these sanctions. As yet there is no definitive research proving the effectiveness of intermediate sanctions. The number of programs to implement these punishments are expanding throughout the country, however, as the criminal justice system seeks to cope with the overall increase in offenders.

## Questions for Review

1 What is the aim of community corrections?
2 What is the nature of probation and how is it organized?
3 What is the purpose of intermediate sanctions?
4 What are the primary forms of intermediate sanctions?
5 Why is net widening a concern of some observers?

## Key Terms and Cases

boot camp/shock incarceration

community service

day reporting center

fine

forfeiture

home confinement

intensive probation supervision

net widening

probation

recidivism

restitution

*Gagnon* v. *Scarpelli* (1973)

*Mempa* v. *Rhay* (1967)

## For Further Reading

Byrne, James M., Arthur J. Lurigio, and Joan Petersilia. *Smart Sentencing: The Emergence of Intermediate Sanctions*. Newbury Park, Calif.: Sage, 1992. A collection of papers exploring various issues in the design and implementation of intermediate sanctions programs.

Clear, Todd R., and Vincent O'Leary. *Controlling the Offender in the Community*. Lexington, Mass.: Lexington Books, 1983. Examination of risk assessment, classification, and supervision in the context of community corrections.

McCarthy, Belinda, and Bernard McCarthy. *Community-Based Corrections*. Pacific Grove, Calif.: Brooks/Cole, 1991. A thorough overview of community corrections and its role in the criminal justice system.

Morris, Norval, and Michael Tonry. *Between Prison and Probation: Intermediate Punishments in a Rational Sentencing System*. New York: Oxford University Press, 1990. Urges development of a range of intermediate punishments that can be used to sanction offenders more severely than probation but less severely than incarceration.

Petersilia, Joan. *Expanding Options for Criminal Sentencing*. Santa Monica, Calif.: Rand Corporation, 1987. A summary of the literature on the effectiveness of intermediate sanctions.

# Notes

1  Quoted in Keven Krajick, "Probation: The Original Community Program," *Corrections Magazine* 6 (December 1980): 7.

2  Randall Guynes, "Difficult Clients, Large Caseloads Plague Probation, Parole Agencies," *Research in Action* (Washington, D.C.: National Institute of Justice, 1988).

3  Todd R. Clear and Vincent O'Leary, *Controlling the Offender in the Community* (Lexington, Mass.: Lexington Books, 1983), 77–100.

4  *New York Times*, 19 June 1990, A–16.

5  *Mempa* v. *Rhay*, 389 U.S. 128 (1967).

6  *Gagnon* v. *Scarpelli*, 411 U.S. 778 (1973).

7  Norval Morris and Michael Tonry, *Between Prison and Probation: Intermediate Punishments in a Rational Sentencing System* (New York: Oxford University Press, 1990), 3.

8  Thomas Blomberg and Karen Lucken, "Intermediate Punishments and the Piling Up of Sanctions," in *Criminal Justice: Law and Politics*, 6th ed., ed. George F. Cole (Belmont, Calif.: Wadsworth, 1993), 470.

9  Sally T. Hillsman, Joyce L. Sichel, and Barry Mahoney, *Fines in Sentencing* (New York: Vera Institute of Justice, 1983).

10  George F. Cole, Barry Mahoney, Roger Hanson, and Marlene Thornton, *Attitudes and Practices of Trial Court Judges toward the Use of Fines* (Denver: Institute for Court Management, 1987).

11  Karla R. Spaulding, " 'Hit Them Where It Hurts': RICO Criminal Forfeitures and White-Collar Crime," *Journal of Criminal Law and Criminology* 80 (1989): 197.

12  *New York Times*, 16 July 1990.

13  *Austin* v. *U.S.*, 61 LW 4811 (1993).

14  Marc Renzema, "Home Confinement Programs: Development, Implementation, and Impact," in *Smart Sentencing: The Emergence of Intermediate Sanctions*, ed. James M. Byrne, Arthur J. Lurigio, and Joan Petersilia (Newbury Park, Calif.: Sage, 1992), 41.

15  Terry L. Baumer and Robert I. Mendelsohn, "Electronically Monitoring Home Confinement: Does It Work?" in *Smart Sentencing*, 54; Terry Baumer, Michael G. Maxfield, and Robert I. Mendelsohn, "Comparative Analysis of Three Electronically Monitored Home Detention Programs," *Justice Quarterly* 10 (March 1993): 120–142.

16  Annesley K. Schmidt, "Electronic Monitoring of Offenders Increases," *Research in Action* (Washington, D.C.: National Institute of Justice, 1989).

17  Renzema, "Home Confinement Programs," 41.

18 Baumer, Maxfield, and Mendelsohn, "Three Electronically Monitored Home Detention Programs," 121.

19 Douglas McDonald, *Punishment Without Walls* (New Brunswick, N.J.: Rutgers University Press, 1986), 38.

20 Jack McDevitt and Robyn Miliano, "Day Reporting Centers: An Innovative Concept in Intermediate Sanctions," in *Smart Sentencing*, 152. Day reporting centers are often called *probation centers* or *alternative incarceration centers*.

21 Dale G. Parent, *Day Reporting Centers for Criminal Offenders: A Descriptive Analysis of Existing Programs* (Washington, D.C.: National Institute of Justice, 1990), 1.

22 See *Crime and Delinquency* 36 (January 1990), an entire issue devoted to intensive probation supervision.

23 Billie S. Erwin and Lawrence A. Bennett, "New Dimensions in Probation: Georgia's Experience with Intensive Probation Supervision," *Research in Brief*, National Institute of Justice, (Washington, D.C.: Government Printing Office, 1987); Joan Petersilia, *Expanding Options for Criminal Sentencing* (Santa Monica, Calif.: Rand Corporation, 1987), 10–32.

24 Joan Petersilia and Susan Turner, "Intensive Probation and Parole," in *Crime and Justice: A Review of Research*, ed. Michael Tonry (Chicago: University of Chicago Press, 1993), 281–335.

25 Joan Petersilia and Susan Turner, *Intensive Supervision for High-Risk Offenders: Findings from Three California Experiments* (Santa Monica, Calif.: Rand Corporation, 1990).

26 Joan Petersilia, "When Probation Becomes More Dreaded Than Prison," *Federal Probation* (March 1990): 24.

27  Todd R. Clear and Patricia L. Hardyman, "The New Intensive Supervision Movement," *Crime and Delinquency* 36 (January 1990): 42; Todd R. Clear and Edward J. Latessa, "Probation Officers' Roles in Intensive Supervision: Surveillance Versus Treatment," *Justice Quarterly* 10 (September 1993): 441–459.

28  Doris Layton MacKenzie, "Boot Camp Prisons in 1993," *National Institute of Justice Journal* (November 1993): 21.

29  Doris Layton MacKenzie and James W. Shaw, "Inmate Adjustment and Change during Shock Incarceration: The Impact of Correctional Boot Camp Programs," *Justice Quarterly* 7 (March 1990): 125–150.

30  *New York Times*, 4 March 1988, B–1, 4.

31  *Newsweek*, 21 February 1994, 26; Doris Layton MacKenzie and James W. Shaw, "The Impact of Shock Incarceration on Technical Violations and New Criminal Activities," *Justice Quarterly* 10 (September 1993): 463–487.

32  Blomberg and Lucken, "Intermediate Punishment and the Piling Up of Sanctions," 470.

33  James Austin and Barry Krisberg, "The Unmet Promise of Alternatives to Incarceration," *Crime and Delinquency* 28 (1982): 374–409.

34  Petersilia and Turner, *Intensive Supervision Probation for High-Risk Offenders*.

35  Joan Petersilia, "Measuring the Performance of Community Corrections," *Performance Measures for the Criminal Justice System* (Washington, D.C.: Bureau of Justice Statistics, 1993), 61.

# Prisons: Their Goals and Management

## 15

**The blue van passes through a small town and then veers**
off the highway onto a secondary road where only
occasional houses punctuate the fields and woods.
We are heading toward a looming fortress. As we
approach it we see gray stone walls, barbed-wire fences,
gun towers, steel bars. The van passes through opened gates and
comes to a stop. Blue-uniformed guards move briskly to the rear doors,
and in a moment four men, linked by wrist bracelets on a chain, stand on
the asphalt and glance about nervously.

Although this description may seem like the beginning of a 1940s "big
house" movie, it could be filmed *today* at Brushy Mountain, Tennessee;
Ossining, New York; or Soledad, California. Certain aspects of incarceration in American prisons for adult felons have changed since the 1940s—
the characteristics of the inmates are different, rehabilitative personnel
are employed in addition to guards, and prisons are more crowded—but
the physical dimensions of the fortress institution remain the same, and
the society of captives within may be changed only slightly.

*Incarceration*—what does it mean to the inmates, the guards, and the public? What goes on in our prisons? In this chapter we examine the general goals of the more than one thousand American prisons in operation today. We will also see how management principles and staff functions have evolved together with those goals and will examine the rights of prisoners while they are incarcerated.

## Questions for Inquiry

- What is the nature of the formal organization of a prison?
- How do contemporary institutions differ from the "big house" prisons?
- What are the assumptions of each model of incarceration?
- How is a prison governed?
- What is the purpose of prison programs?
- What is the role of correctional officers?
- What are the rights of prisoners?

## The Modern Prison: Legacy of the Past

For someone schooled in criminal justice history, entering most contemporary American prisons is like entering a time machine. Elements from each of the major reform movements can be seen within the walls. In accord with the early notion that the prison should be located away from the community, most correctional facilities are in rural areas—Somers, Connecticut; Stateville, Illinois; Attica, New York—far from the urban residences of the inmates' families. The fortress "big house" style, built to secure the population, remains typical of contemporary prison architecture. Many inmates work in prison industries, founded on the principles of the Auburn system. Treatment programs, including vocational education, group therapy, and counseling, are available. But whether it is called a correctional facility or a treatment center, a prison remains a prison.

American correctional institutions have always been more varied than one might suspect from viewing films or reading some of the landmark prison studies. Although big houses predominated in much of the country during the first half of the twentieth century, some prisons, especially in the South, did not conform to this model. There, racial segregation was maintained, prisoners were involved in farm labor, and the massive walled structures were not so dominant a form. In many other states the correctional systems had not emerged from the cruelty and corruption, silence systems, hard labor, and corporal punishment that characterized American prisons during the late nineteenth century.

The typical big house of the 1930s and 1940s was a walled prison with large, tiered cell blocks, a yard, shops, and industries. The prisoners, averaging about twenty-five hundred, came from both urban and rural areas, were poor, and, outside the South, were predominantly white. The prison society was essentially isolated; access to visitors, mail, and other communication was restricted. Prisoners' days were strictly structured, with rules enforced by the guards. There was a basic division between inmates and staff; rank was observed and discipline maintained. In the big house there was little in the way of treatment programs; custody was the primary goal.

Since World War II there have been many changes in American prisons. It is now difficult to find an institution that conforms exactly to the big house depicted in films and analyzed by such social scientists as Donald Clemmer and Gresham Sykes.[1] During the 1950s and early 1960s most penologists accepted the rehabilitation model of corrections. Many states built new facilities and converted others into "correctional institutions." Although the new label was often the principal evidence of an alternative philosophy, treatment programs did become a major part of institutional life. Indeterminate sentences, classification, treatment, and parole, the chief emphases of this approach, brought changes to the prison. In particular, treatment personnel—counselors, educators, and psychologists—were added to the staff. Conflict often erupted over the competing goals of treatment and custody.

During the past thirty years, as the population of the United States changed, so did that of the inmate population. The proportion of African-American and Hispanic inmates increased, and inmates from urban areas became more numerous, as did inmates convicted of drug-related and violent offenses. The average age decreased. The civil rights movement of the early 1960s had a profound effect on minority prisoners. There was an infusion of political activism, with demands that prisoners be more fully integrated into society and that there be greater sensitivity to their needs. The courts began to take notice of the legal rights of prisoners. Former street gangs regrouped inside prisons, disrupting the existing inmate society and raising the level of violence in many institutions. Finally, with the rise of public employees unions, correctional officers were no longer willing to accept the paramilitary work rules of the warden.

As prisons have responded to community influences, they have shifted away from the treatment model of corrections. The rehabilitative programs touted in the 1960s have been either de-emphasized or abandoned. The determinate sentence has replaced the indeterminate sentence in many states; as a consequence, the parole board no longer has as much discretion to return prisoners to the community. In addition to these policy shifts has been a great increase in the number of persons being held in prisons, so that most are overcrowded and under increased tension. Humane incarceration seems to have become the contemporary goal of correctional administrators.

## Models of Incarceration

Various parts of the correctional subsystem tend to emphasize one or a combination of the broad goals of the criminal sanction: punishment, deterrence, incapacitation, and rehabilitation. It is natural to regard security as the dominant purpose of a prison, given the nature of the inmates and the need to protect the staff and the community. High walls, barbed-wire fences, searches, checkpoints, and regular counts of inmates serve the security function: few inmates escape. More importantly, they set the tone and strongly color the daily operations. Thus prisons are expected to be impersonal, quasi-military places where strict discipline, minimal levels of amenities, and restrictions on freedom are thought to serve the goals of the criminal sanction.

Correctional models have been developed to describe the purposes and approaches that should be used in handling prisoners in an institutional setting. Models can provide a set of rationally linked criteria and aims, but the extent to which a model actually works is a question for empirical investigation. As with the stated purpose of the criminal sanction, the plan for a particular model may have little relation to the ongoing process of corrections and the experience of the inmates. New terms may be adopted to describe changes in day-to-day practices, yet actual conditions may differ dramatically from those descriptions.

Three models of incarceration have been prominent since the early 1940s: custodial, rehabilitation, and reintegration. Each summarizes the assumptions and characteristics associated with one style of institutional organization. The **custodial model** is based on the assumption that prisoners have been incarcerated for the protection of society and for the purpose of incapacitation, deterrence, or retribution. It emphasizes maintenance of security and order through the subordination of the prisoner to the authority of the warden. Discipline is strict, and most aspects of behavior are regulated. This model was prevalent within corrections before World War II, and it dominates most maximum security institutions today.

With the onset of the treatment orientation in corrections during the 1950s, the **rehabilitation model** of institutional organization was developed. In prisons organized according to this model, security and housekeeping activities are viewed primarily as a framework for rehabilitative efforts. Professional treatment specialists enjoy a higher status than that accorded other employees, reflecting the idea that all aspects of the organization should be directed toward rehabilitation. Due to the rethinking of the rehabilitative goal since the 1970s, the number of institutions geared toward treatment has declined. Treatment programs still exist in most institutions, but very few prisons can be said to conform to the rehabilitative model.

The **reintegration model** is linked to the structures and goals of community corrections. Although inmates are confined in a prison, that experience is pointed toward later reintegration into society. Prisons that have adopted the reintegration model gradually give inmates greater freedom and responsibility during their confinement and move them to a halfway house, work release program, or community correctional center before they are released under supervision. The reintegration model is based on the assumption that it is important for the offender to maintain or develop ties with the free community. The entire focus of this approach is on the resumption of a normal life in society.

**custodial model**
A model of corrections that emphasizes security, discipline, and order.

**rehabilitation model**
A model of corrections that emphasizes the provision of treatment programs designed to reform the offender.

**reintegration model**
A model of a correctional institution that emphasizes the maintenance of the offender's ties to family and community as a method of reform, in recognition of the fact that the offender will be returning to the community.

It is possible to find correctional institutions that conform to each of these models, but most prisons for men fall much closer to the custodial model than to the rehabilitation or the reintegration model. Treatment programs do exist in prisons but they generally take second place to the requirements of custody. Because almost all inmates return to society at some point, even the most custodial institutions cannot neglect to prepare them for that move. In many correctional systems, regardless of the basic model, inmates spend the last portion of their sentence in a prerelease facility.

We ask a lot of our prisons. As Charles Logan notes, "We ask them to correct the incorrigible, rehabilitate the wretched, deter the determined, restrain the dangerous, and punish the wicked."[2] Prisons are expected to pursue many different and often incompatible goals; hence as institutions they are almost doomed to failure. Logan believes that the mission of prisons should focus on confinement. He argues that the essential purpose of imprisonment is to punish offenders fairly and justly through lengths of confinement proportionate to the gravity of their crimes. If the goal of incarceration is to do justice through confinement, then he summarizes the mission of the prison as "to keep prisoners—to keep them in, keep them safe, keep them in line, keep them healthy, and keep them busy—and to do it with fairness, without undue suffering, and as efficiently as possible."[3] Should confinement be the new goal for incarceration? Many correctional officials, researchers, and policymakers now believe so. If the purpose of prisons is punishment through confinement under fair and just conditions, what are the implications for correctional managers? What measures should be used to evaluate prisons using the criterion of confinement?

In today's crowded prisons there is little to do but watch television. The warehousing of offenders raises questions about the purpose of prison.

# Prison Organization

The prison differs from almost every other institution or organization in modern society. Not only are its physical features different from those of most institutions, but also it is a place where a group of persons devotes itself to managing a group of captives. Prisoners are required to live according to the dictates of their keepers, and their movements are sharply restricted. Unlike managers of other governmental agencies, prison managers:

- cannot select their clients
- have little or no control over the release of their clients
- must deal with clients who are there against their will
- must rely on clients to do most of the work in the daily operation of the institution and to do so by coercion and without fair compensation for their work
- must depend on the maintenance of satisfactory relationships between clients and staff

Given these unique characteristics, how should a prison be run? What rules should guide administrators of this type of institution? As we can see from the description above, wardens and other key personnel are asked to perform a difficult order, one that requires skilled and dedicated managers.

Much research on prisons has assumed that they have the characteristics of a **total institution** as do some other organizations, such as mental hospitals and monasteries.[4] This concept, developed by sociologist Erving Goffman, emphasizes that the prison completely encapsulates the lives of those who work and live there. Whatever prisoners do or do not do begins and ends in the prison; every minute behind bars must be lived according to the institution's rules as enforced by the staff. Adding to the totality of the prison is a basic split between the large group of persons (inmates) who have very limited contact with the outside world and the small group (staff) who supervise on an eight-hour shift within the walls and are socially integrated with the outside world where they live. Each group perceives the other in terms of stereotypes. Staff members view inmates as secretive and untrustworthy, while the inmates view staff as condescending and mean. Staff members may feel superior and righteous, inmates inferior and weak.

Although Goffman's concept of the total institution may have characterized the custodial "big house" of the past, the modern prison is influenced by the outside world. Today's inmates have greater communication with the outside world by way of television, radio, and telephone. The mixture of racial and ethnic cliques among today's inmates discourages the development of a sense of group solidarity in opposition to the staff. Community advocacy groups and the courts have dented the total power of institutional administrators. No longer are the warden and staff so isolated from public view that they can ignore the law. Given these changes, we must use the total institution concept with caution; yet the contemporary prison is still far enough removed from the free world that Goffman's term remains useful for purposes of analysis.

**total institution**
An institution (such as a prison) that completely encapsulates the lives of those who work and live within it. Rules govern behavior, and the group is split into two parts, one of which controls the lives of the other.

## Management

The administrative structure of prisons is organized at even the lowest level. Unlike in factories or the military, where there are separate groups of supervisors and workers or officers and enlisted personnel, the lowest-status prison employee, the correctional officer, is both a supervisor *and* a worker. The correctional officer is seen as a supervisor by the inmates but as a worker by the warden. The warden judges the officers' efficiency on the basis of their ability to manage the prisoners. Since this efficiency often depends largely on being able to secure some cooperation by the inmates, officers are susceptible to corruption by the inmates.

Good management requires that wardens employ a "hands-on" style in order to anticipate problems before they erupt.

Although most prisons have similar organizational structures, management styles vary. Political scientist John DiIulio studied the management of selected prisons in Texas, California, and Michigan.[5] He found differences that were related to the leadership philosophy, political environment, and administrative style of individual wardens. DiIulio argues that the quality of prison life as measured by levels of order, amenity, and service is mainly a function of the management. He believes that prisons can be governed, violence can be minimized, and services can be provided to the inmates if thoughtful leadership is provided by correctional executives and wardens.

DiIulio believes that prison systems will perform well if administrators successfully manage those political and other pressures that make for administrative uncertainty and instability. In particular, management will be successful if prison directors:

1   are in office long enough to learn the job, make plans, and implement them

2   are highly hands-on and proactive, paying close attention to details and not waiting for problems to arise. They must know what is going on inside, yet also recognize the need for outside support. In short, they are strangers neither to the cell blocks nor to the aisles of the state legislature

3   project an appealing image to a wide range of people both inside and outside the organization. They are leaders

4   are dedicated and loyal to the department, seeing themselves as engaged in a noble and challenging profession[6]

From this perspective, making prisons work is a function of administrative leadership and the application of management principles.

## Multiple Goals

Most prisons are expected to fulfill goals related to keeping (custody), using (working), and serving (treating) inmates. Because individual staff members are not equipped to perform all functions, there are separate organizational lines of command for the groups of employees that execute these different tasks. One group is charged with maintaining custody over the prisoners, another group supervises them in their work activities, and a third group attempts to rehabilitate them.

The employees concerned with custody are normally organized along military lines, from warden to captain to officer, with accompanying pay differentials and job titles that follow the chain of command. The professional personnel associated with the using and serving functions, such as clinicians and teachers, are not part of the regular custodial organizational structure, and they have little in common with the others. All employees are responsible to the warden, but the treatment personnel and the civilian supervisors of the workshops have their own salary scales and titles. They are not part of the custodial chain of command, and they do not provide specialized advice to the custodial employees. The formal organization of staff responsibilities in a typical prison for adults is shown in Figure 15.1.

Because of multiple goals and separate employee lines of command, the administration of correctional institutions is often marked by conflict and ambiguity. So how do prisoners and staff meet their own distinct goals in view of the conflicting purposes and the complex set of role relationships within prison society? How do prisons really function? Although the U.S. prison may not conform to the ideal goals of corrections and although the formal organization of staff and inmates may bear little resemblance to the ongoing reality of the informal relations, order *is* kept and a routine *is* followed. We discuss how that happens next.

## Governing a Society of Captives

Much of the public believes that prisons are operated in an authoritarian manner. In such a society of captives, correctional officers *give* orders and inmates *follow* orders. Strictly enforced rules specify what the captives may and may not do. Because the officers have a monopoly on the legal means of enforcing rules and can be backed up by the state police and the National Guard if necessary, many people believe that no question should arise as to how the prison is run. Staff members have the right to grant rewards and to inflict punishment. In theory, any inmate who does not follow the rules should be placed in solitary confinement.

What quality of life should be maintained in prison? According to John DiIulio, a good prison is one that "provides as much order, amenity, and service as possible given the human and financial resources."[7] *Order* is the absence of individual or group misconduct, such as assaults and

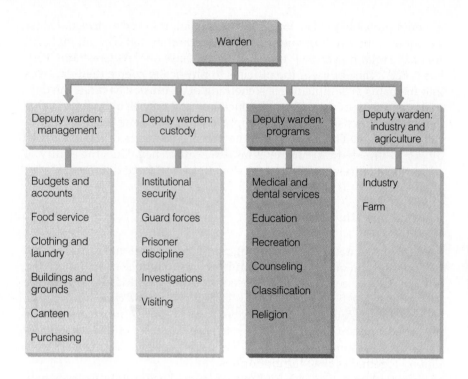

**Figure 15.1**
**Formal organization of a prison for adult felons**
Prison staff are divided into various sections consistent with the goals of the organization. Custodial employees are the most numerous.

rape, that threatens the security of others. *Amenities* are those things that enhance the comfort of the inmates, such as good food, clean cells, recreational opportunities, and the like. Finally, *service* includes programs to improve the lives of inmates: vocational training, remedial education, and work opportunities.

If we accept the premise that well-run prisons are important for the inmates, staff, and society, what are some of the problems that must be faced and solved by correctional administrators? The literature points to four factors that make the governing of prisons different than the administration of other public institutions: (1) the defects of total power; (2) the limited rewards and punishments that can be used by officials; (3) the co-optation of correctional officers; and (4) the strength of inmate leadership. As we review each of these, we should also consider what administrative and leadership styles can best be used by corrections managers to achieve the goal of a prison that is safe, humane, and able to serve the needs of the inmates.

### The Defects of Total Power

Imagine a prison society comprised of hostile and uncooperative captives ruled in an authoritarian manner. Prisoners could be legally isolated from one another, physically abused until they cooperate, and continually placed under surveillance. While such a regime is theoretically possible, it would probably not last long because the public expects correctional institutions to be run humanely. Besides, the notion that correctional officers have total power over the captives is a false one. As Gresham Sykes has noted, "the ability of the officials to physically coerce their captives into the paths of compliance is something of an illusion as far as the day-to-day activities of the prison are concerned and may be of doubtful value in moments of crisis."[8] Forcing people to carry out complex tasks is basically inefficient. The realities and the potential dangers of the usual 1:40 officer-to-inmate ratio further diminishes efficiency. Thus the ability of correctional officers to threaten the use of physical force is limited.

## Rewards and Punishments

**good time**
A reduction of a convict's prison sentence awarded for good behavior at the discretion of the prison administrator.

Faced with the necessity of running a prison, correctional officers often rely on a system of rewards and punishments to induce cooperation. Extensive rules of conduct are imposed on prisoners, and rewards in the form of privileges may be offered for obedience: **good time** allowances, choice job assignments, and favorable parole reports. Informers may be rewarded, and administrators may purposely ignore conflicts among inmates on the assumption that such dissension prevents the prisoners from uniting together against the authorities.

The system of rewards and punishments has limitations, however. One problem is that the punishments for rule breaking do not make a great difference in the status of the prisoners. Because they are already deprived of many freedoms and valued goods—heterosexual relations, money, choice of clothing, and so on—there is little left to take away. The punishment of not being allowed to attend a recreational period may not carry much weight. Furthermore, the system is often defective because the authorized privileges are given to the inmate at the start of the sentence and are taken away only if rules are broken. Thus few additional authorized rewards can be granted for progress or exceptional behavior, although a desired work assignment or transfer to the honor cell block will induce some prisoners to maintain good behavior.

In recent years the ability of correctional officials to discipline prisoners who resist authority has been somewhat weakened by the prisoners' rights movement and the demands of the courts for due process. The extent to which these forces have actually limited official sanctions is not known, but wardens are undoubtedly aware that their actions may be subject to legal action or censure by groups outside the prison.

## Co-optation of Correctional Officers

One way that correctional officers obtain inmates' cooperation is through the types of exchange relationships described in earlier chapters. The housing unit officer is the key official in the exchanges within the custodial bureaucracy:

It is he who must supervise and control the inmate population in concrete and detailed terms. It is he who must see to the translation of the custodial regime from blueprint to reality and engage in the specific battles for conformity. Counting prisoners, periodically reporting to the center of communications, signing passes, checking groups of inmates as they come and go, searching for contraband or signs of attempts to escape—these make up the minutiae of his eight-hour shift.[9]

Thus these officers are in close and intimate association with the prisoners throughout the day—in the cell block, workshop, or recreation area. Although the formal rules stipulate that a social distance must be maintained between officers and inmates and that they speak and act toward each other accordingly, their closeness makes them aware that each depends on the other in many ways. The officers need the cooperation of the prisoners so they will look good to their superiors, and the inmates depend on the guards to relax the rules or occasionally look the other way. Even though the officers are backed by the power of the state and have the formal authority to punish any prisoner who does not follow their orders, they often discover that their best path of action is to make "deals" or "trades" with the captives in their power. As a result, guards exchange or "buy" compliance or obedience in some areas by tolerating violation of the rules in other areas.

Correctional officers must be careful not to pay too high a price for the cooperation of their charges. *Sub rosa* (secret) relationships that turn into manipulation of the guards by the prisoners may result in the smuggling of contraband or in other illegal acts. The officers are under public pressure to be humane and not use coercion—in short, to be "good guys"—yet there are risks in using the carrot rather than the stick.

Increasing numbers of women have become correctional officers in prisons for males. What are the pluses and minuses of having women in these roles?

## Inmate Leadership

In the big-house era, prison administrators enlisted the leaders of the inmate social system—the convict society—in the task of maintaining order. This strategy was described in 1954 by Richard Korn and Lloyd W. McCorkle, who pointed out that administrators gave the inmate hierarchy covert support and recognition by assigning better jobs and quarters to its high-status members—to its "good inmates."[10] In this and other ways the administrators bought peace with the system by avoiding battle with it.

Inmate leaders in the convict society control other inmates. They tend to have extensive prison experience. They have been "tested" through relationships with other inmates so that they are neither pushed around by inmates nor distrusted by them as stool pigeons. Because staff can also rely on them, these leaders serve as the essential communications link between staff and inmates. With the ability to acquire inside information and access to decision makers, inmate leaders command respect from other prisoners. They benefit from the corruption of the formal authority of the staff by receiving illicit privileges and favors from the guards. In turn, they can distribute these benefits to other prisoners, thus bolstering their own influence within the society.

Questions have been raised about the effectiveness of relying on inmate leaders to keep order. In most contemporary institutions there is no longer a homogeneity of the inmate population, so a single leadership structure rarely exists. Rather, the inmate population is divided along racial, ethnic, offense, and hometown lines, resulting in multiple centers of power.

## The Challenge of Governing Prisons

The factors of total power, rewards and punishments, co-optation, and inmate leadership exist in every prison and must be managed. How they are managed greatly influences the quality of prison life. DiIulio's research challenges the common assumption of many correctional administrators that "the cons run the joint." Instead, successful wardens have made their prisons "work" by the application of management principles within the context of their own style of leadership. Prisons can be governed, violence can be minimized, and services can be provided to the inmates if correctional executives and wardens exhibit leadership appropriate to the task. Governing prisons is an extraordinary challenge, but it can be and has been successfully accomplished.

# Prison Programs

A major difference between modern correctional institutions and those of the distant past is the number and variety of programs. Prison industries were a part of such early penitentiaries as Auburn; under the stimulus of the rehabilitative goal, many educational, vocational, and treatment services have subsequently been added to the correctional institution. In some states such programs have not been well developed, and prisoners work at tasks that do not prepare them for jobs on the outside.

Administrators must use institutional programs to manage the problem of time. They know that the more programs they offer, the less likely it is that inmates' idleness and boredom will turn to hostility. The less cell time, the fewer tensions. Activity is the administrator's tool for controlling and stabilizing prison operations.

## Classification of Prisoners

Determining the appropriate program for an individual prisoner is usually made through a **classification** process. This process plays a major role in determining the inmate's life while incarcerated. Most states now have diagnostic and reception centers that are physically separated from the main prison facility. All prison-bound offenders pass through such a center, where they are received for evaluation and classification so that specialized clinical personnel—psychologists, physicians, counselors—can determine the facility to which they will be sent, their treatment needs, work assignments, and eventually their readiness for release. Prisoners may be brought back to the center for reclassification if their needs and goals change or if a transfer to another institution is desired by the staff.

A classification committee usually consists of the deputy warden and the heads of departments for security, treatment, education, industry, and the like. At the hearing caseworkers or counselors present information gathered from the presentence reports, police records, and the reception process. The inmate appears before the committee, personal needs and assignments are discussed, and the committee makes its decision.

Unfortunately, classification decisions are often made on the basis of administrative needs rather than inmate needs. Certain programs are limited, and the demand for them is great. Thus inmates may find that the few places in the electrician's course are filled and that there is a long waiting list. Another problem is that inmates may be excluded from programs because they are needed for the institution's housekeeping work. Inmates from the city may be assigned to farm work—which they are unfamiliar with—because that is where they are needed. What is most upsetting to some prisoners is that release on parole often depends on a good record of participation in treatment or educational programs, some of which may have been unavailable.

**classification**
The act of assigning a new inmate to a type of custody and treatment appropriate to his or her needs.

## Educational Programs

Most correctional facilities offer academic programs in which courses passed by inmates are credited in accordance with state requirements. Since a great majority of adult felons lack a high school diploma, it seems natural that many could use their prison time for academic work. In many institutions, inmates without at least an eighth-grade education are assigned to school as their main occupation. In some facilities, college-level courses are offered through an association with a local community college. Studies have shown that inmates assigned to prison school are good candidates to achieve a conviction-free record after release. Evidence has also suggested, however, that this outcome may be due largely to the type of inmate selected for schooling rather than to the schooling itself.

## Vocational Education

The idea that inmates can be taught a trade that will be helpful to them in the free world has great appeal. Programs in modern facilities are designed to teach a variety of skills: plumbing, automobile mechanics, printing, computer programming. Unfortunately, most such programs are unable to keep abreast of the technological advances and needs of the free market. Too many programs train inmates for trades that already have an adequate labor supply or in which new methods have made the skills taught obsolete. Some vocational programs are even designed to prepare inmates for outside careers that are closed to former felons. The restaurant industry, for example, would seem to be a place where former felons might find employment, yet in many states they are prohibited from working where alcohol is sold.

## Prison Industries

Early prison reformers felt that inmates should develop good work habits and that their productive labor should help pay the costs of their incarceration. Others cited the usefulness of work in keeping inmates out of trouble and declared that work was consistent with the goal of incapacitation. Some scholars now point to the nineteenth-century workshops established at Auburn as reflecting the industrialization of the United States and the need for prison to instill good work habits and discipline in potential members of the labor force (see Chapter 13).

Prisoners have traditionally been required to work at tasks that are necessary to maintain and run their own and other state facilities. Accordingly, food service, laundry, and building maintenance jobs are assigned. In some states, prison farms produce food for the institution. Industry shops make furniture, repair office equipment, and fabricate items. Prisoners receive a nominal fee (perhaps fifty cents an hour) for such work.

The prison industries system has had a checkered career. During the nineteenth century, factories were established in many prisons and inmates manufactured items that were sold on the open market. With the rise of the labor movement, however, state legislatures and Congress passed laws restricting the sale of prison-made goods so that they would not compete with those made by free workers. Whenever unemployment became extensive, political pressures mounted to prevent prisons from engaging in enterprises that might otherwise be conducted by private business and free labor. In 1940 Congress passed the Sumners-Ashurst Act, which prohibited the interstate transportation of convict-made goods for private use. With the outbreak of World War II, however, President Franklin Roosevelt issued an executive order permitting the federal government to procure goods for the military effort from state and federal prisons. Under labor pressure, the wartime order was revoked in 1947 by President Harry Truman, and prisoners returned to idleness.[11] By 1973 the National Advisory Commission found that throughout the correctional system "only a few offenders in institutions have productive work."[12] In 1979 Congress lifted restrictions on the interstate sale of prison-made products and urged correctional administrators to explore with the private sector the possibilities for improving prison industry programs.[13]

In the 1980s there was renewed interest in the channeling of prison labor into industrial programs that would relieve idleness, allow inmates to earn wages that they could save until release, and reduce the costs of incarceration to the state. Initiatives promoted by the federal government have encouraged private-sector companies to set up "factories within fences" in order to use prison labor effectively.

Although the idea of employing inmates sounds attractive, the economic value may be offset by the inefficiencies of prison industries. Turnover among prisoners is great since many are incarcerated for less than two years and are often transferred among several institutions. Supervisors have found that because of the low education levels of inmates and the fact that inmates have not developed steady work habits, it is difficult for prisoners to perform many of the tasks related to modern production. Some prisoners are inefficient. The cost of maintaining security so that materials are not pilfered must also be figured into the business formula. Experiments are being conducted to see if inmate labor can produce goods and services that are competitive in the free market. These activities deserve attention to see whether prison industries can help deal with idleness and inculcate habits and skills that will benefit inmates when they are released.

## Rehabilitative Programs

Rehabilitative programs aim at reforming the offender's behavior by treating defects thought to have produced or triggered the criminality. There is little dispute about the desirability of rehabilitating offenders, but there is much dispute about the degree of emphasis that should be given to these programs and the types that should be offered.

Reports in the mid-1970s cast doubt on the ability of treatment programs to stem recidivism and questioned the ethics of requiring inmates to participate in rehabilitative programs in exchange for the promise of parole. Their findings led to a rethinking of rehabilitation as an element of sentencing decisions. Supporters of treatment programs argue that certain programs work for certain offenders; however, such positive outcomes require more accurate diagnosis and fine-tuned sentencing by judges than are now possible.[14]

In most correctional systems a range of psychological, behavioral, and social services is available to inmates. The extent of their use seems to vary greatly according to the goals of the institution and the attitudes of the administrators. Nationally very little money is spent for treatment services and these programs reach only 5 percent of the inmate population.[15] Rehabilitation programs remain a part of correctional institutions, but their emphasis has diminished. Indeed, incarceration's current goal of humane custody implies no effort to change inmates.

# Correctional Officers

Not many young people consider a career in corrections, which is not surprising because a correctional officer's occupational prestige is tarnished by the company he or (increasingly) she must keep: the adult felon. There is no opportunity to acquire the prestige given to Secret Service agents, for example, who may share in the glamour of those they guard. Furthermore, the prisoner is not pleased at being guarded, and the community—the beneficiary of the correctional officer's activities—seems not to care about the officer's job except when a riot or escape occurs. Officers who are primarily concerned with inmate security comprise more than half of all correctional employees. Their hours are long, pay is low, entry requirements are minimal, and turnover is very high.

## The Officer's Role

**Figure 15.2**
**The officer code reinforces camaraderie among correctional officers**

SOURCE: Adapted from Kelsey Kauffman, *Prison Officers and Their World* (Cambridge, Mass.: Harvard University Press, 1988), 86–114. Reprinted by permission.

Correctional officers are public service workers who must deal with their clients in an organizational environment of scarce resources and who must exercise discretion. The correctional officer must cope with the human problems of inmates on a personal level, that is, the officer must treat prisoners as individuals and help them with their institutional and personal problems. But the officer also functions as a member of a complex bureaucratic organization and is expected to deal with clients impersonally and to follow formal procedures. Fulfilling these contradictory role expectations is difficult in itself, and the difficulty is exacerbated by the physical closeness of the officer and inmate over long periods. Yet John Hepburn and Paul Knepper found that officers who played a human services rather than a purely custody role had greater job satisfaction.[16]

Just as there is an inmate culture that emphasizes certain values and norms, there is a code of behavior that encourages solidarity among officers (see Figure 15.2).[17] Many correctional officers are nostalgic for the days of the "big house" when their purpose was clear, their authority was unchallenged, and they were respected by inmates. In the accompanying Close-Up, a guard tells how he gains respect from and maintains a professional attitude toward prisoners in his care.

The role of the correctional officer has changed greatly since the 1960s. No longer is the officer responsible merely for "guarding." Contemporary officers are crucial to the management of prison because they are in closest contact with the prisoners and are expected to perform a variety of tasks, including counseling, supervising, protecting, and processing the inmates under their care. As the President's Commission noted in 1967,

---

**The Officer Code**

1 Always go to the aid of an officer in distress.

2 Don't "lug" drugs.
   Bringing drugs or alcohol into the prison places fellow officers in danger.

3 Don't rat.
   Never rat on an officer to an inmate.
   Never testify against a fellow officer.

4 Never make a fellow officer look bad in front of inmates.

5 Always support an officer in a dispute with an inmate.

6 Always support officer sanctions against inmates.

7 Don't be a white hat ["bleeding heart"].
   Don't be too lenient or sympathetic to inmates.

8 Maintain officer solidarity versus all outside groups.
   Don't talk about the institution to outsiders.

9 Show positive concern for fellow officers.
   Never leave another officer a problem.
   Help your fellow officer with problems outside the institution.

## Gaining Respect

The hard-nosed, thick-headed, bull correctional officer of the movies in the Jimmy Cagney era doesn't exist. And if he comes in here, he doesn't last very long. Your first goal ought to be to gain the respect of an inmate.

You can't gain respect from an inmate from being an easy mark. They don't respect easy marks. You don't gain respect through bully tactics, then every day he comes into the joint it's going to just wear him down a little bit more. Things just don't work that way anymore.

You gain respect by attempting to treat everyone the same . . . equally . . . no matter what they're in for. As a matter of fact, myself, I try not to find out what a man's in here for. It might change me a little bit. . . . I might not feel that it showed, but it shows. Now, someone will ask me to do something, send a request out to the visiting desk or something like that. . . . His request might sit in my pocket where someone else's request would be expedited right off the bat because of maybe what he did on the street . . . so I try not to even know what he's here for.

SOURCE: Edgar May, "Prison Guards: The Inside Story," *Corrections Magazine*, December 1976, 36. Reprinted by permission of Edna McConnell Clark Foundation.

They can, by their attitude and understanding, reinforce or destroy the effectiveness of almost any correctional program. They can act as effective intermediaries or become insurmountable barriers between the inmates' world and the institution's administrative and treatment personnel.[18]

This quotation identifies a problem that has faced most correctional systems in recent years: the officer is expected to play an unclear role in an institution that combines the goals of keeping, using, and serving. Officers are responsible for preventing escapes, for maintaining order, and for the smooth functioning of the institution. At the same time, they are expected to cooperate with treatment personnel by counseling inmates and assuming an understanding attitude. Not only are those roles incompatible, but also the rehabilitative ideal stresses dealing with each person as a unique being, a task that seems impossible in a large, people-processing institution. Officers are expected to use discretion, yet somehow to behave in both a custodial and a therapeutic manner. As Donald Cressey notes, "if they enforce the rules, they risk being diagnosed as 'rigid,' [on the other hand] if they do not enforce the rules and that failure creates a threat to institutional security, orderliness or maintenance, they are not 'doing their job.' "[19] The Question of Ethics on page 542 poses one dilemma that correctional officers frequently face.

### Recruitment of Officers

As we know, employment as a correctional officer is not a glamorous, sought-after occupation. The work is thought to be boring, the pay is low, and career mobility is almost nonexistent. Studies have shown that one of the primary incentives for becoming involved in correctional work is the security that civil service status provides. In addition, prisons may offer better employment options than other employers in the rural areas where most correctional facilities are located. Because correctional officers are recruited locally, most of them are rural and white, in contrast to the majority of prisoners who are urban and either African-American or Hispanic.

The great increase in the prison population has required more correctional officers. Salaries have been raised so that the yearly average entry level pay runs between $15,000 in some southern and rural states to $30,000 in states such as Colorado and Michigan.[20] Special efforts have been made to recruit women and minorities. Women are no longer restricted to working with female offenders, and the number of correctional officers from minority groups has increased dramatically. For example, 21 percent of Alabama's correctional officers are women and 97 percent work in male institutions.[21]

For most correctional workers a position as a custody officer is a dead-end job. Though officers who perform well may be promoted to higher ranks within the custodial staff, very few ever move into administrative positions. Yet in some states and in the Federal Bureau of Prisons, there are career paths for persons with college degrees to advance to management positions. Increasingly it is possible to achieve these positions without having to move through the ranks of the custodial force.

## Collective Bargaining

Correctional officers have been unionized only fairly recently: it was not until the 1970s, when many states passed laws permitting collective bargaining by public employees, that the unions made inroads in prisons. By 1981 correctional employees in twenty-nine of fifty-two jurisdictions (state, federal, and the District of Columbia) were unionized.[22] Like other labor organizations, unions representing prison employees seek better wages and working conditions for their members. Because the members are public employees, most are prevented by law from engaging in strikes, but work stoppages have occurred in a number of prisons nonetheless. As a result of unionization, relationships between employees and administration are now more formalized, with the rights and obligations of each side stipulated by contract.

Correctional officers are responsible for the smooth functioning of prisons. As they deal with inmates, officers must recognize that the rights of prisoners must be respected, a topic to which we now turn.

## Prisoner Rights

Until the 1960s, the courts, with few exceptions, took the position that the internal administration of prisons was an executive, not a judicial, function. They maintained a **hands-off policy** on corrections. Judges accepted the view that they were not penologists and that their intervention would be disruptive to prison discipline. This view was a continuation of a position taken a century earlier in *Ruffin v. Commonwealth* (1871). In that case, a Virginia court said that the prisoner "has, as a consequence of his crime, not only forfeited his liberty, but all his personal rights except those which the law in its humanity accords to him. He is for the time being the slave of the state."[23] As late as 1951, a federal circuit judge declared: "We think it well settled that it is not the function of the courts to superintend the treatment and discipline of persons in penitentiaries, but only to deliver from imprisonment those who are illegally confined."[24]

But more recently, the courts have become a new factor in the prison management equation. Prisoners now have access to the courts to contest decisions made by officers and aspects of their incarceration that they believe violate basic rights. This change directly affects correctional managers, as we will see.

With the civil rights movement of the 1960s and the expansion of due process by the Supreme Court, prisoner groups and their supporters pushed to secure inmate rights. Some scholars expressed the belief that prisoners were—like blacks, women, gays, and the handicapped—a deprived minority whose rights were not being protected by the government. To achieve such protection, the American Civil Liberties Union, clinic programs for law students, committees of the American Bar Association, and various legal services agencies began to counsel prisoners and to promote the redress of inmates' grievances in the courts.

The most far-reaching departure from the hands-off policy was in 1964 when the Supreme Court ruled in *Cooper v. Pate* that prisoners are entitled to the protections of the Civil Rights Act of 1871.[25] This legislation (designated as Volume 42 United States Code, Section 1983) imposes *civil liability* on any person who deprives another of constitutional rights.

Because of the decision in *Cooper v. Pate* the federal courts now recognize prisoners may sue state officials over the conditions of their confinement, such as brutality by guards, inadequate nutritional and medical care, theft of personal property, and the denial of basic rights. These changes had the effect of decreasing the custodian's power and the prisoners' isolation from the larger society.

**hands-off policy**
Judges should not interfere with the administration of correctional institutions.

*Ruffin v. Commonwealth* (1871)
As a result of his crime, the prisoner is the slave of the state.

*Cooper v. Pate* (1964)
Prisoners are entitled to the protection of the Civil Rights Act of 1871 and may challenge conditions of their confinement in federal courts.

*Johnson* v. *Avery* (1969)
The use of jailhouse lawyers may not be prohibited unless free counsel is provided by the state.

*Bounds* v. *Smith* (1977)
Inmates have the right of access to adequate law libraries or to the assistance of those trained in the law.

The amount of prisoner-inspired litigation in the courts subsequently skyrocketed. For example, in 1969 the Supreme Court ruled in *Johnson v. Avery* that prison officials could not prohibit one inmate from acting as a jailhouse lawyer for another inmate unless the state provided the inmate with free counsel to pursue a claim that rights had been denied.[26] That ruling was followed by *Bounds v. Smith* (1977) in which the Court required that inmates have access to law libraries or to the help of persons trained in the law.[27] By the mid-1970s inmates and wardens had learned that, in the view of the courts, a prisoner is not wholly stripped of constitutional protection when imprisoned.

The first successful cases concerning prisoner rights involved the most excessive of prison abuses: brutality and inhuman physical conditions. Gradually, however, prison litigation has focused more directly on the daily activities of the institution, especially on the administrative rules that regulate inmates' conduct. The result has been a series of court deci-

**Table 15.1**
**Selected interpretations of the First Amendment as applied to prisoners**
The Supreme Court has made numerous decisions affecting prisoners' rights to freedom of speech and expression and freedom of religion.

| Case | Decision |
|------|----------|
| *Procunier* v. *Martinez* (1974) | Censorship of mail is permitted only to the extent necessary to maintain prison security. |
| *Turner* v. *Safley* (1987) | Inmates do not have a right to receive mail from one another, and this mail can be banned if "reasonably related to legitimate penological interests." |
| *Saxbe* v. *Washington Post* (1974) | Rules prohibiting individual interviews with members of the press are justified to prevent some inmates from enhancing their reputations. |
| *Theriault* v. *Carlson* (1977) | The First Amendment does not protect so-called religions that are obvious shams, that tend to mock established institutions, and whose members lack religious sincerity. |
| *Gittlemacker* v. *Prasse* (1970) | The state must give inmates the opportunity to practice their religion but is not required to provide a member of the clergy. |
| *O'Lone* v. *Estate of Shabazz* (1987) | The rights of Black Muslim prisoners are not violated when work assignments make it impossible for them to attend religious services if no alternative exists. |
| *Kahane* v. *Carlson* (1975) | An orthodox Jewish inmate has the right to a diet consistent with his religious beliefs unless the government can show cause why it cannot be provided. |
| *Fulwood* v. *Clemmer* (1962) | The Black Muslim faith must be recognized as a religion and officials may not restrict members from holding services. |
| *Cruz* v. *Beto* (1972) | Prisoners who adhere to other than conventional beliefs may not be denied the opportunity to practice their religion. |

sions concerning the First, Fourth, Eighth, and Fourteenth Amendments to the Constitution. (The full text of these amendments is set forth in Appendix A.) In the remainder of this section, we examine prisoner rights under these amendments.

## First Amendment

Because the Supreme Court has long maintained that the First Amendment holds a special position with respect to the Constitution, it is not surprising that litigation concerning prisoner rights has been most successful under this amendment. The First Amendment guarantees freedom of speech, press, assembly, petition, and religion. Many of the restrictions of prison life—access to reading materials, censorship of mail, and some religious practices—have been successfully challenged by prisoners in the courts.

Since 1970 the federal and state courts have extended the rights of freedom of speech and expression to prisoners and have required correctional administrators to show why restrictions on these rights must be imposed (see Table 15.1). For example, in 1974 the Court said that censorship of mail could be allowed only when there is a substantial governmental interest in maintaining security.[28] The result has been markedly increased communication between inmates and the outside world. The courts have supported these institutional rules only when officials have been able to prove that limitations on speech are necessary because an inmate poses a threat to himself or herself, other inmates, or the staff.

The First Amendment also prevents Congress from making laws respecting the establishment of religion or prohibiting its free exercise. The history of the Supreme Court's interpretation of this clause has been long and complex, and its application to the prison setting is no exception. Although freedom of belief has not been challenged, challenges concerning the free exercise of religion have caused the judiciary some problems, especially when the practice may interfere with prison routine.

The arrival in the 1960s of the Black Muslim religion in prisons holding large numbers of urban blacks set the stage for litigation demanding that this group be granted the same privileges as other faiths (special diets, access to clergy and religious publications, opportunities for group worship). Many prison administrators believed that the Black Muslims were primarily a radical political group posing as a religion, and they did not grant them the benefits accorded to persons who practiced conventional religions.

In a 1962 case (*Fulwood v. Clemmer*) the U.S. District Court of the District of Columbia ruled that correctional officials must recognize the Black Muslim faith as a religion and not restrict members from holding services.[29] In *Cruz v. Beto* (1972), the Supreme Court declared that it was discriminatory and a violation of the Constitution for a Buddhist prisoner to be denied opportunities to practice his faith comparable to the opportunities given to fellow prisoners who belonged to more predominant religions in the United States.[30]

*Fulwood v. Clemmer* (1962)
The Black Muslim faith must be recognized as a religion and officials may not restrict members from holding services.

*Cruz v. Beto* (1972)
Prisoners who adhere to other than conventional beliefs may not be denied the opportunity to practice their religion.

| Case | Decision |
|------|----------|
| *Bell* v. *Wolfish* (1979) | Strip searches, including searches of body cavities after contact visits, may be carried out when the need for such searches outweighs the personal rights invaded. |
| *Lee* v. *Downs* (1981) | Staff members of one sex may not supervise inmates of the opposite sex in toilet and shower areas even if provision of a staff member of the same sex is inconvenient to the administration. |
| *United States* v. *Hitchcock* (1972) | A warrantless search of a cell is not unreasonable and documentary evidence found there is not subject to suppression in court. It is not reasonable to expect a prison cell to be accorded the same level of privacy as a home or automobile. |
| *Hudson* v. *Palmer* (1984) | Officials may search cells without a warrant and seize materials found there. |

**Table 15.2**
**Selected interpretations of the Fourth Amendment as applied to prisoners**
The Supreme Court has often considered the issue of unreasonable searches and seizures.

In many respects, Black Muslims and other prisoners have succeeded in gaining some of the rights considered necessary for the practice of their religion. For example, Native Americans have the right to wear their hair long if it is a sincere expression of religious belief.[31] However, there is no accepted judicial doctrine in this area, and courts have varied in their willingness to order institutional policies changed to meet the requests of minority religions.[32]

### Fourth Amendment

The Fourth Amendment prohibits "unreasonable" searches and seizures and the courts have not been active in extending these protections to prisoners. Thus regulations viewed as reasonable in light of the need for security and order in an institution may be justified. For example, in 1984 the decision in **Hudson v. Palmer** upheld the right of officials to search cells and confiscate any materials found.[33]

*Hudson* v. *Palmer* (1984)
Officials may search cells without a warrant and seize materials found there.

The Supreme Court's opinions with regard to the Fourth Amendment, some of which are outlined in Table 15.2, reveal the fine balance between institutional needs and the right to privacy. Body searches have been harder for administrators to justify than cell searches, for example, but they have been upheld when they are part of a policy clearly related to an identifiable and legitimate institutional need and when they are not intended to humiliate or degrade.[34] These cases illustrate the lack of clear-cut constitutional principles in such matters.

### Eighth Amendment

The Eighth Amendment's prohibition of cruel and unusual punishments has been tied to prisoners' rights in relation to their need for decent treatment and minimal standards of health. Most claims involving the failure of prison administrators to provide minimal conditions necessary for health, to furnish reasonable levels of medical care, and to protect inmates from assault by other prisoners have taken the form of suits against specific officials. The courts have applied three principal tests to determine whether or not conditions violate the protection of the Eighth Amendment: (1) whether the punishment shocks the general conscience of a civilized society, (2) whether the punishment is unnecessarily cruel, and (3) whether the punishment goes beyond legitimate penal aims.

Federal courts have ruled that, although some aspects of prison life may be acceptable, the combination of various factors—the **totality of conditions**—may be such that life in the institution may constitute cruel and unusual punishment. When suits have been brought by pretrial detainees, the totality of conditions in jails have been ruled to constitute unjustifiable punishment without due process of law. The result has been that specific institutions in some states and entire prison systems in other states have been declared in violation of the Constitution.

Wardens have been held liable for maintaining an environment that is suitable to prisoners' health and security, but recovery of damages by inmates is rare. Most often the judge has ruled that specific actions must be taken by correctional administrators to remedy conditions so that they meet constitutional standards.[35] In particular, courts have required that prison populations be reduced to prevent crowding, that treatment programs be instituted, that internal administration be conducted to ensure prisoner safety, and that health or nutritional standards be raised (see Table 15.3).

In several dramatic cases, prison conditions were shown to be so bad that judges have demanded change. On 13 January 1976, Federal Judge Frank M. Johnson, Jr., issued a precedent-setting order listing minimal standards for Alabama prisons and threatened to close all the institutions in that state if the standards were not met. Johnson's opinion was that

**totality of conditions**
Although specific conditions in prisons might not violate the Constitution, the totality of the conditions may violate the cruel and unusual punishment provisions of the Eighth Amendment.

| Case | Decision |
|------|----------|
| *Estelle* v. *Gamble* (1976) | Deliberate indifference to serious medical needs of prisoners constitutes the unnecessary and wanton infliction of pain, and thus violates the Eighth Amendment. |
| *Rhodes* v. *Chapman* (1981) | Double celling and crowding do not necessarily constitute cruel and unusual punishment. It must be shown that the conditions involve "wanton and unnecessary infliction of pain" and are "grossly disproportionate" to the severity of the crime warranting imprisonment. |
| *Whitley* v. *Albers* (1986) | A prisoner shot in the leg during a riot does not suffer cruel and unusual punishment if the action was taken in good faith to maintain discipline rather than for the mere purpose of causing harm. |
| *Ruiz* v. *Estelle* (1980) | Conditions of confinement in the Texas prison system were unconstitutional. |

**Table 15.3**
**Selected interpretations of the Eighth Amendment as applied to prisoners**
In several key cases, the Supreme Court has ruled on whether correctional actions constitute cruel and unusual punishments.

## The Impact of *Ruiz* v. *Estelle*

In December 1980, William W. Justice, federal judge for the Eastern District of Texas, issued a sweeping decree against the Texas Department of Corrections in the case of *Ruiz* v. *Estelle*. He ordered prison officials to change a host of unconstitutional conditions, including overcrowding, unnecessary use of force by personnel, inadequate numbers of guards, poor health-care practices, and a "building-tender" system that allowed some inmates to control others.

The Eastham Unit of the Texas penal system is a large, maximum security institution housing recidivists over the age of twenty-five who have been in prison three or more times. It is tightly managed and has been the depository for troublemakers from other Texas prisons. To help deal with these hard-core criminals, the staff relied upon a select group of inmates known as *building tenders* (BTs). By co-opting the BTs with special privileges, officials were able to use them and their assistants, the "turnkeys," to handle the rank-and-file inmates.

Officially, the building-tender system was an information network. The BTs could help officials penetrate and divide the inmate society. In turn, the BTs and turnkeys had snitches working for them. Information about troublesome inmates, guards, and conditions were passed along by the BTs to officials. With this information, the staff was able to exercise enormous power over the inmates' daily activities. The BTs and turnkeys were rewarded, enjoying power and status far exceed-

ing those of ordinary inmates and even those of lower-ranking guards. Unofficially, the BTs kept order in the cell blocks through intimidation and the physical disciplining of those who broke the rules.

In May 1982, Texas signed a consent decree, agreeing to dismantle the building-tender system by January 1983. BTs were reassigned to ordinary prison jobs; stripped of their power, status, and duties; and moved to separate cell blocks for their protection. At the same time Eastham received 141 new officers, almost doubling the guard force, to help pick up the slack. These reforms were substantial and fundamentally altered the guard and inmate societies.

With the removal of the BTs and turnkeys, with restrictions on the unofficial use of force by guards, and with the institution of a prisoner discipline system emphasizing due process, fairness, and rights, the traditional social structure of Eastham came under severe strain. Criminologists James Marquart and Ben Crouch found that the reforms had brought about three major changes within the prison community: in interpersonal relations between the guards and inmates, reorganization within the inmate society, and the guard subculture and work role.

### Guards and Inmates

Formerly, ordinary inmates had been subject to an all-encompassing, totalitarian system in which they were "dictated to, exploited, and kept in submission." With the new relationship between the keepers and

**Ruiz v. Estelle (1980)**
Conditions of confinement in the Texas prison system were unconstitutional.

imprisonment in Alabama constituted cruel and unusual punishment because prison conditions were barbaric and inhumane.[36] An even more wide-ranging order was issued in December 1980 in the case of *Ruiz* v. *Estelle*, described more fully in the accompanying Close-Up.[37] Judicial supervision of the Texas prison system as a result of this case lasted for a decade and ended on 31 March 1990.

Of particular concern to correctional officials have been rulings that overcrowding is in violation of the Eighth Amendment and must be ended. Among the conditions that the courts have found to violate the Constitution is the crowding of inmates into cells that afford each person less than sixty square feet of floor space. However, in *Rhodes* v. *Chapman* (1981) the Supreme Court upheld double bunking (two beds in a cell

the kept, inmates challenged the authority of correctional officers and were more confrontational and hostile. In response to the verbal and other assaults on their authority, the guards cited inmates for infractions of the rules. The changes in the relationship between guards and inmates resulted from a number of factors: there were more guards, restrictions on the guards meant that physical reprisals were not feared, the guards no longer had the BTs to act as intermediaries, and the social distance between guards and prisoners had diminished.

### Reorganization within the Inmate Society

The purging of the BT-turnkey system created a power vacuum characterized by uncertainty. One outcome was a rise in the amount of inmate-inmate violence. Without the BTs to help settle disputes among inmates, these conflicts more often led to violence in which weapons were used. Self-defense became a social necessity. As personal violence escalated, so did the development of inmate gangs. Gang members know that they will have the assistance of others if they are threatened, assaulted, or robbed. Nongang prisoners must rely upon themselves and avoid contact with inmates known for their toughness.

### Guard Subculture and Work Role

The court-imposed reforms upset the foundations of the guard subculture and work role, making the work no longer well ordered, predictable, or rewarding. Upon removal of the BTs, guards were assigned to cell-block duty for the first time. That placed them in close contact with inmates. The fact that most of the guards were new

to prison work meant that they were hesitant to enforce order. Many officers believe that because they cannot physically punish inmates and their supervisors do not back them up, it is better not to enforce the rules at all. They think that their authority has been undermined and that the new disciplinary process is frustrating. Many would rather look the other way.

### Conclusion

The court-ordered reforms brought Eastham's operations more in line with constitutional requirements of fairness and due process but disrupted an ongoing social system. Before the *Ruiz* decision the prison had been run on the basis of paternalism, coercion, dominance, and fear. Guards exercised much discretion over inmates, and they used the building tenders to help maintain order and as a source of information. During the transition to a new bureaucratic and legal order, levels of violence and personal insecurity increased. Authority was eroded, combative relations between inmates and officers materialized, and inmate gangs developed to provide security and autonomy for members.

An overriding question remains: Can a prison be administered in ways that conform to the requirements of fairness and due process yet maintain security for the inmates and staff?

SOURCE: Adapted from James W. Marquart and Ben M. Crouch, "Judicial Reform and Prison Control: The Impact of *Ruiz* v. *Estelle* on a Texas Penitentiary," *Law and Society Review* 19 (1985): 557–586. Reprinted by permission.

---

designed for one person) in Ohio as not constituting a condition of cruel and unusual punishment.[38] In other cases, courts have ruled overcrowded conditions to be unconstitutional. Judges have issued orders requiring that space be increased or the prison population decreased.

Many conditions that violate the rights of prisoners may be corrected by administrative action, training programs, or a minimal expenditure of funds, but overcrowding requires an expansion of facilities or a dropping of the intake rate. Prison officials have no control over the capacities of their institutions or over the number of offenders that are sent to them by the courts. New facilities are expensive, and they require appropriations by legislatures and, often, approval of bond issues by voters.

*Rhodes* v. *Chapman* (1981)
Double bunking and crowding do not necessarily constitute cruel and unusual punishment. Conditions must involve "wanton and unnecessary infliction of pain" and be "grossly disproportionate to the severity of the crime warranting imprisonment."

## Fourteenth Amendment

Two clauses of the Fourteenth Amendment are relevant to the question of prisoners' rights—those requiring *procedural due process* and *equal protection*—and have produced much litigation in the 1970s. The statutes of many states provide inmates with certain protections with regard to parole release, intraprison transfers, transfers to administrative segregation (solitary confinement), and disciplinary hearings. With regard to due process, however, the Supreme Court has been more cautious in recent years.

**Due Process in Prison Discipline** Administrative discretion in determining disciplinary procedures can usually be exercised within the prison walls without challenge. The prisoner is physically confined, lacks communication with the outside, and is legally in the hands of the state. Furthermore, formal codes stating the rules of prison conduct either do not exist or the rules are written vaguely. Disrespect toward a correctional officer, for example, may be labeled an infraction of the rules without what constitutes disrespect having been defined. Inmates are usually disciplined based on the word of a correctional officer, and an inmate has little opportunity to challenge the charges.

In a series of decisions in the 1970s, the Supreme Court began to insist that procedural fairness be included in the most sensitive of institutional decisions: the process by which inmates are sent to solitary confinement and the method by which "good time" credit may be lost because of misconduct.

*Wolff* v. *McDonnell* (1974)
Basic elements of procedural due process must be present when decisions are made concerning the discipline of an inmate.

In the 1974 case of *Wolff* v. *McDonnell*, certain procedural rights were extended to inmates: to receive notice of the complaint, to have a fair hearing, to confront witnesses, to be assisted in preparing for the hearing, and to be given a written statement of the decision.[39] Yet the Court also said that there is no right to counsel at a disciplinary hearing.[40] The courts have emphasized the need to balance the rights of the prisoner against the interests of the state.

As a result of the Supreme Court decisions, some of which are outlined in Table 15.4, most prisons have established rules that provide some elements of due process in disciplinary proceedings. In many institutions, a disciplinary committee receives the charges, conducts hearings, and de-

**Table 15.4**
**Selected interpretations of the Fourteenth Amendment as applied to prisoners**
The Supreme Court has ruled in several key cases concerning procedural due process and equal protection.

| Case | Decision |
|---|---|
| *Baxter* v. *Palmigiano* (1976) | Although due process must be accorded, an inmate has no right to counsel in a disciplinary hearing. |
| *United States* v. *Bailey* (1980) | An inmate who seeks to justify an escape from prison on the grounds of duress or necessity for self-protection must show having attempted to surrender to an authority. |
| *Wolff* v. *McDonnell* (1974) | The basic elements of procedural due process must be present when decisions are made concerning the disciplining of an inmate. |

Knowing one's way around the law library has become such a marketable skill that some inmates charge other prisoners for legal advice.

cides guilt and punishment. Such committees are usually comprised of administrative personnel, but sometimes inmates or outside citizens are included. Even with these protections, the fact remains that prisoners are powerless and may fear further punishment if they too strongly challenge the disciplinary decisions of the warden.

**Equal Protection**   Institutional practices or conditions that discriminate against prisoners on the basis of race or religion have been held unconstitutional. In 1968 the Supreme Court firmly established that racial discrimination may not be official policy within prison walls.[41] Racial segregation is justified only as a temporary expedient during periods when violence between the races is demonstrably imminent. Equal protection claims have also been upheld in relation to religious freedoms and access to reading materials.

## Redress of Grievances

Decisions of the U.S. Supreme Court make headlines, but they are only the very tip of the iceberg. State prisoners file almost twenty thousand suits annually in the lower federal courts under the Civil Rights Act of 1871 (42 U.S.C. 1983) to contest conditions under which they are being confined. Prisoners claim, for example, that the conditions of their confinement violate their rights, that they are not receiving proper medical care, that the state has lost items of their personal property, that they are not being protected from violent inmates, or that crowding limits their freedom.

Few of these suits are successful. Most petitions to the court are written without the assistance of counsel and are often filed in error because of misinterpretations of the law. Courts have developed screening processes so that clerks evaluate the complaints. Most complaints are returned to the prisoner because of errors and have not been seen by the judge. There have nonetheless been many cases in which individual inmates secured redress of their grievances. Some have received monetary compensation for neglect; others have been given the medical attention they desired; still others have elicited judicial orders that end certain correctional practices.

Courts may respond to prisoners' requests in specific cases, but judges cannot possibly oversee the daily activities within institutional walls. As a result of the increase in conditions-of-confinement cases, correctional authorities have taken steps to ensure that fair procedures are followed and that unconstitutional practices are foregone. Publication of institutional rules, obligations, and procedures is one of the first and most important steps required to meet this goal. In most states, grievance procedures have been developed so that prisoner complaints may be addressed before they result in a suit.

## A Change in Judicial Direction?

**Bell v. Wolfish (1979)**
Strip searches, including body-cavity searches after contact visits, may be carried out when the need for the search outweighs the invasion of personal rights.

Throughout the 1960s and most of the 1970s, the prisoners' rights movement was buoyed by decisions of the U.S. Supreme Court and those of lower federal courts supporting its claims. Beginning in 1979 with **Bell v. Wolfish** and followed by *Rhodes* v. *Chapman* (1981), the Court, under the leadership of Chief Justice Rehnquist, has indicated that it wishes to slow the expansion of rights, if not to return to the hands-off policy.[42] In *Bell* inmates in the Metropolitan Correctional Center (MCC) in New York City, a newly constructed federal detention unit, filed complaints concerning double celling, restrictions against receiving hardcover books from publishers and bookstores, and strip searches. The Supreme Court found no constitutional violations at MCC and said further that the restrictions were a rational response by correctional officials to security concerns. In addition, the Court's majority firmly emphasized that "Prison administrators ... should be accorded wide-ranging deference in the adoption and execution of policies."

In *Rhodes* v. *Chapman* prisoners challenged the double celling at the Ohio maximum security prison. The Court said that in the Ohio situation the conditions did not constitute cruel and unusual punishment because the prisoners were not being deprived of such essentials as food and medical care. Unless the conditions were "deplorable" or "sordid," the courts should defer to correctional authorities.[43]

The Supreme Court under Chief Justice William Rehnquist is less sympathetic to such civil rights claims as evidenced by several cases that limit the ability of prisoners to sue correctional officials. In particular, the Court ruled in 1986 that prisoners could sue for damages in federal court only if officials had inflicted injury intentionally or deliberately.[44] The chief justice wrote for the majority that "the due process clause is simply not implicated by a negligent act of an official causing unintended loss or injury to life, liberty, or property." He said that the due process clause was put into the Constitution only to prevent an "abuse of power" by public officials and that "lack of due care" or carelessness is not included. This reasoning was extended in the 1991 case of *Wilson v. Seiter* when the court ruled that a prisoner's conditions of confinement are not unconstitutional unless it can be shown that prison administrators had acted with "deliberate indifference" to basic human needs.[45] Even with regard to First Amendment rights (inmate to inmate correspondence and attendance at Black Muslim religious services) the Court upheld prison policies.[46]

The pace of prisoners' right cases may be slowed even further by the decision in *McCleskey v. Zant* (1991), which limited access to the federal courts. The Court ruled that all habeas claims must be raised in the initial petition.[47] Thus, although prisoners have a right to access to the courts via law libraries and the assistance of fellow inmates, the reality is that access has been diminished, especially for those prisoners who lack counsel and are likely to be tripped up by the stricter procedural rules.

## Impact of the Prisoners' Rights Movement

The prisoners' rights movement can probably be credited with some general changes in American corrections since the late 1970s.[48] The most obvious are concrete improvements in institutional living conditions and administrative practices. Law libraries and legal assistance are now generally available; communication with the outside is easier; religious practices are protected; inmate complaint procedures have been developed; and due process requirements are emphasized. Prisoners in solitary confinement undoubtedly suffer less neglect than formerly. Although overcrowding is still a major problem in most institutions, many conditions are much improved and the more brutalizing elements of prison life have been diminished.

Individual cases may have made only a dent in correctional bureaucracies, but over time real changes have occurred. The prisoners' rights movement has clearly had an impact on correctional officials. The threat of lawsuits and public exposure has placed many in the correctional bureaucracy on guard. It can be argued that this wariness has merely led to the increased bureaucratization of corrections, with staff now required to prepare extensive and time-consuming documentation of their actions in order to protect themselves from lawsuits. On the other hand, judicial intervention has forced corrections to rethink existing procedures and organizational structures. As part of the wider changes in the "new corrections," new administrators, increased funding, reformulated policies, and improved management procedures were, at least in part, influenced by the prisoners' rights movement.

The extension of constitutional rights to prisoners has by no means been speedy, and the courts have only addressed limited areas of the law. The impact of these decisions on the actual behavior of correctional officials has not yet been measured, but evidence suggests that court decisions have had a broad effect. Wardens and their subordinates may now be refraining from traditional disciplinary actions that might result in judicial intervention. In sum, after two hundred years of judicial neglect of the conditions under which prisoners are held, courts have begun to look more closely at the situation.

**Wilson v. Seiter (1991)**
The standard of review of official conduct is whether state policies or actions by correctional officers constitute "deliberate indifference" to constitutional rights.

**McCleskey v. Zant (1991)**
Limits access to the federal courts since all habeas claims must be raised in the initial petition.

# Summary

The central goals of incarceration and the basic prison facility as depicted in old movies endure, yet many of the characteristics of the convict population, the programs, and the officers have changed. Incarceration takes place in a variety of correctional institutions, none exactly the same as another and each with its own traditions, organization, and environment.

Three models of incarceration have been prominent since 1941. The custodial model emphasizes the maintenance of security through the subordination of the prisoner to the authority of the warden. The rehabilitation model of prison organization views security and housekeeping activities mainly as a framework for treatment efforts. The reintegration model recognizes that prisoners will return to society and thus efforts are made to prepare them for that eventuality. It is possible to find correctional institutions that conform to each of these models, but most prisons for men fall much closer to the custodial model than to the rehabilitation or the reintegration model.

As with other organizations, the management of prisons requires dedication and leadership. Although the public may believe that the warden and officers have total power over the inmates, that belief is outdated. The relationship between the managers and the prisoners is much more fragile and interconnected than any organization chart in the front office would indicate. Good management through effective leadership can be exerted to maintain the quality of prison life as measured by levels of order, amenities, and service.

The correctional officers are the real linchpins in the prison system. They are constantly in close contact with prisoners and are the first to become aware of their problems and needs. The effectiveness of the institution weighs heavily on their shoulders.

Although less emphasized than in the past, treatment, educational, and vocational programs do exist in today's prisons to varying degrees. Efforts to improve prison industries by making them productive have gained prominence in some states.

The prisoners' rights movement has brought about many changes in the administration and conditions of American prisons. Through litigation in the federal courts, prisoners have challenged the conditions of their confinement. In many cases judges have ordered that unconstitutional procedures and conditions be changed.

It seems clear that incarceration will continue to be widely used throughout the coming years. As the National Advisory Commission has said, "the prison ... has persisted, partly because a civilized nation could neither turn back to the barbarism of an earlier time nor find a satisfactory alternative."[49] We can expect that prisons will endure, with varying degrees of success in meeting their goals and with their programs changing as politics and prison population require.

## Questions for Review

1  How do modern prisons differ from those in the past?
2  What are the characteristics of prisons that make them different than other institutions?
3  What must a prison director do to ensure successful management?
4  What is the purpose of inmate classification?
5  What cases by the U.S. Supreme Court are most significant in terms of corrections today? What effect has each had on correctional institutions?

## Key Terms and Cases

classification
custodial model
good time
hands-off policy
rehabilitation model
reintegration model
total institution
totality of conditions
*Bell* v. *Wolfish* (1979)
*Bounds* v. *Smith* (1977)

*Cooper* v. *Pate* (1964)
*Cruz* v. *Beto* (1972)
*Fulwood* v. *Clemmer* (1962)
*Hudson* v. *Palmer* (1984)
*Johnson* v. *Avery* (1969)
*McCleskey* v. *Zant* (1991)

*Rhodes* v. *Chapman* (1981)
*Ruffin* v. *Commonwealth* (1871)
*Ruiz* v. *Estelle* (1980)
*Wilson* v. *Seiter* (1991)
*Wolff* v. *McDonnell* (1974)

## For Further Reading

Cullen, Francis, and Karen Gilbert. *Reaffirming Rehabilitation*. Cincinnati, Ohio: Anderson, 1982. A defense of the effectiveness of rehabilitation.

DiIulio, John J., Jr. *Governing Prisons*. New York: Free Press, 1987. A critique of the sociological perspective on inmate society. DiIulio argues that governance is a central problem with prisons.

Goodstein, Lynne, and Doris Layton MacKenzie, eds. *The American Prison: Issues in Research and Policy*. New York: Plenum Press, 1989. An excellent collection of essays on various prison issues.

Irwin, John, and James Austin. *It's About Time: America's Imprisonment Binge*. Belmont, Calif.: Wadsworth, 1994. Argues that the "grand imprisonment experiment" that has dominated American crime reduction policy has failed miserably and should be abandoned.

Johnson, Robert. *Hard Time: Understanding and Reforming the Prison*. Pacific Grove, Calif.: Brooks/Cole, 1987. A significant contribution to understanding prison society.

Kauffman, Kelsey. *Prison Officers and Their World*. Cambridge, Mass.: Harvard University Press, 1988. Looks at the work of correctional officers, their roles, and their place within the prison environment.

Martin, Steve J., and Sheldon Ekland-Olson. *Texas Prisons: The Walls Came Tumbling Down*. Austin: Texas Monthly Press, 1987. Impact of the federal courts on the Texas prison system.

Useem, Bert, and Peter Kimball. *States of Siege: U.S. Prison Riots, 1971–1986*. New York: Oxford University Press, 1989. Analysis of collective riots in American prisons during the last two decades.

Zimmer, Lynn. *Women Guarding Men*. Chicago: University of Chicago Press, 1986. Exploration of the innovation of women as correctional officers in prisons for men.

## Notes

1  Donald Clemmer, *The Prison Community* (New York: Holt, Rinehart and Winston, 1940); Gresham M. Sykes, *The Society of Captives* (Princeton, N.J.: Princeton University Press, 1958).

2  U.S. Department of Justice, Bureau of Justice Statistics, Charles H. Logan, "Criminal Justice Performance Measures in Prisons," (Washington, D.C.: Government Printing Office, 1993), 5.

3  Ibid.

4  Erving Goffman, *Asylums* (Garden City, N.Y.: Anchor Books, 1961).

5  John DiIulio, Jr., *Governing Prisons* (New York: Free Press, 1987).

6  Ibid., 242. See also DiIulio, *No Escape: The Future of American Corrections* (New York: Basic Books, 1990) and *Barbed Wire Bureaucracy: Leadership and Administration in the Federal Bureau of Prisons* (New York: Oxford University Press, 1991).

7  DiIulio, *Governing Prisons*, 12.

8  Sykes, *Society of Captives*, 49.

9  Ibid., 53.

10  Richard Korn and Lloyd W. McCorkle, "Resocialization within Walls," *Annals* 293 (1954): 191.

11  Gordon Hawkins, "Prison Labor and Prison Industries," in *Crime and Justice*, vol. 5, ed. Michael Tonry and Norval Morris (Chicago: University of Chicago Press, 1983), 90.

12  U.S. National Advisory Committee on Criminal Justice Standards and Goals, *Task Force Report: Corrections* (Washington, D.C.: Government Printing Office, 1973), 188.

13  Justice System Improvement Act of 1979, P.L. 96–157. 93 Stat. 1167, 1215.

14  Ted Palmer, *The Reemergence of Correctional Intervention* (Newbury Park, Calif.: Sage, 1992); Francis Cullen and Karen Gilbert, *Reaffirming Rehabilitation* (Cincinnati, Ohio: Anderson, 1982).

15  Paul Gendreau and Robert R. Ross, "Effective Correctional Treatment: Bibliotherapy for Cynics," in *Effective Correctional Treatment,* ed. Robert R. Ross and Paul Gendreau (Toronto: Butterworths, 1980), 25.

16  John R. Hepburn and Paul E. Knepper, "Correctional Officers as Human Services Workers: The Effect on Job Satisfaction," *Justice Quarterly* 10 (June 1993): 315.

17  Kelsey Kauffman, *Prison Officers and Their World* (Cambridge, Mass.: Harvard University Press, 1988), 86–114.

18  U.S. President's Commission on Law Enforcement and Administration of Justice, *Task Force Report: Corrections* (Washington, D.C.: Government Printing Office, 1967), 96.

19  Donald R. Cressey, "Limitations on Organization of Treatment in the Modern Prison," in *Theoretical Studies in Social Organization of the Prison*, ed. Richard A. Cloward, Donald R. Cressey, George H. Grosser, Richard McCleery, Lloyd E. Ohlin, Gresham M. Sykes, and Sheldon L. Messinger (New York: Social Science Research Council, 1960), 103.

20  U.S. Department of Justice, Bureau of Justice Statistics, *Sourcebook of Criminal Justice Statistics* (Washington, D.C.: Government Printing Office, 1993), 103.

21  Ibid., 102.

22  David Duffee, "Careers in Criminal Justice: Corrections," in *Encyclopedia of Crime and Justice*, ed. Sanford H. Kadish (New York: Free Press, 1983), 1212.

23  *Ruffin* v. *Commonwealth*, 62 Va. 790 (1871).

24  *Stroud* v. *Swope*, 187 F.2d 850 (9th Cir. 1951).

25  *Cooper* v. *Pate*, 378 U.S. 546 (1964).

26  *Johnson* v. *Avery*, 393 U.S. 483 (1969).

27  *Bounds* v. *Smith*, 430 U.S. 817 (1977).

28  *Procunier* v. *Martinez*, 416 U.S. 396 (1974).

29  *Fulwood* v. *Clemmer*, 206 F. Supp. 370 (1962).

30  *Cruz* v. *Beto*, 92 S.Ct. 1079 (1972).

31  *Callahan* v. *Hollyfield*, 516 F. Supp. 1004 (E. D. Va. 1981).

32  *Abdullah* v. *Kinnison*, 769 F.2d 345 (6th Cir. 1985).

33  *Hudson* v. *Palmer*, 52 L.W. 5052 (1984).

34  *Bell* v. *Wolfish*, 441 U.S. 420 (1979).

35  *Estelle* v. *Gamble*, 429 U.S. 97 (1976).

36  *Pugh* v. *Locke*, 406 F. Supp. 318 (1976).

37  *Ruiz* v. *Estelle*, 503 F. Supp. 1265 (S. D. Tex. 1980).

38  *Rhodes* v. *Chapman*, 45 U.S. 337 (1981).

39  *Wolff* v. *McDonnell*, 94 S.Ct. 2963 (1974).

40  *Baxter* v. *Palmigiano*, 425 U.S. 308 (1976).

41  *Lee* v. *Washington*, 390 U.S. 333 (1968).

42  *Bell* v. *Wolfish*, 99 S.Ct. 1861 (1979).

43  *Rhodes* v. *Chapman*, 45 U.S. 337 (1981).

44  *Daniels* v. *Williams*, 54 L.W. 4090 (1986).

45  *Wilson* v. *Seiter*, No. 89–7376 (June 17, 1991).

46 *Turner* v. *Saley*, 107 S.Ct. 2254 (1987); *O'Lone* v. *Shabazz*, 107 S.Ct. 2400 (1987).

47 *McCleskey* v. *Zant*, 222 S.Ct. 1454 (1991).

48 Malcolm M. Feeley and Roger A. Hanson, "The Impact of Judicial Intervention on Prisons and Jails: A Framework of Analysis and a Review of the Literature," in *Courts, Corrections, and the Constitution*, ed. John J. DiIulio, Jr. (New York: Oxford University Press, 1990), 12–46.

49 U.S. National Advisory Committee on Criminal Justice Standards and Goals, *Task Force Report: Corrections* (Washington, D.C.: Government Printing Office, 1973), 343.

# Prison Society

We're crowded into the back of the police van, fifteen convicts en route to the state prison. I'm handcuffed
to two other men, the chains gleaming dully at
wrists and ankles. The man on my right lifts his hand
to smoke, the red eye of his cigarette burning through the
darkness of the van. When he exhales, the man at my left coughs,
the sound in his lungs suggesting that he's old, maybe sick. I want to ask
what he's in for. But I don't speak, restrained by my fear, a feeling that
rises cold up the back of my spine. For a long time no one else speaks
either, each man locked in his own thoughts. It's someone up front, a kid,
his voice brittle with fear, who speaks first. "What's it like down there—
in the joint? Is it as bad as they say?"

"Worse," someone answers. "Cell blocks are dirty. Overcrowded.
Lousy chow. Harassment. Stabbings."

"How do you live there?"

"You don't exactly live. You go through the motions. Eat, sleep, mind
your own business. Do drugs when you can get them. Forget the world
you came from."[1]

This description of the "way in" was written by Michael Knoll, who was incarcerated in the Arizona penal system for seven years. It conveys much of the anxiety not only of the new "fish" but also of the old con. What is it like to be incarcerated? What does it mean to the inmates, the guards, and the administrators? Are the officers in charge or do the prisoners "rule the joint"?

In many ways the interior of the American maximum security prison is like a foreign land. As observers, we need to gain an awareness of the social dimensions of prison life: its traditions, the roles played there, and the prevailing patterns of interpersonal relations. Although the walls and guns may give the impression that everything goes by strict rules and with machinelike precision, a human dimension exists that we may overlook if we study only the formal organization and routes. The lives of the incarcerated are the subjects of this chapter.

## Questions for Inquiry

- What is it like to be in prison, and how do prisoners adapt to life in the joint?
- How are social relationships among female prisoners different from those among male prisoners?
- What is the nature of violence in prisons?
- What can be done about prison violence?

## The Convict World

Because a prison population is comprised of felons, many of whom are prone to violence, we might expect much rebellion if it were not for the discipline imposed by the authorities. As we have seen, however, there are definite limits to the correctional administrators' ability to impose their will on inmates. By examining the convict world, we may begin to understand the prison subculture and the means by which prisoners adapt to their social and physical environments.

Inmates in today's prisons do *not* serve their terms in internal isolation. Rather, prisoners form a society with traditions, norms, and a leadership structure. Some members may choose to associate with only a few close friends; others form cliques along racial or "professional" lines. Still others may be the politicians of the convict society: they attempt to represent convict interests and distribute valued goods in return for support. Just as there is a social culture in the free world, there is a prisoner subculture on the "inside." Membership in a group affords mutual protection from theft and physical assault, serves as the basis of wheeling and dealing activities, and provides a source of cultural identity.

As in any society, the convict world has certain norms and values. Often described as the **inmate code**, the values and norms emerge within the prison social system and help to define the inmate's image of the

**inmate code**
The values and norms of the prison social system that define for inmates the characteristics associated with the model prisoner.

model prisoner. The code also helps to emphasize the solidarity of all inmates against the staff. One feature is that cons are not to interfere with other con's interests; they must, for example, never rat on a con, be nosy, have a loose lip, or put another con on the spot. They must be tough and not trust the officers or the principles that the guards embody. According to the code, guards are hacks or screws; the officials are wrong and the prisoners are right.

Some sociologists believe that the code emerges from within the institution as a way to lessen the pain of imprisonment; others believe that it is part of the criminal culture that prisoners bring with them. The inmate who follows the code can be expected to enjoy a certain amount of admiration from other inmates. He may be thought of as a "right guy" or a "real man." Those who break the code are labeled "rat" or "punk" and will probably spend their prison life at the bottom of the convict social structure, alienated from the rest of the population and preyed upon.[2]

The variety of cultural and subcultural orientations (ethnic, class, and criminal), the variety of preprison experiences, and the intense, open hostility between segments of the prison population today seem to have fractured the code: indeed, a single, overriding inmate code may not exist in some institutions. Instead, race has become a key variable dividing convict society. Perhaps reflecting tensions in the broader community, many prisons now have racially motivated violence, organizations based on race, and voluntary segregation of inmates by race whenever possible (recreation areas, dining halls).

In the absence of a single code accepted by the entire population, administrators find their task more difficult. They must be aware of the variations that exist among the groups, recognize the norms and rules that members hold, and deal with the leaders of many cliques rather than with a few inmates who have risen to top positions in the inmate society.

## Adaptive Roles

On entering prison, a newcomer (a "fish") is confronted by the question: How am I going to do my time? Some may decide to withdraw into their own world and isolate themselves from their fellow prisoners. Others may decide to become full participants in the convict social system, which, "through its solidarity, regulation of activities, distribution of goods and prestige ... helps the individual withstand the 'pains of imprisonment.' "[3] In other words, some inmates may decide to identify mainly with the outside world, and others may orient themselves primarily toward the convict world. This choice of identity is influenced by prisoners' values. Are they interested primarily in achieving prestige according to the norms of the prison culture, or do they try to maintain or realize the values of the free world? Their preference will influence the strategies that they will follow during the prison sentence.

Four categories have been used to describe the life-styles of male inmates as they adapt to prison.[4] "Doing time" and "gleaning" are the choices of those who try to maintain their links with and the perspective of the free world. "Jailing" is the style used by those who cut themselves

Every prisoner must answer the question "How am I going to do my time?" Some will glean as much as they can from prison programs, while others will adopt the role of "jailing" by making the prison their "home."

off from the outside and try to construct a life within the prison. The fourth category, "disorganized criminal," includes those who are unable to develop role orientations to prison life. Each term helps us better understand prison life.

**Doing Time**  The life-style of "doing time" is adopted by those men who regard a prison term as a temporary break in their outside careers. They tend to be professional thieves—that is, criminals who look at their "work" as a legitimate businessman would. A prison sentence to these inmates is one of the risks, or "overhead" costs, of the way they make their living. These inmates try to serve their terms with the least amount of suffering and the greatest amount of comfort they can manage. They avoid trouble by adhering to the inmate code, finding activities to fill their days, forming friendships with only small groups of other convicts, and generally doing what they think is necessary to get out as soon as possible.

**Gleaning**  Some inmates decide to spend their time "gleaning," taking advantage of prison programs to change their lives by trying to improve or "find" themselves. They use every resource at hand: library, correspondence courses, vocational training programs, and school. John Irwin's study of San Quentin, California, a maximum security institution, showed that inmates who adopted this style tended to be those who were not committed to a life of crime.[5]

**Jailing**   Some convicts never acquire a commitment to the outside social world. While in prison, they adopt a "jailing" life-style and make a world for themselves there. They are likely to be "state-raised youth," persons who have been in foster homes, juvenile detention facilities, reformatories, and adult prisons for most of their lives. Because they know the institutional routine, have the skills required to "make it," and view the prison as a familiar place, they often aspire to leadership within the convict society. The jailing life-style has its rewards, from a comfortable routine to an increased prestige in the prison social system.

**Disorganized Criminal**   Often of low intelligence or afflicted with a psychological or physical disability, disorganized criminals have difficulty functioning within the prison society; they are the human putty of the prison social world and are exploited by others.

In considering these roles, we can see that prisoners are not members of an undifferentiated mass; individual members choose to play specific roles in the convict society. These models reflect the physical and social environment of the prison and contribute to the development of the system that maintains the institution's ongoing activities.

## Making It in the Prison Economy

In prison, as in the outside world, individuals desire goods and services that are not freely provided. Although the state feeds, clothes, and houses all prisoners, amenities are sparse; institutional life is a type of enforced destitution. Prisoners are deprived of everything but bare necessities and subjected to monotony in diet and routine, loss of individual identity (due to uniformity of treatment), scarcity of recreational opportunities, and lack of responsibility. Since the mid-1960s, the items that a prisoner may purchase or receive through legitimate channels have increased. In some institutions, for example, inmates may own television sets, civilian clothing, and hot plates. Yet the prison community has been deliberately designated an island of poverty in the midst of a society of relative abundance.

The state has decreed that a life of extreme simplicity is part of the punishment of incarceration. And correctional administrators feel that rules must be enforced so that all prisoners are treated alike and none can gain higher position, status, or comfort because of wealth or access to goods. Thus prisoners are limited as to what they may have in their cells, restrictions are placed on what gifts may be brought into the institution, and money may not be in the inmate's possession.

Recognizing that prisoners do have some needs that are not met, officials have created a formal economic system in the form of a commissary, or "store," from which inmates may, on a scheduled basis, purchase a limited number of items—toilet articles, tobacco, snacks, and other foods—in exchange for credits drawn upon their "bank accounts." The size of a bank account depends on the amount of money deposited on the inmate's entrance, gifts sent by relatives, and amounts earned in the low-paying prison industries. In some prisons, the amount that may be spent weekly is limited.

But the peanut butter, soap, and cigarettes of the typical prison store in no way satisfy the consumer needs and desires of prisoners. In consequence an informal, *sub rosa* economy exists as a major element in the society of captives. Many items taken for granted on the outside are inordinately valued on the inside. For example, talcum powder and deodorant take on added importance because of the limited bathing facilities. Goods and services not consumed at all outside prison may have exaggerated importance inside prison. For example, unable to enjoy their accustomed drink of bourbon, offenders will find that somewhat the same effect can be achieved by sniffing glue. Or, to distinguish themselves from others, offenders may pay laundry workers to iron a shirt in a particular way, a modest version of conspicuous consumption.[6]

David Kalinich has documented the prison economy at the State Prison of Southern Michigan in Jackson.[7] He learned that a complete market economy provided the goods and services not available to prisoners through legitimate sources. This informal economy reinforces the norms and roles of the social system, influences the nature of interpersonal relationships, and is thus one of the principal features of the culture. The extent of the economy and its ability to produce desired goods and services—food, drugs, alcohol, sex, preferred living conditions—vary according to the extent of official surveillance, the demands of the consumers, and the opportunities for entrepreneurship. Much inmate activity revolves around the "hustle."

The standard medium of exchange in the prison economy is cigarettes. Because possession of coins or currency is prohibited and a barter system is somewhat restrictive, "cigarette money" is a useful substitute. Cigarettes are not contraband, are easily transferable, have a stable and well-known standard of value, and come in denominations of singles, packs, and cartons. Furthermore, they are in demand by smokers. Even those who do not smoke keep cigarettes for trading purposes.

Certain positions in the prison society provide opportunities for entrepreneurs. Inmates assigned to work in places such as the kitchen, warehouse, and administrative office have access to food, clothing, materials, and information. As Susan Sheehan found in Green Haven, a New York prison, almost every job offered possibilities for "swagging" (stealing from the state):

Kitchen workers can take far more food than they can eat, and sell it or swap it. One [inmate] who receives five cartons of cigarettes a month from a crime partner he didn't rat on, doesn't smoke but loves to eat. His recent purchases from a kitchen worker have included a dozen eggs (two packs of cigarettes), a pound of rice (one pack), a pound of coffee (one pack), and several steaks (three packs apiece). He also has a contract with his friend in the kitchen for a daily loaf of soft bread (one carton a month). Kitchen workers have access to the various ingredients used at Green Haven to make booze—yeast, raw dough, sugar, fruit, potatoes, cereal—and either sell the raw ingredients or make and sell the finished product.[8]

As the Close-Up on pages 568–569 reveals in more detail, "sales" in the economy are one to one and are also interrelated with other *sub rosa* transactions. Thus the exchange of a dozen eggs for two packs of cigarettes may result in the reselling of the eggs in the form of egg sandwiches made on a hot plate for five cigarettes each, while the kitchen worker who swagged the eggs may use the income to get a laundry worker to starch his shirts or a hospital orderly to provide drugs or to pay a "punk" for sexual favors. The economic transactions wind on and on.

Disruptions of the economy may occur when officials conduct periodic lockdowns (holding inmates in their cells) and inspections. Confiscation of contraband may result in temporary shortages and price readjustments, but gradually hustling will return. The laws of supply and demand will be back in force.

The economy of the prison society meets the members' needs for goods and services. It permits some inmates to live better than others and to exert power over them. Economic transactions may lead to violence when goods are stolen, debts are not paid, or agreements are violated. The guards may also become enmeshed in the prison economy as they, too, see opportunities to provide goods for payment. The prison economy, like that of the outside world, allocates goods and services, rewards and sanctions, and is closely linked to the cultural and social systems of the society it serves.

## Women in Prison

Women constitute only 6 percent (about fifty thousand) of the entire U.S. prison population. This figure is slightly higher than in years past, due in part to increased drug convictions. More important is that since 1980 the rate of growth in the number of incarcerated women has been greater

Compared with the convict society in prisons for males, many female prisoners form pseudofamilies, developing strong bonds with family members.

## A Day in the Life

George Malinow, a self-described "professional criminal," was asked by Susan Sheehan to keep a diary of four ordinary days of incarceration in Green Haven, one of New York State's maximum security prisons. As the following excerpt makes obvious, he knows the ropes of prison life. As he says, "I hustle, I swag, same as on the street."

### Tuesday, August 10

6:30 A.M. Bell rings very loud and long. A certain C.O. [correctional officer or guard] does this (rings bell long) whenever he comes on duty, and I and many other inmates here would like to hit him with a shoe, as he seems to do this on purpose!

God—I hate to get up, I feel so tired!! Serves me right for staying up doing glass painting till 1:55 this morning. But—get up I must and do so. Wash up, shave, and get dressed in my work clothes which is green regulation-issued pants and shirt and work shoes. Put on water to be boiled for my coffee. Have coffee and two donuts. Smoke a cigarette and listen to the news, via earphones.

7:15 A.M. Doors open up. I immediately rush off to the mess hall entrance area on the West Side entrance, being I'm one of the first inmates up—no one is near that area at this time of the morning. Terry, a friend of mine (inmate) who works in the kitchen, is there awaiting me. He hands me a large box which contains 20 dozen fresh eggs, about 20 pounds of raw bacon, and about 20 pounds macaroni, 20 to 30 oranges, 2 large cans orange juice, and one large can of olive oil for cooking. I immediately *rush* back to my cell, to avoid the other inmates about due to start going to the mess hall for their breakfast.

Hide food in my cell and my friend Andy's cell. Andy is just up and washing. We joke together about our sudden good windfall.

7:40 A.M. Andy and I proceed to go to work, the parole-clothing department located at the basement of the administration building. Terry stops us to ask us to please get him some shorts, two white shirts, and black socks. We tell him that we'll give it to him next morning. We reach the checkpoint gate of the administration building, get pat frisked, and sign the logbook to verify at what time we arrived to work. Also left our institutional passes at this checkpoint, as must be done.

We arrive at the basement parole-clothing area where we work. C.O.s Stevens and Barton are there already.

The coffee pot is ready as C.O. Stevens always plugs in this pot early. So Andy, I, and Stevens all have coffee and cake. C.O. Barton is busy checking papers for the inmate he is due to take to the hospital so he doesn't join us. We have the radio playing and listening to the local news broadcast. Meanwhile, there are four men going home on parole this morning and they just arrived and are getting dressed. Andy and I both help and make certain that these inmates have all their clothes and personal property packages. They have cups of coffee and relax in casual and happy conversation—about the steaks, drinks, and women

they'll soon enjoy out there, etc. Does seeing men talk like this and seeing them go home each day bother us? Andy and I feel very glad to see as many as possible leave any prison as prison represents "hell" in all respects!!

7:50 A.M. All the men due to go home now leave with C.O. Stevens to go upstairs to an office where they'll all receive their $40 gate money and whatever's in their inmate account and their release papers. Then C.O. Stevens will escort them out and drive them in the prison van bus to Hopewell Jct. station where they will board a bus for N.Y. City. I sorted out all their state-issued clothing they turned in to our dept. and also gathered all the earphones they brought to our dept. upon departure. Bagged all state clothes to be sent to state shop, their final destination.

8:05 A.M. We have an extra relief C.O. to stay with us, as C.O.s Stevens and Barton are out on assignments. Said relief C.O.'s name is Officer Dover (works in officers' mess from 10 A.M. onward), who is one of the best-natured officers in all respects that I have ever come across. Good sense of humor, always smiling and happy go lucky. Very well mannered, fair, and easy to relate with. Should be made a warden.

Andy and I relax and talk about general topics on the outside.

8:30 A.M. Another three inmates that work with us now arrive to work also. They are Danny, Benno, and Ned.

This morning—we have to take a full inventory of all the stock garments we have and record each item in our general inventory stock so we will know what to order, we are short of. After Danny, Ned, and Benno all have their coffee and buns, all five of us get ready to do the inventory.

8:50 A.M. Andy and I start counting the jackets, slacks, socks, handkerchiefs, belts, shoes, and shirts. Danny and Ned start to count the ties, topcoats, and the other apparel that the men wear to go out on furloughs, death visits, and to courts.

10:35 A.M. We all are caught up on our inventory and go to have coffee again and relax. During inventory taking, Benno sat at the desk to answer all phone calls of general inquiry and also made up lists for calling men the next day—that have to be fitted out with civilian clothes for their due release dates soon.

11:05 A.M. Benno starts to prepare the foods that he will cook for our lunch as we are not going to go to the mess hall as there is only franks for lunch. Benno is making steaks, fried onions, French fried potatoes, sauce gravy, and sweet green peas for our lunch meal. Benno is an exceptional cook! When he cooks, we all leave the kitchen to be out of his way and also, not to distract him then. One or more of us are available to help him—if he calls us, but most times he does it all by himself. Of course, he cooks—so all others of us do the cleaning up and wash the pots and dishes.

11:40 A.M. We are just about ready to start eating. We all are in conversation about how good Benno cooked the steaks, the high price of food outside, etc. The radio is playing a late song hit and we all are enjoying the food and are in a good mood.

12:25 P.M. We are done eating—so Andy, Danny, and I all take out the dishes, silverware, pots to the sink area away from the kitchen and wash and dry all. Meantime, Ned swept out kitchen while Benno went to his desk to relax.

12:45 P.M. No inmates to dress this afternoon so Danny and I recheck all the men due to go home the next morning—on our outgoing releases sheet. We line up all the clothing outfits and their packages containing personal property at the benches where they will get dressed in the morning.

1:15 P.M. We all now sit around the desks and are in conversation about many topics. The parole board's unjust decisions, rehabilitation, politics and prison mismanagement, etc.

2:05 P.M. Phone rings and we have to go to the store house to pick up six large cases containing jackets and slacks. Andy, Danny, and I all take a strong push wagon and check out from the check-out gate at the administration area, get pat frisked, and proceed to go to the store house. Along the way, we stop off at E block, on the East Side, to find out if two of the men locking there will be at our Jaycees meeting tonight? They said they will. We leave for the store house.

We arrive at the store house, load our wagon with all the large cases and pick up a copy of the order form. We arrive at the front administration checkpoint and again are pat frisked. We get all boxes to the rack area. We open all boxes, take out garments, and count them. The total checks out correctly. C.O. Stevens signs the receipt form copy and I take it back to the store house civilian clerk. When I return, Andy, Danny, Benno, and Ned are about halfway done placing the slacks on the shelves in their respective sizes, and the jackets on the line racks, in their respective sizes.

I join them in doing this and I sort the jackets. We stop this work at 2:45 P.M. I check and pull out coffee-pot plug, stove plug, radio plug, and toaster plug. Meanwhile—Andy dumps out all the trash into plastic trash bags due to go out to the dump area, via truck, in the morning. Benno dumps out all water from wash pails in kitchen. Danny washes out coffee pot and prepares it for next morning's use.

2:55 P.M. All of us leave our job area in basement, get pat frisked again at check-out gate, pick up our passes, and proceed to our cells in C block, all except Ned as he locks in J block.

3:05 P.M. I arrive at my cell, change clothes, wash up, and go to the wash room to wash out and hang up the clothes I left there to soak yesterday.

3:25 P.M. Returned to cell, put water on for my thermos bottle to make my coffee. Layed down, smoked a cigar, and relaxed listening to some soft music via earphones.

4:10 P.M. Got up, made cup of coffee, had a ham and Swiss cheese sandwich. Cleaned up table, brushed teeth, and started to get materials ready to do my glass painting. Worked on glass painting until lock in.

5:05 P.M. Bell rings—lock in time. Doors close and two C.O.s walk by and check the doors and count as they walk past my cell. I continue on working on the glass pictures.

5:25 P.M. C.O. stops at my cell and hands me eight letters (personal), two more business letters, and one magazine on real estate. C.O. continues on handing out mail to other cells.

Read three of these letters which come from the Philippines. One from my sweetheart, one from her sister, and the third from her mother. Finish reading all mail and lay down to catch the prison phone bulletin announcements on prison news.

5:55 P.M. Get up, wash up, brush teeth, and get all my papers and materials ready for my Jaycees meeting due tonight at the school class building at J block, from 6 to 8:30 P.M.

6:00 P.M. Doors open up. I proceed to block door exit where many other men are waiting to go to different night classes and program classes. The block C.O. checks each one of us out on his master sheet.

I arrive at my Jaycee classroom and start writing out on the blackboard the agenda for tonight's meeting. An outside male Jaycee coordinator arrives and our Jaycee meeting starts. We discuss various project possibilities. One project involves bringing boys from high schools within a few miles of Haven to the prison to see what it is like so that they will never want to commit crimes and will never wind up in prison. We also form committees for each project. Meeting ends at 8:25 P.M. and all of us leave to return to our blocks.

8:35 P.M. Returned to cell. Wash and make cup of coffee and smoke two cigarettes. Start to work again on my glass pictures and continue until 10 P.M. I stop to eat a salami and cheese with lettuce and tomatoe sandwich. Smoke two cigarettes and relax on my bed.

I start to think of my sweetheart in the Philippines. What's she doing, etc.? That's rather silly since it is a twelve-hour difference in time from N.Y. City, it goes without saying it has to be about 10 A.M. there so of course, she can't be sleeping.

10:20 P.M. I start working on my glass pictures again. I accidently spill over the bottle of drawing paint all over my glass and I am angry as hell at myself for my carelessness! Finally get that particular portion on my glass cleaned and I have to redraw that part of the picture again.

10:55 P.M. The bell rings and that means it's time to lock in for the night. Doors close and the two C.O.s again check the doors and take the count. I continue on working on the glass pictures. I feel very tired tonight so I stop working on these pictures at 11:40 P.M. I clean up all paint brushes, table and put away to a safe area the glass paintings to dry during the night. Have a fast cup of coffee, then wash up, brush teeth, and get undressed.

11:55 P.M. Put on only small night lamp, put on phones to catch midnight news. Light up cigarette and listen to the news on phones. Music (western songs) comes on by some local Poughkeepsie disc jockey and I listen to it until 12:30 A.M.

12:35 A.M. I put out light, pull out phone plug, and go to sleep.

SOURCE: Excerpted from Susan Sheehan, *A Prison and a Prisoner* (Boston: Houghton Mifflin, 1978), 96–102. © 1978 by Susan Sheehan. Reprinted by permission.

than that of men. Between 1980 and 1992, the number of men behind bars rose 163 percent; the number of women, 276 percent.

Perhaps because the number of women both in prison and in corrections research has been so small, the literature on women's institutions is sparse. In general, it compares life in women's prisons with that in men's institutions. Women's prisons are smaller; security is less tight; the relationships between inmates and staff are less structured; physical aggression seems less common; the *sub rosa* economy is not so well developed; and female prisoners appear to be even less committed to the convict code than men. Women serve shorter sentences, and there is perhaps more fluidity in the prison society as new members join and others leave.

Research has shown that incarcerated women are young (average age twenty-nine), poorly educated (less than half have finished high school), and employed at unskilled jobs. In addition, nonwhite women comprise a higher percentage of the prison population than in the general population (see Figure 16.1). Nearly half were caring for dependents when they were admitted, yet most had no male companion. Few had alcohol problems, but about half were drug abusers. Compared to men, a higher proportion of incarcerated women are in prison for property offenses (39 percent vs. 33 percent) and drug-related offenses (11 percent vs. 7 percent).[9]

Although institutional facilities for women are generally smaller, better staffed, and less fortresslike than those for men, these advantages may pale when the problems of remoteness and heterogeneity are considered. Because only three states (Florida, Oklahoma, and Texas) operate more than one prison for women and some operate none, inmates are generally far removed from their families, friends, and attorneys. In addition, because the number of inmates is small, there is less pressure to design programs to meet an individual offender's security and treatment needs. Rehabilitation programs are few, and dangerous inmates are not segregated from those who have committed minor offenses.

**Figure 16.1**
**Characteristics of female prisoners**
As with their male counterparts, female prisoners tend to be young, have low education levels, are frequently members of minority groups, and are predominantly not married.

SOURCE: Adapted from U.S. Department of Justice, Bureau of Justice Statistics, *Special Report* (Washington, D.C.: Government Printing Office, 1991), 2.

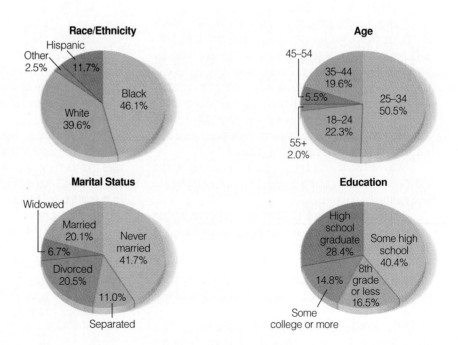

## Social Relationships

What types of social relationships do women prisoners maintain—and how do these differ from those that men maintain in prison? As in all types of penal institutions, homosexual relationships are found, though among women they appear to be more voluntary than coerced. More importantly, female inmates tend to form pseudofamilies in which they adopt various roles—father, mother, daughter, sister—and interact as a unit. Esther Heffernan views these "play" families as a "direct, conscious substitution for the family relationships broken by imprisonment, or…the development of roles that perhaps were not fulfilled in the actual home environment."[10] Such interpersonal links help to relieve the tensions of prison life, to assist the socialization of the new inmate, and to allow individuals to act according to roles and rules that are clearly defined.

Rose Giallombardo believes that in most respects the subcultures of prisons for males and females are similar, with one major exception: the informal social structure of the female prison helps inmates "resist the destructive effects of imprisonment by creating a substitute universe—a world in which the inmates may preserve an identity which is relevant to life outside the prison." The orientation of female inmates is somewhat collectivist, with warmth and mutual aid being offered to an extended network of "family" members. This emphasis, Giallombardo contends, is in sharp contrast to the male strategy of combating the pains of imprisonment through the development of a convict code and by the showing of solidarity with other inmates.[11]

**Adaptive Roles**   Esther Heffernan discovered that three terms in prison slang—"square," "cool," and "in the life"—correspond to the noncriminal, professional, and habitual offenders in women's correctional institutions; these adaptations correspond to identities brought from the outside. *Square* is used, as in the larger community, to describe a person who holds conventional norms and values. A square is a noncriminal who perhaps killed her husband in a moment of rage. She attempts to maintain a conventional life while incarcerated, strives to gain the respect of officers and fellow inmates, and seeks to be a "good Christian woman."

Female prisoners are "cool" if they make a "controlled, pleasurable, manipulative response to a situation." They are the professionals who "keep busy, play around, stay out of trouble, and get out." They attempt to manipulate others and intend to get through this term of incarceration on "easy time" through unity with others in their group, gaining as many amenities as they can without risking a longer stay.

Those who are "in the life"—about 50 percent of women in prison—are the habitual offenders who have been involved in prostitution, drugs, numbers, and shoplifting. They have been in prison previously, interact with others with similar experiences, and find community within the prison. It is important to them to stand firm against authority.[12]

**Male Versus Female Subcultures**   There are many parallels between the subcultures in prisons for men and those for women—and a number of major differences. Comparisons are complicated somewhat by the nature of the research: most studies have been of single-sex institutions. In addition, it seems that theories and concepts have been studied first in male prisons and then replicated in female institutions. Thus the concepts of the inmate code, the prison economy, and so on, are central to this entire body of literature; all have been found to have explanatory value in both types of institution. In both male and female institutions, to "make it" is to adapt to prison life in some way that makes the experience as painless as possible. (For a method that one woman chose, see the Close-Up on the facing page.) Prisoners who cannot come to terms with incarceration can expect to do "hard time" and suffer from the experience.

A principal difference between these two gender-specific societies lies in interpersonal relations. Male prisoners seem to have a greater sense that they act as individuals and that their behavior is evaluated by the yardstick of the prison culture. In a comparative study of four prisons for men and one for women, James Fox noted that male prisoners have their gangs or cliques but not the network of "family" relationships that female prisoners may develop. Men are expected to do their *own* time. The norms stress autonomy, self-sufficiency, and the ability to cope with one's problems. Fox found little sharing among men.[13]

According to Fox, women at the Bedford Hills Correctional Facility in New York were less likely to look toward achievement of status or recognition within the prisoner community or "to impose severe restrictions on the sexual (or emotional) conduct of other members."[14] In prisons for women, close ties seem to exist among small groups of inmates. These extended families, which may include homosexual couple relationships, provide emotional support and emphasize the sharing of resources.

Some researchers have ascribed the distinctive female prison subculture to the nurturing, maternal qualities of women. Others have criticized this analysis as a stereotype of female behavior, imputing to women sex-specific personality characteristics.


## Programs and the Female Role

Two major criticisms of women's prisons are that they do not have the variety of vocational and educational programs available in male institutions and that existing programs for women tend to conform to sexual stereotypes of feminine occupations—cosmetology, food service, housekeeping, sewing. It is suggested that such activities reflect the occupations of women before World War II but have little correspondence to the ones open to women today. Vocational and educational opportunities during incarceration are crucial, both for speeding time in prison and improving life after prison. Upon release most women have to support themselves, and many are financially responsible for children as well; education and training are therefore vital.

Formerly most educational programs for women stopped at the secondary level. The argument given was that the small number of inmates

## Surviving in Prison

I was scared when I went to Bedford Hills. But I knew a few things by then. Like if you act quiet and hostile, people will consider you dangerous and won't bother you. So when I got out of isolation and women came up and talked to me, I said, "I left my feelings outside the gate, and I'll pick 'em up on my way out." I meant I wasn't going to take no junk from anyone. I made a promise if anybody hit me, I was gonna send 'em to the hospital.

When you go in, if you have certain characteristics, you're classified in a certain way. First of all, if you are aggressive, if you're not a dependent kind of woman, you're placed in a position where people think you have homosexual tendencies. If you're in that society long, you play the game if it makes it easier to survive. And it makes it eas-ier if people think you're a stud broad. I played the game to make it easier so they would leave me alone. I didn't have money to use makeup and I couldn't see going through any changes. You're in there and the women are looking for new faces. Since I was quiet and not too feminine-looking, I was placed in a certain box in other people's minds. I let them think that's what box I was in—'cause it was a good way to survive. My good friends knew better. But I had three good friends and they were considered "my women"—so they in turn were safe, too. You have to find ways to survive. You cultivate ways to survive. It's an alien world and it has nothing to do with functioning in society better. What I learned there was to survive there.

SOURCE: Kathryn Watterson Burkhart, *Women in Prison* (New York: Doubleday, 1976), 89–90.

made offering courses at the college level impractical. But recent studies have shown an increase in the number and the variety of educational and vocational programs in women's prisons. Earlier research had emphasized that programs in women's prisons were generally limited as compared to those in male institutions and that they were primarily geared to traditionally "feminine" jobs.[15] When national surveys were conducted in the mid-1980s, educational programs were found in almost all women's institutions; vocational programs existed in about 90 percent of the institutions.[16] Perhaps more important, the range of courses now offered in many prisons for women has increased so that business education, computer training, auto repair, and carpentry have been added to the more traditional offerings.

The lack of medical, nutritional, and recreational services in women's prisons has also been noted. In particular, because of the fewer number of female inmates, most women's institutions share physicians and hospital facilities with male prisons. Because the health-delivery system at Bedford Hills Correctional Facility was deficient—no full-time physician or continuous medical care and inadequate screening for medical problems—a ruling in a lawsuit filed on behalf of the inmates found the institution in violation of the Eighth Amendment's prohibition of cruel and unusual punishments. The court declared that the state had been deliberately indifferent to known medical needs.

## Mothers and Their Children

Of greatest concern to incarcerated women is the fate of their children. The best available data indicate that about 75 percent of women inmates are mothers and that on average they have two dependent children. It is thus estimated that on a typical day 167,000 children in the United States—two-thirds of whom are under ten years of age—have mothers who are in jail or prison.[17] One recent study found that roughly half of these children do not see their mothers while they are in prison.[18]

Few of these mothers have husbands or male partners who are able or willing to maintain a home for the children. In a study of the effects of separation on 133 inmates and their children, Phyllis Jo Baunach found that the children were most often cared for by their maternal grandmothers.[19] An inmate's knowledge that her children were with their grandmother gave her peace of mind. When an inmate had no relative who would care for the children, they were often put up for adoption or placed in state-funded foster care.

Enforced separation of children from their mothers is harmful to the children and to the mothers. It is a stress-producing experience that is not fully shared by male prisoners. Anxiety about the care of their children is felt by all mothers, especially if the children are being cared for by strangers.

Mothers have difficulty maintaining contact with their children because of the distance of prisons from the children's homes, restrictions on visiting hours, intermittent telephone conversations, and the conditions for interacting with offspring when they do visit the institution. In some correctional institutions, children must abide by the same rules governing adult visits: physical contact is not allowed and time is strictly limited.

Programs are increasingly being developed to deal with the problems of mothers and their children. In some states, children may meet with their mothers at almost any time, for extended periods, and in playrooms or nurseries where contact is possible. Transportation for visits is arranged in some states, and in some it is even possible for children to stay overnight. In both South Dakota and Nebraska, for example, children may stay with their mothers for up to five days a month. A few prisons have family visiting programs that allow the inmate, her legal husband, and her children to be together, often in a mobile home or apartment, for periods up to seventy-two hours.[20]

In most states a baby born in prison must be placed with a family member or social agency within three weeks, to the detriment of the early mother-child bonding thought to be important for the development of a baby. Some innovative programs make longer periods possible. The emphasis on community corrections in the 1970s gave rise to programs that permitted mothers and their children to live together in halfway houses. These programs have not expanded as much as first planned in part because the presence of children upset the routine of the facility.

Given the changes in women's roles in the United States during the past twenty years, we might have expected the differences between men's and women's prisons to diminish. The proportion of arrested women who are sent to prison is rising, and their offenses are becoming more like those of men. We can only wonder what a new generation of researchers will find: Will future prisons for women be run differently than they are today? Will women inmates continue to develop pseudofamilies in prison? Will levels of violence in women's prisons increase?

# Violence in Prison

A recipe for violence: confine in cramped quarters a thousand men, some of whom have a history of engaging in violent interpersonal acts, restrict their movement and behavior, allow no contact with women, guard them with guns, and keep them in this condition for an indefinite period. Collective violence, such as the riots at Attica (1971), Santa Fe, New Mexico (1980), and Atlanta (1987), is well known to the public. But few people are aware of the level of interpersonal violence in U.S. prisons. Each year hundreds of prisoners die violent deaths and countless others are assaulted. In 1990, for example, 98 prisoners committed suicide, 49 deaths were "caused by another," and 261 died in circumstances in which it was not clear whether the cause was natural, self-inflicted, accidental, or homicide.[21] Many prisoners live in a state of constant uneasiness, always on the lookout for persons who might subject them to homosexual demands, steal their few possessions, or make their time more painful.

## Assaultive Behavior and Inmate Characteristics

Assaultive behavior in our correctional institutions raises serious questions for administrators, criminal justice specialists, and the general public. What are the nature and causes of prison violence? What can be done to ameliorate the situation? What responsibility does the state have to the prisoners held in these institutions? We consider these questions when we examine the three main categories of prison violence: prisoner-prisoner, prisoner-officer, officer-prisoner. To begin to understand that violence, however, we must first know more about the inmates, for violent behavior in prisons is undoubtedly related in part to the types of people who are incarcerated and the characteristics they bring with them. Three of these characteristics stand out: age, attitudes, and race.

**Age**   Studies have shown that young people, both inside and outside prison, are more prone to violence than their elders.[22] The group most likely to commit violent crimes is comprised of males between the ages of sixteen and twenty-four. Not surprisingly, 96 percent of adult prisoners are males, and their average age at the time of admission is twenty-seven years. Prisoners committed for crimes of violence are generally a year or two younger than the average. Not only do the young have greater physical strength, but they lack those commitments to career and family that are thought to restrict antisocial behavior. In addition, many young men have difficulty defining their position in society; thus many of their interactions with others are interpreted as challenges to their status. *Machismo*, the concept of male honor and the sacredness of one's reputation as a man, has a bearing on violence among the young. To be macho is, for one thing, to have a reputation for physically retaliating against those who make slurs on one's honor. The potential for violence among prisoners with these attributes is obvious.

**Attitudes**    One of the sociological theories advanced to explain crime is that there is a subculture of violence among certain economic, racial, and ethnic groups. According to this theory, developed by Marvin Wolfgang and Franco Ferracuti, this subculture is found in the lower class, and in its value system violence is "tolerable, expected, or required."[23] Arguments are settled and decisions are made by the fist rather than by verbal persuasion. These attitudes are brought into the prison as part of an inmate's heritage.

**Race**    Race has become the major factor that divides the contemporary prison population, reflecting tensions in the larger society. Racist attitudes seem to be acceptable in most institutions and have become part of the convict code. The fact of forced association, having to live with persons with whom one would probably not associate on the outside, exaggerates and amplifies racial conflict. Violence against members of another race may be a way some inmates deal with the frustrations of their lives both inside and outside prison. As we will see, the presence of racially organized gangs contributes to violence in prison. Furthermore, prisoners may be coerced to join the gang of their racial or ethnic group.

### Prisoner-Prisoner Violence

Although prison folklore may attribute violence to brutal guards, most of the violence in prison is inmate to inmate. A study of four Virginia institutions registered a prisoner-prisoner assault rate of 9.96 attacks per 100 inmates per year.[24] These levels of violence are not necessarily related to the size of the prisoner population in a particular facility. The sad fact is that uncounted inmates are injured by assaults. As Hans Toch has observed, the climate of violence in prisons has no free-world counterpart. "Inmates are terrorized by other inmates, and spend years in fear of harm. Some inmates request segregation, others lock themselves in, and some are hermits by choice."[25] Yet it might also be argued that most prisoners come from violent neighborhoods, and perhaps they are safer in prison than they would be on the outside.

This argument may carry less weight given the increased presence of gangs in prison. Racial or ethnic gangs are now linked to acts of violence in many prison systems. In essence the gang wars of the streets are often continued in prison. Gangs are organized primarily with the intention of controlling an institution's drugs, gambling, loan sharking, prostitution, extortion, and debt-collection rackets. In addition, gangs

Racial and ethnic gangs dominate prison society in many institutions.

provide protection for their members from other gangs and instill a sense of macho camaraderie.

Contributing to prison violence is the fact that gang membership is often on a "blood-in, blood-out" basis: A would-be member must stab a gang's enemy to be admitted, and once in cannot drop out without endangering his own life. Given the racial and ethnic foundation of the gangs, violence between them can easily spill into the general prison population.

The only national survey to date on prison gangs found that they existed in the institutions of thirty-four states and in the federal system (see Figure 16.2). The 1985 survey identified 114 individual gangs, with an overall membership of more than 12,000 inmates.[26] Although the gangs are small, they are tightly organized and have even arranged the killing of opposition gang leaders housed in other institutions. Administrators say that prison gangs, like organized crime groups, tend to pursue their "business" interests, yet they are also a major source of inmate-inmate violence as they discipline members, enforce orders, and retaliate against other gangs. The racial composition of prison gangs in Texas is shown in Table 16.1.

**Figure 16.2**
**Prison gangs are reported to exist in most jurisdictions**
The proliferation of prison gangs is a modern phenomenon. They are often street gangs, simply moved "inside," and are a major source of violence and intimidation.

SOURCE: U.S. Department of Justice, Office of Legal Policy, *Prison Gangs: Their Extent, Nature, and Impact on Prisons* (Washington, D.C.: Government Printing Office, 1985).

Prisons with gangs
Prisons without gangs

## Prisoner-Officer Violence

The mass media have focused on riots in which guards are taken hostage, injured, and killed, but most violence in prisons is committed among the inmates; the violence that does take place against officers is situational and individual. Correctional officers do not carry weapons within the walls of the institution because a prisoner may seize them. Prisoners do manage to obtain lethal weapons and can use the element of surprise to inflict injury on an officer. In the course of a workday an officer may encounter situations that require the use of physical force against an inmate—for instance, breaking up a fight or moving a prisoner to segregation. Officers know that such situations are especially dangerous and may enlist the assistance of others to minimize the risk of violence. But it is the unexpected attack against an individual officer that is of greatest concern: a missile thrown from an upper tier by a prisoner who wants to retaliate against an officer he thinks is out to get him, verbal threats and taunts, an officer's "accidental" fall downstairs. The fact that the officer must be constantly watchful against personal attacks adds to the level of stress and keeps many officers at a distance from contact with the inmates.

## Officer-Prisoner Violence

Unauthorized physical violence against inmates by officers to enforce rules, uphold the officer-prisoner relationship, and maintain order is a fact of life in many institutions. Stories abound of guards giving individual prisoners "the treatment" outside the notice of their superiors. Many guards view physical force as a daily operating procedure and consider its use legitimate. In some institutions, authorized "goon squads" com-

| Name of Gang | Racial Composition | Size of Membership | Year Formed |
|---|---|---|---|
| Texas Syndicate | Predominantly Hispanic | 296 | 1975 |
| Texas Mafia | Predominantly white | 110 | 1982 |
| Aryan Brotherhood | All white | 287 | 1983 |
| Mexican Mafia | All Hispanic | 351 | 1984 |
| Nuestro Carneles | All Hispanic | 47 | 1984 |
| Mandingo Warriors | All black | 66 | 1985 |
| Self-Defense Family | Predominantly black | 107 | 1985 |
| Hermanos De Pistolero | All Hispanic | 21 | 1985 |
| Others | | 115 | 1985 |

**Table 16.1**
**Prison gangs in Texas**
Texas has a major problem with prison gangs. As the data show they are racially and ethnically organized. How would you respond to gang membership if you were incarcerated?

SOURCE: Robert S. Fong, "The Organizational Structure of Prison Gangs: A Texas Case Study," *Federal Probation* (March 1990): 36. Reprinted by permission.

prised of physically powerful correctional officers use their muscle to maintain order and the status quo.

When is force legitimate and how is it distinguished from physically harsh violence that is used as punishment? Correctional officers are expected to follow departmental rules in their dealings with prisoners, yet supervisors are generally unable to observe directly staff-prisoner confrontations. Prisoner complaints about officer brutality are often given little credence until an individual officer gains a reputation for harshness. Still, wardens may feel they must uphold the actions of their officers if they are going to maintain their support. It is often difficult to determine what is *excessive* force in the handling of particular situations.

## Decreasing Prison Violence

Having examined the categories of violence that are prevalent in prison, we must consider what management could do to decrease that violence. We must also look deeply at how institutional structure contributes to that violence and why it must be changed.

### The Role of Management

The importance of prison management in limiting violence should not be downplayed. To be effective, every warden and correctional officer must exercise leadership with a full recognition of the types of people with whom they are dealing, the role of prison gangs, and the structure of institutions.

A more effective prison management that provides few opportunities for attacks may decrease the level of assaultive behavior. John DiIulio argues that no group of inmates is "unmanageable," and "no combination of political, social, budgetary, architectural, or other factors makes good management impossible."[27] He identifies varied institutions, such as the California Men's Colony, New York City's Tombs and Rikers Island, the Federal Bureau of Prisons, and the Texas Department of Corrections (under the leadership of George Beto), where good management practices have resulted in prisons and jails in which inmates can "do time" without fearing for their personal safety. Factors related to prison organization and management were the most important determinants of the violence that occurred in the major prison riots from 1971–1986.[28] Wardens who exert leadership and effectively manage their prisons maintain an environment of governance so that problems do not fester and erupt into violent confrontations.

## The Effect of Institutional Structure

In analyzing prison violence, Lee Bowker lists five contributing factors: (1) inadequate supervision by staff members, (2) architectural design that promotes rather than inhibits victimization, (3) the easy availability of deadly weapons, (4) the housing of violence-prone prisoners near relatively defenseless persons, and (5) a general high level of tension produced by close quarters.[29] In addition, variables such as the physical size and condition of the prison and the relations between inmates and staff have a bearing on violence.

The gray walls of the fortress prison certainly do not create a likely atmosphere for normal interpersonal relationships. In addition, the prison that houses up to three thousand inmates presents problems of crowding and management. The massive scale of some institutions provides opportunities for aggressive inmates to hide weapons, carry out private justice, and engage in other illicit activities free from supervision. As the prison population rises and the personal space of each inmate is decreased, we may expect an increase in antisocial behavior.

The degree to which inmate leaders are allowed to take matters into their own hands may have an impact on the amount of violence among inmates. When prison administrators run a tight ship, security is maintained within the institution so that rapes do not occur in dark corners, "shivs" (knives) are not made in the metal shop, and conflict among inmate groups does not occur. According to James Jacobs, "a prison should be the ultimate exemplar of 'defensible space.' It should be an irreducible and primary principle of prison administration that every inmate is entitled to maximum feasible security from physical attack."[30]

In sum, prisons must be made safe places. Because the state puts offenders there, it has a responsibility to prevent violence and maintain order. These purposes may conflict with the goals of correction and restriction of freedom. If violence is to be excluded from prisons, limitations may have to be placed on movement within the institution, contacts with the outside, and the right to choose one's associates. These measures may seem to run counter to the goal of producing men and women who will be accountable when they return to society.

The public hears about prison riots, such as the hostage-taking in Lucasville, Ohio. It knows little about the inmate-to-inmate violence that is a daily fact of prison life in many institutions.

## Summary

No one wants to live in a prison; but for those who must serve their terms for criminal offenses, it is important to adapt to the pains of incarceration. The loss of freedom, privacy, heterosexual relations, and access to goods are characteristics of inmate society. Whereas solidarity among prisoners was a characteristic of institutions in the past, the convict society of today is more heterogeneous, with the result that inmates form friendship groups along racial, ethnic, and neighborhood lines.

Prisoners desire many goods and services not provided by the state, which has decreed that a life of extreme simplicity is part of the punishment of incarceration. To meet the needs of prisoners, an informal, *sub rosa* economy exists as a major element in the society of captives. With cigarettes as the standard medium of exchange, prison entrepreneurs provide many of the goods desired by their fellow inmates.

There has been less research on institutions for women than on those for men. Researchers have found that social relations among women prisoners are closer and are created more for friendship than for protection. Many women form what have been labeled *pseudofamilies* in prison. A primary distinction between female and male convict societies is a woman's responsibility for her children. Concern about children and how they are being cared for causes stress for incarcerated mothers.

Some prisons have greater levels of violence than others. Prison violence can be classified as violence of one prisoner against another prisoner, of a prisoner against an officer, and of an officer against a prisoner.

Characteristics of the inmates, the quality of governance, and the structure of the institutions have been cited as factors causing violence. Violence can be prevented through the exercise of good management principles to ensure that all inmates are secure.

## Questions for Review

1   What is meant by an adaptive role? Which roles are found in male prison society? In female prison society? How do these roles compare?
2   What is the currency of the inmate economy?
3   In what ways is the convict society in institutions for women different from that in institutions for men?
4   What are the major categories of prison violence?
5   What factors contribute to prison violence?

## Key Terms

inmate code

## For Further Reading

Baunach, Phyllis Jo. *Mothers in Prison*. New Brunswick, N.J.: Transaction Books, 1985. A survey of incarcerated mothers and their relationships with their children.

Earley, Pete. *The Hot House: Life Inside Leavenworth Prison*. New York: Bantam Books, 1992. An eyewitness account of daily life in the United States Penitentiary in Leavenworth, Kansas, written by the first journalist given unlimited access to a maximum security institution of the Federal Bureau of Prisons.

Heffernan, Esther. *Making It in Prison*. New York: Wiley, 1972. One of the few studies examining social relations in a prison for women. Examines the roles of the prisoners and their adaptation to institutional life.

Lockwood, Daniel. *Prison Sexual Violence*. New York: Elsevier, 1980. Analysis of the problem of sexual violence within prisons.

Sheehan, Susan. *A Prison and a Prisoner*. Boston: Houghton Mifflin, 1978. A fascinating description of life in Green Haven Prison and the way one prisoner "makes it" through "swagging," "hustling," and "doing time." It contains an excellent discussion of the inmate economy.

Useem, Bert, and Peter Kimball. *States of Siege: U.S. Prison Riots, 1971–1986*. New York: Oxford University Press, 1989. A survey of prison riots with case studies of the upheavals at Attica, Joliet, Santa Fe, Jackson, and Moundsville. Summary chapters consider the nature and causes of prison riots.

## Notes

1 Michael Knoll, "Going In: The Chain," in *American Corrections*, 3d ed., ed. Todd R. Clear and George F. Cole (Belmont, Calif.: Wadsworth, 1994), 260.

2 Gresham M. Sykes, *The Society of Captives* (Princeton, N.J.: Princeton University Press, 1958), 84–90.

3 John Irwin, *The Felon* (Englewood Cliffs, N.J.: Prentice Hall, 1970), 47.

4 Ibid., 67–79.

5 Ibid., 78.

6 Vergil L. Williams and Mary Fish, *Convicts, Codes, and Contraband* (Cambridge, Mass.: Ballinger, 1974), 50.

7 David B. Kalinich, *Power, Stability, and Contraband* (Prospect Heights, Ill.: Waveland, 1980).

8 Susan Sheehan, *A Prison and a Prisoner* (Boston: Houghton Mifflin, 1978), 90.

9 Joycelyn M. Pollock-Byrne, *Women, Prison, and Crime* (Pacific Grove, Calif.: Brooks/Cole, 1990), 57.

10 Esther Heffernan, *Making It in Prison* (New York: Wiley, 1972), 88.

11 Rose Giallombardo, *Society of Women: A Study of a Women's Prison* (New York: Wiley, 1966), 102–103.

12 Heffernan, *Making It in Prison*, 41–42.

13 James G. Fox, *Organizational and Racial Conflict in Maximum Security Prisons* (Lexington, Mass.: Lexington Books, 1982).

14 Ibid., 100.

15 Ruth M. Glick and Virginia V. Neto, U.S. Department of Justice, National Institute of Law Enforcement and Criminal Justice, *National Study of Women's Correctional Programs* (Washington, D.C.: Government Printing Office, 1977).

16 T. E. Ryan, *Adult Female Offenders and Institutional Programs: A State of the Art Analysis* (Washington, D.C.: National Institute of Corrections, 1984), 24; Ralph Weishet, "Trends in Programs for Female Offenders: The Use of Private Agencies As Service Providers," *International Journal of Offender Therapy and Comparative Criminology* 29 (1985): 35–42.

17 *New York Times*, 30 November 1992, 10.

18  *New York Times*, 27 December 1992, D–3.

19  Phyllis J. Baunach, "You Can't Be a Mother and Be in Prison…Can You? Impacts of the Mother-Child Separation," in *The Criminal Justice System and Women*, ed. Barbara Rafel Price and Natalie J. Sokoloff (New York: Clark Boardman, 1982), 155–169.

20  Virginia V. Neto and LaNelle Marie Bainer, "Mother and Wife Locked Up: A Day in the Family," *Prison Journal* 63 (Autumn–Winter, 1983): 124.

21  U.S. Department of Justice, Bureau of Justice Statistics, *Sourcebook of Criminal Justice Statistics* (Washington, D.C.: Government Printing Office, 1992), 701.

22  Leonore M. J. Simon, "Prison Behavior and the Victim-Offender Relationship Among Violent Offenders," *Justice Quarterly* 10 (September 1993): 503.

23  Marvin Wolfgang and Franco Ferracuti, *The Subculture of Violence* (London: Travistock, 1967), 263.

24  Lee H. Bowker, *Prison Victimization* (New York: Elsevier, 1980), 25.

25  Hans Toch, *Peacekeeping: Police, Prisons, and Violence* (Lexington, Mass.: Lexington Books, 1976), 47–48.

26  U.S. Department of Justice, Office of Legal Policy, *Prison Gangs: Their Extent, Nature, and Impact on Prisons* (Washington, D.C.: Government Printing Office, 1985).

27  John J. DiIulio, Jr., *No Escape: The Future of American Corrections* (New York: Basic Books, 1990), 12.

28  Bert Useem and Peter Kimball, *States of Siege: U.S. Prison Riots 1971–1986* (New York: Oxford University Press, 1989).

29  Lee Bowker, "Victimizers and Victims in American Correctional Institutions," in *Pains of Imprisonment*, ed. Robert Johnson and Hans Toch (Newbury Park, Calif.: Sage, 1982), 62.

30  James B. Jacobs, "Prison Violence and Formal Organization," in *Prison Violence*, ed. Albert K. Cohen, George F. Cole, and Robert G. Bailey (Lexington, Mass.: Lexington Books, 1976), 79.

# Release and Supervision in the Community

After three years, three months, and four days in Stanhope Correctional Facility, Ben Brooks was ready to go before the Board of Parole. He woke with butterflies in his stomach, realizing that at nine o'clock he was to walk into the hearing room to confront a roomful of strangers. As he lay on his bunk he rehearsed the answers to the questions he thought the board members might ask: "How do you feel about the person you assaulted? What have you done with your time while incarcerated? Do you think you have learned anything here that will convince the board that you will follow a crime-free life in the community? What are your plans for employment and housing?" According to prison scuttlebutt, these were the types of questions asked and you had to be prepared to answer that you were sorry for your past mistakes, had taken advantage of the prison programs, had a job waiting for you, and that you planned to live with your family. You had to "ring bells" with the board.

At breakfast, friends dropped by Ben's table to reassure him that he had it made. As one said, "Ben, you've done everything they've said to do. What else can they expect?" That was the problem, *What did they expect*?

At eight-thirty Officer Kearney came by the cell. "Time to go, Ben." They walked out of the housing unit and down the long prison corridors to a group of chairs outside the hearing room. Other prisoners were already seated there. "Sit here, Ben. They'll call when they're ready. Good luck."

At ten minutes past nine the door opened and an officer called, "First case, Brooks." Ben got up, walked into the room. "Please take a seat Mr. Brooks," said the black man seated in the center of the table. Ben knew he was Reverend Perry, a man known as being tough but fair. To his left was a white man, Mr. MacDonald, and to his right a Hispanic woman, Ms. Lopez. The white man led the questioning.

"Mr. Brooks. You were convicted of armed robbery and sentenced to a term of six to ten years. Please tell the board what you have learned during your incarceration."

Ben paused and then answered hesitantly, "Well, I learned that to commit such a stupid act was a mistake. I was under a lot of pressure when I pulled the robbery and now am sorry for what I did."

"You severely injured the woman you held up. What might you tell her if she were sitting in this room today?"

"I would just have to say, I'm sorry. It will never happen again."

"But this is not the first time you have been convicted. What makes you think it will never happen again?"

"Well this is the first time I was sent to prison. You see things a lot differently from here."

Ms. Lopez spoke up. "You have a good prison record—member of the Toastmaster's Club, passed your GED, kept your nose clean. Tell the board about your future plans should you be released."

"My brother says I can live with him until I get on my feet, and there is a letter in my file telling you that I have a job waiting at a meat-processing plant. I will be living in my hometown but I don't intend to see my old buddies again. You can be sure that I am now on the straight and narrow."

"But you committed a heinous crime. That woman suffered a lot. Why should the board believe that you won't do it again?"

"All I can say is that I'm different now."

"Thank you Mr. Brooks," said Reverend Perry. "You will hear from us by this evening." Ben got up and walked out of the room. It had only taken eight minutes yet it seemed like hours. Eight minutes during which his future was being decided. Would it be back to the cell or out on the street? It would be about ten hours before he would receive word from the board as to his fate.

Today, scenes similar to this one still occur, but fewer states maintain parole boards or allow boards the wide discretion of the past. In this chapter we examine the mechanisms for prison release and study the supervision of offenders in the community. We will look especially at the problems confronting offenders as they reenter society. Try to imagine yourself as Ben Brooks. He left Stanhope three weeks after his appearance before the board, having been given transportation back to his hometown, a list of rules to follow, and a date to report to his parole officer. What might his first reaction have been to family, friends, and a community he had not seen in years?

## Questions for Inquiry

- What is parole and how does it operate today?

- What effects do mandatory and discretionary release have on the criminal justice system?

- What programs ease the transition of the offender back to society, and how are ex-offenders supervised in the community?

- What purpose does pardon serve?

- What restrictions does society place on ex-offenders?

## Parole: Reentry into Society

Historically, the term **parole** referred to both a release mechanism and a method of community supervision. Parole has meant the conditional release of a prisoner from incarceration but not from the legal custody of the state. It is still used in this general sense, but since adoption of determinate sentencing in some states (discussed in Chapter 12), we must now distinguish between a release mechanism and supervision. Although releasing mechanisms have changed in many states, most former prisoners are still required to serve a period of time under parole supervision.

Only felons are released on parole; adult misdemeanants are usually released directly from local institutions on expiration of their sentences. Every year more than three hundred thousand convicted felons are released from prison and allowed to live in the community. Until the recent advent of determinate sentencing and guidelines to be followed in release decisions, upward of 85 percent of the persons serving prison sentences were returned to society through the discretionary release decision of the parole board. As shown in Figure 17.1, only 40 percent of releases from state prisons in 1990 resulted from a parole board decision. An increasing number of felons are now returned to society through mandatory release as specified by the terms of their sentences.

**parole**

The conditional release of an inmate from incarceration under supervision after a portion of the prison sentence has been served.

### The Origins of Parole

Parole in the United States evolved during the nineteenth century as a result of the English, Australian, and Irish practices of conditional pardon, apprenticeship by indenture, transportation of criminals from one country to another, and the issuance of "tickets-of-leave" or license. The common denominator of all these methods is the movement of criminals out of prison. In most cases, problems such as overcrowding, unemployment, and the cost of incarceration appear to have motivated the practice rather than any rationale linked to a goal of the criminal sanction.

As early as 1587 England had passed the Act of Banishment, which provided for the movement of criminals and "rogues" to the colonies as laborers for the king in exchange for a pardon. The pardons were initially unconditional, but evolved to become conditional on the completion of a

period of service. In later times, especially during the eighteenth century, English convicts were released and indentured to private persons to work in the colonies until the end of a set term, at which time they were freed.

With the independence of the United States, the English were deprived of a major dumping ground for their criminals, and their prisons soon became overcrowded. The colonizing of Australia met the need for a population outlet and a system was developed to transport criminals down under. Under this system the Australian governor was granted the power to pardon felons. Although unconditional pardons were at first given to offenders with good work records and good behavior, problems arose—as before—and the pardons became conditional, that is, with the requirement that prisoners support themselves and remain within a specific district. This method of parole became known as a "ticket-of-leave." It was similar to the modern concept of parole, except that the released prisoner was not supervised by a government agent.

In the development of parole, the names of Captain Alexander Maconochie and Sir Walter Crofton stand out. Maconochie (see Biography) criticized definite prison terms and devised a system of reward for good conduct, labor, and study. He developed a classification procedure by which prisoners could pass through five stages of increasing responsibility and freedom: (1) strict imprisonment, (2) labor on government chain gangs, (3) freedom within a limited area, (4) a ticket-of-leave or parole resulting in a conditional pardon, and (5) full restoration of liberty. Like modern correctional practices, this procedure assumed that prisoners should be prepared gradually for release.

Although Maconochie's idea of requiring prisoners to earn their early release did not gain immediate acceptance in England, it was used in Ireland, where Crofton had built on Maconochie's idea that an offender's progress in prison and a ticket-of-leave were linked. Prisoners who graduated through Crofton's three successive levels of treatment were released on parole with a series of conditions. Most important, parolees were required to submit monthly reports to the police. In Dublin a special civilian inspector helped releasees find jobs, visited them periodically, and supervised their activities. This concept of assistance and supervision is Crofton's main contribution to the modern system of parole.

## The Development of Parole in the United States

In the United States, parole developed during the prison reform movement of the nineteenth century. Relying on the ideas of Maconochie and Crofton, American reformers such as Zebulon Brockway of Elmira, New York (whose Biography appeared in Chapter 13), began to experiment with the concept of parole. Following New York's adoption of indeterminate sentences in 1876, Brockway started to release prisoners on parole. Under the new sentencing law, prisoners could be released when their conduct during incarceration showed they were ready to return to society. The parole system in New York as originally implemented did not require supervision by the police, as in Ireland; rather, responsibility for assisting the parolees was assumed by private reform groups. With increased use of

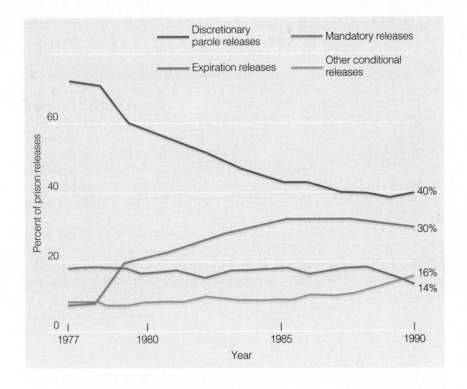

**Figure 17.1**
**Percentage of state prisoners released by various methods, 1977–1990**
With determinate sentences and mandatory release gaining momentum, fewer prisoners are released by parole boards.

SOURCE: U.S. Department of Justice, Bureau of Justice Statistics, *Bulletin* (November 1991), 5.

parole, states replaced the volunteer supervisors with correctional employees who were charged with helping and observing the parolees.

The idea that convicts should be released before they had served a full sentence for their crimes was opposed by many individuals and groups in the United States. Yet by 1900, twenty states had parole systems; by 1932, forty-four states and the federal government had adopted this method. Today all jurisdictions have some mechanism for the release of offenders into the community before the end of their sentences.

Although parole in the United States has been a reality for more than one hundred years, it is still controversial. The general public seems to believe that paroled felons serve much less time than the interests of crime control and justice dictate. These contemporary criticisms have led about half of the states, and the federal government, to restructure their sentencing laws and release mechanisms.

## Release and Release Mechanisms

The use of determinate sentences and parole guidelines (which, like sentencing guidelines, are aimed at limiting discretion) to fix the end of a prisoner's incarceration is referred to as **mandatory release**—mandatory because the correctional authority has little leeway in considering whether the offender is ready to return to society. Determinate sentences are based on the assumption that it is the judge who assigns the offender a specific

**mandatory release**
The required release of an inmate from incarceration upon the expiration of a certain time period, as stipulated by a determinate sentencing law or parole guidelines.

amount of time to serve. Under the older, indeterminate sentencing method, a minimum and maximum period were specified by the judge, allowing the parole board to decide the release date within those limits. With mandatory release the prisoner is automatically discharged to community supervision at the end of the term, less any credited good time.

In states retaining indeterminate sentences, **discretionary release** by the parole board is the manner by which most felons leave prison. This approach is tied to the rehabilitation model and the idea that the parole board should assess the prisoner's fitness for reentry and determine the appropriate release. Discretionary release should be guided by the offender's past, the nature of the offense committed, the inmate's behavior and participation in rehabilitative programs, and the prognosis for a crime-free future.

The formal structures by which felons are released from prison have an enormous impact on other parts of the system: release influences sentencing, plea bargaining, and the size of prison populations. In sum, the actual amount of time that a prisoner serves before release is crucial for maintenance of the links in the criminal justice system.

## The Impact of Discretionary Release on Sentencing

U.S. judges are often said to impose the longest prison sentences in the Western world, but just how much of that time do offenders actually serve? Discretionary release allows an administrative body, the parole board, to shorten a judge's sentence. Even in states that have determinate sentencing or parole guidelines designed to limit discretion, various reductions built into a sentence mean that the full time is rarely served.

To understand the impact of discretionary release on the criminal justice system, we need to compare the amount of time actually served in prison with the sentence specified by the judge. In some jurisdictions up to 80 percent of felons sentenced to prison are released to the community after their first appearance before a parole board. Eligibility for discretionary release is ordinarily determined by the minimum term of the sentence minus good time and jail time. As we have seen, good time allows the minimum sentence to be reduced for good behavior during incarceration or for exceptional performance of assigned tasks or personal achievement. Jail time—credit given for time spent in jail while an offender awaits trial and sentencing—also shortens the period that must be served before an inmate's first appearance before the parole board.

There is considerable variation among the states, but on a national basis it is estimated that felony inmates serve an average of less than two years before release. The amount of time served in prison varies with the nature of the offense. In fact, most people would probably be surprised to learn that the actual time served is much less than the sentences announced in court and in the media.

Figure 17.2 helps to illustrate how the indeterminate sentences, good time, and discretionary release on parole shortened the amount of time that inmates were incarcerated in federal prisons. Although offenders

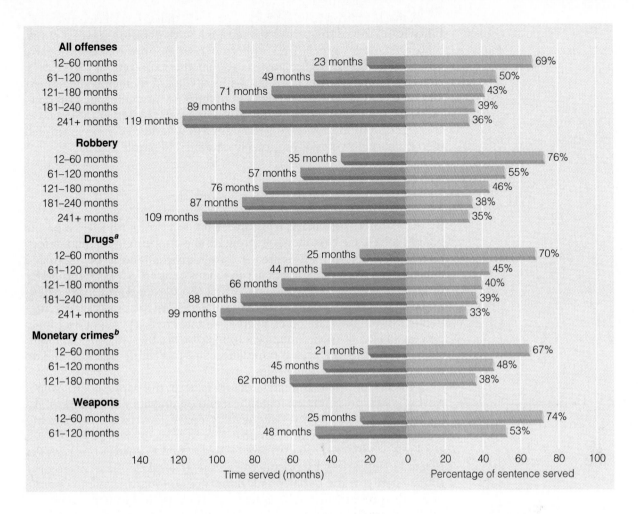

**All offenses**
- 12–60 months: 23 months / 69%
- 61–120 months: 49 months / 50%
- 121–180 months: 71 months / 43%
- 181–240 months: 89 months / 39%
- 241+ months: 119 months / 36%

**Robbery**
- 12–60 months: 35 months / 76%
- 61–120 months: 57 months / 55%
- 121–180 months: 76 months / 46%
- 181–240 months: 87 months / 38%
- 241+ months: 109 months / 35%

**Drugs[a]**
- 12–60 months: 25 months / 70%
- 61–120 months: 44 months / 45%
- 121–180 months: 66 months / 40%
- 181–240 months: 88 months / 39%
- 241+ months: 99 months / 33%

**Monetary crimes[b]**
- 12–60 months: 21 months / 67%
- 61–120 months: 45 months / 48%
- 121–180 months: 62 months / 38%

**Weapons**
- 12–60 months: 25 months / 74%
- 61–120 months: 48 months / 53%

Time served (months) — Percentage of sentence served

who received longer terms did remain in prison for longer periods, note that the percentage of the sentence actually served dropped rapidly as the length of the sentence increased. For example, the robbery offenders who were sentenced to terms of 12 to 60 months actually served 76 percent of their terms; those sentenced to terms of 181 to 240 months actually served only 38 percent. Because a defendant is primarily concerned about when he or she will be freed and because a prosecutor is concerned about a sentence that the public will view as appropriate to the crime but that will still encourage a plea bargain, the impact of parole on the time actually served is in the interests of both sides.

Supporters of discretion for the paroling authority argue that the courts do not adequately dispense justice and that the possibility of parole has invaluable benefits for the system. Discretionary release mitigates the harshness of the penal code, it equalizes disparities inevitable in sentencing behavior, and it assists prison administrators in maintaining order. Supporters also contend that the postponement of sentence determination to the parole stage offers the opportunity for a more detached evaluation than is possible in the trial atmosphere and that early release is economically sensible given the considerable cost of incarceration.

**Figure 17.2**
**Average time served by adults convicted of selected federal offenses**

This figure includes all adult offenders who had their initial hearing between 1 July 1979 and 30 June 1980, and who were released before 1 January 1987 or who had a release date scheduled by the parole commission for a later date. Offenders sentenced to one year or less, and therefore not eligible for parole, are excluded.

SOURCE: Adapted from U.S. Department of Justice, Bureau of Justice Statistics, *Special Report* (June 1987), 4.

[a] Includes marijuana, drug, and controlled substance offenses.
[b] Includes counterfeiting, forgery, mail theft, embezzlement, interstate transportation of stolen securities, and receiving stolen property with intent to sell. Excludes burglary and theft.

A major criticism of the effect of parole is that it has shifted responsibility for many of the primary criminal justice decisions from a judge, who holds legal procedures uppermost, to an administrative board, where discretion rules. In most states that allow discretion, parole decisions are made in secret hearings, with only board members, the inmate, and correctional officers present. Often there are no published criteria to guide decisions, and prisoners are given no reason for either the denial or the granting of their release. We might ask whether such uncontrolled discretionary power is appropriately entrusted to parole boards.

## The Organization of Releasing Authorities

By the statutes they enact, legislatures either grant authority to parole boards to release prisoners or stipulate the conditions for mandatory release by a determinate sentence. Parole boards tend to be organized either as a part of a department of corrections or as an independent agency of government. It has been argued that the parole board must be autonomous so that members can be insulated from the ongoing activities of the institutional staff. Some people feel that an independent decisional process shields the board members from influence by staff considerations, such as reducing the prison population and punishing inmates who do not conform to institutional rules.

Whichever organizational structure is used, the parole board cannot exist in a vacuum, immune to political and organizational influences. An autonomous parole board may develop conflicts with correctional authorities and thus information needed for decision making may be "unavailable" or biased. A board that is closely tied to corrections runs the risk of being viewed by prisoners and the general public as merely the rubber stamp of the department. Both types of boards have to operate under the pressure of public opinion. According to members of one parole board, they had to be very cautious in releasing prisoners because if parolees became involved in further violations of the law, the news media always pointed to the board as having let them out.

Membership on a parole board is often based on the assumption that persons with training in the behavioral sciences are able to discern which candidates have been rehabilitated and are ready to return to society. But in many states political considerations dictate that membership include persons with specific racial or geographical qualifications. In the recent past, for example, the Mississippi board consisted of a contractor, a businessman, a farmer, and a clerk; the Florida board included a journalist, an attorney, and a member with experience in both business and probation; the state of Washington board had persons with training and experience in sociology, government, law, the ministry, and juvenile rehabilitation.

## The Decision to Release

An inmate's eligibility for parole depends on the requirements set by law and the sentence imposed by the court. In the states with determinate

Members of the Massachusetts Board of Parole discuss the possibility of release with a prisoner and his attorney. What factors would you consider if the offender had committed murder? What if the crime was sexual abuse?

sentences or parole guidelines, release from prison to community supervision is mandatory once the offender has served the required amount of time. In these states, mandatory release becomes a matter of bookkeeping to ensure that the correct amount of good time and other credits have been allocated and that the court's sentence has been accurately interpreted so that on expiration of the period, the offender moves automatically into the community. In nearly half the states, however, the decision to release is discretionary, and the parole board has the authority to establish a date on the basis of the sufficiency of rehabilitation and the individual characteristics of each inmate.

As an example of the computation of parole eligibility we may look again at the case of Ben Brooks (see Figure 17.3). At the time of sentencing Brooks had been held in jail for six months awaiting trial and disposition of his case. He was given a sentence of a minimum of five years and a maximum of ten years for robbery with violence. Brooks did well at Stanhope, the maximum security prison to which he was sent. He did not get into trouble and was thus able to amass good time credit at the rate of one day for every four that he spent on good behavior. In addition, he was given meritorious credit of thirty days when he completed his high school equivalency test after attending the prison school for two years. After serving three years, three months, and four days of his sentence, he appeared before the board of parole and was granted release into the community.

In 1933 the American Prison Association asserted that the prisoner's fitness for reentry to the community should determine the release time.

Has the institution accomplished all that it can for him; is the offender's state of mind and attitude toward his own difficulties and problems such that further residence will be harmful or beneficial; does a suitable

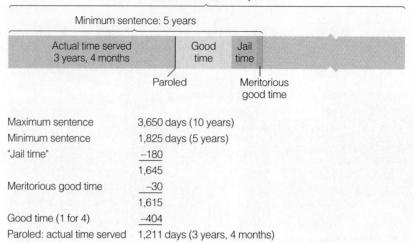

**Figure 17.3**
**Computing parole eligibility for Ben Brooks**
Various good time reductions to the minimum sentence are allowed in most correctional systems. Note how a five-to-ten year sentence can be reduced to a stay of three years, four months.

| | |
|---|---|
| Maximum sentence | 3,650 days (10 years) |
| Minimum sentence | 1,825 days (5 years) |
| "Jail time" | −180 |
| | 1,645 |
| Meritorious good time | −30 |
| | 1,615 |
| Good time (1 for 4) | −404 |
| Paroled: actual time served | 1,211 days (3 years, 4 months) |

environment await him on the outside; can the beneficial effect already accomplished be retained if he is held longer to allow a more suitable environment to be developed?[1]

Although parole boards may subscribe to these principles, the nature of the criteria presents difficulties that cannot be resolved by "hard" data. Some boards have used prediction tables specifying the qualities of an inmate that have been shown over time to correlate with parole success. Not only has the reliability of these data been questioned, but also civil liberty claims have been raised on the ground that the described characteristics do not account for individual differences.

What criteria guide board members as they determine whether inmates can be released? Although a formal statement of standards may list elements such as inmates' attitudes toward their families, their insights into the causes of their past conduct, and the adequacy of their parole plan, the decision is a discretionary act that is probably based on a combination of information and moral judgment. It is frequently said that parole boards release only good risks, but as one parole board member has said, "There are no good-risk men in prison. Parole is really a decision of when to release bad-risk persons."[2] Other considerations, such as internal prison control and morale, public sentiment, and the political implications of their decisions, weigh heavily on board members.

**How to Win Parole**   "If you want to get paroled, you've got to be in a program." This statement reflects one of the most controversial aspects of the rehabilitation model: the link between treatment and discretionary release. Penal authorities emphasize the voluntary nature of most treatment services, clinicians argue that therapy cannot be successful in a coercive atmosphere, yet some parole boards clearly link release to participation in rehabilitative programs. This link causes serious legal and ethical problems, as illustrated by the case of Jim Allen in A Question of Ethics.

Although we may reject the idea that program participation should be a consideration for release, the fact remains that inmates believe they must "play the game" in order to build a record that will look good when they go before the board. Most parole boards stipulate that an inmate's institutional adjustment, including participation and progress in self-improvement programs, is one of the criteria to be considered in a release decision. A Connecticut inmate noted, "The last time I went before the board they wanted to know why I hadn't taken advantage of the programs. Now I go to A.A. and group therapy. I hope they will be satisfied." Playing the "parole board game" may be the dominant motivation for much of the inmate participation in prison programs.

Many offenders come up for parole only to find either they have not done enough to satisfy the board or they have been in the wrong program. This problem may be due to changes in board personnel or to the limited number of places in the educational and rehabilitative programs in American prisons. Offenders report that they often must wait long periods before they can gain admission to a program that fits their needs or that will impress the board.

**Structuring Parole Decisions**   In response to the criticism that the release decisions of parole boards are somewhat arbitrary, many states have adopted parole guidelines to assist their members. As with other guidelines, there is a "severity scale" that ranks crimes according to their seriousness and a "salient factor" score that is based on the offender's characteristics (drug arrests, prior record, age at first conviction, and so on) as they are thought to relate to successful completion of parole (see Tables 17.1 and 17.2). By placing the offender's salient factor score next to his or her particular offense on the severity scale, the board, the inmate, and correctional officials may calculate the **presumptive parole date** soon after the offender enters prison. That is the date by which the inmate can expect to be released if there are no problems during incarceration. The presumptive release date may be modified on a scheduled basis. The date of release may be advanced because of good conduct and superior achievement, or it may be postponed if there are disciplinary infractions or a suitable community supervision plan is not developed.

## A Question of Ethics

The five members of the parole board questioned Jim Allen, an offender with a long history of sex offenses involving teenage boys. Now approaching forty-five and having met the eligibility requirement for a hearing, Allen respectfully answered the board members.

Toward the end of the hearing, Richard Edwards, a dentist who had recently been appointed to the board, spoke up:

"Your institutional record is good, you have a parole plan, a job has been promised, and your sister says she will help you. All of that looks good, but I just can't vote for your parole. You haven't attended the behavior modification program for sex offenders. I think you're going to repeat your crime. I have a thirteen-year-old son, and I don't want him or other boys to run the risk of meeting your kind."

Allen looked shocked. The other members had seemed ready to grant his release.

"But I'm ready for parole. I won't do that stuff again. I didn't go to that program because electroshock to my private area is not going to help me. I've been here five years of the seven-year max and have stayed out of trouble. The judge didn't say I was to be further punished in prison by therapy."

After Jim Allen left the room, the board discussed his case. "You know, Rich, he has a point. He has been a model prisoner and has served a good portion of his sentence," said Brian Lynch, a long-term board member. "Besides we don't know if Dr. Hankin's program works."

"I know, but can we really let someone like that out on the streets?"

Are the results of the behavior-modification program for sex offenders relevant to the parole board's decision? Is the purpose of the sentence to punish Allen for what he did or for what he might do in the future? Would you vote for his release on parole? Would your vote be the same if his case had received media attention?

**presumptive parole date**
The presumed release date stipulated by parole guidelines should the offender serve time without disciplinary or other incidents.

| | Criminal History/Risk Factor | Points | Score |
|---|---|---|---|
| A | No prior felony convictions as an adult or juvenile: | 3 | |
| | One prior felony conviction: | 2 | |
| | Two or three prior felony convictions: | 1 | |
| | Four or more prior felony convictions: | 0 | _____ |
| B | No prior felony or misdemeanor incarcerations (that is, executed sentences of ninety days or more) as an adult or juvenile: | 2 | |
| | One or two prior incarcerations: | 1 | |
| | Three or more prior incarcerations: | 0 | _____ |
| C | Verified period of three years conviction-free in the community prior to the present commitment: | 1 | |
| | Otherwise: | 0 | _____ |
| D | Age at commencement of behavior leading to this incarceration was _____: Date of birth was ____/____/____. | | |
| | Twenty-six or older and at least one point received in A, B, or C: | 2 | |
| | Twenty-six or older and no points received in A, B, or C: | 1 | |
| | Twenty-one to under twenty-six and at least one point received in A, B, or C: | 1 | |
| | Twenty-one to under twenty-six and no points received in A, B, or C: | 0 | |
| | Under twenty-one: | 0 | _____ |
| E | Present commitment does not include parole, probation, failure to appear, release agreement, escape, or custody violation: | 2 | |
| | Present commitment involves probation, release, agreement, or failure to appear violation: | 1 | |
| | Present commitment involves parole, escape, or custody violation: | 0 | _____ |
| F | Has no admitted or documented substance abuse problem within a three-year period in the community immediately preceding the commission of the crime conviction: | 1 | |
| | Otherwise: | 0 | |
| | Total history risk assessment score: | | _____ |

**Table 17.1**
**Criminal history/risk assessment under the Oregon Guidelines for Adult Offenders**
The amount of time to be served is related to the severity of the offense and to the criminal history/risk assessment of the inmate. The criminal history score is determined by adding the points assigned each factor in this table.

SOURCE: Adapted from State of Oregon, Board of Parole, ORS Chapter 144, Rule 255–35–015.

| Offense Severity | Criminal History/Risk Assessment Score | | | |
|---|---|---|---|---|
| | 11–9 Excellent | 8–6 Good | 5–3 Fair | 2–0 Poor |
| *Category 1:* Bigamy, criminal mischief I, dogfighting, incest, possession of stolen vehicle | 6 | 6 | 6–10 | 12–18 |
| *Category 2:* Abandonment of a child, bribing a witness, criminal homicide, perjury, possession of controlled substance | 6 | 6–10 | 10–14 | 16–24 |
| *Category 3:* Assault III, forgery I, sexual abuse, trafficking in stolen vehicles | 6–10 | 10–14 | 14–20 | 22–32 |
| *Category 4:* Aggravated theft, assault II, coercion, criminally negligent homicide, robbery II | 10–16 | 16–22 | 22–30 | 32–44 |
| *Category 5:* Burglary I, escape I, manslaughter II, racketeering, rape I | 16–24 | 24–36 | 40–52 | 56–72 |
| *Category 6:* Arson I, kidnapping I, rape II, sodomy I | 30–40 | 44–56 | 60–80 | 90–130 |
| *Category 7:* Aggravated murder, treason | 96–120 | 120–156 | 156–192 | 192–240 |
| *Category 8:* Aggravated murder (stranger-stranger, cruelty to victim, prior murder conviction) | 20–168 | 168–228 | 228–288 | 288–life |

## Supervision in the Community

Parolees are released from prison on the condition that they do not further violate the law and that they live according to rules designed both to help them readjust to society and to control their movements. These rules may require them to abstain from alcoholic beverages, to avoid bad associates, to maintain good work habits, and not to leave the state without permission. The restrictions are justified on the ground that people who have been incarcerated must gradually readjust to the community with its many temptations and not resume their preconviction habits and associations. This orientation creates problems not only for parolees but also for the administration of community treatment programs. Does the attempt to impose standards of conduct on parolees that are not imposed on law-abiding persons serve a purpose?

When they are first released from prison, the personal and material problems of parolees are staggering. In most states they are given only clothes, a token amount of money, a list of rules governing their conditional release, and the name and address of the parole supervisor to whom they must report within twenty-four hours. Although a promised job is often a condition for release, actually becoming employed may be another matter. Most ex-convicts are unskilled or semiskilled, and the conditions of parole may restrict them from moving to areas where jobs may be available. If the parolee is an African-American male and under thirty, he joins the largest group of unemployed in the country, with the added handicap of having ex-convict status. In most states, laws prevent former prisoners from being employed in certain types of establishments—where alcohol is

**Table 17.2**
**Number of months to be served before release under the Oregon Guidelines**

The presumptive release date is determined by finding the intersection of the criminal history score (Table 17.1) and the category of the offense. Thus an offender with an assessment score between 6 and 8, convicted of a category 3 offense, could expect to serve between 10 and 14 months.

SOURCE: Adapted from State of Oregon, Board of Parole, ORS Chapter 144, Rule 255–75–026 and Rule 255–75–035.

sold, for example—thus placing many jobs automatically off limits. In many trades, union affiliation is a requirement for employment, and there are restrictions on the admission of new members. The situation of the newly released parolee has been described as follows:

> He arrives without a job in an urban area, after years in prison, with perhaps $20 or $30 in his pocket. Surviving is a trick, even if he's a frugal person, not inclined to blow his few dollars on drinks and women. The parole agents—with some remarkable exceptions—don't give a damn. He's deposited in the very middle of the city, where all he can find is a fleabag hotel in the Tenderloin. He has an aching determination to make it on the outside, but there are hustlers all over him; gambling con games, dollar poker.[3]

Reentry problems are very real to parolees; for many, the transition from the highly structured prison life to the open society proves too difficult to manage. Many parolees just do not have the social, psychological, and material resources to adequately cope with the temptations and complications of modern life.

## Community Programs Following Release

Programs have been developed to assist parolees with their reentry to society. Some programs provide employment and housing assistance in the community following release. Other prerelease programs prepare the prisoner for life in the community through evaluation and testing so he or she can steadily move toward reintegration into the community.

In pursuit of prerelease assistance, programs of partial confinement are used to test the readiness of the offender for full release. While the prisoner is still confined, correctional staff ask questions such as the following: "Is it necessary for this offender to be held in a maximum security facility, or is he ready for a less structured environment? With only a year remaining before she appears before the parole board, should this offender be moved to a halfway house? Is work release an option, given the offender's skills?" Notice that community-based corrections assumes that multiple alternatives to incarceration are available; the goal is to choose the least restrictive situation consistent with eventual reintegration.

Among the many programs developed to assist offenders in their return to the community, three are especially important: work and educational release, furloughs, and residential programs. Although they are similar in many ways, each offers a specific approach to helping former inmates reenter the community. This reentry period may be a time of anxiety, as offenders must adjust to societal changes that have taken place while they were in prison. It is believed to be the decisive period with regard to whether the offender returns to crime.

**work and educational release**
The daytime release of inmates from correctional institutions so they may work or attend school.

**Work and Educational Release**   Programs of **work and educational release** were first established in Vermont in 1906, but the Huber Act, passed by the Wisconsin legislature in 1913, is usually cited as the model on which such programs are based. By 1972 most states and the federal government had release programs that allowed inmates to enter the community during the day to work or attend school and to return to the institution at night. Although most of the programs are justifiable in terms of rehabilitation, many correctional administrators and legislators like them because of their lower costs. In some states, a portion of the inmate's employment earnings may be deducted for room and board. One problem of administering the programs is that the person on release is often viewed by other inmates as being privileged, and such perceptions can lead to social discord within the prison. Another problem in some states is that, according to organized labor, jobs are being taken from free citizens. Furthermore, the releasee's contact with the community increases the chances of contraband being brought into the institution. To deal with such bootlegging and to assist in the reintegration process, some states and counties have built special work and educational release facilities in urban areas.

**Furloughs**   Isolation from loved ones is one of the pains of imprisonment. Although conjugal visits have been a part of correctional programs in many countries, they are rare in the United States. Many penologists view the **furlough** as a meaningful alternative. Consistent with the focus of community corrections, brief home furloughs have increased in the United States. In some states efforts are made to ensure that all eligible inmates may have furlough privileges on Thanksgiving and Christmas. In other states, however, the program has been much more restrictive, and often only those about to be released are given furloughs.

Furloughs are thought to be an excellent test of an inmate's ability to cope with the larger society. Through home visits, family ties can be renewed and the tensions of confinement lessened. Most administrators also feel that furloughs are good for a prisoner's morale. To the detriment of the program, the general public is sometimes outraged when an offender on furlough commits another crime or fails to return. The "Willie Horton" syndrome, in which a furloughed offender commits a heinous crime while in the community (which became an issue in the 1988 presidential election), makes correctional authorities nervous about using furloughs.

**Residential Programs**   The **community correctional center** is an institution designed to reduce the inmate's isolation from community services, resources, and support. It may take several forms and serve a variety of offender clients. Halfway houses, prerelease centers, and correctional service centers can be found throughout the country. Most require offenders to live there, although they may work in the community or visit with their families. Others are designed primarily to provide services and programs for parolees. Often these facilities are established in former private homes or small hotels, which permit a less institutional atmosphere. Individual rooms, group dining rooms, and other homelike features are maintained whenever possible.

*Halfway Houses*   The term **halfway house** has been applied to a variety of community correctional facilities and programs. Halfway houses range from secure institutions in the community with programs that assist inmates preparing for release on parole to shelters where parolees, probationers, or persons diverted from the system live with minimal supervision

**furlough**
The temporary release of an inmate from a correctional institution for a brief period, usually one to three days, for a visit home. Such programs are designed to maintain family ties and prepare inmates for release on parole.

**community correctional center**
An institution, usually located in an urban area, that houses inmates soon to be released. Such centers are designed to help inmates establish community ties and thus promote their reintegration with society.

**halfway house**
A correctional facility housing convicted felons who spend a portion of their day at work in the community but reside in the halfway house during nonworking hours.

In community correctional centers offenders released from prison are able to obtain assistance as they adjust to life in the free world.

and direction. Some halfway houses are organized to deliver special treatment services, such as programs that deal with alcohol, drug, or mental problems.

There are no data on the number of halfway houses in the United States or on the number of clients housed in them. In the early 1980s there were approximately eight hundred halfway houses, most operated under contract by private organizations. Their average capacity was twenty-five residents, who stayed eight to sixteen weeks on average.[4] There are three models of release or transfer to halfway houses, as shown in Figure 17.4.

*Problems of Residential Programs*  Not unexpectedly, few neighborhoods want halfway houses or treatment centers for convicts; community resistance has been a primary obstacle and has forced the closing of many facilities. Community corrections, along with programs to deinstitutionalize mental patients and the retarded, has become a major political issue. Many communities, often wealthier ones, have succeeded in blocking placement of halfway houses or treatment centers within their boundaries. One result of this "not in my backyard" attitude is that often the only available facilities are in deteriorating neighborhoods inhabited by the poor, who do not have the same amount of political power or experience as wealthier neighborhoods. But can a center in a poor neighborhood adequately assist a former offender?

The future of residential programs is unclear. Originally advocated for both rehabilitative and financial reasons, they do not seem to be realizing the expected economies. Medical care, education, vocational rehabilitation, and therapy are expensive; it can probably be said that the costs of quality community programs differ little from the costs of incarceration. If recidivism rates of offenders who have been involved in community treatment were proven to be lower, the expenditures might more readily be justified; but the available data are discouraging. For example, one evaluation of a federal prerelease guidance center found a recidivism rate of 37 percent among its clients versus a 32 percent rate among a control group. It seems that the excitement and optimism of the community correctional movement may have been unwarranted.

Community corrections assumes that ex-offenders will be reintegrated into society. In the United States that reintegration is accomplished primarily through government programs such as those described above and through supervision by a parole officer, not necessarily through the "community" itself. By contrast, as the Comparative Perspective on pages 604–605 reveals, citizens in Japan provide assistance to ex-offenders on a voluntary basis. This approach seems to harken back to the idea of probation's founder, John Augustus (see Chapter 14), that citizens should provide guidance and friendship to offenders.

## Parole Officer: Cop or Social Worker?

After release, a parolee's principal contact with the criminal justice system is through the parole officer. The officer is responsible for seeing that the conditions imposed by the parole board are followed. The conditions imposed by Connecticut's Board of Parole are quite substantial and not atypical:

1 Upon release from the institution, you must follow the instructions of the institutional parole officer (or other designated authority of

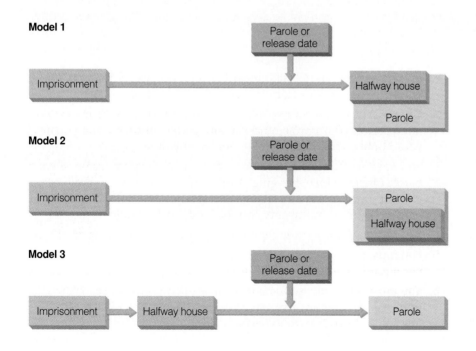

**Model 1**

Imprisonment → Parole or release date → Halfway house → Parole

**Model 2**

Imprisonment → Parole or release date → Parole / Halfway house

**Model 3**

Imprisonment → Halfway house → Parole or release date → Parole

**Figure 17.4**
**Three models of prison release or transfer to a halfway house**
The offender may be released on parole either directly to a halfway house (model 1) or into a community where a halfway house is available should the parolee need its services (model 2). In an increasingly popular alternative (model 3), the halfway house is a way station where the offender stays before being released on parole.

SOURCE: Edward Latessa and Harry Allen, "Halfway Houses and Parole: A National Assessment," *Journal of Criminal Justice* 10 (1982): 156. Copyright © 1982. Reprinted by permission of Elsevier Science, Ltd., The Boulevard, Langford Lane, Kidlington OX5 IGB, UK.

## Community Corrections in Japan

Probation, parole, and aftercare services in Japan are characterized by the extensive participation of community volunteers. When Japan reorganized its correctional services after World War II, it was argued that probation and parole should be developed along the lines of common law countries. The new organization was to be a combination of professional staff and *hogoshi*, volunteer probation workers. A shortage of funds precluded an expanded professional service, and there was a historical record of volunteer services that had contributed to the rehabilitation of offenders. Japan also had a tradition of voluntary social welfare systems firmly rooted in the community. The Offender's Rehabilitation Law called on all people to "render help, in accordance with their position and ability, in order to achieve the goals (of rehabilitation of offenders, etc.)." With passage of the Volunteer Probation Officer Law in 1950, people were nominated to serve in this capacity. They were charged with helping offenders to rehabilitate themselves in society and with fostering a constructive public attitude that would help to promote crime prevention.

Today, 47,000 volunteers work on an individual basis with the two to ten cases assigned to them and are supervised by about 800 professional probation officers. Appointed for two-year terms, vol-

the Division of Parole) with regard to reporting to your supervising parole officer, and/or fulfilling any other obligations.

2 You must report to your parole officer when instructed to do so and must permit your parole officer or any parole officer to visit you at your home and place of employment at any time.

3 You must work steadily, and you must secure the permission of your parole officer before changing your residence or your employment, and you must report any change of residence or employment to your parole officer within twenty-four hours of such change.

4 You must submit written reports as instructed by your parole officer.

5 You must not leave the state of Connecticut without first obtaining permission from your parole officer.

6 You must not apply for a motor vehicle operator's license, or own, purchase, or operate any motor vehicle without first obtaining permission from your parole officer.

unteers are assigned according to their place of residence to one of 764 "rehabilitation areas." The volunteers in each area form an association of officers that is nationally linked to provide for volunteer solidarity, to coordinate training, and to gain resources.

Volunteer officers are from a variety of backgrounds. The largest group (23 percent) comes from such primary industries as agriculture, fishing, and forestry. The second largest category (18 percent) is comprised of individuals officially classified as unemployed but composed mainly of homemakers and the retired. Religious professionals comprise the next largest category. Only five percent of the officers are lawyers, doctors, and other professionals, somewhat in contrast to the community activities of this group in Western countries. Although there is a diversity of backgrounds, most volunteers are middle class.

The volunteer probation officer regularly meets a client at home and also visits the client's family. The volunteer continues to observe the offender in these contacts and tries to advise, assist and support him or her. Assistance is also given to the offender's family, with due respect to the dignity and freedom of the individual. Sometimes the volunteer has to visit the client's place of employment. The greatest concern of the volunteer is how to maintain client contact while at the same time keeping the offender's criminal background from the knowledge of neighbors and employers. The frequency of contact with the client is generally twice a month, but in special cases it occurs almost every day. Volunteers feel they should be readily available to their clients and their families, even during weekends or late at night in case of emergency, particularly in remote areas where professional services are few.

The volunteer probation service in Japan is believed to have unique merits lacked by the professional officer. The nonofficial nature of the relationship between volunteer and offender is thought to be positive. It is believed that through this relationship the offender can regain self-respect and identify with the law-abiding culture. Another merit is the "local" nature of the volunteers. As members of the community where their clients live they know the particular setting and local customs.

The Japanese approach to probation and parole is quite different from the United States. Perhaps it would only be successful in a country where there is not great cultural diversity and where community pressures are a major aspect of social control.

SOURCE: From Yasuyoshi Shiono, "Use of Volunteers in the Non-Institutional Treatment of Offenders in Japan," *International Review of Crime Policy* 27 (1969): 25–31. Reprinted by permission from Kenichi Nakayama, "Japan," in *Major Criminal Justice Systems*, 2d ed., ed. George F. Cole, Stanislaw Frankowski, and Marc G. Gertz (Newbury Park, Calif.: Sage, 1987), 168. Copyright © 1987 by Sage Publications, Inc. Reprinted by permission.

7  You must not marry without first obtaining written permission from your parole officer.

8  You must not own, possess, use, sell, or have under your control at any time, any deadly weapons or firearms.

9  You must not possess, use, or traffic in any narcotic, hallucinatory, or other harmful drugs in violation of the law.

10  You must support your dependents, if any, and assume toward them all moral and legal obligations.

11  (A) You shall not consume alcoholic beverages to excess. (B) You shall totally abstain from the use of alcoholic beverages or liquors. (Strike out either A or B, leaving whichever clause is applicable.)

12  You must comply with all laws and conduct yourself as a good citizen. You must show by your attitude, cooperation, choice of associates, and places of amusement and recreation that you are a proper person to remain on parole.

Parole officers have the dual responsibilities of providing assistance to and supervision of their clients.

Huge caseloads make effective supervision practically impossible in some states. A national survey has shown that parole caseloads range from fifty to seventy—smaller than probation caseloads, but former inmates require more extensive services.

Parole officers are asked to play two different roles: cop and social worker. As police officers, they are given the power to restrict many aspects of the parolee's life, to enforce the conditions of release, and to initiate revocation proceedings if violations occur. Like other officials in the criminal justice system, the parole officer has extensive discretion in low-visibility situations. In many states, parole officers have the authority to search the parolee's house without warning, to arrest him or her without the possibility of bail for suspected violations, and to suspend parole pending a hearing before the board. This authoritative component of the parole officer's role can provoke insecurity in the ex-offender and hamper the development of mutual trust, which is important to the parole officer's other roles in assisting the parolee's readjustment to the community. They must act as social workers by helping the parolee find a job and restore family ties. Parole officers must be prepared to serve as agent-mediators between parolees and the organizations they deal with and to channel them to social agencies, such as psychiatric clinics, where they can obtain help. As caseworkers, parole officers must be able to develop a relationship that allows parolees to feel free to confide their frustrations and concerns. Because parolees are not likely to feel secure if they are constantly aware of the parole officer's ability to send them back to prison, some researchers propose separating the conflicting responsibilities of cop and social worker. Parole officers could maintain the supervisory role and other persons could perform the casework functions. Alternatively, parole officers could be charged solely with the social work role while local police check for violations.

The parole officer works in a bureaucratic environment. In addition, the difficulties faced by many parolees are so complex that the officer's job is difficult. Like most other human service organizations, parole supervision departments are short on resources and expertise. That means they must classify parolees, giving priority to those most in need. Consequently, most parole officers spend more time with the newly released than with those who have been in the community longer. As the officer gains greater confidence in the parolee, the level of supervision can be adjusted to "active" or "reduced" surveillance. Depending on how the parolee has functioned in the community, only check-in periods may be required.

## On the Outside

The reentry problems of parolees are reflected in their rearrest rates. As shown in Figure 17.5, about 25 percent are arrested during the first six months; almost 40 percent within the first year; and 62 percent within three years.[5] About 40 percent of those rearrested will be reincarcerated. With little preparation, the ex-offender moves from the highly structured, authoritarian life of the institution into a world filled with temptations, complicated problems requiring immediate solutions, and unfamiliar responsibilities. The parolee must change roles, suddenly becoming not only an ex-convict but also a worker, parent, spouse, and son or daughter. The expectations, norms, and social relations in the free world are quite different from those learned under the threat of institutional sanction. The parolee's adjustment problems are not only material but also social and psychological. Some problems that parolees encounter when they reenter the community are illustrated in the Close-Up on pages 608–609. As you read about Lloyd Nieman's experience, ask yourself what could have made the difference for him.

It is perhaps not surprising that the recidivism rate, the percentage of former offenders who return to criminal behavior after release, is so high given that the average felon who has served time in prison has been convicted of serious crimes (83 percent for violent or property offenses) and has a criminal record of multiple arrests (8.4 prior arrests) and prior incarcerations (67 percent).[6] Few who have run afoul of the law only once can be characterized as situational offenders; instead, most prisoners have committed serious crimes and have a long history of difficulties with the criminal justice system. A large percentage of today's inmates are career criminals who will resume their old habits upon release.

## Revocation of Parole

Always hanging over the ex-inmate's head is the potential revocation of parole for either committing a crime or failing to live according to the rules of the parole contract. Because the paroled person still has the status of inmate, some scholars believe that parole should be easily revoked without adherence to due process or the rules of evidence. In some states, liberal parole policies have been justified to the public on the ground that revocation is swift and can be imposed before a crime is committed. For example, according to some state statutes if the parole officer has a reasonable cause to believe that the parolee has lapsed, or is probably about to lapse, into criminal activity or company or has violated parole conditions, then these suspicions should be reported to the parole board so that the parolee can

**Figure 17.5**
**Cumulative percentage of state prisoners rearrested, reconvicted, and reincarcerated thirty-six months after release**
The first year after release is the period of greatest probability for recidivism.

SOURCE: U.S. Department of Justice, Bureau of Justice Statistics, *Special Report* (April 1989).

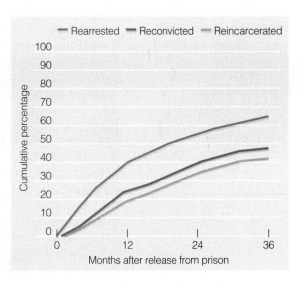

# On His Own

Lloyd Nieman is white and thirty-six years old. He has served two separate terms for forgery and had been on parole for a short time when interviewed. A professional musician, Lloyd was reared by his mother, who worked in a factory. His friends have usually been cons. He attended school through the eighth grade only, which he has regretted most of his life. Although the story itself is more than twenty years old, the problems remain the same. Only the amount of money that parolees receive has changed a bit.

The first few days I was out were about the roughest days of this entire period. I've only been out a short time—five weeks—but the first three days was a hassle . . . no money, no transportation, no job, and no place to live. Now these things have a way of working themselves out in time, but you have to contact the right people, and sometimes it's hard to find the right people. I was lucky enough to make a contact with a fellow at the Service Center and he gave me enough money to tide me over out of a fund that they had. . . .

I was lucky that I had two friends here, too, that could help me. Nick gave me a place to stay, because I was out of money within four days. They give you $60, and out of that you got to buy your own clothes, and I couldn't just move in without paying something, so I gave him $25, you know, for room and board. He didn't want it, but I think there's a lot of guys getting out that don't particularly want charity. They like to pay their own way. Even a convict's got pride.

I'd met Nick four or five times, and he kind of gave me a little coming home party. There was several people there that we'd call "squares." But he explained the whole thing to them and they just kind of accepted me as a person. They didn't shy away from me because I was an ex-con. Everybody was very nice, very friendly. They didn't go out of their way to please, but they were just comfortable, nice. I think that's a big thing, being able to be comfortable.

I put in several job applications when I first got out, and I went through the ex-con bit on the applications. In fact, I thought about going back to music, so I joined a musicians union. I was hired and fired by a club in twenty minutes because I was an ex-con.

Job training is a farce, as far as the institutions are concerned. I was a musician, but they want you to have a manual trade, so they recommended silk screening, which is fine. I have no objection to silk screening, you know. . . . I might as well learn something while I'm

---

be apprehended. The parolee who leaves the state or has been charged with a new offense is usually detained by an arrest warrant until a revocation hearing or a criminal trial is held.

If the parole officer alleges that a technical (noncriminal) violation of the parole contract has occurred, a revocation proceeding will be held. The U.S. Supreme Court, in the case of **Morrissey v. Brewer** (1972), distinguished the requirements of such a proceeding from the normal requirements of the criminal trial but held that many of the due process rights must be accorded the parolee.[7] The Court has required a two-step hearing process whereby the parole board determines whether the contract has been violated. Parolees have the right to be notified of the charges against them, to know the evidence against them, to be heard, to present witnesses, and to confront the witnesses against them.

The number of parole revocations is difficult to determine because the published data do not distinguish between parolees returned to prison for technical violations and those incarcerated for new criminal offenses. Given today's crowded prisons, most revocations occur only after arrest on a serious charge or when the parolee cannot be located by the parole officer. Because of their large caseloads, most parole officers can-

**Morrissey v. Brewer** (1972)
According to due process rights, a prompt, informal inquiry before an impartial hearing officer is required before parole may be revoked. The parolee may present relevant information and question adverse information.

there.... "You got to have this for the [Parole] Board," they say. Well ... all of a sudden, they have an opening at camp. So they send me to camp and tell me, "This training isn't really necessary. You don't need it to go to the Board." They need bodies up at camp, so it's not a question of what's good for you, but of what's good for the institution.

Now I'm at State College on the EOP [Equal Opportunities Program]. Whoever thought I'd go to college at thirty-six? I'm having a hard time studying [because] I've been away from it for so long a time that nothing seems to sink in. Well, I'm going after my B.A., and we'll work on an M.A. from there. But I want to make it through education. I really do.

Financially, I'm not too bad off. I've got enough money now for about another six weeks, and I hope to get a job to supplement that income. I have a few friends and, right now, things are pretty good.

When I was in the joint, I kind of thought I might have to go back to hanging paper [forgery]. I thought, "I'm not going to get what I want. I'll probably go out and get a job. I don't want to go back to playing in the bars if I can get away from it because I think that's part of my problem." I have always put on a front. I have an eighth grade education and the institution should be proud of the fact that I am in college.

But if this [college] had not come to pass, I probably would have gone back to work in the bars and associate with the middle-class crowd or the high-paid bracket crowd, and invariably, I would go to cashing checks to keep up this front, you know.

I didn't expect it to turn out as well as it has. It's getting better all the time. My major disappointment is trying to do too many things too fast and realizing that I can't. The time that you're locked up is gone, you know, and you want to do all the things you've missed. When you get out, you're three or four years behind, or whatever it happens to be, and you try to make these things up. It's a disappointment when you find out that you can't do it, that it's going to take you a while to catch up. You got to go slow.

I have mixed emotions. I'm happy to be out, but I have a thing about being my own man. I realize it is necessary, but I do resent a parole officer telling me what I can do and what I cannot do. I believe that every man is different, every case is different, and there can be no set policy.

*Lloyd didn't make it. Shortly after his interview, he jumped parole and left the state. A year later, he still had not been located.*

SOURCE: Adapted from R. J. Erickson, W. J. Crow, L. A. Zurcher, and A. V. Connett, *Paroled But Not Free* (New York: Behavioral Publications, 1973), 17–21. Copyright © 1973 by Behavioral Publications. Reprinted by permission of Human Services Press, Inc.

not maintain close scrutiny over parolees and, therefore, are unaware of technical violations. Under the new requirements for prompt and fair hearings, parole boards are discouraging the issuance of violation warrants following infractions of parole rules without evidence of serious new crimes.

The effectiveness of corrections is usually measured by the percentage of former offenders who return to criminal behavior after release. It is perhaps not surprising that the recidivism rate is high given that in today's correctional environment, most prisoners have committed serious crimes and have a long history of difficulties with the criminal justice system.

## The Future of Parole

As prison populations rise, demands that felons be allowed to serve part of their time in the community will undoubtedly mount. In states with discretionary release, parole provides one of the few mechanisms available to correctional officials to relieve institutional pressures. In many states where mandatory release is the way out of prison, offenders nearing expiration of their terms are being moved to community facilities so that they can begin the reintegration process.

## Pardon

**pardon**

An action of the executive branch of state or federal government excusing an offense and absolving the offender from the consequences of the crime.

References to **pardon** are found in ancient Hebrew law, and in medieval Europe the church and the monarchies had the power of clemency. Pardon later became known as the "royal prerogative of mercy" in England.

Pardons are executive acts. In the United States, the president or the state governor may grant clemency in individual cases. In each state the executive receives recommendations from the state's board of pardons (often combined with the board of parole) concerning individuals who are thought to be deserving of the act. Pardons serve three main purposes: (1) to remedy a miscarriage of justice, (2) to remove the stigma of a conviction, and (3) to mitigate a penalty. Although full pardons for miscarriages of justice are rare, from time to time society is alerted to the story of some individual who has been released from prison after it has been discovered that he or she was incarcerated by mistake. The more typical activity of pardons boards is to expunge the criminal records of first-time offenders— often young people—so they may enter those professions whose licensing procedures bar former felons, may obtain certain types of employment, and in general will not have to bear the stigma of a single indiscretion.

## Civil Disabilities of Ex-Felons

In theory, once a person has been released from prison, paid a fine, or been discharged from parole or probation, the debt to society is paid and the punishment ended. For many offenders, however, a criminal conviction is a lifetime burden. In most states it is not enough to have served time, to have reestablished family ties, to have gotten a job, and otherwise to have become a law-abiding member of the community; certain civil rights are forever forfeited, some fields of employment may never be entered, and some insurance or pension benefits may be foreclosed.

The extent of civil disabilities varies greatly among the states. In some states, persons who have been convicted of certain crimes are subjected to specific restrictions; forgery, for example, prevents employment in banking or stock-trading fields. In other states, blanket restrictions are placed on all felons regardless of the circumstances of the crime. These restrictions are removed only upon completion of the sentence, after a period subsequent to completion of the sentence, or upon action of the board of pardons. The forfeiture of rights can be traced to the ancient Greeks and Romans, and American courts have generally upheld the constitutionality of such restrictions.

The right to vote and to hold public office are two civil rights that are generally limited upon conviction. Three-fourths of the states return the right to vote after varying lengths of time, while the remainder remove felons from voting lists unless they are pardoned or they apply for the restoration of full citizenship. Nineteen states permanently deny felony offenders the right to hold public office unless pardoned or given back their full citizenship, and twenty-one states return the right following discharge from probation, parole, or prison. Other civil rights such as eligibility to serve on juries and access to public employment are denied felons in many states.[8]

Although most former felons may not believe that restrictions on their civil rights will make it difficult for them to lead normal lives, limitations on entry into certain fields of employment are a problem. As we have seen, many prison vocational programs that promote rehabilitation lead to occupations that may bar former offenders. Occupations that currently restrict the entry of former offenders include nurse, beautician, barber, real estate agent, chauffeur, employee of a place that serves alcoholic beverages, cashier, stenographer, and insurance agent. As Richard Singer has noted, "In all, nearly six thousand occupations are licensed in one or more states; the convicted offender may find the presumption against him either difficult or impossible to overcome."[9] Many observers assert that the restrictions force offenders into menial jobs at low pay and may indirectly lead them back to crime.

Some states provide no procedures for the restoration of rights, others provide discretionary mechanisms—often through the pardoning process—for the expunging of a criminal conviction after the passage of time. But it has not been absolutely determined whether or not a person may legally deny a previous conviction on an employment application even after the conviction has been expunged.

Critics of civil disability laws argue that upon fulfilling the penalty imposed for a crime, the former offender should be assisted to full reintegration into society. They claim that it is counterproductive for government to promote rehabilitation with the goal of reintegration while at the same time preventing offenders from fully achieving that goal. Others, however, say that the possibility of recidivism and the community's need for protection justify these restrictions. In the middle are those who believe that not all persons convicted of felonies should be treated equally and that society can be protected adequately by placing restrictions on only certain individuals.

## Summary

Inmates return to society primarily through release on parole, which is conditional release from incarceration but not from supervision. Parole in the United States evolved as a result of English, Australian, and Irish practices that allowed offenders to leave prison and live in the community under supervision. Today we can distinguish between mandatory release, when offenders leave prison at the end of their determinate sentence minus good time, and discretionary release, when the parole board may decide that release to the community is appropriate.

Parolees are released from prison on the condition that they do not further violate the law and that they live according to rules designed both to help them readjust to society and to control their movements. Parole officers supervise releasees and may request revocation of the parole if the ex-offender is arrested or violates the rules.

Upon release, offenders face a number of problems: they must find housing and employment and reforge links to family and friends. Community corrections assumes that reentry should be a gradual process and that services should be provided to those parolees who require assistance. Halfway houses, work and educational release, furloughs, and community correctional centers are geared to ease the transition. In some states prerelease counseling programs help prisoners prepare for situations that they will face on the street.

Society places restrictions on many ex-felons. State and federal laws prevent offenders from entering certain professions and occupations. The right to vote and hold public office is generally denied to ex-felons. Some offenders are able to obtain pardons for their crimes and have their civil rights reinstated, usually after successfully completing their time on parole.

## Questions for Review

1  What are the basic assumptions of parole?
2  What is the difference between mandatory release and discretionary release?
3  What is the role of the parole officer?
4  What problems confront parolees upon their release?

## Key Terms and Cases

community correctional center

discretionary release

furlough

halfway house

mandatory release

pardon

parole

presumptive parole date

work and educational release

*Morrissey* v. *Brewer* (1972)

## For Further Reading

Glaser, Daniel. *The Effectiveness of a Prison and Parole System*. New York: Bobbs-Merrill, 1964. A classic study of the links between incarceration and parole.

McCleary, Richard. *Dangerous Men: The Sociology of Parole*, 2d ed. Albany, N.Y.: Harrow and Heston, 1992. A study of the bureaucracy of parole supervision.

Rhine, Edward E., William R. Smith, and Ronald W. Jackson. *Paroling Authorities: Recent History and Current Practice*. Laurel, Md.: American Correctional Association, 1991. Results of a national survey conducted by the ACA Task Force on Parole.

Stanley, David. *Prisoners Among Us*. Washington, D.C.: Brookings Institution, 1975. Still the only major published account of parole release decision making. The book emphasizes parole board discretion.

Von Hirsch, Andrew, and Kathleen J. Hanrahan. *The Question of Parole*. Cambridge, Mass.: Ballinger, 1979. Examines parole from the "just deserts" perspective and urges its reform.

## Notes

1   As quoted in Edwin H. Sutherland and Donald R. Cressey, *Criminology* (Philadelphia: Lippincott, 1970), 587.

2   As quoted in Donald J. Newman, "Legal Models for Parole: Future Developments," in *Contemporary Corrections*, ed. Benjamin Frank (Reston, Va.: Reston Publishing Company, 1973), 246.

3   As quoted in Jessica Mitford, *Kind and Usual Punishment* (New York: Knopf, 1973), 217.

4   Edward Latessa and Harry Allen, "Halfway Houses and Parole: A National Assessment," *Journal of Criminal Justice* 10 (1982): 156. See also Edward J. Latessa and Lawrence F. Travis, III, "Residential Community Correctional Programs," in *Smart Sentencing*, ed. James M. Byrne, Arthur J. Lurigio, and Joan Petersilia (Newbury Park, Calif.: Sage, 1992), 166.

5   U.S. Department of Justice, Bureau of Justice Statistics, *Special Report* (April 1989).

6   Ibid.

7   *Morrissey* v. *Brewer*, 408 U.S. 471 (1972).

8   Velmer S. Burton, Jr., Francis T. Cullen, and Lawrence F. Travis, III, "The Collateral Consequences of a Felony Conviction: A National Study of State Statutes," *Federal Probation* 51 (September 1987): 52–60.

9   Richard Singer, "Conviction: Civil Disabilities," in *Encyclopedia of Crime and Justice*, ed. Sanford H. Kadish (New York: Free Press, 1983), 246.

# The Juvenile Justice System

**Crimes committed** by juveniles are a serious national problem. The *Uniform Crime Reports* show that just over a third of the people arrested for an index crime are under eighteen years of age. Children who are charged with crimes, who have been neglected by their parents, or whose behavior is deemed to require official action enter the juvenile justice system, an independent process that is interrelated with the adult system. As Chapter 18 will demonstrate, many of the procedures used in handling juvenile problems are similar to those used with adults, but the overriding philosophy of juvenile justice is somewhat different, and the extent to which the state may intrude into the lives of children is much greater.

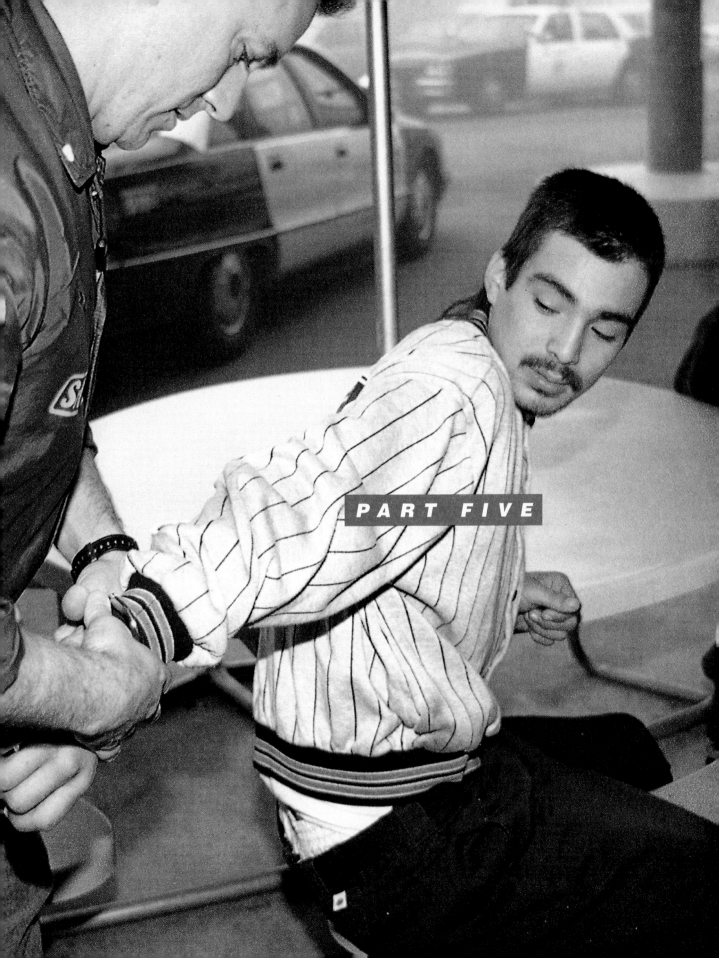

PART FIVE

# Juvenile Justice

At 10:00 A.M. on Monday, 8 June 1964, fifteen-year-old Gerald Gault and his friend Ronald Lewis were taken into custody by the sheriff of Gila County, Arizona, on the complaint of a neighbor about a telephone call to her in which the caller had made lewd and indecent remarks. On her arrival from work late that afternoon, Gerald's mother became alarmed that her son was not home. Neighbors told her that the sheriff's car had been at the house earlier in the day. Because Gerald was on probation as a result of an incident in January 1964, when he had been apprehended in the company of another youth who had stolen a woman's purse, Mrs. Gault anxiously called the sheriff's office and learned that her son was being held at the Children's Detention Home for appearance in Juvenile Court the following day.

At hearings conducted before Judge McGhee on June 9 and 15, Gerald said that he had only dialed the number and that Lewis had done the talking. Attending the hearings were only Gerald, his parents, Judge McGhee, and probation officers Flagg and Henderson. The proceedings were informal, no one was sworn, no transcript was made, and no record was prepared. Mrs. Gault asked why the complaining neighbor was not present "so she could see which boy had done the talking." The judge said her presence was not necessary. The only other item that played a role in the hearing was a "referral report" filed with the court by the probation officers; none of the three Gaults was told what it said.

After the hearing, Judge McGhee announced that he was committing Gerald as a juvenile delinquent to the state industrial school "for the period of his majority [that is, until the age of twenty-one] unless sooner discharged by due process of law." Had he been an adult, the maximum punishment for such a telephone call would have been a fine of five to fifty dollars or imprisonment for not more than two months. As a minor, Gerald Gault was committed to the state school for six years.

With the aid of Amelia Lewis, an attorney and member of the Arizona Civil Liberties Union, the Gaults appealed the decision on the ground that the safeguards of due process had not been accorded. They stated that the juvenile court had not given them adequate notice of the nature of the charges and the hearing; had not advised them of their constitutional rights, including the right to counsel, the right to confront witnesses, and the privilege against self-incrimination; had not made a record of the proceedings; and had used hearsay testimony from unsworn witnesses.

Appealing to the U.S. Supreme Court, Mr. and Mrs. Gault argued that their son had not been accorded the procedural guarantees required by the due process clause of the Fourteenth Amendment. Before focusing on these rights, their brief examined the historical background of juvenile court systems. It argued that *parens patriae*—the legal concept that the state may intervene to protect the welfare of children—had been substituted for procedural due process and had resulted in detrimental effects on many children in juvenile proceedings. Although conceding that the juvenile court movement had led to advances in the treatment accorded juveniles, the brief went on to say that "juvenile court proceedings, which were instituted to protect the young, led in many jurisdictions to findings of delinquency in proceedings that conspicuously failed to protect the child." It further reasoned that neither *parens patriae* nor the theory that a juvenile proceeding was a civil matter dealing with treatment rather than punishment could justify "the refusal to accord Gerald Gault and other juveniles the protection of the Bill of Rights."

On 15 May 1967, almost three years after Gerald Gault had first been sent to the Children's Detention Home, the U.S. Supreme Court reversed the Arizona decision. In its decision *In re Gault* the justices held that a child in a delinquency hearing must be afforded certain procedural rights, including notice of charges, right to counsel, right to confrontation and cross-examination of witnesses, and protection against self-incrimination. Writing for the majority, Justice Abe Fortas emphasized that due process rights and procedures adhere to juvenile justice. "Under our Constitution the condition of being a boy does not justify a kangaroo court."[1] The opinion went on to specify that juveniles had (1) the right to notice, (2) the right to counsel, (3) the right to confront witnesses, (4) the privilege against self-incrimination, (5) the right to transcripts, and (6) the right to appellate review.

Of the two dissenters, Justice Potter Stewart expressed a more traditional conception of juvenile justice:

Juvenile proceedings are not criminal trials. They are not civil trials. They are simply not adversary proceedings. Whether treating a delinquent child, a neglected child, a defective child, or a dependent child, a juvenile proceeding's whole purpose and mission is the very opposite of the mission and purpose of a prosecution in a criminal court. The object of the one is correction of a condition. The object of the other is conviction and punishment for a criminal act.[2]

The Supreme Court decision points to a constant tension within the juvenile justice system between the view that children should be given all the due process guarantees accorded adults and the view that children must be handled in a less adversarial, more treatment-oriented manner so that legal procedures will not interfere with efforts to secure the justice that is in the children's best interest. But since the mid-1960s there has been a trend to "criminalize" the American juvenile court. As noted by Barry Feld, juvenile court procedures increasingly resemble those of adult courts; changes have altered the juvenile justice system's jurisdiction over serious youth offenders who are transferred to adult criminal courts; and the justice system increasingly punishes youths for their offenses rather than treats them for their "real needs."[3]

Readers may wonder why a chapter on juvenile justice appears in this book, which has focused primarily on the justice system that deals with crimes committed by adults. The juvenile justice system is a separate but interrelated part of the broader criminal justice system. While the formal processes of juvenile justice differ from those in the adult system, the differences primarily concern emphasis. Whether involved in policing, courts, or corrections, one cannot be divorced from the problems of youth. With juveniles committing a significant portion of criminal law violations, serious attention must be paid to this system.

## Questions for Inquiry

- What is the extent of youth crime in the United States?
- How did the juvenile justice system develop and what were its assumptions?
- What determines the jurisdiction of the juvenile justice system?
- How does the juvenile justice system operate?
- What are some of the problems facing the American system of juvenile justice?

## Youth Crime in the United States

In Denver a child visiting the zoo was hit by a bullet intended by one teenager for another. A seventeen-year-old Salt Lake City boy was kicked and then shot to death by a group of his fellow high school students. A

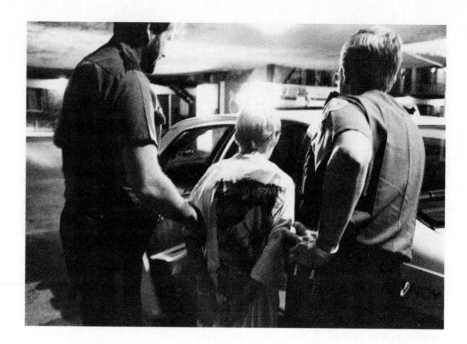

Violence committed by juveniles has become a major national problem. What factors lead young persons, such as this 13-year-old, to attack their parents or other people?

British tourist was killed while at a rest stop; a thirteen-year-old boy was one of the suspects.[4] Such dramatic criminal acts make headlines, but are these only isolated incidents or is the United States facing a major increase in youth crime?

To a great extent, crime in the United States is a phenomenon of youth. Fewer than 12 percent of Americans are aged fifteen to twenty-one, yet this cohort accounts for 31.3 percent of all arrests for violent index crimes and 46.9 percent of all arrests for property index crimes (see Figure 18.1). It is estimated that about one in twenty in the cohort is taken into police custody each year. In all, almost two million juveniles under eighteen years are arrested each year; nearly a million were processed by juvenile courts. Most juvenile crimes are committed by young males; only 24 percent of arrestees under eighteen years of age were females in 1992. The youthfulness of persons prone to crime is underscored by two other facts: about one-third of those arrested each year are under twenty-one and about half are under twenty-five. Some researchers have estimated that one boy in three will be arrested by the police at some point before his eighteenth birthday. More tragic is the fact that homicide is now the leading cause of death for African-American males aged fourteen to forty-four.[5]

The contemporary concern about drugs and its associated violence has again focused attention on juveniles. Data supplied by the National Council of Juvenile and Family Court Judges show that drug abuse is a problem in 60 to 90 percent of the cases referred to them.[6] Although surveys of high school students show that drug use is declining, there remain young people who are either drug users or heavily involved in the sale of drugs. A study of four hundred detained juveniles in Florida showed that 41 percent tested positive for drug use. Of those who tested positive for cocaine, 51 percent were rearrested or referred to juvenile authorities for a property misdemeanor within eighteen months of the testing.[7] The homicide rate among young, urban males engaged in turf battles over drug sales is alarming.

The presence of youth gangs in most large American cities has also focused attention on juvenile crime. There have been periods in the past when gang violence has rocked cities, but during the past twenty years there has been increased gang activity among youth. Gangs such as the Black P Stone Nation, Crips, and Bloods came to police attention in the 1970s, and as Robert Dart, commander of the Gang Section of the Chicago Police Department has written, gangs began to form alliances with other gangs, "not unlike NATO and the (former) Soviet bloc alliances."[8] During the past decade, gangs in many American cities have "spread their wings from a few city blocks of turf into the suburbs inhabited by people who had fled the high-crime cityscape years earlier."[9] Many of the gangs that are now apparent in the adult correctional system have their younger counterparts on the streets. Today's gangs have become a major element in the drug trade with the resulting crimes of violence.

Juvenile delinquency, neglect, and dependency have been concerns since the beginning of the Republic, yet it was not until the early twentieth century that a separate system to deal with these problems evolved. The contemporary juvenile justice system has gone through a major shift of emphasis, as we will see in the next section.

## The Development of Juvenile Justice

The 1967 *Gault* decision was the first major challenge to a system and philosophy of juvenile justice that had its inception in the United States during the late-nineteenth-century period of social reform. The idea that

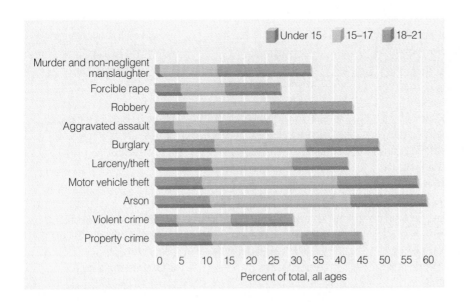

**Figure 18.1**
**Percentage of arrests of persons under twenty-one years**
Although they make up fewer than 12 percent of the population, those age fifteen to twenty-one are arrested for index crimes out of proportion to their numbers. Property offenses are those most often committed by young people, although the number of violent crimes committed by this group is rising.

SOURCE: U.S. Department of Justice, *Crime in the United States* (Washington. D.C.: Government Printing Office, 1993), 233.

children should be treated differently from adults, however, originated in the common law and in the chancery courts of England. The common law had long prescribed that children under seven years of age were incapable of felonious intent and were therefore not criminally responsible. Children aged seven to fourteen could be held accountable only if it could be shown that they understood the consequences of their actions.

Under the doctrine of *parens patriae*, which held the king to be the father of the realm, the chancery courts exercised protective jurisdiction over all children, particularly those involved in questions of dependency, neglect, and property. These courts, however, had civil jurisdiction, and juvenile offenders were dealt with by the criminal courts. But the concept of *parens patriae* was important for the development of juvenile justice, for it legitimized the intervention of the state on behalf of the child.

The English procedures were maintained in the American colonies and continued into the nineteenth century. The earliest attempt by a colony to deal with problem children was passage of the Massachusetts Stubborn Crime Law in 1646. With this law, the theocratic Massachusetts Bay Colony imposed the view that the child was evil and emphasized the need of the family to discipline and raise youths. Those who would not obey their parents were dealt with by the law.

**Table 18.1**
**Juvenile justice developments in the United States**

SOURCE: Adapted from U.S. Department of Justice, *A Preliminary National Assessment of the Status Offender and the Juvenile Justice System*, (Washington, D.C.: Government Printing Office, 1980), 29; Barry Krisberg, Ira M. Schwartz, Paul Litsky, and James Austin, "The Watershed of Juvenile Justice Reform," *Crime and Delinquency* 32 (January 1986): 5–38.

| Period | Major Developments | Causes and Influences | Juvenile Justice System |
|---|---|---|---|
| Puritan 1646–1824 | Massachusetts Stubborn Child Law (1646) | A Puritan view of child as evil<br>B Economically marginal agrarian society | Law provides:<br>A Symbolic standard of maturity<br>B Support for family as economic unit |
| Refuge 1824–1899 | Institutionalization of deviants; House of Refuge in New York established (1825) for delinquent and dependent children | A Enlightenment<br>B Immigration and industrialization | Child seen as helpless, in need of state intervention. |
| Juvenile Court 1899–1960 | Establishment of separate legal system for juveniles; Illinois Juvenile Court Act (1899) | A Reformism and rehabilitative ideology<br>B Increased immigration, urbanization, large-scale industrialization | Juvenile court institutionalized legal irresponsibility of child. |
| Juvenile Rights 1960–1980 | Increased "legalization" of juvenile law; *Gault* decision (1967); Juvenile Justice and Delinquency Prevention Act (1974) calls for deinstitutionalization of status offenders | A Criticism of juvenile justice system on humane grounds<br>B Civil rights movement by disadvantaged groups | Movement to define and protect rights as well as to provide services to children. |
| Crime Control 1980–present | Concern for victims, punishment for serious offenders, transfer to adult court of serious offenders, protection of children from physical and sexual abuse | A More conservative public attitudes and policies<br>B Focus on serious crimes by repeat offenders | System more formal, restrictive, punitive; increased percentage of police referrals to court; incarcerated youths stay longer periods. |

As outlined in Table 18.1, there have been shifts in how the United States has dealt with the problems of youth. During the eighteenth, nineteenth, and twentieth centuries five periods can be defined, each characterized by changes in juvenile justice that reflect the social, intellectual, and political currents of the time. During the past two hundred years, population shifts from rural to urban areas, massive immigration, developments in the social sciences, political reform movements, and the continuing problem of youth crime have all influenced how Americans have treated juveniles. We touched on the Puritan period above; next we examine the refuge period.

## The Refuge Period (1824–1899)

As the population of American cities began to grow in the half century following independence, the problem of youth crime and neglect was a concern for reformers. Just as the Quakers of Philadelphia had been instrumental during the early 1800s in reforming correctional practices, other groups supported changes to educate and protect youths. These reformers focused their efforts primarily on the urban immigrant poor and sought to have parents declared "unfit" if their children roamed the streets and were apparently "out of control." It was not that the children were engaged in criminal acts (although many were), but the reformers believed that children who were not disciplined and trained by their parents to abide by the rules of society would eventually find themselves in prison. The state's power was to be used to prevent delinquency. The solution was to create institutions for these children where they could learn good work and study habits, live in a disciplined and healthy environment, and develop "character."

The first of these institutions was the House of Refuge of New York, which opened in 1825. It was followed by similar facilities in Boston, Philadelphia, and Baltimore. Children were placed in these homes by court order usually because of neglect or vagrancy. They often stayed there until they reached the age of majority.

Recognizing the right of the state to place children in such institutions, the Pennsylvania Supreme Court in 1838 upheld the doctrine of *parens patriae* in a suit brought by a father objecting to the commitment of his daughter (by his wife without his knowledge) to the Philadelphia House of Refuge on the ground that she was "incorrigible." The court said that the courts as guardians of the community could supersede the desires of the natural parents when they were unequal to the task of rearing a child. If the parents fail to fulfill their responsibility of training their children to be productive, law-abiding adults, the state should assume it

In the nineteenth century some states adopted a parental role and placed young people who were deemed "out of control" into institutions such as reform schools to shape their behavior and "character" into socially acceptable modes.

by training the children "to industry (and) by imbuing their minds with the principles of morality and religion."[10]

Some states created "reform schools" to provide the discipline and education needed by wayward youth in a "homelike" atmosphere, usually in rural areas. The first, the Lyman School for Boys, opened in Westboro, Massachusetts, in 1848. A similar school for girls opened in Lancaster, Massachusetts, in 1855. Ohio created the State Reform Farm in 1857, and the states of Maine, Rhode Island, New York, and Michigan soon followed suit.

At the same time that some groups were advocating creation of reform schools, other groups, such as the Children's Aid Society of New York, were emphasizing the need to place neglected and delinquent children in private homes in the country. Like the reform advocates of adult corrections, the children's aid societies of the 1850s emphasized placement in rural areas, away from the crime and bad influences of the city. The additional hands thus acquired provided an economic incentive for farmers to "take in" these juveniles.

## The Juvenile Court Period (1899–1960)

With services to neglected youth widely established in most states by the end of the nineteenth century, juvenile criminality became the focus of attention during the next reform period. Members of the Progressive movement sought to use the power of the state to provide individualized care and treatment to deviants of all kinds—adult criminals, the mentally ill, juvenile delinquents. They pushed for adoption of probation, treatment, indeterminate sentences, and parole for adult offenders and were successful in establishing similar programs for juveniles.

Referred to as the "child savers," these upper-middle class reformers sought to use the power of the state to "save" children from a life of crime.[11] They were stimulated by a concern over the influence of environmental factors on behavior, the rise of the social sciences, which claimed they could treat the problems underlying deviance, and a belief that benevolent state action could rectify social problems.[12]

Juvenile delinquency created a dilemma for the state. The reformers argued that the state could either deal with young accused persons under the adult criminal law, calling upon its full powers to prosecute, try, sentence, and imprison them, or it could refrain from such strictness and merely return them to their parents and the community; both options were viewed as poor policy for juveniles and for society. It was argued that a separate juvenile court system was needed where the problems of individual youth could be treated in an atmosphere in which flexible procedures would, as one reformer said, "banish entirely all thought of crime and punishment."[13] With this stimulus, the Progressives pushed for, and were successful in creating the juvenile court.

Passage of the Juvenile Court Act by Illinois in 1899 established the first comprehensive system of juvenile justice. The act placed under one jurisdiction cases of dependency, neglect, and delinquency ("incorrigibles and children threatened by immoral associations as well as criminal lawbreakers") for children under sixteen. Activists such as Jane Addams and Julia Lathrop, of the settlement house movement, Henry Thurston, a social work educator, and the National Congress of Mothers were successful in promoting the juvenile court concept, so that by 1904 ten states had implemented procedures similar to those of Illinois, and by 1920 all but three states provided for a juvenile court.

Undergirding the philosophy of the juvenile court was the idea that the state should deal with a child who broke the law much as a wise parent would deal with a wayward child. The doctrine of *parens patriae* again helped legitimize the system. Procedures were to be informal and private, records were to be confidential, children were to be detained apart from adults, and probation and social worker staffs were to be appointed. Even the vocabulary and physical surroundings of the juvenile system were changed to emphasize diagnosis and treatment rather than findings of guilt. The term *criminal behavior* was replaced with *delinquent behavior* as it pertained to the acts of children. This shift in terminology underscored the view that although these children were wayward, they could be returned to society as law-abiding citizens. But the new term also emphasized that the juvenile court could deal with behaviors that were not criminal if committed by adults, such as smoking cigarettes, consensual sexual activity, truancy, or living a "wayward, idle, and dissolute life—activities that previously might have been ignored but that the Progressives wished to end because it betokened premature adulthood."[14]

By separating juveniles from the adult criminal justice system and providing them with a rehabilitative alternative to punishment, the juvenile courts rejected not only the criminal law's jurisprudence but also its due process protections. Because procedures were not to be adversarial, lawyers were unnecessary; psychologists and social workers, who could determine the juvenile's underlying behavior problem, were the main professionals attached to the system. Judge Julian Mack (see the Biography), a pioneer of the juvenile justice movement, summarized the questions to be placed before a juvenile court: "The problem for determination by the judge is not, has this boy or girl committed a specific wrong, but what is he, how has he become what he is, and what had best be done in his interest and in the interest of the State to save him from a downward career."[15]

Although the child savers may have been imbued with good intentions, contemporary scholars have noted that the reforms (1) expedited traditional policies rather than created alternatives, (2) assumed the natural dependence of juveniles, (3) maintained a paternalistic approach to youths, and (4) promoted correctional programs designed to inculcate middle-class values and lower-class skills.[16] These reforms were instituted in a system where children lacked the due process rights held by adults.

### The Juvenile Rights Period (1960–1980)

Until the 1960s, the ideology and practices of juvenile justice were dominated by the philosophy expressed by Judge Mack. Very few people questioned the necessity for the sweeping powers given to juvenile justice officials. Then, in the early 1960s, with the due process revolution

challenging the treatment of adult defendants, lawyers and scholars began to criticize the extensive discretion exercised by juvenile justice officials. In essence they believed that the juvenile justice system had failed to fulfill its promise.[17]

Appeals to the U.S. Supreme Court of juvenile court decisions began to grow. In *Kent* v. *United States* (1966) the Court extended due process rights to children. In this case a sixteen-year-old boy was remanded from the juvenile to the adult court without his lawyer present. He was convicted of rape and robbery in the adult court and sentenced to a thirty to ninety year prison term. The Supreme Court found the procedure of transferring the case to the adult court wanting and said that the discretion exercised by the juvenile court meant that the child received the worst of both worlds: "He [the child] gets neither the protections accorded adults nor the solicitous care and treatment postulated for children."[18] The Court ruled that juveniles had the right to counsel at a *waiver hearing*—where a juvenile judge may waive jurisdiction and pass the case to the adult court.

*Kent* was followed by *Gault*, which extended due process rights to juvenile court. In the case of *In re Winship* (1970) the Court held that proof must be established "beyond a reasonable doubt" before a juvenile may be classified as a delinquent for committing an act that would be a crime if it were committed by an adult.[19] Perhaps signifying the extent to which the Court was willing to extend the concept of due process, it held in *McKiever* v. *Pennsylvania* (1971) that "trial by jury in the juvenile court's adjudicative stage is not a constitutional requirement."[20] But in *Breed* v. *Jones* (1975) the Court extended the protection against double jeopardy to juveniles by requiring that before a case is adjudicated in juvenile court, a hearing must be held to determine if it should be transferred to the adult court.[21]

Although the court decisions would seem to have placed the rights of juveniles on a par with those of adults, critics have charged that the states have not fully implemented these rights. The law on the books is different from the law in action. Only thirteen states provide juveniles with a trial by jury;[22] studies of the "beyond a reasonable doubt" requirement have shown that it is still easier to convict in juvenile than in adult court;[23] and "in many states half or less of all juveniles receive the assistance of counsel to which they are constitutionally entitled."[24] The promise of the due process revolution as it applied to juveniles was not fulfilled, yet efforts were made to reform other aspects of the system.

During the civil rights movement efforts to change the juvenile justice system led to the closing of youth correctional institutions in a number of states. Scholars charged that the institutions reinforced delinquent behavior and that too many children were being incarcerated. In 1972, Massachusetts became the first state to close most of its reformatories and place the children in group homes and community treatment centers. Other states less dramatically reduced the number of children held in institutions.

Another area of change concerned status offenders. Status offenders are juveniles who have committed acts that are not illegal if they are committed by an adult. Truancy, running away, or refusing to obey the orders of adults may lead to a correctional term in most states. Congress passed the Juvenile Justice and Delinquency Prevention Act in 1974, which included provisions for the deinstitutionalization of status offenders. Since

---

*In re Winship* (1970)
The standard of proof of beyond a reasonable doubt applies to juvenile delinquency proceedings.

*McKiever* v. *Pennsylvania* (1971)
There is no constitutional right for a jury trial for juveniles.

*Breed* v. *Jones* (1975)
Juveniles cannot be found delinquent in juvenile court and then be waived to adult court without violating double jeopardy.

then efforts have been made to divert such children out of the system, to reduce the possibility of incarceration, and to rewrite **status offense** laws.

As juvenile crime continued to rise during the 1970s, calls were made for tougher approaches in dealing with delinquents. Juvenile justice shifted more directly to crime control policies in the 1980s, parallel to changes in the adult criminal justice system.

**status offense**
Any act committed by a juvenile that is considered unacceptable for a child, such as truancy or running away from home, but that would not be a crime if it were committed by an adult.

## The Crime Control Period (1980–Present)

Much of the reform effort of the 1960s and 1970s focused on infusing the juvenile justice system with due process protections, although juvenile crime continued to be recognized as a serious problem. Since 1980 there has been another revolution in how the United States deals with juvenile offenders. With the public demanding a crackdown on crime, legislators have responded with changes in the system. As Martin Forst and Martha-Elin Blomquist have written, there has been a "renewed interest in public protection, punishment, justice, and accountability."[25]

In *Schall v. Martin* (1984) the Supreme Court significantly departed from the trend toward increased juvenile rights.[26] Noting that any attempt to structure such rights "must be qualified by the recognition that juveniles, unlike adults, are always in some form of custody," the Court confirmed the general notion of *parens patriae* as a primary basis for the juvenile court, equal in importance to the Court's desire to protect the community from crime. Thus juveniles may be detained before trial if they are found to be a "risk" to the community, even though this rationale is not applicable to adult pretrial detention.

*Schall* **v.** *Martin* **(1984)**
Juveniles can be held in preventive detention if there is concern that additional crimes may be committed while awaiting court action.

The *Schall* decision reflects the ambivalence permeating the juvenile justice system. On one side are the liberal reformers, who call for increased procedural and substantive legal protections for juveniles accused of crime; on the other side are the conservatives, who are devoted to crime control policies and alarmed by the rise in juvenile crime. In addition to the Supreme Court, various state courts have considered issues involving the right to treatment, equal protection, and cruel and unusual punishments and have had to acknowledge the vagueness of certain laws affecting juveniles. Greater attention is now being focused on repeat offenders, with policymakers calling for heavier punishment for juveniles who commit crimes. Just as legislators have increased the penalties for adult offenders, juveniles convicted of serious crimes are now spending much longer terms in either youth facilities or adult prisons.

The present crime control policy has resulted in many more juveniles being tried in adult courts. As noted by Alex Kotlowitz, "the crackdown on children has gone well beyond those accused of violent crimes."[27] He notes that between October 1990 and June 1991, 3,248 children were transferred to Florida's adult courts for offenses as serious as murder and as minor as alcohol possession.[28]

Transfer is accomplished either through a **judicial waiver** or by **legislative exclusion**.[29] During a waiver hearing in the past the state had to make a case that the youth was not amenable to rehabilitation in the juvenile system before a transfer to the adult court. Now many states

**judicial waiver**
The juvenile court waives its jurisdiction and transfers the case to the adult criminal court.

**legislative exclusion**
The legislature excludes from juvenile court jurisdiction certain offenses usually either very minor, such as traffic or fishing violations, or very serious, such as murder or rape.

place the burden on the youth to show amenability to treatment.[30] Although many states exclude only murder from juvenile court, others have extended the range to include rape, armed robbery, and other violent crimes.[31]

Public support for a get-tough stance toward older juveniles seems to be growing. The juvenile court, long a bastion of discretion and rehabilitative zeal, has become a system of rules and procedures similar to adult courts. With deserved punishment assuming more prominence as a correctional goal, sentences for juveniles who have been adjudged repeat offenders have become more severe. Before we look at the operations of juvenile justice in the United States, we should examine how Norway deals with youth crime in the Comparative Perspective on pages 630–631.

## The Juvenile Justice System

Juvenile justice operates through a variety of procedures in different states and even in counties within the same states. The offenses committed by juveniles are mostly violations of state laws, so there is very little federal involvement in the juvenile justice system. Still, an overall national pattern can be discerned. In general, the system functions through many of the existing organizations of the state adult criminal justice system but often with specialized structures for juvenile programs. Thus, although some large cities have specialized juvenile sections in their police departments, it is usually the patrol officer who has contact with delinquents when a disturbance or crime has been reported. In many states, special probation officers work with juveniles, but they function as part of the larger probation service. There are even some correctional systems that, although they maintain separate facilities for children, are organized under a commissioner who is responsible for both adult and juvenile institutions.

Even given the differences that exist from state to state or county to county, the juvenile justice system is characterized by two key factors: (1) the age of clients and (2) the categories of cases under juvenile, rather than adult, court jurisdiction. Let us examine each in turn.

**PINS, CINS, JINS**
Acronyms for "person in need of supervision," "child in need of supervision," and "juvenile in need of supervision," which are terms that designate juveniles who are either status offenders or thought to be on the verge of trouble.

**delinquent**
A child who has committed a criminal or status offense.

### Age of Clients

Age normally determines whether a person is processed through the juvenile or adult justice system. The upper age limit for a juvenile varies from sixteen to eighteen: in thirty-eight states and the District of Columbia it is the eighteenth birthday; in eight states, the seventeenth; and in the remainder, the sixteenth. In most states, judges have the discretion to transfer juveniles to adult courts through a waiver hearing. Figure 18.2 shows the age at which juveniles can be transferred to adult court by judicial waiver.

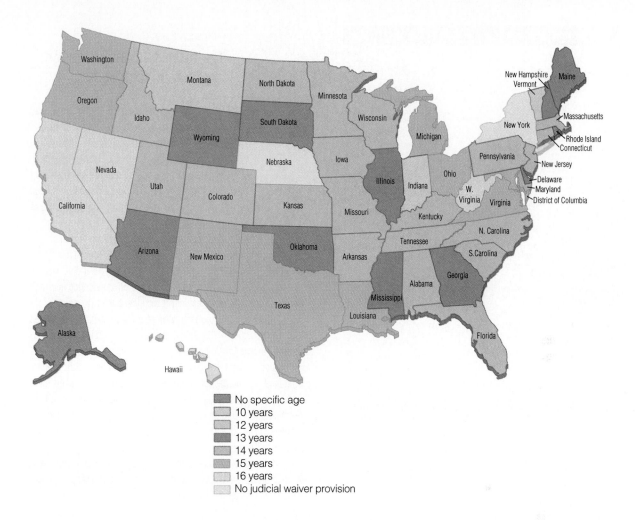

| | No specific age |
| | 10 years |
| | 12 years |
| | 13 years |
| | 14 years |
| | 15 years |
| | 16 years |
| | No judicial waiver provision |

## Categories of Cases under Juvenile Court Jurisdiction

Four types of cases are under the jurisdiction of the juvenile justice system: delinquency, status offenses, neglect, and dependency. Delinquent children have committed acts that if committed by an adult would be criminal—for example, auto theft, robbery, and assault. As we have seen, acts that are illegal only if they are committed by juveniles are known as *status offenses*. Rather than having committed a violation of the penal code, status offenders have been designated as ungovernable or incorrigible: as runaways, truants, or persons in need of supervision (**PINS**).

Some states do not distinguish between delinquent offenders and status offenders and label both as juvenile **delinquents**. Those judged to be ungovernable and those judged to be robbers may be sent to the same correctional institution. Beginning in the early 1960s, many state legislatures attempted to distinguish status offenders and to exempt them from a criminal record. In 1974 Congress required states to remove noncriminal offenders from secure detention and correctional facilities.

**Figure 18.2**
**Youngest age at which juveniles may be transferred to adult criminal court by waiver of juvenile jurisdiction**

The waiver provisions of states vary greatly, and there seems to be no clear regional or other factor that can explain the differences. This inconsistency is perhaps another example of the role of politics in the criminal justice system.

SOURCE: U.S. Department of Justice, Bureau of Justice Statistics, *Sourcebook of Criminal Justice Statistics* (Washington, D.C.: Government Printing Office, 1993), 145.

## The Hidden Juvenile Justice System in Norway

There is no punishment for crimes in Norway for a child who is under fifteen. No special courts have been established with jurisdiction to try criminal cases against juvenile offenders. Older teenagers may be tried in ordinary courts of law and sentenced to prison. Sentences for most crimes, however, consist of only a suspended sentence or probation or several months in an open prison.

In practice, the public prosecutor, who represents the police, will transfer the juvenile case directly to a division of the "social office," the *barnevern*—literally, child protection. Alternatively, the judge, after the trial, will refer the youth to the *barnevern*. Police evidence is turned over to the social workers, not for prosecution, but for "treatment."

The usual first step in treatment is that the *barnevern* takes emergency custody of the child and places the child in a juvenile institution, or *ungdomshjem* (youth home). If the parents or guardians do not give consent, there will be a meeting of the ... child welfare committee. An attorney may represent the parents at this stage; there is no legal fee in serious cases. At the meeting [the social welfare committee] will hear the lawyer's and parents' arguments against the placement. The concern is not with evidence about the crimes but, rather, with appropriate treatment for the child....

The *barnevern* is most often associated in the public mind with handling of cases of child abuse and neglect. In such a case, the board will turn over custody of the child to the *barnevern* social workers who will place the child in a foster home or youth home. Once the custody is removed from the parents, the burden of proof is on the parents to retain custody. Social workers in alcoholism treatment are well aware of numerous such cases of recovering alcoholics who, even after recovery, have been unable to retain custody of their children....

In contrast to the American juvenile court, the Norwegian model is wholly social worker dominated. The function of the judge is to preside over the hearing and to maintain proper legal protocol, but it is the child welfare office that presents the evidence and rec-

The breadth of the law defining status offenses is a matter of concern because the language is often vague and all-encompassing: "growing up in idleness and crime," "engaging in immoral conduct," "in danger of leading an immoral life," "person in need of supervision." A child may be judged incorrigible and therefore delinquent for "refusing to obey the

ommendations and directs the course of the case. The five laypersons who constitute the [social welfare committee] are advised by the child welfare office well before the hearing of the "facts" of the case. Before the hearing, the youth will have been placed in a youth home or mental institution "on an emergency basis"; the parents' rights to custody will have already been terminated.

The process of the hearing itself is thus a mere formality after the fact.... [There] is an overwhelming unanimity among members of the board and between the board and social worker administrators.... [All] the arguments of the clients and of their lawyers [seem to] "fall on deaf ears."...

Proof of guilt brought before the committee will generally consist of a copy of the police report of the offenses admitted by the accused and a school report written by the principal after he or she has been informed of the lawbreaking. Reports by the *barnevern*— appointed psychologist and social worker—are also included. The *barnevern*, in its statement, has summarized the reports from the point of view of its arguments (usually for placement). Otherwise, the reports are ignored.

The hearing itself is a far cry from standard courtroom procedure. The youth and his or her parents may address the board briefly. The attorney sums up the case for a return to the home. Expert witnesses may be called and questioned by the board concerning, for instance, their treatment recommendations.

Following the departure of the parties concerned, the *barnevern* office presents what amounts to "the case for the prosecution." There is no opportunity to rebut the testimony and no opportunity for cross-examination....

Placement in an institution is typically for an indefinite period. No notice of the disposition of the matter is given to the press. This absence of public accountability may serve more to protect the social office than the child.

Children receive far harsher treatments than do adults for similar offenses. For instance, for a young adult first offender the typical penalty for thievery is a suspended sentence. A child, however, may languish in an institution for years for the same offense.

A *barnevern's* first work ought to be to create the best possible childhood. However, the *barnevern* also has a control function in relation to both the parents and the child, and the controller often feels a stronger duty to the community than to the parents and child. The fact of institutionalization of children with behavior problems clearly reflects this social control function. This process has been going on for some time. Approximately half of the 8,174 children under care of the child welfare committee were placed outside the home and the other half placed under protective watch....

The Norwegian *barnevern* is a powerful body vested with the responsibility of child protection. When this department wishes to remove a child from the home, the child welfare committee is called into session. Then with a semblance of legal formality, the decision is put into effect. The child is placed outside the home "until further notice."...

The system of justice for children accused of crimes or behavioral problems is therefore often very harsh in Norway. This is in sharp contrast to the criminal justice system in general, which is strikingly lenient. Where punishment is called *treatment*, however, the right of the state can almost become absolute. The fact that the state is represented by social work administrators creates a sharp ethical conflict for those whose first duty is to the client.

What we see in Norway today is a process of juvenile justice that has not changed substantially since the 1950s. Due to flaws within the system, including the lack of external controls, the best intentions of social workers "have gone awry." Where care and protection were intended, power and secrecy have prevailed. Juvenile justice in Norway today is the justice of America yesterday.

SOURCE: Katherine Van Wormer, "The Hidden Juvenile Justice System in Norway: A Journey Back in Time," *Federal Probation* (March 1990): 57–61.

just and reasonable commands of his or her parents." The jurisdictional net is so broad in many states that almost any child can be described as requiring the protection of the juvenile justice system.

Juvenile justice also deals with problems of neglect and dependency—situations in which children are viewed as being hurt through no

**neglected child**

A child who is not receiving proper care because of some action or inaction of his or her parent(s).

**dependent child**

A child whose parent(s) is unable to give proper care.

fault of their own because their parents have failed to provide a proper environment for them. Such situations have been the concern of most juvenile justice systems since the turn of the century, when the idea that the state should act as a parent to a child whose own parents are unable or unwilling to provide proper care gained attention. Illinois, for example, defines a **neglected child** as one who is neglected as to proper or necessary support, education as required by law, medical or other remedial care recognized under state law, or other care necessary for his well-being; or who is abandoned by his parents, guardians, or custodians; or whose environment is injurious to his welfare; or whose behavior is injurious to his own welfare or that of others. A **dependent child** either is without a parent or guardian or is not receiving proper care because of the physical or mental disability of that person. The jurisdiction here is broad and includes a variety of situations in which the child can be viewed as a victim of adult behavior.

The laws of the state of Connecticut outlining the powers of the juvenile court provide a good example of the range of authority of the system. As the law provides:

Juvenile matters include all proceedings concerning uncared-for, neglected, or dependent children and youth and delinquent children within this state, termination of parental rights of children committed to a state agency, matters concerning families with service needs and contested termination of parental rights transferred from the probate court, but do not include matters of guardianship and adoption or matters affecting property rights of any child or youth over which the probate court has jurisdiction.[32]

**Table 18.2**
**Delinquency and status offenses referred to juvenile court**

The juvenile court is concerned with cases of delinquency, status offenses, and noncriminal matters such as neglect and dependency. Note the distribution of the delinquency and status offense matters in this table.

SOURCE: U.S. Department of Justice, Bureau of Justice Statistics, *Report to the Nation on Crime and Justice*, 2d ed. (Washington, D.C.: Government Printing Office, 1988), 78.

| Percentage of Total Cases Referred | | | |
|---|---|---|---|
| **11% Crimes Against Persons** | | **5% Drug Offenses** | 100% |
| Criminal homicide | 1% | **1% Offenses Against Public Order** | |
| Forcible rape | 2 | Weapons offenses | 6% |
| Robbery | 17 | Sex offenses | 6 |
| Aggravated assault | 20 | Drunkenness and disorderly conduct | 23 |
| Simple assault | 59 | Contempt, probation, and parole violations | 21 |
| | 100% | Other | 44 |
| | | | 100% |
| **46% Crimes Against Property** | | **17% Status Offenses** | |
| Burglary | 25% | Running away | 28% |
| Larceny | 47 | Truancy and curfew violations | 21 |
| Motor vehicle theft | 5 | Ungovernability | 28 |
| Arson | 1 | Liquor violations | 23 |
| Vandalism and trespassing | 19 | | 100% |
| Stolen property offenses | 3 | | |
| | 100% | | |

Cases of child neglect fall within the jurisdiction of the juvenile courts.

Nationally about 75 percent of the cases referred to the juvenile courts are delinquency cases, of which a fifth are concerned with status offenses; about 20 percent are dependency and neglect cases; and about 5 percent involve special proceedings, such as adoption. The system, then, deals with both criminal and noncriminal cases, and a concern has been expressed that juveniles who have done nothing wrong are categorized, either officially or in the public mind, as delinquents. In some states little effort is made in pre-judicial detention facilities or in social service agencies to separate the classes of juveniles. Table 18.2 shows the types of delinquency and status offenses that are referred to juvenile court.

## Juvenile Justice Operations

Underlying the juvenile justice system is the philosophy that the police, judges, and correctional officials should be primarily concerned with the interests of the child. Prevention of delinquency is the system's justification for intervening in the lives of juveniles who are involved in either status or criminal offenses. Action is predicated on the need to prevent further delinquency and a subsequent career as an adult criminal.

Even with the civil rights and crime control changes of the past twenty-five years, it is still assumed that the juvenile proceedings are to be conducted in a nonadversarial environment and that the court should be a place where the judge, social workers, clinicians, and probation officers work together to diagnose the child's problem and select a rehabilitative program to resolve it. As with other aspects of the rehabilitative ideal, officials must exercise discretion.

More discretion is exercised in the juvenile than in the adult justice system. Turn-of-the-century reformers believed that juvenile justice officials should have wide discretion in their efforts to serve the best interests of the child. There are now pressures to narrow the scope of this discretion, yet to a great extent justice is individualized. At the same time, because of the institutional needs of the bureaucracy and the presence of others in the system, juvenile officials must be aware of efficiency, public relations, and the maintenance of harmony and esprit de corps among their underlings.

Juvenile justice is a particular type of bureaucracy that is based on an ideology of social work and is staffed primarily by persons who regard themselves as members of the helping professions. A judge may find in certain cases that the public's demand for punishment conflicts with pressures from probation officers and social workers who blame environmental conditions for deviant behavior and urge treatment for an offender. The juvenile court judge does not have the explicit sanctions described in the criminal law to guide decisions and justify actions.

Like the adult criminal justice system, juvenile justice functions within an organizational and political context in which exchange relationships among officials of various agencies influence decisions. The juvenile court must deal not only with children and their parents but also with patrol officers, probation officers, welfare officials, social workers, psychologists, and the administrators of treatment institutions. These others all have their own goals, their own perceptions of delinquency, and their own concepts of treatment.

## Police Interface

Most complaints against juveniles are brought by the police, although they may be initiated by an injured party, school officials, or even the parents. The police must make three major decisions with regard to the processing of juveniles: (1) whether to take the child into custody, (2) whether to request that the child be detained following apprehension, and (3) whether to refer the child to court.[33]

As might be expected, the police exercise enormous discretion with regard to these decisions. The police do extensive screening and informal adjustment in the street and the station house. In communities and neighborhoods where law enforcement officials have developed close relationships with the residents or where law enforcement policy dictates, the police may deal with violations by warning juveniles and notifying their parents. Figure 18.3 shows that more than half (64.2 percent) of those taken into police custody have their cases referred to the juvenile court; about a third (28.1 percent) are handled within the department and then released; and 7.7 percent are referred to other agencies or to an adult court.

In a study of four communities in the Pittsburgh metropolitan area, a wide variation was found in arrest rates and a corresponding variation in the portion of those arrested who were selected for appearance in juvenile court.[34] Only about half of those who came to the attention of the police for law violations were taken to the station house, and only a small proportion of those officially registered on police records (35.4 percent) were referred to the court for action. Thus whether a child is declared a delinquent is to some extent determined by the police officer in selective reporting of juvenile offenders to the court. This selection process is influenced by the officer's attitude toward the juvenile, the juvenile's family, the offense, and the court; the predominant attitude of the community; and the officer's conception of his or her own role.

In a study of the police in a metropolitan industrial city of 450,000, it was found that the choice of disposition of juvenile cases depended very much on the prior record of the child, but second in importance was the offender's demeanor.[35] Juveniles who had committed minor offenses but were respectful and contrite were defined by the officers as worthy candidates for rehabilitation and were given an informal reprimand. Those who were argumentative or surly were defined as "punks" who needed to be taught a lesson through arrest. The researchers found that only 4 percent of the cooperative youths were arrested in comparison with 67 percent of those who were uncooperative.

To summarize, several key factors influence how the police dispose of a case of juvenile delinquency:

1   The seriousness of the offense.

2   The willingness of the parents to cooperate and to discipline their child.

3   The child's behavioral history as reflected in school and police records.

4   The extent to which the child and his or her parents insist on a formal court hearing.

5   The local political and social norms concerning dispositions in such cases.

Because the law specifies that persons classified as juveniles, usually those under eighteen, be treated differently than adult offenders, and because of the belief that prevention should be a dominant goal of efforts to deal with youth crime, most large police departments have specialized juvenile units. It is generally recommended that a department with more than fifteen employees should have at least one member assigned to deal with youth.

The special juvenile officer is often carefully selected and trained to relate to youths, is knowledgeable about the special laws in such cases, and is sensitive to the special needs of young offenders. Given the importance accorded the goal of diverting juveniles from the justice system, the juvenile officer is also viewed as an important link between police and

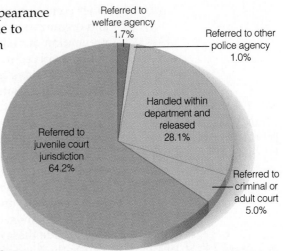

**Figure 18.3**
**Disposition of juveniles taken into police custody**
The police have discretion regarding the disposition of juvenile arrest cases. What factors may influence how a case is disposed?

SOURCE: U.S. Department of Justice, Bureau of Justice Statistics, *Sourcebook of Criminal Justice Statistics* (Washington, D.C.: Government Printing Office, 1993), 455.

other community institutions, such as the schools, recreation facilities, and organizations serving young people. Because of the emphasis on the prevention of delinquency, many authorities urge that juvenile officers not be involved in the investigation of serious juvenile crimes. Other authorities believe that police resources should not be used to enhance recreational activities as a delinquency-prevention strategy.

In dealing with juveniles, police have been confronted by questions on whether or not the *Miranda* warnings and the *Mapp* unreasonable search and seizure rulings apply. Although the language of these court decisions is not explicit, most jurisdictions now provide the Miranda protections, but questions remain as to the ability of juveniles to waive these rights. In 1979 the Court ruled in *Fare* v. *Michael C.* that a child may waive rights to an attorney and to self-incrimination but that juvenile court judges must evaluate the totality of circumstances under which the minor made these decisions.[36]

On the issue of unreasonable searches and seizures as required by the Fourth Amendment, the Court has not been as forthcoming. State courts interpreted *Gault* to extend these provisions, but in 1985 the Supreme Court ruled in *New Jersey* v. *T.L.O.* that school officials can search students and their lockers if they have reasonable suspicion that the search will produce evidence of a school or criminal law violation.[37] The justices recognized that children do have Fourth Amendment rights, yet they also noted that under the concept of *in loco parentis* school officials may act in place of the parent under certain conditions when the child is under their jurisdiction.

Although young people commit many serious crimes, the juvenile function of police work is concerned largely with the maintenance of order. In most incidents of this sort the law is ambiguous, and blame cannot easily be assigned. In terms of physical or monetary damage, many offenses committed by juveniles are minor infractions: breaking windows, hanging around the business district, disturbing the peace, adolescent sexual behavior, and shoplifting. In such instances the function of the investigating officer is not so much to solve crimes as to handle the often legally uncertain complaints involving juveniles. The officer must seek both to satisfy the complainant and to keep the youth from future trouble. Given this emphasis on settling cases within the community—rather than an emphasis upon strict enforcement of the law—the police power to arrest is a weapon that can be used to deter juveniles from criminal activity and to encourage them to conform to the dictates of the law.

### Intake

When the police believe that formal actions should be taken by the juvenile justice system, a complaint is filed with a special division of the juvenile probation department for preliminary screening and evaluation. During this intake stage, an officer reviews the case to determine whether the alleged facts are sufficient to cause the juvenile court to take jurisdiction or whether some other action would be in the child's interest. If it appears that the case warrants formal judicial processing, then a formal petition may be filed with the court. If the police referral does not contain

---

*Fare* v. *Michael C.* **(1979)**
Trial court judges must evaluate the voluntariness of confessions by juveniles by examining the totality of circumstances.

*New Jersey* v. *T.L.O.* **(1985)**
School officials may search a student based on a reasonable suspicion that the search will produce evidence that a school or a civil law has been violated.

sufficient legal evidence or if the juvenile has committed only a minor violation, has no prior record, and is living with a caring parent, then the case may be dismissed. Alternatively, a child may be diverted out of the system to an appropriate mental health, educational, or social agency. In some instances, juveniles are put on informal probation by the intake officer so the department can provide counseling or other services. The intake officer thus has considerable discretion and power. Nationally, between 40 and 50 percent of all referrals from the police are disposed of at this stage, without formal processing by a judge.[38]

The numbers and the types of cases sent to the juvenile court are influenced by the decisions of political and enforcement agencies. The size of the court staff and the resources at its disposal depend on the maintenance of cooperative relations with community leaders. The actions of the juvenile court judge must be consistent with local values. Acts of delinquency that outrage the community will inspire pressures on the court to deal severely with transgressors. Politicians feel that they can gain support by advocating a "get-tough" policy rather than by pushing for the rehabilitation of offenders. When the children of influential persons are charged with delinquency, the informality and the treatment orientation of the system allow a variety of lenient dispositions, including probation, outpatient care at a psychiatric clinic, and incarceration in a therapeutic community. Not all cases result in reform school or industrial school.

In most juvenile justice systems the probation officer plays a crucial role during the intake phase. Because intake is essentially a screening process to determine whether a case should be referred to the court or to a social agency, it often occurs without judicial supervision. Informal discussions among the probation officer, the parents, and the child are important means of learning about the child's social situation, of diagnosing behavioral problems, and of recommending treatment possibilities.

## Diversion

Although there have always been informal methods of diverting alleged delinquents from the courts and toward community agencies, the number and the types of diversion programs have greatly expanded during the past two decades. In keeping with the philosophy of the juvenile court, many people believe that diversion should be promoted as much as possible. Because of the court's extraordinary powers, many think it should intervene only as a last resort. When behavioral problems can be identified early, the child should be given access to the necessary remedial resources without being taken before a judge and labeled "delinquent." Diversion has also been advocated as a way to reduce court workload. Perhaps more important is that children respond more readily to the treatment provided by community-based services than to the correctional services available through the court. Diversion, it is argued, permits the juvenile court to allocate its resources more wisely by concentrating on cases of repeat and serious offenders.

But diversion is not without its critics. Although diversion programs have greatly expanded during the past decade, the number of young people committed to institutions has not decreased appreciably. According to many observers, the increase in diversion programs has widened the juvenile justice net and children who would not have been handled in the past are so handled now.[39]

## Detention

If it is decided to take formal action against a juvenile, then it must also be decided whether or not to place the youth in **detention** until disposition of the case. This decision is usually made by the intake officer.

One early reform of the juvenile justice system was to ensure that children were not held in jails in company with adults who were also awaiting trial or sentencing. To mix juveniles—some of whom are status offenders or under the protection of the court because they are neglected—in the same public facility with adults accused of crimes has long been thought unjust, but in many areas separate detention facilities for juveniles do not exist.

Children are held in detention for a number of reasons. For some, it is to keep them from committing other crimes while awaiting trial. For others, it is the possibility of harm from gang members or parents if they are released. Still others may not appear in court as required if released. Finally, youths are detained when there is no responsible adult who is willing to care for them. These are the formal reasons, but detention may also be used as punishment or to teach a lesson.

Although much attention is focused on the sanctions imposed by juvenile court judges as a result of the formal processes of adjudication, more children are punished through confinement in detention centers and jails before any court action has taken place. An estimated half-million juveniles are detained each year, sometimes for several months, but only about 15 percent are eventually confined to a group home, training school, or halfway house. These figures seem to indicate that detention and intake decisions have a greater impact on future criminality than the decisions of the court. They may also underscore the belief that a brief period of detention is a good device to "shake up the kid and set him straight." The fact remains: juveniles held in detention have not been convicted.

## Adjudication

Barry Feld describes the juvenile courts as a study in contradictions "marked by disjunctions between theory and practice, between rehabilitative rhetoric and punitive reality, and between the law on the books and the law in action."[40] State juvenile court systems also differ substantially both in their jurisdiction and in their processing of young offenders. In different states a juvenile court may be a division of the court of general jurisdiction, a separate court, or a part of a court of limited jurisdiction.[41] As discussed earlier, juvenile systems differ in the age of the accused and the categories of cases under juvenile court jurisdiction.

Differences in the processing of cases have been seen in how judges react to cases in rural and urban areas in the same state. Research in Missouri, for example, found that rural courts seemed to adhere to traditional pre-*Gault*, juvenile court *parens patriae* criteria, while urban courts were more legalistic in their orientation and processed cases more strictly according to offense criteria.[42]

The issues of attaching the label "delinquent" to a juvenile and determining a sanction are the primary matters before the court. In accordance with the Progressives' belief that adjudication should be informal and noncombative, the normal rules of criminal procedure were modified; the rules of evidence were not strictly followed, hearsay testimony could be admitted, there was no prosecutor (a police or probation officer presented the case), and the sessions were closed to the public. From a formal standpoint, the purpose of the hearing was not to determine a child's guilt or innocence of a specific charge but rather to establish the child's status as either delinquent or not delinquent and to help the child become law-abiding.

The role of the juvenile court was described in 1976 by Ted Rubin, a former judge of the Denver Juvenile Court:

This court is a far more complex instrument than outsiders imagine. It is law, and it is social work; it is control, and it is help; it is the good parent and, also, the stern parent; it is both formal and informal. It is concerned not only with the delinquent, but also with the battered child, the runaway and many others.... The juvenile court has been all things to all people.[43]

The changes in criminal proceedings mandated by the due process decisions of the Supreme Court following *Gault* have produced shifts in the philosophy and actions of the juvenile court. Copies of formal petitions with specific charges must be given to the parents and child, counsel may be present and free counsel appointed if the juvenile is indigent, witnesses may be cross-examined, and a transcript of the proceedings must be kept. In about less than half the states, juveniles have a right to a jury trial.

As with other Supreme Court decisions, the reality of local practice may differ sharply from the stipulations in the opinion. Juveniles and their parents often waive their rights in response to suggestions by the judge or the probation officer. The lower social status of the offender's parents, the intimidating atmosphere of the court, and judicial hints that the outcome will be more favorable if a lawyer is not present are reasons the procedures outlined in *Gault* are not demanded. The litany of "treatment," "doing what's right for the child," and "working out a just solution" may sound enticing, especially to people who are unfamiliar with the intricacies of formal legal procedures. In practice, then, juveniles still lack many of the protections accorded adult offenders. Some of the differences between the juvenile and adult criminal justice systems are shown in Table 18.3.

**Adjudicatory Process**  In some jurisdictions the adjudication process is more adversarial than it was before the *Gault* and *Winship* decisions. Like adult cases, however, juvenile cases tend to be adjudicated in a style that conforms to the Crime Control (administrative) Model: Most are settled

| | Adult System | Juvenile System |
|---|---|---|
| Philosophical assumptions | Decisions made as result of adversarial system in context of due process rights | Decisions made as result of inquiry into needs of juvenile within context of some due process elements |
| Jurisdiction | Violations of criminal law | Violations of criminal law, status offenses, neglect, dependency |
| Primary sanctioning goals | Retribution, deterrence, rehabilitation | Retribution, rehabilitation |
| Official discretion | Widespread | Widespread |
| Entrance | Official action of arrest, summons, or citation | Official action, plus referral by school, parents, other sources |
| Role of prosecuting and defense attorneys | Required and formalized | Sometimes required; less structured; poor role definition |
| Adjudication | Procedural rules of evidence in public jury trial required | Less formal structure to rules of evidence and conduct of trial; no right to public jury in most states |
| Treatment programs | Run primarily by public agencies | Broad use of private and public agencies |
| Application of Bill of Rights amendments | | |
| Fourth: Unreasonable searches and seizures | Applicable | Applicable |
| Fifth: Double jeopardy | Applicable | Applicable (re waiver to adult court) |
| Self-incrimination | Applicable (*Miranda* warnings) | Applicable |
| Sixth: Right to counsel | Applicable | Applicable |
| Public Trial | Applicable | Applicable in less than half of states |
| Trial by jury | Applicable | Applicable in less than half of states |
| Eighth: Right to bail | Applicable | Applicable in half of states |
| Fourteenth: Right to treatment | Not Applicable | Applicable |

**Table 18.3**
**The adult and juvenile criminal justice systems**
Compare the basic elements of the adult and juvenile systems. To what extent does a juvenile have the same rights as an adult? Are the different decision-making processes necessary because a juvenile is involved?

in preliminary hearings by a plea agreement, and few go on to formal trial. At the preliminary hearing the youth is notified of the charges and his or her rights, and counsel may be present. In most cases the juvenile has already admitted guilt to the arresting or intake officer, so the focus of the hearing is on the disposition. In contested cases, a prosecutor presents the state's case, and the judge oversees the proceedings, ruling on the admission of evidence and the testimony of witnesses. Because juries are used only sparingly, even in states where they are authorized, guilt or innocence is determined by the judge, who then passes sentence.

Given the increased concern about crime, prosecuting attorneys are taking a more prominent part in the system. In keeping with the traditional child-saver philosophy, prosecuting attorneys rarely appeared in juvenile court before the *Gault* decision. Now, with the presence of a defense attorney, it is felt to be important that the state's interests be represented by legal counsel. In many jurisdictions prosecutors are assigned to deal specifically with juvenile cases by advising the intake officer, administering diversion programs, negotiating pleas, and acting as an advocate during judicial proceedings.

**Disposition**  If the court makes a finding of delinquency, a dispositional hearing is required. This hearing may be held immediately after the entry of a plea or at a later date. The judge typically receives a social history or predispositional report before passing sentence. Few juveniles are found by the court to be not delinquent at trial because the intake and pretrial processes normally filter out cases that cannot prove law violations. In addition to dismissal of a petition, five other choices are available: (1) suspended judgment, (2) probation, (3) community treatment, (4) institutional care, and (5) judicial waiver to an adult court.

The traditional belief of juvenile court advocates was that rehabilitation through treatment was the only goal of the sanction imposed on young people. Throughout most of this century judges have sentenced juveniles to indeterminate sentences so that correctional administrators

Juvenile court judges are expected to act in the interest of the child while at the same time carrying out the law.

would have the discretion to determine when release was appropriate. As with the adult criminal justice system, indeterminate sentences and informal discretion have been under attack since the mid-1970s. A number of states have tightened the sentencing discretion of judges, especially with regard to serious offenses. The state of Washington, for example, has adopted a determinate sentencing law for juveniles. In other states a youth may be transferred to the adult court for adjudication and sentencing. Jurisdictions such as the District of Columbia, Colorado, Florida, and Virginia have passed laws requiring mandatory sentences for certain offenses committed by juveniles.

## Corrections

Many aspects of juvenile corrections are similar or identical to those of adult corrections. Both systems, for example, mix rehabilitative and retributive sanctions. Juvenile corrections differs in many respects from the adult system, however. Some of the differences flow from the *parens patriae* concept and the youthful, seemingly innocent persons with whom the system deals. At times the differences are expressed in formal operational policies, such as contracting for residential treatment; at other times the differences are apparent only in the style and culture of an operation, as in juvenile probation.

One predominant aim of juvenile corrections is to avoid unnecessary incarceration. When children are removed from their homes, they are inevitably damaged emotionally, even when the home is harsh, for they are forced to abandon the only environment they know. Furthermore, placing children in institutions has labeling effects; the children begin to perceive themselves as "bad" because they have received punitive treatment, and children who see themselves as bad are likely to behave that way. Finally, treatment is believed to be more effective when the child is living in a normal, supportive home environment. For these reasons, noninstitutional forms of corrections are seen as highly desirable in juvenile justice, and they have proliferated in recent years.

**Alternative Dispositions**   Although probation and commitment to an institution are the major dispositional alternatives, judges have wide discretion to warn, to fine, to arrange for restitution, to refer a juvenile for treatment at either a public or a private community agency, or to withhold judgment. In making a decision, the judge relies on a social background report, developed by the probation department. Often it includes reports from others in the community, such as school officials or a psychiatrist. When psychological issues are involved, a disposition may be delayed pending further diagnosis.

Judges sometimes suspend judgment, or continue cases without a finding, when they wish to put a youth under supervision but are reluctant to apply the label "delinquent." Judgment may be suspended for a definite or indefinite period. The court thus holds a definitive judgment in abeyance for possible use should a youth misbehave while under the informal supervision of a probation officer or parents.

**Probation**   By far the most common method of handling juvenile offenders is to place them on probation. Juvenile probation operates much the same as adult probation, and it is sometimes carried out by the same agency. In two respects, however, juvenile probation can be very different from adult probation. Traditionally, juvenile probation has been better funded, and hence caseloads of officers are much lighter. Second, juvenile probation itself is often infused with the sense that the offender can change, that the job is enjoyable, and that the clients are worthwhile. Such attitudes make for greater creativity than is possible with adult probation.

The juvenile probation officer can choose from an array of options in working out supervision approaches. A common approach is to pair the juvenile with a "big brother" or "big sister," who spends time with the offender, providing a positive adult role model. Another much-used approach, possible because the officer normally has more discretionary control over the caseload than the adult probation officer, is "contingency contracting," in which something the juvenile hopes for (such as less frequent reporting or termination of supervision) is linked to the juvenile's achievement of some goal (such as passing grades). It is also common for the juvenile probation officer to engage in supervision activities that involve the juvenile's family or school.

**Community Treatment**   Treatment in community-based facilities has greatly expanded since 1970. In particular, the number of private, nonprofit agencies that contract with the states to perform services for troubled youths has grown. Demands for deinstitutionalization emphasized that juveniles could receive better and less costly treatment in the community from private and social service agencies.

Foster homes are families in which juvenile offenders live, usually for a short time. Foster parents often have children of their own, and they treat the foster child more or less as a member of the family. The foster home was developed as a means for implementing a policy of limited intervention into juvenile lives, reflecting the sentiment of the Standard Juvenile Court Act (a model law developed by the National Council on Crime and Delinquency) that when a child "is removed from the control of his parents, the court shall secure for him care as nearly as possible equivalent to [the home]."[44]

Probation officers provide adult role models for juveniles.

Group homes are small, often privately run facilities for groups of juvenile offenders. They are usually older houses that have been remodeled to fit the needs of twelve to twenty juveniles. Each group home has several staff personnel who work as counselors or houseparents on eight-hour or twenty-four-hour shifts. Issues concerning the management of group homes often arise, as posed in A Question of Ethics on page 644.

Group home placements are usually for longer terms than foster home placements, and they may be more suited to seriously delinquent youths because they can allow juveniles to attend local schools, provide individual and group counseling, and otherwise maintain a more structured day than most residents receive in their own homes. Most group homes are nonsecure, in that the residents are expected to abide by rules, including curfews, but staff members take little responsibility for enforcing obedience; juveniles who flout the rules are returned to court for placement elsewhere.

**Institutional Care**   Incarceration of juveniles has traditionally meant commitment to a state institution, often called a training school, reform school, or industrial school. An assumption of the Progressive movement was that juveniles could be helped only if they were removed from "the crowded slum-life of the noisy, disorderly settlement where 70 percent of the population is of foreign parentage." The children were to be "taken away from evil association and temptations, away from the moral and physical filth and contagion, out of the gas light and sewer gas; away out into the woods and fields, free from temptation and contagion; out into the sunlight and the starlight and the pure, sweet air of the meadows."[45] Once in a rural setting, the children were to learn a vocation and be

## A Question of Ethics

Residents of the Lovelock Home had been committed by the juvenile court because they were either delinquent or neglected. All twenty-five boys, aged seven to fifteen, were streetwise, tough, and interested only in getting out. The institution had a staff of social services professionals who tried to deal with the educational and psychological needs of the residents. Because state funding was short, these services looked better in the annual report than to an observer visiting Lovelock. Most of the time the residents watched television, played basketball in the backyard, or just hung out in one another's rooms.

Joe Klegg, the night supervisor, was tired from the eight-hour shift that he had just completed on his "second job" as a daytime convenience store manager. The boys were watching television when he arrived at seven. Everything seemed calm. It should have been, since Joe had placed a tough fifteen year old, Randy Marshall, in charge. Joe had told Randy to keep the younger boys in line. Randy used his muscle and physical presence to intimidate the other residents. He knew that if the home was quiet and there was no trouble, he would be rewarded with special privileges such as a "pass" to go see his girlfriend. Joe wanted no hassles and a quiet house so that he could doze off when the boys went to sleep.

Does the situation at Lovelock Home raise ethical questions, or does it merely raise questions of poor management practices? What are the potential consequences for the residents? For Joe Klegg? What is the state's responsibility?

trained to middle-class standards. That usually meant juveniles were taught outdated farming skills and trades no longer practiced in the urban areas to which they were destined to return. The remoteness of these institutions meant the further loss of meaningful personal and family relationships. Even today, state correctional facilities for children tend to be in rural areas.

Large custodial training schools located in outlying areas remain the typical institutions to which juveniles are committed, although since the late 1970s there has been an increase in the number of privately maintained facilities that accept residents sent to them by the courts. The 1990 census revealed that more than 92,000 juveniles were housed in 3,200 public and private centers; 62 percent of the residents were in public facilities.[46] The census found that the average age in all facilities was approximately fifteen and that boys outnumbered girls three to one. In addition, unknown numbers of children are under the care of the juvenile court but have been placed in noncorrectional private facilities, such as schools for the emotionally disturbed, military academies, and even preparatory schools. Although courts usually maintain jurisdiction over delinquents until they attain the age of majority, data from the training schools indicate that nationally the average length of stay is approximately ten months.

What types of juveniles are placed in public custodial institutions? Results from a national survey showed that 40.7 percent were incarcerated for violent offenses, 60 percent used drugs regularly, and half said that a family member had been in prison at some time in the past. Eighty-eight percent of the residents were male, only 30 percent had grown up in a household with both parents, and the percentages of African-American (42.8 percent) and of Hispanic (15.5 percent) are greater than the portion of those groups in the general population.[47] Figure 18.4 shows the types of offenses and nondelinquency reasons for the placement of juveniles in public correctional facilities.

Placement in the more desirable private treatment centers may be sought for preferred juveniles. Often the availability of treatment alternatives depends upon negotiations between the court and the private agencies. Some private institutions desire referrals in order to maintain and expand their clientele, but they want the "right" type of patients. The private agencies select "motivated" and high-status clients and pass on to public agencies the harder-to-work-with, resistant clients. In return for opening their doors to court referrals, private treatment centers prefer to transfer their troublesome cases to state institutions.[48]

**Institutional Programs**    Because of the emphasis on rehabilitation that has dominated juvenile justice since the late 1940s, a wide variety of treatment programs has been used. Counseling, education, vocational training, and psychotherapy methods have been incorporated into the juvenile correctional programs of most states. Unfortunately, there is much dissatisfaction with the results. For many offenders, incarceration in a juvenile training institution appears mainly to be preparation for entry into adult corrections. John Irwin's concept of the state-raised youth (Chapter 16) provides insight on children who come in contact with institutional life at an early age, lack family relationships and structure, become used to living in a correctional environment, and are unable to move out of this cycle (see the Close-Up on Fernando on pages 646–647).

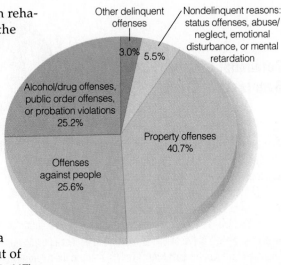

Other delinquent offenses 3.0%

Nondelinquent reasons: status offenses, abuse/ neglect, emotional disturbance, or mental retardation 5.5%

Alcohol/drug offenses, public order offenses, or probation violations 25.2%

Property offenses 40.7%

Offenses against people 25.6%

**Figure 18.4
Juveniles in public facilities: Types of offenses and nondelinquency reasons for placement**

SOURCE: U.S. Department of Justice, Office of Juvenile Justice and Delinquency Prevention, *OJJDP Update on Statistics* (January 1991), 4.

As with adult corrections, rehabilitative programs for juveniles have received critical examination. Reanalysis of research findings often finds that experimental groups were preselected and would probably have been more successful in leading a crime-free life even without treatment. Some critics argue that the manner in which recidivism has been defined and calculated often leads to a misreading of results. Others concede that experimental therapies do produce positive results but claim that when the particular treatment method is incorporated in the regular correctional program, it loses much of its special quality, with the result that resources are diminished, staff become overburdened, and the bureaucratic milieu deadens the enthusiasm of participants. The warehousing of juveniles until they reach the age of majority may become the underlying goal of many institutions.

## Problems of and Perspectives on the Juvenile Justice System

Much criticism of juvenile justice has emphasized the disparity between the treatment ideal and the institutionalized practices of an ongoing bureaucratic system. Commentators have focused on how the language of social reformers has disguised the day-to-day operations in which elements of due process are lacking and custodial incarceration is all too frequent. Other criticisms have stressed the apparent inability of the juvenile justice system to control juvenile crime.

The juvenile court, in both theory and practice, is a remarkably complex institution that must perform a wide variety of functions. Given the range of roles played by the juvenile justice system, it is inevitable that goals and values will collide. In many states the same judges, probation officers, and social workers are asked to deal with both neglected children and young criminals. Although departments of social services may deal primarily with neglect cases, the distinction is often not maintained.

## Fernando, Sixteen, Finds a Sanctuary in Crime

Fernando Morales was glad to discuss his life as a year-old drug dealer, but he had one stipulation owing to his status as a fugitive. He explained that he had recently escaped from Long Lane School, a state correctional institution that became his home after he was caught with $1,100 worth of heroin known as "P."

"The Five-O caught me right here with the bundles of P," he said, referring to a police officer, as he stood in front of a boarded-up house on Bridgeport's East Side. "They sentenced me to eighteen months, but I jetted after four. Three of us got out a bathroom window. We ran through the woods and stole a car. Then we got back here and the Five-O's came to my apartment, and I had to jump out the side window on the second floor."

### What Future?

Since his escape in December, Fernando had been on the run for weeks. He still went to the weekly meetings of his gang, but he was afraid to go back to his apartment, afraid even to go to a friend's place to pick up the three guns he had stashed away. "I would love to get my baby, Uzi, but it's too hot now."

"Could you bring a photographer here?" he asked. "I want my picture in the newspaper. I'd love to have me holding a bundle right there on the front page so the cops can see it. They're going to bug out."

The other dealers on the corner looked on with a certain admiration. They realized that a publicity campaign might not be the smartest long-term career move for a fugitive drug dealer—"Man, you be the one bugging out," another dealer told him—but they also recognized the logic in Fernando's attitude. He was living his life according to a common assumption on these streets: There is no future.

When you ask the Hispanic teenagers selling drugs here what they expect to be doing in five years, you tend to get a lot of bored shrugs. Occasionally they'll talk about being back in school or being a retired drug dealer in a Porsche. But the most common answer is the one that Fernando gave without hesitation or emotion, "Dead or in jail."

The story of how Fernando got that way is a particularly sad one, but the basic elements are fairly typical in the lives of drug dealers and gang members in any urban ghetto. He has grown up amid tenements, housing projects, torched buildings, and abandoned factories. His role models have been adults who use "the city" and "the state" primarily as terms for the different types of welfare checks. His neighborhood is a place where thirteen year olds know by heart the visiting hours at local prisons.

### The Family: A Mother Leaves, A Father Drinks

Fernando Morales was born in Bridgeport, Connecticut, on 16 September 1976, and his mother moved out a few months later. Since then he has occasionally run into her on the street. Neither he nor his relatives can say exactly why she left—or why she didn't take Fernando and her other son with her—but the general assumption is that she was tired of being hit by their father.

The father, Bernabe Morales, who was twenty-four years old and had emigrated from Puerto Rico as a teenager, moved the two boys in with his mother at the P.T. Barnum public housing project. Fernando lived there until the age of eight, when his grandmother died....

After that Fernando and his brother Bernard lived sometimes with their father and his current girlfriend, sometimes with relatives in Bridgeport or Puerto Rico. They eventually settled with their father's cousin, Monserrate Bruno, who already had ten children living in her two-bedroom apartment....

His father, by all accounts, was a charming, generous man when sober but something else altogether when drinking or doing drugs. He was arrested more than two dozen times, usually for fighting for drugs, and spent five years in jail while Fernando was growing up. He lived on welfare, odd jobs, and money from selling drugs, a trade that was taken up by both his sons.

In addition to recognizing the organizational problems of the juvenile system, we must acknowledge that our understanding of the causes of delinquency and its prevention or treatment is extremely limited. Over the years, various social and behavioral theories have been advanced to explain delinquency. Where one generation looked to slum conditions as

## The "Industry": Moving Up in the Drug Trade

Fernando's school days ended two years ago, when he dropped out of ninth grade. "School was corny," he explained. "I was smart, I learned quick, but I got bored. I was just learning things when I could be out making money."

Fernando might have found other opportunities—he had relatives working in fast-food restaurants and repair shops, and one cousin tried to interest him in a job distributing bread that might pay $700 a week—but nothing with such quick rewards as the drug business flourishing on the East Side.

He had friends and relatives in the business, and he started as one of the runners on the street corner making sales or directing buyers to another runner holding the marijuana, cocaine, crack, or heroin. The runners on each block buy their drugs—paying, for instance, $200 for fifty bags of crack that sell for $250—from the block's lieutenant, who supervises them and takes the money to the absentee dealer called the owner of the block.

By this winter Fernando had moved up slightly on the corporate ladder. "I'm not the block lieutenant yet, but I have some runners selling for me," he explained as he sat in a bar near the block. Another teenager came in with money for him, which he proudly added to a thick wad in his pocket. "You see? I make money while they work for me."

Fernando still worked the block himself, too, standing on the corner watching for cars slowing down, shouting "You want P?" or responding to veteran customers for crack who asked, "Got any slab, man?" Fernando said he usually made between $100 and $300 a day and that the money usually went as quickly as it came.

He had recently bought a car for $500 and wrecked it making a fast turn into a telephone pole. He spent money on gold chains with crucifixes, rings, Nike sneakers, Timberland boots, an assortment of Russell hooded sweatshirts called *hoodies*, gang dues, trips to New York City, and his twenty-three-year-old girlfriend.

His dream was to get out of Bridgeport. "I'd be living fat somewhere. I'd go to somewhere hot, Florida or Puerto Rico or somewhere, buy me a house, get six blazing girls with dope bodies." In the meantime, he tried not to think about what his product was doing to his customers.

"Sometimes it bothers me. But see, I'm a hustler. I got to look out for myself. I got to be making money. Forget them. If you put that in your head, you're going to be caught out. You going to be a sucker. You going to be like them." He said he had used marijuana, cocaine, and angel dust himself, but made a point of never using crack or heroin, the drugs that plagued the last years of his father's life....

## The Gangs: "Like a Family" or Drug Dealers

"I cried a little, that's it," was all that Fernando would say about his father's death. But he did allow that it had something to do with his subsequent decision to join a Hispanic gang named *Neta*. He went with friends to a meeting, answered questions during an initiation ceremony, and began wearing its colors, a necklace of red, white, and blue beads.

"It's like a family, and you need that if you've lost your own family," he said. "At the meetings we talk about having heart, trust, and all that. We don't disrespect nobody. If we need money, we get it. If I need anything they're right there to help me."

Neta is allied with Bridgeport's most notorious gang, the Latin Kings, and both claim to be peaceful Hispanic cultural organizations opposed to drug use. But they are financed at least indirectly by the drug trade because many members like Fernando work independently in drug operations, and the drug dealers' disputes can turn into gang wars....

"I like guns, I like stealing cars, I like selling drugs, and I like money," he said. "I got to go to the block. That's where I get my spirit at. When I die, my spirit's going to be at the block, still making money. Booming."...

"I'll be selling till I get my act together. I'm just a little kid. Nothing runs through my head. All I think about is doing crazy things. But when I be big, I know I need education. If I get caught and do a couple of years, I'll come out and go back to school. But I don't have that in my head yet. I'll have my little fun while I'm out."

SOURCE: John Tierney, *New York Times*, 13 April 1993, A–1, B–6. Copyright © 1993 by The New York Times Company. Reprinted by permission.

the cause of juvenile crime, another points to the affluence of the suburbs. Psychologists may stress masculine insecurity in a matriarchal family structure, and some sociologists note the peer group pressures of the gang. The array of theories has occasioned an array of proposed—and often contradictory—treatments. Given this confusion, those interested in the problems of youth may feel despair. What is clear is that additional research is needed to give insights into the causes of delinquency and the treatment of juvenile offenders.

There remains much concern about the serious repeat offender who continues a life of crime as an adult. One key issue is the unavailability of juvenile court records to judges in the adult courts, which means that persons who have already served time on probation and in juvenile institutions are thought to be first offenders when they reach the age of majority. Many believe it important that juvenile records be made available and that efforts be made to treat young criminals more severely in order to deter them from future illegal activity.

What trends may foretell the future of juvenile justice? In many ways the same trends that are found in the adult criminal justice system can be seen in the juvenile counterpart. However, there is often a delay between reform of the adult system and that of the juvenile system. Hence, restriction of the discretion of judges and parole boards, a major thrust of the 1970s, has now surfaced for juvenile justice. The toughening of sentencing standards and increases in the amounts of time served in adult prisons are becoming a part of the juvenile system. Youthful-offender laws have elevated many delinquents to the adult system for adjudication and correction.

Although the future of juvenile justice may reflect the more conservative attitudes of the 1980s and 1990s, it must be recognized that the reforms of the 1970s have had an important impact. These changes have been referred to as the "Big D's" of juvenile justice: diversion, decriminalization, deinstitutionalization, and due process.[49] The Big D's have left a lasting mark on juvenile justice. Lawyers are routinely present at court hearings and other stages of the process, adding a note of formalism that was simply not present twenty years ago. Status offenders seldom are in secure, punitive environments such as training schools. The juvenile justice system looks more like the adult justice system than it formerly did, but it is still less formal. Its stated intention is also less harsh: to keep juveniles in the community whenever possible.

Barry Krisberg, president of the National Council on Crime and Delinquency, however has added a fifth "D"—disarray. He believes that the conservative crime control policies that have hit the adult criminal justice system, with their emphasis on deterrence, retribution, and getting tough, have influenced juvenile justice.[50] He points to growing levels of overcrowding in juvenile institutions, increased litigation challenging the abuse of children in training schools and detention centers, and increased rates of minority youth incarceration. All of these problems have emerged during a period of declining youth populations and fewer arrests of juveniles. With the demographic trend now reversing and the increased concern about drugs, Krisberg sees a surge of adolescents going through their criminally high-risk years in a system and community unable to cope with them.

# Summary

Crimes committed by youths are a major problem in the United States. While the amount of all crimes reported to the police or measured by victimization surveys has remained fairly level since the early 1980s, crimes committed by juveniles has increased.

The history of juvenile justice can be understood as comprising five periods: Puritan, refuge, juvenile court, juvenile rights, and crime control. In each period, social and political developments influenced the criminal justice system. The creation of the juvenile court in 1899 and its extension throughout the nation produced a separate juvenile justice system based on assumptions about the causes of delinquent behavior and the justice processes that should be used to deal with that behavior. Until the 1960s, juvenile justice officials were given wide discretion to fashion processes and sanctions that would serve the best interests of the child.

The Supreme Court decision in the case of Gerald Gault in 1967 and the due process revolution revealed many practices long obscured from public view. As a result, the emphasis on discretion that characterized the juvenile justice of earlier periods has dwindled. At the same time there is renewed concern about youth crime. Legislatures have adopted more of a crime control focus to deal with juvenile delinquency in the 1990s.

Decisions by police officers and juvenile intake officers dispose of a large portion of cases before they are referred to the court for formal processing. The police exercise enormous discretion regarding the disposition of juveniles accused of crime. When they believe that formal actions should be taken, a complaint is filed with a special division of the juvenile probation department for preliminary screening and evaluation. During this intake stage, an officer reviews the case to determine whether the alleged facts are sufficient to cause the juvenile court to take jurisdiction or whether diversion is in the child's interest. If formal action is taken, the juvenile may be detained until disposition of the case. In juvenile court most cases are settled in preliminary hearings by a plea agreement. Few cases go to trial. In contested cases, a prosecutor presents the state's case, and the judge oversees the proceedings. Upon conviction or after a plea, a dispositional hearing is held, and the judge reviews the delinquent's social history and imposes a sentence. The judge may suspend judgment, grant probation, impose community treatment, require institutional care, or waive the offender for further action in adult court. Institutional and noninstitutional programs for those judged to be offenders are available in great variety. A predominant aim of juvenile corrections is to avoid unnecessary incarceration.

According to some observers, past reforms have not addressed the problem of juvenile justice and we are now entering a new era based on a more realistic assessment of the possibilities of dealing with youthful offenders. There seems to be a greater willingness today to confront the problem of violent offenders and to take drastic steps to control those youths.

## Questions for Review

1 What are the major historical periods that characterize juvenile justice in the United States?
2 What is the jurisdiction of the juvenile court system?
3 What are the major processes in the juvenile justice system?
4 What are the sentencing and institutional alternatives for juveniles who are judged delinquent?
5 What due process rights do juveniles possess?

## Key Terms and Cases

delinquent

dependent child

detention

judicial waiver

legislative exclusion

neglected child

*parens patriae*

PINS, CINS, JINS

status offense

*Breed* v. *Jones* (1975)

*Fare* v. *Michael C.* (1979)

*In re Gault* (1967)

*In re Winship* (1970)

*McKiever* v. *Pennsylvania* (1971)

*New Jersey* v. *T.L.O.* (1985)

*Schall* v. *Martin* (1984)

## For Further Reading

Champion, Dean J., and G. Larry Mays. *Transferring Juveniles to Criminal Court: Trends and Implications for Criminal Justice.* New York: Praeger, 1991. A study of the recent movement to shift the adjudication of juveniles accused of serious crimes to the adult criminal court.

Mahoney, Anne Rankin. *Juvenile Justice in Context.* Boston: Northeastern University Press, 1987. A view of juvenile justice in the context of the social and political environment.

Matza, David. *Delinquency and Drift.* New York: Viking, 1974. A classic examination of the role of the juvenile court. Describes the influence of "kadi" justice (in which the judge exercises great discretion) on the system.

Platt, Anthony. *The Child Savers: The Invention of Delinquency.* Chicago: University of Chicago Press, 1970. A history of the Progressive child-saver movement.

Rubin, H. Ted. *Behind the Black Robes.* Beverly Hills, Calif.: Sage, 1985. A juvenile court judge discusses his role and the decision-making process.

# Notes

1   *In re Gault*, 387 U.S. 9 (1967).

2   Ibid.

3   Barry C. Feld, "Criminalizing the American Juvenile Court," in *Crime and Justice: A Review of Research*, vol. 17, ed. Michael Tonry (Chicago: University of Chicago Press, 1993), 197–280.

4   Laura A. Mansnerus, "Treating Teenagers as Adults in Court: A Trend Born of Revulsion," *New York Times*, 3 December 1993, B–7.

5   James D. Wright, Joseph F. Sheley, and M. Dwayne Smith, "Kids, Guns, and Killing Fields," *Society* 30 (November/December 1992): 84.

6   Metropolitan Court Judges Committee Report, "Drugs—The American Family in Crisis" (Reno: University of Nevada, National Council on Juvenile and Family Court Judges, 1988).

7   U.S. Department of Justice, National Institute of Justice, *Research in Brief* (May 1990).

8   Robert Dart, "Street Gang Trends Give Little Cause for Optimism," *CJ the Americas* 5 (December/January 1993): 6.

9   Ibid.

10  *Ex parte Crouse*, 4 Wharton (Pa.) 9 (1838).

11  Anthony Platt, *The Child Savers*, 2d ed. (Chicago: University of Chicago Press, 1977).

12  John Sutton, *Stubborn Children: Controlling Delinquency in the United States* (Berkeley: University of California Press, 1988).

13  David J. Rothman, *Conscience and Convenience* (Boston: Little, Brown, 1980), 213.

14  Feld, "Criminalizing the American Juvenile Court," 203.

15  Julian Mack, "The Juvenile Court," 2 *Harvard Law Review* 119 (1909).

16  Anthony Platt, *The Child Savers: The Invention of Delinquency* (Chicago: University of Chicago Press, 1969), 116.

17  Ormand W. Ketcham, "The Unfulfilled Promise of the American Juvenile Court," in *Justice for the Child*, ed. Margaret K. Rosenheim (New York: Free Press, 1962), 22–43.

18  *Kent* v. *United States*, 383 U.S. 541, 550 (1966).

19  *In re Winship*, 397 U.S. 358 (1970).

20  *McKiever* v. *Pennsylvania*, 403 U.S. 528 (1971).

21  *Breed* v. *Jones*, 421 U.S. 519 (1975).

22  Janet E. Ainsworth, "Re-imaging Childhood and Reconstructing the Legal Order: The Case for Abolishing the Juvenile Court," 69 *North Carolina Law Review* 1083 (1991).

23  Peter Greenwood, Alan Lipson, Allan Abrahamse, and Franklin Zimring, *Youth Crime and Juvenile Justice in California* (Santa Monica, Calif.: Rand Corporation, 1983), 30–31.

24  Feld, "Criminalizing the American Juvenile Court," 222.

25  Martin L. Forst and Martha-Elin Blomquist, "Punishment, Accountability, and the New Juvenile Justice," *Juvenile and Family Court Journal* 43 (1992): 1.

26  *Schall* v. *Martin*, 467 U.S. 253 (1984).

27  Alex Kotlowitz, "Their Crimes Don't Make Them Adults," *New York Times Magazine*, 13 February 1994, 40.

28  Ibid.

29  Dean J. Champion and G. Larry Mays, *Transferring Juveniles to Criminal Courts* (New York: Praeger, 1991), 59–82.

30  Franklin Zimring, "The Treatment of Hard Cases in American Juvenile Justice: In Defense of Discretionary Waiver," *Notre Dame Journal of Law, Ethics, and Public Policy* 5 (1991): 267; Barry C. Feld, "Bad Law Makes Hard Cases: Reflections on Teenaged Axe Murderers, Judicial Activism, and Legislative Default," *Journal of Law and Inequality* 8 (1990): 1.

31  Feld, "Criminalizing the American Juvenile Court," 239.

32  State of Connecticut, General Laws, Sec. 46b–121.

33  H. Ted Rubin, *Juvenile Justice: Policy, Practice, and Law*, 2d ed. (New York: Newbury Award Records, 1985), 87.

34  Nathan Goldman, "The Differential Selection of Juvenile Offenders for Court Appearance," in *The Ambivalent Force: Perspectives on the Police*, ed. Arthur Niederhoffere and Abraham S. Blumberg (Waltham, Mass.: Ginn, 1970), 156.

35  Irving Piliavin and Scott Briar, "Police Encounters with Juveniles," in *Back on the Street*, ed. Robert M. Carter and Malcolm W. Klein (Englewood Cliffs, N.J.: Prentice-Hall, 1976), 197–206.

36  *Fare* v. *Michael C.*, 442 U.S. 707 (1979).

37  *New Jersey* v. *T.L.O.*, 105 S.Ct. 733 (1985).

38  U.S. Department of Justice, Bureau of Justice Statistics, *Report to the Nation on Crime and Justice*, 2d ed. (Washington, D.C.: Government Printing Office, 1988), 79.

39  Scott H. Decker, "A Systematic Analysis of Diversion: Net Widening and Beyond," *Journal of Criminal Justice* 13 (1985): 206–216.

40  Feld, "Criminalizing the American Juvenile Court," 208.

41  Leonard P. Edwards, "The Juvenile Court and the Role of the Juvenile Court Judge," *Juvenile and Family Court Journal* 43 (1992): 72.

42  Kimberly Kempf, Scott H. Decker, and Robert L. Bing, *An Analysis of Apparent Disparities in the Handling of Black Youth within Missouri's Juvenile Justice System* (St. Louis: University of Missouri, Department of Administration of Justice, 1990), 118.

43  H. Ted Rubin, *The Courts: Fulcrum of the Justice System* (Santa Monica, Calif.: Goodyear, 1976), 66.

44  *Standard Juvenile Court Act*, 6th ed. (New York: National Council on Crime and Delinquency, 1959), 4.

45  Ronald Goldfarb and Linda R. Singer, *After Conviction* (New York: Simon and Schuster, 1973), 514.

46  U.S. Department of Justice, Office of Juvenile Justice and Delinquency Prevention, *OJJDP Update on Statistics* (January 1991), 1.

47  Ibid., 2.

48  Richard A. Cloward and Irwin Epstein, "Private Social Welfare's Disengagement from the Poor: The Case of the Family Adjustment Agencies," in *Social Welfare Institutions: A Sociological Reader*, ed. Mayer N. Zald (New York: Wiley, 1965), 626.

49  James O. Finckenauer, *Juvenile Delinquency and Corrections: The Gap Between Theory and Practice* (Orlando, Fl.: Academic Press, 1984), 190.

50  Barry Krisberg, *The Juvenile Court: Reclaiming the Vision* (San Francisco: National Council on Crime and Delinquency, 1988).

# Constitution of the United States
## Criminal Justice Amendments

*The first ten amendments to the Constitution, known as the Bill of Rights, became effective on December 15, 1791.*

**IV**   The right of the people to be secure in their persons, houses, papers, and effects, against unreasonable searches and seizures, shall not be violated, and no warrants shall issue but upon probable cause, supported by oath or affirmation, and particularly describing the place to be searched, and the persons or things to be seized.

**V**   No person shall be held to answer for a capital or otherwise infamous crime, unless on a presentment or indictment of a grand jury, except in cases arising in the land or naval forces or in the militia when in actual service in time of war or public danger; nor shall any person be subject for the same offence to be twice put in jeopardy of life or limb; nor shall be compelled in any criminal case to be a witness against himself, nor be deprived of life, liberty, or property, without due process of law; nor shall private property be taken for public use without just compensation.

**VI**   In all criminal prosecutions the accused shall enjoy the right to a speedy and public trial, by an impartial jury of the State and district wherein the crime shall have been committed, which district shall have been previously ascertained by law, and to be informed of the nature and cause of the accusation; to be confronted with the witnesses against him; to have compulsory process for obtaining witnesses in his favor, and to have the assistance of counsel for his defense.

**VIII**   Excessive bail shall not be required, nor excessive fines imposed, nor cruel and unusual punishments inflicted.

*The Fourteenth Amendment became effective on July 28, 1868.*

**XIV**   Section 1. All persons born or naturalized in the United States, and subject to the jurisdiction thereof, are citizens of the United States and of the State wherein they reside. No State shall make or enforce any law which shall abridge the privileges or immunities of citizens of the United States; nor shall any State deprive any person of life, liberty, or property, without due process of law; nor deny to any person within its jurisdiction the equal protection of the laws.

# Understanding and Using Criminal Justice Data

When it comes to numbers, criminal justice is somewhat like baseball. Both require a wealth of quantitative data in order to answer a variety of questions. Casual baseball fans want to know who has the highest batting average in the league or how many runs a certain pitcher gives up per game. More serious fans might want information that can help them judge whether statistics on various events (home runs, stolen bases, sacrifice bunts) support one or another of the manager's strategies. Similarly, people interested in criminal justice need quantitative data both to describe events and to make inferences about trends or about the effects of different policies. They want to know, for example, how much crime there is; whether or not crime is on the increase and in which categories; whether strong gun control laws are associated with a decrease in violent crime; or what effects different correctional policies have on the likelihood that criminals will break the law in the future.

Researchers constantly gather, analyze, and disseminate quantitative information that helps us understand the dimensions of crime and the workings of the criminal justice system. Both as a student in this course and as an informed citizen, you will need to be able to read about these data intelligently and to make legitimate inferences from them.

In this text, as in most criminal justice books and articles, quantitative data often are reported in graphs and tables that organize the information and highlight certain aspects of it. The way the information is presented reflects the writer's choices about what is important in the raw data that underlie the graphic display. So that you can better interpret and use quantitative information, this appendix provides some pointers both on reading graphic presentations and on interpreting raw data.

## Reading Graphs and Tables

Writers use graphs and tables to organize information so that key factors stand out. Although it's tempting to try to take in the meaning of such displays at a glance, it is important to analyze what is being presented so that you do not misinterpret the material.

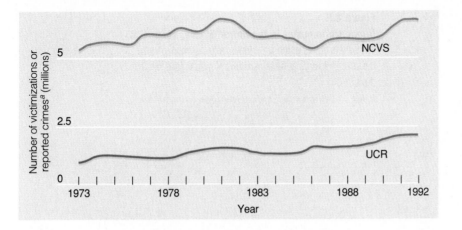

**Figure B.1**
**Violent crime trends measured by *UCR* and NCVS**
Note that these data are for the *number* of violent victimizations reported, not for the victimization rate; from 1973 to 1992.

SOURCE: U.S. Department of Justice, Bureau of Justice Statistics, *Highlights from Twenty Years of Surveying Crime Victims* (August, 1993), 4.

[a] Includes NCVS violent crimes of rape, robbery, aggravated assault, and simple assault, and *UCR* violent crimes of murder and nonnegligent manslaughter, forcible rape, robbery, and aggravated assault.

To begin with, read the title and descriptive caption carefully so that you will understand exactly what the data do and do not represent. For example, consider the title of Figure B.1, "Violent Crime Trends Measured by *UCR* and NCVS," which is reproduced from Chapter 2. The title tells you that the data presented pertain to *violent* crime (not all crime) and that the *sources* of the information are reports to police (the *UCR*) and victimization surveys (NCVS). Knowing the sources of the data is important, since different means of data collection have different strengths and weaknesses. Thus, what this figure presents is not a directly observed picture of crime trends, but a picture that has been filtered through two distinct methods of measuring crime. (For a discussion of these measures of crime, refer to Chapter 2.) In general, always note the sources of data before drawing conclusions from a graphic display.

After reading the title and caption, study the figure itself. In Figure B.1, you will note that the graph compares the number of crimes from 1973 to 1992 as reported by the two types of surveys. As indicated in the caption, the data are presented in terms of the *number* of victimizations, rather than the relative *frequency* of crime (a crime *rate*). For this reason you need to be cautious in making inferences about what the data really show about crime trends. In baseball, a graph showing an increase in the number of home runs struck over a certain period would not prove that home runs were becoming more common if during that same period new teams were added to the league. More teams and more games being played would naturally lead to an increase in the total number of home runs hit. Similarly, given the increases in the U.S. population over the twenty-year period of the data, some of the increase in the *number* of crimes can be attributed to the greater numbers of Americans.

Also note that the data show what has happened over the past two decades. Even though the lines in the graph depict trends during that period, they do *not* in themselves forecast the future. There are statistical procedures that could be used to predict future trends given certain assumptions, but such projections are not a part of this figure.

A final caution about graphic displays in general is that the form in which data are presented can affect or even distort your perception of the

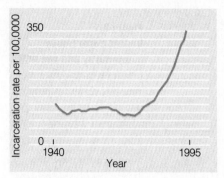

**a**

## Figure B.2
## Incarceration rates in the United States, 1940–1993
The panels of this graph are intentionally distorted to show
the effects of varying the dimensions of graphs (see text
discussion).

SOURCE: U.S. Department of Justice, Bureau of Justice Statistics, *Bulletin* (June 1994).

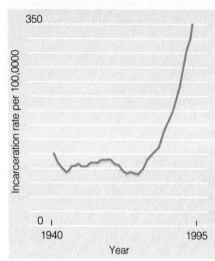

**b**

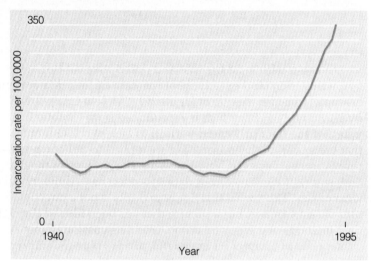

**c**

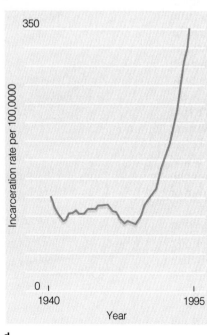

**d**

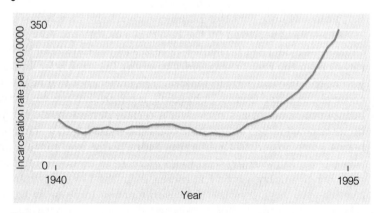

**e**

content. For example, a graph showing incarceration rates in the United States from 1940 to 1993 could be drawn with a shorter or longer time line (see Figure B.2). Figure B.2a shows the graph at normal proportions. If the time line is made shorter in relation to the incarceration rate scale, as in Figure B.2b, the change in incarceration rates will appear to be more drastic than if the line is longer, as in Figure B.2c. By the same token, the height chosen for the vertical axis affects the appearance of the data and can influence the way the data are interpreted. How does your impression of the same data change when you compare Figure B.2d with B.2e?

These brief comments do not exhaust all that can be said about interpreting graphical displays, but they should be sufficient to alert you to the need to carefully review data presented in graphic form. In criminal justice, as in baseball, you need to actively question and think about the information you encounter in order to become a serious student of the game. With these general cautions in mind, let's turn now to some considerations that apply to specific types of graphic presentations.

## Understanding Graphs

You will find three types of graphs in this book: bar graphs, pie graphs (or pie charts), and line graphs. All three are represented in Figure B.3 (reproduced from Chapter 2). Each graph displays information concerning public opinion about crime.

Figure B.3a is a bar graph. Bar graphs compare quantities organized in different categories. In this case, each bar represents the percentage of poll respondents ranking the indicated problem as "the most important problem facing this country today." The lengths of the bars (or their heights, when a bar graph is oriented vertically) allow us to visually compare the quantities associated with each category of response. In this case, you can readily see that when the data were collected in September 1993, health care outranked crime as the public's number one concern by nearly a two to one margin. Of course, the author of a graph of this type needs to take care that the sizes of the bars are visually proportionate to the quantities they represent. A bar graph that is drawn unscrupulously or carelessly can make it appear that the difference in quantities is larger or smaller than it really is. Intentionally or not, graphs that appear in the mass media often exaggerate some effect in this way. The lesson here is to go beyond looking at the shape of the graph. Use the scales provided on the axes to directly compare the numbers being depicted and verify your visual impression.

Figure B.3b is a pie graph. Pie graphs show the relative sizes of the parts of a single whole. Usually these sizes are reported as percentages. In this case, respondents were asked if there is more, less, or about the same amount of violence as there was five years ago. The whole consists of all the responses taken together, and the portions of the "pie" represent the percentage of respondents who chose each option. From the pie graph we can see that a substantial majority (86%) of respondents in this survey believed that violence had increased. The same data could have been reported in a bar graph, but it would not have been as clear that we were seeing a single whole divided into parts.

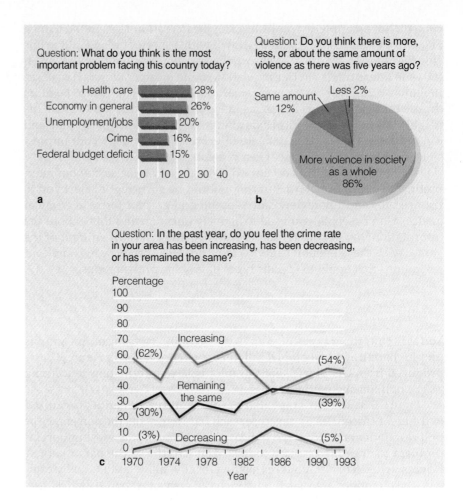

**Figure B.3**
**Crime: In the nation, in our neighborhood**

Crime remains one of the most important problems facing Americans. Over eight in ten people surveyed believe society is more violent than five years ago. A plurality say there is more crime in their neighborhood than a year ago.

SOURCE: "Public Opinion and Demographic Report," *The Public Perspective* 5 (November/December 1993):78.

Whenever data are presented as percentages of a whole—whether in a pie graph, table, or other display—the percentages should add up to 100%. Often, however, the actual sum is slightly over or under 100 because of what is known as *rounding error*. Rounding error can occur when percentages are rounded to the nearest whole number. For instance, suppose the percentage of "more violence" responses were calculated as 86.7%. In that case, the figure might be reported as 87%. Unless rounding of the other percentages compensated for the error, the total of the reported percentages would sum to 101%. Where rounding error occurs, normally there will be a comment associated with the figure or table indicating this fact.

Figure B.3c is a line graph. Line graphs show the relationship between two variables. The variables in question are indicated by the labels on the vertical and longitudinal (horizontal) axes of the graph. In this case, the variable on the vertical axis is the percentage of people who say that crime has been increasing, decreasing, or remaining about the same in the past year. The variable on the longitudinal axis is time, reported as years in which the survey question was asked. In 1970, for instance, 62% of respondents said that crime has been increasing in the past year. Drawing a line through the points that show the percentage associated with each response for each year allows us to see graphically how opinions have changed over time. The same data could have been presented in a table, but it would have been harder to see the direction of change in opinion. Line graphs are especially well suited to showing data about trends.

## Understanding Tables

All the points reviewed so far about graphic presentations in general apply also to tables. When you see a table, read the title and descriptive information carefully; note the source of the data; and be aware of how the presentation itself affects your perception of the content.

Tables relate two or more variables by organizing information in columns and rows. In Table B.1 (a portion of a table from Chapter 2), the columns give data about victimization rates for two categories of crime, violent crime and theft. The rows of the table indicate categories of victims for whom these rates are reported, organized by sex, age, race,

**Table B.1**
**Who are the victims of personal crime?**
NCVS data helps clarify the characteristics of crime victims.

SOURCE: U.S. Department of Justice, Bureau of Justice Statistics, *Highlights from Twenty Years of Surveying Crime Victims* (Washington, D.C.: Government Printing Office, 1993), 18.

[a]Based on 10 or fewer cases.

| | Victims | Rate per 1,000 persons age 12 or over | | | Victims | Rate per 1,000 persons age 12 or over | |
|---|---|---|---|---|---|---|---|
| | | Violence | Theft | | | Violence | Theft |
| **Sex** | Male | 40 | 65 | **Family income** | Less than $7,500 | 59 | 62 |
| | Female | 23 | 58 | | $7,500–$9,999 | 42 | 61 |
| **Age** | 12–15 | 63 | 101 | | $10,000–$14,999 | 43 | 60 |
| | 16–19 | 91 | 94 | | $15,000–$24,999 | 31 | 57 |
| | 20–24 | 75 | 115 | | $25,000–$29,999 | 32 | 57 |
| | 25–34 | 35 | 71 | | $30,000–$49,999 | 25 | 60 |
| | 35–49 | 20 | 56 | | $50,000 or more | 20 | 66 |
| | 50–64 | 10 | 35 | **Education** | 0–4 years | 18 | 16 |
| | 65 and older | 4 | 20 | | 5–7 years | 45 | 67 |
| **Race** | White | 30 | 61 | | 8 years | 28 | 49 |
| | Black | 44 | 61 | | 9–11 years | 49 | 62 |
| | Other | 28 | 52 | | High school graduate | 28 | 49 |
| **Ethnicity** | Hispanic | 36 | 59 | | 1–3 years college | 36 | 83 |
| | Non-Hispanic | 31 | 61 | | College graduate | 18 | 68 |
| **Marital status by sex** | Males | | | **Residence** | Central city | 44 | 75 |
| | Never married | 80 | 97 | | 1,000,000 or more | 39 | 76 |
| | Divorced/separated | 44 | 95 | | 500,000–999,999 | 50 | 80 |
| | Married | 19 | 43 | | 250,000–499,999 | 54 | 70 |
| | Widowed | [a] | 23 | | 50,000–249,999 | 38 | 74 |
| | Females | | | | Suburban | 26 | 61 |
| | Never married | 43 | 90 | | Rural | 25 | 44 |
| | Divorced/separated | 45 | 74 | | | | |
| | Married | 11 | 44 | | | | |
| | Widowed | 6 | 22 | | | | |

ethnicity, and marital status by sex. Reading *down* a column allows us to compare information in the same category of crime (for example, "Theft") for different types of victims. By inspecting each column in turn, you can see that the rates for both types of crime victimization are higher for males versus females; for people aged 16–19 versus those in most other age groups; for blacks than for whites or other racial groups; and so on. Reading *across* a row (for example, "Males, Never married") allows us to compare the different categories of crime victimization for the same type of victim. If you read across all the rows, you can see that nearly all types of crime victims report more incidents of theft than crimes of violence.

Like other types of data displays, tables often require close study beyond the particular information being highlighted by the writer. When you come across a table, read down columns and across rows to discover for yourself the shape of the information being reported. Be careful, however, to notice how the data are organized and to distinguish between the data themselves and any *inferences* you draw from them. In this case, for example, you might be struck by the lower victimization rates reported by males who are married compared to the rates reported by males who are not married. Before you speculate about why married men are less likely to be victims of crime, note that the data for marital status are not broken out by age. We already know that people under age 25 are more likely than those older to be victimized (see the data under "Age"). Since these younger males are far more likely than older males to be unmarried, the difference in victimization rates for married and unmarried males may be largely accounted for by age rather than by marital status. To what extent this might be the case cannot be deduced solely from the information in the table.

In summary, data are presented in tables and graphs so as to be more easily grasped. But before you decide that you have truly understood the information, read the item and accompanying commentary attentively, and be aware of the way the writer has chosen to organize and display the data. By working with graphic presentations and posing questions to yourself as you read them, you'll also make the important information easier to remember.

## Understanding Raw Data

Data presented in graphs and tables have already been sifted and organized. As a student of criminal justice, you will also encounter raw (or "whole") data. For example, the *Sourcebook of Criminal Justice Statistics, 1993*, reports that there were 18,164 arrests for murder in the United States in 1992. Measures of data may also be expressed in terms of *percentage change over time*. The number of murders in 1992 was an increase of 17.7% over 1983. Finally, data often are expressed in terms of the *rate* at which an event occurs per a certain number of people. The murder rate in 1992 was 9 murders per 100,000 people in the United States. The formula for determining the rate is

$$\frac{\text{Number of Murders}}{\text{Total U.S. Population}} \times 100,000 = \text{Rate per 100,000}$$

For some purposes it is important to know the total figures (the raw data). For other purposes, percentages are more informative, and for still other purposes it is most useful to express data as a rate. To illustrate this point, consider the following example of data about incarceration.

Every December 31 the Bureau of Justice Statistics conducts a census of state and federal prisons. The count made on December 31, 1993 (reported in the Bureau of Justice Statistics *Bulletin*, June 1994), found a total of 948,881 inmates in these facilities. The number incarcerated in 1992 was 883,666, from which we can determine that 1993's figure represents a 7.4% increase over the previous year. On a national basis, the number of incarcerated persons represents a rate of 351 prisoners for every 100,000 U.S. residents.

The value of using the appropriate measure can be demonstrated by comparing the data from Louisiana and New Jersey. On December 31, 1993, there were 22,532 offenders held in the prisons of Louisiana and 23,831 in the prisons of New Jersey. How do these states compare? Just knowing the number of prisoners does not allow us to say much about corrections in these states. If, however, we express the numbers as a rate, we allow for the differences in the sizes of the two state populations and get a much clearer picture. In fact, although there are fewer prisoners in Louisiana than in New Jersey, the incarceration rate in Louisiana (499 prisoners per 100,000 population) is considerably higher than in New Jersey (299 per 100,000). From the information presented a moment ago, we can also see that the rate is significantly higher than that for the United States as a whole (351 per 100,000).

## Sources of Criminal Justice Data

To a large extent, criminal justice researchers are dependent on data collected and analyzed by agencies of government. In particular, the Bureau of Justice Statistics of the U.S. Department of Justice produces the *Sourcebook of Criminal Justice Statistics*, an annual compilation of data on most aspects of crime and justice; the *Bulletin*, single-topic issues published on a regular basis that are related to the police, courts, and corrections; and the *Special Report*, a publication presenting findings from specific research projects. The National Institute of Justice, also an arm of the U.S. Department of Justice, publishes *Research in Brief*, summary versions of major research studies. *Crime in the United States*, published each August by the U.S. Department of Justice, contains data collected through the FBI's Uniform Crime Reports system.

The libraries of most colleges and universities hold these publications in the government documents or reference sections. Ask your librarian to help you find them. If you would like to get on the mailing list to receive the free publications of the Bureau of Justice Statistics, fill out the form on the last page of the *Bulletin*.

# GLOSSARY

**accusatory process** The series of events from the arrest of a suspect to the filing of a formal charging instrument (indictment or information) with the court.

**adjudication** The process of determining the guilt or innocence of a defendant.

**administrative regulations** Rules promulgated by governmental agencies to implement specific public policies.

**aggressive patrol** A patrol strategy designed to maximize the number of police interventions and observations in the community.

*Alford* **v.** *North Carolina* **(1970)** A plea of guilty may be accepted for the purpose of a lesser sentence by a defendant who maintains his innocence.

**anomie** A state of normlessness caused by a breakdown in the rules of social behavior.

**appeal** A request to a higher court that it review actions taken in a completed trial.

**appellate court** A court that does not try criminal cases but hears appeals of decisions of lower courts.

**arraignment** The act of calling an accused person before the court to hear the charges lodged against him or her and to enter a plea in response to those charges.

**arrest** The physical taking of a person into custody on the ground that there is probable cause to believe that he or she has committed a criminal offense. Police may use only reasonable physical force in making an arrest. The purpose of arrest is to hold the accused for a court proceeding.

**assigned counsel** An attorney in private practice who is assigned by a court to represent an indigent and whose fee is paid by the government that has jurisdiction over the case.

**bail** An amount of money specified by a judge to be posted as a condition of pretrial release for the purpose of ensuring the appearance of the accused in court as required.

*Barron* **v.** *Baltimore* **(1833)** Bill of Rights applies only to actions of the federal govenment.

*Bell* **v.** *Wolfish* **(1979)** Strip searches, including body-cavity searches after contact visits, may be carried out when the need for the search outweighs the invasion of personal rights.

**bench trial** Trial conducted by a judge who acts as a fact finder and determines issues of law. No jury participates.

**biological explanations** Explanations of crime that emphasize physiological and neurological factors.

**boot camp/shock incarceration** A short-term institutional sentence, usually followed by probation, that puts the offender through a physical regimen designed to develop discipline and respect for authority.

*Bordenkircher* **v.** *Hayes* **(1978)** A defendant's rights were not violated by a prosecutor who warned that not to accept a guilty plea would result in a harsher sentence.

*Bounds* **v.** *Smith* **(1977)** Inmates have the right of access to adequate law libraries or to the assistance of those trained in the law.

*Boykin* **v.** *Alabama* **(1969)** Defendants must make an affirmative statement that they are voluntarily making a plea of guilty.

**Breed v. Jones (1975)** Juveniles cannot be found delinquent in juvenile court and then be waived to adult court without violating double jeopardy.

**Carroll v. United States (1925)** An automobile may be searched if the police have probable cause to believe it contains criminal evidence.

**case law** Legal opinions having the status of law as enunciated by courts.

**challenge for cause** Removal of a prospective juror by showing bias or some other legal disability. The number of such challenges permitted is unlimited.

**circumstantial evidence** Evidence provided by a witness from which a jury must infer a fact.

**citation** A written order issued by a law enforcement officer directing an alleged offender to appear in court at a specified time to answer a criminal charge; referred to as a *summons* in some jurisdictions.

**civil forfeiture** The relinquishing of assets to the state as the consequence of crime.

**civilian review board** A citizen board independent of the police, established to receive and investigate complaints against police officers.

**civil law** Laws regulating the relationships between or among individuals.

**classical criminology** A school of criminology that views behavior as stemming from free will, demands responsibility and accountability of all perpetrators, and stresses the need for punishment sufficiently severe to deter others.

**classification** The act of assigning a new inmate to a type of custody and treatment appropriate to his or her needs.

**clearance rate** The percentage of crimes known to the police that they believe they have solved through an arrest; a statistic used as a measure of a police department's productivity.

**common law** The Anglo-American system of uncodified law, in which judges follow precedent set by earlier decisions when they decide new but similar cases. The substantive and procedural criminal law was originally developed in this manner but was later codified by legislatures.

**community correctional center** An institution, usually located in an urban area, that houses inmates soon to be released. Such centers are designed to help inmates establish community ties and thus to promote their reintegration with society.

**community corrections** A model of corrections based on the assumption that the reintegration of the offender into the community should be the goal of the criminal justice system.

**community service** A sentence requiring the offender to perform a certain amount of labor in the community.

**conflict model** A legal model that asserts that the political power of interest groups and elites influences the content of the criminal law.

**congregate system** A penitentiary system, developed in Auburn, New York, in which each inmate was held in isolation during the night but worked with fellow prisoners during the day under a rule of silence.

**consensus model** A legal model that asserts that criminal law, as an expression of the social consciousness of the whole society, reflects values that transcend the immediate interests of particular groups and individuals.

**constitutions** The basic laws of a country defining the structure of government and the relationship of citizens to that government.

**continuance** An adjournment of a scheduled case until a future date.

**control theories** Theories postulating that criminal behavior occurs when the bonds that tie an individual to others in society are broken or weakened.

**Cooper v. Pate (1964)** Prisoners are entitled to the protection of the Civil Rights Act of 1871 and may challenge conditons of their confinement in federal courts.

**copping out** (slang) Entering a plea of guilty, normally after bargaining. The copping-out ceremony consists of a series of questions that the judge asks the defendant as to the voluntary nature of the plea.

**count** Each separate offense of which a person is accused in an indictment or an information.

**crime** A specific act of commission or omission in violation of the law, for which a punishment is prescribed.

**crime control model** A model of the criminal justice system that assumes that freedom is so important that every effort must be made to repress crime; it emphasizes efficiency and the capacity to apprehend, try, convict, and dispose of a high proportion of offenders.

**crimes without victims** Offenses involving a willing and private exchange of illegal goods or services for which there is a strong demand. Participants do not feel that they are being harmed. Prosecution is justified on the ground that society as a whole is being injured by the act.

**criminal justice wedding cake** A model of the criminal justice process in which criminal cases form a four-tiered hierarchy with a few celebrated cases at the top, and each succeeding layer increasing in size as its importance in the eyes of officials and the public diminishes.

**criminogenic** Factors thought to bring about criminal behavior in an individual.

**criminologist** A scholar who uses the scientific method to study the nature, cause, amount, and control of criminal behavior.

*Cruz* v. *Beto* **(1972)** Prisoners who adhere to other than conventional beliefs may not be denied the opportunity to practice their religion.

**custodial model** A model of corrections that emphasizes security, discipline, and order.

**dark figure of crime** A metaphor that emphasizes the dangerous dimensions of crime that is never reported to the police.

**day reporting center** A community correctional center where an offender reports each day to comply with elements of a sentence.

**defense attorney** The lawyer who represents the accused and the convicted offender in their dealings with criminal justice officials.

**delinquent** A child who has committed a criminal or status offense.

**dependent child** A child whose parent(s) is unable to give proper care.

**detention** A period of temporary custody of a juvenile before disposition of his or her case.

**determinate sentence** A sentence that fixes the term of imprisonment at a specified period of time.

**deterrence** Discouragement of criminal behavior on the part of known offenders (special deterrence) and of the public (general deterrence) by the threat of punishment.

**differential association theory** A theory that people become criminals because they encounter a large number of influences that regard criminal behavior as normal and acceptable, with these influences outnumbering the influences hostile to criminal behavior.

**differential response** A patrol strategy that prioritizes calls for service and assigns various response options.

**directed patrol** A patrol strategy designed to direct resources in a proactive manner against known high-crime areas.

**direct evidence** Eyewitness accounts.

**discovery** A prosecutor's pretrial disclosure to the defense of facts and evidence to be introduced at trial.

**discretion** The authority to make decisions without reference to specific rules or facts, using instead one's own judgment; allows for individualization and informality in the administration of justice.

**discretionary release** The release of an inmate from incarceration at the discretion of the parole board within the boundaries set by the sentence and the penal law.

**diversion** An alternative to adjudication by which the defendant agrees to conditions set by the prosecutor (such as to undergo counseling or drug rehabilitation) in exchange for withdrawal of charges.

**double jeopardy** The subjecting of a person to prosecution more than once for the same offense; prohibited by the Fifth Amendment.

**dual court system** A system consisting of a separate judicial structure for each state in addition to a national structure. Each case is tried in a court of the same jurisdiction as that of the law or laws broken.

**due process (procedural)** The constitutional requirement that all persons be treated fairly and justly by government officials. This means that an accused person can be arrested, prosecuted, tried, and punished only in accordance with procedures prescribed by law.

**due process model** A model of the criminal justice system that assumes that freedom is so important that every effort must be made to ensure that criminal justice decisions are based on reliable information; it emphasizes the adversarial process, the rights of defendants, and formal decision-making procedures.

**Durham Rule** A test of the defense of insanity that requires it to be shown that the accused is not criminally responsible because the act resulted from mental disease or mental defect.

**entrapment** The defense that the individual was induced by the police to commit the criminal act.

*Escobedo v. Illinois* **(1963)** Counsel must be provided when suspects are taken into police custody.

**exchange** A mutual transfer of resources; a balance of benefits and deficits that flow from behavior based on decisions as to the values and costs of alternatives.

**exclusionary rule** The principle that illegally obtained evidence must be excluded from a trial.

*Fare* **v.** *Michael C.* **(1979)** Trial court judges must evaluate the voluntariness of confessions by juveniles by examining the totality of circumstances.

**felony** Serious crime usually carrying a penalty of death or incarceration for more than one year. Persons convicted of felonies lose the right to vote, to hold public elective office, and to practice certain professions and occupations.

**filtering process** A screening operation; a process by which criminal justice officials screen out some cases while advancing others to the next level of decision making.

**fine** A sum of money to be paid to the state by a convicted person as punishment for an offense.

**forfeiture** Seizure by the government of property and other assets derived from or used in criminal activity.

**frankpledge** A system in Old English law whereby members of a tithing, a group of ten families, pledged to be responsible for the good conduct of all members over twelve years of age.

*Fulwood* **v.** *Clemmer* **(1962)** The Black Muslim faith must be recognized as a religion and officials may not restrict members from holding services.

**fundamental fairness** A legal doctrine supporting the idea that so long as a state's conduct maintains the basic elements of fairness, the Constitution has not been violated.

**furlough** The temporary release of an inmate from a correctional institution for a brief period, usually one to three days, for a visit home. Such programs are designed to maintain family ties and prepare inmates for release on parole.

*Furman* **v.** *Georgia* **(1972)** Death penalty, as administered, constituted cruel and unusual treatment.

*Gagnon* **v.** *Scarpelli* **(1973)** Required that before probation may be revoked, a two-stage hearing must be held and the offender provided with specific elements of due process.

**general deterrence** Punishment of criminals intended to serve as an example to the general public and thus to discourage the commission of offenses.

*Gideon* **v.** *Wainwright* **(1963)** Defendants have a right to counsel in felony cases.

**going rate** Local view of the appropriate sentence given the offense, the defendant's prior record, and other characteristics.

**good time** A reduction of a convict's prison sentence awarded for good behavior at the discretion of the prison administrator.

*Gregg* **v.** *Georgia* **(1976)** Upheld death penalty law in which judge and jury considered mitigating and aggravating circumstances in deciding which convicted murderers should be given death.

**grouping** A collective of individuals who interact in the workplace but, because of shifting membership, do not develop into a workgroup.

**habeas corpus**  A writ or judicial order requesting that a person holding another person produce the prisoner and give reasons to justify continued confinement.

**halfway house**  A correctional facility housing convicted felons who spend a portion of their day at work in the community but reside in the halfway house during nonworking hours.

**hands-off policy**  Judges should not interfere with the administration of correctional institutions.

**home confinement**  A sentence requiring the offender to remain inside his or her home during specified periods.

*Hudson* v. *Palmer* **(1984)**  Officials may search cells without a warrant and seize materials found there.

**incapacitation**  Deprivation of capacity to commit crimes against society by detention in prison or capital punishment.

**inchoate offenses**  Conduct made criminal even though it has not yet produced the harm that the law seeks to prevent.

**incorporation**  The extension of the due process clause of the Fourteenth Amendment to make binding on state governments the rights guaranteed in the first ten amendments to the U.S. Constitution (the Bill of Rights).

**indeterminate sentence**  A period set by a judge between the earliest date for a decision on parole eligibility and the latest date for completion of the sentence. In holding that the time necessary for treatment cannot be set, the indeterminate sentence is closely associated with rehabilitation.

**indictment**  A document returned by a grand jury as a "true bill" charging an individual with a specific crime on the basis of a determination of probable cause as presented by a prosecuting attorney.

**information**  A document charging an individual with a specific crime. It is prepared by a prosecuting attorney and presented to a court at a preliminary hearing.

**inmate code**  The values and norms of the prison social system that define for inmates the characteristics associated with the model prisoner.

*In re Gault* **(1967)**  Juveniles have the right to counsel, to confront and examine accusers, and to have adequate notice of charges when there is the possiblity of confinement as a punishment.

*In re Winship* **(1970)**  The standard of proof of beyond a reasonable doubt applies to juvenile delinquency proceedings.

**intensive probation supervision**  Probation granted under conditons of strict reporting to a probation officer with a limited caseload.

**intermediate sanctions**  A variety of punishments that are more restrictive than traditional probation but less stringent and less costly than incarceration.

**internal affairs unit**  A branch of a police department designated to receive and investigate complaints against officers alleging violation of rules and policies.

**irresistible impulse test**  A test of the defense of insanity that requires it to be shown that although the accused knew right from wrong, he or she was unable to control an irresistible impulse to commit the crime.

*Johnson* v. *Avery* **(1969)**  The use of jailhouse lawyers may not be prohibited unless free counsel is provided by the state.

**judicial waiver**  The juvenile court waives its jurisdiction and transfers the case to the adult criminal court.

**jurisdiction**  The territory or boundaries within which control may be exercised; hence, the legal and geographical range of a court's authority.

**jury**  A panel consisting of a statutorily defined number of citizens selected according to law and sworn to determine matters of fact in a criminal action and to render a verdict of guilty or not guilty.

**labeling theories**  Theories emphasizing that the causes of criminal behavior are not found in the individual but in the social process through which certain acts are labeled deviant or criminal.

**law enforcement**  The police function of controlling crime by intervening in situations in which it is clear that the law has been violated and only the identity of the guilty needs to be determined.

**learning theories** Theories postulating that criminal behavior, like legal and normative behavior, is learned.

**legal responsibility** The accountability of an individual for a crime because of the perpetrator's characteristics and the circumstances of the illegal act.

**legal sufficiency** The presence of the minimum legal elements necessary for prosecution of a case. When a prosecutor's decision to prosecute a case is customarily based on legal sufficiency, a great many cases are accepted for prosecution, but the majority of them are disposed of by plea bargaining or dismissal.

**legislative exclusion** The legislature excludes from juvenile court jurisdiction certain offenses usually either very minor, such as traffic or fishing violations, or very serious, such as murder or rape.

**line units** Police components that perform the direct operations and carry out the basic functions of patrol, investigation, traffic, vice, juvenile, and so on.

**local legal culture** Norms shared by members of a court community as to case handling and a participant's behavior in the judicial process.

*mala in se* Offenses that are wrong by their very nature, irrespective of statutory prohibition.

*mala prohibita* Offenses prohibited by statute but not inherently wrong.

**mandatory release** The required release of an inmate from incarceration upon the expiration of a certain time period, as stipulated by a determinate sentencing law or parole guidelines.

**mandatory sentence** A type of sentence determined by statutes, which require that a certain penalty shall be imposed and executed upon certain convicted offenders.

*Mapp v. Ohio* **(1961)** Fourth amendment protects citizens from unreasonable searches and seizures by the states.

*McCleskey v. Kemp* **(1987)** Rejected a challenge of Georgia's death penalty on grounds of racial discrimination.

*McCleskey v. Zant* **(1991)** Limits access to the federal courts since all habeas claims must be raised in the initial petition.

*McKiever v. Pennsylvania* **(1971)** There is no constitutional right for a jury trial for juveniles.

*Mempa v. Rhay* **(1967)** Probationers have the right to counsel at a hearing considering revocation of a suspended sentence.

*mens rea* "Guilty mind," or blameworthy state of mind, necessary for the imputation of responsibility for a criminal offense; criminal, as distinguished from innocent, intent.

*Miranda v. Arizona* **(1966)** Confessions made by suspects who were not notified of their due process rights cannot be admitted as evidence.

**misdemeanor** Offense less serious than a felony and usually punishable by incarceration for no more than a year, probation, or intermediate sanction.

**merit selection** A reform plan in which judges are nominated by a committee and appointed by the governor for a given period. When the term expires, the voters are asked to signify their approval or disapproval of the judge for a succeeding term. If the judge is disapproved, the committee nominates a successor for the governor's appointment.

**mode** A representation; an ideal description of something that cannot be visualized, permitting generalized statements to be made about it and its strengths and weaknesses to be elvaluated.

*Morrissey v. Brewer* **(1972)** According to due process rights, a prompt, informal inquiry before an impartial hearing officer is required before parole may be revoked. The parolee may present relevant information and question adverse information.

**motion** An application to a court requesting that an order be issued to bring about a specified action.

**National Crime Victimization Surveys** Interviews of samples of the U.S. population conducted by the Bureau of Justice Statistics to determine the number and types of criminal victimizations and thus the extent of unreported as well as reported crime.

**National Incident-Based Reporting System** A reporting system in which the police describe each offense in a crime incident together with data describing the offender, victim, and property.

**necessarily included offense** An offense committed for the purpose of committing another offense; for example, trespass committed for the purpose of committing burglary.

**neglected child** A child who is not receiving proper care because of some action or inaction of his or her parent(s).

**net widening** Expansion of the number of people under correctional supervision due to the addition of new sentencing options.

*New Jersey* v. *T.L.O.* **(1985)** School officials may search a student based on a reasonable suspicion that the search will produce evidence that a school or a civil law has been violated.

*nolle prosequi* An entry made by a prosecutor on the record of a case and announced in court to indicate that the charges specified will not be prosecuted. In effect, the charges are thereby dismissed.

*nolo contendere* A defendant's formal answer in court in which it is stated that the charges are not contested and which, while not an admission of guilt, subjects the defendant to the same sentencing consequences as a plea of guilty. Often used to preclude civil action against the accused by the victim.

**nonpartisan election** An election in which candidates who are not endorsed by political parties are presented to the voters for selection.

**norm** Societal expectations concerning behavior.

**occupational crime** Conduct in violation of the law that is committed through opportunities created in the course of a legal occupation.

**order maintenance** The police function of preventing behavior that disturbs or threatens to disturb the public peace or that involves face-to-face conflict between two or more persons. In such situations the police exercise discretion in deciding whether a law has been broken.

**organized crime** A social framework for the perpetration of criminal acts, usually in such fields as gambling, drugs, and prostitution, in which illegal services that are in great demand are provided.

**overcriminalization** The use of criminal sanctions to deter behavior that is acceptable to substantial portions of society.

**pardon** An action of the executive branch of state or federal government excusing an offense and absolving the offender from the consequences of the crime.

*parens patriae* The state as parent; the state as guardian and protector of all citizens (such as juveniles) who are unable to protect themselves.

**parole** The conditional release of an inmate from incarceration under supervision after a portion of the prison sentence has been served.

**partisan election** An election in which candidates endorsed by political parties are presented to the voters for selection.

**penitentiary** An institution intended to isolate prisoners from society and from one another so that they can reflect on their past misdeeds, repent, and thus undergo reformation.

**penology** A branch of criminology dealing with the management of prisons and treatment of offenders.

**peremptory challenge** Removal of a prospective juror without assignment of any cause. The number of such challenges permitted is limited.

**PINS, CINS, JINS** Acronyms for "person in need of supervision," "child in need of supervision," and "juvenile in need of supervision," which are terms used to designate juveniles who either are status offenders or are thought to be on the verge of getting in trouble.

**plea bargaining** A defendant's plea of guilty to a criminal charge with the reasonable expectation of receiving some consideration from the state for doing so, usually a reduction of the charge. The defendant's ultimate goal is a penalty lighter than the one formally warranted by the charged offense.

**political considerations** Matters taken into account in the formulation of public policies and the making of choices among competing values—who gets what portion of the good (justice) produced by the system, when, and how.

**political crimes** Acts that constitute threats against the state (such as treason, sedition, espionage).

**positivist criminology** A school of criminology that views behavior as stemming from social, biological, and psychological factors. It argues that punishment should be tailored to the individual needs of the offender.

*Powell* v. *Alabama* (1932) Counsel must be provided defendants in a capital case.

**presentence report** A report that is prepared by a probation office after an investigation into the background of a convicted offender, and that is designed to help the judge determine an appropriate sentence.

**presumptive parole date** The presumed release date stipulated by parole guidelines should the offender serve time without disciplinary or other incidents.

**preventive detention** The holding of a defendant for trial based on a judge's finding that, if released on bail, he or she would endanger the safety of any other person and the community.

**preventive patrol** Providing regular protection to an area while maintaining a mobile police presence to deter potential criminals from committing crimes.

**proactive** An active search for offenders on the part of the police in the absence of reports of violations of the law. Arrests for crimes without victims are usually proactive.

**probable cause** The evidentiary criteria necessary to uphold an arrest or to support issuance of an arrest or search warrant. Also, facts upholding the belief that a crime has been committed and that the accused committed the offense.

**probation** A sentence allowing the offender to serve the sanctions imposed by the court in the community under supervision.

**problem-oriented policing** An approach to policing in which officers seek to identify, analyze, and respond, on a routine basis, to the underlying circumstances that create the incidents that prompt citizens to call the police.

**procedural criminal law** Law defining the procedures that officials must follow in the enforce-ment, adjudication, and correction portions of the criminal justice system.

**procedural due process** The constitutional requirement that all persons be treated fairly and justly by government officials. An accused person can be arrested, prosecuted, tried, and punished only in accordance with procedures prescribed by law.

**prosecuting attorney** A legal representative of the state with sole responsibility for bringing criminal charges. In some states referred to as district attorney, state's attorney, or county attorney.

**psychological explanations** Explanations of crime that emphasize mental processes and behavior.

**public defender** An attorney employed on a full-time, salaried basis by the government to represent indigents.

**reactive** Occurring in response to a stimulus, such as police activity in response to notification that a crime has been committed.

**real evidence** Physical evidence such as a weapon, records, fingerprints, stolen property.

**reasonable doubt** The standard used by a juror to decide if the prosecution has provided enough evidence for conviction. Jurors should vote for acquittal if they can give a reason to support this position.

**recidivism** A return to criminal behavior.

**rehabilitation** The goal of restoring a convicted offender to a constructive place in society through some form of vocational, educational, or therapeutic treatment.

**rehabilitation model** A model of corrections that emphasizes the provision of treatment programs designed to reform the offender.

**reintegration model** A model of a correctional institution that emphasizes the maintenance of the offender's ties to family and community as a method of reform, in recognition of the fact that the offender will be returning to the community.

**release on recognizance (ROR)** Pretrial release granted on the defendant's promise to appear in court because the judge believes that the defendant's ties in the community are sufficient to guarantee the required appearance.

**restitution** Compensation for injury an offender has inflicted in the form of payment of money to the victim or the performance of service to the community.

**retribution** Punishment inflicted on a person who has infringed on the rights of others and so deserves to be penalized. The severity of the sanction should fit the seriousness of the crime.

*Rhodes* **v.** *Chapman* **(1981)** Double bunking and crowding do not necessarily constitute cruel and unusual punishment. Conditions must involve "wanton and unnecessary infliction of pain" and be "grossly disproportionate to the severity of the crime warranting imprisonment."

*Ricketts* **v.** *Adamson* **(1987)** Defendants must uphold plea agreement or suffer the consequences.

*Ruffin* **v.** *Commonwealth* **(1871)** As a result of his crime, the prisoner is the slave of the state.

*Ruiz* **v.** *Estelle* **(1980)** Conditions of confinement in the Texas prison system were unconstitutional.

*Santobello* **v.** *New York* **(1971)** When a guilty plea rests on a promise of a prosecutor it must be fulfilled.

*Schall* **v.** *Martin* **(1984)** Juveniles can be held in preventive detention if there is concern that additional crimes may be committed while awaiting court action.

**search warrant** An order of a court officer that allows a police officer to search a designated place for specific persons or items to be seized.

**selective incapacitation** Making optimum use of expensive and limited prison space by targeting for incarceration those individuals whose incapacity will do the most to reduce crime.

**self-incrimination** The act of exposing oneself to prosecution by being forced to answer questions that may tend to incriminate one; it is protected against by the Fifth Amendment. In any criminal proceeding the prosecution must prove the charges by means of evidence other than the testimony of the accused.

**sentencing guidelines** An instrument developed to indicate to judges the usual sanctions given previously to particular offenses.

**separate confinement** A penitentiary system, developed in Pennsylvania, in which each inmate was held in isolation from other inmates. All activities, including craft work, were carried on in the cells.

**service** The police function of providing assistance to the public, usually with regard to matters unrelated to crime.

**shock probation** A sentence in which the offender is released after a short incarceration and resentenced to probation.

**social conflict theories** Theories that assume criminal law and the criminal justice system are primarily means of controlling the poor and have-nots.

**socialization** The process by which the rules, symbols, and values of a group or subculture are learned by its members.

**social process theories** Theories that see criminality as normal behavior. Everyone has the potential to become a criminal, depending on the influences that impel one toward or away from crime and how one is regarded by others.

**social structure theories** Theories that blame crime on the creation of a lower-class culture based on poverty and deprivation, and the response of the poor to this situation.

**sociological explanations** Explanations of crime that emphasize the social conditions that bear on the individual as the causes of criminal behavior.

**special deterrence** Punishment inflicted on criminals with the intent to discourage them from committing any future crimes.

*stare decisis* The principle that judges should be bound by precedents (decisions made in previous similar cases) when they decide the cases before them.

**state attorney general** Chief legal officer of a state responsible for both civil and criminal matters.

**status offense** Any act committed by a juvenile that is considered unacceptable for a child, such as truancy or running away from home, but that would not be a crime if it were committed by an adult.

**statutes** Laws passed by legislatures. Statutory definitions of criminal offenses are embodied in penal codes.

**strict liability** An obligation or duty whose breach constitutes an offense that requires no showing of *mens rea* to be adjudged criminal; a principle usually applied to regulatory offenses involving health and safety.

**subculture** The aggregate of symbols, beliefs, and values shared by members of a subgroup within the larger society.

**substantive criminal law** Law defining the behaviors that are subject to punishment, and the sanctions for such offenses.

**sworn officers** Police employees who have taken an oath and been given powers by the state to, for example, make arrests, use force, and transverse property, in accordance with their duties.

**system** A complex whole consisting of interdependent parts whose operations are directed toward goals and are influenced by the environment within which they function.

**system efficiency** Operation of the prosecutor's office in such a way as to effect speedy and early dispositions of cases in response to caseload pressures in the system. Weak cases are screened out at intake, and other nontrial alternatives are used as primary means of disposition.

***Tennessee* v. *Garner* (1985)** Deadly force may not be used against an unarmed and fleeing suspect unless necessary to prevent the escape and the officer has probable cause to believe that the suspect poses a significant threat of death or serious injury to the officers or others.

***Terry* v. *Ohio* (1968)** A police officer may stop and frisk an individual if it is reasonable to suspect that a crime has been committed.

**testimony** Oral evidence provided by a legally competent witness.

**total institution** An institution (such as a prison) that completely encapsulates the lives of those who work and live within it. Rules govern behavior, and the group is split into two parts, one of which controls the lives of the other.

**totality of conditions:** Although specific conditions in prisons might not violate the Constitution, the totality of the conditions may violate the cruel and unusual punishment provisions of the Eighth Amendment.

**trial court of general jurisdiction** A criminal court that has jurisdiction over all offenses, including felonies, and may in some states also hear appeals.

**trial court of limited jurisdiction** A criminal court of which the trial jurisdiction either includes no felonies or is limited to some category of felonies. Such courts have jurisdiction over misdemeanor cases, probable-cause hearings in felony cases, and, sometimes, felony trials that may result in penalties below a specified limit.

**trial sufficiency** The presence of sufficient legal elements to ensure successful prosecution of a case. When a prosecutor's decision to prosecute a case is customarily based on trial sufficiency, only cases that seem certain to result in conviction at trial are accepted for prosecution. Use of plea bargaining is minimal; good police work and court capacity are required.

***Uniform Crime Reports*** An annually published statistical summary of crimes reported to the police, which is based on voluntary reports to the FBI by local, state, and federal law enforcement agencies.

**United States attorneys** Officials responsible for the prosecution of crimes that violate the laws of the United States. Appointed by the president and assigned to a U.S. district jurisdiction.

***United States* v. *Leon* (1984)** Evidence seized using a warrant later found defective is valid if the officer was acting in good faith.

***United States* v. *Salerno* (1987)** Preventive detention provisions of the Bail Reform Act of 1984 upheld; legitimate use of governmental power designed to prevent people from committing crimes while on bail.

**upperworld crime** Conduct in violation of the law engaged in during the course of business activity (like tax evasion, price fixing). Such offenses are often viewed as shrewd business practices that are not really criminal.

**utilitarianism** The doctrine that the aim of all action should be the greatest possible balance of pleasure over pain; hence, the belief that a punishment must achieve enough good to outweigh the pain inflicted on the offender.

**victimology** A subfield of criminology that examines the role played by the victim in precipitating a criminal incident.

**visible crimes** Offenses against persons and property committed primarily by members of the lower class. Often referred to as "street crimes" or "ordinary crimes," these are the offenses most upsetting to the public.

*voir dire* An examination of prospective jurors through which the prosecution and defense screen out persons who might be biased or incapable of rendering a fair verdict.

**warrant** A court order authorizing police officials to take certain actions, for example, to arrest suspects or to search premises.

*Williams v. Florida* **(1970)** Juries of fewer than twelve members are constitutional.

*Wilson v. Seiter* **(1991)** The standard of review of official conduct is whether state policies or actions by correctional officers constitute "deliberate indifference" to constitutional rights.

*Wolf v. McDonnell* **(1974)** Basic elements of procedural due process must be present when decisions are made concerning the discipline of an inmate.

**work and educational release** The daytime release of inmates from correctional institutions so they may work or attend school.

**workgroup** A collectivity of individuals who interact in the workplace on a continuing basis, share goals, develop norms in regard to the way activities should be carried out, and eventually establish a network of roles that serve to differentiate this group from others.

**working personality** The complex of emotional and behavioral characteristics developed by a member of an occupational group in response to the work situation and environmental influences.

**FRONTMATTER**

**i,** © Tim Flach/Tony Stone Worldwide. **ii, v, vii,** George Chan/Tony Stone Images. **viii** (top), Wally McNamee/Woodfin Camp & Associates; (bottom), Alon Reininger/Woodfin Camp & Associates. **ix** (top), Leif Skoogfors/Woodfin Camp & Associates; (bottom); Wide World Photos, Inc. **x** (top), David Portnoy/Black Star; (bottom), AP/Wide World Photos, Inc. **xi** (top), Wide World Photos, Inc.; (bottom), AP/Wide World Photos, Inc. **xii** (top), Charles Gupton/Stock Boston; (bottom), AP/Wide World Photos, Inc. **xiii** (top), Wide World Photos, Inc.; (bottom), Motion Picture & T.V. Photo Archive. **xiv** (top), FourbyFive, Inc.; (bottom), UPI/Bettmann. **xv** (top), Bill Swersey/Liaison International, Inc.; (center), David Butow/Black Star; (bottom), Ferry/Liaison International. **xvi** (top), Ed Kashi; (bottom), Bob Daemmrich/Stock Boston. **xvii** (top), Lester Sloan/Woodfin Camp and Associates; (bottom), Butch Martin/Image Bank. **xviii** (top), Douglas Burrows/Liaison International; (bottom), David Burnett/Woodfin Camp & Associates, Inc. **xix,** FourbyFive, Inc. **xxi,** FourbyFive, Inc. **xxv,** ©Tim Flach/Tony Stone Worldwide.

**PART ONE**

**2,** FourbyFive Inc. **3,** Wally McNamee/Woodfin Camp & Associates.

**CHAPTER 1**

**5,** Alon Reininger/Woodfin Camp & Associates, Inc. **10,** George Chan/Tony Stone Images. **12,** Phil Huber/Black Star. **15,** Phil Huber/Black Star. **17,** Llewellyn/Uniphoto Picture Agency. **19,** David Portnoy/Black Star. **28,** Larry Downing/ Woodfin Camp & Associates, Inc. **29,** Wally McNamee/Woodfin Camp & Associates. **32** (top), Courtesy of the Illinois Department of Corrections; (bottom), L.A. Daily News/Sygma.

**CHAPTER 2**

**41,** Leif Skoogfors/Woodfin Camp & Associates, Inc. **42,** The Bettmann Archive. **43** (left), Wide World Photos, Inc; (right), Culver Pictures, Inc. **46,** The Bettmann Archive. **47,** AP/Wide World Photos, Inc. **50,** Robert Rathe/Stock Boston. **51,** S. McCurry/ Magnum Photos, Inc. **55,** David Woo/Stock Boston. **62,** Alon Reininger/Woodfin Camp & Associates. **69,** Billy E. Barnes/Stock Boston. **71,** Culver Pictures, Inc. **72,** The Bettmann Archive. **75,** Larry Downing/Woodfin Camp & Associates, Inc.

**CHAPTER 3**

**89,** Wide World Photos, Inc. **91,** Archive Photos, Inc. **94** (top), Culver Pictures, Inc; (bottom, left to right), Mark Reinstein/Uniphoto Picture Agency, The Bettmann Archive, David Woo/Stock Boston, FourbyFive, Inc. **96,** Steve Starr/Stock Boston. **103,** Bob Daemmrich/ Stock Boston. **105,** John Curtis. **113** (left), AP/Wide World Photos, Inc.; (right), AP/Wide World Photos, Inc. **114,** John Curtis. **116** (top and bottom), The Bettmann Archive. **119,** Ackad/Collection of the Supreme Court of the United States. **121,** Nubar Alexanian/Woodfin Camp & Associates. **122,** AP/ Wide World Photos, Inc.

**PART TWO**

**130,** Phil Huber/Black Star. **131,** David Portnoy/ Black Star.

**CHAPTER 4**

**133,** AP/Wide World Photos, Inc. **136,** The Bettmann Archive. **139,** UPI/Bettmann. **141,** Detroit Free Press/Black Star. **142** (left), AP/Wide World Photos, Inc; (right), Cary Wolinsky/Stock Boston. **143** (left), Stacy Pick/Stock Boston; (right), Donald Dietz/Stock Boston. **144,** Culver Pictures, Inc. **151** (left), Misha Erwitt/Magnum Photos; (center), Reni Burri/Magnum Photos; (right), Christopher Brown/Stock Boston. **153,** AP/Wide World Photos, Inc. **156,** Herman Kokjan/Black Star. **157,** Sherry Peters/The Hartford Courant.

**CHAPTER 5**

**165,** Wide World Photos, Inc. **169,** Greg English/ Sygma. **171,** David Woo/Stock Boston. **176,** Herman Kokjan/Black Star. **182,** Yvonne Hemsey/Liaison International. **186,** Herman Kokjan/Black Star. **189,** Charles Moore/Black Star. **191,** David Portnoy/

Black Star. **194**, Bill Gallery/Stock Boston. **199**, Richard Falco/Black Star. **203**, Craig Filipacchi/Liaison International.

## CHAPTER 6
**217**, AP/Wide World Photos, Inc. **221**, Dahlgren/ The Stock Market. **224**, Bob Daemmrich/Stock Boston. **225**, Herman Kokjan/Black Star. **227**, Nubar Alexanian/Stock Boston. **230**, Phil Huber/Black Star. **234**, ACey Harper/Reportage Stock. **235**, Herman Kokjan/Black Star. **238**, Doug Menuez/Reportage Stock. **249**, Frances M. Roberts. **255**, Richard Pasley/ Stock Boston.

## PART THREE
**264**, David Sailors/The Stock Market. **265**, Charles Gupton/Stock Boston.

## CHAPTER 7
**267**, AP/Wide World Photos, Inc. **269**, David Burnett/Contact Press Images. **270**, The Bettmann Archive. **271**, John Newbauer/Uniphoto Picture Agency. **274**, John Curtis. **281**, John Curtis. **283**, John Maher/ The Stock Market. **292**, John Curtis. **296**, Bob Daemmrich/Stock Boston.

## CHAPTER 8
**301**, Wide World Photos, Inc. **302**, David Woo/Stock Boston. **304**, UPI/Bettmann. **307**, David Woo/Stock Boston. **315**, John Curtis. **316**, David Woo/Stock Boston. **321**, Bob Daemmrich/Stock Boston.

## CHAPTER 9
**329**, Motion Picture & T.V. Photo Archive. **331**, Douglas Burrows/Gamma-Liaison. **335**, Barry King/Gamma-Liaison. **337**, Cheyenne Rouse/ Photophile. **344**, David Woo/Stock Boston. **345**, Bob Daemmrich/Stock Boston. **351**, Jim Pickerell/Stock Boston. **354**, David Woo/Stock Boston.

## CHAPTER 10
**365**, FourbyFive, Inc. **370**, Culver Pictures, Inc. **373**, C. Zeisse/Magnum Photos. **375**, Frank Fournier/Woodfin Camp & Associates, Inc. **377**, Michal Heron/The Stock Market. **383**, Bob Daemmrich/Stock Boston. **387**, Sygma. **394**, Fred Ward/Black Star.

## CHAPTER 11
**399**, UPI/Bettmann. **401**, Ed Kashi. **405**, Frank Fournier/Woodfin Camp & Associates. **409**, St. Perkins/Magnum Photos. **414**, Archive Photos. **418**, Fred Ward/Black Star. **420**, Stacy Pick/Stock Boston. **422**, Fred Ward/Black Star.

## PART FOUR
**430**, Bill Strode/Woodfin Camp & Associates. **431**, Bill Swersey/Liaison International, Inc.

## CHAPTER 12
**433**, David Butow/Black Star. **435**, David Butow/ Black Star. **436**, Culver Pictures. **437**, UPI/Bettmann. **442**, Wally McNamee/Woodfin Camp & Associates. **445**, AP/Wide World. **448**, Wally McNamee/Woodfin Camp & Associates. **450**, Adam Zettar/Leo deWys Inc. **454**, Paul Fusco/Magnum Photos. **456**, AP/Wide World. **457**, Tex Fuller/Woodfin Camp & Associates. **460**, AP/Wide World Photos.

## CHAPTER 13
**465**, Ferry/Liaison International. **469**, The Bettmann Archive. **470**, Culver Pictures. **473**, Courtesy of the Elmira State Penitentiary. **480**, P. F. Bentley/Black Star. **483**, Culver Pictures. **489**, Stacy Pick/Stock Boston. **491**, Owen Franken/Stock Boston.

## CHAPTER 14
**499**, Ed Kashi. **503**, Courtesy of The Bostonian Society. **512**, J. Chiasson/Liaison International. **517**, Gerd Ludwig/Woodfin Camp & Associates.

## CHAPTER 15
**525**, Bob Daemmrich/Stock Boston. **529**, Irv Rodgers/Stock Boston. **531**, Gilles Peress/Magnum Photos Inc. **535**, Alan Levenson/Tony Stone Images. **541**, Stacy Pick/Stock Boston. **548**, Stacy Pick/Stock Boston. **551**, AP/Wide World Photos.

## CHAPTER 16
**561**, Lester Sloan/Woodfin Camp & Associates. **564**, Bob Daemmrich/Stock Boston. **567**, Neil Leifer/Time Magazine. **568**, Stacy Pick/Stock Boston. **573**, Stacy Pick/Stock Boston. **577**, Alon Reininger/Woodfin Camp & Associates. **581**, Ralf Finn Hestoft/SABA.

## CHAPTER 17
**587**, Butch Martin/Image Bank. **590**, Mary Evans Picture Library. **595**, John Curtis. **602**, Courtesy of Talbert House. Used with permission of ACA. **606**, Marsha Bailey/Used with permission of ACA. **608**, Stacy Pick/Stock Boston.

## PART FIVE
**614**, Tyrone Turner/Times-Picayune/Black Star. **615**, Douglas Burrows/Liaison International.

## CHAPTER 18
**617**, David Burnett/Woodfin Camp & Associates, Inc. **620**, Frank Fournier/Woodfin Camp & Associates, Inc. **623**, Culver Pictures, Inc. **625**, UPI/Bettmann. **633**, Wally McNamee/Woodfin Camp & Associates. **641**, C. Zeisse/Magnum Photos. **643**, Terry Wild Studio. **646**, Renato Rotolo/Liaison International.

*Brown* v. *Mississippi*, 117
Buckey, Raymond, 267–268
Building tenders (BTs), 548
*Burch* v. *Louisiana*, 402
Bureau of Alcohol, Tobacco, and
    Firearms (ATF), 133–134, 144
Bureau of Justice Statistics, 59, 60, 66,
    357, 449, 486
Bureau of Postal Inspection, 144
Bureau of Prisons, 478
Burger, Chief Justice Warren, 118, 346
Burglary, 98
Business, crimes committed in the
    course of, 47–48

# C

California, Victim's Bill of Rights in, 67
Camp, Damon, 106
Capital punishment, 451–458
    controversy over, 457
    as cruel and unusual, 124
    future of, 454–457
    for minors, 455–456
Cardozo, Benjamin, 387
Carlson, Kenneth, 344
*Carroll* v. *United States*, **202**
Carter, Robert, 421
Case law, **93**
Casper, Jonathan, 317, 357
Causation principle, 97
"Celebrated" cases, 32–33
Central Intelligence Agency (CIA), 144
Challenge for cause, **410**
Chambers, Robert, 399–400
Chapper, Joy, 425
Charging
    decisions concerning, 290–295
    process of, 25
Child Protection Act, 106
Children
    criminal behavior by, 108–109
    of women prisoners, 574–575
Children's Aid Society, 624
"Child savers," 624
*Chimel* v. *California*, 201
Chiseling, by police, 239
"Christian burial speech," 206
Cincinnati Declaration, 472–473
CINS (child in need of supervision), **628**
Circuit Courts of Appeal, 367
Circumstantial evidence, **411**
Citations, **340**
Citizen-police encounters, 153–154
Citizen's arrest, 250
Citizens Crime Watch, 232
Civil disability laws, 610–611
Civil forfeiture, **95**
Civilian review boards, 242–244
Civil law, **95**
Civil Rights Act of 1871, 245, 551
Civil rights movement, 140, 527
    juvenile justice and, 625–627
Classical criminology, **70–71**
Classification, **537**
Clearance rate, **154**

Clemmer, Donald, 527
Closing arguments, 413
Coast Guard, 144
Code of Hammurabi, 91
Coercion, as a defense, 108
"Cold" search, 192. *See also* Search and
    seizure
Coleridge, Lord, 108
Collins, Ronald, 126
Commission on Accreditation for Law
    Enforcement Agencies (CALEA),
    244, 245
Common law, **91–92**
Community
    police relations with, 231–233
    prosecutors and, 284
    sanctions administered in, 511–515
Community correctional center, **601**
Community corrections, 23, **475**,
    499–520
    assumptions underlying, 500–502
    intermediate sanctions and, 508–518
    in Japan, 604–605
    in the 1990s, 518–519
    probation and, 502–508
Community model, **475**
Community-oriented policing, 184–185
Community Policing Era, 140–143
Community programs, following pa-
    role, 600–603
Community prosecution, 295–296
Community service, **513**
Community treatment, of juveniles, 645
Comprehensive Crime Control Act of
    1984, 109, 112
Compulsory prosecution, 276–277
Concurrence principle, 97
Confessions, validity of, 120
Conflict model, **44**
Congregate system, **471**
Congress, powers of, 15
Consensus model, **43**
Consent, for search and seizure,
    203–204
Constabularies, creation of, 137
Constitution, U.S., 14, 116–117. *See also*
    Bill of Rights
    death penalty and, 452–454
    Eighth Amendment to, 123–124, 334,
        451, 455, 456, 511, 573
    Fifth Amendment to, 120–121, 200,
        204, 412, 415
    First Amendment to, 544, 545–546
    Fourteenth Amendment to, 117,
        550–551
    Fourth Amendment to, 118–119, 200,
        203–204, 412, 512–513, 546
    police work and, 199
    Sixth Amendment to, 121–123, 200
Constitutions, **92**
"Contingency contracting," 642
Continuance, **392**
Continuing Criminal Enterprise Act
    (CCE), 510
Contract system, of defense services,
    312
Control theories, **76**

Convicts
    prison society of, 561–582
    release and supervision of, 587–612
    release mechanisms for, 591–598
    social system of, 562–567
*Cooper* v. *Pate*, **543**
Copping out, **346**
"Copping-out ceremony," 353
"Cop's world," 225–231. *See also* Police
Corporal punishment, in Singapore,
    444–445
Correctional officers, 540–543
    ethics of, 542
    recruitment of, 541–542
    relationship to prisoners, 535
    role of, 540–541
    unionization of, 542–543
Correctional services, private, 23
Corrections, 28, 465–494. *See also*
    Community corrections
    as a criminal justice agency, 23
    development of, 466–478
    federal, 478–479
    juvenile, 641–645
    local, 481–483
    in the 1990s, 475–478
    organization of, 478–485
    private, 484–485
    state, 479–481
    in Sweden, 476–477
    for women, 483–484
Corruption, police, 236–241
Cosa Nostra, 49
Counsel
    for indigents, 309–313
    during interrogation, 204
    right to, 120, 121–123, 309
Count, **278**
County police agencies, 145
"Courthouse regulars," 312
Courtroom workgroups, 374–380
    impact of, 380–382
    roles in, 379–380
Courts, 365–395. *See also* Juvenile court
    as criminal justice agencies, 22–23
    delay in, 391–394
    felony, 419–420
    functioning of, 372–382
    misdemeanor, 417–419
    structure of, 366–369
    urban versus rural, 373–374
Courts of record, 369
*Covent Garden Journal*, 136
Crawford, William, 470
Cressey, Donald, 541
Crime, **6.** *See also* Crime control; Crime
    prevention; Felonies
    elements of, 98
    extent of, 52–62
    fear of, 187
    as a focus for group feeling, 44
    impact of, 66
    major theories of, 80–81
    perspectives on, 53–54
    as a public policy issue, 6–8
    reporting of, 55
    severity of, 45, 93–95

Retarded persons, execution of, 456
Retribution, **437**
    versus punishment, 436
Rewards, prison system of, 534
*Rhode Island* v. *Innis*, 206
*Rhodes* v. *Chapman*, **549**, 552
Richardson, James, 459
*Ricketts* v. *Adamson*, **353**
"Risk control," 504
Roadblocks, legality of, 202
Robbery rates, 54
Rockefeller drug law, 447
Roper, Robert, 415
Rosenman, Judge Samuel, 389
Rothblat, Henry B., 410
Rothwax, Judge Harold, 394
Rubin, Ted, 639
Ruby, Jack, 15
*Ruffin* v. *Commonwealth*, **543**
*Ruiz* v. *Estelle*, **548**
Rush, Benjamin, 470
Russia, criminal trials in, 406–409

## S

Sanborn, Franklin, 472
Sanctions
    administered by the judiciary, 509–511
    administered in institutions, 515–517
    administered in the community,
        511–515
    criminal, 440–458
    intermediate, 449–450
*Santobello* v. *New York*, **352**
Saratoga Springs, city court in, 418–419
Satter, Judge Robert, 442–443
*Schall* v. *Martin*, **343**, **627**
Schmidt, John, 314
Science, use in aiding investigations, 193
Scopes "monkey trial," 304
Scottsboro case, 117
Search and seizure
    as a police action, 200–204
    unreasonable, 118–119
Searches, types of, 200–201
Search warrant, **200**
Secret Service Division of the Treasury,
    144
Securities and Exchange Commission,
    48
Sedition Act of 1789, 52
Selective incapacitation, **438**
Selective prosecution, 284
Self-defense, 106–107
Self-incrimination, **120**
    protection against, 204, 412
Self-protection, need for, 13
Sentencing, 27, 433–460
    discretionary release and, 592–594
    ethics in, 446
    goals of, 435–439
    process of, 417–423
    reality of, 440
    tendencies in, 420
    versus actual time served, 449
Sentencing guidelines, **422**

Separate confinement, **471**
Service function, **152**
Service style, 149
Sexism, in police work, 224
"Sexual psychopath laws," 74
Shakedown, by police, 239
Sheehan, Susan, 566, 568
Sheriff, position of, 138
Sheriff's office, appointments to, 145
Sherman, Lawrence W., 180, 236
Shock incarceration, **515**. *See also*
    Incarceration
Shock probation, **450**
"Shopping," by police, 239,
Silbey, Susan, 418
*Silence of the Lambs*, 90
Simon, Rita, 78
Singapore, corporal punishment in,
    444–445
Singer, Richard, 611
Single, Eric W., 346
Sing Sing penitentiary, 472
Sixth Amendment, 121–123, 200
*Skinner* v. *Oklahoma*, 72
Skogan, Wesley, 232
Skolnick, Jerome, 46, 232
"Slave patrols," 138
"Slow plea of guilty," 320, 322, 352
Smith, Bruce, 139
Smith Act of 1940, 52
Social conflict theories, **77**
Socialization, **221**
Social process theories, **76**
Social services
    police interface with, 185–186
    as a police responsibility, 22
Social structure theories, **74**
*Sociobiology: The New Synthesis* (Wilson),
    73
Sociological explanations, **74**
"Sociopath," 73
Solitary confinement, 550
"Son of Sam," 90
Sorensen, Jonathan, 234
Sorin, Martin, 343
Souter, Justice David, 125
South, incarceration rate in, 487
Special deterrence, **438**
Specialized operations, police, 196–199
Spelman, William G., 179
Split probation, 450
Spohn, Cassia, 459
Spouse abuse, 155
Standard Juvenile Court Act, 645
*Stanford* v. *Kentucky*, 456
State attorney general, **269**
State corrections systems, 479–481
State courts, 368–369
    management of, 369–371
*State of Prisons in England and Wales, The*
    (Howard), 468
State police agencies, 145
Status offenses, 626–627, 629. *See also*
    Juvenile justice
Statute of Winchester, 135
Statutes, **92**

Stephens, Edwin, 107
Stewart, Justice Potter, 97, 619
"Sting" operations, 183–184
Stoddard, Ellwyn, 238
Stop-and-frisk procedure, 201
"Street crime," 49
Stress, categories of, 229–230
*Strickland* v. *Washington*, 323
Strict liability, **104**
Stuart, Chuck, 165–166
Subculture, **225**
    prison as a, 572
Substantial Capacity Test, 109, 111
Substantive criminal law, **91**, 96–114
"Subway vigilante," 107
Suffet, Frederic, 338
Sumerian Law, 91
Sumners-Ashurst Act, 538
"Suppressible" crimes, 183
Supreme Court, 22, 125–127, 366,
    367–368
    on plea bargaining, 346–347
    "right to counsel" rulings by, 309
    under Warren and Burger, 118
Sutherland, Edwin, 47, 76
"Swagging," 566
Sweden, corrections in, 476–477
Swift justice, importance of, 391
Sworn officers, **174**
Sykes, Gresham, 527, 534
System, **17–18**
System efficiency model, **288**

## T

*Tennessee* v. *Garner*, **235**
*Terry* v. *Ohio*, **201**
Testimony, **411**
Theft
    in Islamic criminal law, 100
    by police, 239
"Thin blue line," 134
Thomas, Justice Clarence, 125
*Thompson* v. *Oklahoma*, 456
"Three-strikes" penal law, 447, 448
Threshold inquiries, 201
Thurman, Tracey, 245
Thurston, Henry, 625
Tickets, 340
"Tickets-of-leave," 589, 590
Tithing, 135
Toch, Hans, 576
Tocqueville, Alexis de, 470
Tonry, Michael, 441, 448, 508
Torts, 95
Total institution, **530**
Totality of conditions, **547**
Traffic control, 196–197
Traffic inspections, searches during, 202
Trial court of general jurisdiction, **368**
Trial court of limited jurisdiction, **368**
Trial judges, responsibilities of, 442–443
Trials, 399–426. *See also* Courts
    majority decisions in, 414
    process in, 405–415
    rules for speedy, 392–393
Trial sufficiency model, **288**

Trojanowicz, Robert, 182
"True bill," 289
Turner, Susan, 449

## U

Unemployment, among parolees,
599–600
Uniform Crime Reporting System, 144
*Uniform Crime Reports* (UCR), **57**, 59, 81,
99, 148
definitions of offenses in, 102
Union brokerage model, 253
United States
corrections in, 478–485
development of parole in, 590–591
youth crime in, 619–621
United States Constitution. *See*
Constitution, U.S.
United States attorneys, **269**
*United States* v. *Brawner*, 111
*United States* v. *Cronic*, 323
*United States* v. *Leon*, **207**
*United States* v. *Ross*, 202
*United States* v. *Salerno and Cafaro*, 123,
**343**
Unreasonable search and seizure,
200–201
Upward Now, Inc., 499
Urban crime, 65
Urban riots, 140
"Us against them" mentality, 238
Utilitarianism, 436

## V

Values
influence of, 34
of judges, 420
law as an expression of, 43–44
prisoner, 563
societal, 42
Van Maanen, John, 219
Vaux, Robert, 470
Vera Institute of Justice, 341
Vernon, Wyman, 241
Vice units, 169, 197
Victimization

probability of, 63–65
vicarious, 66
Victimless crimes, 51, 238
decriminalizing, 488
Victimology, **63**
Victims
compensation programs for, 68,
509–510
in the criminal justice system, 67–68,
280–281
precipitation of crime by, 68–69
Victim's Bill of Rights, 67
in California, 358
Violence
outbreaks of, 53
prison, 575–580
Violent crimes
arrest rate for, 154
in cities, 65
trends for, 61
Visible crimes, **49**
Vocational education, in prison, 538
*Voir dire*, **410**
Vollmer, August, 139
von Bulow, Claus, 33, 400
von Hirsch, Andrew, 436

## W

Wagner, Allen, 241
Waiver hearing, 627–628
Walker, Samuel, 32–33, 142, 222
Walnut Street Jail, 470, 471
Walsh, William, 255
"War on crime" mentality, 232
Warrant, **25**
Warrantless searches, 200–204
Warren, Chief Justice Earl, 118, 119
Watchman style, 148
*Wayward Puritans* (Erikson), 43
*Weekly Pursuit*, 136
*Weeks* v. *United States*, 200
Welch, Susan, 459
Wells, Fargo and Company, 250
Western law, seven principles of, 97–98,
103
Western Penitentiary, 471

White, Justice Byron, 106, 125
"White-collar" crime, 47
Wice, Paul, 305–306, 383
Wilkins, Leslie, 421
*Wilkins* v. *Missouri*, 456
Williams, Edward Bennett, 319
*Williams* v. *Florida*, **402**
*Williams* v. *New York*, 421
"Willie Horton" syndrome, 601
Wilson, Edward O., 73
Wilson, James Q., 73, 140, 148, 150, 154,
183, 202
Wilson, O. W., 139, 180, 241
*Wilson* v. *Seiter*, **553**
Wines, Enoch, 472, 473
*Winship, In re*, **626**
Witchcraft hysteria, 43, 44
Witnesses, presentation of, 412–413
Wolfgang, Marvin, 576
*Wolf* v. *McDonnell*, **550**
Women
battered, 155
criminality among, 77–78
police work and, 222–225
Women's movement, 77–78
effect on rape laws, 103
Women's Prison Association, 484
Women's prisons, 483–484, 567–575
programs in, 572–573
Work and educational release, **600**
Workgroups, **374**
Working personality, **226**
World Trade Center bombing, 52
Wright, J. Skelly, 336–337
Written law, 92–93

## Y

Youth crime, 619–621. *See also* Juvenile
justice
Youth gangs, 623

## Z

Zeisel, Hans, 415

# Can You Help Us Improve This Book?

## A Message from the Author

I hope that you have found *The American System of Criminal Justice*, 7th edition, useful and interesting. So that the publisher and I can improve this text in future editions, would you take the time to complete and return this short questionnaire? I read and value each response received.

1. Your instructor's name _____

2. Your school and department _____

   _____

3. Title of the course in which you used this book _____

   _____

4. What is your general reaction to this textbook? _____

   _____

5. What do you like or value most about the book? _____

   _____

   _____

6. What do you dislike or value least about the book? _____

   _____

   _____

7. How helpful was the book in contributing to your success in the course? _____

   _____

8. In what ways could the text have been more helpful to you? _____

   _____

   _____

9. Which chapters, if any, were *not* assigned for you to read? _____

   _____

   _____

Please write any additional comments, as well as specific suggestions for improving this book, on a separate sheet of paper. All comments and suggestions will be carefully considered.

Thank you!
George Cole

Optional (please complete if you would like a personal response):

Your name _____ Date _____

Your address _____

Your e-mail address _____

May Wadsworth quote you, either in promotion for Cole's *The American System of Criminal Justice*, 7th edition, or in future publishing ventures?

Yes _____   No _____